THE SUPREME COURT
AND THE ALLOCATION
OF CONSTITUTIONAL
POWER

THE SUPREME COURT AND THE ALLOCATION OF CONSTITUTIONAL POWER

Introductory Essays and Selected Cases

Otis H. Stephens
Gregory J. Rathjen
UNIVERSITY OF TENNESSEE, KNOXVILLE

W. H. Freeman and Company
San Francisco

Sponsoring Editor: Richard J. Lamb
Project Editor: Pearl C. Vapnek
Manuscript Editor: Ruth C. Veres
Designer: Marie Carluccio
Production Coordinator: Linda Jupiter
Compositor: Lehigh/Rocappi, Inc.
Printer and Binder: The Maple-Vail Book
Manufacturing Group

Library of Congress Cataloging in Publication Data
Main entry under title:

The Supreme Court and the allocation of constitutional
    power.

    Bibliography: p.
    Includes index.
    1.   Separation of powers—United States—Cases.
2.   Federal government—United States—Cases.
3.   Judicial power—United States—Cases.   4.   United
States.   Supreme Court.   I.   Stephens, Otis H.
II.   Rathjen, Gregory J., 1947–
KF4565.A7S96   342′.73′044   79-26468
ISBN 0-7167-1154-0
ISBN 0-7167-1218-0 pbk.

Printed in the United States of America

9 8 7 6 5 4 3 2 1

To Jane, Linda, Ann, and Carol

CONTENTS

PREFACE   xi

ORGANIZATION CHART OF STATE AND FEDERAL JUDICIAL SYSTEMS   xiii

INTRODUCTION   1

**PART I   ESTABLISHMENT AND DEVELOPMENT
OF JUDICIAL POWER   9**

1   JUDICIAL REVIEW: BASIS OF JUDICIAL POWER   11

Introductory Essay   11
Marbury v. *Madison* (1803)   19
United States v. *Nixon* (1974)   27

2   EXERCISE OF JUDICIAL POWER   34

Introductory Essay   34
*President Franklin D. Roosevelt's Message
   to Congress* (1937)   47
President Franklin D. Roosevelt's "Fireside Chat" (1937)   50
*Chief Justice Charles Evans Hughes' Letter
   to Senator Burton K. Wheeler* (1937)   54
Ex parte McCardle (1869)   57
Cooper v. *Aaron* (1958)   59
President Richard M. Nixon's Message to Congress (1972)   64
Ex parte Grossman (1925)   70
Taylor v. *Hayes* (1974)   74

3   SELF-IMPOSED LIMITATIONS ON THE EXERCISE
OF JUDICIAL POWER   80

Introductory Essay   80
Singleton v. *Wulff* (1976)   93
United States v. *Richardson* (1974)   97
United States v. *Students Challenging
   Regulatory Agency Procedures* (1973)   105

Association of Data Processing Service Organizations
     v. *Camp* (1970)   110
Younger v. *Harris* (1971)   115
Stone v. *Powell* (1976)   122
Baker v. *Carr* (1962)   127
Ashwander v. *Tennessee Valley Authority* (1936)   139

PART II SOURCES AND LIMITS OF CONGRESSIONAL POWER   141

4 POWER TO INVESTIGATE   143

Introductory Essay   143
McGrain v. *Daugherty* (1927)   150
Watkins v. *United States* (1957)   156
Eastland v. *United States Servicemen's Fund* (1975)   166

5 COMMERCE POWER   172

Introductory Essay   172
Gibbons v. *Ogden* (1824)   181
United States v. *E. C. Knight Co.* (1895)   188
National Labor Relations Board
     v. *Jones & Laughlin Steel Corp.* (1937)   195
Wickard v. *Filburn* (1942)   203
Katzenbach v. *McClung* (1964)   208
Goldfarb v. *Virginia State Bar* (1975)   213

6 TAXING AND SPENDING POWER   218

Introductory Essay   218
Pollock v. *Farmers' Loan & Trust Co.* (1895)   226
McCray v. *United States* (1904)   236
Bailey v. *Drexel Furniture Co.* (1922)   242
United States v. *Butler* (1936)   246
Steward Machine Co. v. *Davis* (1937)   256
Buckley v. *Valeo* (1976)   261

PART III SCOPE OF EXECUTIVE POWER   269

7 DOMESTIC AFFAIRS   271

Introductory Essay   271
Youngstown Sheet & Tube Co. v. *Sawyer* (1952)   285
Weiner v. *United States* (1958)   298
Schick v. *Reed* (1974)   302

8 FOREIGN RELATIONS   308

Introductory Essay   308
United States v. *Curtiss–Wright Export Corp.* (1936)   320
Massachusetts v. *Laird* (1970)   325
Korematsu v. *United States* (1944)   329

PART IV DISTRIBUTION OF POWER IN THE FEDERAL SYSTEM   337

9   SHAPING THE FEDERAL SYSTEM: CONSTITUTIONAL
     THEORY AND POLITICAL PRACTICE   339

     Introductory Essay   339
     M'Culloch v. *Maryland* (1819)   349
     Hammer v. *Dagenhart* (1918)   356
     United States v. *Darby* (1941)   360
     National League of Cities v. *Usery* (1976)   366
     Pennsylvania v. *Nelson* (1956)   372

10   STATE POWER TO REGULATE COMMERCE   378

     Introductory Essay   378
     Cooley v. *Board of Wardens* (1852)   386
     South Carolina Highway Department v. *Barnwell* (1938)   390
     Southern Pacific Co. v. *Arizona* (1945)   394
     Hood & Sons v. *DuMond* (1949)   401
     Philadelphia v. *New Jersey* (1978)   406
     Burbank v. *Lockheed Air Terminal* (1973)   411

11   STATE TAXING AND SPENDING POWER   416

     Introductory Essay   416
     New York v. *United States* (1946)   423
     Massachusetts v. *United States* (1978)   429
     Brown v. *Maryland* (1827)   433
     Michelin Tire Corp. v. *Wages* (1976)   438

12   INTERSTATE RELATIONS   442

     Introductory Essay   442
     Estin v. *Estin* (1948)   452
     Sosna v. *Iowa* (1975)   456
     Hicklin v. *Orbeck* (1978)   461
     United States Steel Corp.
          v. *Multistate Tax Commission* (1978)   465

**PART V SCOPE OF ADMINISTRATIVE POWER:
THE BURGEONING BUREAUCRACY   473**

13   DELEGATION OF LEGISLATIVE POWER   475

     Introductory Essay   475
     J. W. Hampton & Co. v. *United States* (1928)   483
     Schechter Poultry Corp. v. *United States* (1935)   486

14   EXERCISE OF ADMINISTRATIVE POWER   494

     Introductory Essay   494
     United States v. *Bisceglia* (1975)   501
     Tennessee Valley Authority v. *Hill* (1978)   507
     Mathews v. *Eldridge* (1976)   516

CHRONOLOGY OF JUSTICES OF THE UNITED STATES SUPREME
     COURT   522

JUSTICES BY APPOINTING PRESIDENT
     AND POLITICAL PARTY AFFILIATION   526

CONSTITUTION OF THE UNITED STATES   529

BIBLIOGRAPHY   545

GLOSSARY   549

TABLE OF CASES   554

PREFACE

This book is designed for political science courses in constitutional law. It analyzes and portrays through introductory essays and leading decisions the function of the United States Supreme Court in allocating constitutional power among the branches of national government and between the national government and the states. Like Congress, the President, and their counterparts at the state level, the Supreme Court formulates public policy. But by deciding cases involving adverse parties, the Court approaches its policymaking responsibility from a perspective that differs from the perspectives of legislators and executives. We do not minimize the importance of a distinction that makes the Supreme Court's role unique in the American system of government. At the same time, we wish to state clearly at the outset our assumption that, in spite of the elaborate interplay of rule, precedent, and judicial doctrine, the Supreme Court functions as an integral part of the political process. Its work merits the careful attention of students of American government and politics.

Supreme Court interpretation of the Constitution falls into two broad categories: (1) decisions recognizing, confirming, or limiting governmental power, and (2) rulings delineating individual rights and freedoms. Most courses in constitutional law deal in detail with these distinct aspects of adjudication. The issues of both power and freedom have proliferated so widely during the past several decades of constitutional development that it is more difficult than ever to deal with them adequately in a single volume of moderate length. Authors of texts on civil liberties have long recognized this problem and have largely divorced their books from the other aspects of constitutional law. Little comparable attention has been given, however, to the utility of considering the issues of power in a separate volume. Hence the rationale for a book that examines those areas of judicial interpretation dealing with the exercise of power by Congress, the President, the bureaucracy, and the Supreme Court in relation to each other; national authority in relation to the states; and the subordination of power to the Constitution.

The reading and understanding of Supreme Court decisions is a complex task.

We have attempted to minimize the problem by omitting all footnotes and most of the citations of precedents and statutes appearing in the cases as published in the *United States Supreme Court Reports.* Where omission of citation occurs, we have placed three asterisks to inform the interested reader that additional information may be obtained by going to the original source. Where we have omitted substantial portions of an opinion (a paragraph or more), we have denoted the omission by centering three dots on a line by themselves.

In writing the essays and editing the cases that make up this volume, we have benefited from the assistance of many persons. Professors Harold J. Spaeth, Michigan State University; Lawrence Baum, Ohio State University; James Magee, University of Delaware; and William P. McLauchlan, Purdue University, read the manuscript and offered invaluable suggestions for its improvement. Graduate and undergraduate assistants helped us with many details of research, manuscript preparation, and proofreading. In particular, we would like to thank Jeffrey Brown, Roger G. Brown, Christopher Cane, Jo Gunderson, Jacqueline Jones, David T. Lewis, Mary Rutherford, Greg L. Sullivan, Susan Tobias, Janet L. Trice, Kathy Windle, Larry Wingate, and Mark J. Wolfson for their help in this regard. Mrs. Lawrence M. Levine and Mrs. Ellie Litt Sokolow of the National Braille Association greatly enhanced access to needed source material by arranging for their transcription into Braille. Linda D. Stephens assisted extensively with proofreading and reference checking. We wish to express our sincere thanks as well to Marilyn Caponetti, who typed early drafts of the manuscript, as did Cathy Adkins, Irene Fansler, Diana Kosier, and Teresa Underwood. We are indebted to Mrs. Kate Leake for her kindness and quality office management; both helped us meet deadlines. Professor Thomas D. Ungs and other members of the political science faculty at the University of Tennessee, Knoxville, proved supportive throughout our writing and editing chores. Finally, we are indebted to the many students in our constitutional law courses at the University of Tennessee. Their strong encouragement and constructive suggestions about early drafts of the introductory essays contributed significantly to the completion of this book.

February 1980   *Otis H. Stephens*
                                                                    Gregory J. Rathjen

ORGANIZATION CHART OF STATE AND FEDERAL JUDICIAL SYSTEMS

Federal Judicial System

State Judicial System(s)

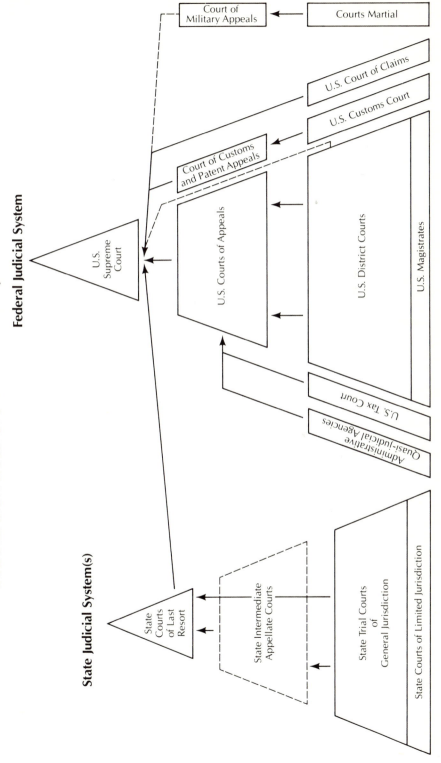

THE SUPREME COURT AND THE ALLOCATION OF CONSTITUTIONAL POWER

INTRODUCTION

The United States Supreme Court occupies a unique place within the American system of government. It is first and foremost a *court of law*. It hears and decides cases between adverse parties and does so within an elaborate framework of rules, procedure, and tradition. At the same time the Supreme Court is a major *political institution*. Like Congress, the President, and the bureaucracy, the Court makes authoritative, conscious choices among competing solutions to public problems, and consequently makes public policy. It does so most obviously when it reconciles differences between the Constitution and less authoritative provisions of law. Yet, it makes policy as well when it interprets the meaning of statutes considered wholly compatible with the Constitution. Because the Court is both a legal and a political entity, its members must be sensitive to the consistency of legal doctrine and other formal requirements of "the law," as well as to the needs of a democratic society and the political realities of the times. A full understanding of the Court's role in American government therefore requires some knowledge of both the legal and the political aspects of Supreme Court decision-making. In the following essays, we focus attention on these components of the judicial process through our efforts to explain and illustrate the Supreme Court's allocation of constitutional power *among* the branches of national government and *between* the national government and the states.

Although most people no doubt have some familiarity with political discourse, the legal world may be rather befuddling. Terms like "injunction," "certiorari," "plaintiff," "*duces tecum*," and "*ex parte*" leave the impression that one must master an entirely new language just to know what is going on, much less understand its broader political import. While we do not believe that a complete mastery of legal terms is an essential prerequisite for gleaning the political from the legal, we recognize that understanding a court decision, particularly a Supreme Court decision, is a complex task. We have tried to minimize this complexity by deleting as much legal paraphernalia as possible without doing damage to the substance of the opinion excerpted. We have also included definitions of legal terms that students might find confusing. To reduce the initial difficulties encountered by students with little if any previous exposure to the work of the Court, we will begin by discussing several characteristics of the legal world and the Supreme Court decision-making process.

Nature of Supreme Court Policymaking

As a court of law, the Supreme Court employs the case mode as the vehicle through which it makes its policy choices. The Court does not enact general statutes, issue executive orders, or promulgate rules and regulations. It does not take note of a given problem, think about it for a while, and then authoritatively state its views about how to solve that problem. Rather the Court must await the presentation of a concrete dispute between two parties, both adversely affected or potentially so, who have framed their dispute in particular ways and brought their struggle to the Court's attention, usually after having traversed a complex maze of lower courts. Once the dispute is presented and the Supreme Court agrees to hear it, the Justices can then resolve it and, in the process of explaining their choice, render broadly based policy. This feature is a key factor distinguishing the policy process of the Supreme Court from the policy process of other branches of government. The Court is essentially a passive institution, depending for its agenda on decisions reached by litigants and lawyers outside its control. True, the Court does possess a wide margin of discretion in selecting which cases it will decide (a matter we turn to in a moment). But that discretion is limited to the selection of cases among those matters brought to the Court and not across the whole range of public problems facing the polity.

Pyramids of Jurisdiction

Courts of Original Jurisdiction

Disputes calling for judicial resolution do not magically appear at the doorstep of the Supreme Court. Most cases begin elsewhere in what are referred to as "courts of original jurisdiction," "courts of first instance," or "trial courts." In the chart on page xiii, these courts are depicted at the base of the pyramid representing the two-court system. They are the courts most familiar to the American public, where TV's Perry Mason and the theater's Clarence Darrow dramatically thrash out the details of life-and-death matters before judge, jury, and spellbound gallery. While everyday life in the trial courts is rarely as exciting as that portrayed on stage and screen, the basics of factual presentation by adverse parties, followed by the jury's verdict or the judge's decision for one side or the other, is fairly accurate.

Legislation and constitutional provisions grant state and federal trial courts the power to hear disputes and decide certain matters initially. These grants of power typically give the courts authority over specified geographic areas. Thus, a state legislature may establish a county court and limit its authority to cases involving residents of that county and controversies occurring there. The grant of judicial power may be over either a broad range of subjects or specialized areas of dispute.

Some states grant certain courts the power to hear and decide only criminal cases while authorizing another set of courts to hear only civil cases. Other states merge these functions in a single set of trial courts of general jurisdiction. Congress has established ninety-four United States District Courts, each with responsibility as the trial court for a given geographic region comprising all or part of a state, and each authorized to hear and decide civil and criminal matters under federal law. In addition, Congress has established several specialized subject matter courts to deal with questions of customs and patents, tax controversies, and claims against the United States government, among other matters.

Appellate Courts

After the initial hearing and decision in any one of the many courts of first instance across the nation, certain aspects of the dispute may proceed for additional consideration to another, "higher" court (one level above the trial courts in the chart). Should a losing party believe that the judge made a mistake in how he or she conducted the trial or interpreted the law, that party may appeal the case to a specified court with "appellate" as opposed to "original" jurisdiction. Appellate courts are empowered to review the transcript of the trial and to hear argument about alleged "errors of law." These courts do not call witnesses and do not retry the "facts" of the dispute. However, the distinction between "law" and "fact" at this level of review is by no means always clear. Appellate courts are primarily authorized to review errors of law and to correct those errors, either by setting aside the lower court's judgment or by sending the case back to that court with orders to retry it free of these errors. In about half of the states and in the federal system, this first appeal from the trial court is handled by an intermediate appellate court. In the remaining states, the appeal goes directly to the highest state court, or "court of last resort." Since 1891 the federal court system has had an established set of intermediate appellate courts, known (since 1948) as United States Courts of Appeals. There are now eleven of these appellate courts: one for the District of Columbia and the remaining ten for designated groups of states.

In most instances, the losing party at a trial has a *right of appeal* to the intermediate appellate court (or, in those states without this tier, to the court of last resort). In most state systems, losing parties at this intermediate level retain the right of appeal to the state's highest tribunal. If the matter in dispute involves only questions of state law, the decision of this latter court is final. If, however, the case involves a question of federal law (that is, if a state law or state action involves an alleged violation of the U.S. Constitution, federal statutes, or federal treaties), or if the case began in the federal courts and was lost in a Court of Appeals or in one of the specialized federal courts, a final option for review remains: a petition to the United States Supreme Court. (These final courts are represented by the triangle atop each pyramid in the chart on page xiii.)

Discretionary Jurisdiction

The term "option" is important here, because unlike the other courts we have been discussing, the Supreme Court's appellate jurisdiction is discretionary. Rather than having an absolute *right* to be heard, the losing party is merely granted an opportunity to request to be heard. The Court, upon review of this request, grants or denies it. Thus, Supreme Court review is a *privilege* rather than a right. There are three means by which a case can be granted Supreme Court review: by writ of certiorari, by writ of appeal, or by certification. Over 90 percent of the requests for review come to the Court via a petition for a writ of certiorari (a Latin term meaning "to be informed, to be made certain in regard to"). The writ, if granted, orders the lower court to send the transcript of the case to the Supreme Court so that it can be "more informed." This sets in motion the review process. Slightly less than 10 percent of the cases in which review is sought come to the Court on petitions of appeal. The difference between appeal and certiorari as modes of access to the Court is largely academic. A litigant under certain circumstances has a statutory right of appeal—a right which, in theory, the Court must recognize. But the Court possesses broad discretion to determine whether a *substantial* federal question is presented by the appeal. If it decides this prerequisite is not met (and the Court alone is authorized to determine whether it is or not), it will deny the appeal. Thus the *right* is in name only. In practice, the writ of appeal, like the writ of certiorari, is discretionary. The final means of securing Supreme Court review is a little-used procedure known as certification. This mode permits lower federal courts to seek instructions from the Supreme Court on questions of law in civil and criminal cases.

Original Jurisdiction of the Supreme Court

In a small number of cases the Supreme Court may also exercise original jurisdiction. The Constitution provides for such jurisdiction in cases "affecting ambassadors, other public ministers, and consuls," and certain cases in which a state is a party. Congress has limited the practical effect of this constitutional language by providing that in most cases the Supreme Court's original jurisdiction is not exclusive but may be exercised by other courts as well. Only cases between two or more states must originate in the Supreme Court. The number of cases the Supreme Court decides each year under its original jurisdiction rarely exceeds 2 percent of the total decided. In the 1977–1978 term only 1 of the 135 cases receiving full-opinion decisions originated in the Court.

Four Stages of Supreme Court Decision-Making

Since most of the Supreme Court's jurisdiction is appellate and discretionary, it is important to take a closer look at how the Justices handle petitions for review and render decisions in the cases they choose to hear. David Rohde and Harold Spaeth (1976) provide a helpful delineation of four stages (or "decision points") of Supreme Court decision-making: (1) the vote on whether or not to accept the case for decision; (2) the vote on the merits; (3) the assignment of the majority opinion; and (4) the bargaining over the contents of the majority opinion. At the first stage, members of the Court decide which cases petitioned to be heard possess sufficient significance to warrant further consideration and ultimate decision. Periodically in the course of the Court's term, the Justices gather in conference to consider this matter. For the most part, the decision to accept a case for review is governed by the "rule of four"; namely, if at least four Justices vote that a case has sufficient merit to be considered, the Court accepts the case for review. Once the Court has accepted a case for review, the Justices read briefs and the record of the case. If the case is to be decided by full opinion, as opposed to a short judicial order requiring no elaboration, oral argument is scheduled. The Court now reaches the second stage of its decision-making. The Justices, meeting in conference, vote to decide which party wins the case; that is, they vote on the merits. The result at this stage is particularistic: The decision applies only to the litigants. A party wins if a majority of the Justices hearing the case vote in his or her favor.

After the vote on the merits, the Chief Justice (or the senior Associate Justice if the Chief Justice is not in the majority) assigns to himself or to another member of the majority the task of writing the Opinion of the Court. This task is of central importance because the opinion's import goes beyond the particular litigants at hand. Ideally, the statement of the Court informs the public of the reason for its choice and communicates the policy position of those Justices constituting the majority in the case. This statement, under rules of precedent, is expected to bind lower courts in their disposition of similar cases. At the same time, the opinion may inform legislative and executive branches, individuals, and groups about constitutional and statutory limitations imposed on future behavior.

Before an opinion can be considered the Opinion of the Court, the Justice assigned the task of preparing the majority opinion must secure the signatures of at least four other Justices. If he fails to obtain such agreement, the result of the case is simply reported in a plurality opinion, the value of which is marginal as either precedent or a guide to other political actors. If he fails to obtain agreement and some Justices change their votes, he may end up on the losing side. Therefore, the majority opinion writer has incentives to write an opinion reflecting the views of a full majority. It is in this context that the fourth and final stage—bargaining over the contents of the majority opinion—takes place. Justices have been known to write notes to each other requesting specific changes and to change their votes or write separate opinions if the opinion writer failed to accede to their requests (see Howard, 1968; Murphy, 1964). The coalitional character of this bargaining may explain the unclear and inconsistent public statements that sometimes emerge in the final opinions signed by a Court majority.

Publication of Opinions

Once the Court has announced its decision, its opinion, together with any concurring or dissenting opinion(s), is published in the official *United States Supreme Court Reports*, prepared and distributed by the U.S. Government Printing Office. The same opinions are published verbatim in two commercial editions of Supreme Court decisions: the *Supreme Court Reporter* by West Publishing Company, and the *Lawyers' Edition* by the Lawyers Cooperative Publishing Company. In the essays that follow, specifically named Supreme Court cases are followed by numbers and abbreviations indicating the volumes and pages where the decisions appear in the official *United States Reports*. For example, the famous reapportionment case of *Baker* v. *Carr* is followed by the designation 369 U.S. 186. The first number refers to the volume of the *United States Reports* in which the case appears. The abbreviation U.S. indicates the official *United States Reports*. The next number refers to the page on which the case begins. In some casebooks and in the Supreme Court opinions themselves the abbreviations S. Ct., L. Ed., and L. Ed. 2d appear as well; these denote the West and Lawyers Cooperative publications respectively. During the early years of its history the Supreme Court had its decisions published under the last names of the persons serving as Court Reporters. Thus, for the famous case of *Marbury* v. *Madison* the official citation of 1 Cranch 137 refers to the first volume of the *United States Reports*, published by Court Reporter Cranch, and the appropiate page.

Evolution of the Prestige, Influence, and Function of the Court

The cases included in this volume cover a time span of more than 180 years. During this long period the Supreme Court has undergone a transformation more striking than that of any other tribunal in modern history. Although it handed down a few important constitutional decisions during the first decade of its existence, it showed little promise of reaching a position of coequality with Congress and the Presidency. But during the Chief Justiceship of John Marshall (1801–1835), the Court's influence and prestige rose dramatically. Even though the Court has sometimes been at the center of national controversy and its authority has occasionally been challenged, its power and prestige have continued to grow. As previously explained, it has gained virtually complete control over its own docket. Since it receives more than 4,000 petitions for review each year, the practical importance of this broad discretion is obvious. But beyond practical considerations of work load, the Court's discretionary review enables it to address significant questions of public policy. When cases involving real people with immediate problems are decided, the results are of immediate concern to the winners and losers. But when questions of public policy are at issue (as they are in each of the cases included in this book), the cases become the instruments through which the Court exercises its authority.

In analyzing the Supreme Court's function with respect to the allocation of power, we have for the most part followed the organizational divisions of most casebooks in constitutional law, giving major attention to judicial review; the constitutional relationships between the Court, Congress, and the President; the sources of national power; and relations between the national government and the states. In addition, we have included a chapter dealing broadly with the question of judicial supervision of federal administrative activity. Since the Supreme Court's increasingly important function in this area requires it to interpret statutes and regulations as well as constitutional provisions, it has been necessary to depart slightly from the conventional constitutional case format. But even in more traditional areas of constitutional interpretation, such as that of the commerce power, the sharp line between constitutional and statutory adjudication is not always clear. Thus, a recent case concerning the scope of legislative power under the Sherman Antitrust Act—a measure based on the Commerce Clause—clearly illustrates the scope of congressional power to regulate commerce, although the case itself poses no formal constitutional question (*Goldfarb* v. *Virginia State Bar*, 421 U.S. 773 [1975]). We have included two cases dealing with questions of administrative procedure: one involving interpretation of the Internal Revenue Code, the other concerning the termination of disability benefits under the Social Security Act. These cases illustrate important issues of bureaucratic power. Their inclusion underscores the fact that the Supreme Court's function in shaping public policy is not confined to constitutional cases. With the proliferation of statutory provisions and administrative regulations, the extraconstitutional dimension of the Court's responsibility has become more prominent. Still, the central function of the Supreme Court in allocating power is governed by provisions of the Constitution, and we emphasize that perspective throughout the text.

PART I

ESTABLISHMENT AND DEVELOPMENT OF JUDICIAL POWER

CHAPTER 1

Judicial Review: Basis of Judicial Power

INTRODUCTORY ESSAY

In size, complexity, and power, American government today bears little resemblance to American government in 1789, 1861, or even 1933. Each of those years marked dramatic changes in the American political system and ultimately in the allocation of constitutional power. For the most part, however, the vast expansion of government, especially the federal bureaucracy, has occurred gradually and with little fanfare. Over the past two centuries the center of political gravity has shifted in varying degrees from state autonomy to national control, from legislative supremacy to presidential leadership, and from limited government to large-scale government engaged in problem-solving efforts touching many aspects of human life.

This transformation has not been accompanied by a corresponding change in political and legal theory. With some notable modifications, such as the shift toward greater national power embodied in the post–Civil War amendments (but not realized until the mid–twentieth century), the principles underlying the structure and process of American government are those of the federal Constitution of 1787 and the Bill of Rights adopted four years later. Two opposing conclusions may be drawn from this apparent dichotomy between theory and practice: (1) that the principles of government on which the system rests are remarkably capable of adaptation to changing conditions; or (2) that the theory is used merely as window dressing, a set of comforting incantations having nothing to do with the real world of jet-age American politics. While it is sometimes tempting to adopt the cynicism of the second of these alternatives, we prefer the view that the first is more in line with an accurate explanation of the American political system. The principles of *separation of powers, checks and balances, federalism, judicial review,* and *rule of law* still exercise great influence on the manner in which power is defined and distributed.

Constitutional Sources of Power

One of the most striking features of the federal Constitution is that it provides for the accommodation of old forms of government to new problems and demands for action. This feature is evident in the broad language outlining legislative, executive, and judicial functions. Article I, for example, gives Congress broad enumerated and implied powers. On the basis of Article II, the President has open-ended authority to "take care" that the laws are faithfully executed. Article III extends judicial power "to all cases in law and equity arising under" the Constitution, laws, and treaties of the United States. These grants of power are underscored by the Supremacy Clause of Article VI, which places the Constitution at the top of a hierarchy of law in which state statutes are subordinate. In a fundamental sense, this clause embodies the principle of "rule of law." In this book we are primarily concerned with the judicial function of interpreting constitutional power, and defining its scope and allocation within the American system of government. The U.S. Supreme Court will receive most of our attention because of the relative finality and general application of its decisions. Although the lower federal courts and state appellate courts also participate significantly in the process of constitutional interpretation, the Supreme Court alone is mentioned by name in the federal Constitution. More importantly, it has come to symbolize, next to the Constitution itself, the highest ideals of legal justice and order in our society.

Roles of the Court

By far the most important of the Supreme Court's many roles are those of (1) interpreting broad constitutional provisions conferring governmental power and (2) safeguarding individual freedoms. Most undergraduate courses in constitutional law analyze these distinct aspects in some detail. Issues focusing on the allocation of power have always been central to the study of constitutional law, but the great drive for civil rights beginning in the mid-1950s turned the spotlight on questions of individual freedom. With internal crises in government, dramatized by the Senate Watergate hearings, the Nixon Tapes Case, and more recently the charges of corruption and malfeasance aimed at Congress and the FBI, renewed attention has been directed to questions of the distribution, allocation, and control of power. We recognize that questions of power cannot be totally differentiated from questions of individual freedom and liberty. The taxing and spending power of Congress and the President's power as Commander in Chief, for example, greatly affect the fundamental rights of millions of individuals. But such constitutional guarantees as freedom of expression, the right to personal privacy, and the safeguards of a fair trial are sufficiently distinct from positive grants of power to permit separate analysis.

Accordingly, we will examine the principal sources of constitutional power that Congress, the President, and the Supreme Court have employed to justify: (1) their respective claims of authority; (2) their coequal status as separate branches of government; (3) their attempted imposition of restrictions on each other; and (4) their mutual assertions of hegemony over the states. In many of the cases reproduced in the following pages, issues of individual rights will be apparent. But before it is possible to consider these issues adequately, it is necessary to have a clear understanding both of the federal Constitution as a conveyer of authoriy and of the methods of interpretation (especially those used by federal judges under the leadership of the Supreme Court) by which the powers of government have been subordinated to constitutional principles.

The Supreme Court has spelled out previously undefined provisions of constitutional authority that affect a number of vital areas of American life, and has defined in varying degrees both the substance and limits of such power. It has also recognized the enormous and still growing scope of legislative, executive, and administrative authority under such provisions as the Commerce Clause, the taxing and spending power, the Necessary and Proper Clause, the war power, and the power of appointment. Moreover, the Court has performed the delicate task of defining its own authority and that of the lower federal courts in relation to other branches and levels of government. A major objective of this introduction and the introductory essays in succeeding chapters is to analyze how the Supreme Court determines the nature and limits of constitutional power in each of these areas.

Judicial Review

A logical starting point in our analysis is the Supreme Court's power of *judicial review*. Often described as the cornerstone of our constitutional system, judicial review has enormous symbolic and practical influence on the American political system. Its character is a blend of the mystical and the practical. In the abstract, the term judicial review may be defined in several ways, but in American constitutional law it has a distinct meaning: It is the power of a court to determine whether an act of government is an exercise of constitutional authority and to strike down that act if it adjudges it to be unconstitutional. Judicial review is most often discussed in relation to the Supreme Court's invalidation of acts of Congress, but it is by no means confined to congressional legislation or to the Supreme Court alone. *Any act of government,* at least in theory, may be declared unconstitutional by any court of competent jurisdiction, if the act is appropriately challenged. Where the act is administrative, review is more likely to be confined to statutory construction. This means that the reviewing court will look first at the question of whether the administrative decision at issue was made within the authority of the administrative agency as defined by the statute that both created it and spelled out its duties. Even if the challenged administrative action is found to be consistent with statutory provisions, it may still be invalidated on constitutional grounds. Court review of administrative acts will be discussed more fully in Part V; it is important at this point simply to note the distinction between review for statutory construction and constitutional judicial review of administrative action. Finally, judicial decisions themselves are, of course, subject to review by higher courts; the Supreme Court may even reconsider and, in rare instances, overturn its own rulings. But this process should not be confused with judicial review as the central doctrine of American constitutional law, in which a court rules on the constitutionality of a legislative, executive, or administrative act at any level of government—national, state, or local—and invalidates or upholds that act.

Judicial Review and the Allocation of Power

Nixon Tapes Case (United States v. Nixon, 418 U.S. 683 [1974])

When the Supreme Court decided in 1974 that President Richard M. Nixon's claim of an absolute executive privilege of confidentiality in communications was subordinate to the constitutional requirements of due process of law in a criminal prosecution, it was exercising judicial review. This ruling, more than any single official pronouncement, proved to be the knockout punch in the impeachment fight and underscored dramatically the Supreme Court's long-recognized authority to declare the law with finality. Writing for a unanimous Court (Justice Rehnquist not participating), Chief Justice Warren E. Burger reminded the country, including the President who had appointed him five years before, that the Court had first asserted this power as early as 1803 with its landmark decision in *Marbury* v. *Madison* (1 Cranch 137). He quoted from the Court's opinion in *Marbury* in which Chief Justice John Marshall found it to be "emphatically the province and duty of the judicial department to say what the law is." It is true that Burger was applying this principle in a very different situation from that in which Marshall first invoked it. Marshall was referring to the Court's duty to declare a law invalid if it conflicted with a constitutional provision. Burger was asserting the exclusive power of the Supreme Court to reject a claim of constitutional power by a coordinate branch of government, in this instance personified by President Richard Nixon. Burger's expanded application of this principle simply served to emphasize the fundamental importance of judicial review as a living source of Supreme Court authority.

Marbury Decision

Ironically, the *Marbury* decision, like the Nixon Tapes controversy, raised the possibility of a head-on collision between the Supreme Court and the executive branch. The principle of judicial review was widely known when *Marbury* v. *Madison* was decided. Prior to the adoption of the federal Constitution, several state courts had used the power to invalidate legislation. This practice had continued after the establishment of the new government in 1789; and in 1796, the Supreme Court itself had in effect recognized the power by upholding a federal carriage tax as a constitutional exercise of congressional authority (*Hylton* v. *United States,* 3 Dall. 171). Nevertheless, *Marbury* v. *Madison* was the first case in which the Supreme Court in a published opinion invalidated an act of Congress on the ground that it violated the Constitution. Marshall reasoned that in light of the Court's "duty" to interpret the law and the proposition that the Constitution is superior to ordinary statutes in the hierarchy of laws, judicial review was inevitable. The Court could not, in other words, recognize the supremacy of the Constitution as provided by Article VI and exercise its judicial duty as prescribed in Article III without sooner or later ruling on the constitutionality of acts of government and striking them down if they conflicted with the basic law. Given his premises, Marshall's conclusions followed logically. But some of his contemporaries, Thomas Jefferson among them, did not accept those premises at all. Early critics of judicial review pointed out that the principle was not explicitly mentioned in the Constitution, even though it was in wide use when the Framers met in Philadelphia in 1787 and a number of them individually favored it. The critics also maintained that the President and Congress, no less than the Supreme Court, were required in their oaths of office to uphold the Constitution of the United States. In one of the most effective refutations of Marshall's position, Justice Gibson of the Pennsylvania Supreme Court contended in 1825 that each branch of government was ultimately responsible to the people for the constitutionality of its own acts (*Eakin* v. *Raub*, 12 Sergeant and Rawle 330). He maintained that the Supreme Court had no more authority to invalidate an act of Congress on constitutional grounds than Congress had to declare a Supreme Court decision unconstitutional. In the realm of logic and language, no final resolution of this issue over the legitimacy of judicial review has ever emerged. The weight of historical evidence seems to favor Marshall's position but it is not conclusive. What eventually established the *Marbury* decision and vindicated Marshall's understanding of the Supreme Court's "duty" was time coupled with experience. The lively academic debate over judicial review continued for well over a century after *Marbury* v. *Madison* was decided, and occasional revivals of the dispute continue to surface, as in the aftermath of the school desegregation decisions of the 1950s. But judicial review has proved to be a convenient mechanism by which Congress and the President can escape the political liability of final decisions on some of the toughest constitutional issues. Under a system of separation of powers, the constitutional escape valve that makes it possible to shift the burden of final decisions, short of constitutional amendment, from elected officials to appointed judges entitled in the subtle phrasing of the Constitution to serve "during good behavior," has proved very useful and attractive. In a broader, more symbolic sense, judicial review has also proved to be an important check upon vast governmental power in an ever-expanding, increasingly complex and impersonal governmental system.

Political Realities of the Power of Enforcement: A Key to Checks and Balances

It is important to recognize that judicial review is not an automatic instrument of government. Under the federal Constitution, the Supreme Court does not hand down advisory opinions. This restriction admittedly does not prevent it from giving advice at great length and on many subjects. However, the essential point is that before the Supreme Court or other courts in the American system can rule on the constitutionality of an act of government, that act must be "appropriately" challenged in an actual case or legal controversy. Most acts of government—legislative, executive, and administrative—are not formally challenged on constitutional grounds in court. But the power of judicial review is not altogether dependent on the frequency with which it is exercised. More important is acknowledgment by all branches of government that when a court—and particularly the United States Supreme Court—declares a law unconstitutional, that decision must be followed unless it is formally overruled by a constitutional amendment.

Nevertheless, as Alexander Hamilton noted in *The Federalist*, No. 78, the Supreme Court lacks the powers of "purse" and "sword." Although it can enforce its decisions against individuals and corporations and, to a lesser extent, against officials of state and local government, it cannot compel a coordinate branch of the national government to comply with its rulings.

Basis of Marshall's Opinion in the Marbury Decision

The point is well illustrated by Marshall's opinion in the *Marbury* decision itself. After the national election of 1800 in which the Federalist Administration of President John Adams was overwhelmingly defeated, it sought to enlarge its control of the federal judiciary. With the ready support of a lame-duck Federalist Congress, the Administration engineered passage of the Judiciary Act of 1801, which, among other things, greatly enlarged the number of judges at all levels of the national judicial system. This act included a provision for the appointment of justices of the peace (JP) for the District of Columbia. William Marbury received one of these JP appointments. Its was duly signed by President Adams and sealed by his Secretary of State John Marshall, but in the last-minute confusion occasioned by the change of administrations, Marshall did not deliver the commission. The new Secretary of State, James Madison, who succeeded to Marshall's old office just as the latter was assuming his new duties as Chief Justice, refused to deliver Marbury's commission as well as those of three other JP appointees for the District of Columbia. These four persons brought a suit in the United States Supreme Court seeking a judicial order, known as a writ of *mandamus,* that would compel Madison to hand over the commissions as part of his official duty.

Chief Justice Marshall did not remove himself from participation in this case even though his own failure to deliver the commissions had made the lawsuit possible. Moreover, he could have chosen to issue the writ of *mandamus,* basing his ruling on well-established principles of equity and the President's constitutional duty to "take care that the laws be faithfully executed." If Marshall had chosen to exercise judicial review in this fashion—that is, to hold that President Jefferson's Secretary of State had acted unconstitutionally as an executive officer in refusing to deliver the commissions—he would in all likelihood have had a losing battle on his hands. Jefferson had made it clear that any attempt to force the delivery of the commissions would be rejected by the new Administration. In fact, it was widely believed that if the Supreme Court issued the writ, impeachment proceedings would be brought against several of its members, including Marshall. The Federalist-dominated Court was already under attack for the statements and actions of at least one of its members, Justice Samuel Chase, in connection with the controversial Alien and Sedition Acts passed during the Adams Administration and assailed by Jefferson and his supporters in the campaign of 1800. (At the time that *Marbury* v. *Madison* was decided, a movement was under way to impeach Chase, and that effort bore fruit in 1804. In that year Chase was impeached, but he was acquitted by a narrow margin in the Senate. See Swisher, 1954, p. 101; Warren, 1926, pp. 279–292.)

Marshall was a political realist as well as a judicial craftsman of great skill. He managed to combine these qualities by asserting the power of judicial review while avoiding a confrontation with his distant cousin and bitter political enemy, President Jefferson. Simply stated, Marshall held that Congress, in giving the Supreme Court the authority to issue writs of *mandamus,* had enlarged by statute the

Court's original jurisdiction as defined by Article III of the Constitution. But, Marshall ruled, the Court lacked jurisdiction in this case because the nature of jurisdiction was determined by the Constitution, not by an act of Congress. Congress could fill in important jurisdictional details and had done so in the Judiciary Act of 1789. But it could not make changes in the basic constitutional distinction drawn by Article III between the Court's original and appellate jurisdiction. Marshall ruled that Section 13 of the 1789 Judiciary Act conflicted with the constitutional specification of the Court's original jurisdiction and was therefore invalid. Many scholars contend that Marshall's reading of Section 13 was contrived—that the words of the statute did not in fact expand the Court's original jurisdiction beyond the limits imposed by Article III of the Constitution. If this viewpoint is correct, Marshall's ability as a political strategist is brought into even sharper focus.

The Supreme Court's power to declare an act of Congress unconstitutional was not exercised again until *Scott* v. *Sanford** in 1857 (19 How. 393). In the meantime, however, Chief Justice Marshall and his colleagues extended the principle of judicial review to state legislation deemed in conflict with the federal Constitution (*Fletcher* v. *Peck,* 6 Cranch 87 [1810]). The Court also established its authority to overrule decisions of the highest appellate state court on questions of federal statutory and constitutional interpretation (*Martin* v. *Hunter's Lessee,* 2 Wheat. 304 [1816]; *Cohens* v. *Virginia,* 6 Wheat. 264 [1821]; see Pritchett, 1977, pp. 52–53, 116 for more detail).

In *Scott* v. *Sanford* Chief Justice Taney and a majority of his colleagues made the serious political blunder of injecting themselves into the center of the slavery controversy and picking what turned out to be the losing side. The pro-slavery decision, authored by the Chief Justice, held that blacks were not citizens under the Constitution and that the Missouri Compromise, by which Congress sought to regulate slavery in United States territories, was unconstitutional. This decision—which produced the resignation of Justice Curtis, one of the two dissenters—quickly became a target of attack by abolitionists and was ultimately undermined by the outcome of the Civil War. It was formally overruled by the adoption of the Thirteenth Amendment, abolishing slavery, and the Fourteenth Amendment, which, among other things, removed race as a factor in determining citizenship.

Even the near disaster of the Dred Scott Case did not destroy the institution of judicial review. Occasionally the Court has been imprudent in exercising this power, as when it departed from precedent in 1895 and declared a federal income tax unconstitutional (*Pollock* v. *Farmers' Loan & Trust Co.,* 158 U.S. 601); that decision was overruled in 1913 by the adoption of the Sixteenth Amendment. Sometimes the Court has failed to discern basic shifts in national values and priorities. Because its exercise of judicial review depends in large part on the willingness of the President and Congress to go along with its decisions, the Court cannot afford to lose touch with major social and political changes within the American polity. It ran into problems of this kind in the mid-1930s when it invalidated most of the economic and social reform measures adopted during the first phase of President Roosevelt's New Deal. The Court's dramatic change of direction in 1937 (discussed in Chapter 2) averted a major presidential challenge to Supreme Court autonomy.

---

* Commonly referred to as the Dred Scott Case.

Far more often the Court has used the power of judicial review with care and self-restraint. Over the years the result has been largely positive from the standpoint of its authority and prestige.

Impact of Judicial Review

With few exceptions, the Supreme Court's use of judicial review has been restricted to issues of public policy outside the fields of international relations and military affairs. In addition, the Court has exercised this power much more often in considering the constitutionality of state legislation than in determining whether acts of Congress are constitutional. As we shall see in Part IV, judicial review has played a critical part in the Supreme Court's work as "arbiter of the federal system"—that is, in determining the allocation of constitutional authority between the states and the national government.

Although used sparingly with respect to national issues, judicial review has figured prominently in many of the controversies dividing the American people during the past 175 years. Besides sharing the limelight in the slavery, income tax, and New Deal controversies, judicial review played a significant role in such issues as: the national regulation of child labor during and immediately after World War I; minimum wage legislation in the 1920s; federal protection of civil rights in the 1960s and 1970s; and the lowering of the minimum voting age to eighteen—resolved with adoption of the Twenty-sixth Amendment in 1971. In all of these areas the Supreme Court had occasion to rule either positively or negatively on the constitutionality of broad vital programs of national policy.

At the state level the Supreme Court's exercise of judicial review has been most important in such fields as economic regulation, freedom of expression, educational policy, criminal procedure, and personal privacy. The public school desegregation cases of 1954 illustrate the importance of judicial review at the state level. In *Brown* v. *Board of Education,* 347 U.S. 483 (1954) and its three companion cases from Delaware, South Carolina, and Virginia, the Supreme Court invalidated state laws requiring racial segregation of public school students on grounds that these statutes violated the Equal Protection Clause of the Fourteenth Amendment. An identical federal requirement for public schools in the District of Columbia was invalidated the same day as a violation of the Due Process Clause of the Fifth Amendment in *Bolling* v. *Sharpe,* 347 U.S. 497. By clear implication, which was not seriously questioned at the time even by the most vocal critics of the decision, the *Brown* ruling condemned school segregation statutes wherever they existed in the country, not merely in the states directly involved in the 1954 litigation. The force of this historic decision was underscored four years later with the dramatic ruling in *Cooper* v. *Aaron,* 358 U.S. 1 (1958): the Court issued a stern rebuke to Arkansas Governor Orville Faubus, who had attempted to block the initial steps to desegregate Central High School in Little Rock.

In the important field of legislative apportionment the Supreme Court's exercise of judicial review has brought about significant changes in the composition of the United States House of Representatives, most state legislatures, and thousands of local elective bodies. For a number of years the Court utilized the "political questions" doctrine (discussed more fully in Chapter 3) as a rationale for avoiding the reapportionment controversy. By the early 1960s, however, controversy over this issue had intensified considerably without producing effective responses from the legislative and executive branches. Sounding the theme of "judicial activism" that characterized the Warren Court of the 1960s, Justice Brennan in the pivotal case of *Baker* v. *Carr,* 369 U.S. 186 (1962) held that the issue of state legislative reapportionment was "justiciable," that is, amenable to judicial decision, and that it involved individual rights protected by the federal Constitution. This conclusion was soon applied to congressional as well as to state legislative redistricting and served as the basis for the "one person, one vote" standard now applied to most representative governing bodies throughout the country (see Cortner, 1970; Dixon, 1968).

In sum, judicial review touches all aspects of American constitutional law. It characterizes the function of the federal judiciary, and in particular the Supreme Court, in formulating public policy by gauging acts of government against the yardstick of the Constitution. In a very real sense, the power of judicial review thus depends on its acceptance by nonjudicial branches of government. But the symbolic authority implicit in this recognition of the Court's legitimating function within the constitutional system merges into practical and immediate authority when familiar institutional patterns appear threatened. This fact was brought home with sharp clarity during the Watergate crisis. The Court's decisive, if limited, ruling in the Tapes Case underscored the fact that judicial review is central to the doctrine of checks and balances and to the Court's pivotal role in giving contemporary meaning to constitutional principles.

Marbury v. *Madison*

1 Cranch 137 (1803)

MR. CHIEF JUSTICE MARSHALL delivered the opinion of the Court.

• • •

In the order in which the court has viewed this subject, the following questions have been considered and decided: 1st. Has the applicant [Marbury] a right to the commission he demands? 2d. If he has a right, and that right has been violated, do the laws of his country afford him a remedy? 3d. If they do afford him a remedy, is it a *mandamus* issuing from this court?

The first object of inquiry is—Has the applicant a right to the commission he demands? His right originates in an act of congress passed in February 1801, concerning the district of Columbia. . . . "that there shall be appointed in and for each of the said counties, such number of discreet persons to be justices of the peace, as the president of the United States shall, from time to time, think expedient, to continue in office for five years."

It appears, from the affidavits, that, in compliance with this law, a commission for William Marbury, as a justice of peace for the county of Washington, was signed by John Adams, then President of the United States; after which, the seal of the United States was affixed to it; but the commission has never reached the person for whom it was made out. In order to determine whether he is entitled to this commission, it becomes necessary to inquire, whether he has been appointed to the office. For if he has been appointed, the law continues him in office for five years, and he is entitled to the possession of those evidences of office, which, being completed, became his property.

[Marshall proceeds to identify the three stages he perceives as necessary to acquire the designation of "officer of the United States": nomination, appointment, and commission. He concludes:]

Mr. Marbury, then, since his commission was signed by the president, and sealed by the secretary of state, was appointed; and as the law creating the office, gave the officer a right to hold for five years, independent of the executive, the appointment was not revocable, but vested in the officer legal rights, which are protected by the laws of his country. To withhold his commission, therefore, is an act deemed by the court not warranted by law, but violative of a vested legal right.

. . . This brings us to the second inquiry; which is: If he has a right, and that right has been violated, do the laws of his country afford him a remedy?

The very essence of civil liberty certainly consists in the right of every individual to claim the protection of the laws, whenever he receives an injury. One of the first duties of government is to afford that protection. In Great Britain, the king himself is sued in the respectful form of a petition, and he never fails to comply with the judgment of his court.

•   •   •

The government of the United States has been emphatically termed a government of laws, and not of men. It will certainly cease to deserve this high appellation, if the laws furnish no remedy for the violation of a vested legal right. . . .

It behooves us, then, to inquire whether there be in its composition any ingredient which shall exempt it from legal investigation, or exclude the injured party from legal redress. . . .

. . . Is the act of delivering or withholding a commission to be considered as a mere political act, belonging to the executive department alone, for the performance of which entire confidence is placed by our constitution in the supreme executive; and for any misconduct respecting which, the injured individual has no remedy? That there may be such cases is not to be questioned; but that every act of duty, to be performed in any of the great departments of government, constitutes such a case, is not to be admitted.

•   •   •

. . . [W]hether the legality of an act of the head of a department be examinable in a court of justice or not, must always depend on the nature of that act. If some acts be examinable, and others not, there must be some rule of law to guide the court in the exercise of its jurisdiction. In some instances, there may be difficulty in applying the rule to particular cases; but there cannot, it is believed, be much difficulty in laying down the rule.

By the constitution of the United States, the president is invested with certain important political powers, in the exercise of which he is to use his own discretion, and is accountable only to his country in his political character, and to his own conscience. To aid him in the performance of these duties, he is authorized to appoint certain officers, who act by his authority, and in conformity with his orders. In such cases, their acts are his acts; and whatever opinion may be entertained of the manner in which executive discretion may be used, still there exists, and can exist, no power to control that discretion. The subjects are political: they respect the nation, not individual rights, and being entrusted to the executive, the decision of the executive is conclusive. . . .

The conclusion from this reasoning is, that where the heads of departments are the political or confidential agents of the executive, merely to execute the will of the president, or rather to act in cases in which the executive possesses a constitutional or legal discretion, nothing can be more perfectly clear, than that their acts are only politically examinable. But where a specific duty is assigned by law, and individual rights depend upon the performance of that duty, it seems equally clear, that the individual who considers himself injured, has a right to resort to the laws of his country for a remedy.

If this be the rule, let us inquire, how it applies to the case under the consideration of the court. The power of nominating to the senate, and the power of appointing the person nominated, are political powers, to be exercised by the president, according to his own discretion. When he has made an appointment, he has exercised his whole power, and his discretion has been completely applied to the case. . . . But as a fact which has existed, cannot be made never to have existed, the appointment cannot be annihilated; . . . the rights he has acquired are protected by the law, and are not resumable by the president. They cannot be extinguished by executive authority, and he has the privilege of asserting them in like manner, as if they had been derived from any other source.

The question whether a right has vested or not, is, in its nature, judicial, and must be tried by the judicial authority. . . .

It is, then, the opinion of the Court: 1st. That by signing the commission of Mr. Marbury, the President of the United States appointed him a justice of peace for the county of Washington, in the district of Columbia; and that the seal of the United States, affixed thereto by the secretary of state, is conclusive testimony of the verity of the signature, and of the completion of the appointment; and that the appointment conferred on him a legal right to the office for the space of five years. 2d. That, having this legal title to the office, he has a consequent right to the commission; a refusal to deliver which is a plain violation of that right, for which the laws of his country afford him a remedy.

. . . It remains to be inquired whether he is entitled to the remedy for which he applies? This depends on—1st. The nature of the writ applied for; and 2d. The power of this court.

[After a lengthy discussion of the nature of the writ of *mandamus* and its historical basis, Marshall continues:]

It is not by the office of the person to whom the writ is directed, but the nature of the thing to be done, that the propriety or impropriety of issuing a *mandamus* is to be determined. Where the head of a department acts in a case, in which executive discretion is to be exercised; in which he is the mere organ of executive will; it is again repeated, that any application to a court to control, in any respect, his conduct would be rejected without hestitation. But where he is directed by law to do a certain act, affecting the absolute rights of individuals, in the performance of which he is not placed under the particular direction of the president, and the performance of which the president cannot lawfully forbid, and therefore, is never presumed to have forbidden; . . . it is not perceived, on what ground the courts of the country are further excused from the duty of giving judgment that right be done to an injured individual, than if the same services were to be performed by a person not the head of a department.

. . .

It is true, that the *mandamus*, now moved for, is not for the performance of an act expressly enjoined by statute. It is to deliver a commission; on which subject, the acts of congress are silent. This difference is not considered as affecting the case. It has already been stated, that the applicant has, to that commission, a vested legal right, of which the executive cannot deprive him. He has been appointed to an office, from which he is not removable at the will of the executive; and being so appointed, he has a right to the commission which the secretary has received from the president for his use. The act of congress does not indeed order the secretary of state to send it to him, but it is placed in his hands for the person entitled to it; and cannot be more lawfully withheld by him, than by any other person.

. . .

This, then, is a plain case for a *mandamus*, either to deliver the commission, or a copy of it from the record; and it only remains to be inquired, whether it can issue from this court?

The act [the Judiciary Act of 1789] to establish the judicial courts of the United States authorizes the supreme court, "to issue writs of *mandamus*, in cases warranted by the principles and usages of law, to any courts appointed or persons holding office, under the authority of the United States" [Section 13]. The secretary of state, being a person holding an office under the authority of the United States, is precisely within the letter of this description; and if this court is not authorized to issue a writ of *mandamus* to such an officer, it must be because the law is unconstitutional, and therefore, absolutely incapable of conferring the authority, and assigning the duties which its words purport to confer and assign.

The constitution vests the whole judicial power of the United States in one supreme court, and such inferior courts as congress shall, from time to time, ordain and establish. This power is expressly extended to all cases arising under the laws of the United States; and consequently, in some form, may be exercised over the present case; because the right claimed is given by a law of the United States.

In the distribution of this power, it is declared, that "the supreme court shall have original jurisdiction, in all cases affecting ambassadors, other public ministers and consuls, and those in which a state shall be a party. In all other cases, the supreme court shall have appellate jurisdiction." It has been insisted, at the bar, that as the original grant of jurisdiction to the supreme and inferior courts, is general, and the clause, assigning original jurisdiction to the supreme court, contains no negative or restrictive words, the power remains to the legislature, to assign original jurisdiction to that court, in other cases than those specified in the article which has been recited; provided those cases belong to the judicial power of the United States.

If it had been intended to leave it in the discretion of the legislature, to apportion the judicial power between the supreme and inferior courts, according to the will of that body, it would certainly have been useless to have proceeded further than to have defined the judicial power, and the tribunals in which it should be vested. The subsequent part of the section is mere surplusage—is entirely without meaning, if such is to be the construction. If congress remains at liberty to give this court appellate jurisdiction, where the constitution has declared their jurisdiction shall be original; and original jurisdiction where the constitution has declared it shall be appellate; the distribution of jurisdiction, made in the constitution, is form without substance. Affirmative words are often, in their operation, negative of other objects than those affirmed; and in this case, a negative or exclusive sense must be given to them, or they have no operation at all.

It cannot be presumed, that any clause in the constitution is intended to be without effect; and therefore, such a construction is inadmissible, unless the words require it. If the solicitude of the convention, respecting our peace with foreign powers, induced a provision that the supreme court should take original jurisdiction in cases which might be supposed to affect them; yet the clause would have proceeded no further than to provide for such cases, if no further restriction on the powers of congress had been intended. That they should have appellate jurisdiction in all other cases, with such exceptions as congress might make, is no restriction; unless the words be deemed exclusive of original jurisdiction.

When an instrument organizing, fundamentally, a judicial system, divides it into one supreme, and so many inferior courts as the legislature may ordain and establish; then enumerates its powers, and proceeds so far to distribute them, as to define the jurisdiction of the supreme court, by declaring the cases in which it shall take original jurisdiction, and that in others it shall take appellate jurisdiction, the plain import of the words seems to be, that in one class of cases, its jurisdiction is original, and not appellate; in the other, it is appellate, and not original. If any other construction would render the clause inoperative, that is an additional reason for rejecting such other construction, and for adhering to their obvious meaning. To enable this court, then, to issue a *mandamus,* it must be shown to be an exercise of appellate jurisdiction, or to be necessary to enable them to exercise appellate jurisdiction.

It has been stated at the bar, that the appellate jurisdiction may be exercised in a variety of forms, and that if it be the will of the legislature that a *mandamus* should be used for that purpose, that will must be obeyed. This is true, yet the jurisdiction must be appellate, not original. It is the essential criterion of appellate jurisdiction, that it revises and corrects the proceedings in a cause already instituted, and does not create that cause. Although, therefore, a *mandamus* may be directed to courts, yet to issue such a writ to an officer, for the delivery of a paper, is, in effect, the same as to sustain an original action for that paper, and therefore, seems not to belong to appellate, but to original jurisdiction. Neither is it necessary in such a case as this, to enable the court to exercise its appellate jurisdiction. The authority, therefore, given to the supreme court by the act establishing the judicial courts of the United States, to issue writs of *mandamus* to public officers, appears not to be warranted by the constitution; and it becomes necessary to inquire, whether a jurisdiction so conferred can be exercised.

The question, whether an act, repugnant to the constitution, can become the law of the land, is a question deeply interesting to the United States; but, happily, not of an intricacy proportioned to its interest. It seems only necessary to recognise certain principles, supposed to have been long and well established, to decide it. That the people have an original right to establish, for their future government, such principles as, in their opinion, shall most conduce to their own happiness, is the basis on which the whole American fabric has been erected. The exercise of this original right is a very great exertion; nor can it, nor ought it, to be frequently repeated. The principles, therefore, so established, are deemed fundamental: and as the authority from which they proceed is supreme, and can seldom act, they are designed to be permanent.

This original and supreme will organizes the government, and assigns to different departments their respective powers. It may either stop here, or establish certain limits not to be transcended by those departments. The government of the United States is of the latter description. The powers of the legislature are defined and limited; and that those limits may not be mistaken or forgotten, the constitution is written. To what purpose are powers limited, and to what purpose is that limitation committed to writing, if these limits may, at any time, be passed by those intended to be restrained? The distinction between a government with limited and unlimited powers is abolished, if those limits do not confine the persons on whom they are imposed, and if acts prohibited and acts allowed, are of equal obligation. It is a proposition too plain to be contested, that the constitution controls any legislative act repugnant to it; or that the legislature may alter the constitution by an ordinary act.

Between these alternatives, there is no middle ground. The constitution is either a superior paramount law, unchangeable by ordinary means, or it is on a level with ordinary legislative acts, and, like other acts, is alterable when the legislature shall please to alter it. If the former part of the alternative be true, then a legislative act, contrary to the constitution, is not law: if the latter part be true, then written constitutions are absurd attempts, on the part of the people, to limit a power, in its own nature, illimitable.

Certainly, all those who have framed written constitutions contemplate them as forming the fundamental and paramount law of the nation, and consequently, the theory of every such government must be, that an act of the legislature, repugnant to the constitution, is void. This theory is essentially attached to a written constitution, and is, consequently, to be considered, by this court, as one of the fundamental principles of our society. It is not, therefore, to be lost sight of, in the further consideration of this subject.

If an act of the legislature, repugnant to the constitution, is void, does it, notwithstanding its invalidity, bind the courts, and oblige them to give it effect? Or, in other words, though it be not law, does it constitute a rule as operative as if it was a law? This would be to overthrow, in fact, what was established in theory; and would seem, at first view, an absurdity too gross to be insisted on. It shall, however, receive a more attentive consideraton.

It is, emphatically, the province and duty of the judicial department, to say what the law is. Those who apply the rule to particular cases, must of necessity expound and interpret that rule. If two laws conflict with each other, the courts must decide on the operation of each. So, if a law be in opposition to the constitution; if both the law and the constitution apply to a particular case, so that the court must either decide that case, conformable to the law, disregarding the constitution; or conformable to the constitution, disregarding the law; the court must determine which of these conflicting rules governs the case: this is of the very essence of judicial duty. If then, the courts are to regard the constitution, and the constitution is superior to any ordinary act of the legislature, the constitution, and not such ordinary act, must govern the case to which they both apply.

Those, then, who controvert the principle, that the constitution is to be considered, in court, as a paramount law, are reduced to the necessity of maintaining that courts must close their eyes on the constitution, and see only the law. This doctrine would subvert the very foundation of all written constitutions. It would declare that an act which, according to the principles and theory of our government, is entirely void, is yet, in practice, completely obligatory. It would declare, that if the legislature shall do what is expressly forbidden, such act, notwithstanding the express prohibition, is in reality effectual. It would be giving to the legislature a practical and real omnipotence, with the same breath which professes to restrict their powers within narrow limits. It is prescribing limits, and declaring that those limits may be passed at pleasure. That it thus reduces to nothing, what we have deemed the greatest improvement on political institutions, a written constitution, would, of itself, be sufficient, in America, where written constitutions have been viewed with so much reverence, for rejecting the constitution. But the peculiar expressions of the constitution of the United States furnish additional arguments in favor of its rejection. The judicial power of the United States is extended to all cases arising under the constitution. Could it be the intention of those who gave this power, to say, that in using it, the constitution should not be looked into? That a case arising under the constitution should be decided, without examining the instrument under which it arises? This is too extravagant to be maintained. In some cases, then, the constitution must be looked into by the judges. And if they can open it at all, what part of it are they forbidden to read or to obey?

. . .

. . . [I]t is apparent, that the framers of the constitution contemplated that instrument as a rule for the government of courts, as well as of the legislature. Why otherwise does it direct the judges to take an oath to support it? This oath certainly applies in an especial manner, to their conduct in their official character. How immoral to impose it on them, if they were to be used as the instruments, and the knowing instruments, for violating what they swear to support!

. . . Why does a judge swear to discharge his duties agreeably to the constitution of the United States, if that constitution forms no rule for his government? if it is closed upon him, and cannot be inspected by him? If such be the real state of things, this is worse than solemn mockery. To prescribe, or to take this oath, becomes equally a crime.

It is also not entirely unworthy of observation, that in declaring what shall be the supreme law of the land, the constitution itself is first mentioned; and not the laws of the United States, generally, but those only which shall be made in pursuance of the constitution, have that rank.

Thus, the particular phraseology of the constitution of the United States confirms and strengthens the principle, supposed to be essential to all written constitutions, that a law repugnant to the constitution is void; and that courts, as well as other departments, are bound by that instrument.

The rule must be discharged.

United States v. Nixon

418 U.S. 683 (1974)

Mr. Chief Justice Burger delivered the opinion of the Court.

[This case presents] for review the denial of a motion, filed on behalf of the President of the United States, . . . to quash a third-party subpoena *duces tecum* issued by the United States District Court for the District of Columbia. * * * The subpoena directed the President to produce certain tape recordings and documents relating to his conversations with aides and advisers. The court rejected the President's claims of absolute executive privilege, of lack of jurisdiction. . . . The President appealed to the Court of Appeals. We granted the United States' petition for certiorari before judgment . . . because of the public importance of the issues presented and the need for their prompt resolution. * * *

On March 1, 1974, a grand jury of the United States District Court for the District of Columbia returned an indictment charging seven named individuals with various offenses, including conspiracy to defraud the United States and to obstruct justice. Although he was not designated as such in the indictment, the grand jury named the President, among others, as an unindicted co-conspirator. On April 18, 1974, upon motion of the Special Prosecutor, . . . a subpoena *duces tecum* was issued * * * to the President by the United States District Court and made returnable on May 2, 1974. This subpoena required the production, in advance of the September 9 trial date, of certain tapes, memoranda, papers, transcripts, or other writings relating to certain precisely identified meetings between the President and others. The Special Prosecutor was able to fix the time, place and persons present at these discussions because the White House daily logs and appointment records had been delivered to him. On April 30, the President publicly released edited transcripts of 43 conversations; portions of 20 conversations subject to subpoena in the present case were included. On May 1, 1974, the President's counsel, filed a "special appearance" and a motion to quash the subpoena. * * * This motion was accompanied by a formal claim of privilege. . . .

May 20, 1974, the District Court denied the motion to quash. . . . It further ordered "the President or any subordinate officer, official or employee with custody or control of the documents or objects subpoenaed," * * * to deliver to the District Court, on or before May 31, 1974, the originals of all subpoenaed items, as well as an index and analysis of those items, together with tape copies of those portions of the subpoenaed recordings for which transcripts had been released to the public by the President on April 30. The District Court rejected jurisdictional challenges based on a contention that the dispute was nonjusticiable because it was between the Special Prosecutor and the Chief Executive and hence "intra-executive" in character; it also rejected the contention that the judiciary was without authority to review an assertion of executive privilege by the President. The court's rejection of the first challenge was based on the authority and powers vested in the Special Prosecutor by the regulation promulgated by the Attorney General; the court concluded that a justiciable controversy was presented. . . .

The District Court held that the judiciary, not the President, was the final arbiter of a claim of executive privilege. The court concluded that, under the circumstances of this case, the presumptive privilege was overcome by the Special Prosecutor's prima facie "demonstration of need sufficiently compelling to warrant judicial examination in chambers . . . ." * * *

. . .

Justiciability

In the District Court, the President's counsel argued that the court lacked jurisdiction to issue the subpoena because the matter was an intra-branch dispute between a subordinate and superior officer of the Executive Branch and hence not subject to judicial resolution. That argument has been renewed in this Court with emphasis on the contention that the dispute does not present a "case" or "controversy" which can be adjudicated in the federal courts. The President's counsel argues that the federal courts should not intrude into areas committed to the other branches of Government. He views the present dispute as essentially a "jurisdictional" dispute within the Executive Branch which he analogizes to a dispute between two congressional committees. Since the Executive Branch has exclusive authority and absolute discretion to decide whether to prosecute a case, * * * it is contended that a President's decision is final in determining what evidence is to be used in a given criminal case. Although his counsel concedes the President has delegated certain specific powers to the Special Prosecutor, he has not "waived nor delegated to the Special Prosecutor the President's duty to claim privilege as to all materials . . . which fall within the President's inherent authority to refuse to disclose to any executive officer." * * * The Special Prosecutor's demand for the items therefore presents, in the view of the President's counsel, a political question under *Baker* v. *Carr,* 369 U.S. 186 (1962), since it involves a "textually demonstrable" grant of power under Art. II.

The mere assertion of a claim of an "intra-branch dispute," without more, has never operated to defeat federal jurisdiction; justiciability does not depend on such a surface inquiry. . . .

Our starting point is the nature of the proceeding for which the evidence is sought—here a pending criminal prosecution. It is a judicial proceeding in a federal court alleging violation of federal laws and is brought in the name of the United States as sovereign. * * * Under the authority of Art. II, § 2, Congress has vested in the Attorney General the power to conduct the criminal litigation of the United States Government. * * * It has also vested in him the power to appoint subordinate officers to assist him in the discharge of his duties. * * * Acting pursuant to those statutes, the Attorney General has delegated the authority to represent the United States in these particular matters to a Special Prosecutor with unique authority and tenure. The regulation gives the Special Prosecutor explicit power to contest the invocation of executive privilege in the process of seeking evidence deemed relevant to the performance of these specially delegated duties. * * *

• • •

. . . So long as this regulation remains in force the Executive Branch is bound by it, and indeed the United States as the sovereign composed of the three branches is bound to respect and to enforce it. Moreover, the delegation of authority to the Special Prosecutor in this case is not an ordinary delegation by the Attorney General to a subordinate officer: with the authorization of the President, the Acting Attorney General provided in the regulation that the Special Prosecutor was not to be removed without the "consensus" of eight designated leaders of Congress. * * *

The demands of and the resistance to the subpoena present an obvious controversy in the ordinary sense, but that alone is not sufficient to meet constitutional standards. In the constitutional sense, controversy means more than disagreement and conflict; rather it means the kind of controversy courts traditionally resolve. Here at issue is the production or nonproduction of specified evidence deemed by the Special Prosecutor to be relevant and admissible in a pending criminal case. It is sought by one official of the Government within the scope of his express authority; it is resisted by the Chief Executive on the ground of his duty to preserve the confidentiality of the communications of the President. Whatever the correct answer on the merits, these issues are "of a type which are traditionally justiciable." . . .

In light of the uniqueness of the setting in which the conflict arises, the fact that both parties are officers of the Executive Branch cannot be viewed as a barrier to justiciability. It would be inconsistent with the applicable law and regulation and the unique facts of this case to conclude other than that the Special Prosecutor has standing to bring this action and that a justiciable controversy is presented for decision.

• • •

The Claim of Privilege

A

. . . [W]e turn to the claim that the subpoena should be quashed because it demands "confidential conversations between a President and his close advisors that it would be inconsistent with the public interest to produce." * * * The first contention is a broad claim that the separation of powers doctrine precludes judicial review of a President's claim of privilege. The second contention is that if he does not prevail on the claim of absolute privilege, the court should hold as a matter of constitutional law that the privilege prevails over the subpoena *duces tecum.*

In the performance of assigned constitutional duties each branch of the Government must initially interpret the Constitution, and the interpretation of its powers by any branch is due great respect from the others. The President's counsel, as we have noted, reads the Constitution as providing an absolute privilege of confidentiality for all presidential communications. Many decisions of this Court, however, have unequivocally reaffirmed the holding of *Marbury* v. *Madison* * * * that "it is emphatically the province and duty of the judicial department to say what the law is." * * *

No holding of the Court has defined the scope of judicial power specifically relating to the enforcement of a subpoena for confidential presidential communications for use in a criminal prosecution, but other exercises of powers by the Executive Branch and the Legislative Branch have been found invalid as in conflict with the Constitution. . . . Since this Court has consistently exercised the power to construe and delineate claims arising under express powers, it must follow that the Court has authority to interpret claims with respect to powers alleged to derive from enumerated powers.

Our system of government "requires that federal courts on occasion interpret the Constitution in a manner at variance with the construction given the document by another branch." *Powell* v. *McCormack* * * * And in *Baker* v. *Carr* * * * the Court stated:

> "[d]eciding whether a matter has in any measure been committed by the Constitution to another branch of government, or whether the action of that branch exceeds whatever authority has been committed, is itself a delicate exercise in constitutional interpretation, and is a responsibility of this Court as ultimate interpreter of the Constitution."

Notwithstanding the deference each branch must accord the others, the "judicial power of the United States" vested in the federal courts by Art. III, § 1 of the Constitution can no more be shared with the Executive Branch than the Chief Executive, for example, can share with the Judiciary the veto power, or the Congress share with the Judiciary the power to override a presidential veto. Any other conclusion would be contrary to the basic concept of separation of powers and the checks and balances that flow from the scheme of a tripartite government. * * * We therefore reaffirm that it is "emphatically the province and the duty" of this Court "to say what the law is" with respect to the claim of privilege presented in this case. * * *

B

In support of his claim of absolute privilege, the President's counsel urges two grounds one of which is common to all governments and one of which is peculiar to our system of separation of powers. The first ground is the valid need for protection of communications between high government officials and those who advise and assist them in the performance of their manifold duties; the importance of this confidentiality is too plain to require further discussion. Human experience teaches that those who expect public dissemination of their remarks may well temper candor with a concern for appearances and for their own interests to the detriment of the decisionmaking process. Whatever the nature of the privilege of confidentiality of presidential communications in the exercise of Art. II powers the privilege can be said to derive from the supremacy of each branch within its own assigned area of constitutional duties. Certain powers and privileges flow from the nature of enumerated powers; the protection of the confidentiality of presidential communications has similar constitutional underpinnings.

The second ground asserted by the President's counsel in support of the claim of absolute privilege rests on the doctrine of separation of powers. Here it is argued that the independence of the Executive Branch within its own sphere * * * insulates a president from a judicial subpoena in an ongoing criminal prosecution, and thereby protects confidential presidential communications.

However, neither the doctrine of separation of powers, nor the need for confidentiality of high level communications, without more, can sustain an absolute, unqualified presidential privilege of immunity from judicial process under all circumstances. The President's need for complete candor and objectivity from advisers calls for great deference from the courts. However, when the privilege depends solely on the broad, undifferentiated claim of public interest in the confidentiality of such conversations, a confrontation with other values arises. Absent a claim of need to protect military, diplomatic or sensitive national security secrets, we find it difficult to accept the argument that even the very important interest in confidentiality of presidential communications is significantly diminished by production of such material for *in camera* inspection with all the protection that a district court will be obliged to provide.

The impediment that an absolute, unqualified privilege would place in the way of the primary constitutional duty of the Judicial Branch to do justice in criminal prosecutions would plainly conflict with the function of the courts under Art. III. In designing the structure of our Government and dividing and allocating the sovereign power among three coequal branches, the Framers of the Constitution sought to provide a comprehensive system, but the separate powers were not intended to operate with absolute independence. . . . To read the Art. II powers of the President as providing an absolute privilege as against a subpoena essential to enforcement of criminal statutes on no more than a generalized claim of the public interest in confidentiality of nonmilitary and nondiplomatic discussions would upset the constitutional balance of "a workable government" and gravely impair the role of the courts under Art. III.

C

Since we conclude that the legitimate needs of the judicial process may outweigh presidential privilege, it is necessary to resolve those competing interests in a manner that preserves the essential functions of each branch. The right and indeed the duty to resolve that question does not free the judiciary from according high respect to the representations made on behalf of the President. * * *

The expectation of a President to the confidentiality of his conversations and correspondence, like the claim of confidentiality of judicial deliberations, for example, has all the values to which we accord deference for the privacy of all citizens and added to those values the necessity for protection of the public interest in candid, objective, and even blunt or harsh opinions in presidential decisionmaking. A President and those who assist him must be free to explore alternatives in the process of shaping policies and making decisions and to do so in a way many would be unwilling to express except privately. These are the considerations justifying a presumptive privilege for presidential communications. The privilege is fundamental to the operation of government and inextricably rooted in the separation of powers under the Constitution. . . .

But this presumptive privilege must be considered in light of our historic commitment to the rule of law. . . . We have elected to employ an adversary system of criminal justice in which the parties contest all issues before a court of law. The need to develop all relevant facts in the adversary system is both fundamental and comprehensive. The ends of criminal justice would be defeated if judgments were to be founded on a partial or speculative presentation of the facts. The very integrity of the judicial system and public confidence in the system depend on full disclosure of all the facts, within the framework of the rules of evidence. To ensure that justice is done, it is imperative to the function of courts that compulsory process be available for the production of evidence needed either by the prosecution or by the defense.

• • •

In this case the President challenges a subpoena served on him as a third party requiring the production of materials for use in a criminal prosecution on the claim that he has a privilege against disclosure of confidential communications. He does not place his claim of privilege on the ground they are military or diplomatic secrets. As to these areas of Art. II duties the courts have traditionally shown the utmost deference to presidential responsibilities. . . . No case of the Court, however, has extended this high degree of deference to a President's generalized interest in confidentiality. Nowhere in the Constitution, as we have noted earlier, is there any explicit reference to a privilege of confidentiality, yet to the extent this interest relates to the effective discharge of a President's powers, it is constitutionally based.

The right to the production of all evidence at a criminal trial similarly has constitutional dimensions. The Sixth Amendment explicitly confers upon every defendant in a criminal trial the right "to be confronted with the witnesses against him" and "to have compulsory process for obtaining witnesses in his favor." Moreover, the Fifth Amendment also guarantees that no person shall be deprived of liberty without due process of law. It is the manifest duty of the courts to vindicate those guarantees and to accomplish that it is essential that all relevant and admissible evidence be produced.

In this case we must weigh the importance of the general privilege of confidentiality of presidential communications in performance of his responsibilities against the inroads of such a privilege on the fair administration of criminal justice. The interest in preserving confidentiality is weighty indeed and entitled to great respect. However, we cannot conclude that advisers will be moved to temper the candor of their remarks by the infrequent occasions of disclosure because of the possibility that such conversations will be called for in the context of a criminal prosecution.

On the other hand, the allowance of the privilege to withhold evidence that is demonstrably relevant in a criminal trial would cut deeply into the guarantee of due process of law and gravely impair the basic function of the courts. A President's acknowledged need for confidentiality in the communications of his office is general in nature, whereas the constitutional need for production of relevant evidence in a criminal proceeding is specific and central to the fair adjudication of a particular criminal case in the administration of justice. Without access to specific facts a criminal prosecution may be totally frustrated. The President's broad interest in confidentiality of communications will not be vitiated by disclosure of a limited number of conversations preliminarily shown to have some bearing on the pending criminal cases.

We conclude that when the ground for asserting privilege as to subpoenaed materials sought for use in a criminal trial is based only on the generalized interest in confidentiality, it cannot prevail over the fundamental demands of due process of law in the fair administration of criminal justice. The generalized assertion of privilege must yield to the demonstrated, specific need for evidence in a pending criminal trial.

CHAPTER **2**

Exercise of Judicial Power

INTRODUCTORY ESSAY

Marshall's position that federal courts possess the power to declare acts of Congress and the Executive null and void, no matter how convincingly argued, rests on the rather thin reed of a loosely interpreted Article III. What the Court asserts in *Marbury* and continues to assert right down through *United States* v. *Nixon* is that such plenipotential power inheres in the mere creation and conferral of judicial power. A first reading of Article III, however, leaves most persons unwilling to concede that Marshall's assertion is self-evident. On its face, the judicial article merely informs us that an entity known as "judicial power" shall be vested in a Supreme Court and in any lesser courts Congress might see fit to create. It also informs us that judges will be insulated from political pressures by a grant of some degree of financial security (a salary cannot be reduced while a judge is serving) and tenure for life (assuming good behavior). Further, it delineates the set of general circumstances under which the judiciary may exercise its power (the majority of circumstances being subject to control by Congress). In the face of all this, Article III still leaves us mostly unenlightened about just what "judicial power" is, what its limits are, and how it is to be used and enforced.

In some respects, this vagueness is a little surprising considering the more elaborate treatment given the scope and limits of the law-making and law-enforcing powers outlined in Articles I and II, respectively. Two related observations help clarify why the Framers left so much to providence in the construction of Article III. In the first place, it is apparent that the source of struggle between the colonies and the British Empire was not judicial in character. In constructing the basic document, the Framers allowed the degree of elaboration of powers, limits, and protections to be in direct proportion to their own perception of which institution(s) had been the most serious sources of political abuse during the colonial experience. The relatively flexible nature of common law remedies and procedures, the limited scope of equity, and the absence of direct judicial interference from British courts served to minimize the perception of the judiciary as a source of political abuse. As a consequence, the Framers expressed little concern over a "tyranny" by judges.

In addition, the Framers ostensibly took for granted what the term "judicial power" meant. To them it was simply the power of a court "to decide and pro-nounce a judgment and carry it into effect between persons and parties who bring a case before it for decision" (Miller, 1891, p. 314). As such, the judiciary posed little threat as an institution likely to aggrandize power in the near or more distant future. Indeed, in *The Federalist,* No. 78, Hamilton went so far as to assert that the judiciary was the weakest of the three constitutionally delineated departments and implied as well that he thought it unlikely it would ever be otherwise. He ex-plained:

> The judiciary . . . has no influence over either the sword or the purse; no direction either of the strength or of the wealth of the society and can take no active resolution whatever. It may be truly said to have neither force nor will, but merely judgment.

The surprising openness of the judicial article stems from the Framers' awareness of the absence of any historical precedent for a judicial tyranny that needed to be protected against and their shared consensus that a future tyrannous exertion of "judicial power" would be highly unlikely.

No one today argues with Hamilton's delineations of judicial weakness as they stand. True, courts have no direct powers of enforcement and, true, they do not control the polity's purse strings. Yet, no one today would deny that the Supreme Court heads a *powerful* institution. What Hamilton failed to foresee was that "mere judgment" would one day hold its own with "force" and "will." Indeed, the almost hallowed character of "mere judgment" makes the Court as likely to secure compliance with its policy pronouncements as institutions possessing very real control over sword and purse. Moreover, these "mere judgments" run the gamut of political issues and affect far more persons than Hamilton ever imagined. Desegre-gation, reapportionment, obscenity, abortion, affirmative action, and a raft of other concerns are all of central importance on the polity's political agenda and are matters for which the Court has served as the key policymaker. The present stature of the judiciary comes from Marshall's expansion of the judicial function to in-clude nullification of congressional, executive, and state actions in the course of deciding and pronouncing judgments between parties bringing cases before the bench. Had there been more precision in the judicial article, it is hard to say whether Marshall could have justified such an expansive power or whether the judiciary would have been able to attain its present coequal status.

The judicial power we know today is not solely the product of a timely judicial assertion based on a liberal interpretation of a loosely defined grant of constitu-tional power. It stems, as well, from the willingness of other political actors to concede that this judicial power embodies what Marshall claimed. While Article III is sufficiently open to allow the Court some play in its interpretation, it also grants ample power to sister departments to severely circumscribe, if not cripple, Court power. The judicial article thus gives the Court grounds to expand its power base while providing external means to limit and control that base. The resulting cre-ative tension serves effectively to control the exercise of judicial power and to protect the polity from a judicial tyranny. What these controls are and how they operate merit our consideration.

Controls on the Exercise of Judicial Power

Congressional Power to Structure and Organize the Federal Judiciary

Article III limits judicial power both directly and indirectly by requiring the judiciary to rely on Congress for a variety of matters. As we noted earlier, the Article leaves it to Congress to fashion a federal court organization beyond the singular Supreme Court directly provided for in the Constitution. In point of fact, the Article makes the creation of other federal courts an altogether optional matter for Congress. Had Congress so chosen, it could easily have left matters as they were by granting existing state courts the power to adjudicate federal law. Rather quickly, though, Congress established a federal court structure with the passage of the Judiciary Act of 1789.

The Act provided for thirteen Federal District Courts, one in each state, designed to function as trial courts or courts of first instance for the federal government. These courts were established with full-time judges and were granted a rather limited authority over federal matters occurring within each court's state boundary. Congress also established three circuit courts to handle some cases as courts of first instance, but also to handle appeals of questions of law in cases rendered by those lower courts within the geographic region over which Congress had granted the "circuit" court control. Rather than staff this tier of courts with full-time judges, Congress specified that each circuit court's judging was to be handled by two Supreme Court justices (riding circuit) and a district court judge from the geographic region of the circuit. Further, the Act more formally established a Supreme Court by designating its size, practice, meeting place, and times of operation, as well as matters of jurisdiction.

This three-tiered schema proved functional and remains the basis for the federal judiciary's organization today. Congress did alter the intermediate appellate court structure in 1891 and 1911 by establishing eleven Courts of Appeals staffed by full-time residential judges. Moreover, the limited authority of the original district courts has progressively been expanded so that they now possess virtually the full authority available under the Constitution. At present there are 94 District Courts with over 500 judges, 11 Courts of Appeals with 132 judges serving, and 1 Supreme Court with 1 Chief Justice and 8 Associate Justices. The power of Congress to establish and alter this federal judicial organization is a potential if somewhat cumbersome means for limiting and controlling the Supreme Court's exertion of judicial power.

Along these lines, considerable attention has been given to a recently proposed structural solution to the problems created by the Supreme Court's burgeoning caseload (Federal Judicial Center, 1972). Each year the Court is called upon to review a greater number of the decisions rendered below. Before 1925 the Supreme Court was required to take and decide most of the cases appealed to it. The resulting unmanageable caseload led Congress in 1925 to pass the Judges Bill, authorizing the Court to use its discretion as to which cases it wished to hear. This procedural change granted the Justices more time to consider the merits of cases believed sufficiently important to require Supreme Court adjudication. It provided, as well, an important measure of tactical flexibility in allowing the Court to set its own agenda. The present proposal would simply shift the greater share of that selection process to a fourth-tier court sandwiched between the Supreme Court and the Courts of Appeals. This "National Court of Review" would screen the 4,000-plus petitions for Supreme Court review, selecting about 10 percent of that number as important enough for the Supreme Court to consider. The National Court would send this 10 percent to the Supreme Court for final selection and review. The remaining 90 percent of the cases would be denied any further consideration, effectively making the decision of the lower court final.

Those advocating this structural change hold that it will increase the amount of time available to members of the Supreme Court to carefully consider the merits of cases, and relieve them of their present obligation to spend an inordinate amount of time and energy just deciding which cases to review. While the proposed reorganization of the federal court structure might create efficiency and administrative effectiveness, it might also serve to dilute the Court's power and control, ultimately having public policy consequences of considerable import. For instance, the Court might be forced to decide matters it would have preferred to delay, which could result in expedient solutions with little tie to broader legal principle or principled decisions with little relation to political reality. Further, judges serving on the National Court of Review (as presently proposed, Courts of Appeals judges selected on a rotating basis) may well drastically shift the proportion of cases to be reviewed in a given area, thereby hamstringing the Court's ability to render coherent policy across that cluster of issues. Despite Chief Justice Burger's continued support for the creation of a National Court of Review, it now seems unlikely that Congress will move to establish one.

Of course, if Congress has the power to establish such a court ostensibly to aid the administration of the judicial resource, it could use that broad power to alter the judicial process in order to control more directly the content of judicial policy. In 1937 Congress was called upon to do just that. Beginning as early as 1934 the Supreme Court had frustrated Roosevelt's efforts to bring the nation out of the Depression. Relying on a political philosophy stressing private rights, particularly private property rights, a variable, but primarily five-member majority of the Court limited federal power to regulate business competition and practices, denied the federal government the power to provide pensions for railroad employees, held legislation fixing prices and regulating hours and wages unconstitutional, and denied unemployment compensation and tax subsidies to disadvantaged individuals. Virtually any social planning that ran counter to laissez-faire economics failed to pass muster with these Justices. After the 1936 election, which Roosevelt won by a substantial margin, rather than wage a direct battle with the Court, Roosevelt proposed to Congress that for every Justice over seventy who did not avail himself of retirement a new Justice be added to the Court. Under this arrangement, Roosevelt would have been able to appoint up to six additional Justices, with the obvious effect of creating a new pro–New Deal majority on the Court.

Roosevelt cloaked his plan in the guise of "neutral" administrative efficiency. The additional Justices were essential to him because most of the sitting Justices were then quite old and the Court, according to the President, needed new blood to make its processing of cases more efficient. No one was really so naive as to assume that Roosevelt's only concern was judicial administration. Much to his chagrin, his attempt to alter the Court's structure in order to change its policy was quickly perceived as too great a blow to the Court's integrity as an institution to be justified as an appropriate means to alter its policy. As a result, many people opposed to the Court's thwarting of the New Deal rose to defend the Court as an institution, including Chief Justice Hughes, who wrote directly to Congress defending the Court and injudiciously intimating that the plan was unconstitutional. (To give a clearer picture of the character of the controversy, both Roosevelt's "plan" and Hughes' letter are reprinted in the readings for this chapter.) Roosevelt's "Court-packing" per se failed to pass in Congress. Indirectly, though, Roosevelt secured his ultimate goal. In 1937 the Court handed down its decision in *National Labor Relations Board* v. *Jones & Laughlin Steel Corp.*, 301 U.S. 1 (1937), ruling constitutional a labor relations act guaranteeing the right of collective bargaining to workers in interstate commerce—a right quite opposed to laissez-faire notions of economic relations but one perceived as central to Roosevelt's plans for economic recovery.

The policy shift apparent in *Jones & Laughlin* emerged with no change in personnel and led pundits to call the case the "switch in time that saved nine." There is considerable uncertainty, though, whether the Court's switch was in any way directly related to Roosevelt's Court-packing effort. Evidence suggests that the switching Justice (Justice Roberts) had done his switching before Roosevelt's message ever reached Congress. At the same time, there are those who suggest that word of Roosevelt's intentions reached the Court before the President went public and before Roberts shifted to support New Deal policy (Rodell, 1955, p. 221). Even if the Court altered the course of its policy independent of executive and congressional pressure, the impression remains in the public's eye, at least, that the Court changed as a direct result of Roosevelt's Court-packing plan. To the extent that such legend remains part of our political mythology, it holds a viable, implicit control over the exertion of a judicial power too long at odds with the "dominant political coalition" of the polity.

Both the proposed National Court of Review and the Court-packing plan illustrate the limits Congress can impose on judicial power through structural manipulation. Technically, Congress could go further than either of these examples suggest. If it wished, it could eliminate the district and appellate courts altogether, cancel Supreme Court terms, and otherwise wreak havoc with the operation of the judicial system, all with quite obvious impact on judicial power. The reaction to Roosevelt's Court-packing plan suggests, though, that Congress is not likely to be so impolitic as to employ such blatant means to secure its preferences. It can burden the courts, in more subtle ways, by refusing to increase judicial salaries, refusing to add needed administrative staff, or refusing to expand the number of courts or justices; it can also show its displeasure with the Supreme Court so as to mitigate judicial power, and do so without alienating public affection.

Congressional Power to Define Federal Judicial Authority

In addition to granting Congress the authority to fashion the federal court organization, the Framers required Congress to play a substantial role in delineating the circumstances under which the judiciary can act. Article III says that judicial power shall extend to all cases in law and equity arising under this Constitution, the laws of the United States, and treaties made, or which shall be made under their authority;

—to all cases affecting ambassadors, other public ministers and consuls;

—to all cases of admiralty and maritime jurisdiction;

—to controversies to which the United States shall be a party;

—to controversies between two or more states;

—between a state and citizens of another state [altered by the Eleventh Amendment];

—between citizens of different states;

—between citizens of the same state claiming lands under grants of different states; and

—between a state, or the citizens thereof, and foreign states, citizens, or subjects [altered by the Eleventh Amendment, as well].

What this provision does is define the types of disputes and litigants over which the federal judiciary can be authorized by legislation to exert judicial power. Whether or not the judiciary is allowed to decide these specified kinds of cases, outside what the Constitution grants the Supreme Court as a court of first instance, depends upon acts of Congress. Article III stipulates that the Supreme Court's appellate jurisdiction shall be made "with such exceptions, and under such regulations as the Congress shall make." The Constitution, then, grants the Supreme Court the authority to decide cases affecting ambassadors and other public ministers and consuls as well as cases in which a state is a party (not a very significant authority in either instance) and grants the Court the power to hear these cases as a court of first instance. All authority to resolve disputes on appeal depends upon positive grants from Congress. The entire scope of lower court authority rests wholly with Congress since Congress ordains these courts in the first place and thus can extend to them whatever portion of constitutionally available jurisdiction it might want.

The congressional power to determine the Supreme Court's appellate jurisdiction, to specify the entire original jurisdiction of district courts, and to designate the entire appellate jurisdiction of Courts of Appeals has an impact on judicial policy, either directly or as an indirect vehicle for shaping future Court policy. Congress made direct use of its jurisdictional control to shape judicial choice between 1868 and 1869 in connection with the Court's hearing and decision in *Ex parte McCardle*, 7 Wall. 506 (1869). After the Civil War, the radical Republican Congress chose to rely on military rule as the most effective means to reconstruct the South. As part of military rule, the reconstruction acts authorized military commissions to try civilians. McCardle, a Southern editor opposed to "Yankee carpetbaggers" and reconstruction in general, was jailed and tried by such a military commission. He ultimately sought release by petitioning for a writ of habeas corpus in the Federal District Court. In 1867 Congress had authorized district courts to hear habeas corpus cases involving anyone held in violation of the federal Constitution or U.S. statutes. The statute authorizing that use of habeas corpus included the option to appeal a lower court denial of the writ to the Supreme Court. McCardle lost his bid for release through habeas corpus in the lower court and appealed the matter to the Supreme Court.

Between the time the arguments were first considered by the Supreme Court and the announcement of the judgment, Congress passed legislation that denied the Supreme Court the authority to hear appeals from denials of writs of habeas corpus. The legislation even went so far as to deny the authority to consider a case already argued, to wit, the *McCardle* case. Congress was quite concerned with the very real possibility that the Supreme Court might rule the reconstruction acts unconstitutional. To avoid that possibility, the legislature turned to this rather drastic means. Interestingly, the Court capitulated, agreeing that by virtue of the sudden denial of jurisdiction, it indeed lacked jurisdiction.

This conclusion suggests that Congress could abolish the appellate jurisdiction of the Supreme Court altogether. Today, however, such a total abolition of appellate jurisdiction would likely be held unconstitutional because it would violate the very concept of the separation of powers. To maintain the coequal status of the legislative and judicial branches, it is essential that Congress not remove so many of the Court's authorizations that the Court would no longer be able to perform its essential function in the constitutional scheme of things (Berger, 1969, Chapter 9). Indeed, Justice Douglas said in 1962: "There is a serious question whether the *McCardle* case could command a majority today" (*Glidden Co.* v. *Zdanok*, 370 U.S. 530). While a drastic full-scale reduction in Court appellate jurisdiction is unlikely, less dramatic jurisdictional manipulations are not out of the question, and, in fact, have been attempted. For instance, the Jenner-Butler Bill, introduced in 1957, was designed to keep the Supreme Court from hearing cases on appeal that dealt with issues of national security. To the more conservative minds in Congress, the Court's decisions in a number of related areas appeared to comfort communism and communists (*Yates* v. *United States,* 354 U.S. 298 [1957]; *Communist Party* v. *Subversive Activities Control Board,* 351 U.S. 115 [1956]; *Pennsylvania* v. *Nelson,* 350 U.S. 497 [1956]; and *Konigsberg* v. *State Bar of California,* 353 U.S. 252 [1957]). By a very narrow margin the Senate tabled Jenner-Butler but not without getting a message to the Supreme Court regarding congressional disgruntlement with this particular set of Court policies. In 1959 the Supreme Court upheld a congressional contempt citation aimed at a witness who had failed to respond before a legislative investigation into communism in education. This action was in stark contradistinction to this same Court's ruling two years earlier to deny a similar contempt citation for a witness who failed to answer legislative investigative questions concerning communism in labor. We will treat this issue more fully in Part II; suffice it to say here that there are many who believe the Court's willingness to sustain the contempt in 1959 and not in 1957 came about as a direct response to Congress' threat to cut off jurisdiction.

Congressional and Executive Responsibilities for Enforcement

Even with a reasonably effective and virtually unassailable federal court structure and a reasonably safe, broad-based judicial authority, the fact remains that the courts must rely on the legislative and executive branches to finance and execute the judgments rendered. Courts do not have, as Hamilton noted, authority over the sword or purse. Congress and the executive must ultimately take responsibility for forcing compliance should resistance arise. Congress plays a role primarily in authorizing expenditures and in enacting laws where Court policy is not self-executing. The executive is, of course, responsible to the Constitution's requirement that he faithfully execute the laws, ostensibly including the Supreme Court's interpretation of those laws.

Andrew Jackson's alleged remark after *Worcester* v. *Georgia,* 6 Pet. 515 (1832), underscores this judicial dependency. The Court ruled Georgia's regulation of the Cherokee Indian Nation contrary to the Constitution and the treaties of the United States. The particulars of the case required Georgia to release the missionaries it held, who had ministered to the Cherokee in violation of the Georgia laws that had now been ruled unconstitutional. Georgia refused to comply with the order, leading President Jackson to aver, "Well, John Marshall has made his decision, now let him enforce it." Despite the potentially explosive character of the setting, the outcome of the case (the Georgia governor pardoned the missionaries in exchange for their promise to leave the state) mitigated what could have been an exasperating executive/judicial confrontation over enforcement.

With some notable exceptions, the Court has secured the necessary help from Congress and the Chief Executive to enforce even unpopular decisions. After a belated entry into the desegregation foray, President Eisenhower did ultimately dispatch federal troops to Little Rock, Arkansas, in 1957 to enforce a Federal District Court's efforts to implement the Supreme Court's *Brown* v. *Board of Education* decisions, 347 U.S. 483 (1954); 349 U.S. 294 (1955). The governor of Arkansas had directly resisted the court-ordered desegregation of Central High School in Little Rock. The Court later sustained this action in *Cooper* v. *Aaron,* 358 U.S. 1 (1958), holding that Court decisions, like any other action of the three branches, function as the supreme law of the land and Presidents must faithfully execute the law of the land as part and parcel of their executive responsibilities.

The Court, as one might expect, asserts an unqualified responsibility on the part of the executive to enforce court orders, yet how and to what extent a Chief Executive must force compliance remains open. Further, a President may use the power of office to thwart enforcement or encourage foot-dragging in matters not directly under his control. Nixon's response to court-ordered busing illustrates the point. By 1972 the Supreme Court had held that court-ordered busing is one of many available, appropriate means to achieve the Court's goal of racial equality in the public schools, a goal first enunciated in *Brown* v. *Board of Education* (1954). Nixon's reaction to these choices implied that the courts were relying solely on this particular means and that such a position was detrimental to children. In addition, Nixon asserted that the Court's busing stance resulted, in his view, from an inaccurate reading of the Constitution. In 1972 Nixon called upon Congress to "impose a moratorium on the implementation of federal court orders" that required the busing of school children to achieve racial balance. Nixon also encouraged Congress to foreclose busing altogether as an option available to the courts to remedy segregation. Instead, Congress simply postponed the effectiveness of Court desegregation orders until all appeals were completed. Nixon's efforts and his clear opposition to the Court (in this and other matters) suggest that a President can hamper the achievement of a Court's policy goals and could ultimately, through a more willing Congress, preclude certain judicial remedies by limiting the enforcement and enforceability of judicial pronouncements. Congressional and executive discretion in enforcement and the flexibility of executive responsibility to encourage compliance with Court judgments diminish judicial power, ultimately placing it at the mercy of others.

Article V's Authority to Amend the Constitution

The limits we have discussed so far are most often not directly targeted to a specific Court pronouncement in a particular case. When the Court interprets a statute in a way not to the liking of Congress, Congress can rewrite the statute in language that leaves no room for doubt about how to interpret it. At the same time, the Court's views on specific *constitutional* matters can be directly overturned only by constitutional amendment. Article V outlines the rather difficult amending process, whose very elaborateness tends to severely circumscribe reliance on the process as a vehicle to alter judicial choice. In only four instances can it reasonably be said that a constitutional amendment was proposed and ratified specifically to alter Court interpretation of the Constitution.

The first such instance followed the Court's decision in *Chisholm* v. *Georgia*, 2 Dall. 419 (1793). The core issue involved the Court's willingness to grant citizens of one state the right to sue the government of another state. By granting Chisholm the right to sue Georgia, the Supreme Court stirred the wrath of those believing strongly in state sovereignty. As a result, the Eleventh Amendment was promptly added to the Constitution, clearly reversing the *Chisholm* holding (and altering portions of Article III from whence the holding came) by denying citizens of one state the right to sue another state. Sixty years later the Supreme Court again ruled in a fashion leading to reversal by amendment. The case in question was *Scott* v. *Sanford*, 19 How. 393 (1857), wherein the Court held that blacks were not citizens. Eleven years and a civil war later the Fourteenth Amendment altered that view.

The Sixteenth Amendment was added to the Constitution in 1913 in direct response to the Court's policy in *Pollock* v. *Farmers' Loan & Trust Co.*, 158 U.S. 601 (1895). Through an elaborate reasoning process, which we will discuss more fully in Part II, the Court ruled a federal income tax unconstitutional for its failure to be apportioned among the states on the basis of population. The Sixteenth Amendment holds that Congress can collect taxes on incomes from whatever source derived and without attention to apportionment among the states. Again some sixty years passed before the Court's policy was altered by amendment. This time, the Twenty-sixth Amendment emerged in response to the Court's holding in *Oregon* v. *Mitchell*, 400 U.S. 112 (1970) that the federal government was powerless to grant the franchise to 18-year-olds in *state*, as opposed to *federal*, elections. Quickly ratified in 1971, the Twenty-sixth Amendment grants 18-year-olds the right to vote in both federal and state elections. That there have been only four instances in almost 200 years of Court history means that amendment to alter judicial policy does not really stand as an ever-present, substantial threat to the Court's prerogatives. Nonetheless, Justices are aware that although their choices are primarily the "final" word on the meaning of the Constitution, there remains a truly *final* word beyond their control.

Executive and Congressional Control of Court Personnel

The exertion of judicial power is not limited solely by congressional control of structure, jurisdiction, and ultimate reversal by amendment. Who sits on the bench, particularly the Supreme Court, may well determine how judicial power is exerted and what judicial policy emerges. Staffing the federal bench is primarily the President's responsibility, though Senate advice and consent is required for final confirmation. Most Presidents will appoint a substantial number of district judges and at least one Supreme Court Justice, if not more, over the course of their terms. No matter what judicial policy may hold sway at a given time or what mode of exercising judicial power may be employed by a given collection of judges, the whole approach can shift drastically because of attrition and subsequent appointment. Nixon may have made his mark as Chief Executive more by virtue of his judicial appointments than by any other action. He largely succeeded in turning a liberal Supreme Court into a somewhat conservative one in four short years. Should a Court assert judicial policy that flies in the face of the popular will, it is likely that the process of personnel change will ultimately turn that abuse around. Of course, there is always the possibility of impeachment as a limitation. To date, Supreme Court Justices have remained free from serious threat of impeachment.* Nonetheless, it does stand in the realm of possibility (more so with the effort to impeach Nixon still in public memory) and could be used to limit judicial power, should such a drastic measure be needed.

Character of the Judicial Process

There are additional matters, endemic to the judicial process itself, that limit judicial power. Courts, for instance, rely on outside participants to bring cases to them for decision. As a result, judges are not entirely free to set their own agenda as other political actors are. This restriction makes it difficult for the Supreme Court to monitor judicial policy. Once the Court announces a policy, it must wait (often for a considerable time) for the return of cases based on that policy, to see if the policy is being followed and what, if any, adjustments need to be made. The adversary process, which pits one side of an issue against another, limits the breadth and scope of information the Court receives (particularly for multifaceted issues) and likely limits policy alternatives as well. While the Court is clearly a policymaking institution, the mode of operation, limiting as it does control of the agenda, effective feedback, and the information received, of necessity forces judges to recognize the limits of judicial policymaking, and thereby serves in its own right to limit judicial power.

In the course of its history, the Supreme Court has been amply aware of the tenuous nature of its power base and has responded by honing its political savvy to a fine edge. The Justices have often brought to legal choice a political awareness to be admired by the best of grass-roots politicians. Indeed, most Justices have been keenly aware of the very real policymaking dimensions of their institution, choosing policies that maximize their preferences while minimizing negative, retributive action from those who must enforce or comply with the policies. (Of course, as our examples have shown, some Justices have been politically inept.) For the most part, though, the Court has preserved its power through a careful, politically sensi-

---

* In 1804 Supreme Court Justice Samuel P. Chase was impeached, but he was later acquitted by the Senate. In 1969, the threat of a Congressional investigation forced Justice Abe Fortas to resign. Otherwise no serious threats have emerged.

tive use of that power. In fact, the awareness of the need to preserve this delicate power balance has led the Court to place further limits on its power by requiring litigants to meet certain conditions before they can have access to the courts. These matters of self-limitation will be taken up in the next chapter. However, before proceeding to an analysis of self-limitation, it is necessary to note and briefly discuss the auxiliary sanctions available to the Supreme Court and lower courts; a court can bring these sanctions to bear on litigants to "carry into effect" the particulars of a given decision.

Auxiliary Judicial Powers

The Contempt Power

As we have noted, much of the power base of the judiciary is symbolic. Indeed, the extensive ritual surrounding the judicial pageant and the norms, mores, and mystery of judge and lawyer are mostly symbolic trappings to enhance the limited authority the courts possess. With these rituals and the attendant public acceptance of the myth of the robe, the courts have successfully secured respect and usually won compliance with their decisions from the particular litigants and other participants before the court in a given case. In those instances, though, where respect or compliance is not forthcoming, judges can exert a little more than symbolic power by charging an individual with contempt of court, finding that person guilty of contempt, and jailing and/or fining the guilty party. Thus in particular instances, judges can "carry into effect" their decisions or retain a necessary dignity and decorum in their courtrooms with actual, tangible sanctions: jail and/or a fine.

As the foregoing suggests, there are really two contempt powers at the disposal of judges. One is a criminal contempt power, the primary purpose of which is to maintain the dignity of the court itself. The other is a civil contempt power, the purpose of which is to secure the rights of one party in a suit by forcing the other party to obey the court's ruling. A charge of criminal contempt is punitive in character; the court seeks to punish immediately for past behavior indicating disrespect for the court. A charge of civil contempt is coercive in character; the court seeks only to force someone to follow its dictates. As a consequence of the differing purpose and character of each form of contempt, the punishment meted out usually differs as well. In contrast to a specified punishment for criminal contempt, civil contempt is punished by a conditional sanction. A party unwilling to obey a court order can be placed in jail until he or she complies. While on first glance this might appear to be cruel and unusual, judges do not appear to feel any qualms about such conditional punishment because the incarcerated person carries the keys to the prison cell: to achieve release, one need only comply with the court's order.

The criminal contempt is usually issued for disorderly behavior in the sight of a judge in or so near to a court of law as to obstruct the administration of justice. When occurring in the presence of a judge, the process is usually summary in character; that is, the judge charges, tries, convicts, and sentences the contemner virtually on the spot without jury or, for the most part, any of the usual procedural protections provided in other criminal trial settings. Indeed, the Supreme Court has gone to great lengths to distinguish this summary process of judicial power to vindicate a court's authority from the actions of the state in enforcing its criminal law. Such a distinction is justified on the basis of the presumed need of a court to act quickly and authoritatively to thwart disrespect so as not to jeopardize the rights of others, which are potentially abridged in an unruly courtroom.

Although the Supreme Court is sympathetic with the need to support the criminal contempt power as an essential tool enabling a judge to control the courtroom, members of the Court have also expressed concern about the potential for abuse the summary character of that power affords. Thus, while the Court does not wish to leave judges powerless to control the courtroom, it has recently decided that notions of elementary fairness could not be ignored for the sake of judicial dignity and authority. Hence, in certain circumstances, it has circumscribed the summary power in criminal contempt proceedings. For instance, in the trial of Narvel Tinsley for murder, Tinsley's lawyer Daniel Taylor apparently conducted his client's defense in a turbulent and unorthodox manner, leading Judge Hayes to summarily find Taylor guilty of contempt of court at the conclusion of the trial. While denying Taylor an opportunity to respond, Hayes sentenced Taylor to four and one-half years in prison, later reducing the sentence to six months. The Court denied Taylor's claim that all contempts of court ought to be tried by a jury, but the majority did find that Judge Hayes' delay until the end of the trial and his denial to Taylor of the option to respond denied Taylor due process of law. The majority also held that if Taylor was to be retried for his contemptuous behavior, the new trial had to be before another judge, Hayes being too personally embroiled to "hold the balance nice, clear, and true between the State and the accused," a requirement of judicial objectivity. Thus, where a judge becomes so personally involved in a controversy in the course of a trial that he or she cannot "maintain the calm detachment necessary for fair adjudication," the contempt must be tried by another judge (*Taylor* v. *Hayes,* 418 U.S. 488 at 506 [1974]; see also *Mayberry* v. *Pennsylvania,* 400 U.S. 455 [1971]). Moreover, if a defendant receives a sentence in excess of six months for contempt, he or she has the right to choose a jury trial (*Cheff* v. *Schnackenberg,* 384 U.S. 373 [1966]; *Bloom* v. *Illinois,* 391 U.S. 194 [1968]; and *Codispoti* v. *Pennsylvania,* 418 U.S. 506 [1974]). When courts (particularly federal courts) impose criminal contempt on actions not occurring in the presence of a judge—called "indirect" criminal contempt—such as refusal to obey a temporary injunction, substantial qualifications to summary power are invoked: notice, hearing, representation by counsel, and if the offense is equivalent to a statutorily proscribed criminal offense, trial by jury. In addition to these court-made protections, it is possible to seek and obtain a presidential pardon for criminal contempt convictions; the purpose of allowing this recourse is to mitigate excessive judicial abuse of the summary power. *Ex parte Grossman,* 267 U.S. 87 (1925), excerpted in this chapter, outlines the rationale for these additional protections.

Similar procedural rights (including the presidential pardon) do *not* apply to civil contempts, since the coercive intent of the punishment provides its own safeguards (that is, the person imprisoned can obtain the keys to the jailhouse door through simple compliance with the court order). Civil contempts have been used by courts, for instance, to coerce testimony from reporters before grand juries. In *Branzburg* v. *Hayes,* 408 U.S. 665 (1972), the Supreme Court held that reporters do not have a First Amendment right to remain silent when questioned by grand juries with respect to their news sources. Should a reporter fail to testify, she or he might be cited with civil contempt, placed in jail, and freed only when agreeing to testify (the incarceration being limited, of course, to the duration of the particular grand jury).

The Power to Issue Writs

In addition to and in conjunction with the contempt power, courts can carry rulings into effect between parties by invoking their power to issue a variety of writs. Under equity jurisdiction, most courts can issue writs that order people or officials to either do particular things (often through a writ of *mandamus*) or refrain from doing particular things (usually by a writ of injunction), all with the intent of precluding continuance of an injury or preventing a possible injury from occurring. Technically, a court can issue these writs only when litigants show that the injury about to occur or any further continuance of the present injury is likely to lead to "irreparable injury" (one that cannot be compensated for at a later date).

As noted in *Marbury,* federal courts were first granted the power to issue writs in the Judiciary Act of 1789, though some believe federal courts could have exercised such powers as an inherent power of courts, without congressional authorization. The courts have, nevertheless, acquiesced to Congress by legitimating legislative limitations on the use of the power to issue writs of injunction, suggesting the view that statutory authorization is necessary for the exercise of this power. Congress has limited the use·of the writ in certain labor disputes, in disputes over the regulation of rates by state public utility commissions, and as a vehicle to restrain tax collection. Furthermore, Congress has required the convening of a three-judge panel before a federal district court can issue an injunction restraining the enforcement of allegedly unconstitutional state or federal statutes, and before restraining an order of the Interstate Commerce Commission.

If someone is ordered to do or refrain from doing something and does not comply, the courts can invoke the contempt power to assure compliance. In conjunction, the writ and contempt powers provide important weapons in the courts' arsenal to secure compliance with court dictates and policy. This is particularly true because a party must follow an injunction (under the ultimate threat of a contempt citation) until the injunction is reversed on appeal even though the party believes the regulations and decisions involved are unconstitutional; this is the reverse of the situation in standard cases.

Aside from *mandamus* and injunction, courts possess substantial powers through their ability to issue writs of habeas corpus. Habeas corpus is basically a judicial instrument designed to protect the citizen against illegal imprisonment. The writ is petitioned for by a person in custody or on behalf of a person in custody. After receiving the petition, the court has several alternatives, but it can ultimately order the person in question to be brought before the bar so it can determine the legality of the detention. If the court determines that the imprisonment is illegal, it can order the release of the prisoner.

Initially the writ was available at the federal level solely to determine the legality of pretrial detention, but in 1867 Congress expanded the writ's applicability to include imprisonments in violation of the laws, treaties, or Constitution of the United States. (This very legislation also authorized appeal to the Supreme Court to challenge a lower court denial of the writ. The explosive character of the issues involved in an appeal based on this authority emerged in the case of *Ex parte McCardle* and gave rise to congressional action to deny appellate jurisdiction for these types of cases.) Some scholars debate the need for congressional authorization of utilization of the writ since the Constitution provides that the writ shall not be suspended except in time of rebellion or invasion. If Congress were to remove all statutory authorization for federal court usage of the writ, Congress would technically thereby suspend the writ. Congressional authorizations do exist and always have existed for the issuance of the writ so the matter is, in part, a moot point. The power to use this writ, like the power to issue contempts and writs of injunction and *mandamus,* facilitates the implementation of policy. Through expansive use of the writ of habeas corpus (to be noted in more detail in subsequent commentary), federal courts during the mid-1960s were able to significantly alter state criminal justice to make it conform to more uniform, federal guidelines.

President Franklin D. Roosevelt's Message to Congress

February 5, 1937

To the Congress of the United States:

. . . The judiciary has often found itself handicapped by insufficient personnel with which to meet a growing and more complex business . . . .

• • •

The simple fact is that today a new need for legislative action arises because the personnel of the Federal judiciary is insufficient to meet the business before them. A growing body of citizens complain of the complexities, the delays, and the expense of litigation in the United States courts.

• • •

A part of the problem of obtaining a sufficient number of judges to dispose of cases is the capacity of the judges themselves. This brings forward the question of aged or infirm judges—a subject of delicacy and yet one which requires frank discussion.

In the Federal courts there are in all 237 life tenure permanent judgeships. Twenty-five of them are now held by judges over 70 years of age and eligible to leave the bench on full pay. Originally no pension or retirement allowance was provided by the Congress. When after 80 years of our national history the Congress made provision for pensions, it found a well-entrenched tradition among judges to cling to their posts, in many instances far beyond their years of physical or mental capacity. Their salaries were small. As with other men, responsibilities and obligations accumulated. No alternative had been open to them except to attempt to perform the duties of their offices to the very edge of the grave.

In exceptional cases, of course, judges, like other men, retain to an advanced age full mental and physical vigor. Those not so fortunate are often unable to perceive their own infirmities. "They seem to be tenacious of the appearance of adequacy." The voluntary retirement law of 1869 provided, therefore, only a partial solution. That law, still in force, has not proved effective in inducing aged judges to retire on a pension.

This result had been foreseen in the debates when the measure was being considered. It was then proposed that when a judge refused to retire upon reaching the age of 70, an additional judge should be appointed to assist in the work of the court. The proposal passed the House but was eliminated in the Senate.

With the opening of the twentieth century, and the great increase of population and commerce, and the growth of a more complex type of litigation, similar proposals were introduced in the Congress. To meet the situation, in 1913, 1914, 1915, and 1916, the Attorneys General then in office recommended to the Congress that when a district or a circuit judge failed to retire at the age of 70, an additional judge be appointed in order that the affairs of the court might be promptly and adequately discharged.

In 1919 a law was finally passed providing that the President "may" appoint additional district and circuit judges, but only upon a finding that the incumbent judge over 70 "is unable to discharge efficiently all the duties of his office by reason of mental or physical disability of permanent character." The discretionary and indefinite nature of this legislation has rendered it ineffective. No President should be asked to determine the ability or disability of any particular judge.

The duty of a judge involves more than presiding or listening to testimony or arguments. It is well to remember that the mass of details involved in the average of law cases today is vastly greater and more complicated than even 20 years ago. Records and briefs must be read; statutes, decisions, and extensive material of a technical, scientific, statistical, and economic nature must be searched and studied; opinions must be formulated and written. The modern tasks of judges call for the use of full energies.

Modern complexities call also for a constant infusion of new blood in the courts, just as it is needed in executive functions of the Government and in private business. A lowered mental or physical vigor leads men to avoid an examination of complicated and changed conditions. Little by little, new facts become blurred through old glasses fitted, as it were, for the needs of another generation; older men, assuming that the scene is the same as it was in the past, cease to explore or inquire into the present or the future.

. . .

Life tenure of judges, assured by the Constitution, was designed to place the courts beyond temptations or influences which might impair their judgments; it was not intended to create a static judiciary. A constant and systematic addition of younger blood will vitalize the courts and better equip them to recognize and apply the essential concepts of justice in the light of the needs and the facts of an ever-changing world.

It is obvious, therefore, from both reason and experience, that some provision must be adopted which will operate automatically to supplement the work of older judges and accelerate the work of the court.

I, therefore, earnestly recommend that the necessity of an increase in the number of judges be supplied by legislation providing for the appointment of additional judges in all Federal courts, without exception, where there are incumbent judges of retirement age who do not choose to retire or to resign. If an elder judge is not in fact incapacitated, only good can come from the presence of an additional judge in the crowded state of the dockets; if the capacity of an elder judge is in fact impaired, the appointment of an additional judge is indispensable. This seems to be a truth which cannot be contradicted.

. . .

These proposals do not raise any issue of constitutional law. They do not suggest any form of compulsory retirement for incumbent judges. Indeed, those who have reached the retirement age, but desire to continue their judicial work, would be able to do so under less physical and mental strain and would be able to play a useful part in relieving the growing congestion in the business of our courts. Among them are men of eminence and great ability whose services the Government would be loath to lose. If, on the other hand, any judge eligible for retirement should feel that his court would suffer because of an increase in its membership, he may retire or resign under already existing provisions of law if he wishes so to do. In this connection let me say that the pending proposal to extend to the Justices of the Supreme Court the same retirement privileges now available to other Federal judges, has my entire approval.

. . .

My desire is to strengthen the administration of justice and to make it a more effective servant of public need. In the American ideal of government the courts find an essential and constitutional place. In striving to fulfill that ideal, not only the judges but the Congress and the Executive as well, must do all in their power to bring the judicial organization and personnel to the high standards of usefulness which sound and efficient government and modern conditions require.

. . .

President Franklin D. Roosevelt's "Fireside Chat"

March 9, 1937

• • •

Tonight, sitting at my desk in the White House, I make my first radio report to the people in my second term of office.

I am reminded of that evening in March 4 years ago, when I made my first radio report to you. We were then in the midst of the great banking crisis.

• • •

In 1933 you and I knew that we must never let our economic system get completely out of joint again—that we could not afford to take the risk of another great depression.

We also became convinced that the only way to avoid a repetition of those dark days was to have a government with power to prevent and to cure the abuses and the inequalities which had thrown that system out of joint.

We then began a program of remedying those abuses and inequalities. . . .

Today we are only part way through that program—and recovery is speeding up to a point where the dangers of 1929 are again becoming possible, not this week or month perhaps, but within a year or two.

National laws are needed to complete that program. Individual or local or State effort alone cannot protect us in 1937 any better than 10 years ago.

• • •

The courts have cast doubts on the ability of the elected Congress to protect us against catastrophe by meeting squarely our modern social and economic conditions.

We are at a crisis in our ability to proceed with that protection. It is a quiet crisis. There are no lines of depositors outside closed banks. But to the far-sighted it is far-reaching in its possibilities of injury to America.

I want to talk with you very simply about the need for present action in this crisis—the need to meet the unanswered challenge of one-third of a nation ill-nourished, ill-clad, ill-housed.

Last Thursday I described the American form of government as a three-horse team provided by the Constitution to the American people so that their field might be plowed. The three horses are, of course, the three branches of government—the Congress, the executive, and the courts. Two of the horses are pulling in unison today; the third is not. Those who have intimated that the President of the United States is trying to drive that team overlook the simple fact that the President, as Chief Executive, is himself one of the three horses.

It is the American people themselves who are in the driver's seat.

It is the American people themselves who want the furrow plowed.

It is the American people themselves who expect the third horse to pull in unison with the other two.

I hope that you have reread the Constitution of the United States. Like the Bible, it ought to be read again and again.

. . . In its preamble the Constitution states that it was intended to form a more perfect Union and promote the general welfare; and the powers given to the Congress to carry out those purposes can be best described by saying that they were all the powers needed to meet each and every problem which then had a national character and which could not be met by merely local action.

But the framers went further. Having in mind that in succeeding generations many other problems then undreamed of would become national problems, they gave to the Congress the ample broad powers "to levy taxes * * * and provide for the common defense and general welfare of the United States."

That, my friends, is what I honestly believe to have been the clear and underlying purpose of the patriots who wrote a Federal Constitution to create a National Government with national power, intended as they said, "to form a more perfect union . . . for ourselves and our posterity."

•   •   •

. . . [S]ince the rise of the modern movement for social and economic progress through legislation, the Court has more and more often and more and more boldly asserted a power to veto laws passed by the Congress and State legislatures. . . .

In the last 4 years the sound rule of giving statutes the benefit of all reasonable doubt has been cast aside. The Court has been acting not as a judicial body, but as a policy-making body.

When the Congress has sought to stabilize national agriculture, to improve the conditions of labor, to safeguard business against unfair competition, to protect our national resources, and in many other ways to serve our clearly national needs, the majority of the Court has been assuming the power to pass on the wisdom of these acts of the Congress—and to approve or disapprove the public policy written into these laws.

That is not only my accusation. It is the accusation of most distinguished Justices of the present Supreme Court. I have not the time to quote to you all the language used by dissenting Justices in many of these cases. But in the case holding the Railroad Retirement Act unconstitutional, for instance, Chief Justice Hughes said in a dissenting opinion that the majority opinion was "a departure from sound principles", and placed "an unwarranted limitation upon the commerce clause." And three other Justices agreed with him.

•   •   •

In the face of these dissenting opinions, there is no basis for the claim made by some members of the Court that something in the Constitution has compelled them regretfully to thwart the will of the people.

In the face of such dissenting opinions, it is perfectly clear that as Chief Justice Hughes has said, "We are under a Constitution, but the Constitution is what the judges say it is."

The Court in addition to the proper use of its judicial functions has improperly set itself up as a third House of the Congress—a superlegislature, as one of the Justices has called it "reading into the Constitution words and implications which are not there, and which were never intended to be there."

We have, therefore, reached the point as a Nation where we must take action to save the Constitution from the Court and the Court from itself. We must find a way to take an appeal from the Supreme Court to the Constitution itself. We want a Supreme Court which will do justice under the Constitution—not over it. In our courts we want a government of laws and not of men.

I want—as all Americans want—an independent judiciary as proposed by the framers of the Constitution. That means a Supreme Court that will enforce the Constitution as written—that will refuse to amend the Constitution by the arbitrary exercise of judicial power—amendment by judicial say-so. It does not mean a judiciary so independent that it can deny the existence of facts universally recognized.

How, then, could we proceed to perform the mandate given us? . . .

. . . I came by a process of elimination to the conclusion that short of amendments the only method which was clearly constitutional, and would at the same time carry out other much needed reforms, was to infuse new blood into all our courts. . . . [W]e must have judges who will bring to the courts a present-day sense of the Constitution—judges who will retain in the courts the judicial functions of a court and reject the legislative powers which the courts have today assumed.

● ● ●

What is my proposal? It is simply this: Whenever a judge or justice of any Federal court has reached the age of 70 and does not avail himself of the opportunity to retire on a pension, a new member shall be appointed by the President then in office, with the approval, as required by the Constitution, of the Senate of the United States.

That plan has two chief purposes: By bringing into the judicial system a steady and continuing stream of new and younger blood, I hope, first, to make the administration of all Federal justice speedier and therefore less costly; secondly, to bring to the decision of social and economic problems younger men who have had personal experience and contact with modern facts and circumstances under which average men have to live and work. This plan will save our National Constitution from hardening of the judicial arteries.

The number of judges to be appointed would depend wholly on the decision of present judges now over 70 or those who would subsequently reach the age of 70.

If, for instance, any one of the six Justices of the Supreme Court now over the age of 70 should retire as provided under the plan, no additional place would be created. Consequently, although there never can be more than 15, there may be only 14, or 13, or 12, and there may be only 9.

There is nothing novel or radical about this idea. It seeks to maintain the Federal bench in full vigor. . . .

•   •   •

The statute would apply to all the courts in the Federal system. There is general approval so far as the lower Federal courts are concerned. The plan has met opposition only so far as the Supreme Court of the United States itself is concerned. If such a plan is good for the lower courts, it certainly ought to be equally good for the highest court, from which there is no appeal.

Those opposing this plan have sought to arouse prejudice and fear by crying that I am seeking to "pack" the Supreme Court and that a baneful precedent will be established.

What do they mean by the words "packing the Court"?

Let me answer this question with a bluntness that will end all honest misunderstanding of my purposes.

If by that phrase "packing the Court" it is charged that I wish to place on the bench spineless puppets who would disregard the law and would decide specific cases as I wished them to be decided, I make this answer: That no President fit for his office would appoint, and no Senate of honorable men fit for their office would confirm, that kind of appointees to the Supreme Court.

But if by that phrase the charge is made that I would appoint and the Senate would confirm Justices worthy to sit beside present members of the Court who understand those modern conditions; that I will appoint Justices who will not undertake to override the judgment of the Congress on legislative policy; that I will appoint Justices who will act as Justices and not as legislators—if the appointment of such Justices can be called "packing the Courts"—then I say that I, and with me the vast majority of the American people, favor doing just that thing—now.

•   •   •

I now propose that we establish by law an assurance against any such ill-balanced Court in the future. I propose that hereafter, when a judge reaches the age of 70, a new and younger judge shall be added to the Court automatically. In this way I propose to enforce a sound public policy by law instead of leaving the composition of our Federal courts, including the highest, to be determined by chance or the personal decision of individuals.

•   •   •

Like all lawyers, like all Americans, I regret the necessity of this controversy. But the welfare of the United States, and indeed of the Constitution itself, is what we all must think about first. Our difficulty with the Court today rises not from the Court as an institution but from human beings within it. But we cannot yield our constitutional destiny to the personal judgment of a few men who, being fearful of the future, would deny us the necessary means of dealing with the present.

This plan of mine is no attack on the Court; it seeks to restore the Court to its rightful and historic place in our system of constitutional government and to have it resume its high task of building anew on the Constitution "a system of living law."

·   ·   ·

During the past half century the balance of power between the three great branches of the Federal Government has been tipped out of balance by the courts in direct contradiction of the high purposes of the framers of the Constitution. It is my purpose to restore that balance. You who know me will accept my solemn assurance that in a world in which democracy is under attack I seek to make American democracy succeed.

Chief Justice Charles Evans Hughes' Letter to Senator Burton K. Wheeler

March 21, 1937

My Dear Senator Wheeler:

In response to your inquiries, I have the honor to present the following statement with respect to the work of the Supreme Court:

1. The Supreme Court is fully abreast of its work. When we rose on March 15 (for the present recess) we had heard argument in cases in which certiorari had been granted only 4 weeks before—February 15.

During the current term, which began last October and which we call "October term, 1936", we have heard argument on merits in 150 cases (180 numbers) and we have 28 cases (30 numbers) awaiting argument. We shall be able to hear all these cases, and such others as may come up for argument, before our adjournment for the term. There is no congestion of cases upon our calendar.

This gratifying condition has obtained for several years. We have been able for several terms to adjourn after disposing of all cases which are ready to be heard.

2. The cases on our docket are classified as original and appellate. Our original jurisdiction is defined by the Constitution and embraces cases to which States are parties. There are not many of these. At the present time they number 13 and are in various stages of progress to submission for determination.

Our appellate jurisdiction covers those cases in which appeal is allowed by statute as a matter of right and cases which come to us on writs of certiorari.

•   •   •

3. The statute relating to our appellate jurisdiction is the act of February 13, 1925. * * * That act limits to certain cases the appeals which come to the Supreme Court as a matter of right. Review in other cases is made to depend upon the allowance by the Supreme Court of a writ of certiorari.

Where the appeal purports to lie as a matter of right, the rules of the Supreme Court (rule 12) require the appellant to submit a jurisdictional statement showing that the case falls within that class of appeals and that a substantial question is involved. We examine that statement, and the supporting and opposing briefs, and decide whether the Court had jurisdiction. As a result, many frivolous appeals are forthwith dismissed and the way is open for appeals which disclose substantial questions.

4. The act of 1925, limiting appeals as a matter of right and enlarging the provisions for review only through certiorari was most carefully considered by Congress. I call attention to the reports of the Judiciary Committees of the Senate and House of Representatives. * * * That legislation was deemed to be essential to enable the Supreme Court to perform its proper function. No single court of last resort, whatever the number of judges, could dispose of all the cases which arise in this vast country and which litigants would seek to bring up if the right of appeal were unrestricted. Hosts of litigants will take appeals so long as there is a tribunal accessible. In protracted litigation, the advantage is with those who command a long purse. Unmeritorious appeals cause intolerable delays. Such appeals clog the calendar and get in the way of those that have merit.

Under our Federal system, when litigants have had their cases heard in the courts of first instance, and the trier of the facts, jury or judge, as the case may require, has spoken and the case on the facts and law has been decided, and when the dissatisfied party has been accorded an appeal to the circuit court of appeals, the litigants, so far as mere private interests are concerned, have had their day in court. If further review is to be had by the Supreme Court it must be because of the public interest in the questions involved. That review, for example, should be for the purpose of resolving conflicts in judicial decisions between different circuit courts of appeals or between circuit courts of appeals and State courts where the question is one of State law; or for the purpose of determining constitutional questions or settling the interpretation of statutes; or because of the importance of the questions of law that are involved. Review by the Supreme

Court is thus in the interest of the law, its appropriate exposition and enforcement, not in the mere interest of the litigants.

It is obvious that if appeal as a matter of right is restricted to certain described cases, the question whether review should be allowed in other cases must necessarily be confided to some tribunal for determination, and, of course, with respect to review by the Supreme Court, that Court should decide.

5. Granting certiorari is not a matter of favor but of sound judicial discretion. It is not the importance of the parties or the amount of money involved that is in any sense controlling. The action of the Court is governed by its rules . . . .

. . .

I should add that petitions of certiorari are not apportioned among the Justices. In all matters before the Court, except in the more routine of administration, all the Justices—unless for some reason a Justice is disqualified or unable to act in a particular case—participate in the decision. This applies to the grant or refusal of petitions for certiorari. Furthermore, petitions for certiorari are granted if four Justices think they should be. A vote by a majority is not required in such cases. Even if two or three of the Justices are strongly of the opinion that certiorari should be alowed, frequently the other Justices will acquiesce in their view, but the petition is always granted if four so vote.

6. The work of passing upon these applications for certiorari is laborious but the Court is able to perform it adequately. Observations have been made as to the vast number of pages of records and briefs that are submitted in the course of a term. The total is imposing but the suggested conclusion is hasty and rests on an illusory basis. Records are replete with testimony and evidence of facts. But the questions on certiorari are questions of law. So many cases turn on the facts, principles of law not being in controversy. It is only when the facts are interwoven with the questions of law which we should review that the evidence must be examined and then only to the extent that it is necessary to decide the questions of law.

This at once disposes of a vast number of factual controversies where the parties have been fully heard in the courts below and have no right to burden the Supreme Court with the dispute which interests no one but themselves.

This is also true of controversies over contracts and documents of all sorts which involve only questions of concern to the immediate parties. The applicant for certiorari is required to state in his petition the grounds for his application and in a host of cases that disclosure itself disposes of his request. So that the number of pages of records and briefs afford no satisfactory criterion of the actual work involved. It must also be remembered that Justices who have been dealing with such matters for years have the aid of a long and varied experience in separating the chaff from the wheat.

I think that it is safe to say that about 60 percent of the applications for certiorari are wholly without merit and ought never to have been made. There are probably about 20 percent or so in addition which have a fair degree of plausibility but which fail to survive critical examination. The remainder, falling short, I believe, of 20 percent, show substantial grounds and are granted. I think that it is the view of the members of the Court that if any error is made in dealing with these applications it is on the side of liberality.

7. An increase in the number of Justices of the Supreme Court, apart from any question of policy, which I do not discuss, would not promote the efficiency of the Court. It is believed that it would impair that efficiency so long as the Court acts as a unit. There would be more judges to hear, more judges to confer, more judges to discuss, more judges to be convinced and to decide. The present number of Justices is thought to be large enough so far as the prompt, adequate, and efficient conduct of the work of the Court is concerned. As I have said, I do not speak of any considerations in view of the appropriate attitude of the Court in relation to questions of policy.

I understand that it has been suggested that with more Justices the Court could hear cases in divisions. It is believed that such a plan would be impracticable. A large proportion of the cases we hear are important and a decision by a part of the Court would be unsatisfactory.

I may also call attention to the provisions of article III, section 1, of the Constitution that the judicial power of the United States shall be vested "in one Supreme Court" and in such inferior courts as the Congress may from time to time ordain and establish. The Constitution does not appear to authorize two or more Supreme Courts or two or more parts of a supreme court functioning in effect as separate courts.

On account of the shortness of time I have not been able to consult with the members of the Court generally with respect to the foregoing statement, but I am confident that it is in accord with the views of the Justices. I should say, however, that I have been able to consult with Mr. Justice Van Devanter and Mr. Justice Brandeis, and I am at liberty to say that the statement is approved by them.

Ex parte McCardle

7 Wall. 506 (1869)

MR. CHIEF JUSTICE CHASE delivered the opinion of the Court.

This cause came here by appeal from the Circuit Court for the Southern District of Mississippi.

A petition for the writ of *habeas corpus* was preferred in that court by [McCardle], alleging unlawful restraint by military force.

The writ was issued and a return was made by the military commander, admitting the restraint, but denying that it was unlawful.

It appeared that the petitioner was not in the military service of the United States, but was held in custody by military authority, for trial before a Military Commission, upon charge founded upon the publication of articles alleged to be incendiary and libelous, in a newspaper of which he was editor.

Upon the hearing, [McCardle] was remanded to military custody; but upon his prayer, an appeal was allowed him to this court, and upon filing the usual appeal bond for costs, he was admitted to bail. . . .

* * *

Subsequently, the case was argued very thoroughly and ably upon the merits, and was taken under advisement. While it was thus held, and before conference in regard to the decision proper to be made, an Act was passed by Congress, * * *, returned, with objections by the President, and repassed by the constitutional majority, which, it is insisted, takes from this court jurisdiction of the appeal.

The 2d section of this Act was as follows:

And be it further enacted, that so much of the Act approved February 5, 1867, . . .
as authorized an appeal from the judgment of the circuit court to the Supreme
Court of the United States, . . . is hereby repealed.

The attention of the court was directed to this statute at the last term, but counsel having expressed a desire to be heard in argument upon its effect, and the Chief Justice being detained from his place here by his duties in the Court of Impeachment, the cause was continued under advisement.

At this term we have heard arguments upon the effect of the repealing Act, and will now dispose of the case.

The first question necessarily is that of jurisdiction; for, if the act . . . takes away the jurisdiction defined by the act of February, 1867, it is useless, if not improper, to enter into any discussion of other questions.

It is quite true, as was argued by the counsel for [McCardle], that the appellate jurisdiction of this court is not derived from acts of Congress. It is, strictly speaking, conferred by the Constitution. But it is conferred "with such exceptions and under such regulations as Congress shall make." . . .

* * *

The exception to appellate jurisdiction in the case before us . . . is not an inference from the affirmation of other appellate jurisdiction. It is made in terms. The provision of the act of 1867, affirming the appellate jurisdiction of this court in cases of *habeas corpus* is expressly repealed. It is hardly possible to imagine a plainer instance of positive exception.

We are not at liberty to inquire into the motives of the legislature. We can only examine into its power under the Constitution; and the power to make exceptions to the appellate jurisdiction of this court is given by express words.

What, then, is the effect of the repealing act upon the case before us? We cannot doubt as to this. Without jurisdiction the court cannot proceed at all in any cause. Jurisdiction is power to declare the law, and when it ceases to exist, the only function remaining to the court is that of announcing the fact and dismissing the cause. And this is not less clear upon authority than upon principle.

Several cases were cited by the counsel for [McCardle] in support of the position that jurisdiction of this case is not affected by the repealing act. But none of them, in our judgment, afford any support to it. They are all cases of the exercise of judicial power by the legislature, or of legislative interference with courts in the exercising of continuing jurisdiction. * * *

On the other hand, the general rule, supported by the best elementary writers * * * is, that "when an act of the legislature is repealed, it must be considered, except as to transactions past and closed, as if it never existed." And the effect of repealing acts upon suits under acts repealed, has been determined by the adjudications of this court. . . .

It is quite clear, therefore, that this court cannot proceed to pronounce judgment in this case, for it has no longer jurisdiction of the appeal; and judicial duty is not less fitly performed by declining ungranted jurisdiction than in exercising firmly that which the Constitution and the laws confer.

Counsel seem to have supposed, if effect be given to the repealing act in question, that the whole appellate power of the court, in cases of *habeas corpus*, is denied. But this is an error. The act of 1868 does not except from that jurisdiction any cases but appeals from Circuit Courts under the act of 1867. It does not affect the jurisdiction which was previously exercised. * * *

The appeal of [McCardle] must be dismissed for want of jurisdiction.

Cooper v. Aaron

358 U.S. 1 (1958)

Opinion of the Court by THE CHIEF JUSTICE, MR. JUSTICE BLACK, MR. JUSTICE FRANKFURTER, MR. JUSTICE DOUGLAS, MR. JUSTICE BURTON, MR. JUSTICE CLARK, MR. JUSTICE HARLAN, MR. JUSTICE BRENNAN, and MR. JUSTICE WHITTAKER.

As this case reaches us it raises questions of the highest importance to the maintenance of our federal system of government. It necessarily involves a claim by the Governor and Legislature of a State that there is no duty on state officials to obey federal court orders resting on this Court's considered interpretation of the United States Constitution. Specifically it involves actions by the Governor and Legislature of Arkansas upon the premise that they are not bound by our holding in Brown v Board of Education. * * * That holding was that the Fourteenth Amendment forbids States to use their governmental powers to bar children on racial grounds from attending schools where there is state participation through any arrangement, management, funds or property. We are urged to uphold a suspension of the Little Rock School Board's plan to do away with segregated public schools in Little Rock until state laws and efforts to upset and nullify our holding in Brown v Board of Education have been further challenged and tested in the courts. We reject these contentions.

. . .

On May 17, 1954, this Court decided that enforced racial segregation in the public schools of a State is a denial of the equal protection of the laws enjoined by the Fourteenth Amendment. Brown v Board of Education. * * * The Court postponed, pending further argument, formulation of a decree to effectuate this decision. That decree was rendered May 31, 1955. * * * In the formulation of that decree the Court recognized that good faith compliance with the principles declared in Brown might in some situations "call for elimination of a variety of obstacles in making the transition to school systems operated in accordance with the constitutional principles set forth in our May 17, 1954, decision." * * *

. . .

. . . [T]he District Courts were directed to require "a prompt and reasonable start toward full compliance," and to take such action as was necessary to bring about the end of racial segregation in the public schools "with all deliberate speed." . . . It was made plain that delay in any guise in order to deny the constitutional rights of Negro children could not be countenanced, and that only a prompt start, diligently and earnestly pursued, to eliminate racial segregation from the public schools could constitute good faith compliance. State authorities were thus duty bound to devote every effort toward initiating desegregation and bringing about the elimination of racial discrimination in the public school system.

. . .

While the School Board was . . . going forward with its preparation for desegregating the Little Rock school system, other state authorities, in contrast, were actively pursuing a program designed to perpetuate in Arkansas the system of racial segregation which this Court had held violated the Fourteenth Amendment. . . .

The School Board and the Superintendent of Schools nevertheless continued with preparations to carry out the first stage of the desegregation program. Nine

Negro children were scheduled for admission in September 1957 to Central High School. . . .

On September 2, 1957, the day before these Negro students were to enter Central High, the school authorities were met with drastic opposing action on the part of the Governor of Arkansas who dispatched units of the Arkansas National Guard to the Central High School grounds and placed the school "off limits" to colored students. As found by the District Court in subsequent proceedings, the Governor's action had not been requested by the school authorities, and was entirely unheralded.

• • •

. . . The Governor's action caused the School Board to request the Negro students on September 2 not to attend the high school "until the legal dilemma was solved." The next day, September 3, 1957, the Board petitioned the District Court for instructions, and the court, after a hearing, found that the Board's request of the Negro students to stay away from the high school had been made because of the stationing of the military guards by the state authorities. The court determined that this was not a reason for departing from the approved plan, and ordered the School Board and Superintendent to proceed with it.

On the morning of the next day, September 4, 1957, the Negro children attempted to enter the high school but . . . [the] National Guard "acting pursuant to the Governor's order, stood shoulder to shoulder at the school grounds and thereby forcibly prevented the 9 Negro students . . . from entering," as they continued to do every school day during the following three weeks. * * *

• • •

. . . After hearings, . . . the District Court found that the School Board's plan had been obstructed by the Governor through the use of National Guard troops, and granted a preliminary injunction . . . enjoining the Governor and the officers of the Guard from preventing the attendance of Negro children at Central High School, and from otherwise obstructing or interfering with the orders of the court in connection with the plan.* * * The National Guard was then withdrawn from the school.

The next school day was Monday, September 23, 1957. The Negro children entered the high school that morning under the protection of the Little Rock Police Department and members of the Arkansas State Police. But the officers caused the children to be removed from the school during the morning because they had difficulty controlling a large and demonstrating crowd which had gathered at the high school. * * * On September 25, however, the President of the United States dispatched federal troops to Central High School and admission of the Negro students to the school was thereby effected. . . .

We come now to the aspect of the proceedings presently before us. . . . [T]he School Board and the Superintendent of Schools filed a petition in the District Court seeking a postponement of their program for desegregation. Their position in essence was that because of extreme public hostility, which they stated had been engendered largely by the official attitudes and actions of the Governor and the Legislature, the maintenance of a sound educational program at Central High School, with the Negro students in attendance, would be impossible. The Board therefore proposed that the Negro students already admitted to the school be withdrawn and sent to segregated schools, and that all further steps to carry out the Board's desegregation program be postponed for a period later suggested by the Board to be two and one-half years.

• • •

One may well sympathize with the position of the Board in the face of the frustrating conditions which have confronted it, but, regardless of the Board's good faith, the actions of the other state agencies responsible for those conditions compel us to reject the Board's legal position. Had Central High School been under the direct management of the State itself, it could hardly be suggested that those immediately in charge of the school should be heard to assert their own good faith as a legal excuse for delay in implementing the constitutional rights of these respondents, when vindication of those rights was rendered difficult or impossible by the actions of other state officials. The situation here is in no different posture because the members of the School Board and the Superintendent of Schools are local officials; from the point of view of the Fourteenth Amendment, they stand in this litigation as the agents of the State.

The constitutional rights of respondents are not to be sacrificed or yielded to the violence and disorder which have followed upon the actions of the Governor and Legislature. . . . Thus law and order are not here to be preserved by depriving the Negro children of their constitutional rights. The record before us clearly establishes that the growth of the Board's difficulties to a magnitude beyond its unaided power to control is the product of state action. . . .

The controlling legal principles are plain. The command of the Fourteenth Amendment is that no "State" shall deny to any person within its jurisdiction the equal protection of the laws. . . . [T]he prohibitions of the Fourteenth Amendment extend to all action of the State denying equal protection of the laws; whatever the agency of the State taking the action. * * * In short, the constitutional rights of children not to be discriminated against in school admission on grounds of race or color declared by this Court in the Brown case can neither be nullified openly and directly by state legislators or state executive or judicial officers, nor nullified indirectly by them through evasive schemes for segregation whether attempted "ingeniously or ingenuously." * * *

What has been said, in the light of the facts developed, is enough to dispose of the case. However, we should answer the premise of the actions of the Governor and Legislature that they are not bound by our holding in the Brown case. It is necessary only to recall some basic constitutional propositions which are settled doctrine.

Article 6 of the Constitution makes the Constitution the "supreme Law of the Land." . . . Chief Justice Marshall . . . declared in Marbury v Madison: * * * "It is emphatically the province and duty of the judicial department to say what the law is." This decision declared the basic principle that the federal judiciary is supreme in the exposition of the law of the Constitution, and that principle has ever since been respected by this Court and the Country as a permanent and indispensable feature of our constitutional system. It follows that the interpretation of the Fourteenth Amendment enunciated by this Court in the Brown Case is the supreme law of the land, and Art 6 of the Constitution makes it of binding effect on the States "any Thing in the Constitution or Laws of any State to the Contrary notwithstanding." Every state legislator and executive and judicial officer is solemnly committed by oath taken pursuant to Art 6, cl 3, "to support this Constitution." . . .

No state legislator or executive or judicial officer can war against the Constitution without violating his undertaking to support it. Chief Justice Marshall spoke for a unanimous Court in saying that: "If the legislatures of the several states may, at will, annul the judgments of the courts of the United States, and destroy the rights acquired under those judgments, the constitution itself becomes a solemn mockery. . . ." * * * A Governor who asserts a power to nullify a federal court order is similarly restrained. . . .

It is, of course, quite true that the responsibility for public education is primarily the concern of the States, but it is equally true that such responsibilities, like all other state activity, must be exercised consistently with federal constitutional requirements as they apply to state action. . . . State support of segregated schools through any arrangement, management, funds, or property cannot be squared with the Amendment's command that no State shall deny to any person within its jurisdiction the equal protection of the laws. . . . The basic decision in Brown was unanimously reached by this Court. . . . Since the first Brown opinion three new Justices have come to the Court. They are at one with the Justices still on the Court who participated in that basic decision as to its correctness, and that decision is now unanimously reaffirmed. The principles announced in that decision and the obedience of the States to them, according to the command of the Constitution, are indispensable for the protection of the freedoms guaranteed by our fundamental charter for all of us. Our constitutional ideal of equal justice under law is thus made a living truth.

MR. JUSTICE FRANKFURTER, concurring.

• • •

The use of force to further obedience to law is a last resort and one not congenial to the spirit of our Nation. But the tragic aspect of this disruptive tactic was that the power of the State was used not to sustain law but as an instrument for thwarting law. The State of Arkansas is thus responsible for disabling one of its subordinate agencies, the Little Rock School Board, from peacefully carrying out the Board's and the State's constitutional duty. Accordingly, while Arkansas is not a formal party in these proceedings and decree cannot go against the State, it is legally and morally before the Court.

We are now asked to hold that the illegal, forcible interference by the State of Arkansas with the continuance of what the Constitution commands, and the consequences in disorder that it entrained, should be recognized as justification for undoing what the School Board had formulated, what the District Court in 1955 had directed to be carried out, and what was in process of obedience. No explanation that may be offered in support of such a request can obscure the inescapable meaning that law should bow to force. To yield to such a claim would be to enthrone official lawlessness, and lawlessness if not checked is the precursor of anarchy. On the few tragic occasions in the history of the Nation, North and South, when law was forcibly resisted or systematically evaded, it has signalled the breakdown of constitutional processes of government on which ultimately rest the liberties of all. Violent resistance to law cannot be made a legal reason for its suspension without loosening the fabric of our society. What could this mean but to acknowledge that disorder under the aegis of a State has moral superiority over the law of the Constitution? For those in authority thus to defy the law of the land is profoundly subversive not only of our constitutional system but of the presuppositions of a democratic society. . . .

•   •   •

President Richard M. Nixon's Message to Congress

March 17, 1972

In this message, I wish to discuss a question which divides many Americans. That is the question of busing.

I want to do so in a way that will enable us to focus our attention on a question which unites all Americans. That is the question of how to ensure a better education for all of our children.

In the furor over busing, it has become all too easy to forget what busing is supposed to be designed to achieve: equality of educational opportunity for all Americans.

Conscience and the Constitution both require that no child should be denied equal educational opportunity. That Constitutional mandate was laid down by the Supreme Court in *Brown* v. *Board of Education* in 1954. The years since have been ones of dismantling the old dual school system in those areas where it existed—a process that has now been substantially completed.

As we look to the future, it is clear that the efforts to provide equal educational opportunity must now focus much more specifically on education: on assuring that the opportunity is not only equal, but adequate, and that in those remaining cases in which desegregation has not yet been completed it be achieved with a greater sensitivity to educational needs.

Acting within the present framework of Constitutional and case law, the lower Federal courts have ordered a wide variety of remedies for the equal protection violations they have found. These remedies have included such plans as redrawing attendance zones, pairing, clustering and consolidation of school districts. Some of these plans have not required extensive additional transportation of pupils. But some have required that pupils be bused long distances, at great inconvenience. In some cases plans have required that children be bused away from their neighborhoods to schools that are inferior or even unsafe.

The maze of differing and sometimes inconsistent orders by the various lower courts has led to contradiction and uncertainty, and often to vastly unequal treatment among regions, States and local school districts. In the absence of statutory guidelines, many lower court decisions have gone far beyond what most people would consider reasonable, and beyond what the Supreme Court has said is necessary, in the requirements they have imposed for the reorganization of school districts and the transportation of school pupils.

All too often, the result has been a classic case of the remedy for one evil creating another evil. In this case, a remedy for the historic evil of racial discrimination has often created a new evil of disrupting communities and imposing hardship on children—both black and white—who are themselves wholly innocent of the wrongs that the plan seeks to set right.

The 14th Amendment to the Constitution—under which the school desegregation cases have arisen—provides that "The Congress shall have power to enforce, by appropriate legislation, the provisions of this article."

Until now, enforcement has been left largely to the courts—which have operated within a limited range of available remedies, and in the limited context of case law rather than of statutory law. I propose that the Congress now accept the responsibility and use the authority given to it under the 14th Amendment to clear up the confusion which contradictory court orders have created, and to establish reasonable national standards.

The legislation I propose today would accomplish this.

It would put an immediate stop to further new busing orders by the Federal courts.

It would enlist the wisdom, the resources and the experience of the Congress in the solution of the vexing problem involved in fashioning school desegregation policies that are true to the Constitutional requirements and fair to the people and communities concerned.

It would establish uniform national criteria, to ensure that the Federal courts in all sections and all States would have a common set of standards to guide them.

• • •

At the same time, these measures would not roll back the Constitution, or undo the great advances that have been made in ending school segregation, or undermine the continuing drive for equal rights.

Specifically, I propose that the Congress enact two measures which together would shift the focus from more transportation to better education, and would curb busing while expanding educational opportunity. They are:

1. *The Equal Educational Opportunities Act of 1972.*

• • •

2. *The Student Transportation Moratorium Act of 1972.*

. . . (This would provide a period of time during which any future, new busing orders by the courts would not go into effect, while the Congress considered legislative approaches—such as the Equal Educational Opportunities Act—to the questions raised by school desegregation cases. This moratorium on new busing would be effective until July 1, 1973, or until the Congress passed the appropriate legislation, whichever was sooner. Its purpose would not be to contravene rights under the 14th Amendment, but simply to hold in abeyance further busing orders while the Congress investigated and considered alternative methods of securing those rights—methods that could establish a new and broader context in which the courts could decide desegregation cases, and that could render busing orders unnecessary.)

Together, these two measures would provide an immediate stop to new busing in the short run, and constructive alternatives to busing in the long run—and they would give the Congress the time it needs to consider fully and fairly one of the most complex and difficult issues to confront the Nation in modern times.

Busing: The Fears and Concerns

Before discussing the specifics of these proposals, let me deal candidly with the controversy surrounding busing itself.

There are some people who fear any curbs on busing because they fear that it would break the momentum of the drive for equal rights for blacks and other minorities. Some fear it would go further, and that it would set in motion a chain of reversals that would undo all the advances so painfully achieved in the past generation.

It is essential that whatever we do to curb busing be done in a way that plainly will not have these other consequences. It is vitally important that the Nation's continued commitment to equal rights and equal opportunities be clear and concrete.

On the other hand, it is equally important that we not allow emotionalism to crowd out reason, or get so lost in symbols that words lose their meaning.

One emotional undercurrent that has done much to make this so difficult an issue is the feeling some people have that to oppose busing is to be anti-black. . . .

There is no escaping the fact that some people oppose busing because of racial prejudice. But to go on from this to conclude that "anti-busing" is simply a code word for prejudice is an exercise in arrant unreason. There are right reasons for opposing busing, and there are wrong reasons—and most people, including large and increasing numbers of blacks and other minorities, oppose it for reasons that have little or nothing to do with race. It would compound an injustice to persist in massive busing simply because some people oppose it for the wrong reasons.

· · ·

In addressing the busing question, it is important that we do so in historical perspective.

Busing for the purpose of desegregation was begun—mostly on a modest scale—as one of a mix of remedies to meet the requirements laid down by various lower Federal courts for achieving the difficult transition from the old dual school system to a new, unitary system.

At the time, the problems of transition that loomed ahead were massive, the old habits deeply entrenched, community resistance often extremely strong. As the years wore on, the courts grew increasingly impatient with what they some-times saw as delay or evasion, and increasingly insistent that, as the Supreme Court put it in the *Green* decision in 1968, desegregation plans must promise "realistically to work, and . . . to work *now*."

But in the past 3 years, progress toward eliminating the vestiges of the dual system has been phenomenal—and so too has been the shift in public attitudes in those areas where dual systems were formerly operated. In State after State and community after community, local civic, business and educational leaders of all races have come forward to help make the transition peacefully and successfully. Few voices are now raised urging a return to the old patterns of enforced segregation.

This new climate of acceptance of the basic Constitutional doctrine is a new element of great importance: for the greater the elements of basic good faith, of desire to make the system work, the less need or justification there is for extreme remedies rooted in coercion.

· · ·

. . . [T]his is not the simple black-white issue that some simplistically present it as being. There are deep divisions of opinion among people of all races—with recent surveys showing strong opposition to busing among black parents as well as among white parents—not because they are against desegregation but because they are for better education.

. . .

In the long, difficult effort to give life to what is in the law, to desegregate the Nation's schools and enforce the principle of equal opportunity, many experiments have been tried. Some have worked, and some have not. We now have the benefit of a fuller fund of experience than we had 18 years ago, or even 2 years ago. It has also become apparent that community resistance—black as well as white—to plans that massively disrupt education and separate parents from their children's schools, makes those plans unacceptable to communities on which they are imposed.

Against this background, the objectives of the reforms I propose are:

—To give practical meaning to the concept of equal educational opportunity.

—To apply the experience gained in the process of desegregation, and also in efforts to give special help to the educationally disadvantaged.

—To ensure the continuing vitality of the principles laid down in *Brown* v. *Board of Education.*

—To downgrade busing as a tool for achieving equal educational opportunity.

—To sustain the rights and responsibilities vested by the States in local school boards.

. . .

The Student Transportation Moratorium Act

. . .

The Congress has both the Constitutional authority and a special capability to debate and define new methods for implementing Constitutional principles. And the educational, financial and social complexities of this issue are not, and are not properly, susceptible of solution by individual courts alone or even by the Supreme Court alone.

This is a moment of considerable conflict and uncertainty; but it is also a moment of great opportunity.

This not a time for the courts to plunge ahead at full speed.

If we are to set a course that enables us to act together, and not simply to do more but to do better, then we must do all in our power to create an atmosphere that permits a calm and thoughtful assessment of the issues, choices and consequences.

I propose, therefore, that the Congress act to impose a temporary freeze on new busing orders by the Federal courts—to establish a waiting period while the Congress considers alternative means of enforcing 14th Amendment rights. I propose that this freeze be effective immediately on enactment, and that it remain in effect until July 1, 1973, or until passage of the appropriate legislation, whichever is sooner.

This freeze would not put a stop to desegregation cases; it would only bar new orders during its effective period, to the extent that they ordered new busing.

This, I recognize, is an unusual procedure. But I am persuaded that the Congress has the Constitutional power to enact such a stay, and I believe the unusual nature of the conflicts and pressures that confront both the courts and the country at this particular time requires it.

· · ·

Conclusion

These measures I have proposed would place firm and effective curbs on busing—and they would do so in a Constitutional way, aiding rather than challenging the courts, respecting the mandate of the 14th Amendment, and exercising the responsibility of the Congress to enforce that Amendment.

Beyond making these proposals, I am directing the Executive departments to follow policies consistent with the principles on which they are based—which will include intervention by the Justice Department in selected cases before the courts, both to implement the stay and to resolve some of those questions on which the lower courts have gone beyond the Supreme Court.

· · ·

I submit these proposals to the Congress mindful of the profound importance and special complexity of the issues they address. It is in that spirit that I have undertaken to weigh and respect the conflicting interests; to strike a balance which is thoughtful and just; and to search for answers that will best serve all of the Nation's children. I urge the Congress to consider them in the same spirit.

· · ·

Ex parte Grossman

267 U.S. 87 (1925)

MR. CHIEF JUSTICE TAFT delivered the opinion of the Court.

. . .

On November 24, 1920, the United States filed a bill in equity against Philip Grossman in the district court of the United States for the northern district of Illinois, under . . . the National Prohibition Act * * * averring that Grossman was maintaining a nuisance at his place of business in Chicago by sales of liquor in violation of the act and asking an injunction to abate the same. Two days later, the district judge granted a temporary order. January 11, 1921, an information was filed against Grossman, charging that after the restraining order had been served on him, he had sold to several persons liquor to be drunk on his premises. He was arrested, tried, found guilty of contempt, and sentenced to imprisonment in the Chicago House of Correction for one year and to pay a fine of $1,000 to the United States, and costs. . . . In December, 1923, the President issued a pardon in which he commuted the sentence of Grossman to the fine of $1,000, on condition that the fine be paid. The pardon was accepted, the fine was paid, and the defendant was released. In May, 1924, however, the district court committed Grossman to the Chicago House of Correction to serve the sentence, notwithstanding the pardon. * * * The only question raised by the pleadings herein is that of the power of the President to grant the pardon.

. . .

Article 2, § 2, clause 1, of the Constitution, dealing with the powers and duties of the President, closes with these words: "And he shall have power to grant reprieves and pardons for offenses against the United States, except in cases of impeachment."

The argument for [holding Grossman] is that the President's power extends only to offenses against the United States and a contempt of court is not such an offense, that offenses against the United States are not common-law offenses, but can only be created by legislative act, that the President's pardoning power is more limited than that of the King of England at common law, which was a broad prerogative and included contempts against his courts chiefly because the judges thereof were his agents and acted in his name; that the context of the Constitution shows that the word "offenses" is used in that instrument only to include crimes and misdemeanors triable by jury, and not contempts of the dignity and authority of the Federal courts, and that to construe the pardon clause to include contempts of court would be to violate the fundamental principle of the Constitution in the division of powers between the legislative, executive, and judicial branches, and to take from the Federal courts their independence and the essential means of protecting their dignity and authority.

The language of the Constitution cannot be interpreted safely except by reference to the common law and to British institutions as they were when the instrument was framed and adopted. The statesmen and lawyers of the Convention, who submitted it to the ratification of the Convention of the thirteen states, were born and brought up in the atmosphere of the common law, and thought and spoke in its vocabulary. They were familiar with other forms of government, recent and ancient, and indicated in their discussions earnest study and consideration of many of them, but when they came to put their conclusions into the form of fundamental law in a compact draft, they expressed them in terms of the common law, confident that they could be shortly and easily understood.

• • •

The King of England, before our Revolution, in the exercise of his prerogative, had always exercised the power to pardon contempts of court, just as he did ordinary crimes and misdemeanors, and as he has done to the present day. In the mind of a common-law lawyer of the eighteenth century the word "pardon" included within its scope the ending by the King's grace of the punishment of such derelictions, whether it was imposed by the court without a jury or upon indictment, for both forms of trial for contempts were had. * * *

. . . [L]ong before our Constitution, a distinction had been recognized at common law between the effect of the King's pardon to wipe out the effect of a sentence for contempt in so far as it had been imposed to punish the contemner for violating the dignity of the court and the King, in the public interest, and its inefficacy to halt or interfere with the remedial part of the court's order necessary to secure the rights of the injured suitor. * * * The same distinction, nowadays referred to as the difference between civil and criminal contempts, is still maintained in English law. * * *

In our own law the same distinction clearly appears. * * * . . . For civil contempts, the punishment is remedial and for the benefit of the complainant, and a pardon cannot stop it. For criminal contempts, the sentence is punitive in the public interest to vindicate the authority of the court and to deter other like derelictions.

• • •

It is said that "offenses against the United States," in the pardon clause, can include only crimes and misdemeanors defined and denounced by congressional act.

• • •

Nothing in the ordinary meaning of the words "offenses against the United States" excludes criminal contempts. That which violates the dignity and authority of Federal courts such as an intentional effort to defeat their decrees justifying punishment violates a law of the United States. * * *

· · ·

The argument is that the word "offenses" is used in the Constitution interchangeably with *crimes and criminal prosecutions.* * * * . . . [W]e have . . . recently held that "while contempt may be an offense against the law and subject to appropriate punishment, certain it is that since the foundation of our government proceedings to punish such offenses have been regarded as . . . criminal prosecutions, within the 6th Amendment, or common understanding." * * * Contempt proceedings . . . are not hedged about with all the safeguards provided in the Bill of Rights for protecting one accused of ordinary crime from the danger of unjust conviction. This is due, of course, to the fact that for years before the American Constitution, courts had been held to be inherently empowered to protect themselves and the function they perform by summary proceedings without a jury to punish disobedience of their orders and disturbance of their hearings. So it is clear to us that the language of the 5th and 6th Amendments and of other . . . parts of the Constitution is not of significance in determining the scope of pardons of "offenses against the United States" in article 2, § 2, clause 1, of the enumerated powers of the President. We think the arguments drawn from the common law, from the power of the King under the British Constitution, which plainly was the prototype of this clause, from the legislative history of the clause in the Convention, and from the ordinary meaning of its words, are much more relevant and convincing.

Moreover, criminal contempts of a Federal court have been pardoned for eighty-five years. In that time the power has been exercised twenty-seven times. . . . Such long practice under the pardoning power and acquiescence in it strongly sustain the construction it is based on. * * *

Finally, it is urged that criminal contempts should not be held within the pardoning power because it will tend to destroy the independence of the judiciary and violate the primary constitutional principle of a separation of the legislative, executive, and judicial powers. . . .

The Federal Constitution nowhere expressly declares that the three branches of the government shall be kept separate and independent. All legislative powers are vested in a Congress. The executive power is vested in a President. The judicial power is vested in one Supreme Court and in such inferior courts as Congress may from time to time establish. The judges are given life tenure and a compensation that may not be diminished during their continuance in office, with the evident purpose of securing them and their courts an independence of Congress and the Executive. Complete independence and separation between the three branches, however, are not attained, or intended, as other provisions of the Constitution and the normal operation of government under it easily demonstrate. By affirmative action through the veto power, the Executive and one more than one third of either House may defeat all legislation. One half of the House and two thirds of the Senate may impeach and remove the members of the Judiciary. The Executive can reprieve or pardon all offenses after their commission, either before trial, during trial, or after trial, by individuals, or by classes, conditionally or absolutely, and this without modification or regulation by Congress. * * * Negatively one House of Congress can withhold all appropriations and stop the operations of government. The Senate can hold up all appointments, confirmation of which either the Constitution or a statute requires, and thus deprive the President of the necessary agents with which he is to take care that the laws be faithfully executed.

These are some instances of positive and negative restraints possibly available under the Constitution to each branch of the government in defeat of the action of the other. They show that the independence of each of the others is qualified and is so subject to exception as not to constitute a broadly positive injunction or a necessarily controlling rule of construction. The fact is that the Judiciary, quite as much as Congress and the Executive, [is] dependent on the co-operation of the other two, that government may go on. Indeed, while the Constitution has made the Judiciary as independent of the other branches as is practicable, it is, as often remarked, the weakest of the three. It must look for a continuity of necessary co-operation, in the possible reluctance of either of the other branches, to the force of public opinion.

Executive clemency exists to afford relief from undue harshness or evident mistake in the operation or enforcement of the criminal law. The administration of justice by the courts is not necessarily always wise or certainly considerate of circumstances which may properly mitigate guilt. To afford a remedy, it has always been thought essential in popular governments, as well as in monarchies, to vest in some other authority than the courts power to ameliorate or avoid particular criminal judgments. It is a check intrusted to the Executive for special cases. To exercise it to the extent of destroying the deterrent effect of judicial punishment would be to pervert it; but whoever is to make it useful must have full discretion to exercise it. Our Constitution confers this discretion on the highest officer in the nation in confidence that he will not abuse it. An abuse in pardoning contempts would certainly embarrass courts, but it is questionable how much more it would lessen their effectiveness than a wholesale pardon of other offenses. . . . The detrimental effect of excessive pardons of completed contempts would be in the loss of the deterrent influence upon future contempts. It is of the same character as that of the excessive pardons of other offenses. The difference does not justify our reading criminal contempts out of the pardon clause by departing from its ordinary meaning, confirmed by its common-law origin and long years of practice and acquiescence.

· · ·

The power of a court to protect itself and its usefulness by punishing contemners is of course necessary, but it is one exercised without the restraining influence of a jury and without many of the guaranties which the Bill of Rights offers to protect the individual against unjust conviction. Is it unreasonable to provide for the possibility that the personal element may sometimes enter into a summary judgment pronounced by a judge who thinks his authority is flouted or denied? May it not be fairly said that in order to avoid possible mistake, undue prejudice or needless severity, the chance of pardon should exist at least as much in favor of a person convicted by a judge without a jury as in favor of one convicted in a jury trial? The pardoning by the President of criminal contempts has been practised more than three quarters of a century, and no abuses during all that time developed sufficiently to invoke a test in the Federal courts of its validity.

• • •

[Grossman] is discharged.

Taylor v. Hayes

418 U.S. 488 (1974)

MR. JUSTICE WHITE delivered the opinion of the Court.

The question in this case concerns the validity of a criminal contempt judgment entered against petitioner by reason of certain events occurring in the course of a criminal trial in the courts of the Commonwealth of Kentucky. [Taylor] was retained counsel for Narvel Tinsley, a Negro, who along with his brother Michael was charged with the murders of two police officers. . . . Trial before [Judge Hayes] began on October 18, 1971, and was completed on October 29.

On nine different occasions during this turbulent trial, [Hayes], out of the hearing of the jury and most often in chambers, informed [Taylor] that he was in contempt of court. The first charge was immediately reduced to a warning and no sentence was imposed at the time of charge in that or any other instance. [Taylor] was permitted to respond to most, but not all, of the charges.

At the conclusion of the trial on October 29 and after a guilty verdict had been returned, [Hayes], in the presence of the jury, made a statement concerning [Taylor's] trial conduct. Refusing [Taylor's] request to respond and declaring that "I have you" on nine counts, [Judge Hayes] proceeded to impose a jail term on each count totalling four and one-half years. . . .

The Kentucky Court of Appeals affirmed, holding that [Taylor] was guilty of each and every contempt charged. In its view, petitioner's actions "were deliberate, delaying or planned disruptive tactics which did in fact create such an atmosphere in the court that he, if permitted to continue, would have appeared to be the star performer in the center ring of a three-ring circus." * * * Petitioner had "committed innumerable acts . . . which clearly reflected his contempt for the court as well as the judicial system of this Commonwealth. . . ."

The Court of Appeals further ruled that . . . [because of Hayes' modification, while on appeal] . . . "the penalty actually imposed on Daniel Taylor [was] six months in jail," and his conviction and sentence without a jury trial was deemed constitutionally permissible. . . . [Taylor] contends that any charge of contempt of court, without exception, must be tried to a jury. Quite to the contrary, however, our cases hold that petty contempt like other petty criminal offenses may be tried without a jury and that contempt of court is a petty offense when the penalty actually imposed does not exceed six months or a longer penalty has not been expressly authorized by statute. * * * Hence, although petitioner was ultimately found guilty and sentenced separately on eight counts of contempt, the sentences were to run concurrently and were, as the Kentucky Court of Appeals held, equivalent to a single sentence of six months. * * * The original sentences imposed on the separate counts were to run consecutively and totaled almost four and one-half years, with two individual counts each carrying a year's sentence. But the trial court itself entered an amended judgment which was understood by the Kentucky Court of Appeals to impose no more than a six-month sentence. The eight contempts, whether considered singly or collectively, thus constituted petty offenses, and trial by jury was not required.

. . . We remain firmly committed to the proposition that "criminal contempt is not a crime of the sort that requires the right to jury trial regardless of the penalty involved." * * *

We are more persuaded by [Taylor's] contention that he was entitled to more of a hearing and notice than he received prior to final conviction and sentence. In each instance during the trial when [Judge Hayes] considered [Taylor] to be in contempt, [Taylor] was informed of that fact and, in most instances, had opportunity to respond to the charge at that time. It is quite true, as the Kentucky Court of Appeals held, that "[t]he contempt citations and the sentences coming at the end of the trial were not and could not have been a surprise to Taylor, because upon each occasion and immediately following the charged act of contempt the court informed Taylor that he was at that time in contempt of court." * * * But no sentence was imposed during the trial, and it does not appear to us that any final adjudication of contempt was entered until after the verdict was returned. It was then that the court proceeded to describe and characterize [Taylor's] various acts during trial as contemptuous, to find him guilty of nine acts of contempt and to sentence him immediately for each of those acts.

It is also plain from the record that when [Taylor] sought to respond to what the Kentucky Court of Appeals referred to as the trial court's "declaration of a charge against Taylor based on the judge's observations" during trial, [Hayes] informed him that "you are not responding to me on anything" and even indicated that [Taylor] might be gagged if he insisted on defending himself. The trial court then proceeded without further formality to impose consecutive sentences totalling almost four and one-half years in the county jail and to bar [Taylor] forever from practicing before the court in which the case at issue had been tried.

This procedure does not square with the Due Process Clause of the Fourteenth Amendment. We are not concerned here with the trial judge's power, for the purpose of maintaining order in the courtroom, to punish summarily and without notice or hearing contemptuous conduct committed in his presence and observed by him. . . .

[W]here conviction and punishment are delayed, "it is much more difficult to argue that action without notice or hearing of any kind is necessary to preserve order and enable [the court] to proceed with its business." * * * . . . This is not to say, however, that a full-scale trial is appropriate. Usually, the events have occurred before the judge's own eyes, and a reporter's transcript is available. But the contemnor might at least urge, for example, that the behavior at issue was not contempt but the acceptable conduct of an attorney representing his client; or, he might present matters in mitigation or otherwise attempt to make amends with the court. * * *

These procedures are essential in view of the heightened potential for abuse posed by the contempt power. * * * The provision of fundamental due process protections for contemnors accords with our historic notions of elementary fairness. While we have no desire "to imprison the discretion of judges within rigid mechanical rules," * * * we remain unpersuaded that "the additional time and expense possibly involved . . . will seriously handicap the effective functioning of the courts." * * * Due process cannot be measured in minutes and hours or dollars and cents. . . .

Because these minimum requirements of due process of law were not extended to [Taylor] in this case, the contempt judgment must be set aside.

We are also convinced that if [Taylor] is to be tried again, he should not be tried by [Judge Hayes]. We agree with the Kentucky Court of Appeals that [Taylor's] conduct did not constitute the kind of personal attack on [Hayes] that, regardless of his reaction or lack of it, he would be "[un]likely to maintain that calm detachment necessary for fair adjudication." * * *

But contemptuous conduct, though short of personal attack, may still provoke a trial judge and so embroil him in controversy that he cannot "hold the balance nice, clear and true between the State and the accused. . . ." * * *

. . . [W]e have examined the record in this case, and it appears to us that [Hayes] did become embroiled in a running controversy with [Taylor]. Moreover, as the trial progressed, there was a mounting display of an unfavorable personal attitude toward [Taylor], his ability and his motives, sufficiently so that the contempt issue should have been finally adjudicated by another judge.

• • •

That [Hayes] had reacted strongly to [Taylor's] conduct throughout the 10-day trial clearly emerged in the statement which he made prior to sentencing petitioner . . . . There he said petitioner had put on "the worst display" he had seen in many years at the bar— "[a]s far as a lawyer is concerned, you're not." * * * Furthermore, [Judge Hayes] denied [Taylor] the opportunity to make any statement at that time, threatened to gag him and forthwith sentenced him to four and one-half years in jail, not to mention later disbarring him from further practice in his court. He also refused to grant him bail pending appeal. We assume for the purposes of this case that each of the charged acts was contemptuous; nevertheless, a sentence of this magnitude reflects the extent to which [Judge Hayes] became personally involved. * * *

From our own reading of the record, we have concluded that "marked personal feelings were present on both sides" and that the marks of "unseemly conduct [had] left personal stings." * * * A fellow judge should have been substituted for the purpose of finally disposing of the charges of contempt made by [Hayes] against [Taylor]. . . .

Nothing we have said here should be construed to condone the type of conduct . . . found by that court to have been engaged in by [Taylor]. Behavior of this nature has no place in the courtroom which, in a free society, is a forum for the courteous and reasoned pursuit of truth and justice.

• • •

Mr. Justice Douglas joined parts of the Court's opinion. [Omitted.]

Mr. Justice Marshall, dissenting in part.

• • •

. . . In my view, [the four and one-half year] sentence marked the contempt charges against petitioner as "serious" rather than "petty" and called into play [Taylor's] Sixth Amendment right to a jury trial.

. . . [T]he trial judge's reduction of [Taylor's] sentence was a transparent effort to circumvent this Court's Sixth Amendment decisions and to save his summary conviction of [Taylor] without the necessity of airing the charges before an impartial jury. . . .

Today's decision represents an extraordinarily rigid and wooden application of the six-month rule that the Court has fashioned to determine when the Sixth Amendment right is applicable. In permitting this obvious device to succeed, I think that the Court changes the nature of the six-month rule from a reasonable effort to distinguish between "serious" and "petty" contempts into an arbitrary barrier behind which judges who wish to protect their summary contempt convictions without exposing their charges to the harsh light of a jury may safely hide. . . . I do not believe that [Taylor] could be deprived of his Sixth Amendment right to jury trial, once it attached through the imposition of a substantial sentence, by the subsequent action of the trial court or an appellate court in reducing the sentence.

• • •

MR. JUSTICE REHNQUIST . . . dissenting.

• • •

The Court's decision today [is] the culmination of a recent trend of constitutional innovation which virtually emasculates [the] historic power of a trial judge. If the Court's holding in this area [was] the product of any new historical insight into the meaning of the Fourteenth Amendment, or if indeed [it] could be regarded as a desirable progression toward a reign of light and law, even though of dubious constitutional ancestry, there would be less occasion for concern. But from the hodge-podge of legal doctrine embodied in [this decision] which [has] irretrievably blended together constitutional guarantees of jury trial in criminal cases, constitutional guarantees of impartial judges, and fragments of the law of contempt . . . the only consistent thread which emerges is this Court's inveterate propensity to second-guess the trial judge.

. . . [The] Court holds, squarely . . . that the . . . trial judge was not entitled to proceed summarily against [Taylor], even though all of the conduct in question occurred in the presence of [Hayes]. The Court apparently concludes that since [Hayes] did not sentence [Taylor] until after the proceedings at issue were completed, and at that point refused to permit [him] to respond, [Taylor's] due process rights were violated.

• • •

Our prior decisions have continuously adhered to the view that "[w]here the contempt is committed directly under the eye or within the view of the court, it may 'proceed upon its knowledge of the facts and punish the offender, without further proof, and without issue or trial in any form.' " * * * It is only when the contempt is not a direct one, i. e., observed by the judge himself, that the power to proceed summarily becomes subject to some qualification. * * *

• • •

Even were I in agreement with the Court's conclusion that Taylor's contempt conviction should be reversed, I nevertheless could not join in the holding that if [he] is to be tried again, he may not be tried by [Hayes]. While conceding that [Taylor's] conduct did not constitute the kind of personal attack on [Hayes] that would prevent the latter from maintaining the calm detachment necessary for fair adjudication, * * * the Court holds that "it appears to us that [Hayes] did become embroiled in a running controversy with [Taylor]." * * *

• • •

. . . [T]oday's decision [teaches us that] a judge *can* be driven out of a case by any counsel sufficiently astute to read the newfound constitutional principles enunciated in [this decision]. Whether as a matter of policy the added procedural rights conferred upon contemptuous lawyers are worth the sacrifice of the historic authority of the trial judge to control proceedings in his court may be open to debate, the total absence of any basis in the Fourteenth Amendment for the result which the Court reaches in Taylor v Hayes, is to me clear beyond any doubt. Accordingly, I dissent from the Court's reversal of the conviction in that case.

CHAPTER 3

Self-Imposed Limitations on the Exercise of Judicial Power

INTRODUCTORY ESSAY

The actual powers of the Supreme Court are relatively minute when compared with its "symbolic" powers; but the distinction between actual and symbolic power is not significant if the policy dictates of the Court are, for the most part, regularly obeyed. In point of fact, the Court has been rather successful in securing compliance from the public at large, state legislatures, Congress, and the President, all in the face of the judiciary's obvious political handicaps vis-à-vis the sources of actual power. What might account for this success? We believe that the Court's present stature as a policymaking institution of considerable authority emanates from the combined effects of acquiescence by state governments, coequal branches, and the public at large to the Court's expanding role and aggrandizement of power and the Court's careful and "judicious" use of the very powers it has acquired in the process. Between 1789 and 1977 the Court ruled only 104 federal provisions unconstitutional (*Congressional Quarterly,* 1977, p. 168), and between 1789 and 1974 it ruled only 848 state laws and 96 municipal ordinances to be at odds with the Constitution (Library of Congress, 1974). (Interestingly, more than a third of those rulings have come since 1940.) Considering the vast number of issues, laws, and ordinances presented to the Court over the years, the blatant exercise of power is the exception rather than the rule.

The Court has not maintained its power base simply by limiting the frequency with which it blatantly exercises its power. Rather than just acting rarely, the Court has developed, or at least attempted to develop, a set of policies restricting the general circumstances under which it and the lower courts will act. Generally a court will act (that is, hear and decide cases) only if it finds that two basic criteria have been met. First the court must determine whether it has the authority to hear and decide a given case. A court's authority, referred to as its *jurisdiction,* is granted and specified by constitution or statute; that authority is subject to some degree of discretionary interpretation by judges. There is a *geographic jurisdiction* specifying the region over which a court's authority extends, a *jurisdiction over the person* specifying the persons subject to court authority, and a *subject matter juris-diction* limiting the subjects of dispute a court can entertain. Finally, there is a *hierarchical jurisdiction* that differentiates a court by its status as a trial court or an appellate court. The first matter of business for a court to decide, then, is whether it is entitled by virtue of geography, party, subject matter, or level of court to hear and decide the case in question.

Once a court determines that it has jurisdiction, it may act if it holds that the case deserves to be heard. This task—usually a determination of whether a litigant has *standing to sue*—is judicially created. The court must ascertain whether the litigant is the "proper" party to bring the dispute and whether the party is in the "proper" forum. What the Supreme Court considers "proper" is defined later in this chapter. Suffice it to say here that before proceeding to the substance or heart of the dispute, a court must determine whether the dispute is deserving of resolution.

The Court has also limited itself publicly by claiming that it will render full-blown constitutional decisions only after all alternative solutions prove unworkable. By making policy assertions regarding (1) access to the decisional forum, and (2) modes of decision once access has been obtained, the Court provides for itself a needed margin of tactical flexibility to pick and choose both the matters it wishes to resolve and the means of resolving them, without relying solely on the enigmatic denial of certiorari. Such flexibility assures compliance with policy choices once they are made while also assuring no loss of credibility if the Court seeks to avoid, on principle or otherwise, making such choices. Policies delimiting access are not promulgated simply for the Supreme Court's advantage. The Court's virtually complete discretion to select which cases it will hear is, of course, unavailable to lower federal courts. Supreme Court policies restricting access to the judicial forum enable lower court judges to exercise some margin of control (thereby providing a limited tactical flexibility) over the cases they entertain. Thus, by limiting the frequency with which it exerts its power and limiting the circumstances under which it and lower courts will act, the Court, oddly enough, increases rather than diminishes its power.

In part, policy controlling access is policy designed to avoid "weakening the courts by embroiling them unnecessarily in the turbulent waters of political controversy" (Cox, 1976, p. 28). As one might imagine, the definition of "unnecessarily" constitutes a political controversy in its own right. For instance, a particular Court's interpretation of various access issues can either widen or narrow the range of cases acceptable for adjudication. The degree of flexibility in these matters is no doubt limited, yet significant consequences emanate from a Court's choices affecting access policy. By careful maneuvering, a Court might succeed in excluding either cases that are politically too difficult to handle or cases that indirectly validate preferred decisions made elsewhere. By contrast, a Court willing to open the courthouse door to just about anyone increases the opportunities for "government by the judiciary," allowing court policy to be imposed directly (Mendelson, 1976). Either way, there is ample opportunity for the Court to utilize access policy for purely political ends (Rathjen and Spaeth, 1979).

This is not to say that the raising or lowering of technical barriers to access is solely a political question. Access policies serve important administrative functions as well (Scott, 1973). Since Congress has yet to provide resources ample enough to enable the judiciary to handle the full range of actual and potential legal conflicts, some mechanism to regulate the flow of cases (size of caseload) has proven necessary to make careful adjudication possible. While the high costs of litigation serve as one means of screening cases, additional technical barriers ostensibly keep dilettante litigants and essentially meaningless but time-consuming cases out of the system. The added screening, undertaken mostly by lawyers and potential litigants, reduces the number of cases requiring the expenditure of judicial resources, thus speeding the meritorious cases through the process and giving judges more time to properly adjudicate.

While choices determining access can be administratively or politically manipulative, the self-imposed barriers and the flexible play allowed among them do give the Court the needed maneuverability to protect, nurture, and enhance its power base. By saying that only certain kinds of matters are appropriate for judicial scrutiny, the Court elevates to a higher plane those cases it does decide; it makes them important enough to warrant attention and enhances compliance with the final choice. As this general discussion suggests, the self-imposed technical barriers to access are important enough to merit extensive consideration.

Self-Imposed Restrictions on Access

Generalizations about Court policy regarding self-imposed limits on access to the federal judicial forum are fraught with difficulties. For every example showing a general line of policy, there are several counterexamples. In fact, many obsevers of the judiciary suggest that general policy in this area is more noticeable in its breach than in its observance. Despite this problem, we will designate the rough contours of Court-made public policy limiting access to the federal judicial forum.

Case or Controversy

The Constitution requires, per Article III, that the judicial power of the Supreme Court be exerted only in "cases" or "controversies." What this has come to mean is that Supreme Court Justices, and lower federal court judges as well, will not decide matters brought to them if they are not real, live, legitimate disputes. The Court will not generally entertain issues that are hypothetical, feigned, or collusive in character, and thus will not render advisory opinions. Requiring adverse litigants keeps the Court's mode of policymaking as "judicial" as possible. While nothing necessarily prevents the Court from entertaining hypothetical cases or rendering advisory opinions, the policy of avoiding both precludes excessive reliance on the judiciary and allows the Court to avoid certain politically touchy issues it might otherwise have to confront.

Mootness

The requirement of a live dispute entails the additional requirement that the live dispute be in existence at the start of the suit and be alive and unresolved until its final *court* resolution. The Court will not waste its resources nor violate the "case or controversy" requirement by resolving cases that have become "moot" as a result of intervening circumstances. For instance, when Marco DeFunis originally sought adjudication of his claim that he had been denied admittance to law school by virtue of his race (an allegation, which, if true, would have violated the Equal Protection Clause of the Fourteenth Amendment), there existed a live, ongoing dispute. But because of the type of relief DeFunis sought, lower courts had ordered his admittance while the adjudication was in process. As a result, by the time the Supreme Court was nearing a final resolution of the case, DeFunis was within a few weeks of graduating from law school. When the Court learned of this, it dismissed the case as moot (*DeFunis* v. *Odegaard,* 416 U.S. 312 [1974]). Since DeFunis was to graduate, his claim that he had been denied equal protection of the law, that is, his dispute with the law school, no longer existed. While some may perceive this as blatant avoidance of a potentially embarrassing and difficult matter (i.e., what to do about "reverse discrimination"), the fact remained that DeFunis' controversy no longer existed and for the Court to decide the matter would have meant deciding in the abstract, outside the context of a set of particulars growing out of a clear-cut, live, ongoing dispute.

There are obvious instances, though, in which a controversy cannot continue through the duration of litigation. For instance, it would have been physically impossible for the women seeking to invalidate the abortion laws to remain pregnant the entire time it would have taken for their cases to reach the Supreme Court. Likewise, people wishing to challenge residency requirements circumscribing voting rights or the ability to secure a divorce would invariably meet those requirements long before the completion of their cases, which the Court could then dismiss as moot. In these time-related cases, the Court could technically never address the alleged injustices since mootness would always intervene to preclude review, while the actions and alleged violations would continue unabated. When these circumstances apply, the Court allows an exception to what might be perceived as a hard-and-fast mootness rule by allowing individuals to bring suits as representatives of those suffering this injury, as representatives of those involved in a controversy that is "capable of repetition" yet able to "evade review." Thus, someone can file what is called a "class action suit." The person filing functions initially as a party presently involved in the ongoing controversy but also serves as a representative of others presently involved, similarly situated, or potentially involved. In this way, even though the person bringing the suit may give birth, become eligible to vote, or secure the very divorce he or she seeks, the fact that other members of the class may presently be prevented from securing an abortion, voting, or divorcing keeps the dispute alive and thus meets the case or controversy requirement.

Direct Injury

The class action suit, while relevant to mootness in the context of case or controversy, is also germane to another condition for access: "proper party." Although they provide a remedy to mootness, class action suits prove to be an exception to the general rule regarding "direct injury." According to this judicial policy, a person may not bring a case to defend or protect the rights of other people. That is, the injury suffered as a result of the actions of others must have happened to the party bringing the case and not just someone else. The Court allows persons to defend the rights of others in the limited class action context when, as just noted, mootness is a problem and when the issues presented in one case are sufficiently similar to all other cases to justify adequate representation by one case and, in turn, spare the Courts relitigation of the same issue for every member of a class or group. Nonetheless, the party bringing the suit as a representative of the class must have been directly injured.

The courts allow defense of other peoples' rights in other circumstances as well. One can hardly expect minors or the mentally incompetent to assert their rights effectively. The courts do allow legal guardians to pursue the legal rights of those parties even though the guardian has personally experienced no injury. In limited circumstances, the Court also allows persons to defend the rights of third parties who are neither incompetent nor under age. For instance, in 1962 Dr. Lee Buxton and Estelle Griswold were arrested and convicted for distributing contraceptives in the state of Connecticut. The law books contained no statute per se that made Buxton and Griswold's actions a criminal offense. Rather, they were convicted under the state's criminal accessory statute, which made a person who gave aid to someone else in the commission of a crime liable to the punishment attached to that crime. In this case, Buxton and Griswold had helped married persons secure and (presumably) use contraceptives, and the use of such devices was defined as a crime in Connecticut. Clearly, both were guilty of aiding married persons in securing and using contraceptives. The only defense against their own criminal liability was not a defense of their own rights but a defense of the rights of others: That is, they had to assert that the law regarding use was a violation of the rights of privacy of married persons. Thus, they were defending third party rights (rights of persons not party to the case) in order to indirectly defend their own rights. In general, the Court would not allow such a defense, but it allowed it here because the situation held substantial obstacles to the third party effectively asserting these rights themselves (*Griswold* v. *Connecticut,* 381 U.S. 479 [1965]). In fact, the extent to which such an obstacle exists underlies the justification for the exception to the general direct injury policy, although the recent case of *Singleton* v. *Wulff,* 428 U.S. 106 (1976) suggests a possible addendum to the proper party policy based on the "character of the relationship" between litigant and third party; such an addition would justify allowing the assertion of third party rights. (In this case the relationship was doctor–patient in the context of abortion law.) These exceptions aside, the general rule still holds: One may not bring a case to defend or protect the rights of other people.

Substantial Injury

While the Court requires that a person possess a personal stake in the matter at issue and that the injury be direct, it will not entertain a case concerning just any individual direct injury. The direct injury must be substantial and not simply a "generalized grievance about the conduct of government" that is shared in an undifferentiated fashion with others in general. Federal taxpayer suits are a case in point. In 1923 in the case of *Frothingham* v. *Mellon,* 262 U.S. 447, the Court refused to entertain Harriet Frothingham's challenge to the Maternity Act of 1921. The Act granted certain monies to states on the condition that they undertake specific programs to reduce maternal and infant mortality. Frothingham alleged that this violated the rights of her state as protected by and reserved to it in the Tenth Amendment. To assure the Court that she was the proper party to bring the suit, she claimed that the tax money used for this purpose (allegedly in violation of the Tenth Amendment) would increase her tax burden and thus would result in the federal government depriving her of property without due process of law. The Court dismissed the case and established that federal taxpayers, solely as taxpayers, did not suffer substantial enough and direct enough injury to qualify as proper parties to bring a suit challenging federal governmental action. The Court contended that a person must show "not only that the statute is invalid but that he has sustained or is immediately in danger of sustaining some direct injury as the result of its enforcement and not merely that he suffers in some indefinite way in common with people generally."

One of the underlying concerns of *Frothingham* was the obvious fear that the courts would be inundated by every dissatisfied taxpayer hoping to overturn congressional action. Indeed, the courts came to apply *Frothingham* as a virtually absolute and unassailable bar to federal taxpayer suits, leaving congressional spending legislation free from review. In 1968, however, in *Flast* v. *Cohen,* 392 U.S. 83, the Court shifted its policy somewhat to allow federal taxpayers standing to sue in a limited set of circumstances. The Court held that a federal taxpayer would be the proper party to challenge congressional spending if the legislation being challenged emanated from the Taxing and Spending Clause and if the taxpayer could show a linkage between that status of the challenged enactment and a specific constitutional limit upon the exercise of the spending power. In this case, Florence Flast, as a taxpayer, challenged expenditures under the Elementary and Secondary Education Act of 1965. The constitutional authorization for such expenditures clearly came from the Taxing and Spending Clause and Flast was thus able to meet the first half of the test. Flast also claimed that specific expenditures in support of parochial schools, authorized by the Act, constituted spending in violation of the First Amendment's specific limitation on Congress' power to spend to establish a religion. By showing a "nexus" between the enactment and a specific limitation on Congress, Flast enabled the Court to claim that she possessed the requisite interest to justify standing to sue. Frothingham, in contrast, had met the Taxing and Spending Clause requirement but had shown no specific limitation on Congress' power to spend as it had. As a general rule, *Frothingham's* prohibition against federal taxpayer standing holds because *Flast* distinguishes only a narrow set of circumstances under which a federal taxpayer can attain standing.

Since *Flast,* the Court has tended toward a strict application of the nexus test. In *United States* v. *Richardson,* 418 U.S. 166 (1974), the Court was faced with a federal taxpayer's effort to obtain information on CIA expenditures. The challenge was directed against the congressional policy of keeping expenditures for the CIA secret, arguably in violation of the Article I, Section 9, Clause 7 requirement that Congress publish from time to time a regular statement of account of the receipts and expenditures of all public money. While William Richardson did not challenge a specific expenditure, it was clear that he could not pursue his case unless he had the information on expenditures available to him. The Court of Appeals felt that although Richardson had not strictly met the requirements of *Flast*, he had shown sufficient nexus to a specific limitation on congressional activities relating to the Taxing and Spending Clause to meet the standing requirement. The Supreme Court disagreed, claiming that *Flast's* first requirement was essential and that without a direct challenge to spending, a taxpayer did not have standing. Taxpayers were also denied standing when they attempted to challenge the fact that members of Congress held positions in the military reserve, arguably in violation of Article I, Section 6, Clause 2 (*Schlesinger* v. *Reservists Committee*, 418 U.S. 208 [1974]). Thus, while *Flast* attempted to limit the extent to which *Frothingham* served as an absolute ban on federal taxpayer suits, the Court's interpretation of *Flast* has not opened the floodgates of federal taxpayer suits, as some predicted it would.

As noted at the outset of the discussion on taxpayer suits, the Court requires a substantial and direct injury as one condition for access. This position was underscored in *Sierra Club* v. *Morton*, 405 U.S. 727 (1972), in which the Court denied the Sierra Club standing to challenge Interior Secretary Morton's decision to allow Disney, Inc., to build a sizable recreation center in the midst of a national forest. The Court allowed that conservational interests could be protected, but argued that those challenging such injury or potential injury to such interests had to be among those suffering or potentially suffering the injury. The Sierra Club had spoken only of its special interest in conservation and had not claimed any direct adverse effect upon its members. One year later, the Court granted an organization calling itself Students Challenging Regulatory Agency Procedures (SCRAP) standing to sue since members alleged injury to their enjoyment of the environment caused by the ICC's allowing an increase in freight surcharges for recyclable material (*United States* v. *Students Challenging Regulatory Agency Procedures*, 412 U.S. 669 [1973]). While the connection between the ICC action and the alleged injury was viewed by some as rather tenuous, the fact that SCRAP alleged and proved to the Court's satisfaction "injury in fact" justified the grant of standing.

"Legal Injury"

The Court, then, will decide only real disputes in which parties to the dispute are directly suffering or are likely to suffer a substantial injury. The Court, however, does not entertain just any conflict or just any injury. Until recently the Court would grant standing only to those conflicts or injuries that involved a legally protected right. That is, the issues in a controversy, the injury one was suffering, had to be specifically tied to a statutory or constitutional provision or to traditional issues in common law involving property or pocketbook. If the matter in question was not specifically protected by statute, tradition, or the Constitution, the matter did not merit judicial resolution. The process of determining whether a "legal injury" was involved appeared to some jurists to entail addressing the merits of the case itself rather than simply determining whether the party bringing the suit merited a hearing. To remedy this, the Court in *Association of Data Processing Service Organizations* v. *Camp* and *Barlow* v. *Collins*, 397 U.S. 150, 159 (1970), replaced the legal injury test with a more flexible two-pronged test. In the first prong, the Court requires a determination of the existence of an "injury in fact, economic or otherwise." Once an injury has been established, the Court will proceed to the second prong: a determination of whether or not the interest sought to be protected is "arguably within the zone of interests to be protected or regulated by the statute or constitutional guarantee in question." Several cases shortly after *Data Processing* and *Barlow* seemed to suggest that the "zone of interest" part of the test is secondary to the "injury in fact" aspect of the test and does not lead to significantly greater access. With the addition of Rehnquist and Powell, the present Burger Court has tightened the injury requirements to include a showing that the injury was in fact caused by the action of the other party (*Linda R. S. v. Richard D.*, 410 U.S. 208 [1973]) and that the Court's actions would actually result in an effective remedy or solution to the controversy (*Simon v. Eastern Kentucky Welfare Rights Organization*, 426 U.S. 26 [1976]).

Exhaustion of Remedies, and Abstention

While the Court sets policy regarding the proper party to bring suit, it also sets policy regarding the proper forum. In a federal system with fifty-plus court systems and an ever-expanding bureaucracy, the "where" of a conflict's appropriate resolution is a difficult issue. Under the general policy referred to as "finality of action," the Court limits access to the federal judicial forum to issues that are "ripe for review." In practice, this means that the federal courts will not entertain a case begun elsewhere until a person has exhausted all remedies available in either the bureaucratic forum or state courts. A conflict over pipeline regulations, for instance, must first go through all the administrative channels for resolution available within the Interstate Commerce Commission before the federal courts will entertain the issue. At the same time, to maintain harmony with state courts and to minimize the federal court work load, the Court relies on what it calls "abstention." Abstention consists in the Court's general reluctance to consider issues whose adjudication has commenced in state courts until the state courts have had an opportunity to render a final authoritative decision. Such a position is viewed as essential, as much out of respect for state court judges as for anything else, because state judges are as obliged as federal judges to honor the U.S. Constitution. Indeed, given this equivalence in obligation, state court judges may resolve issues in such a manner as to minimize the need for federal court adjudication, through the interpretation and clarification of state statutes.

Like many of the policies described so far, the abstention doctrine and the exhaustion of remedies policy are not hard-and-fast, inflexible rules. If a person attacks an agency action as unconstitutional, or if a party can show that an agency is acting beyond its authority, or if one can show the futility of continuing through the available channels, the Court will suspend the exhaustion of remedies rule. Similarly, under certain circumstances the Court will allow federal court intervention in state court proceedings and will allow such intervention long before the state court has handed down an authoritative final ruling. In the 1965 case of *Dombrowski v. Pfister*, 380 U.S. 479, the Court granted the validity of a federal injunction designed to thwart a state prosecutor's improper raids on a civil rights organization. Given the significant "chilling effect" of the prosecutor's actions upon the free speech rights of members of the civil rights organization, the Court held the abstention doctrine inapplicable. Subsequently, because of the Court's perception of overly broad interpretations of the exceptions to the abstention doctrine carved out by *Dombrowski,* it has set stricter requirements. These were most notable in *Younger* v. *Harris,* 401 U.S. 37 (1971), wherein California indicted Harris for allegedly violating its Syndicalism Act. The Act made it a crime to advocate, teach, or aid and abet the commission of crime or the use of unlawful methods of terrorism to accomplish change in industrial ownership or to effect any political change. The statute had originally been sustained as constitutional in the 1927 case of *Whitney* v. *California,* 274 U.S. 357, but a similar Ohio statute had recently been ruled a violation of the First Amendment (*Brandenburg* v. *Ohio,* 395 U.S. 444 [1969]). On the strength of the latter case and the holding in *Dombrowski,* Harris sought a federal court injunction to prevent Younger from prosecuting him. The Court declined to grant the injunction on the basis that federal court intervention required a more clear-cut showing of substantial and immediate irreparable injury coupled with evidence of "bad faith" on the part of state officials and judges. (See also *Rizzo* v. *Goode,* 423 U.S. 362 [1976].)

In the name of stricter attention to abstention, the Burger Court has recently placed tighter limitations on access to the federal courts via the writ of habeas corpus. The writ orders an official to "bring the body" before a federal court so the court can ascertain whether the person (body) is lawfully held. In 1867 Congress extended the writ's applicability to anyone held "in violation of the Constitution, or of any treaty or law of the United States." This broad language allowed federal courts to extend the writ to assessments of the constitutionality of the incarceration of state prisoners. Its use was generally limited to those persons who had exhausted their available state remedies. During the early 1960s the Warren Court allowed state prisoners to secure the writ even when they had failed to exhaust their remedies or were disallowed from doing so by virtue of some procedural error (e.g., *Fay* v. *Noia,* 372 U.S. 391 [1963]). As a consequence of the expansive policy, the number of habeas corpus petitions brought by state prisoners increased at a tremendous rate, creating friction between state and federal courts as well as overloading the already overloaded federal courts. In a series of recent cases, most notably *Stone* v. *Powell,* 428 U.S. 465 (1976), the Burger majority has sought to remedy this problem by denying state prisoners virtually unlimited access to another tier of courts for what had come to be a full-dress retrial of matters that had already been handled in the state courts. In the *Stone* case, the Court decided that state court determinations regarding the exclusion of evidence per the Fourth Amendment need not be considered again in the federal courts via the writ of habeas corpus.

The Fourth Amendment to the Constitution provides a general prohibition against unreasonable searches and seizures. The Amendment, however, contains no implementing language; that is, it makes no provision for penalizing any law enforcement officer who conducts an unreasonable search and seizure. This gap between the recognition and implementation of this right was not addressed until 1914. In that year the Supreme Court held that evidence obtained through a violation of the search-and-seizure restriction was inadmissible in a federal trial (*Weeks* v. *United States,* 232 U.S. 383). This exclusionary rule, as it came to be called, was highly controversial at the time it was announced and has remained a subject of bitter dispute down to the present. In effect, it imposes an indirect penalty on the police by barring the use of any evidence acquired through unreasonable searches and seizures, regardless of its reliability.

In 1961 the Supreme Court greatly extended the exclusionary rule by applying it to state criminal proceedings (*Mapp* v. *Ohio,* 367 U.S. 643). The vast majority of criminal prosecutions in the United States occur at the state level, and the extension of the rule to those cases greatly increased the practical importance and intensity of the controversy characterizing its application. It was at about this time that the Court, under the leadership of Chief Justice Warren, enlarged the scope of federal habeas corpus review of state convictions (noted above). *Stone* v. *Powell* represents, among other things, the Burger Court's retreat from criminal justice commitments of the Warren Court regarding both federal habeas corpus review and faith in the corrective qualities of the exclusionary rule.

Political Questions

Even though a particular case may meet all the requirements of standing, justiciability, and jurisdiction that we have outlined (plus a few more we have not discussed), the Court may still refuse to hear the merits of a case if it so chooses. In this circumstance, the Justices will likely rely on a device we have already alluded to: the "political question doctrine." Exactly what constitutes political question is hard to specify or define (particularly from our perspective, since virtually all the matters federal courts adjudicate, and particularly the matters the Supreme Court entertains, are "political" in the purest sense of the word). According to the Justices, however, some issues are more political than others, and they maintain that such issues must be handled by representative bodies and do not merit a court decision. For example, the Court has left to Congress and the executive the responsibility for guaranteeing to states a republican form of government, per Article IV, Section 4 of the Constitution (*Luther* v. *Borden,* 7 How. 1 [1849]). Anyone who brings to the Court a claim that alleges injury as a result of congressional failure to fulfill those responsibilities entailed in the Guarantee Clause will likely be told that this kind of a dispute is a political question and cannot be decided by the Court. Along the same line, the Court has left to the executive most matters of foreign affairs and the exertion of war powers; left to Congress matters relating to the validity of its enactments and the proper procedures for ratifying constitutional amendments; relied on means other than the injunction to secure presidential compliance; and left to either coequal branch determinations about the recognition and status of Indian tribes—all in the context and name of political questions.

To the chagrin of lawyers and legal scholars, Court policy about what constitutes a political question is anything but clear. For each rule there seem to be exceptions, leading some experts to conclude that a political question is whatever a majority of the Court at a given time is prone to allege a political question is. John Roche has also attacked the doctrine for its circularity: "Political questions are matters not soluble by the judicial process: matters not soluble by the judicial process are political questions" (1955, p. 762). This none-too-clever tautology does not please the legal community.

Seeking to bring some needed clarity, Justice Brennan, in *Baker* v. *Carr,* 369 U.S. 186 (1962), listed six types of issues likely to be considered political questions:

1. Those matters demonstrably committed to some other branch of government by the Constitution.
2. Those matters lacking judicially discoverable and manageable standards applicable to resolution.
3. Those matters requiring initial policy determinations clearly reserved for nonjudicial policymaking discretion.
4. Those matters wherein a decision by the Court would prove to express a lack of respect due a coordinate branch.
5. Those matters in which there appears to be an unusual need for "unquestioning adherence to political decisions already made."
6. Those matters in which there is a danger of embarrassment from multiple pronouncements by various branches on one question, with all the pronouncements leading in different directions.

While Brennan's classifications have proven helpful to some members of the legal community, it is obvious that each is open to a variety of interpretations, leaving the ambiguity surrounding the definition of political questions reduced by very little. Brennan's listing does make one thing clear: Political questions are now limited to matters involving "separation of powers" and thus will function solely as a means of maintaining good public relations with the other national-level branches of government. The addition or clarification of this very element in political question policy allowed the Court in the *Baker* case itself to fly in the face of a decision rendered only some sixteen years earlier. In that decision, *Colegrove* v. *Green,* 328 U.S. 549 (1946), a plurality of the Court came to the conclusion that reapportionment was a dangerous political thicket not to be entered by the Court. The plaintiffs in *Colegrove* had sought reapportionment of congressional districts, while Baker sought to redistrict only the Tennessee state legislature.* Because the issue in *Baker* did not turn on the separation of powers, the Court did not need to avoid it via the political question ploy.

Since *Baker,* the Court has utilized Brennan's six categories to determine whether an issue at hand is a political question, with some surprising results. For instance, in *Powell* v. *McCormack,* 395 U.S. 486 (1969), the Court was called upon to specify the extent of the power of Congress to judge the qualifications of its members. Because of an alleged mishandling of funds and other abuses of power and privilege, Adam Clayton Powell was prevented from taking his seat in the 90th Congress. Members of Congress felt justified in excluding him since Article I granted them the power to determine the qualifications of their members. Powell alleged that while Congress had the power to *expel* members of Congress once seated, it could *exclude* them only if they failed to meet the only qualifications that Article I allowed Congress to judge: age, residency, and citizenship. Lawyers for Congress countered this by arguing that Congress had been granted sole power to

---

* Even so, having entered the reapportionment field, the Court ultimately overruled *Colegrove* in *Wesberry* v. *Sanders,* 376 U.S. 1 (1964).

judge the qualifications of its members and that, as a consequence, final determination of this matter rested with Congress, not the Court.

Referring to Brennan's six points, Chief Justice Warren concluded that only the first was in some measure applicable to this set of circumstances. As far as Warren's majority was concerned, the issues in *Powell* were not beyond judicially manageable and discoverable standards; a judicial decision in this matter did not require a preliminary policy choice not normally made by courts; a decision would not show lack of respect for Congress; the issues raised here did not imply a need to adhere to emergency decisions already made; and there would be no embarrassment from multiple and varied pronouncements. With regard to the first point, Warren asserted that although the authority to judge members' qualifications had been committed to Congress by the Constitution, it was a matter that had been committed to Congress with limitations. Because Congress had exceeded those limitations, the first aspect of the political question did not apply. In a strange fashion, by shifting to a consideration of the merits of a case to determine if the Court ought to decide on those merits, Warren distorted what little clarity Brennan had brought to the political question doctrine. His opinion in *Powell* asserts that if the Constitution commits a matter to some other branch, the Court will call an issue a political question and not decide it, provided it is not shown that the branch to which the matter has been committed has abused its power. Oddly enough, the process of determining whether to resolve a matter (what we have called an access decision) hinges on how the matter is to be resolved once it is decided. Thus, while Brennan strived to clarify the political question doctrine, *Powell* did little to ease the minds of students of the Court regarding an extremely illusive doctrine. Perhaps the Justices really operate the way Justice Stewart does with regard to obscenity: They know a political question when they see one.*

Self-Imposed Limitations Once Access Is Obtained

Once it has resolved a question of access for a particular class of cases or litigants, the Supreme Court continues to limit the range of options available to it in resolving a given dispute. Under long-standing norms of Supreme Court decision-making, the Court will invoke the most important and powerful weapon in its arsenal—judicial review—only in the most propitious of circumstances.

Doctrine of Strict Necessity

When a statute is challenged, for example, the Court alleges that it will do everything in its power to construe that statute so as to render it constitutional. In compliance with this "doctrine of strict necessity," the Court will attempt to inter-

---

* The Supreme Court has struggled since 1956 to formulate a viable definition of obscenity. While the struggle was in full swing, Justice Stewart concluded: "I shall not attempt to . . . define the kinds of material I understand to be embraced within [hard-core pornography]; and perhaps I could never succeed in intelligibly doing so. But I know it when I see it, and the motion picture involved in this case is not that" (*Jacobellis* v. *Ohio*, 378 U.S. 184 [1964]).

pret a statute in the most favorable light. Indeed, in these matters the Court begins by presuming the constitutionality of the legislation. This, of course, places the burden of proof on those challenging the statute as unconstitutional and not on the government seeking to show that it *is* constitutional. (Although this is the general rule, since the 1940s some Justices have held that statutes involving freedom of speech, press, assembly, and religion as well as those that categorize people on the basis of "suspect classifications," like race, are presumptively unconstitutional.)

External Considerations Do Not Apply

The Court also argues that it will not rule a statute unconstitutional on the basis of the alleged motives behind the legislation or the lack of wisdom of the policy choices made by the legislators. The rationale is that as long as the Constitution does not clearly forbid the actions undertaken in the statute as written, the Court cannot of its own volition rule an act unconstitutional on the grounds that evidence suggests that members of Congress intended to accomplish an unconstitutional goal. Thus, the Court allows the taxing and spending power to be used as a surrogate grant of police power to Congress. As long as a taxing measure secures revenue for the federal government, the measure will be constitutional despite the fact that it also regulates people's behaviors. Along the same lines, the Court will not rely on natural law or other matters external to the Constitution as the basis for ruling a statute unconstitutional. (Like exceptions to the strict necessity doctrine, violations of this general rule occurred when the Court relied on "the nature of things" to justify the "separate but equal doctrine" in *Plessy* v. *Ferguson,* 163 U.S. 537 [1896], and later when it relied on sociological data to justify reversing that decision in *Brown* v. *Board of Education,* 347 U.S. 483 [1954].) In addition to its general ban on external considerations, the Court claims the necessity of limiting the breadth of a constitutional decision once it has decided to invoke judicial review. Thus the constitutionally based resolution of the case should not be broader than the facts and issues at hand. These positions are amplified in Justice Brandeis' opinion in *Ashwander* v. *Tennessee Valley Authority,* 297 U.S. 288 (1936), reprinted in this chapter. As the Court noted in *Broadrick* v. *Oklahoma,* 413 U.S. 610 (1973),

> . . . these principles rest on more than the fussiness of judges. They reflect the conviction that under our constitutional system courts are not roving commissions assigned to pass judgment on the validity of the Nation's laws. . . . Constitutional judgments . . . are justified only out of the necessity of adjudicating rights in particular cases between the litigants brought before the Court.

By virtue of this extended discussion of access policy and the various norms of restraint, it should be apparent that the Court possesses a number of means both to protect itself from its powerful coequal branches and to strengthen its own power base in the process. In addition to self-protection and power, much of what underlies the policies of access and restraint noted here arises from the long-standing philosophic uncertainty and discomfort over what is an essentially undemocratic body of nine individuals controlling the destiny of a nation believing it has an essentially democratic governance. As you read the cases that follow, note carefully the strains of deeply held differences among the Justices over the administrative, political, and broadly based philosophic concerns that serve as the motivating factors in choices determining access policy.

Singleton v. Wulff

428 U.S. 106 (1976)

Mr. Justice Blackmun delivered the opinion of the Court. . . .

. . . [T]his case involves a claim of a State's unconstitutional interference with the decision to terminate pregnancy. The particular object of the challenge is a Missouri statute excluding abortions that are not "medically indicated" from the purposes for which Medicaid benefits are available to needy persons. . . . [H]owever, the case presents . . . issues not going to the merits of this dispute.

• • •

. . . [T]wo distinct standing questions are presented . . . and they are these: first, whether [Wulff and other physicians] allege "injury in fact," that is, a sufficiently concrete interest in the outcome of their suit to make it a case or controversy subject to a federal court's Art III jurisdiction, and, second, whether, as a prudential matter, [they] are proper proponents of the particular legal rights on which they base their suit.

A. The first of these questions needs little comment, for there is no doubt now that the . . . physicians suffer concrete injury from the operation of the challenged statute. Their complaint and affidavits . . . allege that they have performed and will continue to perform operations for which they would be reimbursed under the Medicaid program, were it not for the limitation of reimbursable abortions to those that are "medically indicated." If the physicians prevail in their suit to remove this limitation, they will benefit, for they will then receive payment for the abortions. The State (and Federal Government) will be out of pocket by the amount of the payments. The relationship between the parties is classically adverse, and there clearly exists between them a case or controversy in the constitutional sense. * * *

B. The question of what rights the doctors may assert in seeking to resolve that controversy is more difficult. . . . It appears . . . that the Court of Appeals . . . accorded the doctors standing to assert, and indeed granted them relief based partly upon the rights of their patients. We must decide whether this assertion . . . was a proper one.

Federal courts must hesitate before resolving a controversy, even one within their constitutional power to resolve, on the basis of the rights of third persons not parties to the litigation. The reasons are two. First, the courts should not adjudicate such rights unnecessarily, and it may be that in fact the holders of those rights either do not wish to assert them, or will be able to enjoy them regardless of whether the in-court litigant is successful or not. * * * Second, third parties themselves usually will be the best proponents of their own rights. The courts depend on effective advocacy, and therefore should prefer to construe legal rights only when the most effective advocates of those rights are before them. . . . These two considerations underlie the Court's general rule: "Ordinarily, one may not claim standing in this Court to vindicate the constitutional rights of some third party." * * *

Like any general rule, however, this one should not be applied where its underlying justifications are absent. With this in mind, the Court has looked primarily to two factual elements to determine whether the rule should apply in a particular case. The first is the relationship of the litigant to the person whose right he seeks to assert. If the enjoyment of the right is inextricably bound up with the activity the litigant wishes to pursue, the Court at least can be sure that its construction of the right is not unnecessary in the sense that the right's enjoyment will be unaffected by the outcome of the suit. Furthermore, the relationship between the litigant and the third party may be such that the former is fully, or very nearly, as effective a proponent of the right as the latter. . . .

The other factual element to which the Court has looked is the ability of the third party to assert his own right. Even where the relationship is close, the reasons for requiring persons to assert their own rights will generally still apply. If there is some genuine obstacle to such assertion, however, the third party's absence from court loses its tendency to suggest that his right is not truly at stake, or truly important to him, and the party who is in court becomes by the default the right's best available proponent. . . .

Application of these principles to the present case quickly yields its proper result. The closeness of the relationship is patent. . . . A woman cannot safely secure an abortion without the aid of a physician, and an impecunious woman cannot easily secure an abortion without the physician's being paid by the State. The woman's exercise of her right to an abortion, whatever its dimension, is therefore necessarily at stake here. Moreover, the constitutionally protected abortion decision is one in which the physician is intimately involved. * * * Aside from the woman herself, therefore, the physician is uniquely qualified to litigate the constitutionality of the State's interference with, or discrimination against, that decision.

As to the woman's assertion of her own rights, there are several obstacles. For one thing, she may be chilled from such assertion by a desire to protect the very privacy of her decision from the publicity of a court suit. A second obstacle is the imminent mootness, at least in the technical sense, of any individual woman's claim. Only a few months, at the most, after the maturing of the decision to undergo an abortion, her right thereto will have been irrevocably lost, assuming, as it seems fair to assume, that unless the impecunious woman can establish Medicaid eligibility she must forgo abortion. It is true that these obstacles are not insurmountable. Suit may be brought under pseudonym, as so frequently has been done. A woman who is no longer pregnant may nonetheless retain the right to litigate the point because it is " 'capable of repetition yet evading review.' " * * * And it may be that a class could be assembled, whose fluid membership always included some women with live claims. But if the assertion of the right is to be "representative" to such an extent anyway, there seems little loss in terms of effective advocacy from allowing its assertion by a physician.

For these reasons, we conclude that it generally is appropriate to allow a physician to assert the rights of women patients as against governmental interference with the abortion decision. . . .

* * *

MR. JUSTICE STEVENS concurring in part. [Omitted.]

* * *

MR. JUSTICE POWELL, with whom THE CHIEF JUSTICE, MR. JUSTICE STEWART, and MR. JUSTICE REHNQUIST join, concurring in part and dissenting in part.

* * *

. . . [T]he Art III standing inquiry . . . is one of power within our constitutional system, as courts may decide only actual cases and controversies between the parties who stand before the Court. * * * Beyond this question, however, lies the further and less easily defined inquiry of whether it is prudent to proceed to decision on particular issues even at the instance of a party whose Art III standing is clear. This inquiry has taken various forms, including the one presented by this case: whether, in defending against or anticipatorily attacking state action, a party may argue that it contravenes someone else's constitutional rights.

This second inquiry is a matter of "judicial self-governance." * * * The usual—and wise—stance of the federal courts when policing their own exercise of power in this manner is one of cautious reserve. * * * This caution has given rise to the general rule that a party may not defend against or attack governmental action on the ground that it infringes the rights of some third party * * * and to the corollary that any exception must rest on specific factors outweighing the policies behind the rule itself. * * *

[Justice Blackmun's opinion] acknowledges this general rule, but identifies "two factual elements"—thought to be derived from prior cases—that justify the adjudication of the asserted third party rights: (i) obstacles to the assertion by the third party of her own rights, and (ii) the existence of some "relationship" such as the one between physician and patient. In my view these factors do not justify allowing these physicians to assert their patients' rights.

* * *

[Blackmun's opinion] purports to derive . . . the principle that a party may assert another's rights if there is "some genuine obstacle" to the third party's own litigation. * * * But this understates the teaching . . . that such an assertion is proper, not when there is merely some "obstacle" to the rightholder's own litigation, but when such litigation is in all practicable terms impossible. Thus, in its framing of this principle, the [announcement of the Court] has gone far beyond our major precedents.

. . . [T]he litigation of third-party rights cannot be justified in this case. [Blackmun] virtually concedes, as [he] must, that the . . . alleged "obstacles" to the women's assertion of their rights are chimerical. Our docket regularly contains cases in which women, using pseudonyms, challenge statutes that allegedly infringe their right to exercise the abortion decision. . . . In short, in light of experience which we share regularly in reviewing appeals and petitions for certiorari, the "obstacles" identified by [Blackmun] as justifying departure from the general rule simply are not significant. . . .

[Blackmun's opinion] places primary reliance on a second element, the existence of a "confidential relationship" between the rightholder and the party seeking to assert her rights. . . .

With all respect, I do not read [precedent] . . . as merging the physician and his patient for constitutional purposes. . . . In the circumstances of direct interference, I agree that one party to the relationship should be permitted to assert the constitutional rights of the other, for a judicial rule of self-restraint should not preclude an attack on a State's proscription of constitutionally protected activity. * * * But Missouri has not directly interfered with the abortion decision—neither the physicians nor their patients are forbidden to engage in the procedure. The only impact of [the statute] is that, because of the way Missouri chose to structure its Medicaid payments, it causes these doctors financial detriment. . . .

The physicians have offered no special reason for allowing them to assert their patients' rights in an attack on this welfare statute, and I can think of none. Moreover, there are persuasive reasons not to permit them to do so. It seems wholly inappropriate, as a matter of judicial self-governance, for a court to reach unnecessarily to decide a difficult constitutional issue in a case in which nothing more is at stake than remuneration for professional services. And second, this case may well set a precedent that will prove difficult to cabin. No reason immediately comes to mind, after today's holding, why any provider of services should be denied standing to assert his client's or customer's constitutional rights, if any, in an attack on a welfare statute that excludes from coverage his particular transaction.

Putting it differently, the Court's holding invites litigation by those who perhaps have the least legitimate ground for seeking to assert the rights of third parties. Before today I certainly would not have thought that an interest in being compensated for professional services, without more, would be deemed a sufficiently compelling reason to justify departing from a rule of restraint that well serves society and our judicial system. The Court quite recently stated, with respect to the rule against assertion of third-party rights as well as certain other doctrines of judicial self-restraint, that "[t]hese principles rest on more than the fussiness of judges. They reflect the conviction that under our constitutional system courts are not roving commissions assigned to pass judgment on the validity of the Nation's law. . . . Constitutional judgments . . . are justified only out of the necessity of adjudicating rights in particular cases between the litigants brought before the Court." * * * Today's holding threatens to make just such "roving commissions" of the federal courts.

United States v. Richardson

418 U.S. 166 (1974)

Mr. Chief Justice Burger delivered the opinion of the Court.

We granted certiorari in this case to determine whether [Richardson] has standing to bring an action as a federal taxpayer alleging that certain provisions concerning public reporting of expenditures under the Central Intelligence Agency Act * * * violate Art I, § 9, cl 7 of the Constitution which provides:

> "No Money shall be drawn from the Treasury, but in Consequence of Appropriations made by Law; and a regular Statement of Account of the Receipts and Expenditures of all public Money shall be published from time to time."

[Richardson] . . . [made] attempts to obtain from the Government information concerning detailed expenditures of the Central Intelligence Agency. . . . [Richardson] wrote to the Government Printing Office in 1967 and requested that he be provided with the documents "published by the Government in compliance with Article I, section 9, clause (7) of the United States Constitution." The Fiscal Service of the Bureau of Accounts of the Department of the Treasury replied, explaining that it published the document known as the "Combined Statement of Receipts, Expenditures, and Balances of the United States Government." Several copies of the monthly and daily reports . . . were sent with the letter. [Richardson] then wrote to the same office and, quoting part of the CIA Act, asked whether this statute did not "cast reflection upon the authenticity of the Treasury's statement." He also inquired as to how he could receive further information on the expenditures of the CIA. The Bureau of Accounts replied stating that it had no other available information.

. . . [Richardson's] complaint asked the court to "issue a permanent injunction enjoining the defendants from publishing their 'Combined Statement of Receipts, Expenditures, and Balances of the United States Government' and representing it as the fulfillment of the mandates of Article I Section 9 Clause 7 until same fully complies with those mandates." In essence, [Richardson] asked the federal court to declare unconstitutional that provision of the Central Intelligence Agency Act which permits the Agency to account for its expenditures "solely on the certificate of the Director. . . ." * * * The only injury alleged by respondent was that he "cannot obtain a document that sets out the expenditures and receipts" of the CIA but on the contrary was "asked to accept a fraudulent document." . . .

• • •

I

As far back as Marbury v Madison, * * * this Court held that judicial power may be exercised only in a case properly before it—a "case or controversy" not suffering any of the limitations of the political question doctrine, not then moot or calling for an advisory opinion. . . .

• • •

When the Court addressed the question of standing in Flast, Chief Justice Warren traced what he described as the "confusion" following Frothingham as to whether the Court had announced a constitutional doctrine barring suits by taxpayers challenging federal expenditures as unconstitutional or simply a policy rule of judicial self-restraint. In an effort to clarify the confusion and to take into account intervening developments, . . . the Court embarked on "a fresh examination of the limitations upon standing to sue in a federal court and the application of those limitations to taxpayer suits." * * * That re-examination led, however, to the holding that a "taxpayer will have standing *consistent with Article III* to invoke federal judicial power when he alleges that congressional action under the taxing and spending clause is in derogation of those constitutional provisions *which operate to restrict the exercise of the taxing and spending power.*" (Emphasis supplied.) * * * In so holding, the Court emphasized that Art III requirements are the threshold inquiry:

> "The 'gist of the question of standing' is whether the party seeking relief has 'alleged such a personal stake in the outcome of the controversy as to assure that

concrete adverseness . . . upon which the court so largely depends for illumination of difficult constitutional questions.' " * * *

The Court then announced a two-pronged standing test which requires allegations: (a) challenging an enactment under the taxing and spending clause of Art I, § 8 of the Constitution; and (b) claiming that the challenged enactment exceeds specific constitutional limitations imposed on the taxing and spending power. * * * While the "impenetrable barrier to suits against Acts of Congress brought by individuals who can assert only the interest of federal taxpayers" * * * had been slightly lowered, the Court made clear it was reaffirming the principle of Frothingham precluding a taxpayer's use of "a federal court as a forum in which to air his generalized grievances about the conduct of government or the allocation of power in the Federal System." * * * . . .

II

Although the Court made it very explicit in Flast that a "fundamental aspect of standing" is that it focuses primarily on the *party* seeking to get his complaint before the federal court rather than "on the issues he wishes to have adjudicated," * * * it made equally clear that

> "in ruling on [taxpayer] standing, it is both appropriate and necessary to look to the substantive issues for another purpose, namely to determine whether there is a logical nexus between the status asserted and the claim sought to be adjudicated." * * *

We therefore turn to an examination of the issues sought to be raised by respondent's complaint to determine whether he is "a proper and appropriate party to invoke federal judicial power" * * * with respect to those issues.

We need not and do not reach the merits of the constitutional attack on the statute; our inquiry into the "substantive issues" is for the limited purpose indicated above. The mere recital of the respondent's claims and an examination of the statute under attack demonstrates how far he falls short of the standing criteria of Flast and how neatly he falls within the Frothingham holding left undisturbed. Although the status he rests on is that he is a taxpayer, his challenge is not addressed to the taxing or spending power but to the statutes regulating the CIA. * * * That section provides different accounting and reporting requirements and procedures for the CIA, as is also done with respect to other governmental agencies dealing in confidential areas.

[Richardson] makes no claim that appropriated funds are being spent in violation of a "specific constitutional limitation upon the . . . taxing and spending power. . . ." * * * Rather, he asks the courts to compel the government to give him information on precisely how the CIA spends its funds. Thus there is no "logical nexus" between the asserted status of taxpayer and the claimed failure of the Congress to require the Executive to supply a more detailed report of the expenditures of that agency.

The question presented thus is simply and narrowly whether these claims meet the standards for taxpayer standing set forth in Flast; we hold they do not.

[Richardson] is seeking "to employ a federal court as a forum in which to air his generalized grievances about the conduct of the government." * * * Both Frothingham and Flast . . . reject that basis for standing.

III

[Richardson's] claim is that without detailed information on CIA expenditures—and hence its activities—he cannot intelligently follow the actions of Congress or the Executive, nor can he properly fulfill his obligations as a member of the electorate in voting for candidates seeking national office.

This is surely the kind of a generalized grievance described in both Frothingham and Flast since the impact on him is plainly undifferentiated and "common to all members of the public." * * * While we can hardly dispute that this respondent has a genuine interest in the use of funds and that his interest may be prompted by his status as a taxpayer, he has not alleged that, as a taxpayer, he is in danger of suffering any particular concrete injury as a result of the operation of this statute. . . .

· · ·

It can be argued that if [Richardson] is not permitted to litigate this issue, no one can do so. In a very real sense, the absence of any particular individual or class to litigate these claims gives support to the argument that the subject matter is committed to the surveillance of Congress, and ultimately to the political process. Any other conclusion would mean that the Founding Fathers intended to set up something in the nature of an Athenian democracy or a New England town meeting to oversee the conduct of the National Government by means of lawsuits in federal courts. The Constitution created a *representative* Government with the representatives directly responsible to their constituents at stated periods of two, four, and six years; that the Constitution does not afford a judicial remedy does not, of course, completely disable the citizen who is not satisfied with the "ground rules" established by the Congress for reporting expenditures of the Executive Branch. Lack of standing within the narrow confines of Art III jurisdiction does not impair the right to assert his views in the political forum or at the polls. Slow, cumbersome and unresponsive though the traditional electoral process may be thought at times, our system provides for changing members of the political branches when dissatisfied citizens convince a sufficient number of their fellow electors that elected representatives are delinquent in performing duties committed to them.

As our society has become more complex, our numbers more vast, our lives more varied and our resources more strained, citizens increasingly request the intervention of the courts on a greater variety of issues than at any period of our national development. The acceptance of new categories of judicially cognizable injury has not eliminated the basic principle that to invoke judicial power the claimant must have a "personal stake in the outcome," * * * or a "particular concrete injury," * * * "that he has sustained . . . a direct injury . . ." * * * in short, something more than "generalized grievances." * * * Respondent has failed to meet these fundamental tests; accordingly, the judgment of the Court of Appeals is

Reversed.

MR. JUSTICE POWELL, concurring.

I join the opinion of the Court because I am in accord with most of its analysis, particularly insofar as it relies on traditional barriers against federal taxpayer or citizen standing. And I agree that Flast v Cohen, * * * which set the boundaries for the arguments of the parties before us, is the most directly relevant precedent and quite correctly absorbs a major portion of the Court's attention. I write solely to indicate that I would go further than the Court and would lay to rest the approach undertaken in Flast. I would not overrule Flast on its facts, because it is now settled that federal taxpayer standing exists in Establishment Clause cases. I would not, however, perpetuate the doctrinal confusion inherent in the Flast two-part "nexus" test. That test is not a reliable indicator of when a federal taxpayer has standing, and it has no sound relationship to the question whether such a plaintiff, with no other interest at stake, should be allowed to bring suit against one of the branches of the Federal Government. In my opinion, it should be abandoned.

• • •

Relaxation of standing requirements is directly related to the expansion of judicial power. It seems to me inescapable that allowing unrestricted taxpayer or citizen standing would significantly alter the allocation of power at the national level, with a shift away from a democratic form of government. I also believe that repeated and essentially head-on confrontations between the life-tenured branch and the representative branches of government will not, in the long run, be beneficial to either. The public confidence essential to the former and the vitality critical to the latter may well erode if we do not exercise self-restraint in the utilization of our power to negative the actions of the other branches. We should be ever mindful of the contradictions that would arise if a democracy were to permit at large oversight of the elected branches of government by a nonrepresentative, and in large measure insulated, judicial branch. Moreover, the argument that the Court should allow unrestricted taxpayer or citizen standing underestimates the ability of the representative branches of the Federal Government to respond to the citizen pressure that has been responsible in large measure for the current drift toward expanded standing. Indeed, taxpayer or citizen advocacy, given its potentially broad base, is precisely the type of leverage that in a democracy ought to be employed against the branches that were intended to be responsive to public attitudes about the appropriate operation of government.
. . .

Unrestrained standing in federal taxpayer or citizen suits would create a remarkably illogical system of judicial supervision of the coordinate branches of the Federal Government. . . . [S]ince the judiciary cannot select the taxpayers or citizens who bring suit or the nature of the suits, the allowance of public actions would produce uneven and sporadic review, the quality of which would be influenced by the resources and skill of the particular plaintiff. And issues would be presented in abstract form, contrary to the Court's recognition that "judicial review is effective largely because it is not available simply at the behest of a partisan faction, but is exercised only to remedy a particular, concrete injury."
* * *

The power recognized in Marbury v Madison * * * is a potent one. Its prudent use seems to me incompatible with unlimited notions of taxpayer and citizen standing. . . .

. . . [W]e risk a progressive impairment of the effectiveness of the federal courts if their limited resources are diverted increasingly from their historic role to the resolution of public interest suits brought by litigants who cannot distinguish themselves from all taxpayers or all citizens. The irreplaceable value of the power articulated by Chief Justice Marshall lies in the protection it has afforded the constitutional rights and liberties of individual citizens and minority groups against oppressive or discriminatory government action. It is this role, not some amorphous general supervision of the operations of government, that has maintained public esteem for the federal courts and has permitted the peaceful coexistence of the countermajoritarian implications of judicial review and the democratic principles upon which our Federal Government in the final analysis rests.

•   •   •

Mr. Justice Douglas, dissenting.

•   •   •

Respondents in the present case claim that they have a right to "a regular statement and account" of receipts and expenditures of public moneys for the Central Intelligence Agency. As the Court of Appeals noted, Flast recognizes "standing" of a taxpayer to challenge appropriations made in the face of a constitutional prohibition, and it logically asks, ". . . how can a taxpayer make that challenge unless he knows how the money is being spent?" * * *

History shows that the curse of government is not always venality; secrecy is one of the most tempting coverups to save regimes from criticism. . . .

Whatever may be the merits of the underlying claim, it seems clear that the taxpayers in the present case are not making generalized complaints about the operation of government. They do not even challenge the constitutionality of the Central Intelligence Agency Act. They only want to know the amount of tax money exacted from them that goes into CIA activities. Secrecy of government acquires new sanctity when their claim is denied. . . .

. . .

From the history of [Art I, § 9, cl 7] it is apparent that the Framers inserted it in the Constitution to give the public knowledge of the way public funds are expended. No one has a greater "personal stake" in policing this protective measure than a taxpayer. Indeed, if a taxpayer may not raise the question, who may do so? The Court states that discretion to release information is in the first instance "committed to the surveillance of Congress," and that the right of the citizenry to information under Art I, § 9, cl 7 cannot be enforced directly, but only through the "slow, cumbersome and unresponsive" electoral process. One has only to read constitutional history to realize that statement would shock Mason and Madison. Congress of course has discretion; but to say that it has the power to read the clause out of the Constitution when it comes to one or two or three agencies is astounding. That is the bare bone issue in the present case. Does Art I, § 9, cl 7 of the Constitution permit Congress to withhold "a regular statement and account" respecting any agency it chooses? Respecting all federal agencies? What purpose, what function is the clause to perform under the Court's construction? The electoral process already permits the removal of legislators for any reason. Allowing their removal at the polls for failure to comply with Art I, § 9, cl 7, effectively reduces that clause to a nullity, giving it no purpose at all.

The sovereign in this Nation are the people, not the bureaucracy. The statement of accounts of public expenditures goes to the heart of the problem of sovereignty. If taxpayers may not ask that rudimentary question, their sovereignty becomes an empty symbol and a secret bureaucracy is allowed to run our affairs.

The resolution of that issue has not been entrusted to one of the other coordinate branches of government—the test of the "political question." * * * The question is "political" if there is "a textually demonstrable constitutional commitment of the issue to a coordinate political department." * * * The mandate runs to the Congress and to the agencies it creates to make "a regular Statement and Account the Receipts and Expenditures of all public Money." The beneficiaries—as is abundantly clear from the constitutional history—are the public. The public cannot intelligently know how to exercise the franchise unless they have a basic knowledge concerning at least the generality of the accounts under every head of government. No greater crisis in confidence can be generated than today's decision. Its consequences are grave because it relegates to secrecy vast operations of government and keeps the public from knowing what secret plans concerning this or other nations are afoot. The fact that the result is serious does not of course make the issue "justiciable." But resolutions of any doubts or ambiguities should be towards protecting an individual's stake in the integrity of constitutional guarantees rather than turning him away without even a chance to be heard.

I would affirm the judgment below.

Mr. Justice Brennan dissented. [Omitted.]

Mr. Justice Stewart, with whom Mr. Justice Marshall joins, dissenting.

The Court's decisions in Flast v Cohen * * * and Frothingham v Mellon * * * throw very little light on the question at issue in this case. For, unlike . . . those cases, Richardson did not bring this action asking a court to invalidate a federal statute on the ground that it was beyond the delegated power of Congress to enact or that it contravened some constitutional prohibition. Richardson's claim is of an entirely different order. It is that . . . the Statement and Account Clause gives him a right to receive, and imposes on the Government a corresponding affirmative duty to supply, a periodic report of the receipts and expenditures "of all public Money." In support of his standing to litigate this claim, he has asserted his status both as a taxpayer and as a citizen-voter. Whether the Statement and Account Clause imposes upon the Government an affirmative duty to supply the information requested and whether that duty runs to every taxpayer or citizen are questions that go to the substantive merits of this litigation. Those questions are not now before us, but I think that the Court is quite wrong in holding that the respondent was without standing to raise them in the trial court.

. . . When a party is seeking a judicial determination that a defendant owes him an affirmative duty, it seems clear to me that he has standing to litigate the issue of the existence . . . of this duty once he shows that the defendant has declined to honor his claim. If the duty in question involved the payment of a sum of money, I suppose that all would agree that a plaintiff asserting the duty would have standing to litigate the issue of his entitlement to the money upon a showing that he had not been paid. I see no reason for a different result when the defendant is a government official and the asserted duty relates not to the payment of money, but to the disclosure of items of information.

· . . . It seems to me that when the asserted duty is, as here, as particularized, palpable, and explicit as those which courts regularly recognize in private contexts, it should make no difference that the obligor is the government and the duty is embodied in our organic law. . . .

· · ·

The issue in Flast and its predecessor, Frothingham . . . related solely to the standing of a federal taxpayer to challenge allegedly unconstitutional exercises of the taxing and spending power. . . .

Richardson is not asserting that a taxing and spending program exceeds Congress' delegated power or violates a constitutional limitation on such power. Indeed, the constitutional provision that underlies his claim does not purport to limit the power of the Federal Government in any respect, but, according to Richardson, simply imposes an affirmative duty on the Government with respect to all taxpayers or citizen-voters of the Republic. Thus, the nexus analysis of Flast is simply not relevant to the standing question raised in this case.

• • •

On the merits, I presume that the Government's position would be that the Statement and Account Clause of the Constitution does not impose an affirmative duty upon it; that any such duty does not in any event run to Richardson; that any such duty is subject to legislative qualifications, one of which is applicable here; and that the question involved is political and thus not justiciable. Richardson might ultimately be thrown out of court on any one of these grounds, or some other. But to say that he might ultimately lose his lawsuit certainly does not mean that he had no standing to bring it.

For the reasons expressed, I believe that Richardson had standing to bring this action. . . .

United States v. Students Challenging Regulatory Agency Procedures

412 U.S. 669 (1973)

Mr. Justice Stewart delivered the opinion of the Court.

Under the Interstate Commerce Act, the initiative for rate increases remains with the railroads. But in the absence of special permission from the Interstate Commerce Commission, a railroad seeking an increase must provide at least 30 days' notice to the Commission and the public before putting the new rate into effect. * * * During that 30-day period, the Commission may suspend the operation of the proposed rate for a maximum of seven months pending an investigation and decision on the lawfulness of the new rates. * * * At the end of the seven-month period, the carrier may put the suspended rate into effect unless the Commission has earlier completed its investigation and found the rate unlawful.

Proceeding under this regulatory scheme . . . , substantially all of the railroads in the United States requested Commission authorization to file on 5 days' notice a 2.5% surcharge on nearly all freight rates. . . .

As justification for the proposed surcharge, the railroads alleged increasing costs and severely inadequate revenues. . . .

• • •

. . . The Commission authorized the railroads to refile the 2.5% surcharge with not less than 30 days' notice, and an effective date no earlier than February 5, 1972.

On January 5, 1972, the railroads refiled the surcharge to become effective on February 5, 1972. Shippers, competing carriers, and other interested persons requested the Commission to suspend the tariff for the statutory seven-month period. . . .

The Commission issued an order on February 1, 1972 . . . not to suspend the 2.5% surcharge for the seven-month statutory period. . . .

. . . [O]n April 24, 1972, . . . the Commission modified its February 1 order and authorized the railroads to eliminate the June 5 expiration date for the surcharge and to continue collecting the surcharge until November 30, 1972.

I

On May 12, 1972, SCRAP filed the present suit . . . seeking, along with other relief, a preliminary injunction to restrain enforcement of the Commission's . . . orders allowing the railroads to collect the 2.5% surcharge.

SCRAP stated in its amended complaint that it was "an unincorporated association formed by five law students . . . in September, 1971. Its primary purpose is to enhance the quality of the human environment for its members and for all citizens . . . ." To establish standing to bring this suit, SCRAP . . . claimed that each of its members "suffered economic, recreational and aesthetic harm directly as a result of the adverse environmental impact of the railroad freight structure, as modified by the Commission's actions to date. . . ." Specifically SCRAP alleged that each of its members was caused to pay more for finished products, that each of its members "uses the forests, rivers, streams, mountains, and other natural resources surrounding the Washington Metropolitan Area and at his legal residence, for camping, hiking, fishing, sightseeing, and other recreational [and] aesthetic purposes," and that these uses have been adversely affected by the increased freight rates, that each of its members breathes the air within the Washington Metropolitan Area and the area of his legal residence and that this air has suffered increased pollution caused by the modified rate structure, and that each member has been forced to pay increased taxes because of the sums which must be expended to dispose of otherwise reusable waste materials.

The main thrust of SCRAP's complaint was that the Commission's decisions . . . , insofar as they declined to suspend the 2.5% surcharge, were unlawful because the Commission had failed to include a detailed environmental impact statement as required by . . . the National Environmental Policy Act of 1969 (NEPA). * * * NEPA requires such a statement in "every recommendation or report on proposals for legislation and other major Federal actions significantly affecting the quality of the human environment. . . ." * * * SCRAP contended that because of its alleged adverse impact upon recycling, the Commission's action with respect to the surcharge constituted a major federal action significantly affecting the environment.

· · ·

On July 10, 1972, the District Court filed an opinion, * * * and entered an injunction forbidding the Commission "from permitting", and the railroads "from collecting" the 2.5% surcharge "insofar as that surcharge relates to goods being transported for purposes of recycling, pending further order of this court."

· · ·

. . . On December 18, 1972, we noted probable jurisdiction of the appeals filed by the United States, the Commission, and the railroads. * * *

II

The [U.S. and the ICC] challenge [SCRAP's] standing to sue, . . . under our recent decision in Sierra Club v Morton. . . .

The . . . Sierra Club, "a large and long-established organization, with a historic commitment to the cause of protecting our Nation's natural heritage from man's depredations," * * * sought a declaratory judgment and an injunction to restrain federal officials from approving the creation of an extensive ski-resort development. . . . The Sierra Club claimed standing to maintain its "public interest" lawsuit because it had "a special interest in the conservation and the sound maintenance of the national parks, game refuges and forests of the country. . . ." * * * We held those allegations insufficient.

. . . [W]e held that . . . the APA conferred standing to obtain judicial review of agency action only upon those who could show "that the challenged action had caused them 'injury in fact,' and where the alleged injury was to an interest 'arguably within the zone of interests to be protected or regulated' by the statutes that the agencies were claimed to have violated." * * *

In interpreting "injury in fact" we made it clear that standing was not confined to those who could show "economic harm". . . . Nor, we said, could the fact that many persons shared the same injury be sufficient reason to disqualify from seeking review of an agency's action any person who had in fact suffered injury. Rather, we explained: "Aesthetic and environmental well-being, like economic well-being, are important ingredients of the quality of life in our society, and the fact that particular environmental interests are shared by the many rather than the few does not make them less deserving of legal protection through the judicial process." * * * Consequently, neither the fact that [SCRAP] here claimed only a harm to their use and enjoyment of the natural resources of the Washington area, nor the fact that all those who use those resources suffered the same harm, deprives them of standing.

In Sierra Club, though, we went on to stress the importance of demonstrating that the party seeking review be himself among the injured, for it is this requirement that gives a litigant a direct stake in the controversy and prevents the judicial process from becoming no more than a vehicle for the vindication of the value interests of concerned bystanders. No such specific injury was alleged in Sierra Club. . . . [T]he Sierra Club failed to allege that it or its members would be affected in any of their activities or pastimes. . . . Here, by contrast, the appellees claimed that the specific and allegedly illegal action of the Commission would directly harm them in their use of the natural resources of the Washington Metropolitan Area.

*   *   *

But the injury alleged here is also very different from that at issue in Sierra Club because here the alleged injury to the environment is far less direct and perceptible. The petitioner there complained about the construction of a specific project. . . . Here, the Court was asked to follow a far more attenuated line of causation to the eventual injury of which the appellees complained—a general rate increase would allegedly cause increased use of nonrecyclable commodities as compared to recyclable goods, thus resulting in the need to use more natural resources to produce such goods, some of which resources might be taken from the Washington area, and resulting in more refuse that might be discarded in national parks in the Washington area. The railroads protest that the appellees could never prove that a general increase in rates would have this effect, and they contend that these allegations were a ploy to avoid the need to show some injury in fact.

Of course, pleadings must be something more than an ingenious academic exercise in the conceivable. A plaintiff must allege that he has been or will in fact be perceptibly harmed by the challenged agency action, not that he can imagine circumstances in which he could be affected by the agency's action. And it is equally clear that the allegations must be true and capable of proof at trial. But we deal here simply with the pleadings in which the appellees alleged a specific and perceptible harm that distinguished them from other citizens who had not used the natural resources that were claimed to be affected. . . . The District Court was correct in denying the appellants' motion to dismiss the complaint for failure to allege sufficient standing to bring this lawsuit.

[The Court went on to rule that the District Court lacked power to issue a preliminary injunction at such an early stage in the ICC's proceedings.]

Mr. Justice Powell took no part in the consideration or decision of these cases.

Mr. Justice Blackmun, with whom Mr. Justice Brennan joins, concurring.

*   *   *

. . . I would not require that [members of SCRAP], in their individual capacities, prove that they in fact were injured. Rather, I would require only that [SCRAP], as responsible and sincere representatives of environmental interests, show that the environment would be injured in fact and that such injury would be irreparable and substantial.

MR. JUSTICE DOUGLAS, dissenting in part.

•   •   •

Littering is a commonplace phenomenon that affects every person, almost everywhere. By reports and writings we know that littering defaces mountain trails, alpine meadows, and even our highest peaks. Those in the valleys are often almost inundated with litter. Where a river is polluted and a person is dependent on it for drinking water, I suppose there would not be the slightest doubt that he would have standing in court to present his claim. I also suppose there is not the slightest doubt that where smog settles on a city, any person who must breathe that air or feel the sulphuric acid forming in his eyes, would have standing in court to present his claim. I think it is equally obvious that any resident of an area whose paths are strewn with litter, whose parks, or picnic grounds are defaced by it has standing to tender his complaint to the Court. Sierra Club v Morton . . . would seem to cover this case, for littering abetted by the failure to recycle would clearly seem to implicate residents to whom "the aesthetic and recreational values of the area" are important. * * * For the reasons stated in my opinion in Sierra Club v Morton . . . I agree with the Court that [SCRAP members] have standing, but like Mr. Justice Blackmun, I would not require [them], in their individual capacity, to prove injury in fact. As Mr. Justice Blackmun states, it should be sufficient if appellees, "as responsible and sincere representatives of environmental interests, show that the environment would be injured in fact."

•   •   •

MR. JUSTICE WHITE, with whom THE CHIEF JUSTICE and MR. JUSTICE REHNQUIST join, dissenting in part.

I would reverse the judgment of the District Court and order the complaint dismissed because [SCRAP members] lack standing to bring this suit. None of our cases, including inferences that may be drawn from dicta in Sierra Club v Morton, where we denied standing . . . , are sufficient to confer standing . . . in circumstances like these. The allegations here do not satisfy the threshold requirement of injury in fact for constituting a justiciable case or controversy. . . .

The majority acknowledges that these allegations reflect an "attenuated line of causation". . . . To me, the alleged injuries are so remote, speculative and insubstantial in fact that they fail to confer standing. They become no more concrete, real or substantial when it is added that materials will cost more at the marketplace and that somehow the freight rate increase would increase air pollution. Allegations such as these are no more substantial and direct and no more qualify [SCRAP] to litigate than allegations of a taxpayer that governmental expenditures will increase his taxes and have an impact on his pocketbook * * * or allegations that governmental decisions are offensive to reason or morals. The general "right, possessed by every citizen, to require that the Government be administered according to law and that public monies not be wasted" does not confer standing to litigate in federal courts. . . . As I see the allegations in this case, they are in reality little different from the general interest allegations found insufficient and too remote in Sierra Club. If they are sufficient here, we are well on our way to permitting citizens at large to litigate any decisions of the Government which fall in an area of interest to them and with which they disagree.

• • •

Mr. Justice Marshall, concurring in part and dissenting in part. [Omitted.]

Association of Data Processing Service Organizations v. Camp

397 U.S. 150 (1970)

Mr. Justice Douglas delivered the opinion of the Court.

[Association members] sell data processing services to businesses generally. In this suit they seek to challenge a ruling by respondent Comptroller of the Currency that, as an incident to their banking services, national banks, including respondent American National Bank & Trust Company, may make data processing services available to other banks and to bank customers. The District Court dismissed the complaint for lack of standing of petitioners to bring the suit. * * *

Generalizations about standing to sue are largely worthless as such. One generalization is, however, necessary and that is that the question of standing in the federal courts is to be considered in the framework of Article III which restricts judicial power to "cases" and "controversies." . . . "[I]n terms of Article III limitations on federal court jurisdiction, the question of standing is related only to whether the dispute sought to be adjudicated will be presented in an adversary context and in a form historically viewed as capable of judicial resolution." . . .

The first question is whether the plaintiff alleges that the challenged action has caused him injury in fact, economic or otherwise. There can be no doubt but that [Association members] have satisfied this test. [They] not only allege that competition by national banks in the business of providing data processing services might entail some future loss of profits . . . , they also allege that . . . American National Bank & Trust Company was performing or preparing to perform such services for two customers for whom . . . Data Systems, Inc., had previously agreed or negotiated to perform such services. [This] suit was brought not only against the American National Bank & Trust Company, but also against the Comptroller of the Currency. The Comptroller was alleged to have caused [the Association] injury in fact by his 1966 ruling which stated:

> "Incidental to its banking services, a national bank may make available its data processing equipment or perform data processing services on such equipment for other banks and bank customers." * * *

The Court of Appeals viewed the matter differently, stating:

> "[A] plaintiff may challenge alleged illegal competition when as complainant it pursues (1) a legal interest by reason of public charter or contract, . . . (2) a legal interest by reason of statutory protection, . . . or (3) a 'public interest' in which Congress has recognized the need for review of administrative action and plaintiff is significantly involved to have standing to represent the public . . . ." * * *

Those tests were based on prior decisions of this Court, . . . where private power companies sought to enjoin TVA from operating, claiming that the statutory plan under which it was created was unconstitutional. The Court denied the competitors' standing, holding that they did not have that status "unless the right invaded is a legal right,—one of property, one arising out of contract, one protected against tortious invasion, or one founded on a statute which confers a privilege." * * *

The "legal interest" test goes to the merits. The question of standing is different. It concerns, apart from the "case" or "controversy" test, the question whether the interest sought to be protected by the complainant is arguably within the zone of interests to be protected or regulated by the statute or constitutional guarantee in question. Thus the Administrative Procedure Act grants standing to a person "aggrieved by agency action within the meaning of a relevant statute." * * * That interest, at times, may reflect "aesthetic, conservational, and recreational" as well as economic values. * * * A person or a family may have a spiritual stake in the First Amendment values sufficient to give standing to raise issues concerning the Establishment Clause and the Free Exercise Clause. * * * We mention these noneconomic values to emphasize that standing may stem from them as well as from the economic injury on which petitioners rely here. Certainly he who is "likely to be financially" injured * * * may be a reliable private attorney general to litigate the issues of the public interest in the present case.

Apart from Article III jurisdictional questions, problems of standing, as resolved by this Court, have involved a "rule of self-restraint." * * * Congress can, of course, resolve the question one way or another, save as the requirements of Article III dictate otherwise. * * *

Where statutes are concerned, the trend is toward enlargement of the class of people who may protest administrative action. The whole drive for enlarging the category of aggrieved "persons" is symptomatic of that trend. . . . Hardin v Kentucky Utilities Co. * * * involved a section of the TVA Act designed primarily to protect, through area limitations, private utilities against TVA competition. We held that no explicit statutory provision was necessary to confer standing, since the private utility bringing suit was within the class of persons that the statutory provision was designed to protect.

It is argued that the . . . Hardin case [is] relevant here because of . . . the Bank Service Corporation Act of 1962, which provides:

> "No bank service corporation may engage in any activity other than the performance of bank services for banks."

. . .

. . . We do think, however, that [this section] arguably brings a competitor within the zone of interests protected by it.

. . .

We find no evidence that Congress in either the Bank Service Corporation Act or the National Bank Act sought to preclude judicial review of administrative rulings by the Comptroller as to the legitimate scope of activities available to national banks under those statutes. Both Acts are clearly "relevant" statutes within the meaning of [the Administrative Procedure Act]. The Acts do not in terms protect a specified group. But their general policy is apparent; and those whose interests are directly affected by a broad or narrow interpretation of the Acts are easily identifiable. It is clear that petitioners, as competitors of national banks which are engaging in data processing services, are within that class of "aggrieved" persons who . . . are entitled to judicial review of "agency action."

Whether anything in the Bank Service Corporation Act or the National Bank Act gives petitioners a "legal interest" that protects them against violations of those Acts, and whether the actions of respondents did in fact violate either of those Acts, are questions which go to the merits and remain to be decided. . . .

We hold that petitioners have standing to sue and that the case should be remanded for a hearing on the merits.

Reversed and remanded.

MR. JUSTICE BRENNAN, with whom MR. JUSTICE WHITE joins, concurring in the result and dissenting.

• • •

The Court's approach to standing, set out in Data Processing, has two steps: (1) since "the framework of Article III . . . restricts judicial power to 'cases' and 'controversies,' " the first step is to determine "whether the plaintiff alleges that the challenged action has caused him injury in fact"; (2) if injury in fact is alleged, the relevant statute or constitutional provision is then examined to determine "whether the interest sought to be protected by the complainant is arguably within the zone of interests to be protected or regulated by the statute or constitutional guarantee in question."

My view is that the inquiry in the Court's first step is the only one that need be made to determine standing. By requiring a second, nonconstitutional step, the Court comes very close to perpetuating the discredited requirement that conditioned standing on a showing by the plaintiff that the challenged governmental action invaded one of his legally protected interests. . . .

Before the plaintiff is allowed to argue the merits, it is true that a canvass of relevant statutory materials must be made in cases challenging agency action. But the canvass is made, not to determine *standing* but to determine an aspect of *reviewability*, that is, whether Congress meant to deny or to allow judicial review of the agency action at the instance of the plaintiff. The Court in the present case examines the statutory materials for just this purpose but only after making the same examination during the second step of its standing inquiry. Thus in Data Processing the Court determines that the petitioners have standing because they alleged injury in fact and because ". . . [the Bank Service Corporation Act of 1962] arguably brings a competitor within the zone of interests protected by it." The Court then determines that the Comptroller's action is reviewable at the instance of the plaintiffs because "[b]oth [the Bank Service Corporation Act and the National Bank Act] are clearly 'relevant' statutes within the meaning of [the Administrative Procedure Act * * *]. The Acts do not in terms protect a specified group. But their general policy is apparent; and those whose interests are directly affected by a broad or narrow interpretation of the Acts are easily identifiable."
. . .

I submit that in making such examination of statutory materials an element in the determination of standing, the Court not only performs a useless and unnecessary exercise but also encourages badly reasoned decisions, which may well deny justice in this complex field. When agency action is challenged, standing, reviewability, and the merits pose discrete, and often complicated, issues which can best be resolved by recognizing and treating them as such.

• • •

Standing

. . . [S]tanding exists when the plaintiff alleges, as [the Association] . . . alleged, that the challenged action has caused him injury in fact, economic or otherwise. He thus shows that he has the requisite "personal stake in the outcome" of his suit. * * * We may reasonably expect that a person so harmed will, as best he can, frame the relevant questions with specificity, contest the issues with the necessary adverseness, and pursue the litigation vigorously. Recognition of his standing to litigate is then consistent with the Constitution, and no further inquiry is pertinent to its existence.

Reviewability

When the legality of administrative action is at issue, standing alone will not entitle the plaintiff to a decision on the merits. Pertinent statutory language, legislative history, and public policy considerations must be examined to determine whether Congress precluded all judicial review, and, if not, whether Congress nevertheless foreclosed review to the class to which the plaintiff belongs. Under the Administrative Procedure Act (APA), "statutes [may] preclude judicial review" or "agency action [may be] committed to agency discretion by law." * * * In either case, the plaintiff is out of court, not because he had no standing to enter, but because Congress has stripped the judiciary of authority to review agency action. Review may be totally foreclosed * * * or, if permitted, it may nonetheless be denied to the plaintiff's class. But the governing principle . . . is that "judicial review of a final agency action by an aggrieved person will not be cut off unless there is persuasive reason to believe that such was the purpose of Congress."

. . . Where, as in the instant case, there is no express grant of review, reviewability has ordinarily been inferred from evidence that Congress intended the plaintiff's class to be a beneficiary of the statute under which the plaintiff raises his claim. . . .

The Merits

If it is determined that a plaintiff who alleged injury in fact is entitled to judicial review, inquiry proceeds to the merits—to whether the specific legal interest claimed by the plaintiff is protected by the statute and to whether the protested agency action invaded that interest. . . .

. . . [I]n my view alleged injury in fact, reviewability, and the merits pose questions that are largely distinct from one another, each governed by its own considerations. . . . Too often these various questions have been merged into one confused inquiry, lumped under the general rubric of "standing." . . .

The risk of ambiguity and injustice can be minimized by cleanly severing, so far as possible, the inquiries into reviewability and the merits from the determination of standing. Today's decisions, however, will only compound present confusion and breed even more litigation over standing. In the first place, the Court's formulation of its nonconstitutional element of standing is obscure. What precisely must a plaintiff do to establish that "the interest sought to be protected . . . is arguably within the zone of interests to be protected or regulated by the statute"? How specific an "interest" must he advance? Will a broad, general claim, such as competitive interest, suffice, or must he identify a specific legally protected interest? When, too, is his interest "arguably" within the appropriate "zone"? Does a mere allegation that it falls there suffice? If more than an allegation is required, is the plaintiff required to argue the merits? And what is the distinction between a "protected" and a "regulated" interest? Is it possible that a plaintiff may challenge agency action under a statute that unquestionably regulates the interest at stake, but that expressly excludes the plaintiff's class from among the statutory beneficiaries?

. . . The Constitution requires for standing only that the plaintiff allege that actual harm resulted to him from the agency action. Investigation to determine whether the constitutional requirement has been met has nothing in common with the inquiry into statutory language, legislative history, and public policy that must be made to ascertain whether Congress has precluded or limited judicial review. . . . The Court's approach does too little to guard against the possibility that judges will use standing to slam the courthouse door against plaintiffs who are entitled to full consideration of their claims on the merits. The Court's approach must trouble all concerned with the function of the judicial process in today's world. . . .

Younger v. Harris

401 U.S. 37 (1971)

MR. JUSTICE BLACK delivered the opinion of the Court.

Appellee, John Harris, Jr., was indicted in a California state court, charged with violation of the . . . California Criminal Syndicalism Act. . . . He then filed a complaint in the Federal District Court, asking that court to enjoin the appellant, Younger, the District Attorney of Los Angeles County, from prosecuting him, and alleging that the prosecution and even the presence of the Act inhibited him in the exercise of his rights of free speech and press, rights guaranteed him by the First and Fourteenth Amendments. . . . A three-judge Federal District Court . . . held that it had jurisdiction and power to restrain the District Attorney from prosecuting, held that the State's Criminal Syndicalism Act was void for vagueness and overbreadth in violation of the First and Fourteenth Amendments, and accordingly restrained the District Attorney from "further prosecution of the currently pending action against the plaintiff Harris for alleged violation of the Act." * * *

The case is before us on appeal by the State's District Attorney Younger. . . . [W]e have concluded that the judgment of the District Court, enjoining appellant Younger from prosecuting under these California statutes, must be reversed as a violation of the national policy forbidding federal courts to stay or enjoin pending state court proceedings except under special circumstances. We express no view about the circumstances under which federal courts may act when there is no prosecution pending in state courts at the time the federal proceeding is begun.

I

Appellee Harris has been indicted, and was actually being prosecuted by California for a violation of its Criminal Syndicalism Act at the time this suit was filed. He thus has an acute live controversy with the State and its prosecutor. . . . A federal lawsuit to stop a prosecution in a state court is a serious matter. And persons having no fears of state prosecution, except those that are imaginary or speculative, are not to be accepted as appropriate plaintiffs in such cases. * * * Since Harris is actually being prosecuted under the challenged laws, however, we proceed with him as a proper party.

II

Since the beginning of this Country's history Congress has, subject to few exceptions, manifested a desire to permit state courts to try state cases free from interference by federal courts. In 1793 an Act unconditionally provided: ". . . nor shall a writ of injunction be granted to stay proceedings in any court of any state. . . ." * * * A comparison of the 1793 Act with * * * its present-day successor, graphically illustrates how few and minor have been the exceptions granted from the flat, prohibitory language of the old Act. During all this lapse of years from 1793 to 1970 the statutory exceptions to the 1793 congressional enactment have been only three: (1) ". . . except as expressly authorized by Act of Congress . . ."; (2) ". . . where necessary in aid of its jurisdiction . . ."; and (3) ". . . to protect or effectuate its judgments. . . ." In addition, a judicial exception to the long-standing policy evidenced by the statute has been made where a person about to be prosecuted in a state court can show that he will, if the proceeding in the state court is not enjoined, suffer irreparable damages. * * *

The precise reasons for this long-standing public policy against federal court interference with state court proceedings have never been specifically identified but the primary sources of the policy are plain. One is the basic doctrine of equity jurisprudence that courts of equity should not act, and particularly should not act to restrain a criminal prosecution, when the moving party has an adequate remedy at law and will not suffer irreparable injury if denied equitable relief. The doctrine may originally have grown out of circumstances peculiar to the English judicial system and not applicable in this country, but its fundamental purpose of restraining equity jurisdiction within narrow limits is equally important under our Constitution, in order to prevent erosion of the role of the jury and avoid a duplication of legal proceedings and legal sanctions where a single suit would be adequate to protect the rights asserted. This underlying reason for restraining courts of equity from interfering with criminal prosecutions is reinforced by an even more vital consideration, the notion of "comity," that is a proper respect for state functions, a recognition of the fact that the entire country is made up of a Union of separate state governments, and a continuance of the belief that the National Government will fare best if the States and their institutions are left free to perform their separate functions in their separate ways. This, perhaps for lack of a better and clearer way to describe it, is referred to by many as "Our Federalism," and one familiar with the profound debates that ushered our Federal Constitution into existence is bound to respect those who remain loyal to the ideals and dreams of "Our Federalism." The concept does not mean blind deference to "States' Rights" any more than it means centralization of control over every important issue in our National Government and its courts. The Framers rejected both these courses. What the concept does represent is a system in which there is sensitivity to the legitimate interests of both State and National Governments, and in which the National Government, anxious though it may be to vindicate and protect federal rights and federal interests, always endeavors to do so in ways that will not unduly interfere with the legitimate activities of the States. It should never be forgotten that this slogan, "Our Federalism," born in the early struggling days of our Union of States, occupies a highly important place in our Nation's history and its future.

This brief discussion should be enough to suggest some of the reasons why it has been perfectly natural for our cases to repeat time and time again that the normal thing to do when federal courts are asked to enjoin pending proceedings in state courts is not to issue such injunctions. . . .

In all of these cases the Court stressed the importance of showing irreparable injury, the traditional prerequisite to obtaining an injunction. In addition, however, the Court also made clear that in view of the fundamental policy against federal interference with state criminal prosecutions, even irreparable injury is insufficient unless it is "both great and immediate." * * * Certain types of injury, in particular, the cost, anxiety, and inconvenience of having to defend against a single criminal prosecution could not by themselves be considered "irreparable" in the special legal sense of that term. Instead, the threat to the plaintiff's federally protected rights must be one that cannot be eliminated by his defense against a single criminal prosecution. . . .

This is where the law stood when the Court decided *Dombrowski* v. *Pfister* * * * and held that an injunction against the enforcement of certain state criminal statutes could properly issue under the circumstances presented in that case. . . . The appellants in *Dombrowski* had offered to prove that their offices had been raided and all their files and records seized pursuant to search and arrest warrants that were later summarily vacated by a state judge for lack of probable cause. They also offered to prove that despite the state court order quashing the warrants and suppressing the evidence seized, the prosecutor was continuing to threaten to initiate new prosecutions of appellants under the same statutes, was holding public hearings at which photostatic copies of the illegally seized documents were being used, and was threatening to use other copies of the illegally seized documents to obtain grand jury indictments against the appellants on charges of violating the same statutes. These circumstances, as viewed by the Court, sufficiently establish the kind of irreparable injury, above and beyond that associated with the defense of a single prosecution brought in good faith, that had always been considered sufficient to justify federal intervention. . . . [T]he Court in *Dombrowski* went on to say:

> "But the allegations in this complaint depict a situation in which defense of the State's criminal prosecution will not assure adequate vindication of constitutional rights. They suggest that a substantial loss of or impairment of freedoms of expression will occur if appellants must await the state court's disposition and ultimate review in this Court of any adverse determination. These allegations, if true, clearly show irreparable injury." * * *

• • •

The District Court . . . thought that the *Dombrowski* decision substantially broadened the availability of injunctions against state criminal prosecutions and that under that decision the federal courts may give equitable relief, without regard to any showing of bad faith or harassment, whenever a state statute is found "on its face" to be vague or overly broad, in violation of the First Amendment. We recognize that there are some statements in the *Dombrowski* opinion that would seem to support this argument. But as we have already seen, such statements were unnecessary to the decision of that case, because the Court found that the plaintiffs had alleged a basis for equitable relief under the long-established standards. In addition, we do not regard the reasons adduced to support this position as sufficient to justify such a substantial departure from the established doctrines regarding the availability of injunctive relief. It is undoubtedly true, as the Court stated in *Dombrowski*, that "A criminal prosecution under a statute regulating expression usually involves imponderables and contingencies that themselves may inhibit the full exercise of First Amendment freedoms."

* * * But this sort of "chilling effect," as the Court called it, should not by itself justify federal intervention. . . .

Moreover, the existence of a "chilling effect," even in the area of First Amendment rights, has never been considered a sufficient basis, in and of itself, for prohibiting state action. Where a statute does not directly abridge free speech, but—while regulating a subject within the State's power—tends to have the incidental effect of inhibiting First Amendment rights, it is well settled that the statute can be upheld if the effect on speech is minor in relation to the need for control of the conduct and the lack of alternative means for doing so. * * * Just as the incidental "chilling effect" of such statutes does not automatically render them unconstitutional, so the chilling effect that admittedly can result from the very existence of certain laws on the statute books does not in itself justify prohibiting the State from carrying out the important and necessary task of enforcing these laws against socially harmful conduct that the State believes in good faith to be punishable under its laws and the Constitution.

Beyond all this is another, more basic consideration. Procedures for testing the constitutionality of a statute "on its face" in the manner apparently contemplated by *Dombrowski,* and for then enjoining all action to enforce the statute until the State can obtain court approval for a modified version, are fundamentally at odds with the function of the federal courts in our constitutional plan. The power and duty of the judiciary to declare laws unconstitutional is in the final analysis derived from its responsibility for resolving concrete disputes brought before the courts for decision; a statute apparently governing a dispute cannot be applied by judges, consistently with their obligations under the Supremacy Clause, when such an application of the statute would conflict with the Constitution. * * * But this vital responsibility, broad as it is, does not amount to an unlimited power to survey the statute books and pass judgment on laws before the courts are called upon to enforce them. Ever since the Constitutional Convention rejected a proposal for having members of the Supreme Court render advice concerning pending legislation it has been clear that, even when suits of this kind involve a "case or controversy" sufficient to satisfy the requirements of Article III of the Constitution, the task of analyzing a proposed statute, pinpointing its deficiencies, and requiring correction of these deficiencies before the statute is put into effect, is rarely if ever an appropriate task for the judiciary. The combination of the relative remoteness of the controversy, the impact on the legislative process of the relief sought, and above all the speculative and amorphous nature of the required line-by-line analysis of detailed statutes * * * ordinarily results in a kind of case that is wholly unsatisfactory for deciding constitutional questions, whichever way they might be decided. In light of this fundamental conception of the Framers as to the proper place of the federal courts in the governmental processes of passing and enforcing laws, it can seldom be appropriate for these courts to exercise any such power of prior approval or veto over the legislative process.

For these reasons, fundamental not only to our federal system but also to the basic functions of the Judicial Branch of the National Government under our Constitution, we hold that the *Dombrowski* decision should not be regarded as having upset the settled doctrines that have always confined very narrowly the availability of injunctive relief against state criminal prosecutions. We do not think that opinion stands for the proposition that a federal court can properly enjoin enforcement of a statute solely on the basis of showing that the statute "on its face" abridges First Amendment rights. There may, of course, be extraordinary circumstances in which the necessary irreparable injury can be shown even in the absence of the usual prerequisites of bad faith and harassment. . . . Other unusual situations calling for federal intervention might also arise, but there is no point in our attempting now to specify what they might be. It is sufficient for purposes of the present case to hold, as we do, that the possible unconstitutionality of a statute "on its face" does not in itself justify an injunction against good faith attempts to enforce it, and that . . . Harris has failed to make any showing of bad faith, harassment, or any other unusual circumstance that would call for equitable relief. . . .

The judgment of the District Court is reversed, and the case is remanded for further proceedings not inconsistent with this opinion.

Reversed.

MR. JUSTICE STEWART, with whom MR. JUSTICE HARLAN joins, concurring.

The questions the Court decides today are important ones. Perhaps as important, however, is a recognition of the areas into which today's holdings do not necessarily extend. In all of these cases, the Court deals only with the proper policy to be followed by a federal court when asked to intervene by injunction or declaratory judgment in a criminal prosecution which is contemporaneously pending in a state court.

•   •   •

The Court confines itself to deciding the policy considerations that in our federal system must prevail when federal courts are asked to interfere with pending state prosecutions. Within this area, we hold that a federal court must not, save in exceptional and extremely limited circumstances, intervene by way of either injunction or declaration in an existing state criminal prosecution. Such circumstances exist only when there is a threat of irreparable injury "both great and immediate." A threat of this nature might be shown if the state criminal statute in question were patently and flagrantly unconstitutional on its face, * * * or if there has been bad faith and harassment—official lawlessness—in a statute's enforcement. * * * In such circumstances the reasons of policy for deferring to state adjudication are outweighed by the injury flowing from the very bringing of the state proceedings, by the perversion of the very process which is supposed to provide vindication, and by the need for speedy and effective action to protect federal rights. * * *

Mr. Justice Brennan, with whom Mr. Justice White and Mr. Justice Marshall join, concurring in the result. [Omitted.]

Mr. Justice Douglas, dissenting.

The fact that we are in a period of history when enormous extrajudicial sanctions are imposed on those who assert their First Amendment rights in unpopular causes emphasizes the wisdom of *Dombrowski* v. *Pfister*. * * * There we recognized that in times of repression, when interests with powerful spokesmen generate symbolic pogroms against nonconformists, the federal judiciary, charged by Congress with special vigilance for protection of civil rights, has special responsibilities to prevent an erosion of the individual's constitutional rights.

• • •

The special circumstances when federal intervention in a state criminal proceeding is permissible are not restricted to bad faith on the part of state officials or the threat of multiple prosecutions. They also exist where for any reason the state statute being enforced is unconstitutional on its face.

• • •

In *Younger*, "criminal syndicalism" is defined so broadly as to jeopardize "teaching" that socialism is preferable to free enterprise.

Harris' "crime" was distributing leaflets advocating change in industrial ownership through political action. The statute under which he was indicted was the one involved in *Whitney* v. *California*, * * * a decision we overruled in *Brandenburg* v. *Ohio*. * * *

If the "advocacy" which Harris used was an attempt at persuasion through the use of bullets, bombs, and arson, we would have a different case. But Harris is charged only with distributing leaflets advocating political action toward his objective. He tried unsuccessfully to have the state court dismiss the indictment on constitutional grounds. He resorted to the state appellate court for writs of prohibition to prevent the trial, but to no avail. He went to the federal court as a matter of last resort in an effort to keep this unconstitutional trial from being saddled on him.

• • •

The eternal temptation, of course, has been to arrest the speaker rather than to correct the conditions about which he complains. I see no reason why [petitioners like Harris] should be made to walk the treacherous ground of these statutes. They, like other citizens, need the umbrella of the First Amendment as they study, analyze, discuss, and debate the troubles of these days. When criminal prosecutions can be leveled against them because they express unpopular views, the society of the dialogue is in danger.

Stone v. Powell

428 U.S. 465 (1976)

MR. JUSTICE POWELL delivered the opinion of the Court.

Respondents [Powell et al.] in these cases were convicted of criminal offenses in state courts, and their convictions were affirmed on appeal. The prosecution in each case relied upon evidence obtained by searches and seizures alleged by respondents to have been unlawful. Each . . . subsequently sought relief in a Federal District Court by filing a petition for a writ of federal habeas corpus. * * * The question presented is whether a federal court should consider, in ruling on a petition for habeas corpus relief filed by a state prisoner, a claim that evidence obtained by an unconstitutional seach or seizure was introduced at his trial, when he has previously been afforded an opportunity for full and fair litigation of his claim in the state courts. The issue is of considerable importance to the administration of criminal justice.

• • •

The authority of federal courts to issue the writ of habeas corpus . . . was included in the first grant of federal court jurisdiction, made by the Judiciary Act of 1789 * * * with the limitation that the writ extend only to prisoners held in custody by the United States. The original statutory authorization did not define the substantive reach of the writ. . . . The courts defined the scope of the writ in accordance with the common law and limited it to an inquiry as to the jurisdiction of the sentencing tribunal. * * *

In 1867 the writ was extended to state prisoners. * * * Under the 1867 Act federal courts were authorized to give relief in "all cases where any person may be restrained of his or her liberty in violation of the constitution, or of any treaty or law of the United States . . ." But the limitation of federal habeas corpus jurisdiction to consideration of the jurisdiction of the sentencing court persisted. . . .

* * *

The Fourth Amendment assures the "right of the people to be secure in their persons, houses, papers, and effects, against unreasonable searches and seizures." . . .

The exclusionary rule was a judicially created means of effectuating the rights secured by the Fourth Amendment. Prior to the Court's decision in Weeks v United States * * * there existed no barrier to the introduction in criminal trials of evidence obtained in violation of the Amendment. * * *

In Weeks the Court held that the defendant could petition before trial for the return of property secured through an illegal search or seizure conducted by federal authorities. [Later] the Court held broadly that such evidence could not be introduced in a federal prosecution. . . . [T]he exclusionary rule was held applicable to the States in Mapp v Ohio. * * * The Mapp majority justified the application of the rule to the States on several grounds, but relied principally upon the belief that exclusion would deter future unlawful police conduct. * * *

* * *

Mapp involved the enforcement of the exclusionary rule at state trials and on direct review. [Later decisions suggest] the view that implementation of the Fourth Amendment also requires the consideration of search-and-seizure claims upon collateral [additional] review of state convictions [in federal courts via habeas corpus]. But despite the broad deterrent purpose of the exclusionary rule, it has never been interpreted to proscribe the introduction of illegally seized evidence in all proceedings or against all persons. . . .

* * *

We turn now to the specific question presented by these cases. Respondents allege violations of Fourth Amendment rights guaranteed them through the Fourteenth Amendment. The question is whether state prisoners—who have been afforded the opportunity for full and fair consideration of their reliance upon the exclusionary rule with respect to seized evidence by the state courts at trial and on direct review—may invoke their claim again on federal habeas corpus review. The answer is to be found by weighing the utility of the exclusionary rule against the costs of extending it to collateral review of Fourth Amendment claims.

The costs of applying the exclusionary rule even at trial and on direct review are well known; the focus of the trial, and the attention of the participants therein, are diverted from the ultimate question of guilt or innocence that should be the central concern in a criminal proceeding. Moreover, the physical evidence

sought to be excluded is typically reliable and often the most probative information bearing on the guilt or innocence of the defendant. . . . Application of the
rule thus deflects the truthfinding process and often frees the guilty. The disparity in particular cases between the error committed by the police officer and the
windfall afforded a guilty defendant by application of the rule is contrary to the
idea of proportionality that is essential to the concept of justice. Thus, although
the rule is thought to deter unlawful police activity in part through the nurturing
of respect for Fourth Amendment values, if applied indiscriminately it may well
have the opposite effect of generating disrespect for the law and administration of
justice. These long-recognized costs of the rule persist when a criminal conviction
is sought to be overturned on collateral review on the ground that a search-and-
seizure claim was erroneously rejected by two or more tiers of state courts.

Evidence obtained by police officers in violation of the Fourth Amendment is
excluded at trial in the hope that the frequency of future violations will decrease.
Despite the absence of supportive empirical evidence, we have assumed that the
immediate effect of exclusion will be to discourage law enforcement officials from
violating the Fourth Amendment by removing the incentive to disregard it.
More importantly, over the long term, this demonstration that our society at-
taches serious consequences to violation of constitutional rights is thought to
encourage those who formulate law enforcement policies, and the officers who
implement them, to incorporate Fourth Amendment ideals into their value system.

We adhere to the view that these considerations support the implementation
of the exclusionary rule at trial and its enforcement on direct appeal of state-
court convictions. But the additional contribution, if any, of the consideration of
search-and-seizure claims of state prisoners on collateral review is small in relation to the costs. To be sure, each case in which such claim is considered may add
marginally to an awareness of the values protected by the Fourth Amendment.
There is no reason to believe, however, that the overall educative effect of the
exclusionary rule would be appreciably diminished if search-and-seizure claims
could not be raised in federal habeas corpus review of state convictions. Nor is
there reason to assume that any specific disincentive already created by the risk
of exclusion of evidence at trial or the reversal of convictions on direct review
would be enhanced if there were the further risk that a conviction obtained in
state court and affirmed on direct review might be overturned in collateral proceedings often occurring years after the incarceration of the defendant. The view
that the deterrence of Fourth Amendment violations would be furthered rests on
the dubious assumption that law enforcement authorities would fear that federal
habeas review might reveal flaws in a search or seizure that went undetected at
trial and on appeal. Even if one rationally could assume that some additional
incremental deterrent effect would be present in isolated cases, the resulting
advance of the legitimate goal of furthering Fourth Amendment rights would be
outweighed by the acknowledged costs to other values vital to a rational system
of criminal justice.

In sum, we conclude that where the State has provided an opportunity for full and fair litigation of a Fourth Amendment claim, a state prisoner may not be granted federal habeas corpus relief on the ground that evidence obtained in an unconstitutional search or seizure was introduced at his trial. In this context the contribution of the exclusionary rule, if any, to the effectuation of the Fourth Amendment is minimal and the substantial societal costs of application of the rule persist with special force.

Accordingly, the judgments of the Courts of Appeals are reversed.

MR. CHIEF JUSTICE BURGER, concurring. [Omitted.]

MR. JUSTICE BRENNAN, with whom MR. JUSTICE MARSHALL concurs, dissenting.

. . . [This case, despite] the veil of Fourth Amendment terminology employed by the Court, plainly [does] not involve any question of the right of a defendant to have evidence excluded from use against him in his criminal trial when that evidence was seized in contravention of rights ostensibly secured by the Fourth and Fourteenth Amendments. Rather, [it involves] the question of the availability of a *federal forum* for vindicating those federally guaranteed rights. Today's holding portends substantial evisceration of federal habeas corpus jurisdiction, and I dissent.

The Court's opinion does not specify the particular basis on which it denies federal habeas jurisdiction over claims of Fourth Amendment violations brought by state prisoners. The Court insists that its holding is based on the Constitution, * * * but in light of the explicit language of [the habeas corpus statute] (significantly even mentioned by the Court), I can only presume that the Court intends to be understood to hold either that respondents are not, as a matter of statutory construction, "in custody in violation of the Constitution or laws . . . of the United States," or that " 'considerations of comity and concerns for the orderly administration of criminal justice' " * * * are sufficient to allow this Court to rewrite jurisdictional statutes enacted by Congress. Neither ground of decision is tenable; the former is simply illogical, and the latter is an arrogation of power committed solely to the Congress.

• • •

Understandably the Court must purport to cast its holding in constitutional terms, because that avoids a direct confrontation with the incontrovertible facts that the habeas statutes have heretofore always been construed to grant jurisdiction to entertain Fourth Amendment claims of both state and federal prisoners, that Fourth Amendment principles have been applied in decisions on the merits in numerous cases on collateral review of final convictions, and that Congress has legislatively accepted our interpretation of congressional intent as to the necessary scope and function of habeas relief. Indeed, the Court reaches its result without explicitly overruling any of our plethora of precedents inconsistent with that result or even discussing principles of stare decisis. . . . But show of the rhetoric of "interest balancing" used to obscure what is at stake in this case, it is evident that today's attempt to rest the decision on the Constitution must fail so long as Mapp v Ohio * * * remains undisturbed.

Under Mapp, as a matter of federal constitutional law, a state court *must* exclude evidence from the trial of an individual whose Fourth and Fourteenth Amendment rights were violated by a search or seizure that directly or indirectly resulted in the acquisition of that evidence. . . . When a state court admits such evidence, it has committed a *constitutional* error, and unless that error is harmless under federal standards, * * * it follows ineluctably that the defendant has been placed "in custody in violation of the Constitution." . . . In short, it escapes me as to what logic can support the assertion that the defendant's unconstitutional confinement obtains during the process of direct review, no matter how long that process takes, but that the unconstitutionality then suddenly dissipates at the moment the claim is asserted in a collateral attack on the conviction.

• • •

The Court adheres to the holding of Mapp that the Constitution "require[d] exclusion" of the evidence admitted at respondents' trials. * * * However, the Court holds that the Constitution "does not require" that respondents be accorded habeas relief if they were accorded "an opportunity for full and fair litigation of [their] Fourth Amendment claim[s]" in state courts. * * * Yet once the Constitution was interpreted by Mapp to require exclusion of certain evidence at trial, the Constitution became irrelevant to the manner in which that constitutional right was to be enforced in the federal courts; *that* inquiry is only a matter of respecting Congress' allocation of federal judicial power between this Court's appellate jurisdiction and a federal district court's habeas jurisdiction. . . . I can only view the constitutional garb in which the Court dresses its result as a disguise for rejection of the long-standing principle that there are no "second class" constitutional rights for purposes of federal habeas jurisdiction; it is nothing less than an attempt to provide a veneer of respectability for an obvious usurpation of Congress' Art III power to delineate the jurisdiction of the federal courts.

• • •

. . . Employing the transparent tactic that today's is a decision construing the Constitution, the Court usurps the authority—vested by the Constitution in the Congress—to reassign federal judicial responsibility for reviewing state prisoners' claims of failure of state courts to redress violations of their Fourth Amendment rights. Our jurisdiction is eminently unsuited for that task, and as a practical matter the only result of today's holding will be that denials by the state courts of claims by state prisoners of violations of their Fourth Amendment rights will go unreviewed by a federal tribunal. I fear that the same treatment ultimately will be accorded state prisoners' claims of violations of other constitutional rights; thus the potential ramifications of this case for federal habeas jurisdiction generally are ominous. The Court, no longer content just to restrict forthrightly the constitutional rights of the citizenry, has embarked on a campaign to water down even such constitutional rights as it purports to acknowledge by the device of foreclosing resort to the federal habeas remedy for their redress.

I would affirm the judgments of the Courts of Appeals.

Mr. Justice White, dissenting. [Omitted.]

Baker v. Carr

369 U.S. 186 (1962)

Mr. Justice Brennan delivered the opinion of the Court.

. . . [Baker et al.] seek relief in order to protect or vindicate an interest of their own, and of those similarly situated. Their constitutional claim is, in substance, that the 1901 [Tennessee apportionment] statute constitutes arbitrary and capricious state action, offensive to the Fourteenth Amendment in its irrational disregard of the standard of apportionment prescribed by the State's Constitution or of any standard, effecting a gross disproportion of representation to voting population. The injury which appellants assert is that this classification disfavors the voters in the counties in which they reside, placing them in a position of constitutionally unjustifiable inequality vis-à-vis voters in irrationally favored counties. . . .

• • •

In holding that the subject matter of this suit was not justiciable, the District Court relied on Colegrove v Green. * * * . . . We understand the District Court to have read the . . . case as compelling the conclusion that since [Baker] sought to have a legislative apportionment held unconstitutional, [his] suit presented a "political question" and was therefore nonjusticiable. We hold that this challenge to an apportionment presents no nonjusticiable "political question." . . .

Of course the mere fact that the suit seeks protection of a political right does not mean it presents a political question. Such an objection "is little more than a play upon words." * * * Rather, it is argued that apportionment cases, whatever the actual wording of the complaint, can involve no federal constitutional right except one resting on the guaranty of a republican form of government, and that complaints based on that clause have been held to present political questions which are nonjusticiable.

We hold that the claim pleaded here neither rests upon nor implicates the Guaranty Clause and that its justiciability is therefore not foreclosed by our decisions of cases involving that clause. The District Court misinterpreted Colegrove v Green and other decisions of this Court on which it relied. [Baker's] claim that [he is] being denied equal protection is justiciable, and if "discrimination is sufficiently shown, the right to relief under the equal protection clause is not diminished by the fact that the discrimination relates to political rights." * * * . . . [W]e deem it necessary first to consider the contours of the "political question" doctrine.

· · ·

We have said that "In determining whether a question falls within [the political question] category, the appropriateness under our system of government of attributing finality to the action of the political departments and also the lack of satisfactory criteria for a judicial determination are dominant considerations." * * * The nonjusticiability of a political question is primarily a function of the separation of powers. Much confusion results from the capacity of the "political question" label to obscure the need for case-by-case inquiry. Deciding whether a matter has in any measure been committed by the Constitution to another branch of government, or whether the action of that branch exceeds whatever authority has been committed, is itself a delicate exercise in constitutional interpretation, and is a responsibility of this Court as ultimate interpreter of the Constitution. To demonstrate this requires no less than to analyze representative cases and to infer from them the analytical threads that make up the political question doctrine. We shall then show that none of those threads catches this case.

[Brennan here discusses several categories of cases in which the Court has labeled particular controversies as "political." He concludes:]

It is apparent that several formulations which vary slightly according to the settings in which the questions arise may describe a political question, although each has one or more elements which identify it as essentially a function of the separation of powers. Prominent on the surface of any case held to involve a political question is found a textually demonstrable constitutional commitment of the issue to a coordinate political department; or a lack of judicially discoverable and manageable standards for resolving it; or the impossibility of deciding without an initial policy determination of a kind clearly for nonjudicial discretion; or the impossibility of a court's undertaking independent resolution without expressing lack of the respect due coordinate branches of government; or an unusual need for unquestioning adherence to a political decision already made;

or the potentiality of embarrassment from multifarious pronouncements by various departments on one question.

Unless one of these formulations is inextricable from the case at bar there should be no dismissal for nonjusticiability on the ground of a political question's presence. The doctrine of which we treat is one of "political questions," not one of "political cases." The courts cannot reject as "no law suit" a bona fide controversy as to whether some action denominated "political" exceeds constitutional authority. The cases we have reviewed show the necessity for discriminating inquiry into the precise facts and posture of the particular case, and the impossibility of resolution by any semantic cataloguing.

But it is argued that this case shares the characteristics of decisions that constitute a category not yet considered, cases concerning the Constitution's guaranty, in Art 4 § 4, of a republican form of government. A conclusion as to whether the case at bar does present a political question cannot be confidently reached until we have considered those cases with special care. . . .

Republican form of government: [In] Luther v Borden * * * . . . [t]he defendants, admitting an otherwise tortious breaking and entering, sought to justify their action on the ground that they were agents of the established lawful government of Rhode Island. . . . The case arose "out of the unfortunate political differences . . ." which had resulted in a situation wherein two groups laid competing claims to recognition as the lawful government. The plaintiff's right to recover depended upon which of the two groups was entitled to such recognition. . . .

Chief Justice Taney's opinion for the Court reasoned as follows: (1) If a court were to hold the defendants' acts unjustified because the charter government had no legal existence during the period in question, it would follow that all of that government's actions—laws enacted, taxes collected, salaries paid, accounts settled, sentences passed—were of no effect. . . .

(2) No state court had recognized as a judicial responsibility settlement of the issue of the locus of state governmental authority. . . .

(3) Since "[t]he question relates, altogether, to the constitution and laws of [the] . . . State," the courts of the United States had to follow the state courts' decisions unless there was a federal constitutional ground for overturning them.

(4) No provision of the Constitution could be or had been invoked for this purpose except Art 4 § 4, the Guaranty Clause. Having already noted the absence of standards whereby the choice between governments could be made by a court acting independently, Chief Justice Taney now found further textual and practical reasons for concluding that, if any department of the United States was empowered by the Guaranty Clause to resolve the issue, it was not the judiciary:

> "Under this article of the Constitution it rests with Congress to decide what government is the established one in a State. . . . [Its] decision is binding on every other department of the government, and could not be questioned in a judicial tribunal. It is true that . . . Congress was not called upon to decide the controversy. Yet the right to decide is placed there, and not in the courts.

"So, too, . . . the clause . . . [vested] with Congress [the power] to determine upon the means proper to be adopted to fulfill this guarantee. . . . [B]y the act of February 28, 1795, [Congress] provided, that, 'in case of an insurrection in any State against the government thereof, it shall be lawful for the President of the United States, on application of the legislature of such State or of the executive (when the legislature cannot be convened), to call forth such . . . militia . . . as he may judge sufficient to suppress such insurrection.'

"By this act, the power of deciding whether the exigency had arisen upon which the government of the United States is bound to interfere, is given to the President.
. . .

• • •

"It is true that in this case the militia were not called out by the President. But upon the application of the governor under the charter government, the President recognized him as the executive power of the State, and took measures to call out the militia to support his authority if it should be found necessary." . . .

Clearly, several factors were thought by the Court in Luther to make the question there "political": the commitment to the other branches of the decision as to which is the lawful state government; the unambiguous action by the President, in recognizing the charter government as the lawful authority; the need for finality in the executive's decision; and the lack of criteria by which a court could determine which form of government was republican.

But the only significance that Luther could have for our immediate purposes is in its holding that the Guaranty Clause is not a repository of judicially manageable standards which a court could utilize independently in order to identify a State's lawful government. The Court has since refused to resort to the Guaranty Clause—which alone had been invoked for the purpose—as the source of a constitutional standard for invalidating state action. * * *

Just as the Court has consistently held that a challenge to state action based on the Guaranty Clause presents no justiciable question so has it held, and for the same reasons, that challenges to congressional action on the ground of inconsistency with that clause present no justiciable question. . . .

• • •

We come, finally, to the ultimate inquiry whether our precedents as to what constitutes a nonjusticiable "political question" bring the case before us under the umbrella of that doctrine. A natural beginning is to note whether any of the common characteristics which we have been able to identify and label descriptively are present. We find none: The question here is the consistency of state action with the Federal Constitution. We have no question decided, or to be decided, by a political branch of government coequal with this Court. Nor do we risk embarrassment of our government abroad, or grave disturbance at home if we take issue with Tennessee as to the constitutionality of her action here challenged. Nor need [Baker], in order to succeed in this action, ask the Court to enter upon policy determinations for which judicially manageable standards are lacking. Judicial standards under the Equal Protection Clause are well developed and familiar, and it has been open to courts since the enactment of the Fourteenth Amendment to determine, if on the particular facts they must, that a discrimination reflects *no* policy, but simply arbitrary and capricious action.

This case does, in one sense, involve the allocation of political power within a State, and [Baker] might conceivably have added a claim under the Guaranty Clause. Of course, as we have seen, any reliance on that clause would be futile. But because any reliance on the Guaranty Clause could not have succeeded it does not follow that [Baker] may not be heard on the equal protection claim which in fact [he tenders]. True, it must be clear that the Fourteenth Amendment claim is not so enmeshed with those political question elements which render Guaranty Clause claims nonjusticiable as actually to present a political question itself. But we have found that not to be the case here.

• • •

We conclude then that the nonjusticiability of claims resting on the Guaranty Clause which arises from their embodiment of questions that were thought "political," can have no bearing upon the justiciability of the equal protection claim presented in this case. Finally, we emphasize that it is the involvement in Guaranty Clause claims of the elements thought to define "political questions," and no other feature, which could render them nonjusticiable. Specifically, we have said that such claims are not held nonjusticiable because they touch matters of state governmental organization. . . .

. . . [I]n Gomillion v Lightfoot * * * we applied the Fifteenth Amendment to strike down a redrafting of municipal boundaries which effected a discriminatory impairment of voting rights, in face of what a majority of the Court of Appeals thought to be a sweeping commitment to state legislatures of the power to draw and redraw such boundaries.

• • •

. . . [To the argument] that Colegrove v Green, * * * was a barrier to hearing the merits of the case, the Court responded that Gomillion was lifted "out of the so-called 'political' arena and into the conventional sphere of constitutional litigation" because here was discriminatory treatment of a racial minority violating the Fifteenth Amendment.

• • •

We conclude that the complaint's allegations of a denial of equal protection present a justiciable constitutional cause of action upon which [Baker is] entitled to a trial and a decision. The right asserted is within the reach of judicial protection under the Fourteenth Amendment.

The judgment of the District Court is reversed and the cause is remanded for further proceedings consistent with this opinion.

Reversed and remanded.

MR. JUSTICE WHITTAKER did not participate in the decision of this case.

MR. JUSTICE DOUGLAS, concurring.

. . .

There are, of course, some questions beyond judicial competence. Where the performance of a "duty" is left to the discretion and good judgment of an executive officer, the judiciary will not compel the exercise of his discretion one way or the other * * * for to do so would be to take over the office. * * *

Where the Constitution assigns a particular function wholly and indivisibly to another department, the federal judiciary does not intervene. * * * None of those [issues] is relevant here.

. . .

. . . Today's [decision] . . . removes the only impediment to judicial cognizance of the claims stated in the present complaint.

The justiciability of the present claims being established, any relief accorded can be fashioned in the light of well-known principles of equity.

MR. JUSTICE CLARK, concurring.

One emerging from the rash of opinions with their accompanying clashing of views may well find himself suffering a mental blindness. The Court holds that [Baker has] alleged a cause of action. However, it refuses to award relief here—although the facts are undisputed—and fails to give the District Court any guidance whatever. One dissenting opinion, bursting with words that go through so much and conclude with so little, contemns the majority action as "a massive repudiation of the experience of our whole past." Another describes the complaint as merely asserting conclusory allegations that Tennessee's apportionment is "incorrect," "arbitrary," "obsolete," and "unconstitutional." I believe it can be shown that this case is distinguishable from earlier cases dealing with the distribution of political power by a State, that a patent violation of the Equal Protection Clause of the United States Constitution has been shown, and that an appropriate remedy may be formulated.

. . .

. . . The widely heralded case of Colegrove v Green * * * was one not only in which the Court was bobtailed [composed of less than all nine Justices] but in which there was no majority opinion. Indeed, even the "political question" point in Mr. Justice Frankfurter's opinion was no more than an alternative ground.

Moreover, [Colegrove] did not present an equal protection argument. While it has served as a Mother Hubbard to most of the subsequent cases, I feel it was in that respect ill-cast and for all of these reasons put it to one side. Likewise, I do not consider the Guaranty Clause cases based on Art 4 § 4, of the Constitution, because it is not invoked here and it involves different criteria, as the Court's opinion indicates. . . .

•   •   •

Although I find the Tennessee apportionment statute offends the Equal Protection Clause, I would not consider intervention by this Court into so delicate a field if there were any other relief available to the people of Tennessee. But the majority of the people of Tennessee have no "practical opportunities for exerting their political weight at the polls" to correct the existing "invidious discrimination." Tennessee has no initiative and referendum. I have searched diligently for other "practical opportunities" present under the law. I find none other than through the federal courts. The majority of the voters have been caught up in a legislative strait jacket. Tennessee has an "informed, civically militant electorate" and "an aroused popular conscience," but it does not sear "the conscience of the people's representatives." This is because the legislative policy has riveted the present seats in the Assembly to their respective constituencies, and by the votes of their incumbents a reapportionment of any kind is prevented. The people have been rebuffed at the hands of the Assembly; they have tried the constitutional convention route, but since the call must originate in the Assembly it, too, has been fruitless. They have tried Tennessee courts with the same result, and Governors have fought the tide only to flounder. It is said that there is recourse in Congress and perhaps that may be, but from a practical standpoint this is without substance. To date Congress has never undertaken such a task in any State. We therefore must conclude that the people of Tennessee are stymied and without judicial intervention will be saddled with the present discrimination in the affairs of their state government.

•   •   •

In view of the detailed study that the Court has given this problem, it is unfortunate that a decision is not reached on the merits. The majority appears to hold, at least sub silentio, that an invidious discrimination is present, but it remands to the three-judge court for it to make what is certain to be that formal determination. It is true that Tennessee has not filed a formal answer. However, it has filed voluminous papers and made extended arguments supporting its position. At no time has it been able to contradict [Baker's] factual claims; it has offered no rational explanation for the present apportionment; indeed, it has indicated that there are none known to it. As I have emphasized, the case proceeded to the point before the three-judge court that it was able to find an invidious discrimination factually present, and the State has not contested that holding here. In view of all this background I doubt if anything more can be offered or will be gained by the State on remand, other than time. Nevertheless, not being able to muster a court to dispose of the case on the merits, I concur in the opinion of the majority and acquiesce in the decision to remand. . . .

• • •

Mr. Justice Stewart, concurring.

The separate writings of my dissenting and concurring Brothers stray so far from the subject of today's decision as to convey, I think, a distressingly inaccurate impression of what the Court decides. For that reason, I think it appropriate, in joining the opinion of the Court, to emphasize in a few words what the opinion does and does not say.

• • •

The complaint in this case asserts that Tennessee's system of apportionment is utterly arbitrary—without any possible justification in rationality. The District Court did not reach the merits of that claim, and this Court quite properly expresses no view on the subject. Contrary to the suggestion of my Brother Harlan, the Court does not say or imply that "state legislatures must be so structured as to reflect with approximate equality the voice of every voter." * * * The Court does not say or imply that there is anything in the Federal Constitution "to prevent a State, acting not irrationally, from choosing any electoral legislative structure it thinks best suited to the interests, temper, and customs of its people." * * * And contrary to the suggestion of my Brother Douglas, the Court most assuredly does not decide the question, "may a State weight the vote of one county or one district more heavily than it weights the vote in another?" * * *

• • •

. . . [T]he Court today decides only: (1) that the District Court possessed jurisdiction of the subject matter; (2) that the complaint presents a justiciable controversy; (3) that [Baker has] standing. My Brother Clark has made a convincing prima facie showing that Tennessee's system of apportionment is in fact utterly arbitrary—without any possible justification in rationality. My Brother Harlan has, with imagination and ingenuity, hypothesized possibly rational bases for Tennessee's system. But the merits of this case are not before us now. The defendants have not yet had an opportunity to be heard in defense of the State's system of apportionment; indeed, they have not yet even filed an answer to the complaint. As in other cases, the proper place for the trial is in the trial court, not here.

Mr. Justice Frankfurter, whom Mr. Justice Harlan joins, dissenting.

The Court today reverses a uniform course of decision established by a dozen cases. . . . The impressive body of rulings thus cast aside reflected the equally

uniform course of our political history regarding the relationship between population and legislative representation—a wholly different matter from denial of
the franchise to individuals because of race, color, religion or sex. Such a massive
repudiation of the experience of our whole past in asserting destructively novel
judicial power demands a detailed analysis of the role of this Court in our constitutional scheme. Disregard of inherent limits in the effective exercise of the
Court's "judicial Power" not only presages the futility of judicial intervention in
the essentially political conflict of forces by which the relation between population and representation has time out of mind been and now is determined. It
may well impair the Court's position as the ultimate organ of "the supreme Law
of the Land" in that vast range of legal problems, often strongly entangled in
popular feeling, on which this Court must pronounce. The Court's authority—
possessed of neither the purse nor the sword—ultimately rests on sustained public
confidence in its moral sanction. Such feeling must be nourished by the Court's
complete detachment, in fact and in appearance, from political entanglements
and by abstention from injecting itself into the clash of political forces in political
settlements.

· · ·

[In *Colegrove* v. *Green,* now overturned] [t]wo opinions were written by the four
Justices who composed the majority of the seven sitting members of the Court.
Both opinions joining in the result in Colegrove v Green agreed that considerations were controlling which dictated denial or jurisdiction though not in the
strict sense of want of power. While the two opinions show a divergence of view
regarding some of these considerations, there are important points of concurrence. Both opinions demonstrate a predominant concern, first, with avoiding
federal judicial involvement in matters traditionally left to legislative policy
making; second, with respect to the difficulty—in view of the nature of the
problems of apportionment and its history in this country—of drawing on or
devising judicial standards for judgment, as opposed to legislative determinations, of the part which mere numerical equality among voters should play as a
criterion for the allocation of political power; and, third, with problems of finding
appropriate modes of relief—particularly, the problem of resolving the essentially political issue of the relative merits of at-large elections and elections held
in districts of unequal population.

The broad applicability of these considerations—summarized in the loose
shorthand phrase, "political question"—in cases involving a State's apportionment of voting power among its numerous localities has led the Court, since
1946, to recognize their controlling effect in a variety of situations. . . .

· · ·

The Colegrove doctrine, in the form in which repeated decisions have settled
it, was not an innovation. It represents long judicial thought and experience.
From its earliest opinions this Court has consistently recognized a class of contro-

versies which do not lend themselves to judicial standards and judicial remedies. To classify the various instances as "political questions" is rather a form of stating this conclusion than revealing of analysis. . . .

[Frankfurter discusses at length those cases involving "political questions" and concludes:]

The present case involves all of the elements that have made the Guarantee Clause cases non-justiciable. It is, in effect, a Guarantee Clause claim masquerading under a different label. But it cannot make the case more fit for judicial action that [Baker invokes] the Fourteenth Amendment rather than Art. 4 § 4, where, in fact, the gist of their complaint is the same—unless it can be found that the Fourteenth Amendment speaks with greater particularity to their situation. We have been admonished to avoid "the tyranny of labels." . . .

• • •

What, then, is this question of legislative apportionment? Appellants [Baker et al.] invoke the right to vote and to have their votes counted. But they are permitted to vote and their votes are counted. They go to the polls, they cast their ballots, they send their representatives to the state councils. Their complaint is simply that the representatives are not sufficiently numerous or powerful—in short, that Tennessee has adopted a basis of representation with which they are dissatisfied. Talk of "debasement" or "dilution" is circular talk. One cannot speak of "debasement" or "dilution" of the value of a vote until there is first defined a standard of reference as to what a vote should be worth. What is actually asked of the Court in this case is to choose among competing bases of representation—ultimately, really, among competing theories of political philosophy—in order to establish an appropriate frame of government for the State of Tennessee and thereby for all the States of the Union.

In such a matter, abstract analogies which ignore the facts of history deal in unrealities; they betray reason. This is not a case in which a State has, through a device however oblique and sophisticated, denied Negroes or Jews or red-headed persons a vote, or given them only a third or a sixth of a vote. * * * What Tennessee illustrates is an old and still widespread method of representation—representation by local geographical division, only in part respective of population—in preference to others, others, forsooth, more appealing. Appellants contest this choice and seek to make this Court the arbiter of the disagreement. They would make the Equal Protection Clause the charter of adjudication, asserting that the equality which it guarantees comports, if not the assurance of equal weight to every voter's vote, at least the basic conception that representation ought to be proportionate to population, a standard by reference to which the reasonableness of apportionment plans may be judged.

To find such a political conception legally enforceable in the broad and unspecific guarantee of equal protection is to rewrite the Constitution. * * * Certainly, "equal protection" is no more secure a foundation for judicial judgment of the permissibility of varying forms of representative government than is "Republican Form." . . .

The notion that representation proportioned to the geographic spread of population is so universally accepted as a necessary element of equality between man and man that it must be taken to be the standard of a political equality preserved by the Fourteenth Amendment—that it is, in appellants' words "the basic principle of representative government"—is, to put it bluntly, not true. However desirable and however desired by some among the great political thinkers and framers of our government, it has never been generally practiced, today or in the past. It was not the English system, it was not the colonial system, it was not the system chosen for the national government by the Constitution, it was not the system exclusively or even predominantly practiced by the States at the time of adoption of the Fourteenth Amendment, it is not predominantly practiced by the States today. Unless judges, the judges of this Court, are to make their private views of political wisdom the measure of the Constitution—views which in all honesty cannot but give the appearance, if not reflect the reality, of involvement with the business of partisan politics so inescapably a part of apportionment controversies—the Fourteenth Amendment, "itself a historical product," * * * provides no guide for judicial oversight of the representation problem.

•   •   •

Manifestly, the Equal Protection Clause supplies no clearer guide for judicial examination of apportionment methods than would the Guarantee Clause itself. Apportionment, by its character, is a subject of extraordinary complexity, involving—even after the fundamental theoretical issues concerning what is to be represented in a representative legislature have been fought out or compromised—considerations of geography, demography, electoral convenience, economic and social cohesions or divergencies among particular local groups, communications, the practical effects of political institutions like the lobby and the city machine, ancient traditions and ties of settled usage, respect for proven incumbents of long experience and senior status, mathematical mechanics, censuses compiling relevant data, and a host of others. Legislative responses throughout the country to the reapportionment demands of the 1960 Census have glaringly confirmed that these are not factors that lend themselves to evaluations of a nature that are the staple of judicial determinations or for which judges are equipped to adjudicate by legal training or experience or native wit. And this is the more so true because in every strand of this complicated, intricate web of values meet the contending forces of partisan politics. The practical significance of apportionment is that the next election results may differ because of it. Apportionment battles are overwhelmingly party or intra-party contests. It will add a virulent source of friction and tension in federal-state relations to embroil the federal judiciary in them.

Dissenting opinion of MR. JUSTICE HARLAN, whom MR. JUSTICE FRANKFURTER joins.

• • •

Once one cuts through the thicket of discussion . . . there emerges a straightforward issue which, in my view, is determinative of this case. Does the complaint disclose a violation of a federal constitutional right? . . . The majority opinion does not actually discuss this basic question. . . . However, in my opinion, [Baker's] allegations, accepting all of them as true, do not, parsed down or as a whole, show an infringement by Tennessee of any rights assured by the Fourteenth Amendment. Accordingly, I believe the complaint should have been dismissed for "failure to state a claim upon which relief can be granted." * * *

It is at once essential to recognize this case for what it is. . . .

[Baker's] claim . . . ultimately rests entirely on the Equal Protection Clause of the Fourteenth Amendment. . . .

• • •

I can find nothing in the Equal Protection Clause or elsewhere in the Federal Constitution which expressly or impliedly supports the view that state legislatures must be so structured as to reflect with approximate equality the voice of every voter. Not only is that proposition refuted by history, as shown by my Brother Frankfurter, but it strikes deep into the heart of our federal system. Its acceptance would require us to turn our backs on the regard which this Court has always shown for the judgment of state legislatures and courts on matters of basically local concern.

In the last analysis, what lies at the core of this controversy is a difference of opinion as to the function of representative government. It is surely beyond argument that those who have the responsibility for devising a system of representation may permissibly consider that factors other than bare numbers should be taken into account. The existence of the United States Senate is proof enough of that. To consider that we may ignore the Tennessee Legislature's judgment in this instance because that body was the product of an asymmetrical electoral apportionment would in effect be to assume the very conclusion here disputed. Hence we must accept the present form of the Tennessee Legislature as the embodiment of the State's choice, or, more realistically, its compromise, between competing political philosophies. The federal courts have not been empowered by the Equal Protection Clause to judge whether this resolution of the State's internal political conflict is desirable or undesirable, wise or unwise.

• • •

In short, there is nothing in the Federal Constitution to prevent a State, acting not irrationally, from choosing any electoral legislative structure it thinks best suited to the interests, temper, and customs of its people. . . . A State's choice to distribute electoral strength among geographical units, rather than according to a census of population, is certainly no less a rational decision of policy than would be its choice to levy a tax on property rather than a tax on income. Both are legislative judgments entitled to equal respect from this Court.

. . .

In conclusion, it is appropriate to say that one need not agree, as a citizen, with what Tennessee has done or failed to do, in order to deprecate, as a judge, what the majority is doing today. Those observers of the Court who see it primarily as the last refuge for the correction of all inequality or injustice, no matter what its nature or source, will no doubt applaud this decision and its break with the past. Those who consider that continuing national respect for the Court's authority depends in large measure upon its wise exercise of self-restraint and discipline in constitutional adjudication, will view the decision with deep concern.

I would affirm.

Ashwander v. Tennessee Valley Authority
297 U.S. 288 (1936)

[Stockholders in the Alabama Power Company brought suit to block the sale of electric power by the Tennessee Valley Authority (TVA) to the Alabama Power Company. As part of their effort the stockholders challenged the constitutionality of the federal government's building the dam generating the electric power and the constitutionality of contracting to dispose of that power. The Court sustained both powers. The excerpt reproduced below, referred to as the Ashwander Rules, is part of Justice Brandeis' concurring opinion pointing out the centrality of judicial restraint in these matters.]

. . .

Mr. Justice Brandeis, concurring.

The Court has frequently called attention to the "great gravity and delicacy" of its function in passing upon the validity of an act of Congress; and has restricted exercise of this function by rigid insistence that the jurisdiction of federal courts is limited to actual cases and controversies; and that they have no power to give advisory opinions. . . .

The Court developed, for its own governance in the cases confessedly within its jurisdiction, a series of rules under which it has avoided passing upon a large part of all the constitutional questions pressed upon it for decision. They are:

1. The Court will not pass upon the constitutionality of legislation in a friendly, non-adversary proceeding, declining because to decide such questions "is legitimate only in the last resort, and as a necessity in the determination of real, earnest and vital controversy between individuals. It never was the thought that, by means of a friendly suit, a party beaten in the legislature could transfer to the courts an inquiry as to the constitutionality of the legislative act." * * *

2. The Court will not "anticipate a question of constitutional law in advance of the necessity of deciding it." * * * "It is not the habit of the court to decide questions of a constitutional nature unless absolutely necessary to a decision of the case." * * *

3. The Court will not "formulate a rule of constitutional law broader than is required by the precise facts to which it is to be applied." * * *

4. The Court will not pass upon a constitutional question although properly presented by the record, if there is also present some other ground upon which the case may be disposed of. This rule has found most varied application. Thus, if a case can be decided on either of two grounds, one involving a constitutional question, the other a question of statutory construction or general law, the Court will decide only the latter. * * * Appeals from the highest court of a state challenging its decision of a question under the Federal Constitution are frequently dismissed because the judgment can be sustained on an independent state ground. * * *

5. The Court will not pass upon the validity of a statute upon complaint of one who fails to show that he is injured by its operation. * * * Among the many applications of this rule, none is more striking than the denial of the right of challenge to one who lacks a personal or property right. Thus, the challenge by a public official interested only in the performance of his official duty will not be entertained. * * *

6. The Court will not pass upon the constitutionality of a statute at the instance of one who has availed himself of its benefits. * * *

7. "When the validity of an act of the Congress is drawn in question, and even if a serious doubt of constitutionality is raised, it is a cardinal principle that this Court will first ascertain whether a construction of the statute is fairly possible by which the question may be avoided." * * *

• • •

PART II

SOURCES AND LIMITS OF CONGRESSIONAL POWER

CHAPTER **4**

Power to Investigate

INTRODUCTORY ESSAY

In straightforward language Article I of the Constitution confers "lawmaking power" upon a Congress to be composed of a House of Representatives and a Senate. The character of the lawmaking power granted to this Congress is elaborated upon in Section 8 of that Article. At first glance it appears that this list is a rather limiting catalogue of areas in which the Congress might rule. Congress can lay and collect taxes, borrow money, regulate commerce, regulate immigration and naturalization, regulate bankruptcy, coin money, fix standards of weights and measures, establish post offices, regulate patents and copyrights, establish lesser judicial tribunals, declare and wage war, raise and support an army and a navy, regulate the militia and its usage, and perform other, more minor functions. At the outset this listing was considered more than mere window dressing: It was viewed as seriously circumscribing the federal legislative power of the central government. Indeed, at the time of ratification, advocates of the Constitution touted these topical limitations as viable controls on federal power, in the hopes of assuaging the fears of states' righters that the document under consideration would ultimately lead to a centralized, all-powerful government. In practice, however, these specifically delineated powers have proven to be more appearance than viable, substantive limitation—particularly since the Depression. This has been true, in part, because of purely pragmatic considerations that emerged in the face of national change and growth, and has been facilitated by a "catchall" phrase in the Constitution itself, which with liberal interpretation legitimates the exercise of powers well beyond those specifically enumerated. The catchall phrase in question authorizes Congress to pass all laws "necessary and proper" to carry into effect the powers listed in the first seventeen clauses of Section 8. Marshall's view in *M'Culloch* v. *Maryland*, 4 Wheat. 316 (1819), that this clause granted Congress implied powers not specifically outlined, set the groundwork for an expansion of federal legislative power hardly anticipated (or, one would imagine, desired) by the Founding Fathers.

In addition to these substantive powers, Article I delineates the composition of each house, elaborates how members will be chosen to serve, grants fairly broad powers for internal procedural rule-making for each chamber, and allows properly selected members certain "privileges." Thus, members must meet certain minimal requirements of age, residency, and citizenship, must stand for reelection after specified periods of time, must be chosen in a fashion prescribed by statutes, are protected from arrest while in Congress, and are immune from lawsuit for any speech, debate, or legislatively related activity for which they might normally be liable in a court of law. In sum, Article I is fairly elaborate in specifying who shall be members of Congress, how they shall secure office, what they can do once there, what privileges they possess, and how far the collective power of members of Congress extends. Before addressing how the Court has shaped the greater part of these specified matters, we need to focus on an important power exercised by Congress that is not even mentioned in the Constitution—the power to investigate.

Legitimacy of the Power to Investigate

While a legislative investigative power is nowhere explicitly authorized, few have seriously doubted the constitutional legitimacy of its exercise. Indeed, in the first judicial challenge to the power of Congress to investigate, the Supreme Court readily supported that power (*Kilbourn* v. *Thompson,* 103 U.S. 168 [1881]). The case involved a House committee investigation into the financial demise of the Jay Cooke banking firm, a firm with which the United States had deposited federal funds. In the course of the investigation, Hallet Kilbourn was called to testify and bring documents relevant to his "real estate pool" and its dealings with the Jay Cooke Company. Kilbourn, who refused to either testify or provide the records, was cited for contempt of Congress and served forty-five days in jail. Upon his release he brought suit against Thompson, the House sergeant at arms, for false imprisonment. While the Court supported the basic power of Congress to investigate, it clearly stated that this power was not an unlimited one. In *Kilbourn,* Justice Miller informed Congress that it could not justifiably violate the separation of powers by using the investigative power to achieve ends that could only be validly accomplished by the executive or judicial branch. He asserted as well that Congress could only investigate in those areas in which it could validly legislate, and that in setting up an investigation, Congress must stipulate the subject matter and an intent to legislate. In the instant case, the Court vindicated Kilbourn by finding that the investigation had invaded the judicial domain and hence Kilbourn had been falsely imprisoned.

Thus, the *Kilbourn* ruling set the basic policy of the Court with regard to the legislative investigative power: Such a power exists as a necessary and legitimate auxiliary to legislative power and exists despite the absence of express authorization in the Constitution; but although the power of inquiry is broad, it is not unlimited. Congress must use investigations only "in aid of the legislative function" and with respect to matters within its jurisdiction. While these limitations exist, most of the litigation and Court policy in this area have not sought to define what falls within the legislative function and hence grants legitimacy to an investigation; rather, most cases and rulings have dealt with how Congress has exercised the investigative power and particularly how it has exercised that power to inquire into the activities of private citizens.

In Aid of the Legislative Function

In this regard the early and important case of *McGrain* v. *Daugherty,* 273 U.S. 135 (1927) merits our attention. *McGrain* involved Senate efforts to secure testimony from Mally Daugherty, a private citizen, regarding his participation in the Teapot Dome scandal. The central focus of the investigation concerned Mally's brother, Harry, who as Attorney General had allegedly failed to prosecute and secure convictions in the scandal. Mally refused to appear and the Senate issued a warrant to bring him into custody. Mally was taken into custody, but by securing a writ of habeas corpus from a federal district court, he eventually managed to have the court free him on the grounds that Congress had exceeded its constitutional powers in detaining him. In handling the issue, the Supreme Court began by noting that the investigation at hand concerned the Department of Justice (and not solely Harry Daugherty) and that laws and appropriations could, and likely would, be made to correct whatever wrongdoing was found (the finding of wrongdoing per se being incidental to the legislative goal). To the extent that the investigation proved in "aid of the legislative function," the Court would allow Congress to compel testimony from a private citizen. The Court said: "We are of the opinion that the power of inquiry—*with the process to enforce it*—is an essential and appropriate auxiliary to the legislative function." (Emphasis added.) Limiting this power to secure information to mere requests or voluntary compliance would not be enough because testimony might be neither forthcoming nor wholly accurate. Thus, the Court supported the warrant and contempt process as suitable means to secure testimony.

Limitations on the Power to Investigate

Bill of Rights

One might be led to believe that as long as the topic is vaguely within congressional jurisdiction and the inquiry in some fashion aids the legislative function, Congress can call a private citizen before it and insist that he or she answer any question asked in the investigative hearing. A witness who refuses must suffer the consequences of a contempt citation: jail and/or fine. Given that very little falls outside the "jurisdiction" of Congress and that one would be hard-pressed to find an illegitimate inquiry, it would seem that Congress has license to require just about any set of answers to a welter of questions asked of both willing and unwilling witnesses. Several considerations, though, prove to limit the extent to which investigative committee personnel can compel testimony. The Bill of Rights, for instance, holds sway over Congress with respect to laws made and with respect to the procedures used in making those laws. Thus, a witness before a Congressional committee can decline to answer certain questions by invoking the Fifth Amendment right against self-incrimination. Congress is not authorized, as a general rule, to pass laws that require persons to directly incriminate themselves nor can it require public testimony in a committee hearing that would lead to the same result. In this regard Congress has been assiduous in disallowing required testimony when a witness properly pleads the Fifth. Witnesses can rely on the Fifth, however, only in instances of potential *self*-incrimination and cannot use the privilege to protect others or to withhold nonincriminating testimony.

In addition to using the Fifth Amendment, and in part because of its limited applicability, a witness can attempt to avoid answering particular questions by claiming an infringement of his or her First Amendment liberties. To be meaningful, freedom of speech and freedom of association must allow citizens to express ideas, even unpopular ideas, and to join groups, even unpopular groups, without fear of ultimate sanction for doing so. To the extent that testifying before a legislative committee forces one to publicly reveal beliefs and associations whose disclosure could lead to being blacklisted, being socially ostracized, or losing one's job, compelling such testimony infringes one's First Amendment liberties. Moreover, in creating such circumstances for particular individuals, a legislative investigation may create what is called a "chilling effect" on the exercise of these First Amendment rights by others. As Justice Black has noted, people ought to be able to "join organizations, advocate causes, and make political 'mistakes' without later being subjected to governmental penalties for having dared to think for themselves" (*Barenblatt* v. *United States,* 360 U.S. 109 [1959]).

While a proper claim to the Fifth Amendment proves to be virtually unassailable, a witness who refuses to testify on the basis of a First Amendment claim runs considerable risk because the Court argues that "the protections of the First Amendment . . . do not afford a witness the right to resist inquiry in all circumstances. When First Amendment rights are asserted to bar governmental interrogation, resolution of the issue always involves a balancing by the Courts of the competing private and public interests at stake in the particular circumstances shown" (*Barenblatt* v. *United States*). In *Barenblatt,* the Court explicitly weighed the interests of Barenblatt's First Amendment claims to remain silent against the state's interests in learning more about communism in order to legislate to preserve itself. In this instance the Court concluded that the balance fell in favor of the state.

Pertinency

Two years earlier the Court had given lip service to the First Amendment but in the final analysis had supported on altogether different grounds a person's refusal to answer questions. There, in *Watkins* v. *United States,* 354 U.S. 178 (1957), the Court relied on the requirement that a witness need only respond to questions that are pertinent to the matter under inquiry. John Watkins was testifying before the House Un-American Activities Committee (HUAC) investigating communism in labor. Watkins had testified quite willingly about himself and about others he knew to be communists but balked when asked about people who allegedly once were but were no longer involved. Watkins steadfastly refused to answer and did so by asserting:

> I am not going to plead the 5th Amendment but I refuse to answer [questions about former members of the communist party] that I believe are outside the scope of your committee's activities. . . . I do not believe that this committee

has the right to undertake the public exposure of persons because of their past activities.

For so refusing, Watkins was cited with contempt under a statute passed in 1857 that shifted the authority to try contempts of Congress from Congress itself to the federal judiciary. That statute requires that contempts be sustained by the courts only when a witness fails to answer questions pertinent to the matter under inquiry. Thus, rather than rely on the First Amendment in *Watkins,* the majority turned to the pertinency requirement and overturned Watkins' contempt conviction by arguing that the questions asked were not pertinent and Watkins therefore had a right not to answer.

What constitutes pertinency is unfortunately not an easy matter for committee members, witnesses, or a reviewing court to decide. For instance, in the 1953 case of *United States* v. *Rumely,* 345 U.S. 41, the Court addressed the issue of whether questions regarding Edward Rumely's efforts to influence public opinion were pertinent to an investigation of congressional lobbying. The Court held that questions such as those were outside the scope of the committee's authorizing resolution and hence were not pertinent. While suggesting the authorizing resolution as a source for ascertaining pertinency, the case did not fully address the degree to which questions must be pertinent and how this could be determined. In *Watkins,* the Chief Justice more precisely indicated that a witness (and a court) might be informed of the subject matter by looking to the authorizing resolution, the remarks of the committee chairperson, the nature of the proceedings, and the remarks committee members made to explain the line of questioning and its pertinency. To the extent that these sources provided guidance and reasonable clarification as to pertinency, the witness could be expected to answer; in the absence of clarity from these sources, compelled testimony would violate due process. In *Watkins* the Court decided that none of these had been met adequately, whereas in *Barenblatt* it ruled that a sufficient number had been met to justify the contempt.

There are scholars, including the authors, who believe that the rather drastic shift in perspective between *Watkins* and *Barenblatt* hinged on more than a superficial meeting of these standards for determining pertinence. (See Pritchett, 1961; Schubert, 1960; and Spaeth, 1966.) The two cases are rather similar and vary only in that Watkins was initially a cooperative witness and Barenblatt refused to testify altogether. More to the point is the fact that in the late 1950s Congress threatened to cut off the Supreme Court's appellate jurisdiction over contempts of this kind and suggested in other ways its displeasure with the direction the Court had taken regarding the regulation of subversive activities. The *Barenblatt* decision took the wind out of the sails of Congress' attack and allowed the Court to save its appellate jurisdiction and its legitimacy in the eyes of Congress.

Procedural Standards

The Court will also relieve a person from the sanction of contempt if certain, more procedural due process standards are not met. For instance, in *Yellin* v. *United States,* 374 U.S. 109 (1963), Edward Yellin's contempt conviction was overturned because the committee failed to observe its own rules about meeting in executive session rather than in public hearing. This alone, of course, does not serve as a legitimate ground for a witness to refuse to testify.

To summarize, a witness can remain silent and ultimately avoid possible sanction for a contempt citation if he or she (1) makes a proper claim to Fifth Amendment protection, (2) validly alleges an infringement of First Amendment rights, and (3) validly claims the questions asked are not pertinent. However, it is apparent that but for a limited and proper Fifth Amendment claim, none of these options is free of a substantial risk that the witness might be wrong and have to suffer for that miscalculation. In brief, the legislative power of inquiry and the collateral power to coerce testimony are limited in theory but very broad in practice. Essentially the courts will limit Congress in only the most offensive of legislative inquiries and the most offensive instances of witness abuse.

Power of Subpoena

Of course, Congress can obtain information from a private citizen in ways other than through testimony. It has the power to issue a subpoena requiring the production of certain documents. As with oral testimony, citizens so ordered have rights that enable them to refuse to produce such documents. If a person receives a subpoena to provide a legislative committee with documents in his or her possession, the individual can refuse to produce them, be cited with contempt, and then assert in court any of the appropriate protections discussed to avoid the contempt sanction. A recent case, however, raised quite a different set of circumstances (*Eastland* v. *United States Servicemen's Fund,* 421 U.S. 491 [1975]). Instead of directing a subpoena to secure records in the possession of a specific group, a Senate subcommittee subpoenaed the bank records of the organization. The USSF had come to the attention of Senator James O. Eastland's Internal Security subcommittee as a result of the antiwar activities its members engaged in near military bases during the Vietnam War. As part of their authorization to investigate infiltration by persons who are or may be under the control of foreign governments, members of the Senate subcommittee maintained that investigating the financing of the USSF would be appropriate, hence the subpoena for bank records. The USSF, though technically a third party, sought an injunction in Federal District Court to stop the implementation of the subpoena. The organization argued that delivery of their bank records would subject their lists of membership and contributors to public scrutiny, tending to "harass, chill, punish and deter" their members' exercise of First Amendment rights, particularly rights of association. The group also argued that the committee intentionally chose to secure their bank records so as to deprive them of their right to protect their private records.

Speech and Debate Clause Protections

Given the fact that the USSF sought a judicial order to halt the actions of Senator Eastland and other members of the Senate subcommittee, the Court was forced to grapple not only with questions of legislative investigative powers but also with the extent to which Speech and Debate Clause protections extend to this kind of legislative activity. The Speech and Debate Clause holds that "for any speech or debate in either House, they [members of Congress] shall not be questioned in any other place." While appearing on the surface to be a rather self-serving protection (particularly for those at the Constitutional Convention intending to run for Congress), the Speech and Debate Clause serves the valuable function of protecting the integrity of the legislative process by assuring a measure of independence to legislators and putting meat in the constitutional tenet of strict adherence to separation of powers. Over the years the clause has been expanded by Court policy beyond mere speeches and debates to protect virtually all actions of members of Congress falling within what the Court calls the "sphere of legislative activity," making them immune from judicial interference. Thus, in this case the Court needed to determine whether or not the Speech and Debate Clause ought to be used to safeguard legislative investigative activity even though that activity allegedly infringed First Amendment freedoms.

To deal with these matters, the Court began by deciding that this particular investigation met all the requirements of a valid congressional inquiry: The investigation related to and furthered a legitimate task of Congress, the subject fell within the "sphere of legitimate legislative activity," and the investigation involved a subject on which legislation could be enacted. The USSF was deemed an appropriate focus of attention because of its activities and because of the scope of the authorizing resolution for the committee. The Court dealt with the USSF's claimed abridgment of First Amendment rights by noting a minimal connection between scrutiny of the documents in question and the purposes of the investigation and by refusing to look to the motives of the legislators. The Court held that since the investigative power and its compulsory process are an "integral part of the deliberative and communicative processes" and since there was a surface connection between the documents and the legislative purpose, the Speech and Debate Clause barred this kind of judicial interference. Justice Marshall, in concurrence, was quick to point out what the majority opinion left rather ambiguous: The Speech and Debate Clause cannot serve as an absolute bar protecting members of Congress who abuse a citizen's Bill of Rights protections; however, in the case at hand the clause proved determinative. It is thus not clear what circumstances must exist to overcome the protections of the Speech and Debate Clause. Like communicative testimony, the coercive power of the legislative investigative committee to compel production of documents is limited in theory but virtually unrestricted in practice.

Political Dependence Shapes Court Policy

The substance of the Court's public policy regarding legislative investigation is mostly symbolic. The Court notes the outer limits of legislative investigative powers but, except for *Kilbourn,* has never found an instance of violation. The Court also notes in grand libertarian language what limits exist on the use of congressional coercive powers but has chosen only in rare instances to spare citizens from the contempt sanction and has done so only when procedural errors make such a move politically painless. In many respects this pattern illustrates the necessarily timid character of Court efforts to constitutionally shape congressional actions, particularly actions that are, for the most part, perceived as exclusively within the domain of Congress' internal affairs. We say "necessarily timid" because, as we noted earlier, the Court must rely on Congress for much of its power and authority to act. To proceed in a manner that ignores the political dependency of the Court on congressional good will would do little but jeopardize broader legitimacy, authority, and effectiveness. Further, the doctrine of separation of powers compels the Justices to do all within their power to show due respect for a coordinate, coequal branch of the federal government. Too strict and active a Court role in policing legislative investigations could easily be construed as showing a lack of respect, ultimately placing the institutional stature of the Court in less than a preferred light. Thus, the Court allows itself the luxury of stating grand and essentially harmless principles stipulating how the legislature ought to conduct investigations and then busily creates elaborate rationales to show how in each case Congress has met the requirements laid down—a process whereby the Court can show its commitment to broad principle and still maintain its power.

McGrain v. Daugherty

273 U.S. 135 (1927)

Mr. Justice Van Devanter delivered the opinion of the Court.

• • •

Harry M. Daugherty became the Attorney General March 5, 1921, and held that office until March 28, 1924, when he resigned. Late in that period various charges of misfeasance and nonfeasance in the Department of Justice after he became its supervising head were brought to the attention of the Senate by individual senators and made the basis of an insistent demand that the department be investigated to the end that the practices and deficiencies which, according to the charges, were operating to prevent or impair its right administration might be definitely ascertained and that appropriate and effective measures might be taken to remedy or eliminate the evil. The Senate regarded the charges as grave and requiring legislative attention and action. Accordingly it . . . adopted a resolution authorizing and directing a select committee of five senators "to investigate circumstances and facts, and report the same to the Senate, concerning the alleged failure of Harry M. Daugherty, Attorney General of the United States, to prosecute properly violators of the Sherman Antitrust Act and the Clayton Act against monopolies and unlawful restraint of trade; the alleged neglect and failure of the . . . Attorney General to arrest and prosecute Albert B. Fall, Harry F. Sinclair, . . . and . . . co-conspirators in defrauding the Government, as well as the alleged neglect and failure of the said Attorney General to arrest and prosecute many others for violations of Federal statutes. . . .

The resolution also authorized the committee to send for books and papers, to subpoena witnesses, to administer oaths, and to sit at such times and places as it might deem advisable.

In the course of the investigation the committee issued and caused to be duly served on Mally S. Daugherty,—who was a brother of Harry M. Daugherty and president of the Midland National Bank of Washington Court House, Ohio,—a subpoena commanding him to appear before the committee for the purpose of giving testimony bearing on the subject under investigation, and to bring with him the "deposit ledgers of the Midland National Bank since November 1, 1920. . . ." The witness failed to appear.

A little later in the course of the investigation the committee isssued and caused to be duly served on the same witness another subpoena. . . . The witness again failed to appear; and no excuse was offered by him for either failure.

The committee then made a report to the Senate stating that the subpoenas had been issued . . . and that he had failed and refused to appear. After a reading of the report, the Senate adopted a resolution reciting these facts and proceedings as follows.

• • •

"Resolved, That the President of the Senate pro tempore issue his warrant commanding the Sergeant at Arms or his deputy to take into custody . . . M. S. Daugherty . . . and to bring [him] . . . before the bar of the Senate, then and there to answer . . . questions pertinent to the matter under inquiry. . . ."

The deputy, proceeding under the warrant, took the witness into custody at Cincinnati, Ohio, with the purpose of bringing him before the bar of the Senate as commanded; whereupon the witness petitioned the federal district court in Cincinnati for a writ of habeas corpus. . . . After a hearing the court held the attachment and detention unlawful and discharged the witness, the decision being put on the ground that the Senate in directing the investigation and in ordering the attachment exceeded its powers under the Constitution. * * *

We have given the case earnest and prolonged consideration because the principal questions involved are of unusual importance and delicacy. They are (a) whether the Senate—or the House of Representatives, both being on the same plane in this regard—has power, through its own process, to compel a private individual to appear before it or one of its committees and give testimony needed to enable it efficiently to exercise a legislative function belonging to it under the Constitution, and (b) whether it sufficiently appears that the process was being employed in this instance to obtain testimony for that purpose.

* * *

The Constitution provides for a Congress consisting of a senate and House of Representatives and invests it with "all legislative powers" granted to the United States, and with power "to make all laws which shall be necessary and proper" for carrying into execution these powers and "all other powers" vested by the Constitution in the United States or in any department or officer thereof. . . . But there is no provision expressly investing either house with power to make investigations and exact testimony to the end that it may exercise its legislative function advisedly and effectively. So the question arises whether this power is so far incidental to the legislative function as to be implied.

In actual legislative practice power to secure needed information by such means has long been treated as an attribute of the power to legislate. It was so regarded in the British Parliament and in the colonial legislatures before the American Revolution; and a like view has prevailed and been carried into effect in both houses of Congress and in most of the state legislatures.

* * *

Four decisions of this court are cited and more or less relied on, and we now turn to them.

The first decision was in Anderson v. Dunn. * * * The question there was whether, under the Constitution, the House of Representatives has power to attach and punish a person other than a member for contempt of its authority— in fact, an attempt to bribe one of its members. The court regarded the power as essential to the effective exertion of other powers expressly granted, and therefore as implied. . . .

The next decision was in Kilbourn v. Thompson. * * * The question there was whether the House of Representatives had exceeded its power in directing one of its committees to make a particular investigation. The decision was that it had. The principles announced and applied in the case are—that neither house of Congress possesses a "general power of making inquiry into the private affairs of the citizen;" that the power actually possessed is limited to inquiries relating to matters of which the particular house "has jurisdiction," and in respect of which it rightfully may take other action; that if the inquiry relates to "a matter wherein relief or redress could be had only by a judicial proceeding" it is not within the range of this power, but must be left to the courts, conformably to the constitutional separation of governmental powers; and that for the purpose of determining the essential character of the inquiry recourse may be had to the resolution or order under which it is made. . . . [T]he court held that in undertaking the investigation "the House of Representatives not only exceeded the limit of its own authority, but assumed power which could only be properly exercised by another branch of the government, because it was in its nature clearly judicial."

. . .

Next in order is Re Chapman. * * * The inquiry there in question was conducted under a resolution of the Senate and related to charges, published in the press, that senators were yielding to corrupt influences in considering a tariff bill then before the Senate and were speculating in stocks the value of which would be affected by pending amendments to the bill. Chapman appeared before the committee in response to a subpoena, but refused to answer questions pertinent to the inquiry, and was indicted and convicted. . . . [The Court,] after referring to the constitutional provision empowering either house to punish its members for disorderly behavior and by a vote of two-thirds to expel a member, held that the inquiry related to the integrity and fidelity of senators in the discharge of their duties, and therefore to a matter "within the range of the constitutional powers of the Senate," and in respect of which it could compel witnesses to appear and testify. In overruling an objection that the inquiry was without any defined or admissible purpose, in that the preamble and resolution made no reference to any contemplated expulsion, censure, or other action by the Senate, the court held that they adequately disclosed a subject-matter of which the Senate had jurisdiction, that it was not essential that the Senate declare in advance what it meditated doing, and that the assumption would not be indulged that the Senate was making the inquiry without a legitimate object.

The case is relied on here as fully sustaining the power of either house to conduct investigations and exact testimony from witnesses for legislative purposes. . . .

The latest case is Marshall v. Gordon. * * * The question there was whether the House of Representatives exceeded its power in punishing, as for a contempt of its authority, a person—not a member—who had written, published and sent to the chairman of one of its committees an ill-tempered and irritating letter respecting the action and purposes of the committee. Power to make inquiries and obtain evidence by compulsory process was not involved. The court recognized distinctly that the House of Representatives has implied power to punish a person not a member for contempt, * * * but held that its action in this instance was without constitutional justification. The decision was put on the ground that the letter, while offensive and vexatious, was not calculated or likely to affect the House in any of its proceedings or in the exercise of any of its functions—in short, that the act which was punished as a contempt was not of such a character as to bring it within the rule that an express power draws after it others which are necessary and appropriate to give effect to it.

While these cases are not decisive of the question we are considering, they definitely settle two propositions which we recognize as entirely sound and having a bearing on its solution: One, that the two houses of Congress, in their separate relations, possess not only such powers as are expressly granted to them by the Constitution, but such auxiliary powers as are necessary and appropriate to make the express powers effective; and, the other, that neither house is invested with "general" power to inquire into private affairs and compel disclosures, but only with such limited power of inquiry as is shown to exist when the rule of constitutional interpretation just stated is rightly applied. . . .

• • •

We are of opinion that the power of inquiry—with process to enforce it—is an essential and appropriate auxiliary to the legislative function. . . . A legislative body cannot legislate wisely or effectively in the absence of information respecting the conditions which the legislation is intended to affect or change; and where the legislative body does not itself possess the requisite information—which not infrequently is true—recourse must be had to others who do possess it. Experience has taught that mere requests for such information often are unavailing, and also that information which is volunteered is not always accurate or complete; so some means of compulsion are essential to obtain what is needed. All this was true before and when the Constitution was framed and adopted. In that period the power of inquiry—with enforcing process—was regarded and employed as a necessary and appropriate attribute of the power to legislate—indeed, was treated as inhering in it. Thus there is ample warrant for thinking, as we do, that the constitutional provisions which commit the legislative function to the two houses are intended to include this attribute to the end that the function may be effectively exercised.

The contention is earnestly made on behalf of the witness that this power of inquiry, if sustained, may be abusively and oppressively exerted. If this be so, it affords no ground for denying the power. The same contention might be directed against the power to legislate, and of course would be unavailing. We must assume, for present purposes, that neither house will be disposed to exert the power beyond its proper bounds, or without due regard to the rights of witnesses. . . . [A] witness rightfully may refuse to answer where the bounds of the power are exceeded or the questions are not pertinent to the matter under inquiry.

We come now to the question whether it sufficiently appears that the purpose for which the witness's testimony was sought was to obtain information in aid of the legislative function. The court below answered the question in the negative, and put its decision largely on this ground. . . .

• • •

We are of opinion that the court's ruling on this question was wrong, and that it sufficiently appears, when the proceedings are rightly interpreted, that the object of the investigation and of the effort to secure the witness's testimony was to obtain information for legislative purposes.

It is quite true that the resolution directing the investigation does not in terms avow that it is intended to be in aid of legislation; but it does show that the subject to be investigated was the administration of the Department of Justice—whether its functions were being properly discharged or were being neglected or misdirected, and particularly whether the Attorney General and his assistants were performing or neglecting their duties in respect of the institution and prosecution of proceedings to punish crimes and enforce appropriate remedies against the wrongdoers—specific instances of alleged neglect being recited. Plainly the subject was one on which legislation could be had and would be materially aided by the information which the investigation was calculated to elicit. This becomes manifest when it is reflected that the functions of the Department of Justice, the powers and duties of the Attorney General and the duties of his assistants, are all subject to regulation by congressional legislation, and that the department is maintained and its activities are carried on under such appropriations as in the judgment of Congress are needed from year to year.

The only legitimate object the Senate could have in ordering the investigation was to aid it in legislating; and we think the subject-matter was such that the presumption should be indulged that this was the real object. An express avowal of the object would have been better; but in view of the particular subject-matter was not indispensable. . . .

• • •

We conclude that the investigation was ordered for a legitimate object; that the witness wrongfully refused to appear and testify before the committee and was lawfully attached; that the Senate is entitled to have him give testimony pertinent to the inquiry, either at its bar or before the committee; and that the district court erred in discharging him from custody under the attachment.

• • •

Final order reversed.

Mr. Justice Stone did not participate in the consideration or decision of the case.

Watkins v. *United States*

354 U.S. 178 (1957)

MR. CHIEF JUSTICE WARREN delivered the opinion of the Court.

. . . [Watkins] was prosecuted for refusing to make certain disclosures which he asserted to be beyond the authority of the committee to demand. The controversy thus rests upon fundamental principles of the power of the Congress and the limitations upon that power. We approach the questions presented with conscious awareness of the far-reaching ramifications that can follow from a decision of this nature.

On April 29, 1954, [Watkins] appeared as a witness in compliance with a subpoena issued by a Subcommittee of the Committee on Un-American Activities of the House of Representatives. The Subcommittee elicited from [him] a description of his background in labor union activities. . . .

[Watkins'] name had been mentioned by two witnesses who testified before the Committee at prior hearings. . . .

[Watkins] answered . . . freely and without reservation . . . when the questioning turned to the subject of his past conduct, associations and predilections:

"I am not now nor have I ever been a card-carrying member of the Communist Party. . . .

•   •   •

"I would like to make it clear that for a period of time for approximately 1942 to 1947 I cooperated with the Communist Party and participated in Communist activities to such a degree that some persons may honestly believe that I was a member of the party.

"I have made contributions upon occasions to Communist causes. I have signed petitions for Communist causes. . . .

". . . I never carried a Communist Party card. I never accepted discipline and indeed on several occasions I opposed their position."

•   •   •

The Subcommittee . . . was apparently satisfied with [Watkins'] disclosures. After some further discussion elaborating on the statement, counsel for the Committee read [a] list of names to petitioner. [Watkins] stated that he did not know several of the persons. Of those whom he did know, he refused to tell whether he knew them to have been members of the Communist Party. He explained to the Subcommittee why he took such a position:

"I am not going to plead the fifth amendment, but I refuse to answer certain questions that I believe are outside the proper scope of your committee's activities. I will answer any questions which this committee puts to me about myself. I will also answer questions about those persons whom I knew to be members of the Communist Party and whom I believe still are. I will not, however, answer any questions with respect to others with whom I associated in the past. I do not believe that any law in this country requires me to testify about persons who may in the past have been Communist Party members or otherwise engaged in Communist Party activity but who to my best knowledge and belief have long since removed themselves from the Communist movement.

"I do not believe that such questions are relevant to the work of this committee nor do I believe that this committee has the right to undertake the public exposure of persons because of their past activities. I may be wrong, and the committee may have this power, but until and unless a court of law so holds and directs me to answer, I most firmly refuse to discuss the political activities of my past associates."

The Chairman of the Committee submitted a report of petitioner's refusal to answer questions to the House of Representatives. * * * The House directed the Speaker to certify the Committee's report to the United States Attorney for initiation of criminal prosecution. * * * A seven-count indictment was returned. [Watkins] waived his right to jury trial and was found guilty on all counts by the court. The sentence, a fine of $100 and one year in prison, was suspended, and petitioner was placed on probation.

An appeal was taken to the Court of Appeals [and the conviction was reversed.] . . . We granted certiorari because of the very important questions of constitutional law presented. * * *

We start with several basic premises on which there is general agreement. The power of the Congress to conduct investigations is inherent in the legislative process. That power is broad. It encompasses inquiries concerning the administration of existing laws as well as proposed or possibly needed statutes. It includes surveys of defects in our social, economic or political system for the purpose of enabling the Congress to remedy them. It comprehends probes into departments of the Federal Government to expose corruption, inefficiency or waste. But broad as is this power of inquiry, it is not unlimited. There is no general authority to expose the private affairs of individuals without justification in terms of the functions of the Congress. . . . Nor is the Congress a law enforcement or trial agency. These are functions of the executive and judicial departments of government. No inquiry is an end in itself; it must be related to and in furtherance of a legitimate task of the Congress. Investigations conducted solely for the personal aggrandizement of the investigators or to "punish" those investigated are indefensible.

It is unquestionably the duty of all citizens to cooperate with the Congress in its efforts to obtain the facts needed for intelligent legislative action. It is their unremitting obligation to respond to subpoenas, to respect the dignity of the Congress and its committees and to testify fully with respect to matters within the province of proper investigation. This, of course, assumes that the constitutional rights of witnesses will be respected by the Congress as they are in a court of justice. The Bill of Rights is applicable to investigations as to all forms of governmental action. Witnesses cannot be compelled to give evidence against themselves. They cannot be subjected to unreasonable search and seizure. Nor can the First Amendment freedoms of speech, press, religion, or political belief and association be abridged.

· · ·

In the decade following World War II, there appeared a new kind of congressional inquiry unknown in prior periods of American history. Principally this was the result of the various investigations into the threat of subversion of the United States Government, but other subjects of congressional interest also contributed to the changed scene. This new phase of legislative inquiry involved a broad-scale intrusion into the lives and affairs of private citizens. It brought before the courts novel questions of the appropriate limits of congressional inquiry. Prior cases, like Kilbourn, McGrain and Sinclair, had defined the scope of investigative power in terms of the inherent limitations of the sources of that power. In the more recent cases, the emphasis shifted to problems of accommodating the interest of the Government with the rights and privileges of individuals. The central theme was the application of the Bill of Rights as a restraint upon the assertion of governmental power in this form.

It was during this period that the Fifth Amendment privilege against self-incrimination was frequently invoked and recognized as a legal limit upon the authority of a committee to require that a witness answer its questions. Some early doubts as to the applicability of that privilege before a legislative committee never matured. When the matter reached this Court, the Government did not challenge in any way that the Fifth Amendment protection was available to the witness, and such a challenge could not have prevailed. . . .

A far more difficult task evolved from the claim by witnesses that the committees' interrogations were infringements upon the freedoms of the First Amendment. Clearly, an investigation is subject to the command that the Congress shall make no law abridging freedom of speech or press or assembly. While it is true that there is no statute to be reviewed, and that an investigation is not a law, nevertheless an investigation is part of law-making. It is justified solely as an adjunct to the legislative process. The First Amendment may be invoked against infringement of the protected freedoms by law or by law-making.

Abuses of the investigative process may imperceptibly lead to abridgment of protected freedoms. The mere summoning of a witness and compelling him to testify, against his will, about his beliefs, expressions or associations is a measure of governmental interference. And when those forced revelations concern matters that are unorthodox, unpopular, or even hateful to the general public, the reaction in the life of the witness may be disastrous. This effect is even more harsh when it is past beliefs, expressions or associations that are disclosed and judged by current standards rather than those contemporary with the matters exposed. Nor does the witness alone suffer the consequences. Those who are identified by witnesses and thereby placed in the same glare of publicity are equally subject to public stigma, scorn and obloquy. Beyond that, there is the more subtle and immeasurable effect upon those who tend to adhere to the most orthodox and uncontroversial views and associations in order to avoid a similar fate at some future time. That this impact is partly the result of non-governmental activity by private persons cannot relieve the investigators of their responsibility for initiating the reaction.

The Court recognized the restraints of the Bill of Rights upon congressional investigations in United States v Rumely. * * * The magnitude and complexity of the problem of applying the First Amendment to that case led the Court to construe narrowly the resolution describing the committee's authority. It was concluded that, when First Amendment rights are threatened, the delegation of power to the committee must be clearly revealed in its charter.

Accommodation of the congressional need for particular information with the individual and personal interest in privacy is an arduous and delicate task for any court. We do not underestimate the difficulties that would attend such an undertaking. It is manifest that despite the adverse effects which follow upon compelled disclosure of private matters, not all such inquiries are barred. . . . The critical element is the existence of, and the weight to be ascribed to, the interest of the Congress in demanding disclosures from an unwilling witness. We cannot simply assume, however, that every congressional investigation is justified by a public need that overbalances any private rights affected. To do so would be to abdicate the responsibility placed by the Constitution upon the judiciary to insure that the Congress does not unjustifiably encroach upon an individual's right to privacy nor abridge his liberty of speech, press, religion or assembly.

[Watkins] has earnestly suggested that the difficult questions of protecting these rights from infringement by legislative inquiries can be surmounted in this case because there was no public purpose served in his interrogation. His conclusion is based upon the thesis that the Subcommittee was engaged in a program of exposure for the sake of exposure. The sole purpose of the inquiry, he contends, was to bring down upon himself and others the violence of public reaction because of their past beliefs, expressions and associations. . . .

We have no doubt that there is no congressional power to expose for the sake of exposure. The public is, of course, entitled to be informed concerning the workings of its government. That cannot be inflated into a general power to expose where the predominant result can only be an invasion of the private rights of individuals. But a solution to our problem is not to be found in testing the motives of committee members for this purpose. Such is not our function. Their motives alone would not vitiate an investigation which had been instituted by a House of Congress if that assembly's legislative purpose is being served.

. . . The theory of a committee inquiry is that the committee members are serving as the representatives of the parent assembly in collecting information for a legislative purpose. Their function is to act as the eyes and ears of the Congress in obtaining facts upon which the full legislature can act. To carry out this mission, committees and subcommittees, sometimes one Congressman, are endowed with the full power of the Congress to compel testimony. In this case, only two men exercised that authority in demanding information over petitioner's protest.

An essential premise in this situation is that House or Senate shall have instructed the committee members on what they are to do with the power delegated to them. It is the responsibility of the Congress, in the first instance, to insure that compulsory process is used only in furtherance of a legislative purpose. That requires that the instructions to an investigating committee spell out that group's jurisdiction and purpose with sufficient particularity. Those instructions are embodied in the authorizing resolution. That document is the committee's charter. Broadly drafted and loosely worded, however, such resolutions can leave tremendous latitude to the discretion of the investigators. The more vague the committee's charter is, the greater becomes the possibility that the committee's specific actions are not in conformity with the will of the parent House of Congress.

The authorizing resolution of the Un-American Activities Committee was adopted in 1938. . . . Several years later, the Committee was made a standing organ of the House with the same mandate. It defines the Committee's authority as follows:

"The Committee on Un-American Activities, as a whole or by subcommittee, is authorized to make from time to time investigations of (i) the extent, character, and objects of un-American propaganda activities in the United States, (ii) the diffusion within the United States of subversive and un-American propaganda that is instigated from foreign countries or of a domestic origin and attacks the principle of the form of government as guaranteed by our Constitution, and (iii) all other questions in relation thereto that would aid Congress in any necessary remedial legislation."

It would be difficult to imagine a less explicit authorizing resolution. Who can define the meaning of "un-American"? What is that single, solitary "principle of the form of government as guaranteed by our Constitution"? . . .

• • •

Combining the language of the resolution with the construction it has been given, it is evident that the preliminary control of the Committee exercised by the House of Representatives is slight or non-existent. No one could reasonably deduce from the charter the kind of investigation that the Committee was directed to make. As a result, we are asked to engage in a process of retroactive rationalization. Looking backward from the events that transpired, we are asked to uphold the Committee's actions unless it appears that they were clearly not authorized by the charter. As a corollary to this inverse approach, the Government urges that we must view the matter hospitably to the power of the Congress—that if there is any legislative purpose which might have been furthered by the kind of disclosure sought, the witness must be punished for withholding it. No doubt every reasonable indulgence of legality must be accorded to the actions of a coordinate branch of our Government. But such deference cannot yield to an unnecessary and unreasonable dissipation of precious constitutional freedoms.

The Government contends that the public interest at the core of the investigations of the Un-American Activities Committee is the need by the Congress to be informed of efforts to overthrow the Government by force and violence so that adequate legislative safeguards can be erected. From this core, however, the Committee can radiate outward infinitely to any topic thought to be related in some way to armed insurrection. The outer reaches of this domain are known only by the content of "un-American activities." . . . A third dimension is added when the investigators turn their attention to the past to collect minutiae on remote topics, on the hypothesis that the past may reflect upon the present.

The consequences that flow from this situation are manifold. In the first place, a reviewing court is unable to make the kind of judgment made by the Court in United States v Rumely. * * * The Committee is allowed, in essence, to define its own authority, to choose the direction and focus of its activities. In deciding what to do with the power that has been conferred upon them, members of the Committee may act pursuant to motives that seem to them to be the highest. Their decisions, nevertheless, can lead to ruthless exposure of private lives in order to gather data that is neither desired by the Congress nor useful to it. Yet it is impossible in this circumstance, with constitutional freedoms in jeopardy, to declare that the Committee has ranged beyond the area committed to it by its parent assembly because the boundaries are so nebulous.

More important and more fundamental than that, however, it insulates the House that has authorized the investigation from the witnesses who are subjected to the sanctions of compulsory process. There is a wide gulf between the responsibility for the use of investigative power and the actual exercise of that power. This is an especially vital consideration in assuring respect for constitutional liberties. Protected freedoms should not be placed in danger in the absence of a clear determination by the House or the Senate that a particular inquiry is justified by a specific legislative need.

It is, of course, not the function of this Court to prescribe rigid rules for the Congress to follow in drafting resolutions establishing investigating committees. That is a matter peculiarly within the realm of the legislature, and its decisions will be accepted by the courts up to the point where their own duty to enforce the constitutionally protected rights of individuals is affected. An excessively broad charter, like that of the House Un-American Activities Committee, places the courts in an untenable position if they are to strike a balance between the public need for a particular interrogation and the right of citizens to carry on their affairs free from unnecessary governmental interference. . . .

. . .

Since World War II, the Congress has practically abandoned its original practice of utilizing the coercive sanction of contempt proceedings at the bar of the House. The sanction there imposed is imprisonment by the House until the recalcitrant witness agrees to testify or disclose the matters sought, provided that the incarceration does not extend beyond adjournment. The Congress has instead invoked the aid of the federal judicial system in protecting itself against contumacious conduct. It has become customary to refer these matters to the United States Attorneys for prosecution under criminal law.

The appropriate statute . . . provides:

"Every person who having been summoned as a witness by the authority of either House of Congress to give testimony . . . willfully makes default, or who, having appeared, refuses to answer any question pertinent to the question under inquiry, shall be deemed guilty of a misdemeanor, punishable by a fine of not more than $1,000 nor less than $100 and imprisonment in a common jail for not less than one month nor more than twelve months."

In fulfillment of their obligation under this statute, the courts must accord to the defendants every right which is guaranteed to defendants in all other criminal cases. Among these is the right to have available, through a sufficiently precise statute, information revealing the standard of criminality before the commission of the alleged offense. Applied to persons prosecuted under [the statute] * * * this raises a special problem in that the statute defines the crime as refusal to answer "any question pertinent to the question under inquiry." Part of the standard of criminality, therefore, is the pertinency of the questions propounded to the witness.

The problem attains proportion when viewed from the standpoint of the witness who appears before a congressional committee. He must decide at the time the questions are propounded whether or not to answer. . . . An erroneous determination on his part, even if made in the utmost good faith, does not exculpate him if the court should later rule that the questions were pertinent to the question under inquiry.

It is obvious that a person compelled to make this choice is entitled to have knowledge of the subject to which the interrogation is deemed pertinent. That knowledge must be available with the same degree of explicitness and clarity that the Due Process Clause requires in the expression of any element of a criminal offense. The "vice of vagueness" must be avoided here as in all other crimes. There are several sources that can outline the "question under inquiry" in such a way that the rules against vagueness are satisfied. The authorizing resolution, the remarks of the chairman or members of the committee, or even the nature of the proceedings themselves might sometimes make the topic clear.

This case demonstrates, however, that these sources often leave the matter in grave doubt.

• • •

. . . [Watkins] was thus not accorded a fair opportunity to determine whether he was within his rights in refusing to answer, and his conviction is necessarily invalid under the Due Process Clause of the Fifth Amendment.

We are mindful of the complexities of modern government and the ample scope that must be left to the Congress as the sole constitutional depository of legislative power. Equally mindful are we of the indispensable function, in the exercise of that power, of congressional investigations. The conclusions we have reached in this case will not prevent the Congress, through its committees, from obtaining any information it needs for the proper fulfillment of its role in our scheme of government. The legislature is free to determine the kinds of data that should be collected. It is only those investigations that are conducted by use of compulsory process that give rise to a need to protect the rights of individuals against illegal encroachment. That protection can be readily achieved through procedures which prevent the separation of power from responsibility and which provide the constitutional requisites of fairness for witnesses. A measure of added care on the part of the House and the Senate in authorizing the use of compulsory process and by their committees in exercising that power would suffice. That is a small price to pay if it serves to uphold the principles of limited, constitutional government without constricting the power of the Congress to inform itself.

The judgment of the Court of Appeals is reversed, and the case is remanded to the District Court with instructions to dismiss the indictment.

It is so ordered.

MR. JUSTICE BURTON and MR. JUSTICE WHITTAKER took no part in the consideration or decision of this case.

MR. JUSTICE FRANKFURTER, concurring.

I deem it important to state what I understand to be the Court's holding. Agreeing with its holding, I join its opinion.

• • •

. . . [T]he scope of inquiry that a committee is authorized to pursue must be defined with sufficiently unambiguous clarity to safeguard a witness from the hazards of vagueness in the enforcement of the criminal process against which the Due Process Clause protects. The questions must be put with relevance and definiteness sufficient to enable the witness to know whether his refusal to answer may lead to conviction for criminal contempt and to enable both the trial and the appellate courts readily to determine whether the particular circumstances justify a finding of guilt.

. . .

MR. JUSTICE CLARK, dissenting.

As I see it the chief fault in the majority opinion is its mischievous curbing of the informing function of the Congress. While I am not versed in its procedures, my experience in the executive branch of the Government leads me to believe that the requirements laid down in the opinion for the operation of the committee system of inquiry are both unnecessary and unworkable. . . .

It may be that at times the House Committee on Un-American Activities has, as the Court says, "conceived of its task in the grand view of its name." And, perhaps, as the Court indicates, the rules of conduct placed upon the Committee by the House admit of individual abuse and unfairness. But that is none of our affair. So long as the object of a legislative inquiry is legitimate and the questions propounded are pertinent thereto, it is not for the courts to interfere with the committee system of inquiry. To hold otherwise would be an infringement on the power given the Congress to inform itself, and thus a trespass upon the fundamental American principle of separation of powers. The majority has substituted the judiciary as the grand inquisitor and supervisor of congressional investigations. It has never been so.

. . .

I think the Committee here was acting entirely within its scope and that the purpose of its inquiry was set out with "undisputable clarity." In the first place, the authorizing language of the Reorganization Act must be read as a whole, not dissected. It authorized investigation into subversive activity, its extent, character, objects, and diffusion. While the language might have been more explicit than using such words as "un-American," or phrases like "principle of the form of government," still these are fairly well understood terms. We must construe them to give them meaning if we can. Our cases indicate that rather than finding fault with the use of words or phrases, we are bound to presume that the action of the legislative body in granting authority to the Committee was with a legitimate object "if [the action] is *capable* of being so construed." (Emphasis added.) * * * Before we can deny the authority "it must be obvious that" the Committee has "exceeded the bounds of legislative power." * * * The fact that the Committee has often been attacked has caused close scrutiny of its acts by the House as a whole and the House has repeatedly given the Committee its approval. "Power" and "responsibility" have not been separated. But the record in this case does not stop here. It shows that at the hearings involving Watkins, the Chairman made statements explaining the functions of the committee. And, furthermore, Watkins' action at the hearing clearly reveals that he was well acquainted with the purpose of the hearing. It was to investigate Communist infiltration into his union. This certainly falls within the grant of authority from the Reorganization Act and the House has had ample opportunity to limit the investigative scope of the Committee if it feels that the Committee has exceeded its legitimate bounds.

The Court makes much of petitioner's claim of "exposure for exposure's sake" and strikes at the purposes of the Committee through this catch phrase. But we are bound to accept as the purpose of the Committee that stated in the Reorganization Act together with the statements of the Chairman at the hearings involved here. Nothing was said of exposure. The statements of a single Congressman cannot transform the real purpose of the Committee into something not authorized by the parent resolution. * * * The Court indicates that the questions propounded were asked for exposure's sake and had no pertinency to the inquiry. It appears to me that they were entirely pertinent to the announced purpose of the Committee's inquiry. Undoubtedly Congress has the power to inquire into the subjects of communism and the Communist Party. * * * As a corollary of the congressional power to inquire into such subject matter, the Congress, through its committees, can legitimately seek to identify individual members of the Party. * * *

The pertinency of the questions is highlighted by the need for the Congress to know the extent of infiltration of communism in labor unions. This technique of infiltration was that used in bringing the downfall of countries formerly free but now still remaining behind the Iron Curtain. . . . [T]he Party is not an ordinary political party and has not been at least since 1945. Association with its officials is not an ordinary association. Nor does it matter that the questions related to the past. Influences of past associations often linger. . . . The techniques used in the infiltration which admittedly existed here, might well be used again in the future. If the parties about whom Watkins was interrogated were Communists and collaborated with him, as a prior witness indicated, an entirely new area of investigation might have been opened up. Watkins' silence prevented the Committee from learning this information which could have been vital to its future investigation. The Committee was likewise entitled to elicit testimony showing the truth or falsity of the prior testimony of the witnesses who had involved Watkins and the union with collaboration with the Party. If the testimony was untrue a false picture of the relationship between the union and the Party leaders would have resulted. For these reasons there were ample indications of the pertinency of the questions.

. . . [T]he Court honors Watkins' claim of a "right to silence" which brings all inquiries, as we know, to a "dead end." I do not see how any First Amendment rights were endangered here. There is nothing in the First Amendment that provides the guarantees Watkins claims. That Amendment was designed to prevent attempts by law to curtail freedom of speech. * * * It forbids Congress from making any law "abridging the freedom of speech, or of the press." It guarantees

Watkins' right to join any organization and make any speech that does not have an intent to incite to crime. * * * But Watkins was asked whether he knew named individuals and whether they were Communists. He refused to answer on the ground that his rights were being abridged. What he was actually seeking to do was to protect his former associates, not himself, from embarrassment. He had already admitted his own involvement. He sought to vindicate the rights, if any, of his associates. It is settled that one cannot invoke the constitutional rights of another. * * *

• • •

. . . We should afford to Congress the presumption that it takes every precaution possible to avoid unnecessary damage to reputations. Some committees have codes of procedure, and others use the executive hearing technique to this end. The record in this case shows no conduct on the part of the Un-American Activities Committee that justifies condemnation. That there may have been such occasions is not for us to consider here. Nor should we permit its past transgressions, if any, to lead to the rigid restraint of all congressional committees. To carry on its heavy responsibility the compulsion of truth that does not incriminate is not only necessary to the Congress but is permitted within the limits of the Constitution.

Eastland v. United States Servicemen's Fund

421 U.S. 491 (1975)

Mr. Chief Justice Burger delivered the opinion of the Court.

• • •

In early 1970 the Senate Subcommittee on Internal Security was given broad authority by the Senate to "make a complete and continuing study and investigation of . . . the administration, operation and enforcement of the Internal Security Act of 1950. . . ." * * * The authority encompassed discovering the "extent, nature and effect of subversive activities in the United States," and the resolution specifically directed inquiry concerning "infiltration by persons who are or may be under the control of foreign governments. . . ." * * * Pursuant to that mandate the Subcommittee began an inquiry into the activities of . . . the United States Servicemen's Fund, Inc. (USSF).

USSF describes itself as a nonprofit membership corporation supported by contributions. Its stated purpose is "to further the welfare of persons who have served or are presently serving in the military." To accomplish its declared purpose USSF has engaged in various activities directed at United States servicemen. It established "coffeehouses" near domestic military installations, and aided the publication of "underground" newspapers for distribution on American military installations throughout the world. The coffeehouses were meeting places for servicemen, and the newspapers were specialized publications which USSF claims dealt with issues of concern to servicemen. Through these operations USSF attempted to communicate to servicemen its philosophy and attitudes concerning United States involvement in South East Asia. USSF claims the coffeehouses and newspapers "became the focus of dissent and expressions of opposition within the military toward the war in Southeast Asia."

In the course of its investigation of USSF, the Subcommittee concluded that [an adequate] showing had been made of the need for further investigation, and it resolved that appropriate subpoenas, including subpoenas duces tecum [an order that a person bring documents and papers along] could be issued. . . . Eastland, a United States Senator, is, as he was then, Chairman of the Subcommittee. On May 28, 1970, pursuant to the above authority, he signed a subpoena duces tecum, issued on behalf of the Subcommittee, to the bank where USSF has an account. The subpoena commanded the bank to produce on June 4, 1970,

> "any and all records appertaining to or involving the account or accounts of [USSF]. Such records to comprehend papers, correspondence, statements, checks, deposit slips and supporting documentation, or microfilm thereof within [the bank's] control or custody or within [its] means to produce."

. . . USSF and two of its members brought this action to enjoin implementation of the subpoena. . . .

The complaint named as defendants Chairman Eastland, eight other Senators, the Chief Counsel to the Subcommittee, and the bank. The complaint charged that the authorizing resolutions and the Subcommittee's actions implementing them were an unconstitutional abuse of the legislative power of inquiry, that the "sole purpose" of the Subcommittee investigation was to force "public disclosure of beliefs, opinions, expressions and associations of private citizens which may be unorthodox or unpopular," and that the "sole purpose" of the subpoena was to "harass, chill, punish and deter" [USSF and its members] in their exercise of their rights and duties under the First Amendment and particularly to stifle the freedom of the press and association guaranteed by that Amendment. The subpoena was issued to the bank rather than to USSF and its members, the complaint claimed, "in order to deprive [them] of their right to protect their private records, such as the sources of their contributions, as they would be entitled to do if the subpoena had been issued against them directly."

The complaint further claimed that financial support to USSF is obtained exclusively through contributions from private individuals, and if the bank records are disclosed "much of that financial support will be withdrawn, and USSF will be unable to continue its constitutionally protected activities."

For relief USSF and its members, the respondents, sought a permanent injunction restraining the members of the Subcommittee and its Chief Counsel from trying to enforce the subpoena by contempt of Congress or other means and restraining the bank from complying with the subpoena. . . .

* * *

The question to be resolved is whether the actions of [Eastland et al.] fall within the "sphere of legislative activity." If they do, the petitioners "shall not be questioned in any other Place" about those activities since the prohibitions of the Speech or Debate Clause are absolute. * * *

Without exception, our cases have read the Speech or Debate Clause broadly to effectuate its purposes. * * * . . . In our system "the clause serves the additional function of reinforcing the separation of powers so deliberately established by the Founders." * * *

The Clause is a product of the English experience. * * * Due to that heritage our cases make it clear that the "central role" of the Clause is to "prevent intimidation of legislators by the Executive and accountability before a possible hostile judiciary. * * * That role is not the sole function of the Clause, however, and English history does not totally define the reach of the Clause. Rather, it "must be interpreted in light of the American experience, and in the context of the American constitutional scheme of government. . . ." * * * Thus we have long held that when it applies the Clause provides protection against civil as well as criminal actions, and against actions brought by private individuals as well as those initiated by the Executive Branch. * * *

The applicability of the Clause to private civil actions is supported by the absoluteness of the terms "shall not be questioned," and the sweep of the terms "in any other Place." In reading the Clause broadly we have said that legislators acting within the sphere of legitimate legislative activity "should be protected not only from the consequences of litigation's results but also from the burden of defending themselves." * * * Just as a criminal prosecution infringes upon the independence which the Clause is designed to preserve, a private civil action, whether for an injunction or damages, creates a distraction and forces Members to divert their time, energy, and attention from their legislative tasks to defend the litigation. Private civil actions also may be used to delay and disrupt the legislative function. Moreover, whether a criminal action is instituted by the Executive Branch, or a civil action is brought by private parties, judicial power is still brought to bear on Members of Congress and legislative independence is imperiled. We reaffirm that once it is determined that members are acting within the "legitimate legislative sphere" the Speech or Debate Clause is an absolute bar to interference. * * *

In determining whether particular activities other than literal speech or debate fall within the "legitimate legislative sphere" we . . . must determine whether the activities are

"an integral part of the deliberative and communicative processes by which Members participate in committee and House proceedings with respect to the consideration and passage or rejection of proposed legislation or with respect to other matters which the Constitution places within the jurisdiction of either House." * * *

The power to investigate and to do so through compulsory process plainly falls within that definition. This Court has often noted that the power to investigate is inherent in the power to make laws because "[a] legislative body cannot legislate wisely or effectively in the absence of information respecting the conditions which the legislation is intended to affect or change." * * * Issuance of subpoenas such as the one in question here has long been held to be a legitimate use by Congress of its power to investigate. * * * . . . It also has been held that the subpoena power may be exercised by a committee acting, as here, on behalf of one of the Houses. * * * Without such power the subcommittee may not be able to do the task assigned to it by Congress. To conclude that the power of inquiry is other than an integral part of the legislative process would be a miserly reading of the Speech or Debate Clause in derogation of the "integrity of the legislative process." * * *

. . . The issuance of a subpoena pursuant to an authorized investigation is . . . an indispensable ingredient of lawmaking. . . . To hold that Members of Congress are protected for authorizing an investigation, but not for issuing a subpoena in exercise of that authorization, would be a contradiction denigrating the power granted to Congress in Art I and would "indirectly impair the deliberations of Congress." * * *

The particular investigation at issue here is related to and in furtherance of a legitimate task of Congress. * * * On this record the pleadings show that the actions of the Members and the Chief Counsel fall within the "sphere of legitimate legislative activity." The Subcommittee was acting under an unambiguous resolution from the Senate authorizing it to make a complete study of the "administration, operation, and enforcement of the Internal Security Act of 1950. . . ." * * * That grant of authority is sufficient to show that the investigation upon which the Subcommittee had embarked concerned a subject on which "legislation could be had." * * *

The propriety of making USSF a subject of the investigation and subpoena is a subject on which the scope of our inquiry is narrow. * * * Even the most cursory look at the facts presented by the pleadings reveals the legitimacy of the USSF subpoena. Inquiry into the sources of funds used to carry on activities suspected by a Subcommittee of Congress to have a potential for undermining the morale of the armed forces is within the legitimate legislative sphere. Indeed, the complaint here tells us that USSF operated on or near military and naval bases, and that its facilities became the "focus of dissent" to declared national policy. Whether USSF activities violated any statute is not relevant; the inquiry was intended to inform Congress in an area where legislation may be had. USSF asserted it does not know the sources of its funds; in light of the Senate authorization to the Subcommittee to investigate "infiltration by persons who are or may be under the control of foreign governments," . . . and in view of the pleaded facts, it is clear that the subpoena to discover USSF's bank records "may fairly be deemed within [the Subcommittee's] province." * * *

We conclude that the Speech or Debate Clause provides complete immunity for the Members for issuance of this subpoena. . . .

• • •

[USSF] also contend[s] that the subpoena cannot be protected by the speech or debate immunity because the "sole purpose" of the investigation is to "force public disclosure of beliefs, opinions, expressions and associations of private citizens which may be unorthodox or unpopular." * * * Respondents view the scope of the privilege too narrowly. Our cases make clear that in determining the legitimacy of a congressional act we do not look to the motives alleged to have prompted it. * * * . . . If the mere allegation that a valid legislative act was undertaken for an unworthy purpose would lift the protection of the Clause then the Clause simply would not provide the protection historically undergirding it. . . . [T]he legitimacy of a congressional inquiry [is not] to be defined by what it produces. The very nature of the investigative function—like any research—is that it takes the searchers up some "blind alleys" and into nonproductive enterprises. To be a valid legislative inquiry there need be no predictable end result.

Finally, [USSF argues] that the purpose of the subpoena was to "harass, chill, punish and deter them" in the exercise of their First Amendment rights . . . and thus that the subpoena cannot be protected by the Clause. Their theory seems to be that once it is alleged that First Amendment rights may be infringed by congressional action the judiciary may intervene to protect those rights. . . . That approach, however, ignores the absolute nature of the speech or debate protection and our cases which have broadly construed that protection. . . . For us to read the Clause as [USSF] suggest[s] would create an exception not warranted by the language, purposes or history of the Clause. Respondents make the familiar argument that the broad protection granted by the Clause creates a potential for abuse. . . . Our consistently broad construction of the Speech or Debate Clause rests on the belief that it must be so construed to provide the independence which is its central purpose.

This case illustrates vividly the harm that judicial interference may cause. A legislative inquiry has been frustrated for nearly five years during which the Members and their aides have been obliged to devote time to consultation with their counsel concerning the litigation, and have been distracted from the purpose of their inquiry. The Clause was written to prevent the need to be confronted by such "questioning" and to forbid invocation of judicial power to challenge the wisdom of Congress' use of its investigative authority.

• • •

Reversed and remanded.

MR. JUSTICE MARSHALL, with whom MR. JUSTICE BRENNAN and MR. JUSTICE STEWART join, concurring in the judgment.

. . . I write today only to emphasize that the Speech and Debate Clause does not entirely immunize a congressional subpoena from challenge by a party not in a position to assert his constitutional rights by refusing to comply with it.

• • •

Modern legislatures, and particularly the Congress, may legislate on a wide range of subjects. In order to discharge this function, and their related informing function, they may genuinely need a great deal of information in the exclusive possession of persons who would not make it available except under the compulsion of a subpoena. When duly subpoenaed, however, such a person does not shed his constitutional right to withhold certain classes of information. If he refuses to testify or to produce documents and invokes a pertinent privilege, he still runs the risk that the legislature will cite him for contempt. At trial he may defend on the basis of the constitutional right to withhold information from the legislature, and his right will be respected along with the legitimate needs of the legislature. . . .

MR. JUSTICE DOUGLAS, dissenting.

I would affirm the judgment below.

. . . Under our federal regime that delegates, by the Constitution and Acts of Congress, awesome powers to individuals, that power may not be used to deprive people of their First Amendment or other constitutional rights. It is my view that no official, no matter how high or majestic his or her office, who is within the reach of judicial process, may invoke immunity for his actions for which wrongdoers normally suffer. There may be few occasions when, on the merits, it would be appropriate to invoke such a remedy. But no regime of law that can rightfully claim that name may make trustees of these vast powers immune from actions brought by people who have been wronged by official action. * * *

CHAPTER **5**
Commerce Power

INTRODUCTORY ESSAY

The Articles of Confederation contained no provision authorizing the regulation of commerce among the states. This serious deficiency along with the absence of the power to tax and the inability to enforce decisions against either states or individuals greatly limited the effectiveness of the first American national government. The experience of that government was brief and frustrating. Growing commercial rivalries among the thirteen largely independent states could not be resolved by a weak national Congress in which each state, regardless of its population, had an equal vote. No independent executive authority existed to provide national leadership, and there was no national judiciary to establish a uniform legal interpretation of the nature and scope of the power to be exercised by the new government.

Article I, Section 8 of the Constitution of 1787 contains a long list of "enumerated powers." In our discussion of federalism in Part IV we will focus more specifically on the various types of constitutional powers—*enumerated,* or *delegated; implied; reserved; concurrent.* At this point it is sufficient to recognize that the authority of Congress and of the federal bureaucracy that Congress has established over the years, together with a large part of the President's power to propose, sign, or veto legislation, is derived chiefly from the enumerated powers in Article I. This enumeration, deceptively simple in its language, includes the power "to regulate commerce . . . among the several states. . . ." As applied by Congress and interpreted by the Supreme Court, especially in the years following the "judicial revolution" of 1937, this brief phrase has provided a constitutional basis for vast national power in the field of domestic policy. As we shall see, commerce is a broad, open-ended term; and in the absence of more specific powers, its meaning has been expanded as the perceived demands for national governmental action have proliferated.

The Constitution of 1787 was drafted in response to practical problems. It is not and was not intended to be a theoretically cohesive, logically unified, and complete blueprint of government. The quality of practical application, seen in the various compromises out of which the Constitution was forged, has provided it with an adaptability that, in the hands of innovative jurists such as John Marshall, Louis Brandeis, and Earl Warren, has added long life to the Constitution's other attributes. Nowhere is this dynamic quality more apparent than in the broad field

172

of action covered by the Commerce Clause. This clause is important both as a source of national power and as a restriction on state power. In this chapter we are concerned with the former, and in Chapter 10 of Part IV we will consider the latter as part of our discussion of federalism. But the two branches or dimensions of the Commerce Clause—the source of national power and the basis of state restraint—are closely interrelated, and that dual character should be kept in mind.

Constitutional Origins of the Commerce Power

Economic unrest, including the previously noted commercial rivalry among states loosely united under the Articles of Confederation, had reached serious proportions by the mid-1780s. It was just such friction between Virginia and Maryland over fishing rights in Chesapeake Bay that produced the Mount Vernon Conference of 1785. That meeting in turn spawned the abortive Annapolis Convention to which all states were invited the following year to consider similar problems inhibiting trade and commercial development. With delegates from only five states in attendance, it was decided to call for still another meeting of the states to consider broad revision of the Articles of Confederation. Thus the stage was set for the Philadelphia Convention, which met during the late spring and summer of 1787 and produced the federal Constitution. It had become clear that the issue of commercial rivalry among the states was simply part of a larger set of problems stemming from the weakness of the national government.

At the Philadelphia Convention and for many years thereafter, major attention was directed to easing the economic friction among the states. It was the control of interstate rivalry, and not the exercise of national power on a broad scale, that chiefly concerned the Framers of the Constitution. To persuade all the states to give up their autonomy in the field of interstate commerce, it was necessary to make important concessions. One of these was the so-called commerce and slave trade compromise under which several Southern states were persuaded to drop their opposition to the national regulation of commerce in exchange for the assurance that the infamous African slave trade would not be restricted for twenty years. Although it aroused a few objections at the Convention itself, the language adopted by the Framers in dealing with this sensitive issue was delicately evasive: "The migration or importation of *such persons* as any of the states now existing shall think proper to admit, shall not be prohibited by the Congress prior to the year one thousand eight hundred and eight" (Article I, Section 9, Clause 1).

During the first century after adoption of the Constitution, Congress made little use of the Commerce Clause as a source of positive power. It is true that this clause, in combination with other enumerated powers and with the implied powers embraced by the Necessary and Proper Clause, served as authority for the creation of a national bank. Chief Justice John Marshall recognized the constitutionality of the bank legislation in *M'Culloch* v. *Maryland,* 4 Wheat. 316, in 1819 (see Part IV). The range of potential congressional power was thus glimpsed at an early date. Still, the Commerce Clause served primarily as a barrier against state legislation. Neither the states nor the national government engaged in extensive regulation of commerce during this early period, and most of the governmental activity that did occur in this field emanated from the states. It was in this setting that the first major Commerce Clause case reached the Supreme Court.

Early Interpretations of the Commerce Clause

As in most other areas of constitutional interpretation, the starting point is in one of Chief Justice Marshall's opinions. For the Commerce Clause this point of beginning is *Gibbons* v. *Ogden,* 9 Wheat. 1 (1824). As in *Marbury* v. *Madison,* 1 Cranch 137 (1803), and *M'Culloch* v. *Maryland,* Marshall's opinion in the *Gibbons* case is one of those fundamental statements of constitutional jurisprudence whose great influence has grown, not diminished, with the passage of time. Marshall and his colleagues on the Supreme Court of the early 1800s had the advantage of addressing major questions of constitutional law for the first time, unguided, but also uninhibited, by the weight of precedent. Marshall, far more than any other jurist of his era, displayed the ability to put this advantage to effective use.

Plenary Power

At issue in *Gibbons* v. *Ogden* was the constitutionality of New York's grant of a steamboat monopoly to Robert Fulton and James Livingston. Aaron Ogden succeeded to the Fulton-Livingston interest, which extended to commercial steamboat traffic between New York and New Jersey. Thomas Gibbons challenged this exclusive grant on the obvious ground that it interfered with the power of Congress to regulate commerce among the states. It so happened that Gibbons was licensed under *federal* law to engage in what was called the "coasting" trade. He contended that this authorization gave him the rights to engage in commercial activity of an interstate nature within the territory of New York, irrespective of that state's grant of a steamboat monopoly to others. Marshall and his colleagues agreed. In the course of declaring the steamboat monopoly unconstitutional, Marshall wrote expansively about the scope of congressional power embodied in the Commerce Clause. In this instance there was an obvious conflict between the federal licensing provision and the state grant of monopoly. Invoking the Supremacy Clause of Article VI, Marshall resolved this conflict in favor of the national government. He went on to assert that the power of Congress over commerce among the states was plenary, that is, full and complete, and subject to no competing exercise of state power in the same area. The federal law under which Gibbons operated was a modest exercise of that plenary power, but it was enough to warrant invalidation of the state law because the monopoly granted by the state interfered with the commercial privileges provided by the federal government.

It was clear from Marshall's opinion that Congress had acted well within its authority. In fact, he defined commerce so broadly and spoke in such sweeping terms about the plenary power of Congress to regulate it that his opinion came to read as an endorsement of regulatory authority on a grand scale—far beyond anything dreamed of in the 1820s. As Marshall defined it, commerce among the states meant far more than just the movement of goods across state lines. It encompassed a wide range of relationships and transactions summed up in the phrase "commercial intercourse." When Marshall spoke of commerce as *intercourse*, he referred to much more than the isolated movement of an article of trade from a point in state A to a point in state B. He had in mind commercial activity within and between states and saw no way of making realistic distinctions that could be automatically equated with state lines. Marshall acknowledged that some commerce might be altogether internal or *intrastate* in nature; but since that level of commerce was not at issue in *Gibbons*, he did not elaborate on it.

Exclusive Power?

In maintaining that the power of Congress under the Commerce Clause was plenary and superior to any competing state power, Marshall skirted one vitally important question: namely, would state legislation affecting commerce among the states be constitutional in the absence of any conflicting federal law? In a concurring opinion Justice William Johnson answered this question in the negative. In his view the power of Congress was not only plenary but also exclusive. He maintained that the states were absolutely barred from legislating in this broad area. Johnson was not supported in this view by other members of the Court, and his interpretation has never been adopted by a Court majority. Nevertheless, his statement endorsing exclusive congressional control of commerce among the states served to sharpen the underlying issue in *Gibbons* v. *Ogden* and in a long line of cases decided since the announcement of that ruling. The basic issue is this: If the power of Congress is plenary, as Marshall and the other Justices in *Gibbons* believed it to be, does the failure of Congress to regulate a particular aspect of commerce mean that this aspect is not to be regulated at all? And if this question is answered in the negative, does it follow that the states are free to regulate commerce in any area not already covered by federal legislation? Broadly speaking, and with varying degrees of imprecision, the Supreme Court has also answered this question in the negative. The states, as we shall see in Part IV, may, in the absence of conflicting federal law, regulate certain *local* aspects of interstate commerce. But even where no conflict with federal law is present, certain aspects of interstate commerce, which require uniform nationwide regulation, cannot be touched by the states. The problem that remains unresolved in particular cases is where to draw the line between permissible and impermissible state regulation of commerce. It was not necessary in *Gibbons* v. *Ogden* to explore that problem; but as demands for greater governmental regulation at both the state and the national level increased, that problem became ever more perplexing.

Gibbons v. *Ogden* furnished Marshall with an opportunity to lay down an all-encompassing definition of national power under the Commerce Clause. The decision was widely acclaimed by business leaders at the time because it placed restrictions on state grants of commercial monopolies, thus encouraging competitive commercial and industrial activity at a time when the national government played no significant role in regulating the economy. To the advocates of private enterprise in the 1820s it seemed safe enough to talk in the abstract about broad national power to regulate commerce, especially if such talk provided a constitutional justification for curbing state regulation of business. Until late in the nineteenth century that was precisely what the national commerce power symbolized. During this period, the states, under an expanding definition of their *police powers,* adopted an increasing number and variety of economic regulations, many of them aimed at large corporations whose influence in American society was growing. The concept of police power refers to the states' legitimate function in protecting the health, safety, morals, and general welfare of the people. As the application of the concept expanded, it came more and more into conflict with the commerce power of Congress—not the actual exercise of that power, but the domain of potential power that Congress alone could exercise.

Growth of National Regulation

Without going into the almost endless details of the growing conflict between state police power and national commerce power, it should be noted that as the popular demand for effective regulation of business increased and restrictions on state power multiplied, the national government was under greater pressure to use more of its power under the Commerce Clause to limit the concentration of corporate power and reduce economic injustice and exploitation. Congress responded cautiously to this growing demand by passing the Interstate Commerce Act in 1887 and the Sherman Antitrust Act in 1890. The first of these measures established the Interstate Commerce Commission (ICC) and gave it limited initial authority to regulate railroads engaged in commerce among the states. The Sherman Act was aimed at tackling on a national scale the concentration of economic wealth in the form of monopolies, or "combinations in restraint of trade," as the law phrased it.

Counterpart to State Police Power

Both the ICC and the Sherman Act represented the beginnings of a national counterpart to state police power. Both rested squarely on the Commerce Clause of the Constitution, and both encountered rough sledding in the Supreme Court for a number of years. By 1890 the Court had come under the heavy influence of economic theories that stressed the values of individual and corporate freedom and minimized the legitimate sphere of governmental regulation. Although the Court never fully subscribed to the philosophy of economic laissez-faire, its members, some of them former corporation lawyers, were heavily influenced by this perspective. That influence was reflected in the changes that were introduced in the interpretation of the Commerce Clause, together with changes in the interpretation of the Tenth Amendment and the Due Process Clauses of the Fifth and Fourteenth Amendments.

The first major change in the interpretation of the Commerce Clause as applied to the scope of national power came in the 1895 case of *United States* v. *E. C. Knight* Co., 156 U.S. 1. This decision resulted from the government's effort to break up a powerful sugar monopoly. The Court was provided with its first opportunity to interpret the Sherman Act, and the majority found that the Commerce Clause did not apply to certain business activities regulated by this legislation.

By contrast with Marshall's perspective in *Gibbons,* Chief Justice Melville Fuller, writing for the majority in *E. C. Knight,* emphasized the boundaries, not the breadth, of the commerce power. He acknowledged the "evils" of monopoly and conceded that the E. C. Knight Company was indeed engaged in monopolistic practices with respect to the manufacture of refined sugar. He also recognized a connection between control of the manufacture of "a given thing" and "control of its disposition." But he brushed aside this relationship between commerce and manufacturing by maintaining that it was secondary, not primary, in nature. The connection was incidental and indirect. Fuller did not clearly indicate why such a distinction should be drawn or precisely where the cut-off point between manufacturing and commerce could be identified. He simply asserted: "Commerce succeeds to manufacture and is not a part of it." The states, under their police power, were free to regulate monopolies; but according to Fuller the national government had no general police power. Only if the business activity in question came within the rules governing commerce or was itself "a monopoly of commerce," could the national government suppress it. This neat distinction between commerce and manufacturing adopted over the strong dissent of Justice Harlan, effectively gutted the 1890 Sherman Act without formally declaring it unconstitutional. If the government could move only against the postmanufacturing phases of monopolistic activity, rather than against the entire monopolistic enterprise, its hands were effectively tied.

The Court followed similar reasoning in *Hammer* v. *Dagenhart,* 247 U.S. 251 (1918), invalidating by a 5 to 4 margin federal restrictions on child labor. The manufacture of goods by children, even when those goods were clearly destined for shipment in interstate commerce, was not a part of commerce and could not be regulated by Congress. Here the Court, over the scathing dissenting opinion of Justice Holmes, added the observation that there was nothing harmful in the manufactured goods themselves, implying that such a showing would have been necessary to justify their prohibition in interstate commerce.

Ironically, the Court upheld several equally far-reaching exercises of congressional power under the Commerce Clause between its decisions in *E. C. Knight* and *Dagenhart.* In fact, some of these statutes imposed severe criminal penalties in addition to the civil remedies exclusively applied in the latter case. Relying on the Commerce Clause, Congress enacted laws imposing fines and imprisonment for participation in lotteries, prostitution, and the consumption of alcohol and other drugs. Apparently enterprises of this sort, unlike child labor and business monopoly, were widely, if not universally, regarded as immoral. And when it came to punishing what everyone regarded as sinful behavior, the Commerce Clause was seen as an appropriate constitutional weapon (see *Champion* v. *Ames,* 188 U.S. 321 [1903], which upheld the federal antilottery statute, and *Hoke* v. *United States,* 227 U.S. 308 [1913], which upheld the federal law penalizing the transportation of women across state lines for "immoral purposes").

Throughout this period the Court was also willing to uphold national legislation designed to protect consumers against adulterated food shipped across state lines and against the improper processing, packaging, and branding of meat shipped interstate (see *Hipolite Egg Co.* v. *United States,* 220 U.S. 45 [1911], and related cases).

In the field of transportation, particularly with regard to the regulation of railroad freight rates, the scope of national power under the Commerce Clause developed in accordance with the broad language of *Gibbons* v. *Ogden.* Even *intrastate* rates might be regulated by the ICC if states engaged in the creation of rate structures that discriminated against interstate carriers and in favor of their local competitors (see the Shreveport Rate Case, 234 U.S. 342 [1914]). Still, from the 1890s until the late 1930s the Court resisted efforts to expand the Commerce Clause to make it a broad, nonselective basis of national police power.

Outer Limits of the Commerce Power

Instead, the Court developed several broad concepts in attempting to define the outer limits of the commerce power. We identify two of these concepts at this point in our discussion as a means of illustrating the elusiveness and complexity of constitutional doctrine in this field of congressional regulation. The "stream of commerce" concept was first articulated by Justice Holmes in the 1905 case of *Swift and Company* v. *United States,* 196 U.S. 375. Here the Court held that the power of the national government under the Sherman Act extended to conspiracy in restraint of trade among a combination of Chicago meatpackers. Even though the challenged activities—the buying and selling of cattle in Chicago—were local in nature, Holmes found that these transactions were in the "current of commerce among the states." The same rationale was applied by Chief Justice Taft seventeen years later in upholding federal regulation under the Packers and Stockyards Act of 1921 (*Stafford* v. *Wallace,* 258 U.S. 495 [1922]). The second concept is that of the "direct" or "indirect" effect upon commerce. In a number of cases during this period the Court indicated that even though the activity in question might not itself be defined as commerce, it could still be regulated if its *effect* on commerce was "direct." It followed, of course, that a mere "indirect" effect would not alone be sufficient to justify regulatory power under the Commerce Clause. While the "direct-indirect test" was usually applied in such a way as to sustain the regulation under review, the Court used this distinction as a means of indicating that congressional authority was subject to limitation. Indeed, when the National Industrial Recovery Act was declared unconstitutional in *Schechter Poultry Corp.* v. *United States,* 295 U.S. 495 (1935), one of the principal conclusions reached by the Court was that what the government sought to regulate only had an indirect effect upon interstate commerce.

The distinction between manufacturing or production and commerce was reaffirmed in principle and extended to the differentiation between mining and commerce in the 1936 case of *Carter* v. *Carter Coal Co.,* 298 U.S. 238. Between the limited scope of the Commerce Clause and the inherent restrictions of the Tenth Amendment, which recognized reserved powers of the states, a Supreme Court majority throughout this 41-year period (1895–1936) treated the commerce power of Congress as something less than plenary. Then came the confrontation between FDR and the "nine old men" (see Chapter 2). In the aftermath of the President's effort to "pack" it in 1937, the Court moved away from a defense of business toward an affirmation of regulatory power, both national and state. One very important aspect of this transition was a return to the expansive definition of congressional power under the Commerce Clause. The difference between the post-1937 approach and that of Chief Justice Marshall more than a century before was in the specific application of the clause, not in its theoretical restatement. Under President Roosevelt's leadership, the Democratic Congresses of the middle and late 1930s enacted sweeping regulatory measures in such fields as labor relations, agriculture, social insurance, and natural resource development, to cite only a few examples. The Commerce Clause figured prominently as a constitutional source for most of this legislation. Beginning with its decision upholding the National Labor Relations Act (*National Labor Relations Board* v. *Jones & Laughlin Steel Corp.,* 301 U.S. 1 [1937]), the reoriented Supreme Court swept away distinctions between commerce and manufacturing, between direct and indirect burdens on commerce, and between activities that directly or indirectly *affected* commerce. With the decison in *United States* v. *Darby,* 312 U.S. 100 (1941), the Tenth Amendment vanished as a significant restraint on the commerce power, not to be resurrected until 1976 in a case involving the application of federal minimum wage standards to state merit system employees (*National League of Cities* v. *Usery,* 426 U.S. 833).

Modern Scope of the Commerce Power

Prior to the *Usery* case, which many scholars regard as an aberration rather than as an indication of a return to pre-1937 values of federalism, Congress relied on the Commerce Clause as a basis for vast legislative undertakings, some of them well beyond the field of commercial relations. The most important illustration of the commerce power as a source of noncommercial legislation is within the field of race relations. In *Heart of Atlanta Motel* v. *United States,* 379 U.S. 241 (1964), the Supreme Court unanimously upheld the public accommodations section of the 1964 Civil Rights Act as a proper exercise of the commerce power. The motel in question did a substantial volume of business based on the interstate travel of its patrons. The Court ruled that its racially restrictive practices could impede commerce among the states and could be appropriately regulated by Congress.

In the companion case of *Katzenbach* v. *McClung,* 379 U.S. 294 (1964), the Court went even further by recognizing the power of Congress under the Commerce Clause to bar racial discrimination in a restaurant (Ollie's Barbecue in Birmingham, Alabama) patronized almost entirely by local customers. The Court found a connection with interstate commerce in the purchase of food and equipment from sources outside Alabama. Five years later, in *Daniel* v. *Paul,* 395 U.S. 298 (1969), the Court followed the same approach in barring racial discrimination as practiced by the owners of an amusement park near Little Rock, Arkansas. After passage of the 1964 Civil Rights Act, the Pauls, who had been operating their establishment as a public, racially segregated recreational area, began to refer to it as a "private club." They resorted to the additional subterfuge of charging a 25-cent "membership fee" and issuing "membership cards" as a means of excluding black patrons from the snack bar and other park facilities. Writing for the majority, Justice Brennan observed that the Federal District Court, before which this case was tried, took judicial notice of the fact that the "principal ingredients going into the bread were produced and processed in other states" and that "certain ingredients (of the soft drinks) were probably obtained . . . from out-of-state sources." From this, applying the *Katzenbach* rationale, Brennan concluded: "There can be no serious doubt that a 'substantial portion of the food' served at the snack bar [had] moved in interstate commerce." Under such a broad definition of commerce, it is questionable whether any local enterprise that opens its doors to the public could remain outside the scope of the Commerce Clause.

In *Wickard* v. *Filburn*, 317 U.S. 111 (1942), the Court went a long way toward removing any significant distinction between interstate and intrastate commerce as a potential basis for limiting national power. At issue was the constitutionality of a federal acreage allotment for wheat. On its face the question might have seemed easy to resolve in light of the expanded power of Congress in the post–New Deal era. But the specific violation consisted in a farmer's raising a wheat crop in excess of the prescribed allotment, not for sale or distribution in interstate commerce, but for his own consumption. Writing for a unanimous Court, Justice Robert H. Jackson concluded that "even if appellant's activity be local and though it may not be regarded as commerce, it may still, whatever its nature, be reached by Congress if it exerts a substantial economic effect on interstate commerce and this irrespective of whether such effect is what might at some earlier time have been defined as 'direct' or 'indirect' . . . ." A comparison between this sweeping language and the restrictive views of Chief Justice Fuller in the *E. C. Knight* case illustrates the extent to which a single clause of the federal Constitution is subject to contrasting interpretations.

A more recent illustration of the scope of the national regulatory power under the Commerce Clause is provided by *Goldfarb* v. *Virginia State Bar*, 421 U.S. 773 (1975). At issue was the question of whether bar associations violate the Sherman Act by prescribing minimum fees for the performance of routine legal services incident to the purchase of a home. The Goldfarbs contracted to purchase a residence in Fairfax County, Virginia. Before they could borrow money to complete the purchase, they were required to obtain title insurance. This necessitated a title examination, which, under Virginia law, could be performed only by a member of the state bar. The Goldfarbs attempted unsuccessfully to find a lawyer who would charge them less for this service than the amount prescribed in a minimum fee schedule published by the county bar association and enforced by the state bar. They then initiated a class action challenging the legality of the fee schedule and four years later achieved a major Supreme Court victory for consumers of legal services.

Writing for a unanimous Court, Chief Justice Burger held that the publication and enforcement of a minimum fee schedule violated Section 1 of the Sherman Act. He observed:

> Whatever else it may be, the examination of a land title is a service; the exchange of such a service for money is "commerce" in the most common usage of that word. . . . In the modern world it cannot be denied that the activities of lawyers play an important part in commercial intercourse, and that anti-competitive activities by lawyers may exert a restraint on commerce.

He rejected the contention that because the bar was, for certain purposes, a state agency it was shielded from antitrust regulation. He concluded: "Its activities resulted in a rigid price floor from which . . . consumers could not escape if they wished to borrow money to buy a home."

In the cases that follow, you will have an opportunity to discern the conflicting forces underlying the development of one of the most significant sources of national power under the Constitution. You will see that the development is not always logically consistent, not always theoretically cohesive—that it is at times erratic and even contradictory. Always, however, the interpretation of the Commerce Clause, like the language of other constitutional provisions, is undertaken to facilitate the achievement of practical political goals as well as to preserve the continuity of legal institutions.

Gibbons v. Ogden

9 Wheat. 1 (1824)

MR. CHIEF JUSTICE MARSHALL delivered the opinion of the Court.

[Gibbons] contends that [New York's injunction] is erroneous, because the laws [of New York] which purport to give the exclusive privilege (to Ogden to navigate steamboats on New York waters) are repugnant to the constitution and laws of the United States.

They are said to be repugnant . . .—to that clause in the constitution which authorizes Congress to regulate commerce.

• • •

The words are: "Congress shall have power to regulate commerce with foreign nations, and among the several states, and with the Indian tribes."

The subject to be regulated is commerce; and our constitution being, as was aptly said at the bar, one of enumeration, and not of definition, to ascertain the extent of the power it becomes necessary to settle the meaning of the word. The counsel for [Ogden] would limit it to traffic, to buying and selling, or the interchange of commodities, and do not admit that it comprehends navigation. This would restrict a general term, applicable to many objects, to one of its significations. Commerce, undoubtedly, is traffic, but it is something more; it is intercourse. It describes the commercial intercourse between nations, and parts of nations, in all its branches, and is regulated by prescribing rules for carrying on that intercourse. The mind can scarcely conceive a system for regulating commerce between nations, which shall exclude all laws concerning navigation, which shall be silent on the admission of the vessels of the one nation into the ports of the other, and be confined to prescribing rules for the conduct of individuals, in the actual employment of buying and selling or of barter.

If commerce does not include navigation, the government of the Union has no direct power over that subject, and can make no law prescribing what shall constitute American vessels, or requiring that they shall be navigated by American seamen. Yet this power has been exercised from the commencement of the government, has been exercised with the consent of all, and has been understood by all to be a commercial regulation. All America understands, and has uniformly understood, the word "commerce" to comprehend navigation. It was so understood, and must have been so understood, when the constitution was framed. The power over commerce, including navigation, was one of the primary objects for which the people of America adopted their government, and must have been contemplated in forming it. The convention must have used the word in that sense; because all have understood it in that sense, and the attempt to restrict it comes too late.

· · ·

The word used in the constitution, then, comprehends, and has been always understood to comprehend, navigation within its meaning; and a power to regulate navigation is as expressly granted as if that term had been added to the word "commerce."

To what commerce does this power extend? The constitution informs us, to commerce "with foreign nations, and among the several states, and with the Indian tribes."

It has, we believe, been universally admitted that these words comprehend every species of commercial intercourse between the United States and foreign nations. No sort of trade can be carried on between this country and any other, to which this power does not extend. It has been truly said, that commerce, as the word is used in the constitution, is a unit, every part of which is indicated by the term.

If this be the admitted meaning of the word, in its application to foreign nations, it must carry the same meaning throughout the sentence, and remain a unit, unless there be some plain intelligible cause which alters it.

The subject to which the power is next applied, is to commerce "among the several states." The word "among" means intermingled with. A thing which is among others, is intermingled with them. Commerce among the states cannot stop at the external boundary line of each state, but may be introduced into the interior.

It is not intended to say that these words comprehend that commerce which is completely internal, which is carried on between man and man in a state, or between different parts of the same state, and which does not extend to or affect other states. Such a power would be inconvenient, and is certainly unnecessary.

Comprehensive as the word "among" is, it may very properly be restricted to that commerce which concerns more states than one. The phrase is not one which would probably have been selected to indicate the completely interior traffic of a state, because it is not an apt phrase for that purpose; and the enumeration of the particular classes of commerce to which the power was to be extended, would not have been made had the intention been to extend the power to every description. The enumeration presupposes something not enumerated; and that something, if we regard the language or the subject of the sentence, must be the exclusively internal commerce of a state. The genius and character of the whole government seem to be, that its action is to be applied to all the external concerns of the nation, and to those internal concerns which affect the states generally; but not to those which are completely within a particular state, which do not affect other states, and with which it is not necessary to interfere, for the purpose of executing some of the general powers of the government. The completely internal commerce of a state, then, may be considered as reserved for the state itself.

But, in regulating commerce with foreign nations the power of Congress does not stop at the jurisdictional lines of the several states. It would be a very useless power if it could not pass those lines. The commerce of the United States with foreign nations, is that of the whole United States. Every district has a right to participate in it. The deep streams which penetrate our country in every direction, pass through the interior of almost every state in the Union, and furnish the means of exercising this right. If Congress has the power to regulate it, that power must be exercised whenever the subject exists. If it exists within the states, if a foreign voyage may commence or terminate at a port within a state, then the power of Congress may be exercised within a state.

• • •

We are now arrived at the inquiry, What is this power?

It is the power to regulate; that is, to prescribe the rule by which commerce is to be governed. This power, like all others vested in Congress, is complete in itself, may be exercised to its utmost extent, and acknowledges no limitations, other than are prescribed in the constitution. These are expressed in plain terms, and do not affect the questions which arise in this case, or which have been discussed at the bar. If, as has always been understood, the sovereignty of Congress, though limited to specified objects, is plenary as to those objects, the power over commerce with foreign nations, and among the several States, is vested in Congress as absolutely as it would be in a single government, having in its constitution the same restrictions on the exercise of the power as are found in the constitution of the United States. The wisdom and the discretion of Congress, their identity with the people, and the influence which their constituents possess at election, are, in this, as in many other instances, as that, for example, of declaring war, the sole restraints on which they have relied, to secure them from its abuse. They are the restraints on which the people must often rely solely, in all representative governments.

The power of Congress, then, comprehends navigation within the limits of every state in the Union; so far as that navigation may be, in any manner, connected with "commerce with foreign nations, or among the several states, or with the Indian tribes." It may, of consequence, pass the jurisdictional line of New York, and act upon the very waters to which the prohibition now under consideration applies.

But it has been urged with great earnestness, that although the power of Congress to regulate commerce with foreign nations, and among the several states, be co-extensive with the subject itself, and have no other limits than are prescribed in the constitution, yet the states may severally exercise the same power within their respective jurisdictions. In support of this argument, it is said that they possessed it as an inseparable attribute of sovereignty, before the formation of the constitution, and still retain it, except so far as they have surrendered it by that instrument; that this principle results from the nature of the government, and is secured by the tenth amendment; that an affirmative grant of power is not exclusive, unless in its own nature it be such that the continued exercise of it by the former possessor is inconsistent with the grant, and that this is not of that description.

[Gibbons] conceding these postulates, except the last, contends that full power to regulate a particular subject, implies the whole power, and leaves no residuum; that a grant of the whole is incompatible with the existence of a right in another to any part of it.

Both parties have appealed to the constitution, to legislative acts, and judicial decisions; and have drawn arguments from all these sources to support and illustrate the propositions they respectively maintain.

The grant of the power to lay and collect taxes is, like the power to regulate commerce, made in general terms, and has never been understood to interfere with the exercise of the same power by the states; and hence has been drawn an argument which has been applied to the question under consideration. But the two grants are not, it is conceived, similar in their terms or their nature. Although many of the powers formerly exercised by the states, are transferred to the government of the Union, yet the state governments remain, and constitute a most important part of our system. The power of taxation is indispensable to their existence, and is a power which, in its own nature, is capable of residing in, and being exercised by, different authorities at the same time. . . . Congress is authorized to lay and collect taxes, etc., to pay the debts, and provide for the common defense and general welfare of the United States. This does not interfere with the power of the states to tax for the support of their own governments; nor is the exercise of that power by the states an exercise of any portion of the power that is granted to the United States. In imposing taxes for state purposes, they are not doing what Congress is empowered to do. Congress is not empowered to tax for those purposes which are within the exclusive province of the states. When, then, each government exercises the power of taxation, neither is exercising the power of the other. But, when a state proceeds to regulate commerce with foreign nations, or among the several states, it is exercising the very power that is granted to Congress, and is doing the very thing which Congress is authorized to do. There is no analogy, then, between the power of taxation and the power of regulating commerce.

In discussing the question, whether this [commerce] power is still in the states, in the case under consideration, we may dismiss from it the inquiry, whether it is surrendered by the mere grant to Congress, or is retained until Congress shall exercise the power. We may dismiss that inquiry, because it has been exercised, and the regulations which Congress deemed it proper to make, are now in full operation. The sole question is, can a state regulate commerce with foreign nations and among the states, while Congress is regulating it?

• • •

In our complex system, presenting the rare and difficult scheme of one general government, whose action extends over the whole, but which possesses only certain enumerated powers, and of numerous state governments, which retain and exercise all powers not delegated to the Union, contests respecting power must arise. Were it even otherwise, the measures taken by the respective governments to execute their acknowledged powers, would often be of the same description, and might, sometimes, interfere. This, however, does not prove that the one is exercising, or has a right to exercise, the powers of the other.

• • •

Since, . . . in exercising the power of regulating their own purely internal affairs, whether of trading or police, the states may sometimes enact laws, the validity of which depends on their interfering with, and being contrary to, an act of Congress passed in pusuance of the constitution, the court will enter upon the inquiry, whether the laws of New York, as expounded by the highest tribunal of that state, have, in their application to this case, come into collision with an act of Congress, and deprived a citizen of a right to which that act entitles him. Should this collision exist, it will be immaterial whether those laws were passed in virtue of a concurrent power "to regulate commerce with foreign nations and among the several states," or in virtue of a power to regulate their domestic trade and police. In one case and the other, the acts of New York must yield to the law of Congress; and the decision sustaining the privilege they confer, against a right given by a law of the Union, must be erroneous.

. . . [It] has been contended that if a law, passed by a state in the exercise of its acknowleged sovereignty, comes into conflict with a law passed by Congress in pursuance of the constitution, they affect the subject, and each other, like equal opposing powers.

But the framers of our constitution foresaw this state of things, and provided for it, by declaring the supremacy not only of itself, but of the laws made in pursuance of it. The nullity of any act, inconsistent with the constitution, is produced by the declaration that the constitution is the supreme law. The appropriate application of that part of the clause which confers the same supremacy on laws and treaties, is to such acts of the state legislatures as do not transcend their powers, but, though enacted in the execution of acknowledged state powers, interfere with, or are contrary to the laws of Congress, made in pursuance of the constitution, or some treaty made under the authority of the United States. In every such case, the act of Congress, or the treaty, is supreme; and the law of the state, though enacted in the exercise of powers not controverted, must yield to it.

• • •

. . . To the court it seems very clear, that the whole act on the subject of the coasting trade, according to those principles which govern the construction of statutes, implies, unequivocally, an authority to licensed vessels to carry on the coasting trade.

• • •

If the power reside in Congress, as a portion of the general grant to regulate commerce, then acts applying that power to vessels generally, must be construed as comprehending all vessels. If none appear to be excluded by the language of the act, none can be excluded by construction. Vessels have always been employed to a greater or less extent in the transportation of passengers, and have never been supposed to be, on that account, withdrawn from the control or protection of Congress. . . .

• • •

. . . The real and sole question seems to be, whether a steam machine, in actual use, deprives a vessel of the privileges conferred by a license.

In considering this question, the first idea which presents itself, is that the laws of Congress, for the regulation of commerce, do not look to the principle by which vessels are moved. That subject is left entirely to individual discretion; and, in that vast and complex system of legislative enactment concerning it, which embraces everything that the legislature thought it necessary to notice, there is not, we believe, one word respecting the peculiar principle by which vessels are propelled through the water, except what may be found in a single act, granting a particular privilege to steamboats. With this exception, every act, either prescribing duties, or granting privileges, applies to every vessel, whether navigated by the instrumentality of wind or fire, of sails or machinery. . . .

• • •

This act demonstrates the opinion of Congress, that steamboats may be enrolled and licensed, in common with vessels using sails. They are, of course, entitled to the same privileges, and can no more be restrained from navigating waters, and entering ports which are free to such vessels, than if they were wafted on their voyage by the winds, instead of being propelled by the agency of fire. The one element may be as legitimately used as the other, for every commercial purpose authorized by the laws of the Union; and the act of a state inhibiting the use of either to any vessel having a license under the act of Congress, comes, we think, in direct collision with that act.

• • •

MR. JUSTICE JOHNSON [concurring]. The judgment entered by the court in this cause has my entire approbation; but having adopted my conclusions on views of the subject materially different from those of my brethren, I feel it incumbent on me to exhibit those views. . . .

In attempts to construe the constitution, I have never found much benefit resulting from the inquiry, whether the whole, or any part of it, is to be construed strictly, or literally. The simple, classical, precise, yet comprehensive language in which it is couched, leaves, at most, but very little latitude for construction; and when its intent and meaning is discovered nothing remains but to execute the will of those who made it, in the best manner to effect the purposes intended. The great and paramount purpose, was to unite this mass of wealth and power, for the protection of the humblest individual; his rights, civil and political, his interests and prosperity, are the sole end; the rest are nothing but the means. But the principal of those means, one so essential as to approach nearer the characteristics of an end, was the independence and harmony of the states, that they may the better subserve the purposes of cherishing and protecting the respective families of this great republic.

• • •

The "power to regulate commerce," here meant to be granted, was that power to regulate commerce which previously existed in the states. But what was that power? The states were, unquestionably, supreme, and each possessed that power over commerce which is acknowledged to reside in every sovereign state. . . . The power of a sovereign state over commerce, therefore, amounts to nothing more than a power to limit and restrain it at pleasure. And since the power to prescribe the limits to its freedom necessarily implies the power to determine what shall remain unrestrained, it follows that the power must be exclusive; it can reside but in one potentate; and hence, the grant of this power carries with it the whole subject, leaving nothing for the state to act upon.

• • •

It is impossible, with the views which I entertained of the principle on which the commercial privileges of the people of the United States, among themselves, rests, to concur in the view which this court takes of the effect of the coasting license in this cause. I do not regard it as the foundation of the right set up in behalf of [Gibbons]. If there was any one object riding over every other in the adoption of the constitution, it was to keep the commercial intercourse among the states free from all invidious and partial restraints. And I cannot overcome the conviction, that if the licensing act was repealed tomorrow, the rights of [Gibbons] to a reversal of the decision complained of, would be as strong as it is under this license. . . .

United States v. E. C. Knight Co.

156 U.S. 1 (1895)

MR. CHIEF JUSTICE FULLER delivered the opinion of the Court.

By the purchase of the stock of the four Philadelphia refineries, with shares of its own stock, the American Sugar Refining Company acquired nearly complete control of the manufacture of refined sugar within the United States. The bill charged that the contracts under which these purchases were made constituted combinations in restraint of trade, and that in entering into them the defendants combined and conspired to restrain the trade and commerce in refined sugar among the several states and with foreign nations, contrary to the Act of Congress of July 2, 1890.

The relief sought was the cancellation of the agreements under which the stock was transferred; the redelivery of the stock to the parties respectively; and an injunction against the further performance of the agreements and further violations of the Act. . . .

• • •

The fundamental question is whether conceding that the existence of a monopoly in manufacture is established by the evidence, that monopoly can be directly suppressed under the Act of Congress in the mode attempted by this bill.

It cannot be denied that the power of a state to protect the lives, health, and property of its citizens, and to preserve good order and the public morals, "the power to govern men and things within the limits of its dominion," is a power originally and always belonging to the states, not surrendered by them to the general government, nor directly restrained by the Constitution of the United

States, and essentially exclusive. The relief of the citizens of each state from the burden of monopoly and the evils resulting from the restraint of trade among such citizens was left with the states to deal with, and this court has recognized their possession of that power. . . . On the other hand, the power of Congress to regulate commerce among the several states is also exclusive. The Constitution does not provide that interstate commerce shall be free, but, by the grant of this exclusive power to regulate it, it was left free except as Congress might impose restraints. . . . That which belongs to commerce is within the jurisdiction of the United States, but that which does not belong to commerce is within the jurisdiction of the police power of the state. * * *

The argument is that the power to control the manufacture of refined sugar is a monopoly over a necessary of life, to the enjoyment of which by a large population of the United States interstate commerce is indispensable, and that, therefore, the general government in the exercise of the power to regulate commerce may repress such monopoly directly and set aside the instruments which have created it. But this argument cannot be confined to necessaries of life merely, and must include all articles of general consumption. Doubtless the power to control the manufacture of a given thing involves in a certain sense the control of its disposition, but this is a secondary and not the primary sense; and although the exercise of that power may result in bringing the operation of commerce into play, it does not control it, and affects it only incidentally and indirectly. Commerce succeeds to manufacture, and is not a part of it. The power to regulate commerce is the power to prescribe the rule by which commerce shall be governed, and is a power independent of the power to suppress monopoly. But it may operate in repression of monopoly whenever that comes within the rules by which commerce is governed or whenever the transaction is itself a monopoly of commerce.

It is vital that the independence of the commercial power and of the police power, and delimitation between them, however sometimes perplexing, should always be recognized and observed, for while the one furnishes the strongest bond of union, the other is essential to the preservation of the autonomy of the states as required by our dual form of government; and acknowledged evils, however grave and urgent they may appear to be, had better be borne, than the risk be run, in the effort to suppress them, of more serious consequences by resort to expedients of even doubtful constitutionality.

It will be perceived how far reaching the proposition is that the power of dealing with a monopoly directly may be exercised by the general government whenever interstate or international commerce may be ultimately affected. The regulation of commerce applies to the subjects of commerce and not to matters of internal police. Contracts to buy, sell, or exchange goods to be transported among the several states . . . may be regulated, but this is because they form part of interstate trade or commerce. The fact that an article is manufactured for export to another state does not of itself make it an article of interstate commerce, and the intent of the manufacture does not determine the time when the

article or product passes from the control of the state and belongs to commerce.
. . .

•   •   •

Contracts, combinations, or conspiracies to control domestic enterprise in manufacture, agriculture, mining, production in all its forms, or to raise or lower prices or wages might unquestionably tend to restrain external as well as domestic trade, but the restraint would be an indirect result, however inevitable and whatever its extent, and such result would not necessarily determine the object of the contract, combination, or conspiracy.

Again, all the authorities agree that in order to vitiate a contract or combination it is not essential that its result should be a complete monopoly; it is sufficient if it really tends to that end and to deprive the public of the advantages which flow from free competition. Slight reflection will show that if the national power extends to all contracts and combinations in manufacture, agriculture, mining, and other productive industries, whose ultimate result may affect external commerce, comparatively little of business operations and affairs would be left for state control.

It was in the light of well settled principles that the Act of July 2, 1890, was framed. Congress did not attempt thereby to assert the power to deal with monopoly directly as such; or to limit and restrict the rights of corporations created by the states or the citizens of the states in the acquistion, control, or disposition of property; or to regulate or prescribe the price or prices at which such property or the product thereof should be sold; or to make criminal the acts of persons in the acquisition and control of property which the states of their residence or creation sanctioned or permitted. . . . [W]hat the law struck at was combinations, contracts, and conspiracies to monopolize trade and commerce among the several states or with foreign nations; but the contracts and acts of the defendants related exclusively to the acquisition of the Philadelphia refineries and the business of sugar refining in Pennsylvania, and bore no direct relation to commerce between the states or with foreign nations. The object was manifestly private gain in the manufacture of the commodity, but not through the control of interstate or foreign commerce. It is true that the bill alleged that the products of these refineries were sold and distributed among the several states, and that all the companies were engaged in trade or commerce with the several states and with foreign nations; but this was no more than to say that trade and commerce served manufacture to fulfill its function. Sugar was refined for sale, and sales were probably made at Philadelphia for consumption, and undoubtedly for resale by the first purchasers throughout Pennsylvania and other states, and refined sugar was also forwarded by the companies to other states for sale. Nevertheless it does not follow that an attempt to monopolize, or the actual monopoly of, the manufacture was an attempt, whether executory or consummated to monopolize commerce, even though, in order to dispose of the product, the instrumentality of commerce was necessarily invoked. There was nothing in the proofs to indicate any intention to put a restraint upon trade or commerce, and the fact, as we have seen, that trade or commerce might be indirectly affected was not enough to entitle [the government] to a decree. The subject-matter of the sale was shares of manufacturing stock, and the relief sought was the surrender of property which had already passed and the suppression of the alleged monopoly in manufacture by the restoration of the *status quo* before the transfers, yet the Act of Congress only authorized the circuit courts to proceed by way of preventing and restraining violations of the Act in respect of contracts, combinations, or conspiracies in restraint of interstate or international trade or commerce.

• • •

Decree affirmed.

MR. JUSTICE HARLAN dissenting.

Prior to the 4th day of March, 1892, the American Sugar Refining Company, a corporation organized under a general statute of New Jersey for the purpose of buying, manufacturing, refining, and *selling sugar in different parts of the country,* had obtained the control of *all* the sugar refineries in the United States except five, of which four were owned and operated by Pennsylvania corporations—the E. C. Knight Company, the Franklin Sugar Refining Company, Spreckels' Sugar Refining Company, and the Delaware Sugar House—and the other, by the Revere Sugar Refinery of Boston. These five corporations were all in active competition with the American Sugar Refining Company and with each other. The product of the Pennsylvania companies was about thirty-three per cent, and that of the Boston company about two per cent, of the entire quantity of sugar refined in the United States.

In March, 1892, by means of contacts or arrangements with stockholders of the four Pennsylvania companies, the New Jersey corporation—using for that purpose its own stock—purchased the stock of these companies, and thus obtained absolute control of the entire business of sugar refining in the United States except that done by the Boston company, which is too small in amount to be regarded in this discussion.

. . . In its consideration of the important constitutional question presented, this court assumes on the record before us that the result of the transactions disclosed by the pleadings and proof was the creation of a monopoly in the manufacture of a necessary of life. If this combination, so far as its operations necessarily or directly affect interstate commerce, cannot be restrained or suppressed under some power granted to Congress, it will be cause for regret that the patriotic statesmen who framed the Constitution did not foresee the necessity of investing the national government with power to deal with gigantic monopolies holding in their grasp, and injuriously controlling in their own interest, the entire trade *among the states* in food products that are essential to the comfort of every household in the land.

The court holds it to be vital in our system of government to recognize and give effect to both the commercial power of the nation and the police powers of the states, to the end that the Union be strengthened and the autonomy of the states preserved. In this view I entirely concur. Undoubtedly, the preservation of the just authority of the states is an object of deep concern to every lover of his country. No greater calamity could befall our free institutions than the destruction of that authority, by whatever means such a result might be accomplished. . . . But it is equally true that the preservation of the just authority of the general government is essential as well to the safety of the states as to the attainment of the important ends for which that government was ordained by the people of the United States; and the destruction of *that* authority would be fatal to the peace and well-being of the American people. The Constitution which enumerates the powers committed to the nation for objects of interest to the people of all the states should not, therefore, be subjected to an interpretation so rigid, technical and narrow, that those objects cannot be accomplished. . . .

Congress is invested with power to regulate commerce with foreign nations and among the several states. . . .

•   •   •

. . . It is the settled doctrine of this court that interstate commerce embraces something more than the mere physical transportation of articles of property, and the vehicles or vessels by which such transportation is effected. . . . Interstate commerce does not consist in transportation simply. It includes the purchase and sale of articles that are intended to be transported from one state to another— every species of commercial intercourse among the states and with foreign nations.

•   •   •

The fundamental inquiry in this case is, What, in a legal sense, is an unlawful restraint of trade?

•   •   •

. . . [A] general restraint of trade has often resulted from *combinations* formed for the purpose of controlling prices by destroying the opportunity of buyers and sellers to deal with each other upon the basis of fair, open, free competition. Combinations of this character have frequently been the subject of judicial scrutiny, and have always been condemned as illegal because of their necessary tendency to restrain trade. Such combinations are against common right and are crimes against the public. . . .

•   •   •

The power of Congress covers and protects the absolute freedom of such intercourse and trade among the states as may or must succeed manufacture and precede transportation from the place of purchase. This would seem to be conceded; for, the court in the present case expressly declare that "contracts to buy, sell, or exchange goods to be transported among the several states, the transportation and its instrumentalities, and articles, bought, sold, or exchanged for the purpose of such transit among the states, or put in the way of transit, may be regulated, but this is because they form part of interstate trade or commerce." Here is a direct admission—one which the settled doctrines of this court justify— that contracts to buy and the purchasing of goods to be transported from one state to another, and transportation, with its instrumentalities, are all parts of interstate trade or commerce. Each part of such trade is then under the protection of Congress. And yet, by the opinion and judgment in this case, if I do not misapprehend them, Congress is without power to protect the commercial intercourse that such purchasing necessarily involves against the restraints and burdens arising from the existence of combinations that meet purchasers from whatever state they come, with the threat—for it is nothing more nor less than a threat—that they shall not purchase what they desire to purchase, except at the prices fixed by such combinations. A citizen of Missouri has the right to go in person, or send orders, to Pennsylvania and New Jersey for the purpose of purchasing refined sugar. But of what value is that right if he is confronted in those states by a vast combination which absolutely controls the price of that article by reason of its having acquired all the sugar refineries in the United States in order that they may fix prices in their own interest exclusively?

In my judgment, the citizens of the several states composing the Union are entitled, of right, to buy goods in the state where they are manufactured, or in any other state, without being confronted by an illegal combination whose business extends throughout the whole country, which by the law everywhere is an enemy to the public interests, and which prevents such buying, except at prices arbitrarily fixed by it. I insist that the free course of trade among the states cannot coexist with such combinations. When I speak of trade I mean the buying and selling of articles of every kind that are recognized articles of interstate commerce. Whatever improperly obstructs the free course of interstate intercourse and trade, as involved in the buying and selling of articles to be carried from one state to another, may be reached by Congress, under its authority to regulate commerce among the states. The exercise of that authority so as to make trade among the states, in all recognized articles of commerce, absolutely free from unreasonable or illegal restrictions imposed by combinations, is justified by an express grant of power to Congress and would redound to the welfare of the whole country. I am unable to perceive that any such result would imperil the autonomy of the states, especially as that result cannot be attained through the action of any one state.

• • •

While the opinion of the court in this case does not declare the Act of 1890 to be unconstitutional, it defeats the main object for which it was passed. For, it is, in effect, held that the statute would be unconstitutional if interpreted as embracing such unlawful restraints upon the purchasing of goods in one state to be carried to another state as necessarily arise from the *existence* of combinations formed for the purpose and with the effect, not only [of] monopolizing the ownership of all such goods in every part of the country, but of controlling the prices for them in all the states. This view of the scope of the Act leaves the public, so far as national power is concerned, entirely at the mercy of combinations which arbitrarily control the prices of articles purchased to be transported from one state to another state. I cannot assent to that view. In my judgment, the general government is not placed by the Constitution in such a condition of helplessness that it must fold its arms and remain inactive while capital combines, under the name of a corporation, to destroy competition, not in one state only, but throughout the entire country, in the buying and selling of articles—especially the necessaries of life—that go into commerce among the states. The doctrine of the autonomy of the states cannot properly be invoked to justify a denial of power in the national government to meet such an emergency, involving as it does that freedom of commercial intercourse among the states which the Constitution sought to attain.

It is said that there are no proofs in the record which indicate an intention upon the part of the American Sugar Refining Company and its associates to put a restraint upon trade or commerce. Was it necessary that formal proof be made that the persons engaged in this combination admitted, in words, that they intended to restrain trade or commerce? Did any one expect to find in the written agreements which resulted in the formation of this combination a distinct expression of a purpose to restrain interstate trade or commerce? Men who form and control these combinations are too cautious and wary to make such admissions orally or in writing. Why, it is conceded that the object of this combination was to obtain control of the business of making and selling refined sugar throughout the entire country. Those interested in its operations will be satisfied with nothing less than to have the whole population of America pay tribute to them. That object is disclosed upon the very face of the transactions described in the bill. And it is proved—indeed, is conceded—that that object has been accomplished to the extent that the American Sugar Refining Company now controls ninety-eight per cent of all the sugar refining business in the country, and therefore controls the price of that article everywhere. Now, the mere existence of a combination having such an object and possessing such extraordinary power is itself, under settled principles of law—there being no adjudged case to the contrary in this country—a direct restraint of trade in the article for the control of the sales of which in this country that combination was organized. And that restraint is felt in all the states, for the reason, known to all, that the article in question goes, was intended to go, and must always go, into commerce among the several states, and into the homes of people in every condition of life.

• • •

We have before us the case of a combination which absolutely controls, or may, at its discretion, control the price of all refined sugar in this country. Suppose another combination, organized for private gain and to control prices, should obtain possession of all the large flour mills in the United States; another, of all the grain elevators; another, of all the oil territory; another, of all the salt producing regions; another, of all the cotton mills; and another, of all the great establishments for slaughtering animals, and the preparation of meats. What power is competent to protect the people of the United States against such dangers except a national power—one that is capable of exerting its sovereign authority throughout every part of the territory and over all the people of the nation?

To the general government has been committed the control of commercial intercourse among the states, to the end that it may be free at all times from any restraints except such as Congress may impose or permit for the benefit of the whole country. The common government of all the people is the only one that can adequately deal with a matter which directly and injuriously affects the entire commerce of the country, which concerns equally all the people of the Union, and which, it must be confessed, cannot be adequately controlled by any one state. Its authority should not be so weakened by construction that it cannot reach and eradicate evils that, beyond all question, tend to defeat an object which that government is entitled, by the Constitution, to accomplish. . . .

*   *   *

For the reasons stated I dissent from the opinion and judgment of the court.

National Labor Relations Board v. Jones & Laughlin Steel Corp.

301 U.S. 1 (1937)

MR. CHIEF JUSTICE HUGHES delivered the opinion of the Court.

In a proceeding under the National Labor Relations Act of 1935, the National Labor Relations Board found that the respondent, Jones & Laughlin Steel Corporation, had violated the Act by engaging in unfair labor practices affecting commerce. . . . The unfair labor practices charged were that the corporation was discriminating against members of the union with regard to hire and tenure of employment, and was coercing and intimidating its employees in order to interfere with their self-organization. The discriminatory and coercive action alleged was the discharge of certain employees.

The National Labor Relations Board, sustaining the charge, ordered the corporation to cease and desist from such discrimination and coercion, to offer reinstatement to ten of the employees named, to make good their losses in pay, and to post for thirty days notices that the corporation would not discharge or discriminate against members, or those desiring to become members, of the labor union. As the corporation failed to comply, the Board petitioned the Circuit Court of Appeals to enforce the order. The court denied the petition, holding that the order lay beyond the range of federal power. * * * We granted certiorari.

The scheme of the National Labor Relations Act . . . may be briefly stated. The first section sets forth findings with respect to the injury to commerce resulting from the denial by employers of the right of employees to organize and from the refusal of employers to accept the procedure of collective bargaining. There follows a declaration that it is the policy of the United States to eliminate these causes of obstruction to the free flow of commerce. The Act then defines the terms it uses, including the terms "commerce" and "affecting commerce." * * * It creates the National Labor Relations Board and prescribes its organization. * * * It sets forth the right of employees to self-organization and to bargain collectively through representatives of their own choosing. * * * It defines "unfair labor practices." * * * It lays down rules as to the representation of employees for the purpose of collective bargaining. * * * The Board is empowered to prevent the described unfair labor practices affecting commerce and the Act prescribes the procedure to that end. The Board is authorized to petition designated courts to secure the enforcement of its orders. The findings of the Board as to the facts, if supported by evidence, are to be conclusive. If either party on application to the court shows that additional evidence is material and that there were reasonable grounds for the failure to adduce such evidence in the hearings before the Board, the court may order the additional evidence to be taken. Any person aggrieved by a final order of the Board may obtain a review in the designated courts with the same procedure as in the case of an application by the Board for the enforcement of its order. * * * The Board has broad powers of investigation. * * * Interference with members of the Board or its agents in the performance of their duties is punishable by fine and imprisonment. * * * Nothing in the Act is to be construed to interfere with the right to strike. . . .

The procedure in the instant case followed the statute. . . .

Contesting the ruling of the Board, [Jones & Laughlin] argues (1) that the Act is in reality a regulation of labor relations and not of interstate commerce; [and] (2) that the Act can have no application to the respondent's relations with its production employees because they are not subject to regulation by the federal government. . . .

* * *

First. The scope of the Act.—The Act is challenged in its entirety as an attempt to regulate all industry, thus invading the reserved powers of the States over their local concerns. It is asserted that the references in the Act to interstate and foreign commerce are colorable at best; that the Act is not a true regulation of such commerce or of matters which directly affect it but on the contrary has the fundamental object of placing under the compulsory supervision of the federal government all industrial labor relations within the nation. . . .

If this conception of terms, intent and consequent inseparability were sound, the Act would necessarily fall by reason of the limitation upon the federal power which inheres in the constitutional grant, as well as because of the explicit reservation of the Tenth Amendment. * * * The authority of the federal government may not be pushed to such an extreme as to destroy the distinction, which the commerce clause itself establishes, between commerce "among the several States" and the internal concerns of a State. That distinction between what is national and what is local in the activities of commerce is vital to the maintenance of our federal system. * * *

But we are not at liberty to deny effect to specific provisions, which Congress has constitutional power to enact, by superimposing upon them inferences from general legislative declarations of an ambiguous character, even if found in the same statute. The cardinal principle of statutory construction is to save and not to destroy. We have repeatedly held that as between two possible interpretations of a statute, by one of which it would be unconstitutional and by the other valid, our plain duty is to adopt that which will save the act. . . .

We think it clear that the National Labor Relations Act may be construed so as to operate within the sphere of constitutional authority. . . .

* * *

There can be no question that the commerce . . . contemplated by the Act . . . is interstate and foreign commerce in the constitutional sense. The Act also defines the term "affecting commerce." * * *

* * *

This definition is one of exclusion as well as inclusion. The grant of authority to the Board does not purport to extend to the relationship between all industrial employees and employers. Its terms do not impose collective bargaining upon all industry regardless of effects upon interstate or foreign commerce. It purports to reach only what may be deemed to burden or obstruct that commerce and, thus qualified, it must be construed as contemplating the exercise of control within constitutional bounds. It is a familiar principle that acts which directly burden or obstruct interstate or foreign commerce, or its free flow, are within the reach of the congressional power. Acts having that effect are not rendered immune because they grow out of labor disputes. * * * It is the effect upon commerce, not the source of the injury, which is the criterion. * * * Whether or not particular action does affect commerce in such a close and intimate fashion as to be subject to federal control, and hence to lie within the authority conferred upon the Board, is left by the statute to be determined as individual cases arise. We are thus to inquire whether in the instant case the constitutional boundary has been passed.

Second. The unfair labor practices in question. . . .

• • •

. . . [I]n its present application, the statute goes no further than to safeguard the right of employees to self-organization and to select representatives of their own choosing for collective bargaining or other mutual protection without restraint or coercion by their employer.

That is a fundamental right. Employees have as clear a right to organize and select their representatives for lawful purposes as the respondent has to organize its business and select its own officers and agents. Discrimination and coercion to prevent the free exercise of the right of employees to self-organization and representation is a proper subject for condemnation by competent legislative authority. Long ago we stated the reason for labor organizations. We said that they were organized out of the necessities of the situation; that a single employee was helpless in dealing with an employer; that he was dependent ordinarily on his daily wage for the maintenance of himself and family; that if the employer refused to pay him the wages that he thought fair, he was nevertheless unable to leave the employ and resist arbitrary and unfair treatment; that union was essential to give laborers opportunity to deal on an equality with their employer. * * * . . . Fully recognizing the legality of collective action on the part of employees in order to safeguard their proper interests, we said that Congress was not required to ignore this right but could safeguard it. Congress could seek to make appropriate collective action of employees an instrument of peace rather than of strife. We said that such collective action would be a mockery if representation were made futile by interference with freedom of choice. Hence the prohibition by Congress of interference with the selection of representatives for the purpose of negotiation and conference between employers and employees, "instead of being an invasion of the constitutional right of either, was based on the recognition of the rights of both." * * *

Third. The application of the Act to employees engaged in production.—The principle involved.—Respondent [Jones & Laughlin Steel Corp.] says that whatever may be said of employees engaged in interstate commerce, the industrial relations and activities in the manufacturing department . . . are not subject to federal regulation. The argument rests upon the proposition that manufacturing in itself is not commerce. * * *

. . . The various parts of respondent's enterprise are described as interdependent and as thus involving "a great movement of iron ore, coal and limestone along well-defined paths to the steel mills, thence through them, and thence in the form of steel products into the consuming centers of the country—a definite and well-understood course of business." It is urged that these activities constitute a "stream" or "flow" of commerce . . . and that industrial strife at [the central manufacturing plant of Jones & Laughlin] would cripple the entire movement. * * * . . .

. . .

We do not find it necessary to determine whether these features of [Jones & Laughlin's] business dispose of the asserted analogy to the "stream of commerce" cases. The instances in which that metaphor has been used are but particular, and not exclusive, illustrations of the protective power which the Government invokes in support of the present Act. The congressional authority to protect interstate commerce from burdens and obstructions is not limited to transactions which can be deemed to be an essential part of a "flow" of interstate or foreign commerce. Burdens and obstructions may be due to injurious action springing from other sources. The fundamental principle is that the power to regulate commerce is the power to enact "all appropriate legislation" for "its protection and advancement"; * * * to adopt measures "to promote its growth and insure its safety"; * * * "to foster, protect, control and restrain." * * * That power is plenary and may be exerted to protect interstate commerce "no matter what the source of the dangers which threaten it." * * * Although activities may be intrastate in character when separately considered, if they have such a close and substantial relation to interstate commerce that their control is essential or appropriate to protect that commerce from burdens and obstructions, Congress cannot be denied the power to exercise that control. * * * Undoubtedly the scope of this power must be considered in the light of our dual system of government and may not be extended so as to embrace effects upon interstate commerce so indirect and remote that to embrace them, in view of our complex society, would effectually obliterate the distinction between what is national and what is local and create a completely centralized government. * * * The question is necessarily one of degree. . . .

That intrastate activities, by reason of close and intimate relation to interstate commerce, may fall within federal control is demonstrated in the case of carriers who are engaged in both interstate and intrastate transportation. There federal control has been found essential to secure the freedom of interstate traffic from interference or unjust discrimination and to promote the efficiency of the interstate service. * * * It is manifest that intrastate rates deal *primarily* with a local activity. But in rate-making they bear such a close relation to interstate rates that effective control of the one must embrace some control over the other. . . .

The close and intimate effect which brings the subject within the reach of federal power may be due to activities in relation to productive industry although the industry when separately viewed is local. . . .

• • •

It is . . . apparent that the fact that the employees here concerned were engaged in production is not determinative. The question remains as to the effect upon interstate commerce of the labor practice involved. In the *Schechter* case, * * * we found that the effect there was so remote as to be beyond the federal power. To find "immediacy or directness" there was to find it "almost everywhere," a result inconsistent with the maintenance of our federal system. In the *Carter* case, * * * the Court was of the opinion that the provisions of the statute relating to production were invalid upon several grounds,—that there was improper delegation of legislative power, and that the requirements not only went beyond any sustainable measure of protection of interstate commerce but were also inconsistent with due process. These cases are not controlling here.

Fourth. Effects of the unfair labor practice in respondent's enterprise.— . . . [T]he stoppage of [Jones & Laughlin] operations by industrial strife would have a most serious effect upon interstate commerce. In view of respondent's far-flung activities, it is idle to say that the effect would be indirect or remote. It is obvious that it would be immediate and might be catastrophic. We are asked to shut our eyes to the plainest facts of our national life and to deal with the question of direct and indirect effects in an intellectual vacuum. Because there may be but indirect and remote effects upon interstate commerce in connection with a host of local enterprises throughout the country, it does not follow that other industrial activities do not have such a close and intimate relation to interstate commerce as to make the presence of industrial strife a matter of the most urgent national concern. When industries organize themselves on a national scale, making their relation to interstate commerce the dominant factor in their activities, how can it be maintained that their industrial labor relations constitute a forbidden field into which Congress may not enter when it is necessary to protect interstate commerce from the paralyzing consequences of industrial war? We have often said that interstate commerce itself is a practical conception. It is equally true that interferences with that commerce must be appraised by a judgment that does not ignore actual experience.

Experience has abundantly demonstrated that the recognition of the right of employees to self-organization and to have representatives of their own choosing for the purpose of collective bargaining is often an essential condition of industrial peace. Refusal to confer and negotiate has been one of the most prolific causes of strife. This is such an outstanding fact in the history of labor disturbances that it is a proper subject of judicial notice and requires no citation of instances. . . .

These questions have frequently engaged the attention of Congress and have been the subject of many inquiries. The steel industry is one of the great basic industries of the United States, with ramifying activities affecting interstate commerce at every point. . . . It is not necessary again to detail the facts as to respondent's enterprise. Instead of being beyond the pale, we think that it presents in a most striking way the close and intimate relation which a manufacturing industry may have to interstate commerce and we have no doubt that Congress had constitutional authority to safeguard the right of [Jones & Laughlin's] employees to self-organization and freedom in the choice of representatives for collective bargaining.

• • •

Our conclusion is that the order of the Board was within its competency and that the Act is valid as here applied. The judgment of the Circuit Court of Appeals is reversed and the cause is remanded for further proceedings in conformity with this opinion.

Reversed.

• • •

MR. JUSTICE MCREYNOLDS delivered the following dissenting opinion. . . .

MR. JUSTICE VAN DEVANTER, MR. JUSTICE SUTHERLAND, MR. JUSTICE BUTLER and I are unable to agree with the [decision] just announced.

• • •

Considering [its] far-reaching import . . . , the departure from what we understand has been consistently ruled here, and the extraordinary power confirmed to a Board of three, the obligation to present our views becomes plain.

• • •

Any effect on interstate commerce by the discharge of employees shown here, would be indirect and remote in the highest degree, as consideration of the facts will show. In [this case] ten men out of ten thousand were discharged. . . . The immediate effect in the factory may be to create discontent among all those employed and a strike may follow, which, in turn, may result in reducing production, which ultimately may reduce the volume of goods moving in interstate commerce. By this chain of indirect and progressively remote events we finally reach the evil with which it is said the legislation under consideration undertakes to deal. A more remote and indirect interference with interstate commerce or a more definite invasion of the powers reserved to the states is difficult, if not impossible, to imagine.

The Constitution still recognizes the existence of states with indestructible powers; the Tenth Amendment was supposed to put them beyond controversy.

We are told that Congress may protect the "stream of commerce" and that one who buys raw material without the state, manufactures it therein, and ships the output to another state is in that stream. Therefore it is said he may be prevented from doing anything which may interfere with its flow.

This, too, goes beyond the constitutional limitations heretofore enforced. If a man raises cattle and regularly delivers them to a carrier for interstate shipment, may Congress prescribe the conditions under which he may employ or discharge helpers on the ranch? The products of a mine pass daily into interstate commerce; many things are brought to it from other states. Are the owners and the miners within the power of Congress in respect of the miners' tenure and discharge? May a mill owner be prohibited from closing his factory or discontinuing his business because so to do would stop the flow of products to and from his plant in interstate commerce? May employees in a factory be restrained from quitting work in a body because this will close the factory and thereby stop the flow of commerce? May arson of a factory be made a Federal offense whenever this would interfere with such flow? If the business cannot continue with the existing wage scale, may Congress command a reduction? If the ruling of the Court just announced is adhered to, these questions suggest some of the problems certain to arise.

And if this theory of a continuous "stream of commerce" as now defined is correct, will it become the duty of the Federal Government hereafter to suppress every strike which by possibility may cause a blockade in that stream? * * * Moreover, since Congress has intervened, are labor relations between most manufacturers and their employees removed from all control by the state? * * *

• • •

There is no ground on which reasonably to hold that refusal by a manufacturer, whose raw materials come from states other than that of his factory and whose products are regularly carried to other states, to bargain collectively with employees in his manufacturing plant, directly affects interstate commerce. In such business, there is not one but two distinct movements or streams in interstate transportation. The first brings in raw material and there ends. Then follows manufacture, a separate and local activity. Upon completion of this, and not before, the second distinct movement or stream in interstate commerce begins and the products go to other states. Such is the common course for small as well as large industries. It is unreasonable and unprecedented to say the commerce clause confers upon Congress power to govern relations between employers and employees in these local activities. * * * In *Schechter's* case we condemned as unauthorized by the commerce clause assertion of federal power in respect of commodities which had come to rest after interstate transportation. And, in *Carter's* case, we held Congress lacked power to regulate labor relations in respect of commodities before interstate commerce has begun.

It is gravely stated that experience teaches that if an employer discourages membership in "any organization of any kind" "in which employees participate, and which exists for the purpose in whole or in part of dealing with employers concerning grievances, labor disputes, wages, rates of pay, hours of employment or conditions of work," discontent may follow and this in turn may lead to a strike, and as the outcome of the strike there may be a block in the stream of interstate commerce. Therefore Congress may inhibit the discharge! Whatever effect any cause of discontent may ultimately have upon commerce is far too indirect to justify Congressional regulation. Almost anything—marriage, birth, death—may in some fashion affect commerce.

That Congress has power by appropriate means, not prohibited by the Constitution, to prevent direct and material interference with the conduct of interstate commerce is settled doctrine. But the interference struck at must be direct and material, not some mere possibility contingent on wholly uncertain events; and there must be no impairment of rights guaranteed. . . .

. . .

The right to contract is fundamental and includes the privilege of selecting those with whom one is willing to assume contractual relations. This right is unduly abridged by the Act now upheld. A private owner is deprived of power to manage his own property by freely selecting those to whom his manufacturing operations are to be entrusted. We think this cannot lawfully be done in circumstances like those here disclosed.

It seems clear to us that Congress has transcended the powers granted.

Wickard v. Filburn

317 U.S. 111 (1942)

MR. JUSTICE JACKSON delivered the opinion of the Court.

. . .

[Filburn] for many years past has owned and operated a small farm in Montgomery County, Ohio, maintaining a herd of dairy cattle, selling milk, raising poultry, and selling poultry and eggs. It has been his practice to raise a small acreage of winter wheat, sown in the Fall and harvested in the following July; to sell a portion of the crop; to feed part to poultry and livestock on the farm, some of which is sold; to use some in making flour for home consumption; and to keep the rest for the following seeding. The intended disposition of the crop here involved has not been expressly stated.

In July of 1940, pursuant to the Agricultural Adjustment Act of 1938, as then amended, there were established for [Filburn's] 1941 crop a wheat acreage allotment of 11.1 acres and a normal yield of 20.1 bushels of wheat an acre. He was given notice of such allotment in July of 1940 before the Fall planting of his 1941 crop of wheat, and again in July of 1941, before it was harvested. He sowed, however, 23 acres, and harvested from his 11.9 acres of excess acreage 239 bushels, which under the terms of the Act . . . constituted farm marketing excess, subject to a penalty of 49 cents a bushel, or $117.11 in all. [Filburn] has not paid the penalty and he has not postponed or avoided it by storing the excess under regulations of the Secretary of Agriculture. . . .

The general scheme of the Agricultural Adjustment Act of 1938 as related to wheat is to control the volume moving in interstate and foreign commerce in order to avoid surpluses and shortages and the consequent abnormally low or high wheat prices and obstructions to commerce. Within prescribed limits and by prescribed standards the Secretary of Agriculture is directed to ascertain and proclaim each year a national acreage allotment for the next crop of wheat, which is then apportioned to the states and their counties, and is eventually broken up into allotments for individual farms. Loans and payments to wheat farmers are authorized in stated circumstances.

The Act provides further that whenever it appears that the total supply of wheat as of the beginning of any marketing year . . . will exceed a normal year's domestic consumption and export . . . a compulsory national marketing quota shall be in effect with respect to the marketing of wheat. . . . [T]he Secretary must . . . conduct a referendum of farmers who will be subject to the quota to determine whether they favor or oppose it; and if more than one third of the farmers voting in the referendum do oppose, the Secretary must prior to the effective date of the quota by proclamation suspend its operation.

· · ·

Pursuant to the Act, the referendum of wheat growers was held on May 31, 1941. According to the required published statement of the Secretary of Agriculture, 81 per cent of those voting favored the marketing quota, with 19 per cent opposed.

· · ·

It is urged that under the Commerce Clause of the Constitution, Article 1, § 8, clause 3, Congress does not possess the power it has in this instance sought to exercise. The question would merit little consideration since our decision in United States v. Darby, * * * sustaining the federal power to regulate production of goods for commerce except for the fact that this Act extends federal regulation to production not intended in any part for commerce but wholly for consumption on the farm. The Act includes a definition of "market" and its derivatives so that as related to wheat in addition to its conventional meaning it also means to dispose of "by feeding (in any form) to poultry or livestock which, or the products of which, are sold, bartered, or exchanged, or to be so disposed of." Hence, marketing quotas not only embrace all that may be sold without penalty but also what may be consumed on the premises. Wheat produced on excess acreage is designated as "available for marketing" as so defined and the penalty is imposed thereon. Penalties do not depend upon whether any part of the wheat either within or without the quota is sold or intended to be sold. The sum of this is that the Federal Government fixes a quota including all that the farmer may harvest for sale or for his own farm needs, and declares that wheat produced on excess acreage may neither be disposed of nor used except upon payment of the penalty or except it is stored as required by the Act or delivered to the Secretary of Agriculture.

[Filburn] says that this is a regulation of production and consumption of wheat. Such activities are, he urges, beyond the reach of congressional power under the Commerce Clause, since they are local in character, and their effects upon interstate commerce are at most "indirect." In answer the Government argues that the statute regulates neither production nor consumption, but only marketing; and, in the alternative, that if the Act does go beyond the regulation of marketing it is sustainable as a "necessary and proper" implementation of the power of Congress over interstate commerce.

The Government's concern lest the Act be held to be a regulation of production or consumption rather than of marketing is attributable to a few dicta and decisions of this Court which might be understood to lay it down that activities such as "production," "manufacturing," and "mining" are strictly "local" and, except in special circumstances which are not present here, cannot be regulated under the commerce power because their effects upon interstate commerce are, as matter of law, only "indirect." Even today, when this power has been held to have great latitude, there is no decision of this Court that such activities may be regulated where no part of the product is intended for interstate commerce or intermingled with the subjects thereof. We believe that a review of the course of decision under the Commerce Clause will make plain, however, that questions of the power of Congress are not to be decided by reference to any formula which would give controlling force to nomenclature such as "production" and "indirect" and foreclose consideration of the actual effects of the activity in question upon interstate commerce.

At the beginning Chief Justice Marshall described the federal commerce power with a breadth never yet exceeded. He made emphatic the embracing and penetrating nature of this power by warning that effective restraints on its exercise must proceed from political rather than from judicial processes.
* * *

For nearly a century, however, decisions of this Court under the Commerce Clause dealt rarely with questions of what Congress might do in the exercise of its granted power under the Clause and almost entirely with the permissibility of state activity which it was claimed discriminated against or burdened interstate commerce. During this period there was perhaps little occasion for the affirmative exercise of the commerce power, and the influence of the Clause on American life and law was a negative one, resulting almost wholly from its operation as a restraint upon the powers of the states. In discussion and decision the point of reference, instead of being what was "necessary and proper" to the exercise by Congress of its granted power, was often some concept of sovereignty thought to be implicit in the status of statehood. Certain activities such as "production," "manufacturing," and "mining" were occasionally said to be within the province of state governments and beyond the power of Congress under the Commerce Clause.

It was not until 1887 with the enactment of the Interstate Commerce Act that the interstate commerce power began to exert positive influence in American law and life. This first important federal resort to the commerce power was followed in 1890 by the Sherman Anti-trust Act and, thereafter, mainly after 1903, by many others. These statutes ushered in new phases of adjudication, which required the Court to approach the interpretation of the Commerce Clause in the light of an actual exercise by Congress of its power thereunder.

When it first dealt with this new legislation, the Court adhered to its earlier pronouncements, and allowed but little scope to the power of Congress. * * *

Even while important opinions in this line of restrictive authority were being written, however, other cases called forth broader interpretations of the Commerce Clause destined to supersede the earlier ones,—and to bring about a return to the principles first enunciated by Chief Justice Marshall in Gibbons v. Ogden. * * *

．　．　．

The Court's recognition of the relevance of the economic effects in the application of the Commerce Clause . . . has made the mechanical application of legal formulas no longer feasible. Once an economic measure of the reach of the power granted to Congress in the Commerce Clause is accepted, questions of federal power cannot be decided simply by finding the activity in question to be "production" nor can consideration of its economic effects be foreclosed by calling them "indirect." . . .

Whether the subject of the regulation in question was "production," "consumption," or "marketing" is, therefore, not material for purposes of deciding the question of federal power before us. That an activity is of local character may help in a doubtful case to determine whether Congress intended to reach it. The same consideration might help in determining whether in the absence of congressional action it would be permissible for the state to exert its power on the subject matter, even though in so doing it to some degree affected interstate commerce. But even if [Filburn's] activity be local and though it may not be regarded as commerce, it may still, whatever its nature, be reached by Congress if it exerts a substantial economic effect on interstate commerce, and this irrespective of whether such effect is what might at some earlier time have been defined as "direct" or "indirect."

*   *   *

The wheat industry has been a problem industry for some years. . . . The decline in the export trade has left a large surplus in production which in connection with an abnormally large supply of wheat and other grains in recent years caused congestion in a number of markets; tied up railroad cars; and caused elevators in some instances to turn away grains, and railroads to institute embargoes to prevent further congestion.

*   *   *

In the absence of regulation the price of wheat in the United States would be much affected by world conditions. . . .

*   *   *

The effect of consumption of home-grown wheat on interstate commerce is due to the fact that it constitutes the most variable factor in the disappearance of the wheat crop. Consumption on the farm where grown appears to vary in an amount greater than 20 per cent of average production. The total amount of wheat consumed as food varies but relatively little, and use as seed is relatively constant.

The maintenance by government regulation of a price for wheat undoubtedly can be accomplished as effectively by sustaining or increasing the demand as by limiting the supply. The effect of the statute before us is to restrict the amount which may be produced for market and the extent as well to which one may forestall resort to the market by producing to meet his own needs. That [Filburn's] own contribution to the demand for wheat may be trivial by itself is not enough to remove him from the scope of federal regulation where, as here, his contribution, taken together with that of many others similarly situated, is far from trivial. * * *

It is well established by decisions of this Court that the power to regulate commerce includes the power to regulate the prices at which commodities in that commerce are dealt in and practices affecting such prices. One of the primary purposes of the Act in question was to increase the market price of wheat and to that end to limit the volume thereof that could affect the market. It can hardly be denied that a factor of such volume and variability as home-consumed wheat would have a substantial influence on price and market conditions. This may arise because being in marketable condition such wheat overhangs the market and if induced by rising prices tends to flow into the market and check price increases. But if we assume that it is never marketed, it supplies a need of the man who grew it which would otherwise be reflected by purchases in the open market. Home-grown wheat in this sense competes with wheat in commerce. The stimulation of commerce is a use of the regulatory function quite as definitely as prohibitions or restrictions thereon. This record leaves us in no doubt that Congress may properly have considered that wheat consumed on the farm where grown if wholly outside the scheme of regulation would have a substantial effect in defeating and obstructing its purpose to stimulate trade therein at increased prices.

It is said, however, that this Act, forcing some farmers into the market to buy what they could provide for themselves, is an unfair promotion of the markets and prices of specializing wheat growers. It is of the essence of regulation that it lays a restraining hand on the self-interest of the regulated and that advantages from the regulation commonly fall to others. The conflicts of economic interest between the regulated and those who advantage by it are wisely left under our system to resolution by the Congress under its more flexible and responsible legislative process. Such conflicts rarely lend themselves to judicial determination. And with the wisdom, workability, or fairness, of the plan of regulation we have nothing to do.

Katzenbach v. McClung

379 U.S. 294 (1964)

Mr. Justice Clark delivered the opinion of the Court.

. . .

The Facts

Ollie's Barbecue is a family-owned restaurant in Birmingham, Alabama, specializing in barbecued meats and homemade pies, with a seating capacity of 220 customers. It is located on a state highway 11 blocks from an interstate . . . and a somewhat greater distance from railroad and bus stations. The restaurant caters to a family and white-collar trade with a take-out service for Negroes. It employs 36 persons, two-thirds of whom are Negroes.

In the 12 months preceding the passage of the [Civil Rights Act of 1964], the restaurant purchased locally approximately $150,000 worth of food, . . . 46% of which was meat that it bought from a local supplier who had procured it from outside the State. The District Court expressly found that a substantial portion of the food served in the restaurant had moved in interstate commerce. The restaurant has refused to serve Negroes in its dining accommodations since its original opening in 1927, and since July 2, 1964, it has been operating in violation of the Act. The court below concluded that if it were required to serve Negroes it would lose a substantial amount of business.

On the merits, the District Court held that the Act could not be applied under the Fourteenth Amendment because it was conceded that the State of Alabama was not involved in the refusal of the restaurant to serve Negroes. . . . As to the Commerce Clause, the court found that it was "an express grant of power to Congress to regulate interstate commerce, which consists of the movement of persons, goods or information from one state to another"; and it found that the clause was also a grant of power "to regulate intrastate activities, but only to the extent that action on its part is necessary or appropriate to the effective execution of its expressly granted power to regulate interstate commerce." There must be, it said, a close and substantial relation between local activities and interstate commerce which requires control of the former in the protection of the latter. The court concluded, however, that the Congress, rather than finding facts sufficient to meet this rule, had legislated a conclusive presumption that a restaurant affects interstate commerce if it serves or offers to serve interstate travelers or if a substantial portion of the food which it serves has moved in commerce. This, the court held, it could not do because there was no demonstrable connection between food purchased in interstate commerce and sold in a restaurant and the conclusion of Congress that discrimination in the restaurant would affect that commerce.

The basic holding in *Heart of Atlanta Motel*, answers many of the contentions made by the appellees. There we outlined the overall purpose and operational plan of Title II and found it a valid exercise of the power to regulate interstate commerce insofar as it requires hotels and motels to serve transients without regard to their race or color. In this case we consider its application to restaurants which serve food a substantial portion of which has moved in commerce.

The Act As Applied

. . . Title II [of the Civil Rights Act of 1964] commands that all persons shall be entitled to the full and equal enjoyment of the goods and services of any place of public accommodation without discrimination or segregation on the ground of race, color, religion, or national origin; and * * * defines establishments as places of public accommodation if their operations affect commerce or segregation by them is supported by state action. * * * [Further, specific sections] place any "restaurant . . . principally engaged in selling food for consumption on the premises" under the Act "if . . . it serves or offers to serve interstate travelers or a substantial portion of the food which it serves . . . has moved in commerce."

Ollie's Barbecue admits that it is covered by these provisions of the Act. The Government makes no contention that the discrimination at the restaurant was supported by the State of Alabama. There is no claim that interstate travelers frequented the restaurant. The sole question, therefore, narrows down to whether Title II, as applied to a restaurant annually receiving about $70,000 worth of food which has moved in commerce, is a valid exercise of the power of Congress. The Government has contended that Congress had ample basis upon which to find that racial discrimination at restaurants which receive from out of state a substantial portion of the food served does, in fact, impose commercial burdens of national magnitude upon interstate commerce. The appellees' major argument is directed to this premise. They urge that no such basis existed. It is to that question that we now turn.

The Congressional Hearings

. . . [B]oth Houses of Congress conducted prolonged hearings on the Act. And . . . while no formal findings were made, . . . it is well that we make mention of the testimony at these hearings the better to understand the problem before Congress and determine whether the Act is a reasonable and appropriate means toward its solution. The record is replete with testimony of the burdens placed on interstate commerce by racial discrimination in restaurants. A comparison of per capita spending by Negroes in restaurants, theaters, and like establishments indicated less spending, after discounting income differences, in areas where discrimination is widely practiced. This condition, which was especially aggravated in the South, was attributed in the testimony of the Under Secretary of Commerce to racial segregation. * * * This diminutive spending springing from a refusal to serve Negroes and their total loss as customers has, regardless of the absence of direct evidence, a close connection to interstate commerce. The fewer customers a restaurant enjoys the less food it sells and consequently the less it buys. * * * In addition, the Attorney General testified that this type of discrimination imposed "an artificial restriction on the market" and interfered with the flow of merchandise. * * * In addition, there were many references to discriminatory situations causing wide unrest and having a depressant effect on general business conditions in the respective communities. * * *

Moreover there was an impressive array of testimony that discrimination in restaurants had a direct and highly restrictive effect upon interstate travel by Negroes. This resulted, it was said, because discriminatory practices prevent Negroes from buying prepared food served on the premises while on a trip, except in isolated and unkempt restaurants and under most unsatisfactory and often unpleasant conditions. This obviously discourages travel and obstructs interstate commerce for one can hardly travel without eating. Likewise, it was said, that discrimination deterred professional, as well as skilled, people from moving into areas where such practices occurred and thereby caused industry to be reluctant to establish there. * * *

We believe that this testimony afforded ample basis for the conclusion that established restaurants in such areas sold less interstate goods because of the discrimination, that interstate travel was obstructed directly by it, that business in general suffered and that many new businesses refrained from establishing there as a result of it. Hence the District Court was in error in concluding that there was no connection between discrimination and the movement of interstate commerce. The court's conclusion that such a connection is outside "common experience" flies in the face of stubborn fact.

It goes without saying that, viewed in isolation, the volume of food purchased by Ollie's Barbecue from sources supplied from out of state was insignificant when compared with the total foodstuffs moving in commerce. But, as our late Brother Jackson said for the Court in *Wickard* v. *Filburn* * * *

"That [Filburn's] own contribution to the demand for wheat may be trivial by itself is not enough to remove him from the scope of federal regulation where, as here, his contribution, taken together with that of many others similarly situated, is far from trivial." * * *

. . .

The Power of Congress to Regulate Local Activities

Article I, § 8, cl. 3, confers upon Congress the power "[t]o regulate Commerce . . . among the several States" and Clause 18 of the same Article grants it the power "[t]o make all Laws which shall be necessary and proper for carrying into Execution the foregoing Powers. . . ." This grant, . . . "extends to those activities intrastate which so affect interstate commerce, or the exertion of the power of Congress over it, as to make regulation of them appropriate means to the attainment of a legitimate end, the effective execution of the granted power to regulate interstate commerce." * * * Much is said about a restaurant business being local but "even if appellee's activity be local and though it may not be regarded as commerce, it may still, whatever its nature, be reached by Congress if it exerts a substantial economic effect on interstate commerce. . . ." * * * The activities that are beyond the reach of Congress are "those which are completely within a particular State, which do not affect other States, and with which it is not necessary to interfere, for the purpose of executing some of the general powers of the government." * * * This rule is as good today as it was when Chief Justice Marshall laid it down almost a century and a half ago.

This Court has held time and again that this power extends to activities of retail establishments, including restaurants, which directly or indirectly burden or obstruct interstate commerce. . . .

. . .

[The McClungs] contend that Congress has arbitrarily created a conclusive presumption that all restaurants meeting the criteria set out in the Act "affect commerce." Stated another way, they object to the omission of a provision for a case-by-case determination—judicial or administrative—that racial discrimination in a particular restaurant affects commerce.

But Congress' action in framing this Act was not unprecedented. . . .

Here . . . Congress has determined for itself that refusals of service to Negroes have imposed burdens both upon the interstate flow of food and upon the movement of products generally. Of course, the mere fact that Congress has said when particular activity shall be deemed to affect commerce does not preclude further examination by this Court. But where we find that the legislators, in light of the facts and testimony before them, have a rational basis for finding a chosen regulatory scheme necessary to the protection of commerce, our investigation is at an end. The only remaining question—one answered in the affirmative by the court below—is whether the particular restaurant either serves or offers to serve interstate travelers or serves food a substantial portion of which has moved in interstate commerce.

• • •

Confronted as we are with the facts laid before Congress, we must conclude that it had a rational basis for finding that racial discrimination in restaurants had a direct and adverse effect on the free flow of interstate commerce. Insofar as the sections of the Act here relevant are concerned, * * * Congress prohibited discrimination only in those establishments having a close tie to interstate commerce, i. e., those, like the McClungs', serving food that has come from out of the State. We think in so doing that Congress acted well within its power to protect and foster commerce in extending the coverage of Title II only to those restaurants offering to serve interstate travelers or serving food, a substantial portion of which has moved in interstate commerce.

The absence of direct evidence connecting discriminatory restaurant service with the flow of interstate food, a factor on which the [McClungs] place much reliance, is not, given the evidence as to the effect of such practices on other aspects of commerce, a crucial matter.

The power of Congress in this field is broad and sweeping; where it keeps within its sphere and violates no express constitutional limitation it has been the rule of this Court, going back almost to the founding days of the Republic, not to interfere. The Civil Rights Act of 1964, as here applied, we find to be plainly appropriate in the resolution of what the Congress found to be a national commercial problem of the first magnitude. We find it in no violation of any express limitations of the Constitution and we therefore declare it valid.

The judgment is therefore

Reversed.

MR. JUSTICE DOUGLAS, concurring.

Though I join the Court's opinions, I am somewhat reluctant here * * * to rest solely on the Commerce Clause. My reluctance is not due to any conviction that Congress lacks power to regulate commerce in the interests of human rights. It is rather my belief that the right of people to be free of state action that discriminates against them because of race, like the "right of persons to move freely from State to State" * * * "occupies a more protected position in our constitutional system than does the movement of cattle, fruit, steel and coal across state lines." . . .

Hence I would prefer to rest on the assertion of legislative power contained in § 5 of the Fourteenth Amendment which states: "The Congress shall have power to enforce, by appropriate legislation, the provisions of this article"—a power which the Court concedes was exercised at least in part in this Act.

A decision based on the Fourteenth Amendment would have a more settling effect, making unnecessary litigation over whether a particular restaurant or inn is within the commerce definitions of the Act or whether a particular customer is an interstate traveler. Under my construction, the Act would apply to all customers in all the enumerated places of public accommodation. And that construction would put an end to all obstructionist strategies and finally close one door on a bitter chapter in American history.

•   •   •

MR. JUSTICE BLACK and MR. JUSTICE GOLDBERG also concurred. [Both omitted.]

Goldfarb v. Virginia State Bar

421 U.S. 773 (1975)

MR. CHIEF JUSTICE BURGER delivered the opinion of the Court.

•   •   •

I

In 1971 petitioners, husband and wife, contracted to buy a home in Fairfax County, Virginia. The financing agency required them to secure title insurance; this required a title examination, and only a member of the Virginia State Bar could legally perform that service. [The Goldfarbs] therefore contacted a lawyer who quoted them the precise fee suggested in a minimum fee schedule published by respondent Fairfax County Bar Association; the lawyer told them that it was his policy to keep his charges in line with the minimum fee schedule which provided for a fee of 1% of the value of the property involved. Petitioners then tried to find a lawyer who would examine the title for less than the fee fixed by the schedule. They sent letters to 36 other Fairfax County lawyers requesting their fees. Nineteen replied, and none indicated that he would charge less than the rate fixed by the schedule; several stated that they knew of no attorney who would do so.

The fee schedule the lawyers referred to is a list of recommended minimum prices for common legal services. . . . Fairfax County Bar Association published the fee schedule although, as a purely voluntary association of attorneys, the County Bar has no formal power to enforce it. Enforcement has been provided by . . . [the] Virginia State Bar which is the administrative agency through which the Virginia Supreme Court regulates the practice of law in that State; membership in the State Bar is required in order to practice in Virginia. Although the State Bar has never taken formal disciplinary action to compel adherence to any fee schedule, it has published reports condoning fee schedules, and has issued two ethical opinions indicating fee schedules cannot be ignored. The most recent opinion states that "evidence that an attorney *habitually* charges less than the suggested minimum fee schedule adopted by his local bar association raises a presumption that such lawyer is guilty of misconduct . . . ."

Because petitioners could not find a lawyer willing to charge a fee lower than the schedule dictated they had their title examined by the lawyer they had first contacted. They then brought this class action against the State Bar and the County Bar alleging that the operation of the minimum fee schedule, as applied to fees for legal services relating to residential real estate transactions, constitutes price fixing in violation of § 1 of the Sherman Act. [The Goldfarbs] sought both injunctive relief and damages.

After a trial solely on the issue of liability the District Court held that the minimum fee schedule violated the Sherman Act. * * * The court viewed the fee schedule system as a significant reason for petitioners' failure to obtain legal services for less than the minimum fee, and it rejected the County Bar's contention that as a "learned profession" the practice of law is exempt from the Sherman Act.

• • •

The Court of Appeals reversed as to liability * * * . . . and held the Fairfax Bar immune because the practice of law is not "trade or commerce" under the Sherman Act. There has long been judicial recognition of a limited exclusion of "learned professions" from the scope of the antitrust laws, the court said. . . .

. . . [T]he Court of Appeals held that [the Bar Associations'] activities did not have sufficient effect on interstate commerce to support Sherman Act jurisdiction. [The Goldfarbs] had argued that the fee schedule restrained the business of financing and insuring home mortgages by inflating a component part of the total cost of housing, but the court concluded that a title examination is generally a local service, and even where it is part of a transaction which crosses state lines its effect on commerce is only "incidental," and does not justify federal regulation.

We granted certiorari * * * and are thus confronted for the first time with the question of whether the Sherman Act applies to services performed by attorneys in examining titles in connection with financing the purchase of real estate.

II

Our inquiry can be divided into [three] steps: did [the Bar Associations] engage in price fixing? If so, are their activities in interstate commerce or do they affect interstate commerce? If so, are the activities exempt from the Sherman Act because they involve a "learned profession"? . . .

A

The County Bar argues that because the fee schedule is merely advisory, the schedule and its enforcement mechanism do not constitute price fixing. Its purpose, the argument continues, is only to provide legitimate information to aid member lawyers in complying with Virginia professional regulations. Moreover, the County Bar contends that in practice the schedule has not had the effect of producing fixed fees. The facts found by the trier belie these contentions, and nothing in the record suggests these findings lack support.

A purely advisory fee schedule issued to provide guidelines, or an exchange of price information without a showing of an actual restraint on trade, would present us with a different question. * * * The record here, however, reveals a situation quite different from what would occur under a purely advisory fee schedule. Here a fixed, rigid price floor arose from [the Bar Associations'] activities: every lawyer who responded to [the Goldfarbs'] inquiries adhered to the fee schedule, and no lawyer asked for additional information in order to set an individualized fee. . . . The fee schedule was enforced through the prospect of professional discipline from the State Bar, and the desire of attorneys to comply with announced professional norms, . . . the motivation to conform was reinforced by the assurance that other lawyers would not compete by underbidding. This is not merely a case of an agreement that may be inferred from an exchange of price information * * * for here a naked agreement was clearly shown, and the effect on prices is plain. * * *

. . . On this record [the Bar Associations'] activities constitute a classic illustration of price fixing.

B

The County Bar argues, as the Court of Appeals held, that any effect on interstate commerce caused by the fee schedule's restraint on legal services was incidental and remote. In its view the legal services, which are performed wholly intrastate, are essentially local in nature and therefore a restraint with respect to them can never substantially affect interstate commerce. Further, the County Bar maintains, there was no showing here that the fee schedule and its enforcement mechanism increased fees, and that even if they did there was no showing that such an increase deterred any prospective homeowner from buying in Fairfax County.

These arguments misconceive the nature of the transactions at issue and the place legal services play in those transactions. . . . [I]n this class action the transactions which create the need for the particular legal services in question frequently are interstate transactions. The necessary connection between the interstate transactions and the restraint of trade provided by the minimum fee schedule is present because, in a practical sense, title examinations are necessary in real estate transactions to assure a lien on a valid title of the borrower. In financing realty purchases lenders require, "as a condition of making the loan, that the title to the property involved be examined . . . ." Thus a title examination is an integral part of an interstate transaction and this Court has long held that

> "there is an obvious distinction to be drawn between a course of conduct wholly within a state and conduct which is an inseparable element of a larger program dependent for its success upon activity which affects commerce between the states." * * *

Given the substantial volume of commerce involved, and the inseparability of this particular legal service from the interstate aspects of real estate transactions we conclude that interstate commerce has been sufficiently affected. * * *

The fact that there was no showing that home buyers were discouraged by the challenged activities does not mean that interstate commerce was not affected. Otherwise, the magnitude of the effect would control, and our cases have shown that, once an effect is shown, no specific magnitude need be proved. * * * Nor was it necessary for [the Goldfarbs] to prove that the fee schedule raised fees. [They] clearly proved that the fee schedule fixed fees. . . .

Where, as a matter of law or practical necessity, legal services are an integral part of an interstate transaction, a restraint on those services may substantially affect commerce for Sherman Act purposes. . . .

C
. . .

In arguing that learned professions are not "trade or commerce" the County Bar seeks a total exclusion from antitrust regulation. Whether state regulation is active or dormant, real or theoretical, lawyers would be able to adopt anticompetitive practices with impunity. We cannot find support for the proposition that Congress intended any such sweeping exclusion. The nature of an occupation, standing alone, does not provide sanctuary from the Sherman Act, * * * nor is the public service aspect of professional practice controlling in determining whether § 1 includes professions. * * * Congress intended to strike as broadly as it could in § 1 of the Sherman Act, and to read into it so wide an exemption as that urged on us would be at odds with that purpose.

... In the modern world it cannot be denied that the activities of lawyers play an important part in commercial intercourse, and that anticompetitive activities by lawyers may exert a restraint on commerce.

• • •

III

We recognize that the States have a compelling interest in the practice of professions within their boundaries, and that as part of their power to protect the public health, safety, and other valid interests they have broad power to establish standards for licensing practitioners and regulating the practice of professions. We also recognize that in some instances the State may decide that "forms of competition usual in the business world may be demoralizing to the ethical standards of a profession." * * * The interest of the States in regulating lawyers is especially great since lawyers are essential to the primary governmental function of administering justice, and have historically been "officers of the courts." * * * In holding that certain anticompetitive conduct by lawyers is within the reach of the Sherman Act we intend no diminution of the authority of the State to regulate its professions.

The judgment of the Court of Appeals is reversed and the case is remanded to the Court of Appeals with orders to remand to the District Court for further proceedings consistent with this opinion.

Reversed and remanded.

MR. JUSTICE POWELL took no part in the consideration or decision of this case.

CHAPTER **6**

Taxing and Spending Power

INTRODUCTORY ESSAY

The limited scope of national government under the Articles of Confederation is underscored by the fact that this government existed for eight years without the power to tax. It subsisted precariously on requisitions from the states proportioned on the largely indeterminate basis of land values. But Congress lacked the power to require even these uncertain payments. If absence of the power to regulate commerce stifled economic growth, the inability to tax and, by implication, to spend, threatened the continued existence of the government itself. The Framers of the Constitution proposed to remedy this weakness by providing in the very first clause of Article I, Section 8, the following *enumerated* power: "to lay and collect taxes, duties, imposts and excises, to pay the debts and provide for the common defense and general welfare of the United States." The vast taxing and spending powers exercised by the national government today are based squarely on this open-ended constitutional provision. In the following pages we will examine in broad outline the Supreme Court's function in defining the scope of these powers.

Turning first to taxation as a source of congressional power, it is necessary to distinguish between two important functions: (1) the most basic and obvious function of raising revenue; and (2) the less direct but often equally important function of economic or social regulation. It is in the second of these areas that the most enduring and important questions of constitutional power have been debated. Although the modern Supreme Court accords wide scope to both the revenue-raising and regulatory aspects of national taxation, it is at least theoretically more likely to entertain constitutional objections to the latter.

The taxing power is independent of any of the specific regulatory powers listed in other provisions of the Constitution. However, through linkage with the Necessary and Proper Clause, the taxing power can be used far beyond the limits of its own enumeration, to implement or carry out various regulatory programs. In other words, the taxing power is not confined to the objectives set forth in Section 8, Clause 1; that is, those of paying the debts and providing "for the common defense and general welfare of the United States." Congress, as Justice Frankfurter pointed out, may also "make an oblique use of the taxing power in relation to activities with which [it] may deal directly, as, for instance, commerce between the states" (*United States* v. *Kahriger,* 345 U.S. 22 at 37 [1953], dissenting).

218

The national taxing power, like the taxing power of the states, is exercised on the people directly. But, within strict limits, both state and national governments may also impose taxes on each other, so long as fundamental considerations of sovereignty, as determined on a case-by-case basis, are not threatened. The doctrine of reciprocal immunity has historically imposed some limits on intergovernmental taxation. Its rise and gradual decline will be discussed in Chapter 11.

Direct and Indirect Taxes

The Constitution distinguishes between *direct* and *indirect* taxes but leaves those vague categories largely undefined. Two separate provisions in Article I specify that direct taxes shall be apportioned among the states on the basis of population (Section 2, Clause 3, and Section 9, Clause 4). The second of these provisions refers to "capitation or other direct tax," suggesting through this linkage that the Framers had in mind a distinction between *direct* taxes such as those imposed on persons without regard to particular activities and *indirect* taxes such as those levied on businesses, goods, services, and various privileges. Nevertheless, the distinction between direct and indirect taxes was and is a muddy one. Fortunately, it is of little constitutional significance today.

However, the Supreme Court's failure to differentiate consistently between those categories posed serious problems in early constitutional development. In fact, one of the first constitutional questions about the scope of congressional power turned on this distinction. At issue in the 1796 case of *Hylton* v. *United States* (3 Dall. 171) was the constitutionality of a national tax on carriages. This measure exacted the payment of $16.00 per carriage and was challenged as a direct tax that had not been apportioned among the states in accordance with constitutional requirements. As noted in Part I, this case afforded the Court an opportunity to rule on the constitutionality of an act of Congress several years prior to *Marbury* v. *Madison*. But, in upholding the tax, the Court did not expound on the principle of judicial review. It is clear from the unusual circumstances out of which *Hylton* v. *United States* arose that the new government was anxious to obtain a favorable ruling on the constitutionality of the tax. To meet the minimum "amount in controversy" requirement of $2,000 for a federal case, a figure set by Congress in the Judiciary Act of 1789 and raised on several subsequent occasions, it was necessary to stipulate falsely Daniel Hylton's ownership of 125 carriages. Alexander Hamilton, former Secretary of the Treasury and an original proponent of this tax measure, participated in the government's argument of the case before the Supreme Court. The three Justices (Chase, Patterson, and Iredell) who took part in the decision agreed that by its nature a tax on carriages could not be justly apportioned among the states. The number of carriages in a given state would roughly reflect wealth, not population. The tax was thus defined as an *indirect* tax and was held to be a valid exercise of congressional power. The only direct taxes that the Court identified in the *Hylton* decision were capitation or poll taxes and taxes on land—neither of these designations being clearly explained. (For background, see Goebel, 1971, pp. 778–782.)

Income Tax Cases and the Sixteenth Amendment

In 1881 a unanimous Supreme Court upheld a Civil War income tax (*Springer* v. *United States,* 102 U.S. 586), concluding that this measure was an indirect excise tax that need not be apportioned among the states according to population. But four-teen years later the Court abruptly changed directions, striking down by a 5 to 4 vote, a peacetime tax of 2 percent on incomes above $4,000 a year (*Pollock* v. *Farmers' Loan & Trust Co.,* 158 U.S. 601 [1895]). The majority was obviously influ-enced by the imposing briefs of such eminent counsel as Joseph H. Choate and James C. Carter, who, as representatives of corporate wealth, branded the tax as a populistic assault on the institutions of private property and capitalism. Choate condemned it as part of the "communist march" that, if not blocked at once, would lead to further incursions on private property, "the very keystone of the arch upon which all civilized government rests." (For background, see Swisher, 1954, Chapter 20; and King, 1967, Chapter 15.) The Court's vehement reaction to what a congressional majority regarded as progressive legislation in the national interest is portrayed in the unrestrained language of Justice Field's concurring opinion: "The present assault upon capital is but the beginning. It will be the stepping-stone to others, larger and more sweeping, till our political contests will become a war of the poor against the rich; a war constantly growing in intensity and bitterness."

In his majority opinion Chief Justice Fuller concluded, among other things, that insofar as this tax was levied on income derived from land, it was a direct tax and thus invalid because not apportioned among the states on the basis of population. For several reasons this decision was highly controversial. It was an example of the Court's use of judicial review to invalidate a popular measure and to align itself openly with vested economic interests. Moreover, in reaching a final disposition of the case, the Court exhibited sharp internal division. With one of its members not participating because of illness, the Court was evenly divided when the case was first argued. Prior to reargument before a full Court later in the year, one of the Justices changed his position. For these reasons the *Pollock* decision was a shaky precedent at best. Some observers were convinced that if Congress enacted an-other income tax measure, the Court would return to the *Springer* rationale and declare it constitutional. This belief was encouraged by several personnel changes in the late 1890s, including the retirement of that staunch defender of economic individualism, Justice Stephen J. Field. In 1900 the Court sustained a graduated inheritance tax (*Knowlton* v. *Moore,* 178 U.S. 41), and in 1911 a tax levied on corporations was sustained as an excise tax on the privilege of doing business, although it was measured by income (*Flint* v. *Stone Tracy Co.,* 220 U.S. 107). Before this ruling, however, Congress had proposed the Sixteenth Amendment, specifical-ly authorizing taxation of income from any source and without the prerequisite of apportionment among the states on the basis of population. The formal ratification process was completed early in 1913, thus overruling the income tax decision of 1895 and, for all practical purposes, ending the confusion over the distinction between direct and indirect taxes.

Requirement of Geographic Uniformity

Apart from the income tax question, most constitutional issues in this field involve levies on virtually all aspects of business and an endless array of other activities. The indirect nature of such taxes can be seen in the capacity of those taxed to pass the ultimate burden on to consumers of the business or activity in question. The only limitation that the Constitution imposes on indirect taxes is that of geographic uniformity. They must be "uniform throughout the United States," that is, uniform in their application *among* the states, not identical as applied to each individual.

Taxation as a Regulatory Device

The Supreme Court has always given wide latitude to the taxing power as a source of regulatory authority when used in combination with other enumerated powers. The 1869 case of *Veazie Bank* v. *Fenno,* 8 Wall. 531, provides a classic example. There the Court upheld a tax of 10 percent on notes issued by state banks, a measure specifically designed to drive this unstable form of currency out of existence. Because the tax was linked to the congressional power to regulate currency, a power that emanates from several provisions in Article I, Section 8, Chief Justice Salmon P. Chase, Lincoln's former Secretary of the Treasury, expressed no doubts regarding its constitutionality: "Having thus, in the exercise of undisputed constitutional power, undertaken to provide a currency for the whole country, it cannot be questioned that Congress may, constitutionally, secure the benefit of it to the people by appropriate legislation."

Oleomargarine Case

Historically, the Court has expressed less certainty about the use of the taxing power as an independent regulatory device. By the mid-1930s two conflicting lines of constitutional precedent bearing on this question had emerged—one endorsing and the other denying broad congressional authority. In *McCray* v. *United States,* 195 U.S. 27 (1904), a divided Court upheld an act under which Congress, responding to strong pressure from the dairy industry, levied a tax of ten cents a pound on oleomargarine colored to look like butter and a tax of only one-fourth of a cent per pound on uncolored oleomargarine. The majority conceded that both the Fifth Amendment Due Process Clause and the Tenth Amendment recognition of the states' reserved powers imposed limits on the taxing power of Congress. But, according to Justice Edward D. White, who wrote the majority opinion, those limits had not been violated by this tax. If it were "plain to the judicial mind" that the taxing power was not being used to raise revenue "but solely for the purpose of destroying rights" implicit in constitutional principles of freedom and justice, courts would be duty-bound to declare that Congress had acted beyond the authority conferred by the Constitution. The difference between the abuse of legislative power and the exercise of reasonable discretion was simply a matter of judgment, to be made in each case. Applying this flexible standard, White concluded that "the manufacture of artificially colored oleomargarine may be prohibited by a free government without a violation of fundamental rights." It should be noted that, unlike other exercises of the national police power in the first decade of the twentieth century, this law was not clearly identified with the promotion of public health, safety, or morality. At best, it discouraged the deceptive marketing of a food product with which the dairy industry did not want to compete.

The *McCray* decision served as a precedent for using the taxing power to regulate the sale of narcotics and firearms (*United States* v. *Doremus,* 249 U.S. 86 [1919]; *Sonzinsky* v. *United States,* 300 U.S. 506 [1937]). But it was held not to apply to the regulation of child labor (*Bailey* v. *Drexel Furniture Co.,* 259 U.S. 20 [1922]) or to the regulation of agricultural production (*United States* v. *Butler,* 297 U.S. 1 [1936]). In the *United States* v. *Doremus* and *Sonzinsky* cases, the Court chose to recognize the validity of the revenue of the taxes in question and to view their regulatory features as fully consistent with the constitutional exercise of congressional power. In *Bailey* and *United States* v. *Butler,* the Court did just the opposite, choosing to interpret the taxes not as revenue measures (although they obviously produced revenue) but as penalties or coercive regulations infringing either individual liberty or the reserved powers of the states.

Child Labor Tax Case

Thus in the Child Labor Tax Case, Chief Justice Taft maintained that Congress through the taxing power was attempting to regulate an activity properly within the scope of state authority. He noted the Court's previous recognition in *Hammer* v. *Dagenhart,* 247 U.S. 251 (1918), of state autonomy regarding the control of child labor. Congress could not accomplish through the taxing power an objective previously denied it as an unconstitutional exercise of the commerce power. The tax amounted to 10 percent of the annual net income of mills, factories, mines, and quarries employing children under designated ages. This act singled out certain employment practices for tax purposes, just as the oleomargarine law singled out a particular marketing practice. Both were designed to discourage specific activities through the application of differential tax burdens. Yet the Court saw one as an appropriate revenue measure and the other as an impermissible use of the taxing power.

Butler Case

The Court invalidated the Agricultural Adjustment Act of 1933 in *United States* v. *Butler.* This nullification of a major piece of New Deal legislation is of constitutional importance for several reasons. It rejected Congress' use of the taxing power as a basis for regulating agricultural production. In fact, the Court's condemnation of the processing tax at issue in this case is, to this day, the last repudiation of national legislative authority based on the distinction between the regulatory and revenue-raising features of a tax. In this respect the *Butler* case simply repeated the rationale applied in the Child Labor Tax case; but its constitutional importance is substantially greater because it provided the Court with its first opportunity to consider the scope of the spending power as well.

The Spending Power

The source of the spending power is found in the same clause of the Constitution that confers on Congress the power to tax. The language is deceptively simple: "Congress shall have the power to . . . pay the debts and provide for the common defense and general welfare of the United States." The latter phrase—known as the General Welfare Clause (not to be confused with the "general welfare" referred to in the Preamble to the Constitution)—has been used in combination with other enumerated powers since the 1936 decision in *United States* v. *Butler* as the basis for vast governmental programs.

Under the Agricultural Adjustment Act of 1933, proceeds from the processing tax were used to pay farmers in exchange for their promise to reduce crop acreage. Thus, the scheme of regulation at issue embodied both taxing and spending features and rested squarely on Article I, Section 8, Clause 1 as its constitutional source. Justice Roberts, writing one of his most influential but puzzling majority opinions, recognized that Congress could use appropriations for regulatory purposes by making them conditional—that is, by withholding them until the potential recipients either performed or failed to perform specified actions. In this way the spending power could serve the same indirect regulatory function as the taxing power. He found the Act objectionable primarily because both its taxing and spending aspects sought to regulate agricultural production, an area then regarded as reserved to the states by the Tenth Amendment. His detailed analysis of the spending power, however, did not necessarily point to this result.

Roberts adopted the view widely held by constitutional scholars that the General Welfare Clause was not an unrestricted grant of power, but was linked to the taxing power granted in the same constitutional provision. According to this view, the General Welfare Clause conferred no independent regulatory power as such but only a power to spend. However, he rejected the narrow interpretation advanced by Madison that the taxing and spending power was to be exercised only in furtherance of other enumerated congressional powers. He reasoned that each of the other enumerated powers incidentally involved the expenditure of money and that if the provisions of Section 8, Clause 1 were to be used only in combination with them, the taxing and spending power was "mere tautology." Roberts accepted the broader alternative view first articulated by Hamilton and later endorsed by Justice Story in his influential *Commentaries* on the Constitution. According to this interpretation, the taxing and spending power, while not unrestricted, is subject to limitations found within the General Welfare Clause itself rather than in other enumerated powers. Roberts in effect recognized an independent source of congressional power to tax and spend and at the same time attempted to place internal limits on the exercise of that power. He was drawing what he regarded as a crucial distinction between special, enumerated powers and a broad, unrestricted grant of national authority. Considerations of classical federalism—the division of power between the national government and the states—were of key importance in his analysis. This is evident from the structure of his opinion. After commenting on the internal limits of the taxing and spending power, he shifted abruptly to a consideration of the broad regulatory scheme contemplated by the statute, concluding that it violated the domain of powers reserved to the states.

Roberts' opinion has a quality of ambivalence that reflects his uncertainty about the emergence of sweeping regulatory power at the national level—an uncertainty shared by other Justices during this chaotic period in the Court's history. In any event, his interpretation of the General Welfare Clause proved untenable as a standard for assessing the constitutionality of other federal programs based on the taxing and spending power. Beginning with two 1937 decisions upholding the newly enacted social security program, the Court abandoned the *Butler* rationale (*Steward Machine Co. v. Davis,* 301 U.S. 548; and *Helvering v. Davis,* 301 U.S. 619). Justice Stone, dissenting in *Butler,* had accused the majority of second-guessing Congress on the "wisdom" of the Agricultural Adjustment Act, remarking caustically: "Courts are not the only agency of government that must be assumed to have capacity to govern."

He was obviously unimpressed by Justice Roberts' disingenuous claim that in reviewing the constitutionality of an act of Congress, "the judicial branch of the government has only one duty: to lay the article of the Constitution which is invoked beside the statute which is challenged and to decide whether the latter squares with the former." In Stone's view the *Butler* majority was exercising far more doctrinaire judicial authority than this merely mechanical description of judicial review implied. His call for the imposition of greater judicial self-restraint became a central theme of majority opinions in the fields of commerce and taxing and spending after 1937. In 1939 the Court underscored this new and greatly diminished involvement with national economic policy by sustaining the second Agricultural Adjustment Act (*Mulford v. Smith,* 307 U.S. 38). Since Justice Cardozo's opinion in the *Steward Machine Co.* case, upholding the unemployment compensation features of the Social Security Act, the Court has accorded broad scope to the spending power of Congress. This latitude is based on an interpretation of the General Welfare Clause as a source of plenary power.

An illustration of the broad scope now accorded the national spending power under the General Welfare Clause is provided by the 1976 decision of *Buckley v. Valeo* (424 U.S. 1). One of the many issues raised in this multifaceted case was the constitutionality of certain provisions of the Internal Revenue Code calling for public financing of presidential campaigns. The Court rejected the contention that the General Welfare Clause placed limits on the spending power in this regard. Rather, it viewed the clause as a "grant of power the scope of which is quite expansive, particularly in view of the enlargement of power by the Necessary and Proper Clause." Since, according to well-established precedent, Congress could regulate presidential elections and primaries, it followed that "public financing of presidential elections as a means to reform the electoral process was clearly a choice within the granted power." It was up to Congress "to decide which expenditures [would] promote the general welfare."

With the expansion of the commerce and taxing and spending powers since the late 1930s, the distinction between the regulatory and revenue functions served by taxing and spending has ceased to be of great practical importance. It remains significant at the theoretical level and could be invoked at any time as a restraint on governmental prerogatives. But as long as Congress is accorded primary responsibility for enacting national economic and social policy into law, the old distinction, once so pivotal, is likely to be ignored.

The Taxing Power and the Bill of Rights

The potential limits imposed by various provisions of the Bill of Rights remain important in determining the outer limits of the taxing and spending power. Due process standards impose significant procedural requirements on all legislation, including that in the field of taxation. As a practical matter, however, the Fifth Amendment protection against compulsory self-incrimination has served as the primary basis in recent years for invalidating congressional exercise of the taxing power. Justice Black first articulated this source of constitutional restraint in a dissenting opinion in a case sustaining the wagering tax provisions of the Revenue Act of 1951 (*United States* v. *Kahriger*). He read the registration provisions of the act as requiring persons to confess that they were engaged in the illegal "business of gambling." In his view, such compulsion, however indirect, was condemned by the Self-Incrimination Clause of the Fifth Amendment. In the years following the *Kahriger* decision the Supreme Court, under the Chief Justiceship of Earl Warren, greatly expanded the constitutional rights of persons accused of crime. Consistent with this trend, Justice Black's dissenting view was adopted in 1968 and *Kahriger* was expressly overruled (*Marchetti* v. *United States,* 390 U.S. 39; and *Grosso* v. *United States,* 390 U.S. 62). Writing for the majority in the *Marchetti* case, Justice Harlan was careful to distinguish between the scope of the taxing power, which he did not wish to diminish, and the specific individual safeguards of the Fifth Amendment, which he wished to recognize. The issue as he saw it was "whether the methods employed by Congress in the Federal Wagering Tax statutes [were] in this situation consistent with the limitations created by the privilege against self-incrimination." Since the registration requirements forced gamblers to expose their own illegal activity, he concluded that the Fifth Amendment was violated.

The Court made it clear in a 1976 decision, however, that even this procedural protection required the positive assertion of the right in question (*Garner* v. *United States,* 424 U.S. 648). Thus, it rejected a defendant's contention that the introduction into evidence of his income tax return, which listed his occupation as that of "professional gambler," violated his immunity against compulsory self-incrimination. In another recent attempt to strike a balance between procedural safeguards and the exercise of substantive powers, the Court recognized that the taxing power cannot be used in such a way as to undermine Fourth Amendment restrictions against unreasonable searches and seizures. Thus in *General Motors Leasing Corp.* v. *United States,* 429 U.S. 338 (1977), it held that a warrantless entry into a business office under the purported authority of the Internal Revenue Code was, under the circumstances, an invasion of the right of privacy.

The vast dimensions of the constitutional power to tax remain unlimited as a substantive grant of congressional authority. The Court seems inclined to require only that the means by which this power is exercised conform to the guarantees of the Bill of Rights. As in the national commerce field, the Supreme Court's principal role in dealing with the taxing and spending power has been to broaden the scope of constitutional authority so as to bring it into accord with the practical demands of proliferating governmental activity.

Pollock v. *Farmers' Loan & Trust Co.*

158 U.S. 601 (1895)

[As a stockholder in Farmers' Loan & Trust Co., Charles Pollock brought suit for himself and all other stockholders to prevent the company from paying particular taxes to the United States. In this case the tax involved an 1894 tax act that placed a 2 percent tax on income from real estate and municipal bonds, among other things. Pollock argued that the tax was unconstitutional. The Court agreed.]

MR. CHIEF JUSTICE FULLER delivered the opinion of the Court.

· · ·

. . . [T]he Constitution divided Federal taxation into two great classes, the class of direct taxes, and the class of duties, imposts, and excises; and prescribed two rules which qualified the grant of power as to each class.

The power to lay direct taxes apportioned among the several states in proportion to their representation in the popular branch of Congress, a representation based on population as ascertained by the census, was plenary and absolute; but to lay direct taxes without apportionment was forbidden. The power to lay duties, imposts, and excises was subject to the qualification that the imposition must be uniform throughout the United States.

Our previous decision was confined to the consideration of the validity of the tax on the income from real estate, and on the income from municipal bonds. The question thus limited was whether such taxation was direct or not, in the meaning of the Constitution; and the court went no farther, as to the tax on the income from real estate, than to hold that it fell within the same class as the source whence the income was derived, that is, that a tax upon the realty and a tax upon the receipts therefrom were alike direct; while, as to the income from municipal bonds, that could not be taxed because of want of power to tax the source, and no reference was made to the nature of the tax as being direct or indirect.

We are now permitted to broaden the field of inquiry, and to determine to which of the two great classes a tax upon a person's entire income, whether derived from rents, or products, or otherwise, of real estate, or from bonds, stocks, or other forms of personal property, belongs; and we are unable to conclude that the enforced subtraction from the yield of all the owner's real or personal property, in the manner prescribed, is so different from a tax upon the property itself, that it is not a direct, but an indirect tax, in the meaning of the Constitution.

· · ·

Whatever the speculative views of political economists or revenue reformers may be, can it be properly held that the Constitution, taken in its plain and obvious sense, and with due regard to the circumstances attending the formation of the government, authorizes a general unapportioned tax on the products of the farm and the rents of real estate, although imposed merely because of ownership and with no possible means of escape from payment, as belonging to a totally different class from that which includes the property from whence the income proceeds?

There can be but one answer, unless the constitutional restriction is to be treated as utterly illusory and futile, and the object of the framers defeated. We find it impossible to hold that a fundamental requisition, deemed so important as to be enforced by two provisions, one affirmative and one negative, can be refined away by forced distinctions between that which gives value to property, and the property itself.

Nor can we perceive any ground why the same reasoning does not apply to capital in personalty held for the purpose of income or ordinarily yielding income, and to the income therefrom. All the real estate of the country, and all its invested personal property, are open to the direct operation of the taxing power if an apportionment be made according to the Constitution. The Constitution does not say that no direct tax shall be laid by apportionment on any other property than land; on the contrary, it forbids all unapportioned direct taxes; and we know of no warrant for exempting personal property from the exercise of the power, or any reason why an unapportioned direct tax cannot be laid and assessed . . . "upon the same objects of taxation on which the direct taxes levied under the authority of the state are laid and assessed."

Personal property of some kind is of general distribution; and so are incomes, though the taxable range thereof might be narrowed through large exemptions.

· · ·

The stress of the argument is thrown, however, on the assertion that an income tax is not a property tax at all; that it is not a real estate tax, or a crop tax, or a bond tax; that it is an assessment upon the taxpayer on account of his money spending power as shown by his revenue for the year preceding the assessment; that rents received, crops harvested, interest collected, have lost all connection with their origin, and although once not taxable have become transmuted in their new form into taxable subject matter; in other words, that income is taxable irrespective of the source from whence it is derived.

.   .   .

We have unanimously held in this case that, so far as this law operates on the receipts from municipal bonds, it cannot be sustained, because it is a tax on the power of the states, and on their instrumentalities to borrow money, and consequently repugnant to the Constitution. But if, as contended, the interest when received has become merely money in the recipient's pocket, and taxable as such without reference to the source from which it came, the question is immaterial whether it could have been originally taxed at all or not. This was admitted by the Attorney General with characteristic candor; and it follows that, if the revenue derived from municipal bonds cannot be taxed because the source cannot be, the same rule applies to revenue from any other source not subject to the tax; and the lack of power to levy any but an apportioned tax on real and personal property equally exists as to the revenue therefrom.

Admitting that this Act taxes the income of property irrespective of its source, still we cannot doubt that such a tax is necessarily a direct tax in the meaning of the Constitution.

.   .   .

Being direct, and therefore to be laid by apportionment, is there any real difficulty in doing so? Cannot Congress, if the necessity exists of raising thirty, forty, or any other number of million dollars for the support of the government, in addition to the revenue from duties, imposts, and excises, apportion the quota of each state upon the basis of the census, and thus advise it of the payment which must be made, and proceed to assess that amount on all the real and personal property and the income of all persons in the state, and collect the same? . . . Inconveniences might possibly attend the levy of an income tax, . . . but that it is apportionable is hardly denied, although it is asserted that it would operate so unequally as to be undesirable.

.   .   .

We are not here concerned with the question whether an income tax be or be not desirable, nor whether such a tax would enable the government to diminish taxes on consumption and duties on imports, and to enter upon what may be believed to be a reform of its fiscal and commercial system. Questions of that character belong to the controversies of political parties, and cannot be settled by judicial decision. In these cases our province is to determine whether this income tax on the revenue from property does or does not belong to the class of direct taxes. If it does, it is, being unapportioned, in violation of the Constitution, and we must so declare.

.   .   .

If it be true that the Constitution should have been so framed that a tax of this kind could be laid, the instrument defines the way for its amendment. In no part of it was greater sagacity displayed. Except that no state, without its consent, can be deprived of its equal suffrage in the Senate, the Constitution may be amended upon the concurrence of two thirds of both houses, and the ratification of the legislatures or conventions of the several states, or through a Federal convention when applied for by the legislatures of two thirds of the states, and upon like ratification. The ultimate sovereignty may be thus called into play by a slow and deliberate process, which gives time for mere hypothesis and opinion to exhaust themselves, and for the sober second thought of every part of the country to be asserted.

We have considered the Act only in respect of the tax on income derived from real estate, and from invested personal property, and have not commented on so much of it as bears on gains or profits from business, privileges, or employments, in view of the instances in which taxation on business, privileges, or employments, has assumed the guise of an excise tax and been sustained as such.

Being of opinion that so much of the sections of this law as lays a tax on income from real and personal property is invalid, we are brought to the question of the effect of that conclusion upon these sections as a whole.

It is elementary that the same statute may be in part constitutional and in part unconstitutional, and if the parts are wholly independent of each other, that which is constitutional may stand while that which is unconstitutional will be rejected. And in the case before us there is no question as to the validity of this Act, except sections . . . which relate to the subject which has been under discussion; and as to them we think the rule . . . is applicable, that if the different parts "are so mutually connected with and dependent on each other, as conditions, considerations or compensations for each other, as to warrant a belief that the legislature intended them as a whole, and that, if all could not be carried into effect, the legislature would not pass the residue independently, and some parts are unconstitutional, all the provisions which are thus dependent, conditional or connected, must fall with them." . . .

• • •

. . . [I]t is evident that the income from realty formed a vital part of the scheme for taxation embodied therein. If that be stricken out, and also the income from all invested personal property, bonds, stocks, investments of all kinds, it is obvious that by far the largest part of the anticipated revenue would be eliminated, and this would leave the burden of the tax to be borne by professions, trades, employments, or vocations, and in that way what was intended as a tax on capital would remain in substance a tax on occupations and labor. We cannot believe that such was the intention of Congress. We do not mean to say that an Act laying by apportionment a direct tax on all real estate and personal property, or the income thereof, might not also lay excise taxes on business, privileges, employments, and vocations. But this is not such an Act; and the scheme must be considered as a whole. Being invalid as to the greater part, and falling, as the tax would, if any part were held valid, in a direction which could not have been contemplated except in connection with the taxation considered as an entirety, we are constrained to conclude that sections twenty-seven to thirty-seven, inclusive, of the Act, which became a law without the signature of the President on August 28, 1894, are wholly inoperative and void.

Our conclusions may, therefore, be summed up as follows:

First. We adhere to the opinion already announced that, taxes on real estate being indisputably direct taxes, taxes on the rents or income of real estate are equally direct taxes.

Second. We are of opinion that taxes on personal property, or on the income of personal property, are likewise direct taxes.

Third. The tax imposed by sections twenty-seven to thirty-seven, inclusive, of the Act of 1894, so far as it falls on the income of real estate and of personal property, being a direct tax within the meaning of the Constitution, and, therefore, unconstitutional and void because not apportioned according to representation, all those sections, constituting one entire scheme of taxation, are necessarily invalid.

The decrees hereinbefore entered in this court will be vacated; the decrees below will be reversed, and the cases remanded, with instructions to grant the relief prayed.

Mr. Justice Harlan dissenting.

At the former hearing of these causes it was adjudged that, within the meaning of the Constitution, a duty on incomes arising from rents was a direct tax on the lands from which such rents were derived, and, therefore, must be apportioned among the several states on the basis of population, and not by the rule of uniformity, throughout the United States, as prescribed in the case of duties, imposts, and excises. And the court, eight of its members being present, was equally divided upon the question whether *all* the other provisions of the statute relating to incomes would fall in consequence of that judgment.

It is appropriate now to say that however objectionable the law would have been, after the provision for taxing incomes arising from rents was stricken out, I did not then, nor do I now, think it within the province of the court to annul the provisions relating to incomes derived from other specified sources, and take from the government the entire revenue contemplated to be raised by the taxation of incomes, simply because the clause relating to rents was held to be unconstitutional. The reasons for this view will be stated in another connection.

• • •

From [the] history of legislation and of judicial decisions it is manifest—

That, in the judgment of the members of this court as constituted when the Hylton case was decided . . . the only taxes that could certainly be regarded as direct taxes, within the meaning of the Constitution, were capitation taxes and taxes on lands;

That, in their opinion, a tax on real estate was properly classified as a direct tax; . . .

• • •

That, in the judgment of all the judges in the Hylton case, no tax was a direct one, that could not be apportioned among the states, on the basis of numbers, with some approach to justice and equality among the people of the several states who owned the property or subject taxed; . . .

That by the judgment in the Hylton case, a tax on specific personal property, owned by the taxpayer and used or let to hire, was not a direct tax to be apportioned among the states on the basis of numbers;

• • •

That in 1861 and subsequent years Congress imposed, without apportionment among the states on the basis of numbers, but by the rule of uniformity, duties on *income* derived *from every kind of property, real and personal,* including income derived from *rents,* and from trades, professions, and employments, etc.; and, lastly,

That upon every occasion when it has considered the question whether a duty on *incomes* was a direct tax within the meaning of the Constitution, this court has, *without a dissenting voice,* determined it in the negative, always proceeding on the ground that capitation taxes and taxes on land were the only direct taxes contemplated by the framers of the Constitution.

• • •

. . . I have a deep, abiding conviction, which my sense of duty compels me to express, that it is not possible for this court to have rendered any judgment more to be regretted than the one just rendered.

• • •

In my judgment a tax on *income* derived from real property ought not to be, and until now has never been, regarded by any court as a direct tax on such property within the meaning of the Constitution. As the great mass of lands in most of the states do not bring any rents, and as incomes from rents vary in the different states, such a tax cannot possibly be apportioned among the states on the basis merely of numbers with any approach to equality of right among taxpayers, any more than a tax on carriages or other personal property could be so apportioned. And, in view of former adjudications, . . . a decision now that a tax on income from real property can be laid and collected only by apportioning the same among the states, on the basis of numbers, may, not improperly, be regarded as a judicial revolution, that may sow the seeds of hate and distrust among the people of different sections of our common country.

• • •

In determining whether a tax on income from rents is a direct tax, within the meaning of the Constitution, the inquiry is not whether it may in some way indirectly affect the land or the land owner, but whether it is a *direct* tax *on the thing taxed, the land.* The circumstance that such a tax may possibly have the effect to diminish the value of the use of the land is neither decisive of the question nor important. While a tax *on the land* itself, whether at a fixed rate applicable to all lands without regard to their value, or by the acre or according to their market value, might be deemed a direct tax within the meaning of the Constitution, . . . a duty on rents is a duty on something distinct and entirely separate from, although issuing out of, the land.

. . .

In my judgment—to say nothing of the disregard of the former adjudications of this court, and of the settled practice of the government—this decision may well excite the gravest apprehensions. It strikes at the very foundations of national authority, in that it denies to the general government a power which is, or may become, vital to the very existence and preservation of the Union in an emergency, such as that of war with a great commercial nation, during which the collection of all duties upon imports will cease or be materially diminished. It tends to re-establish that condition of helplessness in which Congress found itself during the period of the Articles of Confederation, when it was without authority by laws operating directly upon individuals, to lay and collect, through its own agents, taxes sufficient to pay the debts and defray the expenses of government, but was dependent, in all such matters, upon the good will of the states, and their promptness in meeting requisitions made upon them by Congress.

. . .

. . . The decision now made may provoke a contest in this country from which the American people would have been spared if the court had not overturned its former adjudications, and had adhered to the principles of taxation under which our government . . . has always been administered. Thoughtful, conservative men have uniformly held that the government could not be safely administered except upon principles of right, justice, and equality—without discrimination against any part of the people because of their owning or not owning visible property, or because of their having or not having incomes from bonds and stocks. But by its present construction of the Constitution, the court, for the first time in all its history, declares that our government has been so framed that, in matters of taxation for its support and maintenance, those who have incomes derived from the renting of real estate, or from the leasing or using of tangible personal property, or who own invested personal property, bonds, stocks, and investments, of whatever kind, have privileges that cannot be accorded to those having incomes derived from the labor of their hands, or the exercise of their skill, or the use of their brains. . . . If this new theory of the Constitution, as I believe it to be, if this new departure from the same way marked out by the fathers and so long followed by this court, is justified by the fundamental law, the American people cannot too soon amend their Constitution.

It was said in argument that the passage of the statute imposing this income tax was an assault by the poor upon the rich, and by much eloquent speech this court has been urged to stand in the breach for the protection of the just rights of property against the advancing hosts of Socialism. With the policy of legislation of this character, the court has nothing to do. That is for the legislative branch of the government. It is for Congress to determine whether the necessities of the government are to be met, or the interests of the people subserved, by the taxation of incomes. With that determination, so far as it rests upon grounds of expediency or public policy, the courts can have no rightful concern. The safety and permanency of our institutions demand that each department of government shall keep within its legitimate sphere as defined by the supreme law of the land. We deal here only with questions of law. . . .

If it were true that this legislation, in its important aspects and in its essence, discriminated against the rich, because of their wealth, the court, in vindication of the equality of all before the law, might well declare that the statute was not an exercise of the power of *taxation*, but was repugnant to those principles of natural right upon which our free institutions rest, and, therefore, was legislative spoilation, under the guise of taxation. But it is not of that character. There is no foundation for the charge that this statute was framed in sheer hostility to the wealth of the country. . . .

• • •

I am of opinion that with the exception of capitation and land taxes, and taxes on exports from the states and on the property and instrumentalities of the states, the government of the Union, in order to pay its debts and provide for the common defense and the general welfare, and under its power to lay and collect taxes, duties, imposts, and excises, may reach, under the rule of uniformity, all property and property rights in whatever state they may be found. This is as it should be, and as it must be, if the national government is to be administered upon principles of right and justice, and is to accomplish the beneficent ends for which it was established by the people of the United States. The authority to sustain itself, and, by its own agents and laws, to execute the powers granted to it, are the features that particularly distinguish the present government from the confederation which Washington characterized as "a half-starved, limping government," that was "always moving upon crutches and tottering at every step." The vast powers committed to the present government may be abused, and taxes may be imposed by Congress which the public necessities do not in fact require, or which may be forbidden by a wise policy. But the remedy for such abuses is to be found at the ballot-box and in a wholesome public opinion which the representatives of the people will not long, if at all, disregard, and not in the disregard by the judiciary of powers that have been committed to another branch of the government.

· · ·

. . . [T]he serious aspect of the present decision is that by a new interpretation of the Constitution, it so ties the hands of the legislative branch of the government, that without an amendment of that instrument, or unless this court, at some future time, should return to the old theory of the Constitution, Congress cannot subject to taxation—however great the needs or pressing the necessities of the government—either the invested personal property of the country, bonds, stocks, and investments of all kinds, or the income arising from the renting of real estate, or from the yield of personal property, except by the grossly unequal and unjust rule of apportionment among the states. Thus, undue and disproportioned burdens are placed upon the many, while the few, safely entrenched behind the rule of apportionment among the states on the basis of numbers, are permitted to evade their share of responsibility for the support of the government ordained for the protection of the rights of all.

I cannot assent to an interpretation of the Constitution that impairs and cripples the just powers of the national government in the essential matter of taxation, and at the same time discriminates against the greater part of the people of our country.

The practical effect of the decision to-day is to give to certain kinds of property a position of favoritism and advantage inconsistent with the fundamental principles of our social organization, and to invest them with power and influence that may be perilous to that portion of the American people upon whom rests the larger part of the burdens of the government, and who ought not to be subjected to the dominion of aggregated wealth any more than the property of the country should be at the mercy of the lawless.

I dissent from the opinion and judgment of the court.

MR. JUSTICE BROWN dissenting.

· · ·

It is difficult to overestimate the importance of these cases. I certainly cannot overstate the regret I feel at the disposition made of them by the court. It is never a light thing to set aside the deliberate will of the legislature, and in my opinion it should never be done, except upon the clearest proof of its conflict with the fundamental law. Respect for the Constitution will not be inspired by a narrow and technical construction which shall limit or impair the necessary powers of Congress. Did the reversal of these cases involve merely the striking down of the inequitable features of this law, or even the whole law, for its want of uniformity, the consequences would be less serious; but as it implies a declaration that every income tax must be laid according to the rule of apportionment, the decision involves nothing less than a surrender of the taxing power to the moneyed class.

By resuscitating an argument that was exploded in the Hylton case, and has lain practically dormant for a hundred years, it is made to do duty in nullifying, not this law alone, but every similar law that is not based upon an impossible theory of apportionment. Even the spectre of socialism is conjured up to frighten Congress from laying taxes upon the people in proportion to their ability to pay them. It is certainly a strange commentary upon the Constitution of the United States and upon the democratic government that Congress has no power to lay a tax which is one of the main sources of revenue of nearly every civilized state. It is a confession of feebleness in which I find myself wholly unable to join.

While I have no doubt that Congress will find some means of surmounting the present crisis, my fear is that in some moment of national peril this decision will rise up to frustrate its will and paralyze its arm. I hope it may not prove the first step toward the submergence of the liberties of people in a sordid despotism of wealth.

As I cannot escape the conviction that the decision of the court in this great case is fraught with immeasurable danger to the future of the country, and that it approaches the proportion of a national calamity, I feel it my duty to enter my protest against it.

Mr. Justice Jackson dissenting.

• • •

The decision disregards the well established canon of construction to which I have referred, that an Act passed by a co-ordinate branch of the government has every presumption in its favor, and should never be declared invalid by the courts unless its repugnancy to the Constitution is clear beyond all reasonable doubt. It is not a matter of conjecture; it is the established principle that it must be clear beyond a reasonable doubt. I cannot see, in view of the past, how this case can be said to be free of doubt.

Again, the decision not only takes from Congress its rightful power of fixing the rate of taxation, but substitutes a rule incapable of application without producing the most monstrous inequality and injustice between citizens residing in different sections of their common country, such as the framers of the Constitution never could have contemplated, such as no free and enlightened people can ever possibly sanction or approve.

The practical operation of the decision is not only to disregard the great principles of equality in taxation, but the further principle that in the imposition of taxes for the benefit of the government the burdens thereof should be imposed upon those having most *ability* to bear them. This decision, in effect works out a directly opposite result, in relieving the citizens having the greater *ability*, while the burdens of taxation are made to fall most heavily and oppressively upon those having the least ability. It lightens the burden upon the larger number, in some states subject to the tax, and places it most unequally and disproportionately on the smaller number in other states. Considered in all its bearings, this decision is, in my judgment, the most disastrous blow ever struck at the constitutional power of Congress. It strikes down an important portion of the most vital and essential power of the government in practically excluding any recourse to incomes from real and personal estate for the purpose of raising needed revenue to meet the government's wants and necessities under any circumstances.

I am therefore compelled to enter my dissent to the judgment of the court.

MR. JUSTICE WHITE dissenting. [Omitted.]

McCray v. United States

195 U.S. 27 (1904)

MR. JUSTICE WHITE . . . delivered the opinion of the Court.

As the controversy in every aspect involves the acts of Congress concerning the taxation of oleomargarine, a summary of those acts becomes essential.

The original act was passed in 1886. * * * The 1st section provided:

"That for the purposes of this act the word 'butter' shall be understood to mean the food product usually known as butter, and which is made exclusively from milk or cream. . . ."

The 2d thus defined oleomargarine:

"That for the purposes of this act certain manufactured substances, certain extracts . . . shall be known and designated as 'oleomargarine,' namely: All substances heretofore known as oleomargarine . . . ; all mixtures and compounds of oleomargarine, oleo, oleomargarine oil . . . ; and all mixtures and compounds of tallow, beef fat, suet, lard, . . . intestinal fat and offal fat made in imitation or semblance of butter, or, when so made, calculated or intended to be sold as butter or for butter."

The 3d, 4th, 5th, 6th, and 7th sections imposed a license on manufacturers and dealers in oleomargarine, and contained many requirements controlling the packing, marketing, and supervision of the manufacture and sale of the taxed article. The 8th section provided as follows:

"That upon oleomargarine which shall be manufactured and sold, or removed for consumption or use, there shall be assessed and collected a tax of two cents per pound, to be paid by the manufacturer thereof. . . . The tax levied by this section shall be represented by coupon stamps, and the provisions of existing

laws governing the engraving, issue, sale, accountability, effacement, and destruction of stamps relating to tobacco and snuff, as far as applicable, are hereby
made to apply to stamps provided for by this section."

. . . In 1902 further provisions were made on the subject, and the act of 1886
was, in many respects, expressly amended. * * *

. . .

. . . Section 3 amends § 8 of the act of 1886 by increasing the tax on oleomargarine from two (2) to ten (10) cents per pound, with this proviso: "*Provided,*
When oleomargarine is free from artificial coloration that causes it to look like
butter of any shade of yellow, said tax shall be one fourth of one cent per pound.
The tax levied by this section shall be represented by coupon stamps. . . ."

Section 4 [as amended] reiterates the definition of butter contained in the 1st
section of the act of 1886, and besides gives a definition of "adulterated butter,"
"process butter," or "renovated butter," and imposes taxes upon the manufacture and sale of these articles, the tax upon adulterated butter being at the rate
of 10 cents a pound.

. . .

The summary which follows embodies . . . the substance of the elaborate
argument. . . . Not denying the general power of Congress to impose excise taxes,
and conceding that the acts in question, on their face, purport to levy taxes of
that character, the propositions are these:

(*a*) That the power of internal taxation which the Constitution confers on
Congress is given to that body for the purpose of raising revenue, and that the tax
on artificially colored oleomargarine is void because it is of such an onerous
character as to make it manifest that the purpose of Congress in levying it was
not to raise revenue, but to suppress the manufacture of the taxed article.

(*b*) The power to regulate the manufacture and sale of oleomargarine being
solely reserved to the several states, it follows that the acts in question, enacted by
Congress for the purpose of suppressing the manufacture and sale of oleomargarine, when artificially colored, are void, because usurping the reserved power of
the states, and therefore exerting an authority not delegated to Congress by the
Constitution.

(*c*) Whilst it is true—so the argument proceeds—that Congress, in exerting
the taxing power conferred upon it, may use all means appropriate to the exercise of such power, a tax which is fixed at such a high rate as to suppress the
production of the article taxed is not a legitimate means to the lawful end, and is
therefore beyond the scope of the taxing power.

(*d*) As the tax levied by the acts which are assailed discriminates against
oleomargarine . . . and creates an unwarranted and unreasonable distinction
between the oleomargarine which is artificially colored and that which is not,
and as the necessary operation and effect of the tax is to suppress the manufacture of artificially colored oleomargarine, and to aid the butter industry, there-

fore the acts are void. And with this proposition in mind it is insisted that wherever the judiciary is called upon to determine whether a power which Congress has exerted is within the authority conferred by the Constitution, the duty is to test the validity of the act, not merely by its face, or, to use the words of the argument, "by the label placed upon it by Congress," but by the necessary scope and effect of the assailed enactment.

(*e*) Admitting that the power to tax, as delegated to Congress by the Constitution as originally adopted, was subject to no limitation except as expressed in that instrument, the amendments to the Constitution, it is urged, have imposed limitations on the taxing power not expressed in the original Constitution. Under this assumption it is insisted that the acts in question are void, because the burdens which they impose are repugnant to both the 5th and 10th Amendments. To the 5th Amendment, because the amount of the tax is so out of proportion to the value of the property taxed as to destroy that property, and thus amount to a taking thereof without due process of law. To the 10th Amendment, because the necessary operation and effect of the acts is to destroy the oleomargarine industry, and thus exert a power not delegated to Congress, but reserved to the several states.

(*f*) Although, as a general rule, it be true that the power of Congress to tax, conferred by the Constitution, is unlimited, except as otherwise expressed in that instrument, . . . it is urged that, as the burdens which the acts impose are so onerous and so unjust as to be confiscatory, the acts are void, because they amount to a violation of those fundamental rights which it is the duty of every free government to protect.

. . . [W]e . . . come, first, to ascertain how far, if at all, the motives or purposes of Congress are open to judicial inquiry in considering the power of that body to enact the laws in question. Having determined the question of our right to consider motive or purpose, we shall then approach the propositions relied on by the light of the correct rule on the subject of purpose or motive.

[While] . . . it is axiomatic that the judicial department of the government is charged with the solemn duty of enforcing the Constitution . . . no instance is afforded from the foundation of the government where an act which was within a power conferred, was declared to be repugnant to the Constitution, because it appeared to the judicial mind that the particular exertion of constitutional power was either unwise or unjust. To announce such a principle would amount to declaring that, in our constitutional system, the judiciary was not only charged with the duty of upholding the Constitution, but also with the responsibility of correcting every possible abuse arising from the exercise by the other departments of their conceded authority. . . .

It is, however, argued, if a lawful power may be exerted for an unlawful purpose, and thus, by abusing the power, it may be made to accomplish a result not intended by the Constitution, all limitations of power must disappear, and the grave function lodged in the judiciary, to confine all the departments within the authority conferred by the Constitution, will be of no avail. This, when reduced to its last analysis, comes to this: that, because a particular department of the government may exert its lawful powers with the object or motive of reaching an end not justified, therefore it becomes the duty of the judiciary to restrain the exercise of a lawful power wherever it seems to the judicial mind that such lawful power has been abused. But this reduces itself to the contention that, under our constitutional system, the abuse by one department of the government of its lawful powers is to be corrected by the abuse of its powers by another department.

The proposition, if sustained, would destroy all distinction between the powers of the respective departments of the government, would put an end to that confidence and respect for each other which it was the purpose of the Constitution to uphold, and would thus be full of danger to the permanence of our institutions. . . .

• • •

It is, of course, true, as suggested, that if there be no authority in the judiciary to restrain a lawful exercise of power by another department of the government, where a wrong motive or purpose has impelled to the exertion of the power, that abuses of a power conferred may be temporarily effectual. The remedy for this, however, lies, not in the abuse by the judicial authority of its functions, but in the people, upon whom, after all, under our institutions, reliance must be placed for the correction of abuses committed in the exercise of a lawful power. . . .

The decisions of this court from the beginning lend no support whatever to the assumption that the judiciary may restrain the exercise of lawful power on the assumption that a wrongful purpose or motive has caused the power to be exerted. . . .

• • •

It being thus demonstrated that the motive or purpose of Congress in adopting the acts in question may not be inquired into, we are brought to consider the contentions relied upon to show that the acts assailed were beyond the power of Congress, putting entirely out of view all considerations based upon purpose or motive.

1. Undoubtedly, in determining whether a particular act is within a granted power, its scope and effect [are] to be considered. Applying this rule to the acts assailed, it is self-evident that on their face they levy an excise tax. That being their necessary scope and operation, it follows that the acts are within the grant of power. The argument to the contrary rests on the proposition that, although the tax be within the power, as enforcing it will destroy or restrict the manufacture of artificially colored oleomargarine, therefore the power to levy the tax did not obtain. This, however, is but to say that the question of power depends, not upon the authority conferred by the Constitution, but upon what may be the consequence arising from the exercise of the lawful authority.

Since . . . the taxing power conferred by the Constitution knows no limits except those expressly stated in that instrument, it must follow, if a tax be within the lawful power, the exertion of that power may not be judicially restrained because of the results to arise from its exercise. . . .

. . .

Of course, where a state law is assailed as repugnant to the Constitution of the United States, and on its face such act was seemingly within the power of the state to adopt, but its necessary effect and operation is to usurp a power granted by the Constitution to the government of the United States, it must follow, from the paramount nature of the Constitution of the United States, that the act is void. In such a case the result of the test of necessary operation and effect is to demonstrate the want of power, because of the controlling nature of the limitations imposed by the Constitution of the United States on the states.

. . .

2. The proposition that where a tax is imposed which is within the grant of powers, and which does not conflict with any express constitutional limitation, the courts may hold the tax to be void because it is deemed that the tax is too high, is absolutely disposed of by the opinions in . . . cases . . . which expressly hold . . . that "The judicial department cannot prescribe to the legislative department limitations upon the exercise of its acknowledged powers. The power to tax may be exercised oppressively upon persons; but the responsibility of the legislature is not to the courts, but to the people by whom its members are elected."

3. [While] undoubtedly both the 5th and 10th Amendments qualify, in so far as they are applicable, all the provisions of the Constitution, nothing in those amendments operates to take away the grant of power to tax conferred by the Constitution upon Congress. The contention on this subject rests upon the theory that the purpose and motive of Congress in exercising its undoubted powers may be inquired into by the courts, and the proposition is therefore disposed of by what has been said on that subject.

The right of Congress to tax within its delegated power being unrestrained, except as limited by the Constitution, it was within the authority conferred on Congress to select the objects upon which an excise should be laid. It therefore follows that, in exerting its power, no want of due process of law could possibly result, because that body chose to impose an excise on artificially colored oleomargarine, and not upon natural butter artificially colored. The judicial power may not usurp the functions of the legislative in order to control that branch of the government in the performance of its lawful duties. . . .

. . .

4. Lastly we come to consider the argument that, even though as a general rule a tax of the nature of the one in question would be within the power of Congress, in this case the tax should be held not to be within such power, because

of its effect. This is based on the contention that, as the tax is so large as to destroy the business of manufacturing oleomargarine artificially colored to look like butter, it thus deprives the manufacturers of that article of their freedom to engage in a lawful pursuit, and hence, irrespective of the distribution of powers made by the Constitution, the taxing laws are void, because they violate those fundamental rights which it is the duty of every free government to safeguard, and which, therefore, should be held to be embraced by implied, though none the less potential, guaranties, or, in any event, to be within the protection of the due process clause of the 5th Amendment.

* * *

. . . [I]t has been conclusively settled by this court that the tendency of [artificially colored oleomargarine] to deceive the public into buying it for butter is such that the states may, in the exertion of their police powers, without violating the due process clause of the 14th Amendment, absolutely prohibit the manufacture of the article. It hence results, that, even although it be true that the effect of the tax in question is to repress the manufacture of artificially colored oleomargarine, it cannot be said that such repression destroys rights which no free government could destroy, and, therefore, no ground exists to sustain the proposition that the judiciary may invoke an implied prohibition, upon the theory that to do so is essential to save such rights from destruction. . . . From this it follows, as we have also previously declared, that the judiciary is without authority to avoid an act of Congress exerting the taxing power, even in a case where, to the judicial mind, it seems that Congress had, in putting such power in motion, abused its lawful authority by levying a tax which was unwise or oppressive, or the result of the enforcement of which might be to indirectly affect subjects not within the powers delegated to Congress.

Let us concede that if a case was presented where the abuse of the taxing power was so extreme as to be beyond the principles which we have previously stated, and where it was plain to the judicial mind that the power had been called into play, not for revenue, but solely for the purpose of destroying rights which could not be rightfully destroyed consistently with the principles of freedom and justice upon which the Constitution rests, that it would be the duty of the courts to say that such an arbitrary act was not merely an abuse of a delegated power, but was the exercise of an authority not conferred. This concession, however, . . . must be without influence upon the decision of this cause for the reasons previously stated; that is, that the manufacture of artificially colored oleomargarine may be prohibited by a free government without a violation of fundamental rights.

Affirmed.

THE CHIEF JUSTICE, MR. JUSTICE BROWN, and MR. JUSTICE PECKHAM dissent.

Bailey v. Drexel Furniture Co.

259 U.S. 20 (1922)

MR. CHIEF JUSTICE TAFT delivered the opinion of the Court.

This case presents the question of the constitutional validity of the Child Labor Tax Law. . . . [T]he Drexel Furniture Company is engaged in the manufacture of furniture in the western district of North Carolina. On September 20, 1921, it received a notice from Bailey, United States collector of internal revenue for the district, that it had been assessed $6,312.79 for having, during the taxable year 1919, employed and permitted to work in its factory a boy under fourteen years of age, thus incurring the tax of 10 per cent on its net profits for that year. The company paid the tax under protest, and, after rejection of its claim for a refund, brought this suit. . . .

The Child Labor Tax Law . . . begins with § 1200 . . . as follows:

"Sec. 1200. That every person . . . operating (a) any mine or quarry situated in the United States in which children under the age of sixteen years have been employed or permitted to work during any portion of the taxable year; or (b) any mill, cannery, workshop, factory, or manufacturing establishment situated in the United States in which children under the age of fourteen years have been employed or permitted to work, or children between the ages of fourteen and sixteen have been employed or permitted to work more than eight hours in any day or more than six days in any week, or after the hour of seven o'clock [PM] or before the hour of six o'clock [AM] during any portion of the taxable year, shall pay . . . an excise tax equivalent to 10 per centum of the entire net profits received or accrued for such year. . . ."

Section 1203 relieves from liability to the tax anyone who employs a child, believing him to be of proper age. . . .

Section 1206 gives authority to the Commissioner of Internal Revenue or any other person authorized by him, "to enter and inspect at any time any mine, quarry, mill, cannery, workshop, factory or manufacturing establishment." The Secretary of Labor, or any person whom he authorizes, is given like authority in order to comply with a request of the Commissioner to make such inspection and report the same. Any person who refuses entry or obstructs inspection is made subject to fine or imprisonment or both.

The law is attacked on the ground that it is a regulation of the employment of child labor in the states,—an exclusively state function under the Federal Constitution and within the reservations of the 10th Amendment. It is defended on the ground that it is a mere excise tax, levied by the Congress of the United States under its broad power of taxation conferred by § 8, article 1, of the Federal

Constitution. We must construe the law and interpret the intent and meaning of Congress from the language of the act. The words are to be given their ordinary meaning unless the context shows that they are differently used. Does this law impose a tax with only that incidental restraint and regulation which a tax must inevitably involve? Or does it regulate by the use of the so-called tax as a penalty? If a tax, it is clearly an excise. If it were an excise on a commodity or other thing of value we might not be permitted, under previous decisions of this court, to infer, solely from its heavy burden, that the act intends a prohibition instead of a tax. But this act is more. It provides a heavy exaction for a departure from a detailed and specified course of conduct in business. That course of business is that employers shall employ in mines and quarries, children of an age greater than sixteen years; in mills and factories, children of an age greater than fourteen years; and shall prevent children of less than sixteen years in mills and factories from working more than eight hours a day or six days in the week. If an employer departs from this prescribed course of business, he is to pay to the government one tenth of his entire net income in the business for a full year. The amount is not to be proportioned in any degree to the extent or frequency of the departures, but is to be paid by the employer in full measure whether he employs five hundred children for a year, or employs only one for a day. Moreover, if he does not know the child is within the named age limit, he is not to pay; that is to say, it is only where he knowingly departs from the prescribed course that payment is to be exacted. Scienters [parts of an indictment or pleading wherein a defendant's previous knowledge is made known] are associated with penalties, not with taxes. The employer's factory is to be subject to inspection at any time not only by the taxing officers of the Treasury, the Department normally charged with the collection of taxes, but also by the Secretary of Labor and his subordinates, whose normal function is the advancement and protection of the welfare of the workers. In the light of these features of the act, a court must be blind not to see that the so-called tax is imposed to stop the employment of children within the age limits prescribed. Its prohibitory and regulatory effect and purpose are palpable. All others can see and understand this. How can we properly shut our minds to it?

It is the high duty and function of this court in cases regularly brought to its bar to decline to recognize or enforce seeming laws of Congress, dealing with subjects not intrusted to Congress, but left or committed by the supreme law of the land to the control of the states. We cannot avoid the duty even though it require us to refuse to give effect to legislation designed to promote the highest good. The good sought in unconstitutional legislation is an insidious feature because it leads citizens and legislators of good purpose to promote it without thought of the serious breach it will make in the ark of our covenant, or the harm which will come from breaking down recognized standards. In the maintenance of local self-government, on the one hand, and the national power, on the other, our country has been able to endure and prosper for near a century and a half.

Out of a proper respect for the acts of a co-ordinate branch of the government, this court has gone far to sustain taxing acts as such, even though there has been ground for suspecting, from the weight of the tax, it was intended to destroy its subject. But in the act before us, the presumption of validity cannot prevail, because the proof of the contrary is found on the very face of its provisions. Grant the validity of this law, and all that Congress would need to do hereafter, in seeking to take over to its control any one of the great number of subjects of public interest, jurisdiction of which the states have never parted with, and which are reserved to them by the 10th Amendment, would be to enact a detailed measure of complete regulation of the subject and enforce it by a so-called tax upon departures from it. To give such magic to the word "tax" would be to break down all constitutional limitation of the powers of Congress and completely wipe out the sovereignty of the states.

The difference between a tax and a penalty is sometimes difficult to define, and yet the consequences of the distinction in the required method of their collection often are important. Where the sovereign enacting the law has power to impose both tax and penalty, the difference between revenue production and mere regulation may be immaterial; but not so when one sovereign can impose a tax only, and the power of regulation rests in another. Taxes are occasionally imposed in the discretion of the legislature on proper subjects with the primary motive of obtaining revenue from them, and with the incidental motive of discouraging them by making their continuance onerous. They do not lose their character as taxes because of the incidental motive. But there comes a time in the extension of the penalizing features of the so-called tax when it loses its character as such and becomes a mere penalty, with the characteristics of regulation and punishment. Such is the case in the law before us. Although Congress does not invalidate the contract of employment, or expressly declare that the employment within the mentioned ages is illegal, it does exhibit its intent practically to achieve the latter result by adopting the criteria of wrongdoing, and imposing its principal consequence on those who transgress its standard.

The case before us cannot be distinguished from that of Hammer v. Dagenhart. * * *

* * *

The analogy of the Dagenhart Case is clear. The congressional power over interstate commerce is, within its proper scope, just as complete and unlimited as the congressional power to tax; and the legislative motive in its exercise is just as free from judicial suspicion and inquiry. Yet when Congress threatened to stop interstate commerce in ordinary and necessary commodities, unobjectionable as subjects of transportation, and to deny the same to the people of a state, in order to coerce them into compliance with Congress's regulation of state concerns, the court said this was not in fact regulation of interstate commerce, but rather that of state concerns, and was invalid. So here the so-called tax is a penalty to coerce people of a state to act as Congress wishes them to act in respect of a matter completely the business of the state government under the Federal Constitution. . . .

[I]t is pressed upon us that this court has gone so far in sustaining taxing measures the effect and tendency of which was to accomplish purposes not directly within congressional power that we are bound by authority to maintain this law.

The first of these is Veazie Bank v. Fenno. * * * In that case, the validity of a law which increased a tax on the circulating notes of persons and state banks from 1 per centum to 10 per centum was in question. . . .

• • •

. . . [T]he sole objection to the tax . . . was its excessive character. Nothing else appeared on the face of the act. It was an increase of a tax admittedly legal to a higher rate, and that was all. There were no elaborate specifications on the face of the act, as here, indicating the purpose to regulate matters of state concern and jurisdiction through an exaction so applied as to give it the qualities of a penalty for violation of law rather than a tax.

• • •

But more than this, what was charged to be the object of the excessive tax was within the congressional authority. . . . After having pointed out the legitimate means taken by Congress to secure a national medium or currency, the court said * * *

"Having thus, in the exercise of undisputed constitutional powers, undertaken to provide a currency for the whole country, it cannot be questioned that Congress may, constitutionally, secure the benefit of it to the people by appropriate legislation. . . . Congress may restrain, by suitable enactments, the circulation as money of any notes, not issued under its own authority. Without this power, indeed, its attempts to secure a sound and uniform currency for the country must be futile."

The next case is that of McCray v. United States. * * * This court held that the discretion of Congress in the exercise of its constitutional powers to levy excise taxes could not be controlled or limited by the courts because the latter might deem the incidence of the tax oppressive or even destructive. . . . In neither of these cases did the law objected to show on its face, as does the law before us, the detailed specifications of a regulation of a state concern and business with a heavy exaction to promote the efficacy of such regulation.

• • •

The [final] case is United States v. Doremus. * * * That involved the validity of the Narcotic Drug Act * * * which imposed a special tax on the manufacture, importation, and sale or gift of opium or coca leaves or their compounds or derivatives. It required every person subject to the special tax to register with the collector of internal revenue his name and place of business, and forbade him to sell except upon the written order of the person to whom the sale was made, on a form prescribed by the Commissioner of Internal Revenue. . . . The validity of a special tax in the nature of an excise tax on the manufacture, importation, and sale of such drugs was, of course, unquestioned. The provisions for subjecting the sale and distribution of the drugs to official supervision and inspection were held to have a reasonable relation to the enforcement of the tax, and were therefore held valid.

The court said that the act could not be declared invalid just because another motive than taxation, not shown on the face of the act, might have contributed to its passage. This case does not militate against the conclusion we have reached in respect to the law now before us. The court, there, made manifest its view that the provisions of the so-called taxing act must be naturally and reasonably adapted to the collection of the tax, and not solely to the achievement of some other purpose plainly within state power.

For the reasons given, we must hold the Child Labor Tax Law invalid, and the judgment of the District Court is affirmed.

MR. JUSTICE CLARKE dissents.

United States v. Butler

297 U.S. 1 (1936)

MR. JUSTICE ROBERTS delivered the opinion of the Court.

In this case we must determine whether certain provisions of the Agricultural Adjustment Act, 1933, conflict with the federal Constitution.

• • •

On July 14, 1933, the Secretary of Agriculture, with the approval of the President, proclaimed that he had determined rental and benefit payments should be made with respect to cotton; that the marketing year for that commodity was to begin August 1, 1933; and calculated and fixed the rates of processing and floor taxes on cotton in accordance with the terms of the [Agricultural Adjustment Act].

The United States presented a claim to [Butler et al.] as receivers of the Hoosac Mills Corporation for processing and floor taxes on cotton levied under [provisions] of the act. The receivers recommended that the claim be disallowed. The District Court found the taxes valid and ordered them paid. Upon appeal the Circuit Court of Appeals reversed the order. . . .

First. At the outset the United States contends that [Butler has] no standing to question the validity of the tax. The position is that the act is merely a revenue measure levying an excise upon the activity of processing cotton,—a proper subject for the imposition of such a tax,—the proceeds of which go into the federal treasury and thus become available for appropriation for any purpose. It is said that what [Butler is] endeavoring to do is to challenge the intended use of the money pursuant to Congressional appropriation when, by confession, that money will have become the property of the Government and the taxpayer will no longer have any interest in it. [Frothingham v. Mellon] is claimed to foreclose litigation by [Butler] or other taxpayers, as such, looking to restraint of the expenditure of government funds. That case might be an authority in the [Government's] favor if we were here concerned merely with a suit by a taxpayer to restrain the expenditure of the public moneys. . . . Obviously the asserted interest of a taxpayer in the federal government's funds and the supposed increase of the future burden of taxation are minute and indeterminable. But here [Butler, who is] called upon to pay moneys as taxes, resist[s] the exaction as a step in an unauthorized plan. This circumstance clearly distinguishes the case. . . .

The tax can only be sustained by ignoring the avowed purpose and operation of the act, and holding it a measure merely laying an excise upon processors to raise revenue for the support of government. Beyond cavil the sole object of the legislation is to restore the purchasing power of agricultural products to a parity with that prevailing in an earlier day; to take money from the processor and bestow it upon farmers who will reduce their acreage for the accomplishment of the proposed end, and, meanwhile, to aid these farmers during the period required to bring the prices of their crops to the desired level.

The tax plays an indispensable part in the plan of regulation. . . . A tax automatically goes into effect for a commodity when the Secretary of Agriculture determines that rental or benefit payments are to be made for reduction of production of that commodity. The tax is to cease when rental or benefit payments cease. The rate is fixed with the purpose of bringing about crop-reduction and price-raising. . . . If the Secretary finds the policy of the act will not be promoted by the levy of the tax for a given commodity, he may exempt it. * * * The whole revenue from the levy is appropriated in aid of crop control; none of it is made available for general governmental use. The entire agricultural adjustment program * * * is to become inoperative when, in the judgment of the President, the national economic emergency ends. . . .

The statute not only avows an aim foreign to the procurement of revenue for the support of government, but by its operation shows the exaction laid upon processors to be the necessary means for the intended control of agricultural production.

· · ·

It is inaccurate and misleading to speak of the exaction from processors prescribed by the challenged act as a tax, or to say that as a tax it is subject to no infirmity. A tax, in the general understanding of the term, and as used in the Constitution, signifies an exaction for the support of the Government. The word has never been thought to connote the expropriation of money from one group for the benefit of another. We may concede that the latter sort of imposition is constitutional when imposed to effectuate regulation of a matter in which both groups are interested and in respect of which there is a power of legislative regulation. But manifestly no justification for it can be found unless as an integral part of such regulation. The exaction cannot be wrested out of its setting, denominated an excise for raising revenue and legalized by ignoring its purpose as a mere instrumentality for bringing about a desired end. To do this would be to shut our eyes to what all others than we can see and understand. * * *

We conclude that the act is one regulating agricultural production; that the tax is a mere incident of such regulation and that [Butler has] standing to challenge the legality of the exaction.

It does not follow that as the act is not an exertion of the taxing power and the exaction not a true tax, the statute is void or the exaction uncollectible. . . . [I]f this is an expedient regulation by Congress, of a subject within one of its granted powers, "and the end to be attained is one falling within that power, the act is not void, because, within a loose and more extended sense than was used in the Constitution," the exaction is called a tax.

Second. The Government asserts that even if [Butler] may question the propriety of the appropriation embodied in the statute their attack must fail because Article 1, § 8 of the Constitution authorizes the contemplated expenditure of the funds raised by the tax. This contention presents the great and the controlling question in the case. We approach its decision with a sense of our grave responsibility to render judgment in accordance with the principles established for the governance of all three branches of the Government.

There should be no misunderstanding as to the function of this court in such a case. It is sometimes said that the court assumes a power to overrule or control the action of the people's representatives. This is a misconception. The Constitution is the supreme law of the land ordained and established by the people. All legislation must conform to the principles it lays down. When an act of Congress is appropriately challenged in the courts as not conforming to the constitutional mandate the judicial branch of the Government has only one duty,—to lay the article of the Constitution which is invoked beside the statute which is challenged and to decide whether the latter squares with the former. All the court does, or can do, is to announce its considered judgment upon the question. The only power it has, if such it may be called, is the power of judgment. This court neither approves nor condemns any legislative policy. Its delicate and difficult office is to ascertain and declare whether the legislation is in accordance with, or in contravention of, the provisions of the Constitution; and, having done that, its duty ends.

The question is not what power the federal Government ought to have but what powers in fact have been given by the people. . . . Each State has all governmental powers save such as the people, by their Constitution, have conferred upon the United States, denied to the States, or reserved to themselves. The federal union is a government of delegated powers. It has only such as are expressly conferred upon it and such as are reasonably to be implied from those granted. In this respect we differ radically from nations where all legislative power, without restriction or limitation, is vested in a parliament or other legislative body subject to no restrictions except the discretion of its members.

Article I, § 8, of the Constitution vests sundry powers in the Congress. . . .

*   *   *

The clause thought to authorize the legislation,—the first,—confers upon the Congress power "to lay and collect Taxes, Duties, Imposts and Excises, to pay the Debts and provide for the common Defence and general Welfare of the United States. . . ." It is not contended that this provision grants power to regulate agricultural production upon the theory that such legislation would promote the general welfare. The Government concedes that the phrase "to provide for the general welfare" qualifies the power "to lay and collect taxes." The view that the clause grants power to provide for the general welfare, independently of the taxing power, has never been authoritatively accepted. Mr. Justice Story points out that if it were adopted "it is obvious that under color of the generality of the words, to 'provide for the common defence and general welfare,' the government of the United States is, in reality, a government of general and unlimited powers, notwithstanding the subsequent enumeration of specific powers." The true construction undoubtedly is that the only thing granted is the power to tax for the purpose of providing funds for payment of the nation's debts and making provision for the general welfare.

Nevertheless the Government asserts that warrant is found in this clause for the adoption of the Agricultural Adjustment Act. The argument is that Congress may appropriate and authorize the spending of moneys for the "general welfare"; that the phrase should be liberally construed to cover anything conducive to national welfare; that decision as to what will promote such welfare rests with Congress alone, and the courts may not review its determination; and finally that the appropriation under attack was in fact for the general welfare of the United States.

The Congress is expressly empowered to lay taxes to provide for the general welfare. Funds in the Treasury as a result of taxation may be expended only through appropriation. * * * They can never accomplish the objects for which they were collected unless the power to appropriate is as broad as the power to tax. The necessary implication from the terms of the grant is that the public funds may be appropriated "to provide for the general welfare of the United States." These words cannot be meaningless, else they would not have been used. The conclusion must be that they were intended to limit and define the granted power to raise and to expend money. How shall they be construed to effectuate the intent of the instrument?

Since the foundation of the nation sharp differences of opinion have persisted as to the true interpretation of the phrase. Madison asserted it amounted to no more than a reference to the other powers enumerated in the subsequent clauses of the same section; that, as the United States is a government of limited and enumerated powers, the grant of power to tax and spend for the general national welfare must be confined to the enumerated legislative fields committed to the Congress. In this view the phrase is mere tautology, for taxation and appropriation are or may be necessary incidents of the exercise of any of the enumerated legislative powers. Hamilton, on the other hand, maintained the clause confers a power separate and distinct from those later enumerated, is not restricted in meaning by the grant of them, and Congress consequently has a substantive power to tax and to appropriate, limited only by the requirement that it shall be exercised to provide for the general welfare of the United States. Each contention has had the support of those whose views are entitled to weight. This court has noticed the question, but has never found it necessary to decide which is the true construction. Mr. Justice Story, in his Commentaries, espouses the Hamiltonian position. We shall not review the writings of public men and commentators or discuss the legislative practice. Study of all these leads us to conclude that the reading advocated by Mr. Justice Story is the correct one. While, therefore, the power to tax is not unlimited, its confines are set in the clause which confers it, and not in those of § 8 which bestow and define the legislative powers of the Congress. It results that the power of Congress to authorize expenditure of public moneys for public purposes is not limited by the direct grants of legislative power found in the Constitution.

But the adoption of the broader construction leaves the power to spend subject to limitations.

As Story says:

"The Constitution was, from its very origin, contemplated to be the frame of a national government, of special and enumerated powers, and not of general and unlimited powers."

Again he says:

"A power to lay taxes for the common defence and general welfare of the United States is not in common sense a general power. It is limited to those objects. It cannot constitutionally transcend them."

That the qualifying phrase must be given effect all advocates of broad construction admit. Hamilton, in his well known Report on Manufactures, states that the purpose must be "general, and not local." . . . Story says that if the tax be not proposed for the common defence or general welfare, but for other objects wholly extraneous, it would be wholly indefensible upon constitutional principles. And he makes it clear that the powers of taxation and appropriation extend only to matters of national, as distinguished from local, welfare.

• • •

We are not now required to ascertain the scope of the phrase "general welfare of the United States" or to determine whether an appropriation in aid of agriculture falls within it. Wholly apart from that question, another principle embedded in our Constitution prohibits the enforcement of the Agricultural Adjustment Act. The act invades the reserved rights of the states. It is a statutory plan to regulate and control agricultural production, a matter beyond the powers delegated to the federal government. The tax, the appropriation of the funds raised, and the direction for their disbursement, are but parts of the plan. They are but means to an unconstitutional end.

From the accepted doctrine that the United States is a government of delegated powers, it follows that those not expressly granted, or reasonably to be implied from such as are conferred, are reserved to the states or to the people. To forestall any suggestion to the contrary, the Tenth Amendment was adopted. The same proposition, otherwise stated, is that powers not granted are prohibited. None to regulate agricultural production is given, and therefore legislation by Congress for that purpose is forbidden.

It is an established principle that the attainment of a prohibited end may not be accomplished under the pretext of the exertion of powers which are granted.

• • •

The power of taxation, which is expressly granted, may, of course, be adopted as a means to carry into operation another power also expressly granted. But resort to the taxing power to effectuate an end which is not legitimate, not within the scope of the Constitution, is obviously inadmissible.

• • •

Third. If the taxing power may not be used as the instrument to enforce a regulation of matters of state concern with respect to which the Congress has no authority to interfere, may it, as in the present case, be employed to raise the money necessary to purchase a compliance which the Congress is powerless to command? The Government asserts that whatever might be said against the validity of the plan, if compulsory, it is constitutionally sound because the end is accomplished by voluntary cooperation. There are two sufficient answers to the contention. The regulation is not in fact voluntary. The farmer, of course, may refuse to comply, but the price of such refusal is the loss of benefits. The amount offered is intended to be sufficient to exert pressure on him to agree to the proposed regulation. The power to confer or withhold unlimited benefits is the power to coerce or destroy. If the cotton grower elects not to accept the benefits, he will receive less for his crops; those who receive payments will be able to undersell him. The result may well be financial ruin. . . . This is coercion by economic pressure. The asserted power of choice is illusory.

· · ·

But if the plan were one for purely voluntary co-operation it would stand no better so far as federal power is concerned. At best it is a scheme for purchasing with federal funds submission to federal regulation of a subject reserved to the states.

· · ·

Congress has no power to enforce its commands on the farmer to the ends sought by the Agricultural Adjustment Act. It must follow that it may not indirectly accomplish those ends by taxing and spending to purchase compliance. The Constitution and the entire plan of our government negative any such use of the power to tax and to spend as the act undertakes to authorize. It does not help to declare that local conditions throughout the nation have created a situation of national concern; for this is but to say that whenever there is a widespread similarity of local conditions, Congress may ignore constitutional limitations upon its own powers and usurp those reserved to the states. If, in lieu of compulsory regulation of subjects within the states' reserved jurisdiction, which is prohibited, the Congress could invoke the taxing and spending power as a means to accomplish the same end, clause 1 of § 8 of Article I would become the instrument for total subversion of the governmental powers reserved to the individual states.

· · ·

Hamilton himself, the leading advocate of broad interpretation of the power to tax and to appropriate for the general welfare, never suggested that any power granted by the Constitution could be used for the destruction of local self-government in the states. Story countenances no such doctrine. It seems never to have occurred to them, or to those who have agreed with them, that the general welfare of the United States, . . . might be served by obliterating the constituent members of the Union. But to this fatal conclusion the doctrine contended for would inevitably lead. And its sole premise is that, though the makers of the Constitution, in erecting the federal government, intended sedulously to limit and define its powers, so as to reserve to the states and the people sovereign power, to be wielded by the states and their citizens and not to be invaded by the United States, they nevertheless by a single clause gave power to the Congress to tear down the barriers, to invade the states' jurisdiction, and to become a parliament of the whole people, subject to no restrictions save such as are self-imposed. The argument when seen in its true character and in the light of its inevitable results must be rejected.

· · ·

The judgment is affirmed.

Mr. Justice Stone, dissenting.

I think the judgment should be reversed. The present stress of widely held and strongly expressed differences of opinion of the wisdom of the Agricultural Adjustment Act makes it important, in the interest of clear thinking and sound result, to emphasize at the outset certain propositions which should have controlling influence in determining the validity of the Act. They are:

1. The power of courts to declare a statute unconstitutional is subject to two guiding principles of decision which ought never to be absent from judicial consciousness. One is that courts are concerned only with the power to enact statutes, not with their wisdom. The other is that while unconstitutional exercise of power by the executive and legislative branches of the government is subject to judicial restraint, the only check upon our own exercise of power is our own sense of self-restraint. For the removal of unwise laws from the statute books appeal lies not to the courts but to the ballot and to the processes of democratic government.

2. The constitutional power of Congress to levy an excise tax upon the processing of agricultural products is not questioned. The present levy is held invalid, not for any want of power in Congress to lay such a tax to defray public expenditures, including those for the general welfare, but because the use to which its proceeds are put is disapproved.

3. As the present depressed state of agriculture is nation-wide in its extent and effects, there is no basis for saying that the expenditure of public money in aid of farmers is not within the specifically granted power of Congress to levy taxes to "provide for the . . . general welfare." The opinion of the Court does not declare otherwise.

•   •   •

It is with these preliminary and hardly controverted matters in mind that we should direct our attention to the pivot on which the decision of the Court is made to turn. It is that a levy unquestionably within the taxing power of Congress may be treated as invalid because it is a step in a plan to regulate agricultural production and is thus a forbidden infringement of state power. The levy is not any the less an exercise of taxing power because it is intended to defray an expenditure for the general welfare rather than for some other support of government. Nor is the levy and collection of the tax pointed to as effecting the regulation. While all federal taxes inevitably have some influence on the internal economy of the states, it is not contended that the levy of a processing tax upon manufacturers using agricultural products as raw material has any perceptible regulatory effect upon either their production or manufacture. The tax is unlike the penalties which were held invalid in the Child Labor Tax Case * * * because they were themselves the instruments of regulation by virtue of their coercive effect on matters left to the control of the states. Here regulation, if any there be, is accomplished not by the tax but by the method by which its proceeds are expended, and would equally be accomplished by any like use of public funds, regardless of their source.

* * *

It is upon the contention that state power is infringed by purchased regulation of agricultural production that chief reliance is placed. It is insisted that, while the Constitution gives to Congress, in specific and unambiguous terms, the power to tax and spend, the power is subject to limitations which do not find their origin in any express provision of the Constitution and to which other expressly delegated powers are not subject.

The Constitution requires that public funds shall be spent for a defined purpose, the promotion of the general welfare. . . . The power of Congress to spend is inseparable from persuasion to action over which Congress has no legislative control. Congress may not command that the science of agriculture be taught in state universities. But if it would aid the teaching of that science by grants to state institutions, it is appropriate, if not necessary, that the grant be on the condition * * * that it be used for the intended purpose. Similarly it would seem to be compliance with the Constitution, not violation of it, for the government to take and the university to give a contract that the grant would be so used. It makes no difference that there is a promise to do an act which the condition is calculated to induce. Condition and promise are alike valid since both are in furtherance of the national purpose for which the money is appropriated.

These effects upon individual action, which are but incidents of the authorized expenditure of government money, are pronounced to be themselves a limitation upon the granted power, and so the time-honored principle of constitutional interpretation that the granted power includes all those which are incident to it is reversed. . . .

* * *

. . . The spending power of Congress is in addition to the legislative power and not subordinate to it. This independent grant of the power of the purse, and its very nature, involving in its exercise the duty to insure expenditure within the granted power, presuppose freedom of selection among divers ends and aims, and the capacity to impose such conditions as will render the choice effective. It is a contradiction in terms to say that there is power to spend for the national welfare, while rejecting any power to impose conditions reasonably adapted to the attainment of the end which alone would justify the expenditure.

The limitation now sanctioned must lead to absurd consequences. The government may give seeds to farmers, but may not condition the gift upon their being planted in places where they are most needed or even planted at all. The government may give money to the unemployed, but may not ask that those who get it shall give labor in return, or even use it to support their families. It may give money to sufferers from earthquake, fire, tornado, pestilence or flood, but may not impose conditions—health precautions designed to prevent the spread of disease, or induce the movement of population to safer or more sanitary areas. All that, because it is purchased regulation infringing state powers, must be left for the states, who are unable or unwilling to supply the necessary relief. . . . Do all its activities collapse because, in order to effect the permissible purpose, in myriad ways the money is paid out upon terms and conditions which influence action of the recipients within the states, which Congress cannot command? The answer would seem plain. If the expenditure is for a national public purpose, that purpose will not be thwarted because payment is on condition which will advance that purpose. The action which Congress induces by payments of money to promote the general welfare, but which it does not command or coerce, is but an incident to a specifically granted power, but a permissible means to a legitimate end. If appropriation in aid of a program of curtailment of agricultural production is constitutional, and it is not denied that it is, payment to farmers on condition that they reduce their crop acreage is constitutional. It is not any the less so because the farmer at his own option promises to fulfill the condition.

That the governmental power of the purse is a great one is not now for the first time announced. Every student of the history of government and economics is aware of its magnitude and of its existence in every civilized government. Both were well understood by the framers of the Constitution when they sanctioned the grant of the spending power to the federal government, and both were recognized by Hamilton and Story, whose views of the spending power as standing on a parity with the other powers specifically granted, have hitherto been generally accepted.

The suggestion that it must now be curtailed by judicial fiat because it may be abused by unwise use hardly rises to the dignity of argument. So may judicial power be abused. "The power to tax is the power to destroy," but we do not, for that reason, doubt its existence, or hold that its efficacy is to be restricted by its incidental or collateral effects upon the states. * * * The power to tax and spend is not without constitutional restraints. One restriction is that the purpose must be truly national. Another is that it may not be used to coerce action left to state control. Another is the conscience and patriotism of Congress and the Executive.
. . .

A tortured construction of the Constitution is not to be justified by recourse to extreme examples of reckless congressional spending which might occur if courts could not prevent—expenditures which, even if they could be thought to effect any national purpose, would be possible only by action of a legislature lost to all sense of public responsibility. Such suppositions are addressed to the mind accustomed to believe that it is the business of courts to sit in judgment on the wisdom of legislative action. Courts are not the only agency of government that must be assumed to have capacity to govern. Congress and the courts both unhappily may falter or be mistaken in the performance of their constitutional duty. But interpretation of our great charter of government which proceeds on any assumption that the responsibility for the preservation of our institutions is the exclusive concern of any one of the three branches of government, or that it alone can save them from destruction, is far more likely, in the long run, "to obliterate the constituent members" of "an indestructible union of indestructible states" than the frank recognition that language, even of a constitution, may mean what it says: that the power to tax and spend includes the power to relieve a nation-wide economic maladjustment by conditional gifts of money.

Mr. Justice Brandeis and Mr. Justice Cardozo join in this opinion.

Steward Machine Co. v. Davis

301 U.S. 548 (1937)

Mr. Justice Cardozo delivered the opinion of the Court.

The validity of the tax imposed by the Social Security Act on employers of eight or more is here to be determined.

[Steward Machine Co.] paid a tax in accordance with the statute, filed a claim for refund with the Commissioner of Internal Revenue, and sued to recover the payment ($46.14), asserting a conflict between the statute and the Constitution of the United States. . . . An important question of constitutional law being involved, we granted certiorari. * * *

The Social Security Act * * * is divided into eleven separate titles, of which only titles IX. and III. are so related to this case as to stand in need of summary.

. . . [Under Title IX] every employer (with stated exceptions) is to pay for each calendar year "an excise tax, with respect to having individuals in his employ," the tax to be measured by prescribed percentages of the total wages payable by the employer during the calendar year with respect to such employment. * * *

Under [Title III] certain sums of money are "authorized to be appropriated" for the purpose of assisting the states in the administration of their unemployment compensation laws. . . . The appropriations when made were not specifically out of the proceeds of the employment tax, but out of any moneys in the Treasury. Other sections of the title prescribe the method by which the payments are to be made to the state * * * and also certain conditions to be established. . . . They are designed to give assurance to the Federal Government that the moneys granted by it will not be expended for purposes alien to the grant, and will be used in the administration of genuine unemployment compensation laws.

The assault on the statute proceeds on an extended front. Its assailants take the ground that the tax is not an excise; that it is not uniform throughout the United States as excises are required to be; that its exceptions are so many and arbitrary as to violate the Fifth Amendment; that its purpose was not revenue, but an unlawful invasion of the reserved powers of the states; and that the states in submitting to it have yielded to coercion and have abandoned governmental functions which they are not permitted to surrender.

. . .

First: The tax, which is described in the statute as an excise, is laid with uniformity throughout the United States as a duty, an impost or an excise upon the relation of employment.

1. We are told that the relation of employment is one so essential to the pursuit of happiness that it may not be burdened with a tax. Appeal is made to history. From the precedents of colonial days we are supplied with illustrations of excises common in the colonies. They are said to have been bound up with the enjoyment of particular commodities. . . .

. . . Doubtless there were many excises in colonial days and later that were associated, more or less intimately, with the enjoyment or the use of property. This would not prove, even if no others were then known, that the forms then accepted were not subject to enlargement. * * * But in truth other excises *were* known, and known since early times. . . . Our colonial forbears knew more about ways of taxing than some of their descendants seem to be willing to concede.

The historical prop failing, the prop or fancied prop of principle remains. We learn that employment for lawful gain is a "natural" or "inherent" or "inalienable" right, and not a "privilege" at all. But natural rights, so called, are as much subject to taxation as rights of less importance. An excise is not limited to vocations or activities that may be prohibited altogether. It is not limited to those that are the outcome of a franchise. It extends to vocations or activities pursued as of common right. What the individual does in the operation of a business is amenable to taxation just as much as what he owns, at all events if the classification is not tyrannical or arbitrary. . . .

The subject matter of taxation open to the power of the Congress is as comprehensive as that open to the power of the states, though the method of apportionment may at times be different. . . . The statute books of the states are strewn with illustrations of taxes laid on occupations pursued of common right. We find no basis for a holding that the power in that regard which belongs by accepted practice to the legislatures of the states, has been denied by the Constitution to the Congress of the nation.

2. The tax being an excise, its imposition must conform to the canon of uniformity. There has been no departure from this requirement. According to the settled doctrine the uniformity exacted is geographical, not intrinsic. * * *

Second: The excise is not invalid under the provisions of the Fifth Amendment by force of its exemptions.

The statute does not apply . . . to employers of less than eight. It does not apply to agricultural labor, or domestic service in a private home or to some other classes of less importance. [Steward Machine Co.] contends that the effect of these restrictions is an arbitrary discrimination vitiating the tax.

The Fifth Amendment unlike the Fourteenth has no equal protection clause. * * * But even the states, though subject to such a clause, are not confined to a formula of rigid uniformity in framing measures of taxation. * * * They may tax some kinds of property at one rate, and others at another, and exempt others altogether. * * * They may lay an excise on the operations of a particular kind of business, and exempt some other kind of business closely akin thereto. * * * If this latitude of judgment is lawful for the states, it is lawful . . . in legislation by the Congress, which is subject to restraints less narrow and confining. * * *

The classifications and exemptions directed by the statute now in controversy have support in considerations of policy and practical convenience that cannot be condemned as arbitrary. The classifications and exemptions would therefore be upheld if they had been adopted by a state and the provisions of the Fourteenth Amendment were invoked to annul them. . . . The act of Congress is therefore valid, so far at least as its system of exemptions is concerned, and this though we assume that discrimination, if gross enough, is equivalent to confiscation and subject under the Fifth Amendment to challenge and annulment.

Third: The excise is not void as involving the coercion of the States in contravention of the Tenth Amendment or of restrictions implicit in our federal form of government.

The proceeds of the excise when collected are paid into the Treasury at Washington, and thereafter are subject to appropriation like public moneys generally. * * * No presumption can be indulged that they will be misapplied or wasted. Even if they were collected in the hope or expectation that some other and collateral good would be furthered as an incident, that without more would not make the act invalid. * * * . . .

To draw the line intelligently between duress and inducement there is need to remind ourselves of facts as to the problem of unemployment that are now matters of common knowledge. * * * Of the many available figures a few only will be mentioned. During the years 1929 to 1936, when the country was passing through a cyclical depression, the number of the unemployed mounted to unprecedented heights. Often the average was more than 10 million; at times a peak was attained of 16 million or more. Disaster to the breadwinner meant disaster to dependents. Accordingly the roll of the unemployed, itself formidable enough, was only a partial roll of the destitute or needy. The fact developed quickly that the states were unable to give the requisite relief. The problem had become national in area and dimensions. There was need of help from the nation if the people were not to starve. It is too late today for the argument to be heard with tolerance that in a crisis so extreme the use of the moneys of the nation to relieve the unemployed and their dependents is a use for any purpose narrower than the promotion of the general welfare. * * * . . .

In the presence of this urgent need for some remedial expedient, the question is to be answered whether the expedient adopted has overleapt the bounds of power. The assailants of the statute say that its dominant end and aim is to drive the state legislatures under the whip of economic pressure into the enactment of unemployment compensation laws at the bidding of the central government. Supporters of the statute say that its operation is not constraint, but the creation of a larger freedom, the states and the nation joining in a cooperative endeavor to avert a common evil. . . .

The Social Security Act is an attempt to find a method by which all these public agencies may work together to a common end. Every dollar of the new taxes will continue in all likelihood to be used and needed by the nation as long as states are unwilling, whether through timidity or for other motives, to do what can be done at home. At least the inference is permissible that Congress so believed, though retaining undiminished freedom to spend the money as it pleased. On the other hand fulfilment of the home duty will be lightened and encouraged by crediting the taxpayer upon his account with the Treasury of the nation to the extent that his contributions under the laws of the locality have simplified or diminished the problem of relief and the probable demand upon the resources of the fisc. . . .

Who then is coerced through the operation of this statute? Not the taxpayer. He pays in fulfilment of the mandate of the local legislature. Not the state. Even now she does not offer a suggestion that in passing the unemployment law she was affected by duress. * * * For all that appears she is satisfied with her choice, and would be sorely disappointed if it were now to be annulled. The difficulty with the petitioner's contention is that it confuses motive with coercion. "Every tax is in some measure regulatory. To some extent it interposes an economic impediment to the activity taxed as compared with others not taxed." * * * In like manner every rebate from a tax when conditioned upon conduct is in some measure a temptation. But to hold that motive or temptation is equivalent to coercion is to plunge the law in endless difficulties. The outcome of such a doctrine is the acceptance of a philosophical determinism by which choice becomes impossible. Till now the law has been guided by a robust common sense which assumes the freedom of the will as a working hypothesis in the solution of its problems. The wisdom of the hypothesis has illustration in this case. Nothing in the case suggests the exertion of a power akin to undue influence, if we assume that such a concept can ever be applied with fitness to the relations between state and nation. Even on that assumption the location of the point at which pressure turns into compulsion, and ceases to be inducement, would be a question of degree,—at times, perhaps, of fact. . . .

In ruling as we do, we leave many questions open. We do not say that a tax is valid, when imposed by act of Congress, if it is laid upon the condition that a state may escape its operation through the adoption of a statute unrelated in subject matter to activities fairly within the scope of national policy and power. No such question is before us. . . .

Fourth: The statute does not call for a surrender by the states of powers essential to their quasi-sovereign existence.

•   •   •

The judgment is affirmed.

Separate opinion of Mr. Justice McReynolds (dissenting).

That portion of the Social Security legislation here under consideration, I think, exceeds the power granted to Congress. It unduly interferes with the orderly government of the State by her own people and otherwise offends the Federal Constitution.

•   •   •

The doctrine thus announced and often repeated, I had supposed was firmly established. Apparently the States remained really free to exercise governmental powers, not delegated or prohibited, without interference by the Federal Government through threats of punitive measures or offers of seductive favors. Unfortunately, the decision just announced opens the way for practical annihilation of this theory. . . .

•   •   •

No defense is offered for the legislation under review upon the basis of emergency. The hypothesis is that hereafter it will continuously benefit unemployed members of a class. Forever, so far as we can see, the States are expected to function under federal direction concerning an internal matter. By the sanction of this adventure, the door is open for progressive inauguration of others of like kind under which it can hardly be expected that the States will retain genuine independence of action. And without independent States a Federal Union as contemplated by the Constitution becomes impossible.

•   •   •

Ordinarily, I must think, a denial that the challenged action of Congress and what has been done under it amount to coercion and impair freedom of government by the people of the State would be regarded as contrary to practical experience. Unquestionably our federate plan of government confronts an enlarged peril.

Separate opinion of Mr. Justice Sutherland (dissenting in part).

•   •   •

If we are to survive as the United States, the balance between the powers of the nation and those of the states must be maintained. There is grave danger in permitting it to dip in either direction, danger—if there were no other—in the precedent thereby set for further departures from the equipoise. The threat implicit in the present encroachment upon the administrative functions of the states is that greater encroachments, and encroachments upon other functions, will follow.

For the foregoing reasons, I think the judgment below should be reversed.

Mr. Justice Van Devanter joins in this opinion.

Mr. Justice Butler (dissenting). [Omitted.]

Buckley v. Valeo

424 U.S. 1 (1976)

[Per curiam.]

* * *

Public Financing of Presidential Election Campaigns

A series of statutes for the public financing of Presidential election campaigns produced the scheme now found in * * * Subtitle H * * * of the Internal Revenue Code. . . . Both the District Court * * * and the Court of Appeals * * * sustained Subtitle H against a constitutional attack. [Buckley et al.] renew their challenge here, contending that the legislation violates the First and Fifth Amendments. We find no merit in their claims and affirm.

A. Summary of Subtitle H

[Subtitle H] establishes a Presidential Election Campaign Fund, financed from general revenues in the aggregate amount designated by individual taxpayers * * * who on their income tax returns may authorize payment to the Fund of one dollar of their tax liability in the case of an individual return or two dollars in the case of a joint return. The Fund consists of three separate accounts to finance (1) party nominating conventions, * * * (2) general election campaigns, * * * and (3) primary campaigns. * * *

[The section of the statute], which concerns financing of party nominating conventions and general election campaigns, distinguishes among "major," "minor," and "new" parties. . . .

Major parties are entitled to $2,000,000 to defray their national committee Presidential nominating convention expenses, must limit total expenditures to that amount, * * * and they may not use any of this money to benefit a particular candidate or delegate. * * * A minor party receives a portion of the major-party entitlement determined by the ratio of the votes received by the party's candidate in the last election to the average of the votes received by the major-parties' candidates. . . .

For expenses in the general election campaign, [the law] . . . entitles each major-party candidate to $20,000,000. . . . Minor-party candidates are also entitled to funding, again based on the ratio of the vote received by the party's candidate in the preceding election to the average of the major-party candidates. . . .

B. Constitutionality of Subtitle H

[Buckley argues] that Subtitle H is invalid (1) as "contrary to the 'general welfare,' " Art I, § 8, (2) because any scheme of public financing of election campaigns is inconsistent with the First Amendment, and (3) because Subtitle H invidiously discriminates against certain interests in violation of the Due Process Clause of the Fifth Amendment. We find no merit in these contentions.

[Buckley's] "general welfare" contention erroneously treats the General Welfare Clause as a limitation upon congressional power. It is rather a grant of power, the scope of which is quite expansive, particularly in view of the enlargement of power by the Necessary and Proper Clause. * * * Congress has power to regulate Presidential elections and primaries, * * * and public financing of Presidential elections as a means to reform the electoral process was clearly a choice within the granted power. It is for Congress to decide which expenditures will promote the general welfare: "[T]he power of Congress to authorize expenditure of public moneys for public purposes is not limited by the direct grants of legislative power found in the Constitution." * * * Any limitations upon the exercise of that granted power must be found elsewhere in the Constitution. In this case, Congress was legislating for the "general welfare"—to reduce the deleterious influence of large contributions on our political process, to facilitate communication by candidates with the electorate, and to free candidates from the rigors of fundraising. * * * Whether the chosen means appear "bad," "unwise," or "unworkable" to us is irrelevant; Congress has concluded that the means are "necessary and proper" to promote the general welfare, and we thus decline to find this legislation without the grant of power in Art I, § 8.

[Buckley's] challenge to the dollar check-off provision * * * fails for the same reason. [He maintains] that Congress is required to permit taxpayers to designate particular candidates or parties as recipients of their money. But the appropriation to the Fund * * * is like any other appropriation from the general revenue except that its amount is determined by reference to the aggregate of the one- and two-dollar authorization on taxpayers' income tax returns. This detail does not constitute the appropriation any less an appropriation by Congress. The fallacy of appellants' argument is therefore apparent; every appropriation made by Congress uses public money in a manner to which some taxpayers object.

[Buckley et al.] next argue that "by analogy" to the religion clauses of the First Amendment public financing of election campaigns, however meritorious, violates the First Amendment. We have of course held that the Religion Clauses—"Congress shall make no law respecting an establishment of religion, or prohibiting the free exercise thereof"—require Congress, and the States through the Fourteenth Amendment, to remain neutral in matters of religion. * * * The Government may not aid one religion to the detriment of others or impose a burden on one religion that is not imposed on others, and may not even aid all religions. * * * But the analogy is patently inapplicable to our issue here. Although "Congress shall make no law . . . abridging the freedom of speech, or of the press," Subtitle H is a congressional effort, not to abridge, restrict, or censor speech, but rather to use public money to facilitate and enlarge public discussion and participation in the electoral process, goals vital to a self-governing people. Thus, Subtitle H furthers, not abridges, pertinent First Amendment values. [Buckley argues], however, that as constructed public financing invidiously discriminates in violation of the Fifth Amendment.

. . . In several situations concerning the electoral process, the principle has been developed that restrictions on access to the electoral process must survive exacting scrutiny. The restriction can be sustained only if it furthers a "vital" governmental interest * * * that is "achieved by a means that does not unfairly or unnecessarily burden either a minority party's or an individual candidate's equally important interest in the continued availability of political opportunity." * * * [These matters], however, dealt primarily with state laws requiring a candidate to satisfy certain requirements in order to have his name appear on the ballot. These were of course direct burdens not only on the candidate's ability to run for office but also on the voter's ability to voice preferences regarding representative government and contemporary issues. In contrast, the denial of public financing to some Presidential candidates is not restrictive of voters' rights and less restrictive of candidates'. Subtitle H does not prevent any candidate from getting on the ballot or any voter from casting a vote for the candidate of his choice; the inability, if any, of minority-party candidates to wage effective campaigns will derive not from lack of public funding but from their inability to raise private contributions. Any disadvantages suffered by operation of the eligibility formulae under Subtitle H is thus limited to the claimed denial of the enhancement of opportunity to communicate with the electorate that the formula affords eligible candidates. But eligible candidates suffer a countervailing denial. . . . [A]cceptance of public financing entails voluntary acceptance of an expenditure ceiling. Noneligible candidates are not subject to that limitation. Accordingly, we conclude that public financing is generally less restrictive of access to the electoral process than the ballot-access regulations. . . . In any event, Congress enacted Subtitle H in furtherance of sufficiently important governmental interests and has not unfairly or unnecessarily burdened the political opportunity of any party or candidate.

It cannot be gainsaid that public financing as a means of eliminating the improper influence of large private contributions furthers a significant governmental interest. * * * In addition, the limits on contributions necessarily increase the burden of fundraising, and Congress properly regarded public financing as an appropriate means of relieving major-party Presidential candidates from the rigors of soliciting private contributions. . . . Congress' interest in not funding hopeless candidacies with large sums of public money * * * necessarily justifies the withholding of public assistance from candidates without significant public support. Thus, Congress may legitimately require "some preliminary showing of a significant modicum of support" * * * as an eligibility requirement for public funds. This requirement also serves the important public interest against providing artificial incentives to "splintered parties and unrestrained factionalism." * * *

At the same time Congress recognized the constitutional restraints against inhibition of the present opportunity of minority parties to become major political entities if they obtain widespread support. * * * . . .

General Election Campaign Financing

. . . [P]rovisions [for financing the general election], it is argued, are fatal to the validity of the scheme, because they work invidious discrimination against minor and new parties in violation of the Fifth Amendment. We disagree.

. . . [T]he Constitution does not require Congress to treat all declared candidates the same for public financing purposes. . . . Third parties have been completely incapable of matching the major parties' ability to raise money and win elections. Congress was of course aware of this fact of American life, and thus was justified in providing both major parties full funding and all other parties only a percentage of the major-party entitlement. Identical treatment of all parties, on the other hand, "would not only make it easy to raid the United States Treasury, it would also artificially foster the proliferation of splinter parties." * * * . . .

• • •

. . . Without any doubt a range of formulations would sufficiently protect the public fisc and not foster factionalism, and also recognize the public interest in the fluidity of our political affairs. We cannot say that Congress' choice falls without the permissible range.

• • •

Mr. Chief Justice Burger, concurring in part, and dissenting in part.

Public Financing

I dissent from . . . sustaining the constitutionality of the public financing provisions of the Act.

Since the turn of this century when the idea of Government subsidies for political campaigns first was broached, there has been no lack of realization that the use of funds from the public treasury to subsidize political activity of private individuals would produce substantial and profound questions about the nature of our democratic society. . . .

The Court chooses to treat this novel public financing of political activity as simply another congressional appropriation whose validity is "necessary and proper" to Congress' power to regulate and reform elections and primaries. * * * No holding of this Court is directly in point, because no federal scheme allocating public funds in a comparable manner has ever been before us. The uniqueness of the plan is not relevant, of course, to whether Congress has power to enact it. Indeed, I do not question the power of Congress to regulate elections; nor do I challenge the broad proposition that the General Welfare Clause is a grant, not a limitation, of power. * * *

I would, however, fault the Court for not adequately analyzing and meeting head-on the issue whether public financial assistance to the private political activity of individual citizens and parties is a legitimate expenditure of public funds. The public monies at issue here are not being employed simply to police the integrity of the electoral process or to provide a forum for the use of all participants in the political dialog, as would, for example, be the case if free broadcast time were granted. Rather, we are confronted with the Government's actual financing, out of general revenues, a segment of the political debate itself. As Senator Howard Baker remarked during the debate on this legislation:

> "I think there is something politically incestuous about the Government financing and, I believe, inevitably then regulating, the day to day procedures by which the Government is selected . . . . I think it is extraordinarily important that the Government not control the machinery by which the public expresses the range of its desires, demands, and dissent." * * *

If this "incest" affected only the issue of the wisdom of the plan, it would be none of the concern of judges. But, in my view, the inappropriateness of subsidizing, from general revenues, the actual political dialog of the people—the process which begets the Government itself—is as basic to our national tradition as the separation of church and state also deriving from the First Amendment, * * * or the separation of civilian and military authority, * * * neither of which is explicit in the Constitution but which have developed through case by case adjudication of express provisions of the Constitution.

Recent history shows dangerous examples of systems with a close, "incestuous" relationship between "government" and "politics"; the Court's opinion simply dismisses possible dangers by noting that:

"Subtitle H is a congressional effort, not to abridge, restrict or censor speech, but rather to use public money to facilitate and enlarge public discussion and participation in the electoral process, goals vital to a self-governing people."

. . . [T]he Court points to no basis for predicting that the historical pattern of "varying measures of control and surveillance" * * * which usually accompany grants from Government will not also follow in this case. Up to now, the Court has always been extraordinarily sensitive, when dealing with First Amendment rights, to the risk that the "flag-tends-to-follow-the-dollars." Yet, here, where the Act specifically requires the auditing of records of political parties and candidates by Government inspectors, the Court shows little sensitivity to the danger it has so strongly condemned in other contexts. * * * Up to now, this Court has scrupulously refrained, absent claims of invidious discrimination, from entering the arena of intra-party disputes concerning the seating of convention delegates. * * * An obvious underlying basis for this reluctance is that delegate selection and the management of political conventions have been considered a strictly private political matter, not the business of Government inspectors. But once the Government finances these national conventions by the expenditure of millions of dollars from the public treasury, we may be providing a springboard for later attempts to impose a whole range of requirements on delegate selection and convention activities. Does this foreshadow judicial decisions allowing the federal courts to "monitor" these conventions to assure compliance with court orders or regulations?

Assuming . . . that Congress could validly appropriate public money to subsidize private political activity, it has gone about the task in this Act in a manner which is not, in my view, free of constitutional infirmity. I do not question that Congress has "wide discretion in the manner of prescribing details of expenditures" in some contexts. * * * Here, however, Congress has not itself appropriated a specific sum to attain the ends of the Act but has delegated to a limited group of citizens—those who file tax returns—the power to allocate general revenue for the Act's purposes—and of course only a small percentage of that limited group has exercised the power. There is nothing to assure that the "fund" will actually be adequate for the Act's objectives. Thus, I find it difficult to see a rational basis for concluding that this scheme would, in fact, attain the stated purposes of the Act when its own funding scheme affords no real idea of the amount of the available funding.

. . . [T]he scheme approved by the Court today invidiously discriminates against minor parties. Assuming . . . the constitutionality of the overall scheme, there is a legitimate governmental interest in requiring a group to make a "preliminary showing of a significant modicum of support." * * * But the present system could preclude or severely hamper access to funds before a given election by a group or an individual who might, at the time of the election, reflect the views of a major segment or even a majority of the electorate. The fact that there have been few drastic realignments in our basic two-party structure in 200 years is no constitutional justification for freezing the status quo of the present major parties at the expense of such future political movements. * * * When and if some minority party achieves majority status, Congress can readily deal with any problems that arise. In short, I see grave risks in legislation, enacted by incumbents of the major political parties, which distinctly disadvantage minor parties or independent candidates. This Court has, until today, been particularly cautious when dealing with enactments that tend to perpetuate those who control legislative power. * * *

• • •

MR. JUSTICE REHNQUIST also dissented from this part of the decision. [Omitted.]

PART III

SCOPE OF EXECUTIVE POWER

CHAPTER **7**

Domestic Affairs

INTRODUCTORY ESSAY

Article II of the Constitution creates the office of President of the United States and grants to that office executive power. Unlike Article I, which opens with the stipulation that the following list of legislative powers belongs to a Congress, Article II announces rather straightforwardly that "executive power shall be vested in a President of the United States." While some may not place much stock in what appears to be a minor stylistic turn of phrase, the difference between each Article's stipulation of authority has given rise to considerable debate over the breadth of executive power. The debate stems from the fact that from one perspective this grant of power is simply one of designation: The phrase tells us only who has the power and requires the reader to look to the remainder of Article II for the particulars of that power (much as the reader must ostensibly do regarding the powers of Congress). In contrast, the beginning phrase may well be interpreted as a grant of power in its own right, leaving what follows in Article II as merely a partial delineation. From this perspective, the stipulations of the presidential power to nominate and appoint ambassadors, other public ministers, judges, and the like (many with Senate approval); to receive ambassadors; to command the army and the navy; to veto bills of Congress; to inform Congress of the State of the Union; to call Congress into special session; and to make sure the laws are faithfully executed serve only to emphasize *some* powers, not all of them; the remaining "residual" or "inherent" powers must be fleshed out in practice.

These issues greatly concerned Madison and Hamilton at the outset. Hamilton advocated the second interpretation and argued that "the difficulty of a complete enumeration of all cases of executive authority would naturally dictate the use of general terms and would render it improbable that a specification of certain particulars was designed as a substitute for the term (executive power) . . ." (Hamilton, 1851, p. 76). This position led Hamilton to hold that the "general doctrine of our Constitution then is that the *executive power* of the nation is vested in the President; subject only to the *exceptions* and *qualifications* which are expressed in that instrument" (*ibid.*). In contrast, Madison rejected Hamilton's view that the opening clause of Article II created powers other than those granted in subsequent enumerations. To Madison, if power after power could ultimately be justified as inherently or concurrently executive, "no citizen could any longer guess at the character of the government under which he lives; the most penetrating jurist would be unable to scan the extent of constructive prerogative" (Madison, 1865, p. 621).

Constitutional versus Stewardship Theory of Executive Power

Madison and Hamilton's debate finds more modern expression in two competing twentieth-century theories of executive power: a constitutional theory and a stewardship theory (Mason and Beaney, 1964, p. 57). In the constitutional theory, based on Madison's perspective, the presidential exercise of executive power is severely circumscribed by the Constitution directly or by constitutionally authorized grants of power from Congress. As President Taft argued, to act in accordance with constitutional theory, a President can "exercise no power which cannot be fairly and reasonably traced to some specific grant of power or justly implied and included within such express grant as proper and necessary to its exercise" (Taft, 1916, p. 139). In other words, the President must be able to justify each act by showing that it emanates from constitutional grants of authority or from statutory grants of power by Congress. In contrast, the stewardship theory of executive power allows the President, as President Theodore Roosevelt once said, "to do anything that the needs of the nation [demand] unless such action [is] forbidden by the Constitution or by the laws" (Roosevelt, 1913, p. 389). According to this perspective, the President functions as a steward in doing all that is necessary (save what is clearly forbidden) to further the public interest. The theory of the stewardship presidency, then, simply puts the constitutional thesis on its head; rather than seek out positive grants of authority, it looks for clear prohibitions and limitations on the exercise of presidential power.

Stewardship Prevails

The views of Hamilton and Teddy Roosevelt have prevailed over the course of the American experience. This has been particularly true in the President's handling of foreign affairs (a matter we take up in the following chapter) and in his direction of domestic matters in times of crisis. Even today, after the abuses of power perpetrated by Nixon, few voices call for replacing the expansive stewardship presidency with a constitutional one. The exigencies of modernization, the complexities of living in a technological age, and the very vagueness of Article II itself have helped secure the stewardship view of executive power as a necessary interpretation of the presidency. The courts have done little to alter this development. In fact, in those few instances in which the Court has been called upon or has chosen to grapple directly with these competing conceptions, the Justices have generally supported the stewardship theory in one form or another.

Oddly enough, the first case bearing on these matters forced the Justices to deal with the abstract theories of executive power in a context involving the not-so-abstract issue of their own personal safety and welfare while riding circuit (*In re Neagle*, 135 U.S. 1 [1890]). In 1890 a U.S. Marshall by the name of David Neagle was charged under California law with first-degree murder for having killed an individual while carrying out what Neagle believed to be his responsibility to protect a U.S. Supreme Court Justice. At the time, Supreme Court Justices were required to ride circuit; that is, they had to travel extensively over particular geographic areas when the Supreme Court was not in session and preside at trials of the first instance as well as participate in intermediate appellate hearings. On one such circuit riding, Justice Field so dismayed a particular litigant, a David Terry, that Terry threatened to take Field's life should Field return to California. Given this clear threat to Field's security, Neagle was assigned to protect the Justice on his next circuit ride through California. Upon Field's return, Terry appeared and attempted to attack the Justice. Neagle intervened and killed Terry. Neagle was arrested by California authorities for the murder of Field's alleged assailant.

Soon after Neagle was placed in custody, the United States initiated a habeas corpus action to free Neagle. Neagle could secure release if he could show that he was being held "in custody for an act done or omitted in pursuance of a law of the United States." The problem for Neagle stemmed from the fact that he had been assigned to protect Field without specific statutory authorization. Therefore, in the strictest sense, Neagle had acted on his own and not in "pursuance of a law of the United States."

The Court, opting for the stewardship view, held that the President was not "limited to enforcement of acts of Congress . . . according to their express terms . . ."; rather, since the Constitution vests the government and particularly the executive with the obligation to protect the "peace of the United States," the executive is authorized to do whatever is necessary to fulfill that obligation (and that authorization is equivalent to a law). The President can, then, take necessary action to secure the peace (indeed, must do so under the obligation to faithfully execute the "laws") and appropriately did so in the instant case. Thus, the Court read Hamilton's view of Article II into Supreme Court policy: Presidential power grows not only out of the Constitution and statutes but also out of the requirements of protecting the public peace implicit in the very nature of government itself.

Judicial Efforts to Restrict Executive Power

Although the Court had several occasions to define the scope of an inherent executive power after *Neagle* (for instance, see *In re Debs*, 158 U.S. 564 [1895]; *United States* v. *Midwest Oil Co.*, 236 U.S. 459 [1915]; and *Korematsu* v. *United States*, 323 U.S. 214 [1944]), it did not deal with the issue in detail until events in the winter and spring of 1951–1952 forced the Court to consider the limits of a stewardship presidency (*Youngstown Sheet & Tube Co.* v. *Sawyer*, 343 U.S. 579). In December 1951 President Truman was notified of the breakdown of negotiations between the steelworkers and the steel industry. Fearful of the negative impact of a steel stoppage on both the economy and the Korean War effort, Truman proceeded to delay the strike by referring the issue to the Wage Stabilization Board for extended negotiations. By April of 1952, though, negotiations had still failed to produce a settlement and the steelworkers announced their intent to strike. Rather than allow the strike, Truman ordered Secretary of Commerce Sawyer to seize the steel plants and keep the steel industry in full operation. In rather short order, the Supreme Court was called upon to determine whether Truman's actions were constitutional.

Much to Truman's dismay, the Court rejected the argument that the opening clause of Article II granted him power to seize the steel mills without specific authorization from Congress. Five of the six Justices in the majority technically signed the "opinion of the Court" (written by Justice Black), but several of the nonseparate concurrences suggest more disagreement than agreement over the extent of inherent executive power. The opinion of the Court accepts the strict constitutional theory of the executive and does so in the face of precedent to the contrary. This strict view argues that in areas where the legislature is authorized to legislate, no independent power exists per Article II allowing a President to act on his own. Invoking a strict interpretation of the separation of powers, which precludes an executive from "legislating," Black required this limitation to hold even in the ostensible emergency at hand.

Despite Black's efforts to reduce the issue to a clash between an inherent executive power and the demands of a separation of powers, matters proved more complex because the other Justices in the majority believed that Congress had expressly declined to authorize seizure as a means of handling work stoppages. To the five remaining members of the majority, this refusal had substantial import. Indeed, had Congress not expressly refused to grant the President the power to seize the mills, the outcome of the case may well have been more consistent with the Court's stewardship policies of the past.

In this regard, Justice Jackson, while concurring with Black's opinion, implied that an inherent executive power did exist. He maintained that although the Framers wanted a separation of powers to insure individual liberty, they also contemplated an integration of powers to make government workable. From this perspective, executive power had to be expansive. However, even though he supported the stewardship theory, Jackson expressed the belief that when a President "takes measures incompatible with the expressed or implied will of Congress," executive power is at its lowest ebb and is most susceptible to exceeding its constitutional limits. For Jackson, the fact that Congress had expressly denied seizure as a means of dealing with the situation made Truman's actions unconstitutional. Justices Frankfurter and Burton both concurred with the majority opinion and clearly believed that the President possessed more flexible powers than Black's opinion allowed, but in the instant case they held that Truman had exceeded even those flexible powers primarily because Congress had spoken quite clearly against seizure as a means of handling labor disputes. Justice Clark, concurring separately, took a more pragmatic view of the matter. His position limited the President where Congress had acted, but allowed presidential action free of congressional authorization if the gravity of the situation warranted such action. In the case at hand, however, the specific prohibitions were clear, and thus, to Clark, Truman had acted improperly.

Justices Vinson, Minton, and Reed supported Truman's actions. Vinson, writing for all three, believed that Truman had to seize the steel mills in order not to jeopardize the competing congressionally authorized Korean War effort and congressional economic policy. Furthermore, Vinson was quick to point out that when Truman issued the seizure order, he had at the same time sent a message to Congress asking approval of his action. To Vinson this suggested that Truman's actions were only temporary, pending congressional approval, and were designed to further (or at least not to jeopardize) competing, if not more important, congressional goals in a very grave emergency. Under the circumstances, Truman had no choice but to seize, given his duty to faithfully execute the laws.

While the majority clearly rebuked Truman (acting with assurances that Truman would willingly abide by any decision rendered by the Court), the Supreme Court did not dispense with the notion of an inherent executive power. In fact, only two of the Justices (Black and Douglas) asserted what amounts to an inflexible constitutional theory of executive power while five (Vinson, Minton, Reed, Clark, and Jackson) clearly accepted the stewardship thesis, and two (Frankfurter and Burton) refused to comment beyond the facts at hand. Even so, the Court's action here was important. The Justices placed the Chief Executive on notice that he is no longer immune from judicial scrutiny when it comes to domestic policymaking, and, by so doing, set at least an outer limit on the extent to which a President can pursue goals believed in the public interest, without congressional authorization.

Impoundment

While theory is intriguing, the practice of the American presidency has proven to be clearly stewardship, in fact, an expansive stewardship in the face of the holding in *Youngstown*. Indeed, since Franklin Roosevelt, executive power has grown by leaps and bounds, in part by congressional abdication of power through delegations (to be discussed), in part by presidential aggrandizement of power in more subtle ways than Truman's seizure. One subtle means of exerting and expanding power is the impoundment of congressionally appropriated funds. The validity of this practice was severely circumscribed by Congress in 1974 through passage of the Congressional Budget and Impoundment Control Act and by the Court in 1975 in *Train* v. *City of New York*, 420 U.S. 35. Both of these actions were inspired by a misuse of that presidential power, a power not provided for in the Constitution but one in which Congress and the Court had generally acquiesced as a necessary part of the pragmatics of a workable government.

Impoundment consists in the presidential practice of withholding or refusing to allow the expenditure of certain monies appropriated by Congress. The Constitution grants the power of appropriation to Congress per Article I, Section 9, Clause 7 ("No money shall be drawn from the Treasury, but in consequence of appropriations made by law"), and allows a presidential role only through a broad veto power. Clearly, whoever has the final say over the spending of federal funds exerts substantial (if not complete) political control over the shape of public policy. While the Constitution grants that shaping power to Congress only, if Congress appropriates and a President refuses to spend, the President, by indirection, becomes the appropriating power in place of Congress, and, as a consequence, the President becomes the primary shaper of public policy. In this fashion, Presidents can and have used impoundment as an important vehicle for the expansion of executive power.

The first instance of impoundment occurred in 1803 when Jefferson withheld $50,000 that Congress had appropriated to build gunboats to patrol and defend the Mississippi River. Jefferson's purpose was merely to delay the expenditure, mainly because the Louisiana Purchase had been transacted between passage of the defense appropriation and the intended executive outlay; that transaction had minimized the need for defense buildups along the Mississippi, which Congress had intended the expenditures to facilitate. For the remainder of the nineteenth century, executives rarely impounded funds. Then, in 1905 Congress gave legal authority for presidential play in the allocation of appropriated funds to minimize departmental deficits before the end of the fiscal year. And, in 1921 Congress allowed the withholding of funds to save money should Congress authorize more than necessary to secure the goal in question.

These rather minor adjustments through congressional concessions to the executive did not undermine the basic power of the purse vested in Congress. Beginning with FDR, however, Presidents increasingly used impoundment to effect executive policy goals. Roosevelt consistently spent less than had been allotted by Congress in order to further both his economic recovery goals and his war effort. Truman, Eisenhower, and Johnson justified refusals to spend the full amount authorized for certain defense projects on the basis of their powers as Commander in Chief. While these actions occasioned squabbles with Congress, their magnitude was not sufficient to raise the ire of the public or bring the issue to court for constitutional adjudication (see Mullen, 1976).

Nixon, however, extended the impoundment power beyond acceptable limits and did so for clear policy purposes; his actions gave rise to the aforementioned efforts by Congress as well as to a substantial number of anti-impoundment decisions by lower courts and the Supreme Court. Nixon not only shaped domestic spending to suit his preferences, he also sought to abolish programs authorized and appropriated by refusing to spend altogether. Disgruntled with the Office of Economic Opportunity (OEO), for instance, Nixon tried to dismantle it by refusing to spend the monies Congress had designated for the office. Public and congressional outcries forced Nixon to capitulate on the matter and OEO continued. In one of his more far-reaching uses of impoundment to further policy goals, Nixon ordered Environmental Protection Agency (EPA) head Russell Train to withhold substantial expenditures for sewage treatment plants that had been authorized by the Federal Water Pollution Control Act of 1972. What was particularly disturbing about this effort was that Congress had overridden Nixon's original veto of the measure, thereby making "perfectly clear" to Nixon and the EPA what congressional policy was. In withholding the funds, Nixon was attempting to get his way in the face of a two-thirds congressional mandate to the contrary. The City of New York, not securing the revenues it needed and was entitled to for sewage treatment, brought suit to force Train to release those monies. In *Train* v. *City of New York,* the Court could not see that any interpretation of the Act granted the President a "seemingly limitless power to withhold funds from allotment and obligation."

While this case was pending, Congress passed the Congressional Budget and Impoundment Act in an effort to curb Nixon's abuses and correct some of the weaknesses in the congressional budgetary process itself—a process that justified much presidential impoundment in the first place. Congress now requires Presidents to inform the legislature of the reasons for an intended impoundment. If within forty-five days Congress adopts a resolution (not subject to presidential veto) disapproving the proposed deferral of funds, such a resolution has the power to force their expenditure. Without the resolution, the President may impound the funds. To rescind funding altogether (as Nixon tried to do with the OEO), a President must win the approval of both the House and the Senate within forty-five days of his announcement of the action; otherwise the money must be spent. In addition to the provisions circumscribing the power of impoundment, Congress revised its budgetary process by creating budget committees in each house and a congressional budget office comparable to the Office of Management and Budget under the President. It remains to be seen whether these actions will enable Congress to reassert budgetary and policy control, conceivably by allowing it to "harmonize" conflicting laws, "fine tune" spending policies, and minimize waste through legislation rather than through abdication to presidential impoundment.

Executive Appointment and Removal Powers

Whether acting from a constitutional or stewardship perspective, Presidents do not fulfill nor could they be expected to fulfill their duties alone. As presidential power has expanded, so too has the size and complexity of the executive branch and its bureaucracy. At the outset, Congress provided for only three cabinet departments—State, War, and Treasury—to aid the President in the execution and administration of the law. Now, thirteen cabinet departments and a raft of independent agencies, boards, and commissions ostensibly facilitate the presidential task. From the handful of federal employees that made up the bureaucracy in the 1790s, federal civilian employment has grown to where now it exceeds 2 million. Since the advent and expansion of the civil service, the President directly appoints about 2,000 upper-level officials, of whom only about 500 have any real effect on policy-making. The power to appoint these executive officials, as with judicial officers, emanates from Article II, Section 2, which provides that the President

> . . . shall nominate, and by and with the advice and consent of the Senate, shall appoint ambassadors, other public ministers and consuls, judges of the Supreme Court, and all other officers of the United States, whose appointments are not herein otherwise provided for, which shall be established by law; but the Congress may by law vest the appointment of such inferior officers, as they think proper, in the President alone, in the courts of law, or in the heads of departments.

These provisions allow some upper-level officials in the executive branch to be appointed solely at the discretion of the President and some to be appointed solely by heads of departments; the ostensibly more important federal officers are to be appointed by the President with the advice and consent of the Senate. While the President and heads of departments have a large measure of control over the persons selected to fill those offices not requiring Senate confirmation, the fact that Congress creates the offices and can set particular qualifications for holding them means that Congress indirectly influences those appointments. The Senate's role in giving advice and consent for specific appointments is more direct. For positions requiring Senate confirmation, the President nominates a candidate, awaits Senate approval of the nominee (usually by a majority vote of those present), and then commissions the confirmed nominee as an "officer of the United States."

The Supreme Court has made it clear that this process of nomination, confirmation, and commission is mandatory and that the task of nomination is exclusively presidential. As part of the Federal Election Campaign Act of 1972, Congress established a Federal Election Commission to oversee enforcement of the Act's limitations on campaign spending. Aware of the potential for partisan abuse of the Commission through selection of commissioners, Congress sought to play a role in the appointment process itself. Accordingly, the Act allowed the President to appoint two members, the president *pro tempore* of the Senate to appoint two, and the Speaker of the House to appoint the remaining two, with all six ultimately being confirmed, not by the Senate alone, but by a majority of both houses of Congress. In *Buckley* v. *Valeo,* 424 U.S. 1 (1976), the Court held, among other things, that since the commissioners were "officers of the United States," an appointment process not left completely to the President (with the advice and consent of the Senate alone) violated the Appointments Clause.

Although the Constitution is fairly clear regarding the question of appointments, the matter of removing a properly appointed officer has raised a number of constitutional issues, the most significant of which concern the extent of the removal power and who wields it. The Constitution addresses removal only in the context of the cumbersome impeachment process. It is hard to imagine, though, that the Founding Fathers intended officeholders serving under a given President to remain in office until the end of that President's term, no matter what, save impeachment. Such a state of affairs could easily paralyze a President's program and work at cross-purposes with the President's commitment to faithfully execute the laws.

Most political observers agree that officers of the United States can be removed by means other than impeachment—except for judges, of course, whose tenure is assured by Article III. The problem centers on the role Congress can play in the removal of executive officers. Given the need for Senate advice and consent at the time of appointment, some believe it is not unreasonable to require Senate advice and consent for removal. They also argue it would be reasonable to allow Congress to place limitations on what grounds a President might use to justify removing an officer. These matters were first addressed by the Court (a Court, incidently, headed by a former President) in the case of *Myers* v. *United States,* 272 U.S. 52 (1926).

The *Myers* case brought into question provisions of an 1876 act requiring Senate approval for the removal of first-, second-, and third-class postmasters. In 1920, President Wilson had removed Frank Myers, a first-class postmaster in Portland, Oregon, before his term expired, without abiding by the Act's consent provisions. Myers sued for the wages lost between the time of his removal and the end of his term, alleging his right to these monies since his removal was not in accordance with the law. In a rather lengthy opinion, Taft averred that the removal of Myers was constitutional and that the advice and consent portions of the Act were invalid. *Myers* holds that purely executive officials performing executive functions may be removed at will by a President, untrammeled by Congress. For Taft, removal was incident to the power to appoint and was a purely executive function. Given the President's duty to faithfully execute the laws, it would be unreasonable, according to Taft, to expect a President to keep someone upon whom he could no longer rely to follow orders.

The argument holds sway when applied to the removal of those exercising presidential discretion and duty, but it seems less persuasive the farther one gets from high-level policymaking. Taft could see nothing in the Constitution, though, to indicate differences in levels of offices and thus held that a President's power to remove was unlimited and certainly included carte blanche to remove a nondiscretionary officer like a postmaster.

Taft went beyond the situation at hand in *Myers,* however, and argued that a President could also remove, at will, those appointed to independent regulatory agencies and commissions like the Interstate Commerce Commission (ICC). This assertion flew in the face of the existing statutory language establishing such commissions. While the statutes did not require Senate consent to remove a commissioner, they did stipulate that the executive had to show cause (inefficiency, neglect of duty, malfeasance) for removal. In 1935, in the case of *Humphrey's Executor* v. *United States,* 295 U.S. 602, the Court was called upon to determine whether this kind of limitation on the executive power of removal was constitutional. In 1931 President Hoover had appointed William E. Humphrey as a Federal Trade Commissioner; his seven-year term was subject to presidential removal only for inefficiency, neglect of duty, or malfeasance. When Roosevelt took office, he removed Humphrey solely because he believed the political goals of his administration could be carried out better with personnel of his own selection. Humphrey died soon after his removal, leaving the executor of his estate to sue for wages from the time of removal to the time of death.

In *Humphrey,* the Court limited the breadth of Taft's theory of an unbridled executive power of removal. The Justices agreed with Taft's assertion that citizens appointed to perform exclusively executive functions, even as menial as those of postmaster, serve subject to executive will and must therefore be subject to executive removal in order for a President to fulfill the duty to faithfully execute the laws. However, when an officer's duties entail furthering congressional policies "without executive leave," removal can be limited to cause. Thus, in creating "quasi-judicial or quasi-legislative" agencies designed to perform tasks independent of executive control, Congress can limit the executive power to remove agency officers to "removal for cause."

In 1958 in *Weiner* v. *United States,* 357 U.S. 349, the Court expanded upon *Humphrey* by holding that the unique functions of independent agencies require that removal must be for cause alone, whether or not Congress so stipulates. Myron Weiner had been removed from the War Claims Commission by Eisenhower, simply for partisan reasons. Weiner challenged the action, even though the statute that established the commission placed no limitations on the reasons for removal. The Court proved sympathetic to Weiner's claim for wages from the time of his removal to the ending of the Commission, on the basis of the agency's function. Congress, the Court concluded, had intended the agency to make final "quasi-judicial" decisions regarding remunerations for damages suffered during the war by private citizens and groups; those decisions were to be made free from executive interference. Writing for the majority, Frankfurter noted that this function suggested Congress' preference not to have "hanging over the Commission the Damocles sword of removal by the President for no reason other than that he preferred to have on that Commission men of his own choosing."

Court policy thus holds that the function performed by an officer appointed by the President will determine the legality of any removal: Officers performing purely executive functions may be removed at will, while officers performing quasi-judicial or quasi-legislative functions can be removed only if a President shows cause. In shaping these policies, the Court was fortunate that each litigant sought only back pay. The term of office for Myers had expired, Humphrey had died, and Weiner's job had been phased out. The resolution of the issues would have been more complex had each litigant been seeking reinstatement instead of just back pay. Indeed, a removal instance of this kind may yet reach the Court, making resolution of the matter rather difficult, particularly if a new officer has been installed in the course of the lawsuit.

The issues surrounding the executive power of removal are not obscure matters affecting only the internal workings of the executive branch. This fact was brought into sharp focus in 1973 when Nixon fired Archibald Cox as special prosecutor. Cox was planning to subpoena tapes and documents of the President in order to prosecute key figures in the Watergate affair. Nixon ordered Cox not to pursue the subpoenas. Cox persisted and Nixon ordered his attorney general to remove the special prosecutor. Attorney General Richardson and Assistant Attorney General Ruckelshaus both refused to carry out Nixon's order and were both summarily fired. Eventually Solicitor General Robert Bork agreed to fire Cox. While perfectly legal, this instance points up the reverse side of Taft's *Myers* thesis: Although a President may need the freedom to remove those who frustrate efforts to *faithfully* execute the laws, a President may also use the removal power to safeguard the *improper* and *unfaithful* execution of the laws and to protect his own wrongdoing.

Removal of the Chief Executive

No doubt Taft would have argued that congressional tinkering with the removal power is not the appropriate means to combat this kind of misuse. Rather the impeachment process would be the appropriate means of handling such executive impropriety. The Constitution, per Article II, Section 4, states:

> The President, Vice President and all civil officers of the United States shall be removed from office on impeachment for and conviction of treason, bribery, or other high crimes and misdemeanors.

Under these provisions and additional ones in Article I, the House of Representatives serves as a grand jury of sorts to determine whether there is cause to believe a President ought to be removed. After the "articles of impeachment" are drafted and agreed upon by the House, a trial before the Senate is required to determine whether, in fact, to remove (convict). Andrew Johnson is the only President to have been impeached and tried before the Senate. Johnson retained his office by a narrow margin: The Senate was only one vote shy of the two-thirds required for conviction. Nixon's resignation from office precluded what would have been an impeachment with Senate trial, and most likely removal.

Until Nixon's actions raised the real possibility of impeachment, most scholars and politicians saw impeachment as a cumbersome and unlikely device with which to control presidential excess and, hence, as no real threat to presidential prerogative. Now, of course, it is likely that most executive action is taken with some awareness of the possibility of impeachment proceedings.

While there is no doubt some political awareness of the potential for impeachment, the tool of impeachment is an awkward and not very effective means of limiting presidential power; even with the extensive debates of the summer of 1974, what constitutes an impeachable offense remains an open, problematic question. Given the historical uncertainty concerning the very nature of executive power itself, it is little wonder that the essence of "high crimes and misdemeanors" remains ambiguous as well. Members of the House Judiciary Committee debated the definitional issue at length during the Nixon impeachment hearings. The central question in the debates was whether the terms "high crimes and misdemeanors" meant only specifically indictable criminal offenses or whether they covered actions beyond that narrow view. The majority of the House Committee held the view that removal did not have to be based on acts potentially indictable as criminal offenses. They believed a President could be removed for "undermining the integrity of office, disregard of constitutional duties and oath of office, arrogation of power, abuse of the governmental process, and adverse impact on the system of government" (House Judiciary Committee, 1974). Indeed, they maintained that the terms "high crimes and misdemeanors" could be construed to allow room to deal with the substantial inadequacies of a set of criminal statutes not designed to cope with the unique position of President. In contrast, Nixon's defenders argued for the narrower view in which "high crimes and misdemeanors" specifically denotes indictable offenses as the only offenses justifying removal. Their argument relies on the thesis of a clear separation of powers, which holds that if it is possible to institute impeachment proceedings for a virtually limitless range of presidential actions—even for good faith actions sincerely taken by a President to enhance his stewardship—Presidents will be subject to a constant impeachment scrutiny that will ultimately dominate or destroy the executive as a coequal branch of the national government (*Congressional Quarterly,* 1974).

The Court, of course, has not been called upon to resolve matters of this kind; if it were, it would probably rely on the "political question" doctrine to decline to do so. Raoul Berger (1973) has proposed, though, that the Court's willingness to limit to age, residency, and citizenship the criteria by which Congress can exclude its members (*Powell* v. *McCormack,* 395 U.S. 486 [1969]) suggests that the Justices would be legally able to enter the foray to define "high crimes and misdemeanors." However, there is no doubt that the Court would severely jeopardize the delicate balance of its coequal power were it to take a case of an impeached, tried, and convicted President refusing to leave office pending a definitive Supreme Court decision.

Executive Privilege

In addition to confronting the definitional quandary raised by the 1974 impeachment effort, the House Judiciary Committee was forced to grapple with Nixon's claim that executive privilege allowed him to withhold information. Executive privilege consists in the authority a President has to refuse to produce the documents or provide the information demanded through the compulsory process of either the legislative or the judicial branch. Unlike the privilege against self-incrimination, the Constitution does not specifically grant executive privilege against revealing information, but it is inferable from the very notion of the separation of powers. Moreover, the privilege is viewed as a necessary, practical prerogative essential to a President's efforts to carry out his constitutional duties; that is, an assured, protected confidentiality in discussion is essential to effective channels for giving and receiving advice and to meaningful deliberations in the process of presidential decision-making.

Presidents have long asserted the privilege (though the term "executive privilege" itself was first used during the Eisenhower Administration) but never in the context of an impeachment hearing. Andrew Johnson freely opened his files and even his personal bank records in the course of his impeachment investigation. Polk, while asserting the privilege in a general inquiry, was quick to note his belief that the privilege would not apply in an impeachment proceeding (Labovitz, 1978, pp. 211–213). In the face of this precedent, Nixon alleged that executive privilege extended even to an impeachment hearing so as to protect the executive branch from becoming subservient to the legislative branch:

> If the institution of an impeachment inquiry against a President were permitted to override restraints of separation of powers, this would spell the end of the doctrine of separation of powers; it would be an open invitation to future Congresses to use an impeachment inquiry, however frivolously, as a device to assert their own supremacy over the Executive and to reduce Executive confidentiality to a nullity. . . . the Executive, no less than the Legislative or Judicial branches, must be immune from unlimited search and seizure by the other co-equal branches. (Quoted in Labovitz, 1978, p. 206.)

On the basis of these arguments, Nixon refused to comply with the Judiciary Committee's subpoena. His failure to comply became part of the articles of impeachment against him reported out of the House Committee. There is considerable doubt about the validity of Nixon's assertion of the privilege in the context of an impeachment hearing but not about its valid assertion in more general congressional and judicial inquiries. In some respects, however, Nixon's self-serving use of the privilege has muddled its important and valid exertion elsewhere.

While Congress was busy dealing with these matters, the judiciary undertook similar actions to secure information it believed pertinent to the criminal prosecutions of the Watergate principals. Ultimately the Supreme Court was called upon to deal with executive privilege in the judicial context in the case of *United States* v. *Nixon*, 418 U.S. 683 (1974). Here, special prosecutor Leon Jaworski sought and obtained from a lower court a subpoena requiring Nixon to deliver certain tapes of conversations between the President and his aides. Jaworski believed the tapes contained crucial evidence of the culpability of Mitchell, Haldeman, Erlichman, and others and as such were important to the effective prosecution of those officials.

The Supreme Court concurred with Jaworski and ordered the delivery of the evidence held by the President, despite claims of executive privilege. However, the Court also recognized the constitutional status of executive privilege, holding that the concept was "inextricably rooted in the separation of powers under the Constitution." Basing its argument on a concern for protecting presidential confidentiality, the Court declared: "A President and those who assist him must be free to explore alternatives in the process of shaping policies and making decisions and to do so in a way many would be unwilling to express except privately." Absent this protection a President could not effectively and independently exercise those powers conferred by the Constitution.

The Court, in granting the validity of the privilege, was quick to point out, however, that such a privilege was not without limits. The mere assertion of privilege could not stand as a bar to the judiciary's need for evidence in criminal trials in particular circumstances. To this Court in this setting, the demands of due process required giving evidence in a criminal trial, and such demands outweighed a claim of a broad, undifferentiated executive privilege. The Court also made it clear that the judiciary, not the executive, had the power to determine what was needed in a criminal prosecution. While asserting these interpretations, the Court stated that more specific claims of executive privilege, particularly ones related to the military or international relations, would serve to justify withholding information. Thus, the Court granted executive privilege a constitutional status, limited its use with regard to the judiciary, and left the Court as final arbiter in disputes over claims of executive privilege. Still open to resolution is the degree to which these limitations on executive privilege apply or do not apply in congressional inquiries.

The Pardoning Power

As is apparent, the Nixon presidency brought to the forefront of political awareness a number of major constitutional issues: the limits of a stewardship presidency, impoundment, executive privilege, appointment and removal powers, and impeachment. In his departure, Nixon brought yet another question of presidential power to the public eye when Gerald Ford granted him a full and unconditional pardon for any and all offenses related to his presidency. While this move may have been humane, it proved politically unwise (so unwise, in fact, that Ford's election efforts were directly and negatively affected by it). Even so, Ford's action was perfectly constitutional. Article II, Section 2, Clause 1, states that the President shall have the power to "grant reprieves and pardons for offenses against the United States, except in cases of impeachment." The pardon power then is constitutionally unencumbered, save its impropriety in impeachment matters. The President cannot only grant full pardons, but can also commute sentences, remit fines, penalties, and forfeitures, and grant conditional pardons. Further, he can carry out each of these types of pardon either before or after conviction and sentencing.

The Court has held that a pardon is a private transaction that must be accepted by the recipient before it becomes valid (*Burdick* v. *United States,* 236 U.S. 79 [1915]). Thus, while a President may grant the pardon, it must be accepted before it is in effect. This notion of a personal, private transaction implies that a President cannot grant broad amnesties. This inference, however, has not been substantiated, as evidenced by Carter's amnesty for Vietnam War deserters and draft evaders. Nor does the power of a President to grant amnesty preclude a congressional power to pass amnesty laws of its own (Schwartz, 1972, p. 161).

A President can pardon a person receiving punishment for contempt of court, providing the contempt in question is criminal not civil. Because criminal contempts punish abuses of court dignity while civil contempts are a means of enforcing court edicts, a pardon of the latter would violate the separation of powers by usurping judicial prerogatives, whereas a pardon of the former would not. *Ex parte Grossman,* 267 U.S. 87 (1925), allowed the pardon in criminal contempts as a conceivable means to soften punishments meted out by a vengeful judge but, in *dicta,* denied the power to pardon civil contempts. Although this distinction may appear to limit the President's power to pardon, it is necessary to point out that constitutionally the pardon power extends only to offenses against the United States and civil contempts are not technically in that category.

An unqualified pardon fully restores the recipient's civil rights. In *Ex parte Garland,* 4 Wall. 333 (1867), the Court ruled that a pardon makes an individual as innocent as if he or she had never committed the crime. For A. H. Garland this meant that he could practice before the Supreme Court without having to first take a statutorily required oath attesting to the fact that he had never voluntarily borne arms against the United States. Garland had indeed borne arms as a Confederate during the Civil War, but the Court ruled that Johnson's full pardon absolved him of the need to take the oath.

The presidential power to pardon is not limited to full pardons. A "conditional" pardon is considered a constitutionally valid exercise of the pardoning power. As the Court said in *Schick* v. *Reed,* 419 U.S. 256 (1974):

> The plain purpose of the broad power conferred . . . was to allow . . . the President to "forgive" the convicted person in part or entirely, to reduce a penalty in terms of a specified number of years, or to alter it with conditions which are in themselves constitutionally unobjectionable.

President Eisenhower had commuted Maurice Shick's death sentence for murder to life imprisonment, subject to the condition that Schick be ineligible for parole. Between the 1960 conditional pardon and the 1974 case, the Supreme Court had ruled in *Furman* v. *Georgia,* 408 U.S. 256 (1972), that in certain instances the death penalty was cruel and unusual punishment and therefore unconstitutional. Schick argued that in light of *Furman* and the fact that the decision had been applied retroactively to set aside other death sentences, his death sentence should be set aside as well, which would make his no-parole condition no longer applicable. The Court concluded that the pardon was lawful when made and that the decision in *Furman* did not alter its validity.

Legislative Duties

The presidential powers discussed so far relate primarily to the execution and administration of laws. The Constitution requires the President to perform certain "legislative" duties as well. For instance, the President may call Congress into session on extraordinary occasions and may adjourn Congress when both houses cannot agree on a time of adjournment (not surprisingly, an event that has yet to occur). The President also performs an important lawmaking role by virtue of his duty to give Congress information on the state of the union and his responsibility to recommend measures for congressional consideration. This element of the executive's legislative activity has evolved to the point where the President has now become the primary force in setting the agenda for the legislative branch—a policymaking power of no small importance.

More importantly, though, the President has a direct effect on lawmaking through the presidential veto power provided for in Article I, Section 7. The veto provisions of the Constitution require executive approval of most legislative actions on an all-or-nothing basis that precludes an "item veto." By refusing to approve, the President precludes a law from becoming effective, at least temporarily. Congress can override a veto by a two-thirds vote of both houses. To veto a bill formally, a President returns the bill unsigned to the house of origin within ten days, with objections attached. Less formally, a President can veto a bill by holding onto it as Congress adjourns before the ten-day period expires, thereby precluding return of the bill. Known as a "pocket veto," this tactic was validated by the Court in the Pocket Veto Case, 279 U.S. 655 (1929); the Justices ruled that even recesses and temporary adjournments can serve to kill a bill. Recent decisions have cast doubt on the broad scope of the Court's 1929 ruling, but the Supreme Court has not yet been called upon to alter its earlier policy (see, for example, *Kennedy* v. *Sampson,* 511 F. 2d 430 [1974]).

As this brief canvass of Court policy and political practice suggests, executive power in the domestic domain is both broad and far-reaching. For whatever reason—historical accident, judicial consent, congressional abdication, or the persuasive powers of unique presidential personalities—the modern Chief Executive is held largely responsible for the public peace, the national security, and our economic prosperity; these matters were most likely not envisioned as duties of the Chief Executive by those who framed Article II. The cases excerpted here and in the next chapter show the role the Court has played in the creation of the twentieth-century presidency.

Youngstown Sheet & Tube Co. v. *Sawyer*

343 U.S. 579 (1952)

Mr. Justice Black delivered the opinion of the Court.

We are asked to decide whether the President was acting within his constitutional power when he issued an order directing the Secretary of Commerce to take possession of and operate most of the Nation's steel mills. The mill owners argue that the President's order amounts to lawmaking, a legislative function which the Constitution has expressly confided to the Congress and not to the President. The Government's position is that the order was made on findings of the President that his action was necessary to avert a national catastrophe which would inevitably result from a stoppage of steel production, and that in meeting this grave emergency the President was acting within the aggregate of his constitutional powers as the Nation's Chief Executive and the Commander in Chief of the Armed Forces of the United States. The issue emerges here from the following series of events:

In the latter part of 1951, a dispute arose between the steel companies and their employees over terms and conditions that should be included in new collective bargaining agreements. Long-continued conferences failed to resolve the dispute. On December 18, 1951, the employees' representative, United Steelworkers of America, C. I. O., gave notice of an intention to strike when the existing bargaining agreements expired on December 31. The Federal Mediation and Conciliation Service then intervened in an effort to get labor and management to agree. This failing, the President on December 22, 1951, referred the dispute to the Federal Wage Stabilization Board to investigate and make recommendations for fair and equitable terms of settlement. This Board's report resulted in no settlement. On April 4, 1952, the Union gave notice of a nation-wide strike called to begin at 12:01 a.m. April 9. The indispensability of steel as a component of substantially all weapons and other war materials led the President to believe that the proposed work stoppage would immediately jeopardize our national defense and that governmental seizure of the steel mills was necessary in order to assure the continued availability of steel. Reciting these considerations for his action, the President, a few hours before the strike was to begin, issued Executive Order 10340. . . . The order directed the Secretary of Commerce to take possession of most of the steel mills and keep them running. The Secretary immediately issued his own possessory orders, calling upon the presidents of the various seized companies to serve as operating managers for the United States. They were directed to carry on their activities in accordance with regulations and directions of the Secretary. The next morning the President sent a message to Congress reporting his action. * * * Twelve days later he sent a second message. * * * Congress has taken no action.

Obeying the Secretary's orders under protest, the companies brought proceedings against him in the District Court. Their complaints charged that the seizure was not authorized by an act of Congress or by any constitutional provisions. The District Court was asked to declare the orders of the President and the Secretary invalid and to issue preliminary and permanent injunctions restraining their enforcement. Opposing the motion for preliminary injunction, the United States asserted that a strike disrupting steel production for even a brief period would so endanger the well-being and safety of the Nation that the President had "inherent power" to do what he had done—power "supported by the Constitution, by historical precedent, and by court decisions." The Government also contended that in any event no preliminary injunction should be issued because the companies had made no showing that their available legal remedies were inadequate or that their injuries from seizure would be irreparable. Holding against the Government on all points, the District Court on April 30 issued a preliminary injunction restraining the Secretary from "continuing the seizure and possession of the plants . . . and from acting under the purported authority of Executive Order No. 10340." * * * On the same day the Court of Appeals stayed the District Court's injunction. * * * Deeming it best that the issues raised be promptly decided by this Court, we granted certiorari on May 3 and set the cause for argument on May 12. * * *

. . .

The President's power, if any, to issue the order must stem either from an act of Congress or from the Constitution itself. There is no statute that expressly authorizes the President to take possession of property as he did here. Nor is there any act of Congress to which our attention has been directed from which such a power can fairly be implied. Indeed, we do not understand the Government to rely on statutory authorization for this seizure. There are two statutes which do authorize the President to take both personal and real property under certain conditions. However, the Government admits that these conditions were not met and that the President's order was not rooted in either of the statutes. The Government refers to the seizure provisions of one of these statutes * * * (the Defense Production Act) as "much too cumbersome, involved, and time-consuming for the crisis which was at hand."

Moreover, the use of the seizure technique to solve labor disputes in order to prevent work stoppages was not only unauthorized by any congressional enactment; prior to this controversy, Congress had refused to adopt that method of settling labor disputes. When the Taft-Hartley Act was under consideration in 1947, Congress rejected an amendment which would have authorized such governmental seizures in cases of emergency. Apparently it was thought that the technique of seizure, like that of compulsory arbitration, would interfere with the process of collective bargaining. Consequently, the plan Congress adopted in that Act did not provide for seizure under any circumstances. Instead, the plan sought to bring about settlements by use of the customary devices of mediation, conciliation, investigation by boards of inquiry, and public reports. In some instances temporary injunctions were authorized to provide cooling-off periods. All this failing, unions were left free to strike after a secret vote by employees as to whether they wished to accept their employers' final settlement offer.

It is clear that if the President had authority to issue the order he did, it must be found in some provision of the Constitution. And it is not claimed that express constitutional language grants this power to the President. The contention is that presidential power should be implied from the aggregate of his powers under the Constitution. Particular reliance is placed on provisions in Article II which say that "The executive Power shall be vested in a President . . ."; that "he shall take Care that the Laws be faithfully executed"; and that he "shall be Commander in Chief of the Army and Navy of the United States."

The order cannot properly be sustained as an exercise of the President's military power as Commander in Chief of the Armed Forces. The Government attempts to do so by citing a number of cases upholding broad powers in military commanders engaged in day-to-day fighting in a theater of war. Such cases need not concern us here. Even though "theater of war" be an expanding concept, we cannot with faithfulness to our constitutional system hold that the Commander in Chief of the Armed Forces has the ultimate power as such to take possession of private property in order to keep labor disputes from stopping production. This is a job for the Nation's lawmakers, not for its military authorities.

Nor can the seizure order be sustained because of the several constitutional provisions that grant executive power to the President. In the framework of our Constitution, the President's power to see that the laws are faithfully executed refutes the idea that he is to be a lawmaker. The Constitution limits his functions in the lawmaking process to the recommending of laws he thinks wise and the vetoing of laws he thinks bad. And the Constitution is neither silent nor equivocal about who shall make laws which the President is to execute. The first section of the first article says that "All legislative Powers herein granted shall be vested in a Congress of the United States . . . ." After granting many powers to the Congress, Article I goes on to provide that Congress may "make all Laws which shall be necessary and proper for carrying into Execution the foregoing Powers, and all other Powers vested by this Constitution in the Government of the United States, or in any Department or Officer thereof."

The President's order does not direct that a congressional policy be executed in a manner prescribed by Congress—it directs that a presidential policy be executed in a manner prescribed by the President. The preamble of the order itself, like that of many statutes, sets out reasons why the President believes certain policies should be adopted, proclaims these policies as rules of conduct to be followed, and again, like a statute, authorizes a government official to promulgate additional rules and regulations consistent with the policy proclaimed and needed to carry that policy into execution. The power of Congress to adopt such public policies as those proclaimed by the order is beyond question. It can authorize the taking of private property for public use. It can make laws regulating the relationships between employers and employees, prescribing rules designed to settle labor disputes, and fixing wages and working conditions in certain fields of our economy. The Constitution does not subject this lawmaking power of Congress to presidential or military supervision or control.

It is said that other Presidents without congressional authority have taken possession of private business enterprises in order to settle labor disputes. But even if this be true, Congress has not thereby lost its exclusive constitutional authority to make laws necessary and proper to carry out the powers vested by the Constitution "in the Government of the United States, or any Department or Officer thereof."

The Founders of this Nation entrusted the lawmaking power to the Congress alone in both good and bad times. It would do no good to recall the historical events, the fears of power and the hopes for freedom that lay behind their choice. Such a review would but confirm our holding that this seizure order cannot stand.

The judgment of the District Court is

Affirmed.

• • •

Mr. Justice Frankfurter.

• • •

The issue before us can be met, and therefore should be, without attempting to define the President's powers comprehensively. I shall not attempt to delineate what belongs to him by virtue of his office beyond the power even of Congress to contract; what authority belongs to him until Congress acts; what kind of problems may be dealt with either by the Congress or by the President or by both; * * * what power must be exercised by the Congress and cannot be delegated to the President. It is as unprofitable to lump together in an undiscriminating hotch-potch past presidential actions claimed to be derived from occupancy of the office, as it is to conjure up hypothetical future cases. The judiciary may, as this case proves, have to intervene in determining where authority lies as between the democratic forces in our scheme of government. But in doing so we should be wary and humble. Such is the teaching of this Court's role in the history of the country.

• • • •

The question before the Court comes in this setting. Congress has frequently—at least 16 times since 1916—specifically provided for executive seizure of production, transportation, communications, or storage facilities. In every case it has qualified this grant of power with limitations and safeguards. . . . The power to seize has uniformly been given only for a limited period or for a defined emergency, or has been repealed after a short period. Its exercise has been restricted to particular circumstances such as "time of war or when war is imminent," the needs of "public safety" or of "national security or defense," or "urgent and impending need." . . .

• • •

By the Labor Management Relations Act of 1947, Congress said to the President, "You may not seize. Please report to us and ask for seizure power if you think it is needed in a specific situation." . . . But it is now claimed that the President has seizure power by virtue of the Defense Production Act of 1950 and its Amendments. And the claim is based on the occurrence of new events—Korea and the need for stabilization, etc.—although it was well known that seizure power was withheld by the Act of 1947, and although the President, whose specific requests for other authority were in the main granted by Congress, never suggested that in view of the new events he needed the power of seizure which Congress in its judgment had decided to withhold from him. . . .

No authority that has since been given to the President can by any fair process of statutory construction be deemed to withdraw the restriction or change the will of Congress as expressed by a body of enactments, culminating in the Labor Management Relations Act of 1947 . . . .

• • •

It is one thing to draw an intention of Congress from general language and to say that Congress would have explicitly written what is inferred, where Congress has not addressed itself to a specific situation. It is quite impossible, however, when Congress did specifically address itself to a problem, as Congress did to that of seizure, to find secreted in the interstices of legislation the very grant of power which Congress consciously withheld. To find authority so explicitly withheld is not merely to disregard in a particular instance the clear will of Congress. It is to disrespect the whole legislative process and the constitutional division of authority between President and Congress.

• • •

MR. JUSTICE DOUGLAS, concurring.

There can be no doubt that the emergency which caused the President to seize these steel plants was one that bore heavily on the country. But the emergency did not create power; it merely marked an occasion when power should be exercised. And the fact that it was necessary that measures be taken to keep steel in production does not mean that the President, rather than the Congress, had the constitutional authority to act. The Congress, as well as the President, is trustee of the national welfare. The President can act more quickly than the Congress. The President with the armed services at his disposal can move with force as well as with speed. All executive power—from the reign of ancient kings to the rule of modern dictators—has the outward appearance of efficiency.

• • •

The great office of President is not a weak and powerless one. The President represents the people and is their spokesman in domestic and foreign affairs. The office is respected more than any other in the land. It gives a position of leadership that is unique. The power to formulate policies and mould opinion inheres in the Presidency and conditions our national life. The impact of the man and the philosophy he represents may at times be thwarted by the Congress. Stalemates may occur when emergencies mount and the Nation suffers for lack of harmonious, reciprocal action between the White House and Capitol Hill. That is a risk inherent in our system of separation of powers. The tragedy of such stalemates might be avoided by allowing the President the use of some legislative authority. The Framers with memories of the tyrannies produced by a blending of executive and legislative power rejected that political arrangement. Some future generation may, however, deem it so urgent that the President have legislative authority that the Constitution will be amended. We could not sanction the seizures and condemnations of the steel plants in this case without reading Article II as giving the President not only the power to execute the laws but to make some. Such a step would most assuredly alter the pattern of the Constitution.

. . .

Mr. Justice Jackson, concurring in the judgment and opinion of the Court.

That comprehensive and undefined presidential powers hold both practical advantages and grave dangers for the country will impress anyone who has served as legal adviser to a President in time of transition and public anxiety. While an interval of detached reflection may temper teachings of that experience, they probably are a more realistic influence on my views than the conventional materials of judicial decision which seem unduly to accentuate doctrine and legal fiction. . . . The tendency is strong to emphasize transient results upon policies—such as wages or stabilization—and lose sight of enduring consequences upon the balanced power structure of our Republic.

A judge, like an executive adviser, may be surprised at the poverty of really useful and unambiguous authority applicable to concrete problems of executive power as they actually present themselves. Just what our forefathers did envision, or would have envisioned had they foreseen modern conditions, must be divined from materials almost as enigmatic as the dreams Joseph was called upon to interpret for Pharaoh. A century and a half of partisan debate and scholarly speculation yields no net result but only supplies more or less apt quotations from respected sources on each side of any question. They largely cancel each other. And court decisions are indecisive because of the judicial practice of dealing with the largest questions in the most narrow way.

The actual art of governing under our Constitution does not and cannot conform to judicial definitions of the power of any of its branches based on isolated clauses or even single Articles torn from context. While the Constitution diffuses power the better to secure liberty, it also contemplates that practice will integrate the dispersed powers into a workable government. It enjoins upon its branches separateness but interdependence, autonomy but reciprocity. Presidential powers are not fixed but fluctuate, depending upon their disjunction or conjunction with those of Congress. We may well begin by a somewhat over-simplified grouping of practical situations in which a President may doubt, or others may challenge, his powers, and by distinguishing roughly the legal consequences of this factor of relativity.

1. When the President acts pursuant to an express or implied authorization of Congress, his authority is at its maximum, for it includes all that he possesses in his own right plus all that Congress can delegate. In these circumstances, and in these only, may he be said (for what it may be worth) to personify the federal sovereignty. . . .

2. When the President acts in absence of either a congressional grant or denial of authority, he can only rely upon his own independent powers, but there is a zone of twilight in which he and Congress may have concurrent authority, or in which its distribution is uncertain. . . . In this area, any actual test of power is likely to depend on the imperatives of events and contemporary imponderables rather than on abstract theories of law.

3. When the President takes measures incompatible with the expressed or implied will of Congress, his power is at its lowest ebb, for then he can rely only upon his own constitutional powers minus any constitutional powers of Congress over the matter. . . . Presidential claim to a power at once so conclusive and preclusive must be scrutinized with caution, for what is at stake is the equilibrium established by our constitutional system.

Into which of these classifications does this executive seizure of the steel industry fit? It is eliminated from the first by admission, for it is conceded that no congressional authorization exists for this seizure. . . .

Can it then be defended under flexible tests available to the second category? It seems clearly eliminated from that class because Congress has not left seizure of private property an open field but has covered it by three statutory policies inconsistent with this seizure. . . .

This leaves the current seizure to be justified only by the severe tests under the third grouping. . . . In short, we can sustain the President only by holding that seizure of such strike-bound industries is within his domain and beyond control by Congress. Thus, this Court's first review of such seizures occurs under circumstances which leave presidential power most vulnerable to attack and in the least favorable of possible constitutional postures.

I did not suppose, and I am not persuaded, that history leaves it open to question, at least in the courts, that the executive branch, like the Federal Government as a whole, possesses only delegated powers. . . . Some clauses could be made almost unworkable, as well as immutable, by refusal to indulge some latitude of interpretation for changing times. I have heretofore, and do now, give to the enumerated powers the scope and elasticity afforded by what seem to be reasonable, practical implications instead of the rigidity dictated by a doctrinaire textualism.

· · ·

[One] clause on which the Government . . . relies is that "The President shall be Commander in Chief of the Army and Navy of the United States . . . ." These cryptic words have given rise to some of the most persistent controversies in our constitutional history. Of course, they imply something more than an empty title.
. . .

• • •

That military powers of the Commander in Chief were not to supersede representative government of internal affairs seems obvious from the Constitution and from elementary American history. . . .

• • •

We should not use this occasion to circumscribe, much less to contract, the lawful role of the President as Commander in Chief. I should indulge the widest latitude of interpretation to sustain his exclusive function to command the instruments of national force, at least when turned against the outside world for the security of our society. But, when it is turned inward, not because of rebellion but because of a lawful economic struggle between industry and labor, it should have no such indulgence. His command power is not such an absolute as might be implied from that office in a militaristic system but is subject to limitations consistent with a constitutional Republic whose law and policy-making branch is a representative Congress. The purpose of lodging dual titles in one man was to insure that the civilian would control the military, not to enable the military to subordinate the presidential office. No penance would ever expiate the sin against free government of holding that a President can escape control of executive powers by law through assuming his military role. What the power of command may include I do not try to envision, but I think it is not a military prerogative, without support of law, to seize persons or property because they are important or even essential for the military and naval establishment.

• • •

The Solicitor General lastly grounds support of the seizure upon nebulous, inherent powers never expressly granted but said to have accrued to the office from the customs and claims of preceding administrations. The plea is for a resulting power to deal with a crisis or an emergency according to the necessities of the case, the unarticulated assumption being that necessity knows no law.

Loose and irresponsible use of adjectives colors all nonlegal and much legal discussion of presidential powers. "Inherent" powers, "implied" powers, "incidental" powers, "plenary" powers, "war" powers and "emergency" powers are used, often interchangeably and without fixed or ascertainable meanings.

The vagueness and generality of the clauses that set forth presidential powers afford a plausible basis for pressures within and without an administration for presidential action beyond that supported by those whose responsibility it is to defend his actions in court. . . .

. . .

In view of the ease, expedition and safety with which Congress can grant and has granted large emergency powers, certainly ample to embrace this crisis, I am quite unimpressed with the argument that we should affirm possession of them without statute. Such power either has no beginning or it has no end. If it exists, it need submit to no legal restraint. I am not alarmed that it would plunge us straightway into dictatorship, but it is at least a step in that wrong direction.

As to whether there is imperative necessity for such powers, it is relevant to note the gap that exists between the President's paper powers and his real powers. The Constitution does not disclose the measure of the actual controls wielded by the modern presidential office. That instrument must be understood as an Eighteenth-Century sketch of a government hoped for, not as a blueprint of the Government that is. Vast accretions of federal power, eroded from that reserved by the States, have magnified the scope of presidential activity. Subtle shifts take place in the centers of real power that do not show on the face of the Constitution.

. . .

But I have no illusion that any decision by this Court can keep power in the hands of Congress if it is not wise and timely in meeting its problems. . . . We may say that power to legislate for emergencies belongs in the hands of Congress, but only Congress itself can prevent power from slipping through its fingers.

. . .

Mr. Justice Burton, concurring. [Omitted.]

. . .

Mr. Justice Clark, concurring in the judgment of the Court.

. . .

The limits of presidential power are obscure. However, Article II, no less than Article I, is part of "a constitution intended to endure for ages to come, and, consequently, to be adapted to the various *crises* of human affairs." Some of our Presidents, such as Lincoln, "felt that measures otherwise unconstitutional might become lawful by becoming indispensable to the preservation of the Constitution through the preservation of the nation." Others, such as Theodore Roosevelt, thought the President to be capable, as a "steward" of the people, of exerting all power save that which is specifically prohibited by the Constitution or the Congress. In my view . . . the Constitution does grant to the President extensive authority in times of grave and imperative national emergency. In fact, to my thinking, such a grant may well be necessary to the very existence of the Constitution itself. . . . In describing this authority I care not whether one calls it "residual," "inherent," "moral," "implied," "aggregate," "emergency," or otherwise. . . .

I conclude that where Congress has laid down specific procedures to deal with the type of crisis confronting the President, he must follow those procedures in meeting the crisis; but that in the absence of such action by Congress, the President's independent power to act depends upon the gravity of the situation confronting the nation. I cannot sustain the seizure in question because here * * * Congress had prescribed methods to be followed by the President in meeting the emergency at hand.

· · ·

Mr. Chief Justice Vinson, with whom Mr. Justice Reed and Mr. Justice Minton join, dissenting.

· · ·

In passing upon the question of Presidential powers in this case, we must first consider the context in which those powers were exercised.

Those who suggest that this is a case involving extraordinary powers should be mindful that these are extraordinary times. A world not yet recovered from the devastation of World War II has been forced to face the threat of another and more terrifying global conflict.

Accepting in full measure its responsibility in the world community, the United States was instrumental in securing adoption of the United Nations Charter. . . . In 1950, when the United Nations called upon member nations "to render every assistance" to repel aggression in Korea, the United States furnished its vigorous support. . . .

Further efforts to protect the free world from aggression are found in the congressional enactments of the Truman Plan for assistance to Greece and Turkey and the Marshall Plan for economic aid needed to build up the strength of our friends in Western Europe. In 1949, the Senate approved the North Atlantic Treaty under which each member nation agrees that an armed attack against one is an armed attack against all. . . . The concept of mutual security recently has been extended by treaty to friends in the Pacific.

· · ·

Even this brief review of our responsibilities in the world community discloses the enormity of our undertaking. Success of these measures may, as has often been observed, dramatically influence the lives of many generations of the world's peoples yet unborn. Alert to our responsibilities, which coincide with our own self-preservation through mutual security, Congress has enacted a large body of implementing legislation. . . .

[Vinson here discusses these legislative acts as well as the seizure authorizations included in the statutes. In addition, the Chief Justice chronicles instances of seizures, both based on these statutes and deriving their legitimacy from other sources.]

Focusing now on the situation confronting the President on the night of April 8, 1952, we cannot but conclude that the President was performing his duty under the Constitution to "take Care that the Laws be faithfully executed." . . .

The President reported to Congress the morning after the seizure that he acted because a work stoppage in steel production would immediately imperil the safety of the Nation by preventing execution of the legislative programs for procurement of military equipment. And, while a shutdown could be averted by granting the price concessions requested by [Youngstown Sheet & Tube Co.], granting such concessions would disrupt the price stabilization program also enacted by Congress. Rather than fail to execute either legislative program, the President acted to execute both.

Much of the argument in this case has been directed at straw men. We do not now have before us the case of a President acting solely on the basis of his own notions of the public welfare. Nor is there any question of unlimited executive power in this case. The President himself closed the door to any such claim when he sent his Message to Congress stating his purpose to abide by any action of Congress, whether approving or disapproving his seizure action. Here, the President immediately made sure that Congress was fully informed of the temporary action he had taken only to preserve the legislative programs from destruction until Congress could act.

The absence of a specific statute authorizing seizure of the steel mills as a mode of executing the laws—both the military procurement program and the anti-inflation program—has not until today been thought to prevent the President from executing the laws. . . . Flexibility as to mode of execution to meet critical situations is a matter of practical necessity. . . .

• • •

. . . [A]s of December 22, 1951, the President had a choice between alternate procedures for settling the threatened strike in the steel mills: one route [the Taft-Hartley Act] created to deal with peacetime disputes; the other route [the Defense Production Act] specially created to deal with disputes growing out of the defense and stabilization program. There is no question of bypassing a statutory procedure because both of the routes available to the President in December were based upon statutory authorization. Both routes were available in the steel dispute. The Union, by refusing to abide by the defense and stabilization program, could have forced the President to invoke Taft-Hartley at that time to delay the strike a maximum of 80 days. Instead, the Union agreed to cooperate with the defense program and submit the dispute to the Wage Stabilization Board [WSB].

• • •

When the President acted on April 8, he had exhausted the procedures for settlement available to him. Taft-Hartley was a route parallel to, not connected with, the WSB procedure. The strike had been delayed 99 days as contrasted with the maximum delay of 80 days under Taft-Hartley. There had been a hearing on the issues in dispute and bargaining which promised settlement up to the very hour before seizure had broken down. Faced with immediate national peril through stoppage in steel production on the one hand and faced with destruction of the wage and price legislative programs on the other, the President took temporary possession of the steel mills as the only course open to him consistent with his duty to take care that the laws be faithfully executed.

. . . The President's action has thus far been effective, not in settling the dispute, but in saving the various legislative programs at stake from destruction until Congress could act in the matter.

The diversity of views expressed in the six opinions of the majority, the lack of reference to authoritative precedent, the repeated reliance upon prior dissenting opinions, the complete disregard of the uncontroverted facts showing the gravity of the emergency and the temporary nature of the taking all serve to demonstrate how far afield one must go to affirm the order of the District Court.

The broad executive power granted by Article II to an officer on duty 365 days a year cannot, it is said, be invoked to avert disaster. Instead, the President must confine himself to sending a message to Congress recommending action. Under this messenger-boy concept of the Office, the President cannot even act to preserve legislative programs from destruction so that Congress will have something left to act upon. There is no judicial finding that the executive action was unwarranted because there was in fact no basis for the President's finding of the existence of an emergency for, under this view, the gravity of the emergency and the immediacy of the threatened disaster are considered irrelevant as a matter of law.

Seizure of [the steel companies'] property is not a pleasant undertaking. Similarly unpleasant to a free country are the draft which disrupts the home and military procurement which causes economic dislocation and compels adoption of price controls, wage stabilization and allocation of materials. The President informed Congress that even a temporary Government operation of [the steel mills] was "thoroughly distasteful" to him, but was necessary to prevent immediate paralysis of the mobilization program. Presidents have been in the past, and any man worthy of the Office should be in the future, free to take at least interim action necessary to execute legislative programs essential to survival of the Nation. A sturdy judiciary should not be swayed by the unpleasantness or unpopularity of necessary executive action, but must independently determine for itself whether the President was acting, as required by the Constitution, to "take Care that the Laws be faithfully executed."

As the District Judge stated, this is no time for "timorous" judicial action. But neither is this a time for timorous executive action. Faced with the duty of executing the defense programs which Congress had enacted and the disastrous effects that any stoppage in steel production would have on these programs, the President acted to preserve those programs by seizing the steel mills. There is no question that the possession was other than temporary in character and subject to congressional direction—either approving, disapproving or regulating the manner in which the mills were to be administered and returned to the owners. The President immediately informed Congress of his action and clearly stated his intention to abide by the legislative will. No basis for claims of arbitrary action, unlimited powers or dictatorial usurpation of congressional power appears from the facts of this case. On the contrary, judicial, legislative and executive precedents throughout our history demonstrate that in this case the President acted in full conformity with his duties under the Constitution. Accordingly, we would reverse the order of the District Court.

Weiner v. *United States*

357 U.S. 349 (1958)

MR. JUSTICE FRANKFURTER delivered the opinion of the Court.

This is a suit for back pay, based on [Weiner's] alleged illegal removal as a member of the War Claims Commission. The facts are not in dispute. By the War Claims Act of 1948, * * * Congress established that Commission with "jurisdiction to receive and adjudicate according to law" * * * claims for compensating internees, prisoners of war, and religious organizations * * * who suffered personal injury or property damage at the hands of the enemy in connection with World War II. The Commission was to be composed of three persons, at least two of whom were to be members of the bar, to be appointed by the President, by and with the advice and consent of the Senate. The Commission was to wind up its affairs not later than three years after the expiration of the time for filing claims, originally limited to two years but extended by successive legislation. . . . This limit on the Commission's life was the mode by which the tenure of the Commissioners was defined, and Congress made no provision for removal of a Commissioner.

Having been duly nominated by President Truman, [Weiner] was confirmed on June 2, 1950, and took office on June 8. . . . On his refusal to heed a request for his resignation, he was, on December 10, 1953, removed by President Eisenhower in the following terms: "I regard it as in the national interest to complete the administration of the War Claims Act of 1948, as amended, with personnel of my own selection." The following day, the President made recess appointments to the Commission, including petitioner's post. After Congress assembled, the President, on February 15, 1954, sent the names of the new appointees to the Senate. The Senate had not confirmed these nominations when the Commission was abolished, July 1, 1954. * * * Thereupon, [Weiner] brought this proceeding in the Court of Claims for recovery of his salary as a War Claims Commissioner from December 10, 1953, the day of his removal by the President, to June 30, 1954, the last day of the Commission's existence. . . . We brought the case here * * * . . .

Controversy pertaining to the scope and limits of the President's power of removal fills a thick chapter of our political and judicial history. The long stretches of its history, beginning with the very first Congress, with early echoes in the Reports of this Court, were laboriously traversed in Myers v United States * * * and need not be retraced. President Roosevelt's reliance upon the pronouncements of the Court in that case in removing a member of the Federal Trade Commission on the ground that "the aims and purposes of the Administration with respect to the work of the Commission can be carried out most effectively with personnel of my own selection" reflected contemporaneous professional opinion regarding the significance of the Myers decision. Speaking through a Chief Justice who himself had been President, the Court did not restrict itself to the immediate issue before it, the President's inherent power to remove a post-master, obviously an executive official. As of set purpose and not by way of parenthetic casualness, the Court announced that the President had inherent constitutional power of removal also of officials who have "duties of a quasi-judicial character . . . whose decisions after hearing affect interests of individuals, the discharge of which the President can not in a particular case properly influence or control." * * * This view of presidential power was deemed to flow from his "constitutional duty of seeing that the laws be faithfully executed." * * *

The assumption was short-lived that the Myers case recognized the President's inherent constitutional power to remove officials, no matter what the relation of the executive to the discharge of their duties and no matter what restrictions Congress may have imposed regarding the nature of their tenure. . . . Within less than ten years a unanimous Court, in Humphrey's Exr. v United States, * * * narrowly confined the scope of the Myers decision to include only "all purely executive officers." * * * The Court explicitly "disapproved" the expressions in Myers supporting the President's inherent constitutional power to remove members of quasi-judicial bodies. * * * Congress had given members of the Federal Trade Commission a seven-year term and also provided for the removal of a Commissioner by the President for inefficiency, neglect of duty or malfeasance in office. . . .

•   •   •

Humphrey's case was a cause célèbre—and not least in the halls of Congress. And what is the essence of the decision in Humphrey's case? It drew a sharp line of cleavage between officials who were part of the Executive establishment and were thus removable by virtue of the President's constitutional powers and those who are members of a body "to exercise its judgment without the leave or hindrance of any other official or any department of the government" * * * as to whom a power of removal exists only if Congress may fairly be said to have conferred it. This sharp differentiation derives from the difference in functions between those who are part of the Executive establishment and those whose tasks require absolute freedom from Executive interference. "For it is quite evident," again to quote Humphrey's Executor, "that one who holds his office only during the pleasure of another, cannot be depended upon to maintain an attitude of independence against the latter's will." * * *

Thus, the most reliable factor for drawing an inference regarding the President's power of removal in our case is the nature of the function that Congress vested in the War Claims Commission. What were the duties that Congress confided to this Commission? And can the inference fairly be drawn from the failure of Congress to provide for removal that these Commissioners were to remain in office at the will of the President? For such is the assertion of power on which [Weiner's] removal must rest. The ground of President Eisenhower's removal . . . was precisely the same as President Roosevelt's removal of Humphrey. Both Presidents desired to have Commissioners, one on the Federal Trade Commission, the other on the War Claims Commission, "of my own selection." They wanted these Commissioners to be their men. The terms of removal in the two cases are identical and express the assumption that the agencies of which the two Commissioners were members were subject in the discharge of their duties to the control of the Executive. An analysis of the Federal Trade Commission Act left this Court in no doubt that such was not the conception of Congress in creating the Federal Trade Commission. The terms of the War Claims Act of 1948 leave no doubt that such was not the conception of Congress regarding the War Claims Commission.

The history of this legislation emphatically underlines this fact. The short of it is that the origin of the Act was a bill * * * passed by the House that placed the administration of a very limited class of claims by Americans against Japan in the hands of the Federal Security Administrator and provided for a Commission to inquire into and report upon other types of claims. * * * The Federal Security Administrator was indubitably an arm of the President. When the House bill reached the Senate, it struck out all but the enacting clause, rewrote the bill, and established a Commission with "jurisdiction to receive and adjudicate according to law". . . . The Commission was established as an adjudicating body with all the paraphernalia by which legal claims are put to the test of proof, with finality of determination "not subject to review by any other official of the United States or by any court, by mandamus or otherwise." * * * Awards were to be paid out of a War Claims Fund in the hands of the Secretary of the Treasury, whereby such claims were given even more assured collectability than adheres to judgments rendered in the Court of Claims. * * * With minor amendment * * * this Senate bill became law. . . . For Congress itself to have made appropriations for the claims with which it dealt under the War Claims Act was not practical in view of the large number of claimants and the diversity in the specific circumstances giving rise to the claims. The House bill in effect put the distribution of the narrow class of claims that it acknowledged into Executive hands, by vesting the procedure in the Federal Security Administrator. The final form of the legislation, as we have seen, left the widened range of claims to be determined by adjudication. Congress could, of course, have given jurisdiction over these claims to the District Courts or to the Court of Claims. The fact that it chose to establish a Commission to "adjudicate according to law" the classes of claims defined in the statute did not alter the intrinsic judicial character of the task with which the Commission was charged. The claims were to be "adjudicated according to law," that is, on the merits of each claim, supported by evidence and governing legal considerations, by a body that was "entirely free from the control or coercive influence, direct or indirect," * * * of either the Executive or the Congress. If, as one must take for granted, the War Claims Act precluded the President from influencing the Commission in passing on a particular claim, a fortiori must it be inferred that Congress did not wish to have hang over the Commission the Damocles' sword of removal by the President for no reason other than that he preferred to have on that Commission men of his own choosing.

For such is this case. We have not a removal for cause involving the rectitude of a member of an adjudicatory body, nor even a suspensory removal until the Senate could act upon it by confirming the appointment of a new Commissioner or otherwise dealing with the matter. Judging the matter in all the nakedness in which it is presented, . . . we are compelled to conclude that no such power is given to the President directly by the Constitution, and none is impliedly conferred upon him by statute simply because Congress said nothing about it. The philosophy of Humphrey's Executor, in its explicit language as well as its implications, precludes such a claim.

The judgment is

Reversed.

Schick v. Reed

419 U.S. 256 (1974)

Mr. Chief Justice Burger delivered the opinion of the Court.

. . .

The pertinent facts are undisputed. In 1954 [Schick], then a master sergeant in the United States Army stationed in Japan, was tried before a court-martial for the brutal murder of an eight-year-old girl. He admitted the killing, but contended that he was insane at the time that he committed it. Medical opinion differed on this point. . . . The court-martial rejected [Schick's] defense and he was sentenced to death on March 27, 1954, pursuant to * * * the Uniform Code of Military Justice * * *. . . .

The case was then forwarded to President Eisenhower for final review. . . . The President acted on March 25, 1960:

> "[P]ursuant to the authority vested in me as President of the United States by Article II, Section 2, Clause 1, of the Constitution, the sentence to be put to death is hereby commuted to dishonorable discharge, forfeiture of all pay and allowances becoming due on and after the date of this action, and confinement at hard labor for the term of his . . . natural life. This commutation of sentence is expressly made on the condition that the said Maurice L. Schick shall never have any rights, privileges, claims, or benefits arising under the parole and suspension or remission of sentence laws of the United States and the regulations promulgated thereunder governing Federal prisoners confined in any civilian or military penal institution * * *. . . ."

. . . [Schick] was accordingly discharged from the Army and transferred to the Federal Penitentiary at Lewisburg, Pa. He has now served 20 years of his sentence. Had he originally received a sentence of life imprisonment he would have been eligible for parole consideration in March 1969; the condition in the President's order of commutation barred parole at any time.

. . .

When the death sentence was imposed in 1954 it was, as [Schick] concedes, valid under the Constitution of the United States and subject only to final action by the President. Absent the commutation of March 25, 1960, the sentence could, and in all probability would, have been carried out prior to 1972. Only the President's action in commuting the sentence under his Art II powers, on the conditions stipulated, prevented execution of the sentence imposed by the court-martial.

The essence of [Schick's] case is that, in light of this Court's holding in Furman v Georgia [1972], * * * which he could not anticipate, he made a "bad bargain" by accepting a no-parole condition in place of a death sentence. He does not cast his claim in those terms, of course. Rather, he argues that the conditions attached to the commutation put him in a worse position than he would have been in had he contested his death sentence—and remained alive—until the Furman case was decided 18 years after that sentence was originally imposed.

It is correct that pending death sentences not carried out prior to Furman were thereby set aside without conditions such as were attached to [Schick's] commutation. However, [Schick's] death sentence was not pending in 1972 because it had long since been commuted. The question here is whether Furman must now be read as nullifying the condition attached to that commutation when it was granted in 1960. Alternatively, [Schick] argues that even in 1960 President Eisenhower exceeded his powers under Art II by imposing a condition not expressly authorized by the Uniform Code of Military Justice.

In sum, [Schick's] claim gives rise to [these] questions: . . . was the conditional commutation of his death sentence lawful in 1960; . . . if so, did Furman retroactively void such conditions. . . .

The express power of Art II, § 2, cl 1, from which the Presidential power to commute criminal sentences derives, is to "grant Reprieves and Pardons . . . except in Cases of Impeachment." Although the authors of this clause surely did not act thoughtlessly, neither did they devote extended debate to its meaning. This can be explained in large part by the fact that the draftsmen were well acquainted with the English Crown authority to alter and reduce punishments as it existed in 1787. The history of that power, which was centuries old, reveals a gradual contraction to avoid its abuse and misuse. Changes were made as potential or actual abuses were perceived. . . .

At the time of the drafting and adoption of our Constitution it was considered elementary that the prerogative of the English Crown could be exercised upon conditions. . . .

Various types of conditions, both penal and nonpenal in nature, were employed. For example, it was common for a pardon or commutation to be granted on condition that the felon be transported to another place, and indeed our own Colonies were the recipients of numerous subjects of "banishment." This practice was never questioned despite the fact that British subjects generally could not be forced to leave the realm without an Act of Parliament and banishment was rarely authorized as a punishment for crime. . . . In short, by 1787 the English prerogative to pardon was unfettered except for a few specifically enumerated limitations.

The history of our executive pardoning power reveals a consistent pattern of adherence to the English common-law practice. . . .

. . . [T]he draftsmen of Art II, § 2, spoke in terms of a "prerogative" of the President, which ought not be "fettered or embarrassed." In light of the English common law from which such language was drawn, the conclusion is inescapable that the pardoning power was intended to include the power to commute sentences on conditions which do not in themselves offend the Constitution, but which are not specifically provided for by statute.

The few cases decided in this area are consistent with the view of the power described above. . . .

● ● ●

. . . [T]his Court has long read the Constitution as authorizing the President to deal with individual cases by granting conditional pardons. The very essence of the pardoning power is to treat each case individually. . . . Presidents throughout our history as a Nation have exercised the power to pardon or commute sentences upon conditions that are not specifically authorized by statute. Such conditions have generally gone unchallenged and, . . . attacks have been firmly rejected by the courts. * * * These facts are not insignificant for our interpretation of Art II, § 2, cl 1, because, as observed by Mr. Justice Holmes: "If a thing has been practised for two hundred years by common consent, it will need a strong case" to overturn it. * * *

A fair reading of the history of the English pardoning power, from which our Art II, § 2, cl 1, derives, of the language of that clause itself, and of the unbroken practice since 1790 compels the conclusion that the power flows from the Constitution alone, not from any legislative enactments, and that it cannot be modified, abridged, or diminished by the Congress. Additionally, considerations of public policy and humanitarian impulses support an interpretation of that power so as to permit the attachment of any condition which does not otherwise offend the Constitution. The plain purpose of the broad power conferred by § 2, cl 1, was to allow plenary authority in the President to "forgive" the convicted person in part or entirely, to reduce a penalty in terms of a specified number of years, or to alter it with conditions which are in themselves constitutionally unobjectionable. If we were to accept [Schick's] contentions, a commutation of his death sentence to 25 to 30 years would be subject to the same challenge as is now made, i.e., that parole must be available to [Schick] because it is to others. That such an interpretation of § 2, cl 1, would in all probability tend to inhibit the exercise of the pardoning power and reduce the frequency of commutations is hardly open to doubt. We therefore hold that the pardoning power is an enumerated power of the Constitution and its limitations, if any, must be found in the Constitution itself. It would be a curious logic to allow a convicted person who petitions for mercy to retain the full benefit of a lesser punishment with conditions, yet escape burdens readily assumed in accepting the commutation which he sought.

[Schick's] claim must therefore fail. The no-parole condition attached to the commutation of his death sentence is similar to sanctions imposed by legislatures such as mandatory minimum sentences or statutes otherwise precluding parole; it does not offend the Constitution. Similarly, the President's action derived solely from his Art II powers; it did not depend upon * * * any . . . statute fixing a death penalty for murder. . . .

We are not moved by [Schick's] argument that it is somehow "unfair" that he be treated differently from persons whose death sentences were pending at the time that Furman was decided. Individual acts of clemency inherently call for discriminating choices because no two cases are the same. Indeed, as noted earlier, [Schick's] life was undoubtedly spared by President Eisenhower's commutation order of March 25, 1960. Nor is [Schick] without further remedies since he may, of course, apply to the present or future Presidents for a complete pardon, commutation to time served, or relief from the no-parole condition. We hold only that the conditional commutation of his death sentence was lawful when made and that intervening events have not altered its validity.

Affirmed.

Mr. Justice Marshall, with whom Mr. Justice Douglas and Mr. Justice Brennan join, dissenting.

• • •

I

The Court misconstrues [Schick's] retroactivity argument. Schick does not dispute the constitutional validity of the death penalty in 1954 under then-existing case law. Nor does he contend that he was under sentence of death in 1972 when the decision issued in Furman, invalidating "the imposition and carrying out" of discretionary death sentences. * * * Rather he argues that the retroactive application of Furman to his no-parole commutation is required because the imposition of the death sentence was the indispensable vehicle through which he became subject to his present sentence. In other words, the no-parole condition could not now exist had the court-martial before which Schick was tried not imposed the death penalty.

• • •

Since Furman is fully retroactive [Schick's] case should be simple to resolve. . . . A death sentence was imposed by the court-martial and affirmed by the Board of Review and the United States Court of Military Appeals. * * * The death sentence so imposed was declared unconstitutional by Furman and is therefore null and void as a matter of law. The only legal alternative—simple life imprisonment—must be substituted. Concomitantly, the adverse consequence of the death sentence—the no-parole condition of [Schick's] 1960 commutation—must also be voided, as it exceeds the lawful alternative punishment that should have been imposed. [He] should now be subject to treatment as a person sentenced to life imprisonment on the date of his original sentence and eligible for parole.

. . .

II

Since the majority devotes its opinion to a discussion of the scope of Presidential power, I am compelled to comment. I have no quarrel with the proposition that the source of the President's commutation power is found in Art II, § 2, cl 1, of the Constitution. . . .

. . . I take issue with the Court's conclusion that annexation of the "no-parole condition . . . does not offend the Constitution." * * * In my view the President's action exceeded the limits of the Art II pardon power. In commuting a sentence the Chief Executive is not embued with the constitutional power to create unauthorized punishments.

The congressionally prescribed parameters of punishment mark the boundaries within which the Executive must exercise his authority. By virtue of the pardon power the Executive may abstain from enforcing a judgment by judicial authorities; he may not, under the aegis of that power, engage in lawmaking or adjudication. . . .

While the clemency function of the Executive in the federal criminal justice system is consistent with the separation of powers, the attachment of punitive conditions to grants of clemency is not. Prescribing punishment is a prerogative reserved for the lawmaking branch of government, the legislature. As a consequence, President Eisenhower's addition to Schick's commutation of a condition that did not coincide with punishment prescribed by the legislature for *any* military crime, much less this specific offense, was a usurpation of a legislative function. While the exercise of the pardon power was proper, the imposition of this penal condition was not embraced by that power.

. . .

In conclusion I note that where a President chooses to exercise his clemency power he should be mindful that

"The punishment appropriate for the diverse federal offenses is a matter for the discretion of Congress, subject only to constitutional limitations, more particularly the Eighth Amendment." * * *

* * * The Congress has not delegated such authority to the President. I do not challenge the right of the President to issue pardons on nonpenal conditions, but where the Executive elects to exercise the Presidential power for commutation, the clear import of the Constitution mandates that the lesser punishment imposed be sanctioned by the legislature.

In sum, the no-parole condition is constitutionally defective in the face of the retrospective application of Furman and the extra-legal nature of the Executive action. I would nullify the condition, and direct the lower court to remand the case for resentencing to the only alternative available—life with the opportunity for parole—and its attendant benefits.

CHAPTER **8**

Foreign Relations

INTRODUCTORY ESSAY

Anyone casually reading the Constitution in the hopes of discovering to which branch of the national government it delegates the primary responsibility for managing United States foreign policy would likely come away unenlightened. The Constitution is not at all clear about which branch is the principal agent responsible for the conduct of international affairs. Article II gives the President power over the armed forces by naming the Chief Executive Commander in Chief; yet Article I grants to Congress the power to raise, support, provide for, and maintain an army and a navy, the power to tax and spend for defense, and the power to declare war. Moreover, the Constitution gives the President the power to negotiate treaties, but requires Senate advice and consent before any such document stands as a formal international commitment (requiring, as well, that Congress enact laws to put certain kinds of treaty provisions into effect). The Constitution also allows the President to recognize foreign emissaries, ministers, and ambassadors, but requires Senate approval of all ambassadors a President might wish to send.

Executive Dominance in the Face of Constitutional Ambiguity

One might conclude from this analysis that the Founding Fathers intended to have Congress and the Chief Executive either formally share the power to make and implement foreign policy or dramatically struggle for control of that power. Whatever the intent of the Framers may have been, the primary responsibility for the management of foreign relations now rests with the President (aided by the National Security Council and the State Department). He conducts those affairs with occasional cooperation and struggle from Congress, but there is no established, formal sharing of control over international relations between the two branches.

Extraconstitutional Bases of Presidential Authority

Several related factors help us understand the emergence of executive dominance despite constitutional provisions suggesting a wholly different plan. In the first place, the management of foreign affairs, encompassing as it does a need for secrecy, dispatch, and massive information processing, does not easily lend itself to cooperative efforts between an executive and a 535-member legislature. At the same time, most members of Congress have little incentive to invest the time and effort necessary to bring the legislature to a coequal status in the area of foreign policy. Because reelection often hinges on the ability of members to secure direct and perceptible benefits for their constituencies, and because foreign policy decisions rarely provide direct benefits to domestic localities, it is no wonder that international affairs prove of only peripheral concern to most members of Congress. While the impracticality of cooperative efforts and congressional inertia have no doubt contributed to executive primacy, long-standing traditions in the international community relying on single heads of state have also facilitated the development of the executive's centrality. Further, the advent of the nuclear age has given an urgency and importance to world peace that has served to foster a perceived need to rely on a central, presumably rational, individual as sole spokesperson in national security emergencies and international matters generally. Those factors, as well as the fact that the Supreme Court has done little to maintain whatever constitutional design for shared foreign policy management there might have been, have catapulted the Chief Executive into a position of primacy in the international sphere of American policymaking.

Presidential "primacy," of course, does not mean that Congress is powerless. The legislature can influence executive management of foreign relations, and has done so. Indeed, a President would be foolhardy not to make foreign policy with an eye toward both international consequences and congressional reaction. Should Congress wish, it could easily bring to bear on foreign policy those powers it clearly possesses. In a few instances, Congress has done just that. For the most part though, Congress has deferred to the executive. Aside from those factors already mentioned, there is the generally held belief that executive power in foreign affairs is based on more than what the Framers allocated to the President in Article II. Most political observers concede a set of vague extraconstitutional or inherent powers in foreign affairs that emanate from the concept of nationhood itself. These inherent powers have been conferred upon or assumed by the President by virtue of tradition, practice, and an executive centrality in American politics that make the President the most visible, viable agent to function as a national representative abroad.

Inherent Powers and the Conduct of Foreign Affairs

The Court recognized the additional, inherent executive powers rather explicitly in the 1936 case of *United States* v. *Curtiss-Wright Export Corp.,* 299 U.S. 304. In May 1934, Congress, by a joint resolution, authorized the President to forbid American munitions firms from selling arms (with such limitations and exceptions as the President might determine) to the belligerent nations of Paraguay and Bolivia. Shortly after passage of the resolution, Roosevelt issued an embargo order to be enforced by the Secretary of State; the order remained in effect for eighteen months. In 1936 the Curtiss-Wright Corporation was indicted for conspiring to sell arms to Bolivia against the President's orders. Curtiss-Wright sought to avoid prosecution by arguing that the resolution unconstitutionally delegated legislative power to the Chief Executive, and hence the specific rules devised by Roosevelt (and not Congress) to control arms shipments abroad were illegal and inapplicable. The Supreme Court did not concur with Curtiss-Wright that the nondelegability doctrine applies equally to both foreign matters and domestic concerns. In internal domestic matters, the Court was quick to point out, Congress can act only if the Constitution so specifies or if one can reasonably hold that the Constitution implies an action is necessary and proper to carry into effect specified powers. And true, once a set of specified powers has been assigned to Congress, those powers cannot be cavalierly delegated to the President. In the domestic sphere, Justice Sutherland argued for the majority, powers enumerated for the national government were taken from those already possessed by each state and because of this source, the enumerated powers are very limited. In the area of foreign relations, however, since the separate states never possessed the power to deal in foreign matters, the authority over foreign affairs was not lifted from the states and was therefore not limited to a constitutional basis. Rather, the Court argued, the source of power to deal internationally lay in the colonial separation from Great Britain, which created a necessary transfer of sovereignty from the Crown to the united colonies, not the colonies separately. From this elaborate reasoning Sutherland concluded:

> . . . The investment of the federal government with the powers of external sovereignty did not depend upon the affirmative grants of the Constitution. The powers to declare and wage war, to conclude peace, to make treaties, to maintain diplomatic relations with other sovereignties, if they had never been mentioned in the Constitution would have vested in the federal government as a necessary concomitant of nationality.

Thus, for the Court, the management of foreign relations was an exclusively federal power whose exercise did not depend upon enumerations in the Constitution. The majority believed as well that the President plays a special, expansive role in international matters which allows the executive to exercise powers in this sphere beyond those outlined in Article II. The President alone has the power to speak or listen for the nation and therefore serves as the "sole organ of the federal government in the field of international relations." All of these rationales made it clear to the Court that Roosevelt's limitation of arms shipments to South America derived from powers belonging exclusively to the federal government and granted substantially to the President; those powers were beyond the Constitution, and hence the question of an illegal delegation of congressional lawmaking power to the President (possessed as he was of independent powers to so act anyway) was an irrelevant issue.

The majority's assertion in Curtiss-Wright of the expansive inherent power a President wields in the management of foreign affairs has been taken to task as altogether too broad. Most jurists agree that the President is not wholly free to handle foreign affairs as he sees fit. Indeed, Justice Jackson noted in the Steel Seizure Case, 343 U.S. 579 (1952), that while the President has expansive inherent powers in the area of foreign relations (clearly more expansive in foreign relations than in domestic affairs), he cannot exercise those powers in blatant contradistinction to the express wishes of Congress. In the Pentagon Papers Case, 403 U.S. 713 (1971), the Supreme Court refused to grant the executive the authority to institute prior restraint on the press solely on the basis of an inherent power in foreign affairs. Even so, the Court has granted the President an "executive privilege" to withhold national security information from public scrutiny, but it has denied the same privilege on the domestic side—a position based mainly on inherent powers in foreign affairs (*United States* v. *Nixon,* 418 U.S. 683 [1974]). Similarly, the Justices have upheld wiretap limitations imposed by the Fourth Amendment in domestic matters but supported their suspension in cases where the concern was with foreign subversives believed to endanger national security (*United States* v. *United States District Court,* 407 U.S. 297 [1972]).

Specifics of Conducting Foreign Affairs

Recognition of Foreign Governments

Although the President's authority in international relations rests in part on inherent powers, the Constitution does provide a sizable power base for independent executive action in foreign affairs. One section grants the power to recognize foreign governments. Article II authorizes the President to receive ambassadors, ministers, and emissaries from other nations. The Chief Executive has the discretion to employ this power to significant advantage in international diplomacy. In so doing, he determines who the government of a foreign nation will be for legal purposes within the United States; he also determines with whom the United States will exchange communications and reach agreements or treaties. Such power is of obvious importance in international affairs as Roosevelt's recognition of the Soviet Union in the early 1930s, Truman's recognition of the newly created state of Israel in the late 1940s, Kennedy's severance of ties with Cuba in the early 1960s, and Carter's severance of ties with Taiwan and recognition of mainland China in the 1970s all attest.

The Constitution grants the President this power independently of Congress or the Court. The Court stays out of the politics of recognition by claiming that such matters are "political questions." Thus, the Court will only entertain suits for, say, recovery of property from nations recognized by the executive. In fact, under what is called the "act of state doctrine," the Court has generally declined to adjudicate matters in which the central legal issue in dispute concerns decisions bearing on foreign affairs, particularly which foreign government is a nation's legitimate government. Congress, too, remains apart from this process, in large part to avoid embarrassment should each branch present differing views on recognition. The ability of a President to act unilaterally in this area may easily put Congress at a disadvantage in exerting its foreign relations prerogatives.

Treaty-Making

In addition to exerting his authority to recognize foreign governments as a vehicle of international relations, the Chief Executive is empowered by the Constitution to make treaties with other nations, subject of course to the advice and consent of two-thirds of the Senate. A treaty is an agreement between two or more nations specifying intentions to behave in certain ways. The recent Panama Canal Treaty is a good example of two nations, the United States and Panama, agreeing to transfer ownership of a given property by a certain date, with specifications of rights of access as a condition of the transfer. As with all treaty provisions, these provisions are ostensibly binding on both parties (ostensibly, because in international law there are no real enforcement powers nor is there a single authority empowered to invoke sanctions should one party or the other fail to fulfill the terms of the treaty). A treaty obviously places some form of obligation on the United States in the international community. Treaties also impose domestic obligations because a treaty is the constitutional equivalent of a federal statute in that it is also considered the supreme law of the land.

The fact that the terms of a treaty potentially affect the domestic policy of the nation can be problematic. In fact, the decision in *Missouri* v. *Holland,* 252 U.S. 416 (1920), raised serious constitutional questions along these very lines. The case concerned the constitutionality of a statute passed to further obligations incurred by a migratory bird treaty between the United States and Great Britain (Canada). The treaty, designed to limit the shooting of certain birds during their migration across Canada and the United States, required each nation to pass laws to limit the hunting seasons and to establish other protections for the migratory bird population. In 1918 Congress passed a federal migratory bird act to put the terms of the treaty into effect. Missouri challenged the statute as an invasion of its rights to deal with its fowl as it saw fit, claiming that in enacting the statute Congress had exceeded its power and usurped powers reserved to the states by the Tenth Amendment. Interestingly, this particular argument had proven successful in getting a lower court to rule that an earlier migratory bird act, based on commerce powers and not in furtherance of a treaty, was unconstitutional. The lower court, applying the "dual federalism" view of the nation-state relationship in vogue at the time (see Part IV), held that the Tenth Amendment limited the scope of congressional commerce powers. Of course, what made the 1920 case different from the earlier litigation was the fact that Congress did not rely on the Commerce Clause for justification of the recent law but rather on the necessity to fulfill international commitments under the federal treaty power.

The Supreme Court upheld the 1918 statute against the claimed interference with states rights. To some extent the Court relied on the questionable character of Missouri's claim to ownership of birds in transit. The primary argument in support of the statute, however, rested on the fact that the statute was in furtherance of a treaty obligation. Given the national character of the problem, the Justices could not see how some "invisible radiation from the general terms of the Tenth Amendment" precluded an effective solution. While the treaty power was not without some constitutional qualification, "there may be matters of the sharpest exigency for the national well-being that an act of Congress could not deal with but that a treaty followed by such an act could." Thus, a statute that would not have been legitimate under the Commerce Clause (as applied in the period under question) became valid when passed to fulfill the requirements of a treaty.

Missouri v. *Holland* made clear the close interconnection between the foreign and domestic spheres of power and revealed the potential problems of maintaining a government whose domestic authority emanates from a constitution but whose power to deal externally has its source elsewhere. Indeed, the holding in this case raised the possibility of using the treaty power to greatly expand the congressional power to legislate domestically. At the time of the decision, the Court had denied Congress the authority under the Commerce Clause to regulate child labor and minimum wages and hours. Now *Missouri* v. *Holland* raised the possibility that such legislation could be legitimized under the treaty power. No such legislation followed, but some officials and political observers considered the idea as well as more extreme possibilities regarding the potential misuse and abuse of the treaty power.

In response to the most extreme view that virtually all constitutional limitations could be swept away by reliance on the treaty power, Senator Bricker in the early 1950s proposed a constitutional amendment to correct perceived problems in the conduct of foreign relations (see Kallenbach, 1966, pp. 510–512). In Section 1 of the proposal, Bricker required the nullification of any treaty provision that conflicted with the Constitution—it could have no force or effect. Section 2 maintained that a treaty could become effective as internal law only through legislation that would have been valid had there been no treaty. The proposed amendment was never sent to the states for ratification because supporters fell one vote short of the two-thirds majority required for approval in the Senate. Even so, interest in the proposal lasted through much of the decade. However, by 1957, support for Bricker's amendment had been undermined by commentary in *Reid* v. *Covert,* 351 U.S. 487 (1956). Justice Black addressed the fundamental fears underlying the amendment drive by saying:

> . . . No agreement with a foreign nation can confer power on the Congress or on any other branch of government which is free from the restraints of the Constitution. . . . It would be manifestly contrary to the objectives of those who created the Constitution, as well as those who were responsible for the Bill of Rights—let alone to our entire constitutional history and tradition—to . . . [permit] the United States to exercise power under an international agreement without observing constitutional prohibitions.

Black's assurances are clear: The Constitution cannot be altered by virtue of an interpretation of the treaty-making power that was allegedly conferred by the Court in 1920.

Executive Agreements

Support for the Bricker proposal, though, was not wholly based on fears that the treaty power could ultimately be used to usurp the Constitution. The amendment also sought to curtail the increasing presidential tendency to bypass Congress altogether through the use of executive agreements. Since the 1850s the importance and centrality of the treaty as an instrument for conducting foreign affairs had diminished considerably as the executive agreement evolved to take its place. Executive agreements, like treaties, entail commitments among nations to interact with one another in certain ways, but they are concluded through heads of state acting independently of their lawmaking bodies. Most such agreements involve relatively minor details of international concern such as specifications for the details of postal relations or the use of radio airwaves. However, the executive agreement has emerged as a vital tool of foreign policy and is presently used for far more important matters than was once the case. This development was encouraged by a policy announced by the Supreme Court in *United States* v. *Belmont,* 301 U.S. 324 (1937), and *United States* v. *Pink,* 315 U.S. 203 (1942). Both cases challenged the domestic effect of the Litvinov Agreements that FDR had reached with the Soviet Union without congressional authorization. Aside from recognizing the nation, the Agreement granted the Soviet claim to properties that had been nationalized but had remained in American hands. In *Belmont* the claim involved assets of the Petrograd Metal Works Company that were still deposited in a New York bank. After the Bolshevik Revolution the Soviet government had nationalized the metal works and as a consequence held title to those assets remaining in the United States. The United States brought suit to secure the assets in order to transfer them to the Soviet Union as agreed to in the Litvinov Agreements. A lower court held that the confiscation was contrary to New York policy and that New York therefore did not need to transfer the funds. The Supreme Court overruled the decision, holding that the executive agreement was essentially equivalent to a treaty and as such was the supreme law of the land, New York's policy notwithstanding. In *Pink* similar results were obtained regarding the assets of a Soviet insurance company. The Court supported the *Belmont* policy of a virtual identity between executive agreements and treaties.

Both decisions granted an equivalency between treaty and executive agreement that obviously had the effect of making executive agreements all the more enticing to Presidents. Given the uncertainty of treaty ratification in the Senate, the executive agreement seemed the more reliable procedure as a vehicle for foreign policy.

As the Senate's role in important areas of foreign relations appeared to decline, support for the Bricker proposal increased. Proponents of the amendment were able to marshal support particularly for that part of the proposal requiring congressional approval of executive agreements before they could have any effect domestically.

Not all executive agreements were of concern to supporters of the Bricker amendment. A substantial number of agreements were, and still are, initially authorized by Congress through statutes granting the President the power to reach subsequent agreements virtually independently. For example, in the Reciprocal Trade Agreements Act of 1934, Congress allowed the President to modify tariffs, as needed, by executive agreement rather than through a full-dress statute or treaty. Since the Truman administration, the lion's share of international commitment has been made by executive agreement pursuant to statutory authorization. Even so, a small but important share of commitments are made by the President independently of congressional consideration. Nevertheless, members of Congress have increasingly felt that the few agreements reached by the executive alone are of sufficient importance to warrant congressional participation. This consideration of the importance and impact of agreements served as the primary impetus for the Bricker effort. However, in the late 1950s and early 1960s, many of the factors that inspired the amendment proposal and its reasonably strong coalition of support dissipated with shifts in international concern, transformations in domestic belief, and the development of the Cold War, as much as with the defeat of Senator Bricker. Nonetheless, the Vietnam era brought these concerns to the surface again, although no proposals for constitutional amendment have been forthcoming. In the midst of the Vietnam War Senator Fulbright brought the issue into sharp focus when he noted that while the Senate was being convened to approve by a two-thirds vote a treaty to preserve cultural artifacts in a friendly neighboring country, the President was moving American men and material "around the globe like so many pawns in a chess game" and doing so without express congressional authorization" (quoted in Johnson and McCormick, 1978, p. 470n).

War Powers

As Senator Fulbright's remark suggests, presidential power in international affairs is not limited to the diplomatic formalities and niceties of recognition and treaty-making. An integral part of foreign relations is the power to use or threaten armed force against another nation or set of nations. The use of force is often justified as the only way to protect American interests abroad, enforce the terms of earlier treaty commitments, maintain national security against possible attack, or defend the nation against an actual attack. The success of American foreign policy would, no doubt, be severely circumscribed if the nation's fundamental law limited the ability to back up ultimatums in the international community or defend the nation in the event of armed attack.

Recognizing this, the Framers granted a divided war power, vesting Congress with the authority to declare war and the President with the responsibility of commanding the armed forces. This separation has generated ample debate over the proper role of each branch. Because the Chief Executive has primacy in foreign affairs and is also Commander in Chief, the power to make (and hence, for all practical purposes, declare) war has actually resided with him alone, until recently.

Since the nation's beginning Congress has declared war only five times, and in only two of those instances (the War of 1812 and the Spanish-American War) did Congress do more than simply recognize that a state of war already existed. The United States has been enmeshed in far more than five military conflicts, several of which are clearly classifiable as "war" despite the absence of a congressional declaration. United States operations in Korea, Cuba, Vietnam, and Cambodia were all military actions engaged in under presidential order without a congressional declaration of war. In initiating and sustaining these actions, the Chief Executive relied on powers conferred as Commander in Chief and powers conferred as "sole organ of foreign affairs" to justify sending troops into battle.

The Vietnam controversy raised a number of constitutional questions, the most central of which concerned the role Congress should play in the commitment of troops to foreign soil in the name of national security. Revitalizing a strict interpretation of the Constitution, proponents of a divided war power argued that any and all commitment of troops must rest on express authorization by Congress. The response to such an assertion usually noted that in the event of attack, a President cannot allow the nation to go down to defeat while awaiting congressional approval (that is, declaration of war) to fight back. This specific matter of emergency war powers was raised and resolved in favor of the executive in the Prize Cases, 2 Bl. 635 (1863). The case involved the disposition of Confederate vessels captured by the Union navy during that navy's blockade of Southern ports. The challenge before the courts questioned the legality of the blockade because there had been no congressional declaration of war. Under the international "laws of war," the vessels would be legally in the hands of the Union if the conflict were a declared war and illegally held if no war had been declared. The politics of the Civil War forced the Court to find the captures legal without an express congressional declaration of war. The Court held that "the President is not only authorized, but bound to resist force by force. He does not initiate the war, but is bound to accept the challenge without waiting for any special legislative authority." In addition, Justice Grier noted that the "President was bound to meet [the Civil War] in the shape it presented itself, without waiting for Congress to baptize it with a name; and no name given to it by him or them could change the fact." The Court went on to aver that the judiciary must rely on the political departments in the executive and must defer to the President's determination of what degree of force a given crisis demands.

Lincoln's views of the war power, sustained by the Prize Cases, serve to grant the executive inherent powers in military matters that allow the President to make the final determination of when the demands of national security require the use of troops. Indeed, much of the justification for the Vietnam War (a war fought without direct congressional authorization) emanated from such a posture. State Department documents during the Vietnam War asserted that the duty of the Commander in Chief and other presidential responsibility for conducting foreign affairs included

> the power to deploy American forces abroad and commit them to military operations when the President deems such action necessary to maintain the security and defense of the United States. . . . If he considers that deployment of U.S. Forces to South Vietnam is required, and that military measures against the source of communist aggression in North Vietnam are necessary, he is constitutionally empowered to take these measures. (Meeker, 1966, p. 474)

While the Court had ample opportunity during the Vietnam era to grapple with the validity of this State Department view, it studiously sought to avoid the issue by claiming that those who brought such cases lacked standing to sue or that the matter was a political question. In the most unusual of the efforts to secure a judicial pronouncement, the Supreme Court simply refused, without comment, to allow Massachusetts to file a suit directly challenging the constitutionality of the Vietnam War. The Massachusetts legislature had passed a bill in 1970 that held that no Massachusetts serviceman could be required to fight in Vietnam. The legislation also authorized the state attorney general to bring an original jurisdiction action in the U.S. Supreme Court on behalf of the state and its citizens who were required to serve. The purpose of the bill was simply to secure a ruling on the constitutionality of the large-scale undeclared war in Southeast Asia. A six-member Court majority concurred in the terse denial of Massachusett's motion to file, while Justices Douglas, Harlan, and Stewart dissented. The views of the dissenters are reprinted in this chapter (*Massachusetts* v. *Laird,* 400 U.S. 886 [1970]).

As the Court's reluctance to deal with the matter became quite clear, Congress began to question the executive's justifications and to consider reasserting some of the legislature's war-making prerogatives. In 1973 Congress passed the War Powers Resolution over the veto of then President Nixon. The Resolution was designed to limit the President's ability to unilaterally send troops into foreign combat. It required the President to make a full report to Congress when he sent troops into foreign areas, limited how long combat could continue without congressional authorization, and provided a means for Congress to require the ending of hostilities even before the allotted grace period had expired. Under these provisions a President can send military troops into battle only when there is a declared war, when Congress has provided specific statutory authorization, or when actual attack on the United States, its territories, or possessions has occurred. When troops are committed in the absence of a declaration of war, the President must report the details to Congress within forty-eight hours and must withdraw troops from combat within a maximum of ninety days should Congress not act to affirm the move or specifically act to require that the troops be removed.

Whether this resolution will prove effective in limiting the executive power to commit troops abroad remains to be seen. In some circles the Resolution is seen as doing just the opposite because Congress actually sanctions the unilateral executive power to engage in combat for ninety days (Mullen, 1976, p. 103). Not only does the Resolution provide a specific grant of power, in contrast to the vagaries of the Constitution, it poses problems of enforcement as well. A future Chief Executive could simply refuse to comply with the provisions of the Resolution and thereby force Congress to test the matter in the courts.

While it is difficult to determine who possesses the power to initiate war, an equally difficult constitutional matter is the proper manner of exercising the war powers. Once a state of emergency is in effect, particularly one in which the very survival of the nation depends, clear, almost dictatorial leadership often proves a necessity. What constitutional limitations still apply in such a context? In the exigencies of war, it is easy to see how one might justify ignoring the dictates of the Constitution in favor of the "laws of necessity" or virtual martial law to preserve the very society itself.

The Court's stance on the extent of acceptable emergency powers and martial law is rather mixed. Whatever policy has emerged has stemmed from the clash between the demands of military necessity and respect for the civil rights of the individual. One of the earliest cases dealing with this issue, though not a Supreme Court case per se, was *Ex parte Merryman,* 17 Fed. Cas. 144 (1861). John Merryman was a resident of Maryland with clear Southern sympathies who made those views known quite openly. Fearing that Merryman's statements and potential actions might affect the Union campaign, military officials arrested him under the auspices of a presidential directive. Merryman sought a writ of habeas corpus from Justice Taney soon after his detention. The writ was never formally honored because the general in charge of the fort where Merryman was detained refused to consider it since Lincoln had suspended the writ. Chief Justice Taney, on circuit duty, cited the general with contempt and ultimately conceded the legitimacy of Merryman's release. At the same time, he informed Lincoln that only Congress could suspend the writ and that Lincoln's unilateral action was therefore unconstitutional. Lincoln never replied directly to Taney. He did, however, without mentioning Taney, inform Congress that Taney's insistence that only Congress had the power to suspend the writ was inaccurate. Lincoln maintained that since the Constitution was silent on which branch possessed the power to suspend the privilege of the writ, he was justified in proceeding as he did.

Although the Court did not entertain the *Merryman* case, it did have an opportunity to expound on the constitutional limitations of executive power during wartime in the case of *Ex parte Milligan*, 4 Wall. 2 (1866), which it heard after the Civil War had ended. Lambdin P. Milligan, like John Merryman, had been a Southern sympathizer and active collaborator. In 1864 he had been arrested in Indiana and tried by a military commission established by Lincoln. He was found guilty and sentenced to be hanged. In 1865 Milligan sought a writ of habeas corpus. In his petition he asserted that the trial by military commission was an unconstitutional violation of his right to a trial by jury in a nonmilitary courtroom. He had been denied a jury trial by virtue of Lincoln's suspension of the privilege of the writ.

A crucial matter for the Court in Milligan's case was the fact that Milligan's trial had been held before a military commission even though the civil courts were still in operation at the time. The Supreme Court, in releasing Milligan, condemned the President's assertion that executive war powers granted him the right to institute military trials of civilian personnel when civil courts were open and functioning. Five Justices went one step further and argued that even Congress could never authorize suspension of the writ when the regular courts were operating. Although there is no mistaking the intent of the *Milligan* ruling that even in time of war certain constitutional limitations must obtain, the Court was spared the difficulty of enforcing such an order during the conflict because the fighting had ceased by the time the majority handed down its opinion.

By contrast, during World War II the operations of civil courts in the territory of Hawaii were suspended for a considerable period of time. During the suspension military commissions undertook the normal business of the federal courts. Unlike Milligan's circumstance, the Hawaiian action drew its authority from the Hawaii Organic Act, which granted the institution of martial law under certain conditions. Even though the dangers that had initially inspired the Hawaiian governor to institute martial law (with President Roosevelt's consent) had subsided, military trials of civilians continued. Ultimately a federal judge issued a writ of habeas corpus to secure the release of a prisoner held under military detention. In *Duncan* v. *Kahanamoku*, 327 U.S. 304 (1944), the Court held that Congress had not intended the Hawaii Organic Act to "authorize the supplanting of courts by military tribunals." This ruling was in line with the policy formulated in *Milligan*.

While *Milligan* and *Duncan* provide judicial support for the constitutional protection of rights even against the demands of war, the holding in *Korematsu* v. *United States,* 323 U.S. 214 (1944), is striking in its contrary view. Early in World War II Roosevelt issued an executive order that authorized the Secretary of War to establish "military areas" from which military personnel could restrict, exclude, or expel ostensibly dangerous persons. Legislation passed by Congress in support of this order established punishments for violations of the orders. These combined executive and legislative actions resulted in the indiscriminate forced evacuation and incarceration of Japanese and Japanese Americans from those West Coast states denoted as military areas.

In *Korematsu* the Court was faced with a direct challenge to the constitutionality of such a blatantly discriminatory procedure exercised in the name of the war power. The Court, in what some have considered a "total judicial surrender to an outrage against individual liberties committed under a claim of executive discretion to meet military necessities" (Shapiro and Hobbs, 1974, p. 433), deferred to military opinion that the Japanese were potentially dangerous, that efforts to determine loyalty were impractical, and that the actions were therefore constitutional. Three Justices dissented. Justice Murphy took the majority to task by claiming that longstanding prejudices against Japanese Americans inspired the evacuation and prison camps, not any demonstrated public necessity. Justices Jackson and Roberts felt that the Court ought not to give constitutional approval to a "military expedient that has no place in law under the Constitution."

The limits of the executive's power under conditions of warfare or public emergency are difficult to pinpoint, and it is not likely that the Supreme Court will be able to pinpoint them with much precision. Many of the expansive exercises of war powers by Lincoln during the Civil War and by Roosevelt during World War II were never tested in the Court and were never really considered in need of testing. Both Presidents asserted the need to exercise extraordinary power to cope with extraordinary circumstances.

Oddly enough, many of the war powers exerted during World War II continued in effect well beyond the ending of hostilities. This situation gave rise to fears that a loosely defined "war power" turned "emergency power" could mitigate the binding quality of the Constitution. Indeed, since 1970 Congress has delegated numerous powers to the President to cope with the emergencies of an energy shortage and an inflationary economy. There is a danger in granting extraordinary powers such as these. Many people are capable of turning simple problems into "emergency" problems to justify extraordinary action.

Executive Centrality: A Look to the Future

Considering the thesis of inherent powers in foreign affairs as expressed in *Curtiss-Wright,* the constitutionally based and judicially broadened grounds for executive primacy in the management of foreign affairs, the expansion of executive power under the authority of the Commander in Chief, and the scope of the war powers, it is not unreasonable to assert that executive centrality will continue as the principal characteristic of American foreign policymaking. Again, the Court's role has been more passive than aggressive, but its actions have nonetheless been important in contributing to the executive's emergence as the "sole organ" of foreign affairs.

United States v. Curtiss–Wright Export Corp.

299 U.S. 304 (1936)

MR. JUSTICE SUTHERLAND delivered the opinion of the Court.

On January 27, 1936, an indictment was returned in the court below, the first count of which charges that [Curtiss-Wright], beginning with the 29th day of May, 1934, conspired to sell in the United States certain arms of war, namely fifteen machine guns, to Bolivia, a country then engaged in armed conflict in the Chaco, in violation of the Joint Resolution of Congress approved May 28, 1934, and the provisions of a proclamation issued on the same day by the President of the United States pursuant to authority conferred by * * * the resolution. . . . The Joint Resolution * * * follows:

"*Resolved by the Senate and House of Representatives of the United States of America in Congress assembled,* That if the President finds that the prohibition of the sale of arms and munitions of war in the United States to those countries now engaged in armed conflict in the Chaco may contribute to the reestablishment of peace between those countries, and if after consultation with the governments of other American Republics and with their cooperation, as well as that of such other governments as he may deem necessary, he makes proclamation to that effect, it shall be unlawful to sell, except under such limitations and exceptions as the President prescribes, any arms or munitions of war in any place in the United States to the countries now engaged in that armed conflict, or to any person, company, or association acting in the interest of either country, until otherwise ordered by the President or by Congress.

" . . . Whoever sells any arms or munitions of war in violation of section 1 shall, on conviction, be punished by a fine not exceeding $10,000 or by imprisonment not exceeding two years, or both."

The President's proclamation [May 28, 1934] * * * after reciting the terms of the Joint Resolution [barred the sale of arms to Bolivia and Paraguay].

• • •

On November 14, 1935, this proclamation was revoked. * * *

• • •

. . . It is contended that by the Joint Resolution, the going into effect and continued operation of the resolution was conditioned (a) upon the President's judgment as to its beneficial effect upon the reestablishment of peace between the countries engaged in armed conflict in the Chaco; (b) upon the making of a proclamation, which was left to his unfettered discretion, thus constituting an attempted substitution of the President's will for that of Congress; (c) upon the making of a proclamation putting an end to the operation of the resolution, which again was left to the President's unfettered discretion; and (d) further, that the extent of its operation in particular cases was subject to limitation and exception by the President, controlled by no standard. In each of these particulars, [Curtiss-Wright urges] that Congress abdicated its essential functions and delegated them to the Executive.

Whether, if the Joint Resolution had related solely to internal affairs it would be open to the challenge that it constituted an unlawful delegation of legislative power to the Executive, we find it unnecessary to determine. The whole aim of the resolution is to affect a situation entirely external to the United States, and falling within the category of foreign affairs. The determination which we are called to make, therefore, is whether the Joint Resolution, as applied to that situation, is vulnerable to attack under the rule that forbids a delegation of the law-making power. In other words, assuming (but not deciding) that the challenged delegation, if it were confined to internal affairs, would be invalid, may it nevertheless be sustained on the ground that its exclusive aim is to afford a remedy for a hurtful condition within foreign territory?

It will contribute to the elucidation of the question if we first consider the differences between the powers of the Federal government in respect of foreign or external affairs and those in respect of domestic or internal affairs. That there are differences between them, and that these differences are fundamental, may not be doubted.

The two classes of powers are different, both in respect of their origin and their nature. The broad statement that the Federal government can exercise no powers except those specifically enumerated in the Constitution, and such implied powers as are necessary and proper to carry into effect the enumerated powers, is categorically true only in respect of our internal affairs. In that field, the primary purpose of the Constitution was to carve from the general mass of legislative powers *then possessed by the states* such portions as it was thought desirable to vest in the Federal government, leaving those not included in the enumeration still in the states. * * * That this doctrine applies only to powers which the states had, is self-evident. And since the states severally never possessed international powers, such powers could not have been carved from the mass of state powers but obviously were transmitted to the United States from some other source. During the colonial period, those powers were possessed exclusively by and were entirely under the control of the Crown. By the Declaration of Independence, "the Representatives of the United States of America" declared the United [not the several] Colonies to be free and independent states, and as such to have "full Power to levy War, conclude Peace, contract Alliances, establish Commerce and to do all other Acts and Things which Independent States may of right do."

As a result of the separation from Great Britain by the colonies, acting as a unit, the powers of external sovereignty passed from the Crown not to the colonies severally, but to the colonies in their collective and corporate capacity as the United States of America. Even before the Declaration, the colonies were a unit in foreign affairs, acting through a common agency—namely the Continental Congress, composed of delegates from the thirteen colonies. That agency exercised the powers of war and peace, raised an army, created a navy, and finally adopted the Declaration of Independence. Rulers come and go; governments end and forms of government change; but sovereignty survives. A political society cannot endure without a supreme will somewhere. Sovereignty is never held in suspense. When, therefore, the external sovereignty of Great Britain in respect of the colonies ceased, it immediately passed to the Union. * * *. . . .

The Union existed before the Constitution, which was ordained and established among other things to form "a more perfect Union." Prior to that event, it is clear that the Union, declared by the Articles of Confederation to be "perpetual," was the sole possessor of external sovereignty, and in the Union it remained without change save in so far as the Constitution in express terms qualified its exercise. . . .

.   .   .

It results that the investment of the Federal government with the powers of external sovereignty did not depend upon the affirmative grants of the Constitution. The powers to declare and wage war, to conclude peace, to make treaties, to maintain diplomatic relations with other sovereignties, if they had never been mentioned in the Constitution, would have vested in the Federal government as necessary concomitants of nationality. . . .

.   .   .

Not only . . . is the Federal power over external affairs in origin and essential character different from that over internal affairs, but participation in the exercise of the power is significantly limited. In this vast external realm, with its important, complicated, delicate and manifold problems, the President alone has the power to speak or listen as a representative of the nation. He *makes* treaties with the advice and consent of the Senate; but he alone negotiates. Into the field of negotiation the Senate cannot intrude; and Congress itself is powerless to invade it. . . .

.   .   .

It is important to bear in mind that we are here dealing not alone with an authority vested in the President by an exertion of legislative power, but with such an authority plus the very delicate, plenary and exclusive power of the President as the sole organ of the Federal government in the field of international relations—a power which does not require as a basis for its exercise an act of Congress, but which, of course, like every other governmental power, must be exercised in subordination to the applicable provisions of the Constitution. It is quite apparent that if, in the maintenance of our international relations, embarrassment—perhaps serious embarrassment—is to be avoided and success for our aims achieved, congressional legislation which is to be made effective through negotiation and inquiry within the international field must often accord to the President a degree of discretion and freedom from statutory restriction which would not be admissible were domestic affairs alone involved. Moreover, he, not Congress, has the better opportunity of knowing the conditions which prevail in foreign countries, and especially is this true in time of war. He has his confidential sources of information. He has his agents in the form of diplomatic, consular and other officials. Secrecy in respect of information gathered by them may be highly necessary, and the premature disclosure of it productive of harmful results. . . .

•   •   •

The marked difference between foreign affairs and domestic affairs in this respect is recognized by both houses of Congress in the very form of their requisitions for information from the executive departments. In the case of every department except the Department of State, the resolution *directs* the official to furnish the information. In the case of the State Department, dealing with foreign affairs, the President is requested to furnish the information "if not incompatible with the public interest." A statement that to furnish the information is not compatible with the public interest rarely, if ever, is questioned.

When the President is to be authorized by legislation to act in respect of a matter intended to affect a situation in foreign territory, the legislator properly bears in mind the important consideration that the form of the President's action—or, indeed, whether he shall act at all—may well depend, among other things, upon the nature of the confidential information which he has or may thereafter receive, or upon the effect which his action may have upon our foreign relations. This consideration, in connection with what we have already said on the subject, discloses the unwisdom of requiring Congress in this field of governmental power to lay down narrowly definite standards by which the President is to be governed. . . .

In the light of the foregoing observations, it is evident that this court should not be in haste to apply a general rule which will have the effect of condemning· legislation like that under review as constituting an unlawful delegation of legislative power. The principles which justify such legislation find overwhelming support in the unbroken legislative practice which has prevailed almost from the inception of the national government to the present day.

•   •   •

Practically every volume of the United States Statutes contains one or more acts or joint resolutions of Congress authorizing action by the President in respect of subjects affecting foreign relations, which either leave the exercise of the power to his unrestricted judgment, or provide a standard far more general than that which has always been considered requisite with regard to domestic affairs. . . .

• • •

The result of holding that the joint resolution here under attack is void and unenforceable as constituting an unlawful delegation of legislative power would be to stamp this multitude of comparable acts and resolutions as likewise invalid. And while this court may not, and should not, hesitate to declare acts of Congress, however many times repeated, to be unconstitutional if beyond all rational doubt it finds them to be so, an impressive array of legislation such as we have just set forth, enacted by nearly every Congress from the beginning of our national existence to the present day, must be given unusual weight in the process of reaching a correct determination of the problem. A legislative practice such as we have here, evidenced not by only occasional instances, but marked by the movement of a steady stream for a century and a half of time, goes a long way in the direction of proving the presence of unassailable ground for the constitutionality of the practice, to be found in the origin and history of the power involved, or in its nature, or in both combined.

• • •

The uniform, long-continued and undisputed legislative practice just disclosed rests upon an admissible view of the Constitution which, even if the practice found far less support in principle than we think it does, we should not feel at liberty at this late day to disturb.

. . . It is enough to summarize by saying that, both upon principle and in accordance with precedent, we conclude there is sufficient warrant for the broad discretion vested in the President to determine whether the enforcement of the statute will have a beneficial effect upon the reestablishment of peace in the affected countries; whether he shall make proclamation to bring the resolution into operation; whether and when the resolution shall cease to operate and to make proclamation accordingly; and to prescribe limitations and exceptions to which the enforcement of the resolution shall be subject.

• • •

The judgment of the court below must be reversed and the cause remanded for further proceedings in accordance with the foregoing opinion.

Reversed.

MR. JUSTICE McREYNOLDS does not agree. He is of opinion that the court below reached the right conclusion and its judgment ought to be affirmed.

MR. JUSTICE STONE took no part in the consideration or decision of this case.

Massachusetts v. Laird

400 U.S. 886 (1970)

Memorandum. . . .

* * *

The motion for leave to file a bill of complaint is denied.

MR. JUSTICE DOUGLAS, dissenting.

This motion was filed by the Commonwealth of Massachusetts against the Secretary of Defense, a citizen of another State. It is brought pursuant to a mandate contained in an act of the Massachusetts Legislature. * * * Massachusetts seeks to obtain an adjudication of the constitutionality of the United States' participation in the Indochina war. It requests that the United States' participation be declared "unconstitutional in that it was not initially authorized or subsequently ratified by Congressional declaration"; it asks that the Secretary of Defense be enjoined "from carrying out, issuing, or causing to be issued any further orders which would increase the present level of United States troops in Indochina"; and it asks that, if appropriate congressional action is not forthcoming within 90 days of this Court's decree, that the Secretary of Defense be enjoined "from carrying out, issuing, or causing to be issued any further order directing any inhabitant of the Commonwealth of Massachusetts to Indochina for the purpose of participating in combat or supporting combat troops in the Vietnam war." Today this Court denies leave to file the complaint. I dissent.

The threshold issues for granting leave to file a complaint in this case are standing and justiciability. I believe that Massachusetts has standing and the controversy is justiciable. At the very least, however, it is apparent that the issues are not so clearly foreclosed as to justify a summary denial of leave to file.

Standing

In Massachusetts v. Mellon * * * the Court held a State lacked standing to challenge, as parens patriae [as guardian of its citizens], a federal grant-in-aid program under which the Federal Government was allegedly usurping powers reserved to the States. . . .

. . . [T]he ruling of the Court in that case is not dispositive of this one. The opinion states "We need not go so far as to say that a state may never intervene by suit to protect its citizens against any form of enforcement of unconstitutional acts of Congress; but we are clear that the right to do so does not arise here." * * * Thus the case did not announce a per se rule to bar all suits against the Federal Government as parens patriae. . . .

Mellon relates to an Act of Congress signed by the Executive, a distinction noted in other original actions. * * *

Massachusetts attacks no federal statute. In fact, the basis of Massachusetts' complaint is the absence of congressional action.

It is said that the Federal Government "represents" the citizens. Here the complaint is that only one representative of the people, the Executive, has acted and the other representatives of the citizens have not acted, although, it is argued, the Constitution provides that they must act before an overseas "war" can be conducted.

• • •

In South Carolina v Katzenbach, * * * . . . we denied standing to South Carolina to assert claims under the Bill of Attainder Clause of Article I and the principle of separation of powers which were regarded "only as protections for individual persons and private groups who are particularly vulnerable to nonjudicial determinations of guilt." * * * Yet we went on to allow South Carolina to challenge the Voting Rights Act of 1965 as beyond congressional power under the Fifteenth Amendment.

The main interest of South Carolina was in the continuing operation of her election laws. Massachusetts' claim to standing in this case is certainly as strong as South Carolina's was in the Katzenbach case.

Massachusetts complains, as parens patriae, that her citizens are drafted and sent to fight in an unconstitutional overseas war. Their lives are in jeopardy. Their liberty is impaired. . . . The allegation in . . . Mellon . . . was that Congress had exceeded the general powers delegated to it by Art I, § 8, and invaded the reserved powers of the States under the Tenth Amendment. The claim was not specific. . . . Here Massachusetts points to a specific provision of the Constitution. Congress by Art I, § 8, has the power "To declare War." . . .

[Case law] has been settled at least since 1901 that "if the health and comfort of the inhabitants of a State are threatened, the State is the proper party to represent and defend them." * * * Those cases involved injury to inhabitants of one State by water or air pollution of another State, by interference with navigation, by economic losses caused by an out-of-state agency, and the like. The harm to citizens of Massachusetts suffered by being drafted for a war are certainly of no less a magnitude. Massachusetts would clearly seem to have standing as parens patriae to represent, as alleged in its complaint, its male citizens being drafted for overseas combat in Indochina.

Justiciability

A question that is "political" is opposed to one that is "justiciable." In reviewing the dimensions of the "political" question we said in Baker v Carr, * * *

". . . Prominent on the surface of any case held to involve a political question is found a textually demonstrable constitutional commitment of the issue to a coordinate political department; or a lack of judicially discoverable and manageable standards for resolving it; or the impossibility of deciding without an initial policy determination of a kind clearly for nonjudicial discretion; or the impossibility of a court's undertaking independent resolution without expressing lack of the respect due coordinate branches of government; or an unusual need for unquestioning adherence to a political decision already made; or the potentiality of embarrassment from multifarious pronouncements by various departments on one question."

1. *A textually demonstrable constitutional commitment of the issue to a coordinate political department.* At issue here is the phrase in Art I, § 8, cl 11: "To declare War." Congress definitely has that power. The Solicitor General argues that only Congress can determine whether it has declared war. He states, " 'To declare War' includes a power to determine, free of judicial interference, the form which its authorization of hostilities will take." This may be correct. But as we stated in Powell v. McCormack, * * * the question of a textually demonstrable commitment and "what is the *scope* of such commitment are questions [this Court] . . . must resolve . . ." * * * (emphasis added). It may well be that it is for Congress, and Congress alone, to determine the form of its authorization, but if that is the case we should only make that determination after full briefs on the merits and oral argument.

2. *A lack of judicially discoverable and manageable standards for resolving the issue.* The standards that are applicable are not elusive. The case is not one where the Executive is repelling a sudden attack. The present Indochina "war" has gone on for six years. The question is whether the Gulf of Tonkin Resolution was a declaration of war or whether other Acts of Congress were its equivalent.

3. *The impossibility of deciding without an initial policy determination of a kind clearly for nonjudicial discretion.* In Ex parte Milligan * * * (concurring opinion), it was stated that "neither can the President, in war more than in peace, intrude upon the proper authority of Congress. . . ." That issue in this case is not whether we ought to fight a war in Indochina, but whether the Executive can authorize it without congressional authorization. This is not a case where we would have to determine the wisdom of any policy.

4. *The impossibility of a court's undertaking independent resolution without expressing lack of respect due coordinate branches of government.* The Solicitor General argues it would show disrespect of the Executive to go behind his statements and determine his authority to act in these circumstances. Both Powell and the Steel Seizure Case * * *, however, demonstrate that the duty of this Court is to interpret the Constitution, and in the latter case we did go behind an executive order to determine his authority. * * *

• • •

It is far more important to be respectful to the Constitution than to a coordinate branch of government.

5. *An unusual need for unquestioning adherence to a political decision already made.* This test is essentially a reference to a commitment of a problem and its solution to a coordinate branch of government. . . .

6. *The potentiality of embarrassment from multifarious pronouncements by various departments of government on one question.* Once again this relates back to whether the problem and its solution are committed to a given branch of government.

We have never ruled, I believe, that when the Federal Government takes a person by the neck and submits him to punishment, imprisonment, taxation, or submission to some ordeal, the complaining person may not be heard in court. The rationale in cases such as the present is that government cannot take life, liberty, or property of the individual and escape adjudication by the courts of the legality of its action.

That is the heart of this case. It does not concern the wisdom of fighting in Southeast Asia. Likewise no question of whether the conflict is either just or necessary is present. We are asked instead whether the Executive has power, absent a congressional declaration of war, to commit Massachusetts citizens in armed hostilities on foreign soil. Another way of putting the question is whether under our Constitution presidential wars are permissible. Should that question be answered in the negative we would then have to determine whether Congress has declared war. That question which Massachusetts presents is in my view justiciable.

*   *   *

"The war power of the United States like its other powers . . . is subject to constitutional limitations." * * * No less than the war power—the greatest leveler of them all—is the power of the Commander-in-Chief subject to constitutional limitations. . . .

This Court has previously faced issues of presidential war making. The legality of Lincoln's blockade was considered in the Prize Cases * * * and although the Court narrowly split in supporting the President's position, the split was on the merits, not on whether the claim was justiciable. And even though that war was the Civil War and not one involving an overseas expedition, the decision was 5 to 4.

In the Steel Seizure Case members of this Court wrote seven opinions and each reached the merits of the Executive's seizure. In that case, as here, the issue related to the President's powers as Commander-in-Chief and the fact that all nine Justices decided the case on the merits and construed the powers of a coordinate branch at a time of extreme emergency should be instructive. . . .

*   *   *

If we determine that the Indochina conflict is unconstitutional because it lacks a congressional declaration of war, the Chief Executive is free to seek one, as was President Truman free to seek congressional approval after our Steel Seizure decision.

There is, of course, a difference between this case and the Prize Cases and the Steel Seizure Case. In those cases a private party was asserting a wrong to him: his *property* was being taken and he demanded a determination of the legality of the taking. Here the *lives* and *liberties* of Massachusetts citizens are in jeopardy. Certainly the Constitution gives no greater protection to *property* than to *life* and *liberty*. It might be argued that the authority in the Steel Seizure Case was not textually apparent in the Constitution, while the power of the Commander-in-Chief to commit troops is obvious and therefore a different determination on justiciability is needed. The Prize Cases, however, involved Lincoln's exercise of power in ordering a blockade by virtue of his powers as the Commander-in-Chief.

Since private parties—represented by Massachusetts as parens patriae—are involved in this case the teaching of the Prize Cases and the Steel Seizure Case is that their claims are justiciable.

• • •

Today we deny a hearing to a State which attempts to determine whether it is constitutional to require its citizens to fight in a foreign war absent a congressional declaration of war. . . . The question of an unconstitutional war is neither academic nor "political." . . . It should be settled here and now.

I would set the motion for leave to file down for argument and decide the merits only after full argument.

MR. JUSTICE HARLAN and MR. JUSTICE STEWART dissent. They would set this motion for argument on the questions of standing and justiciability.

Korematsu v. United States

323 U.S. 214 (1944)

MR. JUSTICE BLACK delivered the opinion of the Court.

The petitioner [Korematsu], an American citizen of Japanese descent, was convicted in a federal district court for remaining in San Leandro, California, a "Military Area," contrary to Civilian Exclusion Order No. 34 . . . which directed that after May 9, 1942, all persons of Japanese ancestry should be excluded from that area. No question was raised as to [Korematsu's] loyalty to the United States. The Circuit Court of Appeals affirmed, and the importance of the constitutional question involved caused us to grant certiorari.

It should be noted, to begin with, that all legal restrictions which curtail the civil rights of a single racial group are immediately suspect. That is not to say that all such restrictions are unconstitutional. It is to say that courts must subject them to the most rigid scrutiny. Pressing public necessity may sometimes justify the existence of such restrictions; racial antagonism never can.

In the instant case prosecution of [Korematsu] was begun by information charging violation of an Act of Congress, of March 21, 1942, * * * which provides that ". . . whoever shall enter, remain in, leave, or commit any act in any military area or military zone prescribed, under the authority of an Executive order of the President, . . . contrary to the restrictions applicable to any such area or zone . . . shall, if it appears that he knew or should have known of the existence and extent of the restrictions or order and that his act was in violation thereof, be guilty of a misdemeanor and upon conviction shall be liable to a fine of not to exceed $5,000 or to imprisonment for not more than one year, or both, for each offense."

Exclusion Order No. 34, which [Korematsu] knowingly and admittedly violated, was one of a number of military orders and proclamations, all of which were substantially based upon Executive Order No. 9066. * * * That order, issued after we were at war with Japan, declared that "the successful prosecution of the war requires every possible protection against espionage and against sabotage to national-defense material, national-defense premises, and national-defense utilities. . . ."

One of the series of orders and proclamations, a curfew order, . . . subjected all persons of Japanese ancestry in prescribed West Coast military areas to remain in their residences from 8 p.m. to 6 a.m. As is the case with the exclusion order here, that prior curfew order was designed as a "protection against espionage and against sabotage." In *Hirabayashi* v. *United States* * * * we sustained a conviction obtained for violation of the curfew order. . . .

The 1942 Act was attacked in the *Hirabayashi* case as an unconstitutional delegation of power; it was contended that the curfew order and other orders on which it rested were beyond the war powers of the Congress, the military authorities and of the President, as Commander in Chief of the Army; and finally that to apply the curfew order against none but citizens of Japanese ancestry amounted to a constitutionally prohibited discrimination solely on account of race. . . .

In the light of the principles we announced in the *Hirabayashi* case, we are unable to conclude that it was beyond the war power of Congress and the Executive to exclude those of Japanese ancestry from the West Coast war area at the time they did. True, exclusion from the area in which one's home is located is a far greater deprivation than constant confinement to the home from 8 p.m. to 6 a.m. Nothing short of apprehension by the proper military authorities of the gravest imminent danger to the public safety can constitutionally justify either. But exclusion from a threatened area, no less than curfew, has a definite and close relationship to the prevention of espionage and sabotage. The military authorities, charged with the primary responsibility of defending our shores, concluded that curfew provided inadequate protection and ordered exclusion. They did so, as pointed out in our *Hirabayashi* opinion, in accordance with Congressional authority to the military to say who should, and who should not, remain in the threatened areas.

In this case [Korematsu] challenges the assumptions upon which we rested our conclusions in the *Hirabayashi* case. He also urges that by May 1942, when Order No. 34 was promulgated, all danger of Japanese invasion of the West Coast had disappeared. After careful consideration of these contentions we are compelled to reject them.

Here, as in the *Hirabayashi* case * * * ". . . we cannot reject as unfounded the judgment of the military authorities and of Congress that there were disloyal members of that population, whose number and strength could not be precisely and quickly ascertained. We cannot say that the war-making branches of the Government did not have grounds for believing that in a critical hour such persons could not readily be isolated and separately dealt with, and constituted a menace to the national defense and safety, which demanded that prompt and adequate measures be taken to guard against it."

Like curfew, exclusion of those of Japanese origin was deemed necessary because of the presence of an unascertained number of disloyal members of the group, most of whom we have no doubt were loyal to this country. It was because we could not reject the finding of the military authorities that it was impossible to bring about an immediate segregation of the disloyal from the loyal that we sustained the validity of the curfew order as applying to the whole group. In the instant case, temporary exclusion of the entire group was rested by the military on the same ground. The judgment that exclusion of the whole group was for the same reason a military imperative answers the contention that the exclusion was in the nature of group punishment based on antagonism to those of Japanese origin. That there were members of the group who retained loyalties to Japan has been confirmed by investigations made subsequent to the exclusion. Approximately five thousand American citizens of Japanese ancestry refused to swear unqualified allegiance to the United States and to renounce allegiance to the Japanese Emperor, and several thousand evacuees requested repatriation to Japan.

We uphold the exclusion order as of the time it was made and when [Korematsu] violated it. * * * In doing so, we are not unmindful of the hardships imposed by it upon a large group of American citizens. * * * But hardships are part of war, and war is an aggregation of hardships. All citizens alike, both in and out of uniform, feel the impact of war in greater or lesser measure. Citizenship has its responsibilities as well as its privileges, and in time of war the burden is always heavier. Compulsory exclusion of large groups of citizens from their homes, except under circumstances of direst emergency and peril, is inconsistent with our basic governmental institutions. But when under conditions of modern warfare our shores are threatened by hostile forces, the power to protect must be commensurate with the threatened danger.

•   •   •

It is said that we are dealing here with the case of imprisonment of a citizen in a concentration camp solely because of his ancestry, without evidence or inquiry concerning his loyalty and good disposition towards the United States. Our task would be simple, our duty clear, were this a case involving the imprisonment of a loyal citizen in a concentration camp because of racial prejudice. Regardless of the true nature of the assembly and relocation centers—and we deem it unjustifiable to call them concentration camps with all the ugly connotations that term implies—we are dealing specifically with nothing but an exclusion order. To cast this case into outlines of racial prejudice, without reference to the real military dangers which were presented, merely confuses the issue. Korematsu was not excluded from the Military Area because of hostility to him or his race. He *was* excluded because we are at war with the Japanese Empire, because the properly constituted military authorities feared an invasion of our West Coast and felt constrained to take proper security measures, because they decided that the military urgency of the situation demanded that all citizens of Japanese ancestry be segregated from the West Coast temporarily, and finally, because Congress, reposing its confidence in this time of war in our military leaders—as inevitably it must—determined that they should have the power to do just this. There was evidence of disloyalty on the part of some, the military authorities considered that the need for action was great, and time was short. We cannot—by availing ourselves of the calm perspective of hindsight—now say that at that time these actions were unjustified.

Affirmed.

Mr. Justice Frankfurter, concurring.

•   •   •

The provisions of the Constitution which confer on the Congress and the President powers to enable this country to wage war are as much part of the Constitution as provisions looking to a nation at peace. And we have had recent occasion to quote approvingly the statement of former Chief Justice Hughes that the war power of the Government is "the power to wage war successfully." * * * Therefore, the validity of action under the war power must be judged wholly in the context of war. That action is not to be stigmatized as lawless because like action in times of peace would be lawless. To talk about a military order that expresses an allowable judgment of war needs by those entrusted with the duty of conducting war as "an unconstitutional order" is to suffuse a part of the Constitution with an atmosphere of unconstitutionality. The respective spheres of action of military authorities and of judges are of course very different. But within their sphere, military authorities are no more outside the bounds of obedience to the Constitution than are judges within theirs. . . . To recognize that military orders are "reasonably expedient military precautions" in time of war and to deny them constitutional legitimacy makes of the Constitution an instrument for dialectic subtleties not reasonably to be attributed to the hard-headed Framers, of whom a majority had had actual participation in war. If a military order such as that under review does not transcend the means appropriate for conducting war, such action by the military is as constitutional as would be any authorized action by the Interstate Commerce Commission within the limits of the constitutional power to regulate commerce. And being an exercise of the war power explicitly granted by the Constitution for safeguarding the national life by prosecuting war effectively, I find nothing in the Constitution which denies to Congress the power to enforce such a valid military order by making its violation an offense triable in the civil courts. * * * To find that the Constitution does not forbid the military measures now complained of does not carry with it approval of that which Congress and the Executive did. That is their business, not ours.

MR. JUSTICE ROBERTS.

I dissent, because I think the indisputable facts exhibit a clear violation of Constitutional rights.

This is not a case of keeping people off the streets at night * * * nor a case of temporary exclusion of a citizen from an area for his own safety or that of the community, nor a case of offering him an opportunity to go temporarily out of an area where his presence might cause danger to himself or to his fellows. On the contrary, it is the case of convicting a citizen as a punishment for not submitting to imprisonment in a concentration camp, based on his ancestry, and solely because of his ancestry, without evidence or inquiry concerning his loyalty and good disposition towards the United States. If this be a correct statement of the facts disclosed by this record, and facts of which we take judicial notice, I need hardly labor the conclusion that Constitutional rights have been violated.

•   •   •

The judicial test of whether the Government, on a plea of military necessity, can validly deprive an individual of any of his constitutional rights is whether the deprivation is reasonably related to a public danger that is so "immediate, imminent, and impending" as not to admit of delay and not to permit the intervention of ordinary constitutional processes to alleviate the danger. * * * Civilian Exclusion Order No. 34, banishing from a prescribed area of the Pacific Coast "all persons of Japanese ancestry, both alien and non-alien," clearly does not meet that test. Being an obvious racial discrimination, the order deprives all those within its scope of the equal protection of the laws as guaranteed by the

Fifth Amendment. It further deprives these individuals of their constitutional rights to live and work where they will, to establish a home where they choose and to move about freely. In excommunicating them without benefit of hearings, this order also deprives them of all their constitutional rights to procedural due process. Yet no reasonable relation to an "immediate, imminent, and impending" public danger is evident to support this racial restriction which is one of the most sweeping and complete deprivations of constitutional rights in the history of this nation in the absence of martial law.

· · ·

That this forced exclusion was the result in good measure of [the] erroneous assumption of racial guilt rather than bona fide military necessity is evidenced by the Commanding General's Final Report on the evacuation from the Pacific Coast area. In it he refers to all individuals of Japanese descent as "subversive," as belonging to "an enemy race" whose "racial strains are undiluted," and as constituting "over 112,000 potential enemies . . . at large today" along the Pacific Coast. In support of this blanket condemnation of all persons of Japanese descent, however, no reliable evidence is cited to show that such individuals were generally disloyal, or had generally so conducted themselves in this area as to constitute a special menace to defense installations or war industries, or had otherwise by their behavior furnished reasonable ground for their exclusion as a group.

Justification for the exclusion is sought, instead, mainly upon questionable racial and sociological grounds not ordinarily within the realm of expert military judgment, supplemented by certain semi-military conclusions drawn from an unwarranted use of circumstantial evidence. . . .

The main reasons relied upon by those responsible for the forced evacuation, therefore, do not prove a reasonable relation between the group characteristics of Japanese Americans and the dangers of invasion, sabotage and espionage. The reasons appear, instead, to be largely an accumulation of much of the misinformation, half-truths and insinuations that for years have been directed against Japanese Americans by people with racial and economic prejudices—the same people who have been among the foremost advocates of the evacuation. A military judgment based upon such racial and sociological considerations is not entitled to the great weight ordinarily given the judgments based upon strictly military considerations. . . .

The military necessity which is essential to the validity of the evacuation order thus resolves itself into a few intimations that certain individuals actively aided the enemy, from which it is inferred that the entire group of Japanese Americans could not be trusted to be or remain loyal to the United States. . . . But to infer that examples of individual disloyalty prove group disloyalty and justify discriminatory action against the entire group is to deny that under our system of law individual guilt is the sole basis for deprivation of rights. . . . To give constitutional sanction to that inference in this case, however well-intentioned may have been the military command on the Pacific Coast, is to adopt one of the cruelest of the rationales used by our enemies to destroy the dignity of the individual and to encourage and open the door to discriminatory actions against other minority groups in the passions of tomorrow.

No adequate reason is given for the failure to treat these Japanese Americans on an individual basis by holding investigations and hearings to separate the loyal from the disloyal, as was done in the case of persons of German and Italian ancestry.

• • •

I dissent, therefore, from this legalization of racism. Racial discrimination in any form and in any degree has no justifiable part whatever in our democratic way of life. It is unattractive in any setting but it is utterly revolting among a free people who have embraced the principles set forth in the Constitution of the United States. All residents of this nation are kin in some way by blood or culture to a foreign land. Yet they are primarily and necessarily a part of the new and distinct civilization of the United States. They must accordingly be treated at all times as the heirs of the American experiment and as entitled to all the rights and freedoms guaranteed by the Constitution.

Mr. Justice Jackson, dissenting.

• • •

. . . [I]f any fundamental assumption underlies our system, it is that guilt is personal and not inheritable. Even if all of one's antecedents had been convicted of treason, the Constitution forbids its penalties to be visited upon him, for it provides that "no attainder of treason shall work corruption of blood, or forfeiture except during the life of the person attainted." But here is an attempt to make an otherwise innocent act a crime merely because this prisoner is the son of parents as to whom he had no choice, and belongs to a race from which there is no way to resign. If Congress in peace-time legislation should enact such a criminal law, I should suppose this Court would refuse to enforce it.

• • •

It would be impracticable and dangerous idealism to expect or insist that each specific military command in an area of probable operations will conform to conventional tests of constitutionality. When an area is so beset that it must be put under military control at all, the paramount consideration is that its measures be successful, rather than legal. The armed services must protect a society, not merely its Constitution. The very essence of the military job is to marshal physical force, to remove every obstacle to its effectiveness, to give it every strategic advantage. Defense measures will not, and often should not, be held within the limits that bind civil authority in peace. . . .

But if we cannot confine military expedients by the Constitution, neither would I distort the Constitution to approve all that the military may deem expedient. That is what the Court appears to be doing, whether consciously or not. . . .

• • •

. . . [O]nce a judicial opinion rationalizes . . . an order [such as the Civilian Exclusion Order] to show that it conforms to the Constitution, or rather rationalizes the Constitution to show that the Constitution sanctions such an order, the Court for all time has validated the principle of racial discrimination in criminal procedure and of transplanting American citizens. The principle then lies about like a loaded weapon ready for the hand of any authority that can bring forward a plausible claim of an urgent need. Every repetition imbeds that principle more deeply in our law and thinking and expands it to new purposes. All who observe the work of courts are familiar with what Judge Cardozo described as "the tendency of a principle to expand itself to the limit of its logic." A military commander may overstep the bounds of constitutionality, and it is an incident. But if we review and approve, that passing incident becomes the doctrine of the Constitution. There it has a generative power of its own, and all that it creates will be in its own image. Nothing better illustrates this danger than does the Court's opinion in this case.

• • •

I should hold that a civil court cannot be made to enforce an order which violates constitutional limitations even if it is a reasonable exercise of military authority. The courts can exercise only the judicial power, can apply only law, and must abide by the Constitution, or they cease to be civil courts and become instruments of military policy.

• • •

My duties as a justice as I see them do not require me to make a military judgment as to whether General DeWitt's evacuation and detention program was a reasonable military necessity. I do not suggest that the courts should have attempted to interfere with the Army in carrying out its task. But I do not think they may be asked to execute a military expedient that has no place in law under the Constitution. I would reverse the judgment and discharge the prisoner.

PART **IV**

DISTRIBUTION OF POWER IN THE FEDERAL SYSTEM

CHAPTER **9**

Shaping the Federal System: Constitutional Theory and Political Practice

INTRODUCTORY ESSAY

The tension between constitutional theory and political practice is nowhere more apparent than in that bundle of relationships implicit in the concept of *American federalism*. As an applied principle of government, federalism in the United States reflects an ongoing attempt by legislators, Chief Executives, and judges to balance a welter of competing interests and values: individual liberty and public order; local diversity and the "national interest"; limited government and social justice—to mention only a few. In this chapter we will examine the constitutional basis and evolving meaning of American federalism, giving special attention to the contribution of the Supreme Court in defining the relationships and marking the boundaries between national and state functions.

There is a sharp distinction between the classical theoretical definition of federalism and its practical meaning in American politics. As a formal legal principle, federalism connotes a division of powers between coordinate, largely independent, units of government—one having nationwide authority, each of the others having authority within a particular region. In a purely legal sense each unit or sphere of government exists independently of the others. Each is supreme within its own designated area of authority. The relationship between national and regional governments stresses the coequality, not the subordination, of the latter.

National Primacy Versus State Sovereignty

In its original form the federal Constitution is largely consistent with this formal type of federalism. Although the Supremacy Clause of Article VI recognizes the primacy of national authority in areas of national activity, those areas are specifically enumerated in Article I, with the implication (later made explicit in the Tenth Amendment) that the states retain autonomy in all other areas. However, the Constitution is ambiguous on the basic question of where ultimate sovereign power resides. Hamilton, Marshall, Webster, and other proponents of national supremacy easily resolved the issue in favor of the central government. One of the clearest statements of this position appears in the landmark decision *M'Culloch* v. *Maryland,* 4 Wheat. 316 (1819), in which Marshall broadly interpreted the Necessary and Proper Clause as conferring on Congress the *implied* power to establish a national bank. He went on to hold that a Maryland tax of $15,000 a year on the Baltimore branch of this bank was barred by the Supremacy Clause.

For Jefferson, Madison, and Calhoun, the countervailing claims of state sovereignty were much more persuasive. Marshall's great nationalistic opinions in *M'Culloch* v. *Maryland, Gibbons* v. *Ogden,* 9 Wheat. 1 (1824), and *Cohens* v. *Virginia,* 6 Wheat. 264 (1821), were offset by the states' rights doctrines of interposition and nullification and by decisions such as *Scott* v. *Sanford,* 19 How. 393 (1857). Sharp regional divisions, accentuated by the constitutionally sanctioned but increasingly unacceptable institution of slavery ultimately split the nation into two armed camps and produced the greatest bloodbath in American history. After the loss of more than 600,000 lives and the destruction of billions of dollars worth of property, it was decided that a state could not withdraw from the federal Union and that where state and national governments collided in their exercise of legal authority, the former must be subordinate. In 1868 adoption of the Fourteenth Amendment placed substantial restraint upon the states by prohibiting them either from depriving "any person of life, liberty, or property, without due process of law" or from denying to persons within their jurisdiction "the equal protection of the laws." Congress was authorized to enforce the provisions of this Amendment as well as those of the two other Civil War Amendments (Thirteenth and Fifteenth) "by appropriate legislation." With its decision in *Texas* v. *White,* 7 Wall. 700 (1869), handed down four years after Lee's surrender at Appomattox, the Supreme Court added its constitutional endorsement to the new order by solemnly proclaiming that a state could not withdraw from the Union without violating the basic law. The Court perhaps contributed a measure of legal authority to the military verdict of the Civil War, but in so doing (after the fact), it underscored the limits of judicial power in dealing with questions that fundamentally divide the American people.

Although the Civil War and adoption of the Thirteenth, Fourteenth, and Fifteenth Amendments basically altered the original federal structure of American government, they did not destroy the federal character of the system. The states retained relative independence from national control in many areas, while many questions of competing national and state authority remained unsettled. The system continued to change in response to conflicting forces of centralization and decentralization—moving toward national dominance during the Reconstruction Era, then wavering between the claims of states' rights and national supremacy from the 1880s well into the 1930s, and finally shifting to still greater national dominance in the decades beginning with the New Deal and World War II. Despite current efforts (through federal statutes and judicial decisions) to revitalize the status of the states as active partners in the federal relationship, the role of the national government remains pervasive.

Basic Characteristics of the Federal System

Taking into account both the constitutional basis and the political dimensions of American federalism, it is possible to identify those characteristics that appear most basic to this particular system of government. The first characteristic is the continuing division of legal authority between two levels of government, national and state. Each level has its own independent mechanism of government through which it enacts, interprets, and administers law. Considerable overlapping occurs, of course, but the construct of two legally distinct spheres of government, each with its own constitution, legislature, chief executive, judiciary, and administrative bureaucracy remains intact. A second characteristic of the American federal system is that the two levels of government exercise direct authority simultaneously over persons within their territory. Dual citizenship is a fundamental part of the system, and a wide range of rights, privileges, and immunities accrue from both national and state citizenship. A third characteristic is the subordination of state to national authority in fields such as taxation and the regulation of interstate commerce where both levels of government concurrently exercise broad legal power. Fourth is a growing area of cooperative activity in which the national government and the states jointly undertake programs in education, highway construction, public health, social security, unemployment compensation, and environmental protection, to cite but a few examples. This joint effort, popularly known as *cooperative federalism,* continues to expand. A fifth characteristic is the recognized authority of one tribunal, the United States Supreme Court, to mark the boundaries and allocate constitutional power between the national government and the states. The fact that the federal Constitution is the supreme law of the land does not, of course, always mean that claims of national power prevail over counterclaims on behalf of the states. In adjusting this type of competing claim, the Supreme Court performs one of its most important functions. Because its decisions in this area have come to be accepted with finality, subject to reversal only by constitutional amendment, the Court serves as "arbiter of the federal system."

Expansion of Governmental Power

More significant than the growth of national power at the expense of the states has been the expansion of governmental power at all levels. It is true that in the past half century the Supreme Court has often resolved conflicts between state and national assertions of power in favor of the latter. But far more frequently the Court has found ways to permit both levels of government to expand their respective spheres of activity. State financial dependence on the national government has increased sharply in recent decades, but the states have not been downgraded to mere administrative units. In this respect they differ sharply from counties and cities in the hierarchy of governmental organization. Counties and cities, existing as "creatures" of the state, do not participate in the same type of relationship with the states as the states themselves have with the national government.

Although its powers are vast, the national government (at least outside the areas of foreign relations and war) is a government of enumerated powers. These powers are supplemented by the Supreme Court's generous interpretation of implied powers, through which the enumerated powers may be carried out. Still, the listing of enumerated powers in Article I, Section 8, of the Constitution, together with other restrictive language, places restraints on the national government. Moreover, the Tenth Amendment recognizes a largely open-ended, unspecified category of powers reserved to the states and, in the abstract, to the people. This Amendment, adopted as part of the original Bill of Rights in 1791, not only underscores the principle of limited national government but also provides a constitutional basis for the broad functions of state government. Although its scope was sharply narrowed in the aftermath of the Court's 1937 conflict with FDR, the Tenth Amendment is still accorded significance by the Supreme Court (see *Fry* v. *United States,* 421 U.S. 542 [1975], and *National League of Cities* v. *Usery,* 426 U.S. 833 [1976]).

Chief Justice Marshall developed his concept of nationalism in large part as a constitutional rationale for limiting the broad base of power reserved to the states. His Court invalidated various state commercial and financial restrictions opposed by business interests, citing infringements on federal authority. But this federal authority was almost entirely dormant during the Marshall era. Marshall did not anticipate a vigorous national regulatory policy; and, in fact, no such policy emerged until well into the twentieth century. Marshall's nationalism went hand in hand with the growth of private enterprise. By placing restrictions on state power in the name of abstract principles of national supremacy, his Court, during the first two decades of the nineteenth century, cleared the way for early commercial and industrial expansion.

Growth of State Police Power

As this economic development proceeded, basic changes took place within the political environment. Jacksonian democracy, with its emphasis on broader political participation (among white males) swept away most of the property qualifications for voting that existed when the Constitution was written. With the drive toward greater political equality came attacks on economic privilege—attacks carried out in large part in the state legislatures through the adoption of measures for both debtor relief and more extensive regulation of business in the name of the general welfare. More and more legislation of this kind came up for review before the Supreme Court, and some softening of the Court's earlier negative position was apparent even before Marshall's death in 1835. For example, over Marshall's lone dissenting opinion (his only recorded dissent in a constitutional case), the Court upheld an Ohio law making bankruptcy procedures available to persons contracting debts after its passage (*Ogden* v. *Saunders,* 12 Wheat. 213 [1827]). A similar law, applicable to *all* debtors within its jurisdiction, had been enacted by New York a few years earlier, but had been declared unconstitutional by the Marshall Court as an infringement on the Contract Clause of the Constitution (*Sturgis* v. *Crowninshield,* 14 Wheat. 122 [1819]). In 1832 Marshall joined his colleagues in recognizing the power of a state to protect the public health by draining disease-infested marshlands (*Willson* v. *Blackbird Creek Marsh Co.,* 2 Pet. 245 [1829]). The dam constructed for this purpose interfered with commercial navigation, but in this instance the Court held that the public health objective was a basic aspect of the state's police power and as such it outweighed the private interests opposing the dam. This was a limited, but significant, victory for proponents of state regulation.

During the Chief Justiceship of John Marshall's successor, Roger B. Taney (1836-1864), the police power of the states—part of the broad power reserved to them by the Tenth Amendment—was greatly expanded. In addition to protecting public health and safety, the police power served in specific cases as a rationale for a variety of state laws, justified on the basis that they promoted the "morals" and general welfare of the community (*New York* v. *Miln,* 11 Pet. 102 [1837]). The constitutional changes wrought by the Civil War did not impede the further growth of the state police power. The rapid accumulation and concentration of corporate wealth, stimulated by the upheaval and dislocation of war, drew an even more active regulatory response from state legislatures during the 1860s and 1870s. Farmers organized and brought enough pressure to bear on the political process to achieve the enactment of laws regulating the freight rates charged by the nation's growing railroad combines. And for a time the Supreme Court continued, in the tradition of the Taney Court, to uphold these and similar exercises of state police power (see, for example, *Munn* v. *Illinois,* 94 U.S. 113 [1877]).

Limitations on Regulatory Power and the Emergence of Dual Federalism

Only with the rise of organized labor in the 1880s and the appearance of the Populist Party in the 1890s did a marked change in this permissive view toward state regulatory power take place. Identifying with an economic establishment that saw the specter of socialism in these movements, the Supreme Court began to use the Due Process Clause of the Fourteenth Amendment and the Commerce Clause as justification for restricting the police power of the states in some, but by no means all, areas of economic activity. This tendency was but one aspect of a far larger trend of constitutional interpretation through which the Court set limits on regulatory power at all levels of government. While placing restrictions on state police power, the Court also imposed similar curbs on the emerging *national* police power through invocation of the Tenth Amendment. That provision, together with the Due Process Clause of the Fifth Amendment, which applies directly to the national government, contributed to the rise of *dual federalism* after 1890. Proponents of this perspective not only sought a balance between state and national power, but also contemplated a kind of constitutional twilight zone into which neither the states nor the central government could intrude.

Governmental Centralization

Dual federalism remained a major factor in American constitutional development until the beginning of the judicial revolution in 1937. But it was not the only factor at work during the half century preceding its eventual downfall. The accelerated growth of corporate industry and organized labor in conjunction with the social pressures of population growth and urbanization increased the pressure toward governmental centralization. As noted in Part II, the Court sanctioned piecemeal extensions of national power under the Commerce Clause, particularly to protect public morality, health, and safety. Even during the pre–New Deal period the growing number of problems demanding a national response threatened to upset the balance implicit in the dualist approach.

As government assumed a more positive and pervasive role in American society during the Great Depression, the Court haltingly began to provide constitutional legitimation. Thus in 1934 a narrow majority sustained state legislation giving relief to home buyers through a moratorium on mortgage foreclosures, rejecting the assertion that this Minnesota law impaired the obligation of contracts (*Home Building & Loan Association* v. *Blaisdell,* 290 U.S. 398). In the same year a New York statute establishing a milk control board with authority to set minimum and maximum retail prices was upheld against the contention that this exercise of police power deprived persons of liberty in violation of due process (*Nebbia* v. *New York,* 291 U.S. 502).

However, during the next two years the Court, through narrow interpretations of the commerce and taxing powers, dismantled a large part of the New Deal program of national legislation that had been enacted in 1933 (see, for example, *Carter* v. *Carter Coal Co.,* 298 U.S. 238 [1936], and *United States* v. *Butler,* 297 U.S. 1 [1936]). And in 1936 it reaffirmed earlier restrictions on state legislation by striking down a New York minimum wage law (*Morehead* v. *New York ex rel. Tipaldo,* 298 U.S. 587). These negative rulings, along with others that limited both the President's removal power and congressional discretion to delegate power to the executive branch, made the Court itself an object of controversy in the 1936 election campaign. FDR's sweeping reelection victory that November was followed in the spring of 1937 by his abortive Court-packing proposal, discussed in Chapter 2. A sudden change in the positions of Chief Justice Hughes and Justice Roberts made further attempts to force a change in the Court's stance unnecessary. These two "moderates" joined the "liberal wing," consisting of Justices Brandeis, Stone, and Cardozo, in stressing the affirmative aspects of the commerce, taxing, and spending powers. Facilitated by the appointment of several new Justices, whose pro–New Deal credentials were impeccable, the Court over the next several years sanctioned the exercise of national regulatory power and social welfare programs of vast scope.

Eclipse of the Tenth Amendment

In sharp conflict with this expansion of enumerated powers, but consistent with the policy implications of the new approach, the Tenth Amendment went into eclipse. The change is graphically illustrated by a comparison of the anti–child-labor legislation decision of *Hammer* v. *Dagenhart,* 247 U.S. 251 (1918), with the decision in *United States* v. *Darby,* 312 U.S. 100 (1941), which overruled it twenty-three years later. In *Hammer,* the Tenth Amendment provided the *basic* rationale for blocking Congress in its attempt to curb the abuses of child labor. By 1941 Justice Stone, writing for a unanimous Court in *Darby,* found nothing in the Tenth Amendment that barred expansion of the national police power under the Commerce Clause. In upholding the Fair Labor Standards Act with its minimum wage and anti–child-labor provisions, Stone relegated the Tenth Amendment to the status of a historical monument. Ignoring the emphasis accorded the Amendment only a few years earlier, he said that it stated "a mere truism that all is retained which has not been surrendered." He found "nothing in the history of its adoption" suggesting "that it was more than declaratory of the relationship between the national and state governments" as established by the original Constitution. The purpose of the Tenth Amendment was simply "to allay fears that the new national government might seek to exercise powers not granted, and that the states might not be able to exercise fully their reserved powers." By contrast with his expansive interpretation of the commerce power in the same case, Stone confined the Tenth Amendment to narrow limits, stressing the supposed intent of those who adopted it. He conveniently omitted consideration of intervening judicial interpretation, especially that of the preceding generation, through which the scope of that Amendment had been enlarged as a means of balancing state and national authority. Stone's approach in the *Darby* case reveals much about the nature of constitutional decision-making. His emphasis on "original intent" as a yardstick for determining the narrow scope of the Tenth Amendment did not carry over to his analysis of the Commerce Clause and the great national power exercised in its name 150 years after the Philadelphia Convention. Stone's selective emphasis on such variables as original intent and the changing conditions of society is by no means unique in Supreme Court annals. Reference to it at this point serves only to illustrate the inconsistency of the human dimension of constitutional interpretation.

Cooperative Federalism

Before approving the Fair Labor Standards Act, the Supreme Court had upheld equally far-reaching economic and social measures, all of which eroded the concept of dual federalism and encouraged the trend toward cooperative federalism. The cooperative dimension was a prominent feature of the Social Security Act of 1935. A narrow Court majority sustained this legislation two years later as a constitutional exercise of the national taxing and spending power (*Steward Machine Co. v. Davis*, 301 U.S. 548 [1937]). Dissenting Justices contended that tax credits allowed to employers who contributed to state unemployment funds had the effect of forcing the states to participate in the social security program and that such coercion violated the Tenth Amendment. The argument did not prevail, and with the passage of time it became apparent that cooperative arrangements between nation and state would proliferate. After World War II the demand for national programs in many areas continued to grow. Problems plaguing the cities were compounded by the large-scale movement of mostly white, middle-class residents to the suburbs and their replacement in the inner cities by less affluent residents, many of them poorly educated blacks from the rural South. The resulting erosion of the property tax base undermined a major source of local revenue; and yet demands for local government services, like those for their state and national counterparts, continued to grow. Cities found it expedient to turn directly to the national government for assistance. Although technically "creatures of the state," municipal governments found it possible to use the political process to work closely with the national government in such areas as urban renewal and law enforcement. This partnership was facilitated in the 1960s by the Court-led revolution in legislative reapportionment, which, among other things, ostensibly increased the relative influence of urban constituencies in the United States House of Representatives. Although by no means out of the picture, the states themselves were to some extent bypassed in the administration of many nationally financed programs aimed at meeting the "urban crisis."

Federal Status of States and the New Federalism

A century after the Civil War the question was not whether the nation would remain unified but whether the states comprising its legal and political subdivisions would remain full partners in the federal system. In 1968 the Court upheld an extension of the wage and hour provisions of the Fair Labor Standards Act to state employees in schools and hospitals (*Maryland* v. *Wirtz,* 392 U.S. 138). In his majority opinion Justice Harlan noted that "labor conditions in the schools and hospitals can affect commerce." Accordingly, he found a "rational basis" for "congressional action prescribing minimum labor standards" here, just as for other enterprises importing goods and services from other states. He flatly rejected the contention of Maryland and twenty-seven other states that the act as amended interfered with "state sovereignty in the performance of governmental functions." Justice Douglas, joined by Justice Stewart, filed what proved to be a prophetic dissent. In his view this extension of national wage and hour coverage, even to a limited category of state employees, disrupted the fiscal policy of the states and interfered with their traditional police powers in regulating health and education.

Demands for governmental services continued to grow in the 1970s. In attempting to meet these demands, states and cities became vulnerable to the added pressures of inflation and recession. Concern about state autonomy could no longer be dismissed as a mere expression of reactionary political or racial views. In the aftermath of Vietnam and Watergate, this concern was coupled with growing skepticism about the competence and integrity of national leadership. Presumptions of the superior wisdom of national, as opposed to state, policy in such fields as law enforcement, public health, and education were no longer dominant, even among political liberals.

The growing cost of government at all levels contributed to changes in public attitudes toward the capacity and commitment of government to solve social and economic problems. A "new federalism" emerged as one political response to what was preceived as a basic change in the mood of the electorate.

Part of the new federalism took the form of less restrictive national financial grants to the states. Another aspect of it was political rhetoric about a "viable partnership" between the national government and the states. All of this was merely a variation on the familiar theme of cooperative federalism, but more fundamental changes were at work. In 1976 the Supreme Court, in *National League of Cities* v. *Usery,* struck down provisions of the 1974 amendments to the Fair Labor Standards Act that extended minimum wage coverage to virtually all state and local employees. In so doing, the Court overruled *Maryland* v. *Wirtz* (1968). Writing for the 5 to 4 majority, Justice Rehnquist held that the national commerce power must yield to the Tenth Amendment when the former infringes upon "traditional aspects of state sovereignty." He did not define with precision the exact nature or scope of those "traditional aspects." Nevertheless, he made it clear that, at least for a majority of the Burger Court, the Tenth Amendment would not be regarded as a "mere truism." Acknowledging the broad power of Congress to regulate commerce among the states, Rehnquist drew a sharp distinction between that authority as applied to business activity on the one hand and to the function of "states as states" on the other. It is difficult to discern the specific Tenth Amendment interests that, for Rehnquist, justified restricting the commerce power. We share Professor Laurence Tribe's view that, at bottom, the majority was attempting to protect individual rights to essential governmental services, such as police and fire protection, which the states and their subdivisions have traditionally provided (1978, p. 309). Rehnquist voiced concern about the adverse economic impact the 1974 amendments would have on already overburdened state and local governments. Blanket minimum wage requirements would not only be costly, but the national law that imposed them would also displace "state policies regarding the manner in which they will structure delivery of those governmental services which their citizens require." The bitter dissent of Justice Brennan assailed the *Usery* ruling as an irresponsible departure from modern views regarding the national commerce power and the federal relationship. Others praised the decision as a welcome reassertion of the principle of balance inherent in the federal system. At this writing it remains unclear whether the decision represents a major shift or a mere aberration in constitutional development.

National Preemption

There is one final issue related to the distribution of power within the federal system. *Pennsylvania* v. *Nelson,* 350 U.S. 497 (1956), illustrates the controversy in an important political context. The question posed by that case was whether Pennsylvania's prosecution of Steve Nelson, a member of the Communist Party, for violation of its Sedition Act was foreclosed by the existence of national legislation against "subversive activities." In a long line of decisions the Supreme Court has held that national law preempts state law if considerations of national policy warrant it, so long as those considerations are consistent with either enumerated powers or broader national security interests. Without using the terminology of the "preemption doctrine" per se, Chief Justice Warren held in the *Nelson* case that through a series of statutes beginning with the Smith Act of 1940, Congress had "occupied the field to the exclusion of parallel state legislation." Even though Congress had not condemned state legislation in the field of subversion, dominant national interest in maintaining internal security precluded state intervention. Presumably Congress is free to sanction state activity in a field covered by national policy; but when Congress is silent on the question, as it was with regard to subversion, the Court does not always assume that silence means consent. Many members of Congress reacted strongly to what they saw as the unwarranted and misguided use of the preemption doctrine. The Court was already under attack from some political leaders for its 1954 school desegregation decision (*Brown* v.

Board of Education, 347 U.S. 483). For the more extreme critics of the Warren Court, *Pennsylvania* v. *Nelson* suggested that the Court was "soft on Communism." A serious but ultimately unsuccessful effort was made to overturn the decision (for background, see Lytle, 1968; Murphy, 1964).

Federalism in the Context of Checks and Balances

In spite of the enormous changes that have taken place within the structure and ongoing operation of the American federal system, the Supreme Court's rulings have always supported the values implicit in the distribution of powers. Although it has at times stressed the importance of national interests at the expense of the states and occasionally done just the reverse, the Court has approached problems of federalism within the context of the principle of checks and balances and that principle's underlying commitment to individual liberty. Thus while the Court restricted state power in *M'Culloch* v. *Maryland* with the warning that "the power to tax involves the power to destroy," it applied the same rationale a half century later in holding that a state judge's salary was not subject to a national income tax (*Collector* v. *Day,* 11 Wall. 113 [1871]). The doctrine of reciprocal tax immunity, established by these early decisions and narrowed in the post–New Deal era, will be discussed more fully in Chapter 11. The issues of federalism cut across many areas determining the allocation of power and continue to command a major share of the Court's attention.

Until very recently the states' rights position was almost exclusively identified with economic conservatism, opposition to the enlargement of civil rights protections, and resistance to social legislation on a national scale. Even with the mounting skepticism about the efficacy of many national domestic programs, the states have by no means undergone a renaissance of vitality and leadership. They have often been extolled as important laboratories for governmental experimentation, but this innovative capacity has been more apparent in theory than in practice. If there is a renewal of interest in preserving the governmental autonomy of the states, it is not because of any deep conviction that the states are better able to perform and provide answers to the country's pressing questions than is the national government. Rather, the reemphasis on traditional postulates of federalism, as exemplified by the *Usery* case, is more likely a response to the problem of controlling national power, especially bureaucratic power, in the late twentieth century. The Supreme Court has been particularly mindful of maintaining the balance between the federal and state judicial systems. Of course, in matters of ultimate constitutional authority the Supreme Court asserted early in its history the power to reverse decisions of the highest state courts (*Martin* v. *Hunter's Lessee,* 1 Wheat. 304 [1816], and *Cohens* v. *Virginia.* But state courts and state systems of law are given great deference by federal judges in the many areas of the legal system not routinely affected by such constitutional provisions as the Supremacy Clause and the commerce power. In fact, judicial federalism more closely approximates the classical pattern than the cooperative federalism characteristic of so many legislative and administrative programs.

M'Culloch v. Maryland

4 Wheat. 316 (1819)

[The First Bank of the United States was created by Congress in 1791 and given a twenty-year charter. Congress failed to extend the expiration date, and in 1811 the bank went out of business. Five years later, and after intensive controversy, Congress established the Second Bank of the United States, again granting it a charter for twenty years. This bank, like its predecessor, was bitterly opposed by many local economic interests identified first with the Jeffersonian Republican party and later with its successor, the Democratic party under the leadership of Andrew Jackson. The bitter struggle over the issue of rechartering the Second Bank of the United States was of central importance during Jackson's Administration. It is against this background of partisan politics that the decision in *M'Culloch* v. *Maryland* should be read.

One of the branches of the Second Bank of the United States was located in Baltimore, and in 1818 the Maryland legislature imposed a tax on all banks not chartered by the state. The act imposed an annual fee of $15,000 payable in advance or a 2 percent tax on the value of notes issued by such banks. A penalty of $500 was imposed for each violation of this tax measure, which, as everyone recognized, was aimed squarely at the Bank of the United States. M'Culloch, the cashier of the Baltimore branch, refused to comply with the state law. His subsequent conviction was upheld by the Maryland Court of Appeals.]

MR. CHIEF JUSTICE MARSHALL delivered the opinion of the court.

. . .

The first question made in the cause is, has Congress power to incorporate a bank?

. . .

The power now contested was exercised by the first Congress elected under the present constitution. . . . Its principle was completely understood, and was opposed with equal zeal and ability. After being resisted, first in the fair and open field of debate, and afterwards in the executive cabinet, . . . it became a law. The original act was permitted to expire; but a short experience of the embarrassments to which the refusal to revive it exposed the government, convinced those who were most prejudiced against the measure of its necessity and induced the passage of the present law.

. . .

This government is acknowledged by all to be one of enumerated powers. The principle, that it can exercise only the powers granted to it, would seem too apparent to have required to be enforced by all those arguments which its enlightened friends, while it was depending before the people, found it necessary to urge. That principle is now universally admitted. But the question respecting the extent of the powers actually granted, is perpetually arising, and will probably continue to arise, as long as our system shall exist.

In discussing these questions, the conflicting powers of the general and state governments must be brought into view, and the supremacy of their respective laws, when they are in opposition, must be settled.

If any one proposition could command the universal assent of mankind, we might expect it would be this—that the government of the Union, though limited in its powers, is supreme within its sphere of action. This would seem to result necessarily from its nature. It is the government of all; its powers are delegated by all; it represents all, and acts for all. Though any one state may be willing to control its operations, no state is willing to allow others to control them. The nation, on those subjects on which it can act, must necessarily bind its component parts. But this question is not left to mere reason; the people have, in express terms, decided it by saying, "this constitution, and the laws of the United States, which shall be made in pursuance thereof," "shall be the supreme law of the land," and by requiring that the members of the state legislatures, and the officers of the executive and judicial departments of the states shall take the oath of fidelity to it.

The government of the United States, then, though limited in its powers, is supreme; and its laws, when made in pursuance of the constitution, form the supreme law of the land, "anything in the constitution or laws of any state to the contrary notwithstanding."

Among the enumerated powers, we do not find that of establishing a bank or creating a corporation. But there is no phrase in the instrument which, like the articles of confederation, excludes incidental or implied powers; and which requires that everything granted shall be expressly and minutely described. Even the 10th amendment, which was framed for the purpose of quieting the excessive jealousies which had been excited, omits the word "expressly," and declares only that the powers "not delegated to the United States, nor prohibited to the states, are reserved to the states or to the people:" thus leaving the question, whether the particular power which may become the subject of contest has been delegated to the one government, or prohibited to the other, to depend on a fair construction of the whole instrument. . . . A constitution, to contain an accurate detail of all the subdivisions of which its great powers will admit, and of all the means by which they may be carried into execution, would partake of a prolixity of a legal code, and could scarcely be embraced by the human mind. It would probably never be understood by the public. Its nature, therefore, requires, that only its great outlines should be marked, its important objects designated, and the minor ingredients which compose those objects be deduced from the nature of the objects themselves. . . . In considering this question, then, we must never forget that it is a constitution we are expounding.

Although, among the enumerated powers of government, we do not find the word "bank" or "incorporation," we find the great powers to lay and collect taxes; to borrow money; to regulate commerce; to declare and conduct a war; and to raise and support armies and navies. The sword and the purse, all the external relations, and no inconsiderable portion of the industry of the nation, are entrusted to its government. . . . [I]t may with great reason be contended, that a government, entrusted with such ample powers, on the due execution of which the happiness and prosperity of the nation so vitally depends, must also be entrusted with ample means for their execution. The power being given, it is the interest of the nation to facilitate its execution. It can never be their interest, and cannot be presumed to have been their intention, to clog and embarrass its execution by withholding the most appropriate means. . . .

· · ·

The government which has a right to do an act, and has imposed on it the duty of performing that act, must, according to the dictates of reason, be allowed to select the means; and those who contend that it may not select any appropriate means, that one particular mode of effecting the object is excepted, take upon themselves the burden of establishing that exception.

But the constitution of the United States has not left the right of Congress to employ the necessary means for the execution of the powers conferred on the government to general reasoning. To its enumeration of powers is added that of making "all laws which shall be necessary and proper, for carrying into execution the foregoing powers, and all other powers vested by this constitution, in the government of the United States, or in any department thereof."

The counsel for the State of Maryland have urged various arguments, to prove that this clause, though in terms a grant of power, is not so in effect. . . . In support of this proposition, they have found it necessary to contend, that this clause was inserted for the purpose of conferring on Congress the power of making laws. That, without it, doubts might be entertained whether Congress could exercise its powers in the form of legislation.

But could this be the object for which it was inserted? A government is created by the people, having legislative, executive, and judicial powers. Its legislative powers are vested in a Congress. . . . That a legislature, endowed with legislative powers, can legislate, is a proposition too self-evident to have been questioned.

But the argument on which most reliance is placed, is drawn from the peculiar language of this clause. Congress is not empowered by it to make all laws, which may have relation to the powers conferred on the government, but such only as may be "necessary and proper" for carrying them into execution. The word "necessary" is considered as controlling the whole sentence, and as limiting the right to pass laws for the execution of the granted powers, to such as are indispensable, and without which the power would be nugatory. That it excludes the choice of means, and leaves to Congress, in each case, that only which is most direct and simple.

Is it true that this is the sense in which the word "necessary" is always used? Does it always import an absolute physical necessity, so strong that one thing, to which another may be termed necessary, cannot exist without that other? We think it does not. . . . To employ the means necessary to an end, is generally understood as employing any means calculated to produce the end, and not as being confined to those single means, without which the end would be entirely unattainable. Such is the character of human language, that no word conveys to the mind, in all situations, one single definite idea. . . .

It is, we think, impossible to compare the sentence which prohibits a state from laying "imposts or duties on imports or exports, except what may be absolutely necessary for executing its inspection laws," with that which authorizes Congress "to make all laws which shall be necessary and proper for carrying into execution" the powers of the general government, without feeling a conviction that the convention understood itself to change materially the meaning of the word "necessary," by prefixing the word "absolutely." This word, then, like others, is used in various senses; and, in its construction, the subject, the context, the intention of the person using them, are all to be taken into view.

Let this be done in the case under consideration. The subject is the execution of those great powers on which the welfare of a nation essentially depends. It must have been the intention of those who gave these powers, to insure, as far a human prudence could insure, their beneficial execution. This could not be done by confiding the choice of means to such narrow limits as not to leave it in the power of Congress to adopt any which might be appropriate, and which were conducive to the end. This provision is made in a constitution intended to endure for ages to come, and, consequently, to be adapted to the various crises of human affairs.

· · ·

The result of the most careful and attentive consideration bestowed upon this clause is, that if it does not enlarge, it cannot be construed to restrain the powers of Congress, or to impair the right of the legislature to exercise its best judgment in the selection of measures to carry into execution the constitutional powers of the government. If no other motive for its insertion can be suggested, a sufficient one is found in the desire to remove all doubts respecting the right to legislate on that vast mass of incidental powers which must be involved in the constitution, if that instrument be not a splendid bauble.

We admit, as all must admit, that the powers of the government are limited, and that its limits are not to be transcended. But we think the sound construction of the constitution must allow to the national legislature that discretion, with respect to the means by which the powers it confers are to be carried into execution, which will enable that body to perform the high duties assigned to it, in the manner most beneficial to the people. Let the end be legitimate, let it be within the scope of the constitution, and all means which are appropriate, which are plainly adapted to that end, which are not prohibited, but consist with the letter and spirit of the constitution, are constitutional.

That a corporation must be considered as a means not less usual, not of higher dignity, not more requiring a particular specification than other means, has been sufficiently proved. . . . [W]e find no reason to suppose that a constitution, omitting, and wisely omitting, to enumerate all the means for carrying into execution the great powers vested in government, ought to have specified this. . . .

• • •

If a corporation may be employed indiscriminately with other means to carry into execution the powers of the government, no particular reason can be assigned for excluding the use of a bank, if required for its fiscal operations. To use one, must be within the discretion of Congress, if it be an appropriate mode of executing the powers of government. That it is a convenient, a useful, and essential instrument in the prosecution of its fiscal operations, is not now a subject of controversy.

. . .[W]ere its necessity less apparent, none can deny its being an appropriate measure; and if it is, the degree of its necessity, as has been very justly observed, is to be discussed in another place. Should Congress, in the execution of its powers, adopt measures which are prohibited by the constitution; or should Congress, under the pretext of executing its powers pass laws for the accomplishment of objects not entrusted to the government, it would become the painful duty of this tribunal, should a case requiring such a decision come before it, to say that such an act was not the law of the land. But where the law is not prohibited, and is really calculated to effect any of the objects entrusted to the government, to undertake here to inquire into the degree of its necessity, would be to pass the line which circumscribes the judicial department, and to tread on legislative ground. This court disclaims all pretensions to such a power.

• • •

After the most deliberate consideration, it is the unanimous and decided opinion of this court that the act to incorporate the bank of the United States is a law made in pursuance of the constitution, and is a part of the supreme law of the land.

• • •

It being the opinion of the court that the act incorporating the bank is constitutional, . . . we proceed to inquire:

Whether the state of Maryland may, without violating the constitution, tax that branch?

That the power of taxation is one of vital importance; that it is retained by the states; that it is not abridged by the grant of a similar power to the government of the Union: that it is to be concurrently exercised by the two governments: are truths which have never been denied. But, such is the paramount character of the constitution that its capacity to withdraw any subject from the action of even this power, is admitted. The states are expressly forbidden to lay any duties on imports or exports, except what may be absolutely necessary for executing their inspection laws. If the obligation of this prohibition must be conceded—if it may restrain a state from the exercise of its taxing power on imports and exports—the same paramount character would seem to restrain, as it certainly may restrain, a state from such other exercise of this power, as is in its nature incompatible with, and repugnant to, the constitutional laws of the Union. A law, absolutely repugnant to another, as entirely repeals that other as if express terms of repeal were used.

• • •

This great principle is, that the constitution and the laws made in pursuance thereof are supreme; that they control the constitution and laws of the respective states, and cannot be controlled by them. From this, which may be almost termed an axiom, other propositions are deduced as corollaries, on the truth or error of which, and on their application to this case the cause has been supposed to depend. These are, 1st. that a power to create implies a power to preserve. 2d. That a power to destroy, if wielded by a different hand, is hostile to, and incompatible with these powers to create and to preserve. 3d. That where this repugnancy exists, that authority which is supreme must control, not yield to that over which it is supreme.

• • •

That the power to tax involves the power to destroy; that the power to destroy may defeat and render useless the power to create; that there is a plain repugnance, in conferring on one government a power to control the constitutional measures of another, which other, with respect to those very measures, is declared to be supreme over that which exerts the control, are propositions not to be denied. . . .

• • •

If the states may tax one instrument, employed by the government in the execution of its powers, they may tax any and every other instrument. They may tax the mail; they may tax the mint; they may tax patent-rights; they may tax the papers of the custom-house; they may tax judicial process; they may tax all the means employed by the government, to an excess which would defeat all the ends of government. This was not intended by the American people. . . .

. . . The question is, in truth, a question of supremacy; and if the right of the states to tax the means employed by the general government be conceded, the declaration that the constitution, and the laws made in pursuance thereof, shall be the supreme law of the land, is empty and unmeaning declamation.

· · ·

It has also been insisted, that, as the power of taxation in the general and state governments is acknowledged to be concurrent, every argument which would sustain the right of the general government to tax banks chartered by the states, will equally sustain the right of the states to tax banks chartered by the general government.

But the two cases are not on the same reason. The people of all the states have created the general government, and have conferred upon it the general power of taxation. The people of all the states, and the states themselves, are represented in Congress, and, by their representatives, exercise this power. When they tax the chartered institutions of the states, they tax their constituents; and these taxes must be uniform. But, when a state taxes the operations of the government of the United States, it acts upon institutions created, not by their own constituents, but by people over whom they claim no control. It acts upon the measures of a government created by others as well as themselves, for the benefit of others in common with themselves. The difference is that which always exists, and always must exist, between the action of the whole on a part, and the action of a part on the whole—between the laws of a government declared to be supreme, and those of a government which, when in opposition to those laws, is not supreme.

But if the full application of this argument could be admitted, it might bring into question the right of Congress to tax the state banks, and could not prove the right of the states to tax the Bank of the United States.

The court has bestowed on this subject its most deliberate consideration. The result is a conviction that the states have no power, by taxation or otherwise, to retard, impede, burden, or in any manner control the operations of the constitutional laws enacted by Congress to carry into execution the powers vested in the general government. This is, we think, the unavoidable consequence of that supremacy which the constitution has declared.

We are unanimously of opinion that the law passed by the legislature of Maryland, imposing a tax on the Bank of the United States, is unconstitutional and void.

This opinion does not deprive the states of any resources which they originally possessed. It does not extend to a tax paid by the real property of the bank, in common with the other real property within the state, nor to a tax imposed on the interest which the citizens of Maryland may hold in this institution, in common with other property of the same description throughout the state. But this is a tax on the operations of the bank, and is, consequently, a tax on the operation of an instrument of the Union to carry its powers into execution. Such a tax must be unconstitutional.

Hammer v. Dagenhart

247 U.S. 251 (1918)

MR. JUSTICE DAY delivered the opinion of the court.

A bill was filed in the United States district court for the western district of North Carolina by a father in his own behalf and as next friend of his two minor sons, one under the age of fourteen years and the other between the ages of fourteen and sixteen years, employees in a cotton mill at Charlotte, North Carolina, to enjoin the enforcement of the act of Congress intended to prevent interstate commerce in the products of child labor. * * *

The district court held the act unconstitutional. . . . This appeal brings the case here. . . .

• • •

The controlling question for decision is: Is it within the authority of Congress in regulating commerce among the states to prohibit the transportation in interstate commerce of manufactured goods, the product of a factory in which, within thirty days prior to their removal therefrom, children under the age of fourteen have been employed or permitted to work, or children between the ages of fourteen and sixteen years have been employed or permitted to work, more than eight hours in any day, or more than six days in any week, or after the hour of 7 o'clock P.M. or before the hour of 6 o'clock A.M.?

The power essential to the passage of this act, the government contends, is found in the commerce clause of the Constitution, which authorizes Congress to regulate commerce with foreign nations and among the states.

. . . [The commerce] power is one to control the means by which commerce is carried on, which is directly the contrary of the assumed right to forbid commerce from moving and thus destroy it as to particular commodities. But it is insisted that adjudged cases in this court establish the doctrine that the power to regulate given to Congress incidentally includes the authority to prohibit the movement of ordinary commodities, and therefore that the subject is not open for discussion. The cases demonstrate the contrary. They rest upon the character of the particular subjects dealt with and the fact that the scope of governmental authority, state or national, possessed over them, is such that the authority to prohibit is, as to them, but the exertion of the power to regulate.

. . . [It has been held that] Congress might pass a law having the effect to keep the channels of commerce free from use in the transportation of tickets used in the promotion of lottery schemes; . . . [prohibiting] the introduction into the states by means of interstate commerce of impure foods and drugs; . . . [forbidding] transportation of a woman in interstate commerce for the purpose of prostitution; . . . [prohibiting] the transportation of women in interstate commerce for the purposes of debauchery and kindred purposes; . . . [and barring] the transportation of intoxicating liquors. . . .

. . .

In each of these instances the use of interstate transportation was necessary to the accomplishment of harmful results. In other words, although the power over interstate transportation was to regulate, that could only be accomplished by prohibiting the use of the facilities of interstate commerce to effect the evil intended.

This element is wanting in the present case. The thing intended to be accomplished by this statute is the denial of the facilities of interstate commerce to those manufacturers in the states who employ children within the prohibited ages. The act in its effect does not regulate transportation among the states, but aims to standardize the ages at which children may be employed in mining and manufacturing within the states. The goods shipped are of themselves harmless. The act permits them to be freely shipped after thirty days from the time of their removal from the factory. When offered for shipment, and before transportation begins, the labor of their production is over, and the mere fact that they were intended for interstate commerce transportation does not make their production subject to Federal control under the commerce power.

Commerce "consists of intercourse and traffic . . . and includes the transportation of persons and property, as well as the purchase, sale and exchange of commodities." The making of goods and the mining of coal are not commerce, nor does the fact that these things are to be afterwards shipped, or used in interstate commerce, make their production a part thereof. * * *

Over interstate transportation, or its incidents, the regulatory power of Congress is ample, but the production of articles intended for interstate commerce is a matter of local regulation. . . . If it were otherwise, all manufacture intended for interstate shipment would be brought under Federal control to the practical exclusion of the authority of the states,—a result certainly not contemplated by the framers of the Constitution when they vested in Congress the authority to regulate commerce among the states. * * *

It is further contended that the authority of Congress may be exerted to control interstate commerce in the shipment of child-made goods because of the effect of the circulation of such goods in other states where the evil of this class of labor has been recognized by local legislation, and the right to thus employ child labor has been more rigorously restrained than in the state of production. In other words, that the unfair competition thus engendered may be controlled by closing the channels of interstate commerce to manufacturers in those states where the local laws do not meet what Congress deems to be the more just standard of other states.

There is no power vested in Congress to require the states to exercise their police power so as to prevent possible unfair competition. Many causes may co-operate to give one state, by reason of local laws or conditions, an economic advantage over others. The commerce clause was not intended to give to Congress a general authority to equalize such conditions. . . .

The grant of power to Congress over the subject of interstate commerce was to enable it to regulate such commerce, and not to give it authority to control the states in their exercise of the police power over local trade and manufacture.

The grant of authority over a purely Federal matter was not intended to destroy the local power always existing and carefully reserved to the states in the 10th Amendment to the Constitution.

Police regulations relating to the internal trade and affairs of the states have been uniformly recognized as within such control. . . .

* * *

That there should be limitations upon the right to employ children in mines and factories in the interest of their own and the public welfare, all will admit. That such employment is generally deemed to require regulation is shown by the fact that the brief of counsel states that every state in the Union has a law upon the subject, limiting the right to thus employ children. In North Carolina, the state wherein is located the factory in which the employment was had in the present case, no child under twelve years of age is permitted to work.

* * *

In interpreting the Constitution it must never be forgotten that the nation is made up of states, to which are intrusted the powers of local government. And to them and to the people the powers not expressly delegated to the national government are reserved. The power of the states to regulate their purely internal affairs by such laws as seem wise to the local authority is inherent, and has never been surrendered to the general government. * * * To sustain this statute would not be, in our judgment, a recognition of the lawful exertion of congressional authority over interstate commerce, but would sanction an invasion by the Federal power of the control of a matter purely local in its character, and over which no authority has been delegated to Congress in conferring the power to regulate commerce among the states.

We have neither authority nor disposition to question the motives of Congress in enacting this legislation. The purposes intended must be attained consistently with constitutional limitations, and not by an invasion of the powers of the states. This court has no more important function than that which devolves upon it the obligation to preserve inviolate the constitutional limitations upon the exercise of authority, Federal and state, to the end that each may continue to discharge, harmoniously with the other, the duties intrusted to it by the Constitution.

. . . [T]he act in a twofold sense is repugnant to the Constitution. It not only transcends the authority delegated to Congress over commerce, but also exerts a power as to a purely local matter to which the Federal authority does not extend. The far-reaching result of upholding the act cannot be more plainly indicated than by pointing out that if Congress can thus regulate matters intrusted to local authority by prohibition of the movement of commodities in interstate commerce, all freedom of commerce will be at an end, and the power of the states over local matters may be eliminated, and thus our system of government be practically destroyed.

For these reasons we hold that this law exceeds the constitutional authority of Congress. It follows that the decree of the District Court must be affirmed.

MR. JUSTICE HOLMES, dissenting.

. . . [I]f an act is within the powers specifically conferred upon Congress, it seems to me that it is not made any less constitutional because of the indirect effects that it may have, however obvious it may be that it will have those effects; and that we are not at liberty upon such grounds to hold it void.

The first step in my argument is to make plain what no one is likely to dispute,—that the statute in question is within the power expressly given to Congress if considered only as to its immediate effects, and that if invalid it is so only upon some collateral ground. The statute confines itself to prohibiting the carriage of certain goods in interstate or foreign commerce. Congress is given power to regulate such commerce in unqualified terms. It would not be argued to-day that the power to regulate does not include the power to prohibit. Regulation means the prohibition of something, and when interstate commerce is the matter to be regulated I cannot doubt that the regulations may prohibit any part of such commerce that Congress sees fit to forbid. . . .

The question, then, is narrowed to whether the exercise of its otherwise constitutional power by Congress can be pronounced unconstitutional because of its possible reaction upon the conduct of the states in a matter upon which I have admitted that they are free from direct control. I should have thought that that matter had been disposed of so fully as to leave no room for doubt. I should have thought that the most conspicuous decisions of this court had made it clear that the power to regulate commerce and other constitutional powers could not be cut down or qualified by the fact that it might interfere with the carrying out of the domestic policy of any state.

[Holmes reviews in a slightly different light the same set of cases supporting the prohibition of supposedly "harmful" products, discussed by Justice Day in the majority opinion, and continues:]

The notion that prohibition is any less prohibition when applied to things now thought evil I do not understand. But if there is any matter upon which civilized countries have agreed,—far more unanimously than they have with regard to intoxicants and some other matters over which this country is now emotionally aroused,—it is the evil of premature and excessive child labor. I should have thought that if we were to introduce our own moral conceptions where, in my opinion, they do not belong, this was pre-eminently a case for upholding the exercise of all its powers by the United States.

But I had thought that the propriety of the exercise of a power admitted to exist in some cases was for the consideration of Congress alone, and that this court always had disavowed the right to intrude its judgment upon questions of policy or morals. It is not for this court to pronounce when prohibition is neces-sary to regulation if it ever may be necessary,—to say that it is permissible as against strong drink, but not as against the product of ruined lives.

The act does not meddle with anything belonging to the states. They may regulate their internal affairs and their domestic commerce as they like. But when they seek to send their products across the state line they are no longer within their rights. If there were no Constitution and no Congress their power to cross the line would depend upon their neighbors. Under the Constitution such commerce belongs not to the states, but to Congress to regulate. It may carry out its views of public policy whatever indirect effect they may have upon the activi-ties of the states. Instead of being encountered by a prohibitive tariff at her boundaries, the state encounters the public policy of the United States which it is for Congress to express. The public policy of the United States is shaped with a view to the benefit of the nation as a whole. . . . The national welfare as under-stood by Congress may require a different attitude within its sphere from that of some self-seeking state. It seems to me entirely constitutional for Congress to enforce its understanding by all the means at its command.

Mr. Justice McKenna, Mr. Justice Brandeis, and Mr. Justice Clarke concur in this opinion.

United States v. Darby

312 U.S. 100 (1941)

Mr. Justice Stone delivered the opinion of the Court.

The two principal questions raised by the record in this case are, *first*, whether Congress has constitutional power to prohibit the shipment in interstate com-merce of lumber manufactured by employees whose wages are less than a pre-scribed minimum or whose weekly hours of labor at that wage are greater than a prescribed maximum, and, *second*, whether it has power to prohibit the employment of workmen in the production of goods "for interstate commerce" at other than prescribed wages and hours. . . .

• • •

The Fair Labor Standards Act [FLSA] set up a comprehensive legislative scheme for preventing the shipment in interstate commerce of certain products and commodities produced in the United States under labor conditions as respects wages and hours which fail to conform to standards set up by the Act. Its purpose, as we judicially know from the declaration of policy, * * * is to exclude from interstate commerce goods produced for the commerce and to prevent their production for interstate commerce, under conditions detrimental to the maintenance of the minimum standards of living necessary for health and general well-being; and to prevent the use of interstate commerce as the means of competition in the distribution of goods so produced, and as the means of spreading and perpetuating such substandard labor conditions among the workers of the several states. . . .

. . .[T]he statute * * * prohibits certain specified acts and punishes willful violation of it by a fine of not more than $10,000 and punishes each conviction after the first by imprisonment of not more than six months or by the specified fine or both. [The Act makes it unlawful to ship in interstate commerce goods produced by employees working for less than a minimum wage of twenty-five cents per hour or for more than forty-four hours a week.]

• • •

The indictment charges that [Darby] is engaged, in the state of Georgia, in the business of acquiring raw materials, which he manufactures into finished lumber with the intent, when manufactured, to ship it in interstate commerce to customers outside the state, and that he does in fact so ship a large part of the lumber so produced. There are numerous counts charging [him] with the shipment in interstate commerce from Georgia to points outside the state of lumber in the production of which, for interstate commerce, [Darby] has employed workmen at less than the prescribed minimum wage or more than the prescribed maximum hours without payment to them of any wage for overtime. . . .

• • •

The case comes here on assignments by the Government that the district court erred in so far as it held that Congress was without constitutional power to penalize the acts set forth in the indictment, and [Darby] seeks to sustain the decision below on the grounds that the prohibition by Congress of those Acts is unauthorized by the commerce clause. . . .

The prohibition of shipment of the proscribed goods in interstate commerce. [The FLSA] prohibits, and the indictment charges, the shipment in interstate commerce, of goods produced for interstate commerce by employees whose wages and hours of employment do not conform to the requirements of the Act. . . . [T]he only question arising under the commerce clause with respect to such shipments is whether Congress has the constitutional power to prohibit them.

While manufacture is not of itself interstate commerce the shipment of manufactured goods interstate is such commerce and the prohibition of such shipment by Congress is indubitably a regulation of the commerce. The power to regulate commerce is the power "to prescribe the rule by which commerce is governed." * * * It extends not only to those regulations which aid, foster and protect the commerce, but embraces those which prohibit it. * * * It is conceded that the power of Congress to prohibit transportation in interstate commerce includes noxious articles, * * * and articles such as intoxicating liquor or convict made goods, traffic in which is forbidden or restricted by the laws of the state of destination. * * *

But it is said that the present prohibition falls within the scope of none of these categories; that while the prohibition is nominally a regulation of the commerce its motive or purpose is regulation of wages and hours of persons engaged in manufacture, the control of which has been reserved to the states and upon which Georgia and some of the states of destination have placed no restriction; that the effect of the present statute is not to exclude the prescribed articles from interstate commerce in aid of state regulation, * * * but instead, under the guise of a regulation of interstate commerce, it undertakes to regulate wages and hours within the state contrary to the policy of the state which has elected to leave them unregulated.

The power of Congress over interstate commerce "is complete in itself, may be exercised to its utmost extent, and acknowledges no limitations other than are prescribed in the Constitution." * * * That power can neither be enlarged nor diminished by the exercise or nonexercise of state power. * * * Congress, following its own conception of public policy concerning the restrictions which may appropriately be imposed on interstate commerce, is free to exclude from the commerce articles whose use in the states for which they are destined it may conceive to be injurious to the public health, morals or welfare, even though the state has not sought to regulate their use. * * *

Such regulation is not a forbidden invasion of state power merely because either its motive or its consequence is to restrict the use of articles of commerce within the states of destination and is not prohibited unless by other constitutional provisions. It is no objection to the assertion of power to regulate interstate commerce that its exercise is attended by the same incidents which attend the exercise of the police power of the states. * * *

The motive and purpose of the present regulation are plainly to make effective the Congressional conception of public policy that interstate commerce should not be made the instrument of competition in the distribution of goods produced under substandard labor conditions, which competition is injurious to the commerce and to the states from and to which the commerce flows. The motive and purpose of a regulation of interstate commerce are matters for the legislative judgment upon the exercise of which the Constitution places no restriction and over which the courts are given no control. * * * . . . Whatever their motive and purpose, regulations of commerce which do not infringe some constitutional prohibition are within the plenary power conferred on Congress by the Commerce Clause. Subject only to that limitation, presently to be considered, we conclude that the prohibition of the shipment interstate of goods produced under the forbidden substandard labor conditions is within the constitutional authority of Congress.

In the more than a century which has elapsed since the decision of Gibbons v. Ogden, these principles of constitutional interpretation have been so long and repeatedly recognized by this Court as applicable to the Commerce Clause, that there would be little occasion for repeating them now were it not for the decision of this Court twenty-two years ago in Hammer v. Dagenhart. * * * In that case it was held by a bare majority of the Court over the powerful and now classic dissent of Mr. Justice Holmes setting forth the fundamental issues involved that Congress was without power to exclude the products of child labor from interstate commerce. The reasoning and conclusion of the Court's opinion there cannot be reconciled with the conclusion which we have reached, that the power of Congress under the Commerce Clause is plenary to exclude any article from interstate commerce subject only to the specific prohibitions of the Constitution.

Hammer v. Dagenhart has not been followed. The distinction on which the decision was rested that Congressional power to prohibit interstate commerce is limited to articles which in themselves have some harmful or deleterious property—a distinction which was novel when made and unsupported by any provision of the Constitution—has long since been abandoned. * * * The thesis of the opinion that the motive of the prohibition or its effect to control in some measure the use or production within the states of the article thus excluded from the commerce can operate to deprive the regulation of its constitutional authority has long since ceased to have force. * * *

The conclusion is inescapable that Hammer v. Dagenhart was a departure from the principles which have prevailed in the interpretation of the Commerce Clause both before and since the decision and that such vitality, as a precedent, as it then had has long since been exhausted. It should be and now is overruled.

Validity of the wage and hour requirements.

• • •

. . .[W]e must at the outset determine whether the particular acts charged in the counts, . . . as they were construed below, constitute "production for commerce" within the meaning of the statute. As the Government seeks to apply the statute in the indictment, and as the court below construed the phrase "produced for interstate commerce," it embraces at least the case where an employer engaged, as is [Darby], in the manufacture and shipment of goods in filling orders of extrastate customers, manufactures his product with the intent or expectation that according to the normal course of his business all or some part of it will be selected for shipment to those customers.

Without attempting to define the precise limits of the phrase, we think the acts alleged in the indictment are within the sweep of the statute. The obvious purpose of the Act was not only to prevent the interstate transportation of the proscribed product, but to stop the initial step toward transportation, production with the purpose of so transporting it. Congress was not unaware that most manufacturing businesses shipping their product in interstate commerce make it in their shops without reference to its ultimate destination and then after manufacture select some of it for shipment interstate and some intrastate according to the daily demands of their business, and that it would be practically impossible, without disrupting manufacturing businesses, to restrict the prohibited kind of production to the particular pieces of lumber, cloth, furniture or the like which later move in interstate rather than intrastate commerce. * * *

. . .

There remains the question whether such restriction on the production of goods for commerce is a permissible exercise of the commerce power. The power of Congress over interstate commerce is not confined to the regulation of commerce among the states. It extends to those activities intrastate which so affect interstate commerce or the exercise of the power of Congress over it as to make regulation of them appropriate means to the attainment of a legitimate end, the exercise of the granted power of Congress to regulate interstate commerce. * * *

While this Court has many times found state regulations of interstate commerce, when uniformity of its regulation is of national concern, to be incompatible with the Commerce Clause even though Congress has not legislated on the subject, the Court has never implied such restraint on state control over matters intrastate not deemed to be regulations of interstate commerce or its instrumentalities even though they affect the commerce. * * * In the absence of Congressional legislation on the subject state laws which are not regulations of the commerce itself or its instrumentalities are not forbidden even though they affect interstate commerce. * * *

But it does not follow that Congress may not by appropriate legislation regulate intrastate activities where they have a substantial effect on interstate commerce. * * * . . .

In such legislation Congress has sometimes left it to the courts to determine whether the intrastate activities have the prohibited effect on the commerce, as in the Sherman Act. It has sometimes left it to an administrative board or agency to determine whether the activities sought to be regulated or prohibited have such effect, as in the case of the Interstate Commerce Act and the National Labor Relations Act, or whether they come within the statutory definition of the prohibited Act as in the Federal Trade Commission Act. And sometimes Congress itself has said that a particular activity affects the commerce as it did in the present act, the Safety Appliance Act and the Railway Labor Act. In passing on the validity of legislation of the class last mentioned the only function of courts is to determine whether the particular activity regulated or prohibited is within the reach of the federal power. * * *

Congress, having by the present Act adopted the policy of excluding from interstate commerce all goods produced for the commerce which do not conform to the specified labor standards, it may choose the means reasonably adapted to the attainment of the permitted end, even though they involve control of intra-state activities. Such legislation has often been sustained with respect to powers, other than the commerce power granted to the national government, when the means chosen, although not themselves within the granted power, were never-theless deemed appropriate aids to the accomplishment of some purpose within an admitted power of the national government. * * * A familiar like exercise of power is the regulation of intrastate transactions which are so commingled with or related to interstate commerce that all must be regulated if the interstate commerce is to be effectively controlled. * * * . . .

. . . [T]he evils aimed at by the [FLSA] are the spread of substandard labor conditions through the use of the facilities of interstate commerce for competition by the goods so produced with those produced under the prescribed or better labor conditions; and the consequent dislocation of the commerce itself caused by the impairment or destruction of local businesses by competition made effective through interstate commerce. The Act is thus directed at the suppression of a method or kind of competition in interstate commerce which it has in effect condemned as "unfair," as the Clayton Act has condemned other "unfair meth-ods of competition" made effective through interstate commerce. * * *

The Sherman Act and the National Labor Relations Act are familiar exam-ples of the exertion of the commerce power to prohibit or control activities wholly intrastate because of their effect on interstate commerce. * * *

The means adopted . . . for the protection of interstate commerce by the suppression of the production of the condemned goods for interstate commerce is so related to the commerce and so affects it as to be within the reach of the commerce power. * * * Congress, to attain its objective in the suppression of nationwide competition in interstate commerce by goods produced under sub-standard labor conditions, has made no distinction as to the volume or amount of shipments in the commerce or of production for commerce by any particular shipper or producer. It recognized that in present day industry, competition by a small part may affect the whole and that the total effect of the competition of many small producers may be great. * * * The legislation aimed at a whole embraces all its parts. * * *

Our conclusion is unaffected by the Tenth Amendment which provides: "The powers not delegated to the United States by the Constitution nor prohibited by it to the states are reserved to the states respectively or to the people." The amendment states but a truism that all is retained which has not been surren-dered. There is nothing in the history of its adoption to suggest that it was more than declaratory of the relationship between the national and state governments as it had been established by the Constitution before the amendment or that its purpose was other than to allay fears that the new national government might seek to exercise powers not granted, and that the states might not be able to exercise fully their reserved powers. * * *

From the beginning and for many years the amendment has been construed as not depriving the national government of authority to resort to all means for the exercise of a granted power which are appropriate and plainly adapted to the permitted end. * * * Whatever doubts may have arisen of the soundness of that conclusion they have been put at rest by the decisions under the Sherman Act and the National Labor Relations Act. . . .

• • •

The Act is sufficiently definite to meet constitutional demands. One who employs persons, without conforming to the prescribed wage and hour conditions, to work on goods which he ships or expects to ship across state lines, is warned that he may be subject to the criminal penalties of the Act. No more is required. * * *

• • •

Reversed.

National League of Cities v. Usery

426 U.S. 833 (1976)

Mr. Justice Rehnquist delivered the opinion of the Court.

Nearly 40 years ago Congress enacted the Fair Labor Standards Act, and required employers covered by the Act to pay their employees a minimum hourly wage and to pay them at one and one-half times their regular rate of pay for hours worked in excess of 40 during a work week. . . . This Court unanimously upheld the Act as a valid exercise of congressional authority under the commerce power in United States v Darby * * * . . . .

The original Fair Labor Standards Act passed in 1938 specifically excluded the States and their political subdivisions from its coverage. In 1974, however, Congress enacted the most recent of a series of broadening amendments to the Act. By these amendments Congress has extended the minimum wage and maximum hour provisions to almost all public employees employed by the States and by their various political subdivisions. Appellants in these cases include individual cities and States, the National League of Cities, and the National Governors' Conference; they brought an action . . . which challenged the validity of the 1974 amendments. They asserted in effect when Congress sought to apply the Fair Labor Standards Act provisions virtually across the board to employees of state and municipal governments it "infringed a constitutional prohibition" running in favor of the States *as States*. The gist of their complaint was not that the conditions of employment of such public employees were beyond the scope of the commerce power had those employees been employed in the private sector, but that the established constitutional doctrine of intergovernmental immunity consistently recognized in a long series of our cases affirmatively prevented the exercise of this authority in the manner which Congress chose in the 1974 amendments.

· · ·

[The League] in no way challenge[s] . . . the breadth of authority granted Congress under the commerce power. Their contention, on the contrary, is that when Congress seeks to regulate directly the activities of States as public employers, it transgresses an affirmative limitation on the exercise of its power akin to other commerce power affirmative limitations contained in the Constitution. Congressional enactments which may be fully within the grant of legislative authority contained in the Commerce Clause may nonetheless be invalid because found to offend against the right to trial by jury contained in the Sixth Amendment * * * or the Due Process Clause of the Fifth Amendment. * * * [The League's] essential contention is that the 1974 amendments to the Act, while undoubtedly within the scope of the Commerce Clause, encounter a similar constitutional barrier because they are to be applied directly to the States and subdivisions of States as employers.

This Court has never doubted that there are limits upon the power of Congress to override state sovereignty, even when exercising its otherwise plenary powers to tax or to regulate commerce which are conferred by Art I of the Constitution. . . . [T]he Court [has] recognized that an express declaration of this limitation is found in the Tenth Amendment:

> While the Tenth Amendment has been characterized as a 'truism,' stating merely that 'all is retained which has not been surrendered,' * * * it is not without significance. The Amendment expressly declares the constitutional policy that Congress may not exercise power in a fashion that impairs the States' integrity or their ability to function effectively in a federal system. * * *

· · ·

[Usery] argues that the cases in which this Court has upheld sweeping exercises of authority by Congress, even though those exercises pre-empted state regulation of the private sector, have already curtailed the sovereignty of the States quite as much as the 1974 amendments to the Fair Labor Standards Act. We do not agree. It is one thing to recognize the authority of Congress to enact laws regulating individual businesses necessarily subject to the dual sovereignty of the government of the Nation and of the State in which they reside. It is quite another to uphold a similar exercise of congressional authority directed, not to private citizens, but to the States as States. We have repeatedly recognized that there are attributes of sovereignty attaching to every state government which may not be impaired by Congress, not because Congress may lack an affirmative grant of legislative authority to reach the matter, but because the Constitution prohibits it from exercising the authority in that manner. . . .

One undoubted attribute of state sovereignty is the States' power to determine the wages which shall be paid to those whom they employ in order to carry out their governmental functions, what hours those persons will work, and what compensation will be provided where these employees may be called upon to work overtime. The question we must resolve here, then, is whether these determinations are "'functions essential to separate and independent existence,'" * * * so that Congress may not abrogate the States' otherwise plenary authority to make them.

· · ·

Quite apart from the substantial costs imposed upon the States and their political subdivisions, the Act displaces state policies regarding the manner in which they will structure delivery of those governmental services which their citizens require. The Act, speaking directly to the States qua States, requires that they shall pay all but an extremely limited minority of their employees the minimum wage rates currently chosen by Congress. It may well be that as a matter of economic policy it would be desirable that States, just as private employers, comply with these minimum wage requirements. But it cannot be gainsaid that the federal requirement directly supplants the considered policy choices of the States' elected officials and administrators as to how they wish to structure pay scales in state employment. The State might wish to employ persons with little or no training, or those who wish to work on a casual basis, or those who for some other reason do not possess minimum employment requirements, and pay them less than the federally prescribed minimum wage. It may wish to offer part-time or summer employment to teenagers at a figure less than the minimum wage, and if unable to do so may decline to offer such employment at all. But the Act would forbid such choices by the States. The only "discretion" left to them under the Act is either to attempt to increase their revenue to meet the additional financial burden imposed upon them by paying congressionally prescribed wages to their existing complement of employees, or to reduce that complement to a number which can be paid the federal minimum wage without increasing revenue.

This dilemma presented by the minimum wage restrictions may seem not immediately different from that faced by private employers, who have long been covered by the Act and who must find ways to increase their gross income if they are to pay higher wages while maintaining current earnings. The difference, however, is that a State is not merely a factor in the "shifting economic arrangements" of the private sector of the economy, * * * but is itself a coordinate element in the system established by the Framers for governing our Federal Union.

This congressionally imposed displacement of state decisions may substantially restructure traditional ways in which the local governments have arranged their affairs. Although at this point many of the actual effects under the proposed amendments remain a matter of some dispute among the parties, enough can be satisfactorily anticipated for an outline discussion of their general import. The requirement imposing premium rates upon any employment in excess of what Congress has decided is appropriate for a governmental employee's workweek, for example, appears likely to have the effect of coercing the States to structure work periods in some employment areas, such as police and fire protection, in a manner substantially different from practices which have long been commonly accepted among local governments of this Nation. . . .

Our examination of the effect of the 1974 amendments, as sought to be extended to the States and their political subdivisions, satisfies us that both the minimum wage and the maximum hour provisions will impermissibly interfere with the integral governmental functions of these bodies. . . . If Congress may withdraw from the States the authority to make those fundamental employment decisions upon which their systems for performance of these functions must rest, we think there would be little left of the States' "'separate and independent existence.'" * * * Thus, even if appellants may have overestimated the effect which the Act will have upon their current levels and patterns of governmental activity, the dispositive factor is that Congress has attempted to exercise its Commerce Clause authority to prescribe minimum wages and maximum hours to be paid by the States in their capacities as sovereign governments. In so doing, Congress has sought to wield its power in a fashion that would impair the States' "ability to function effectively in a federal system." * * * This exercise of congressional authority does not comport with the federal system of government embodied in the Constitution. We hold that insofar as the challenged amendments operate to directly displace the States' freedom to structure integral operations in areas of traditional governmental functions, they are not within the authority granted Congress by Art I, § 8, cl 3.

· · ·

The judgment of the District Court is accordingly reversed and the case is remanded for further proceedings consistent with this opinion.

Mr. Justice Blackmun, concurring. [Omitted.]

Mr. Justice Brennan, with whom Mr. Justice White and Mr. Justice Marshall join, dissenting.

. . .

My Brethren do not successfully obscure today's patent usurpation of the role reserved for the political process by their purported discovery in the Constitution of a restraint derived from sovereignty of the States on Congress' exercise of the commerce power. . . . [T]here is no restraint based on state sovereignty requiring or permitting judicial enforcement anywhere expressed in the Constitution; our decisions over the last century and a half have explicitly rejected the existence of any such restraint on the commerce power.

. . .

My Brethren have today manufactured an abstraction without substance, founded neither in the words of the Constitution nor on precedent. An abstraction having such profoundly pernicious consequences is not made less so by characterizing the 1974 amendments as legislation directed against the "States qua States." * * * . . .

The reliance of my Brethren upon the Tenth Amendment as "an express declaration of [a state sovereignty] limitation" * * * not only suggests that they overrule governing decisions of this Court that address this question but must astound scholars of the Constitution. . . . [A]s the Tenth Amendment's significance was summarized:

> "The amendment states but a truism that all is retained which has not been surrendered. *There is nothing in the history of its adoption to suggest that it was more than declaratory of the relationship between the national and state governments as it had been established by the Constitution before the amendment* or that its purpose was other than to allay fears that the new national government might seek to exercise powers not granted, and that the states might not be able to exercise fully their reserved powers. . . .
>
> "From the beginning and for many years the amendment has been construed as not depriving the national government of authority to resort to all means for the exercise of a granted power which are appropriate and plainly adapted to the permitted end." * * * (emphasis added)

. . .

Today's repudiation of [an] unbroken line of precedents that firmly reject my Brethren's ill-conceived abstraction can only be regarded as a transparent cover for invalidating a congressional judgment with which they disagree. The only analysis even remotely resembling that adopted today is found in a line of opinions dealing with the Commerce Clause and the Tenth Amendment that ultimately provoked a constitutional crisis for the Court in the 1930's. * * * We tend to forget that the Court invalidated legislation during the Great Depression, not solely under the Due Process Clause, but also and primarily under the Commerce Clause and the Tenth Amendment. It may have been the eventual abandonment of that overly restrictive construction of the commerce power that spelled defeat for the Court-packing plan, and preserved the integrity of this institution, . . . but my Brethren today are transparently trying to cut back on that recognition of the scope of the commerce power.

• • •

My Brethren do more than turn aside longstanding constitutional jurisprudence that emphatically rejects today's conclusion. More alarming is the startling restructuring of our federal system, and the role they create therein for the federal judiciary. This Court is simply not at liberty to erect a mirror of its own conception of a desirable governmental structure. If the 1974 amendments have any "vice," * * * my Brother Stevens is surely right that it represents "merely . . . a policy issue which has been firmly resolved by the branches of government having power to decide such questions." * * * It bears repeating "that effective restraints on . . . exercise [of the commerce power] must proceed from political rather than from judicial processes." * * *

It is unacceptable that the judicial process should be thought superior to the political process in this area. Under the Constitution the Judiciary has no role to play beyond finding that Congress has not made an unreasonable legislative judgment respecting what is "commerce." . . .

Judicial restraint in this area merely recognizes that the political branches of our Government are structured to protect the interests of the States, as well as the Nation as a whole, and that the States are fully able to protect their own interests in the premises. Congress is constituted of representatives in both the Senate and House elected from the States. * * * Decisions upon the extent of federal intervention under the Commerce Clause into the affairs of the States are in that sense decisions of the States themselves. Judicial redistribution of powers granted the National Government by the terms of the Constitution violates the fundamental tenet of our federalism that the extent of federal intervention into the States' affairs in the exercise of delegated powers shall be determined by the States' exercise of political power through their representatives in Congress. * * * . . . Any realistic assessment of our federal political system, dominated as it is by representatives of the people *elected from the States,* yields the conclusion that it is highly unlikely that those representatives will ever be motivated to disregard totally the concerns of these States. * * *

• • •

We are left with a catastrophic judicial body blow at Congress' power under the Commerce Clause. Even if Congress may nevertheless accomplish its objectives—for example, by conditioning grants of federal funds upon compliance with federal minimum wage and overtime standards * * * —there is an ominous portent of disruption of our constitutional structure implicit in today's mischievous decision. I dissent.

MR. JUSTICE STEVENS, dissenting.

The Court holds that the Federal Government may not interfere with a sovereign State's inherent right to pay a substandard wage to the janitor at the state capitol. The principle on which the holding rests is difficult to perceive.

The Federal Government may, I believe, require the State to act impartially when it hires or fires the janitor, to withhold taxes from his paycheck, to observe safety regulations when he is performing his job, to forbid him from burning too much soft coal in the capitol furnace, from dumping untreated refuse in an adjacent waterway, from overloading a state-owned garbage truck, or from driving either the truck or the governor's limousine over 55 miles an hour. Even though these and many other activities of the capitol janitor are activities of the State qua State, I have no doubt that they are subject to federal regulation.

• • •

My disagreement with the wisdom of this legislation may not, of course, affect my judgment with respect to its validity. On this issue there is no dissent from the proposition that the Federal Government's power over the labor market is adequate to embrace these employees. Since I am unable to identify a limitation on that federal power that would not also invalidate federal regulation of state activities that I consider unquestionably permissible, I am persuaded that this statute is valid. Accordingly, with respect and a great deal of sympathy for the views expressed by the Court, I dissent from its constitutional holding.

Pennsylvania v. Nelson

350 U.S. 497 (1956)

MR. CHIEF JUSTICE WARREN delivered the opinion of the Court.

. . . Steve Nelson, an acknowledged member of the Communist Party, was convicted in the Court of Quarter Sessions of Allegheny County, Pennsylvania, of a violation of the Pennsylvania Sedition Act and sentenced to imprisonment for twenty years and to a fine of $10,000 and to costs of prosecution in the sum of $13,000. The Superior Court affirmed the conviction. * * * The Supreme Court of Pennsylvania, . . . decided the case on the narrow issue of supersession of the state law by the Federal Smith Act. . . .

The precise holding of the court, and all that is before us for review, is that the Smith Act of 1940, as amended in 1948, which prohibits the knowing advocacy of the overthrow of the Government of the United States by force and violence, supersedes the enforceability of the Pennsylvania Sedition Act which proscribes the same conduct.

· · ·

It should be said at the outset that the decision in this case does not affect the right of States to enforce their sedition laws at times when the Federal Government has not occupied the field and is not protecting the entire country from seditious conduct. . . . Nor does it limit the jurisdiction of the States where the Constitution and Congress have specifically given them concurrent jurisdiction, as was done under the Eighteenth Amendment and the Volstead Act [Prohibition]. * * * Neither does it limit the right of the State to protect itself at any time against sabotage or attempted violence of all kinds. Nor does it prevent the State from prosecuting where the same act constitutes both a federal offense and a state offense under the police power. . . .

Where . . . Congress has not stated specifically whether a federal statute has occupied a field in which the States are otherwise free to legislate, different criteria have furnished touchstones for decision. . . .

· · ·

First, "[t]he scheme of federal regulation [is] so pervasive as to make reasonable the inference that Congress left no room for the States to supplement it." * * * The Congress determined in 1940 that it was necessary for it to re-enter the field of antisubversive legislation, which had been abandoned by it in 1921. In that year, it enacted the Smith Act which proscribes advocacy of the overthrow of any government—federal, state or local—by force and violence and organization of and knowing membership in a group which so advocates. Conspiracy to commit any of these acts is punishable under the general criminal conspiracy provisions. * * * The Internal Security Act of 1950 is aimed more directly at Communist organizations. It distinguishes between "Communist-action organizations" and "Communist-front organizations," requiring such organizations to register and to file annual reports with the Attorney General giving complete details as to their officers and funds. Members of Communist-action organizations who have not been registered by their organization must register as individuals. Failure to register . . . is punishable by a fine of not more than $10,000 for an offending organization and by a fine of not more than $10,000 or imprisonment for not more than five years or both for an individual offender—each day of failure to register constituting a separate offense. And the Act imposes certain sanctions upon both "action" and "front" organizations and their members. The Communist Control Act of 1954 declares "that the Communist Party of the

United States, although purportedly a political party, is in fact an instrumental-ity of a conspiracy to overthrow the Government of the United States" and that "its role as the agency of a hostile foreign power renders its existence a clear present and continuing danger to the security of the United States." It also contains a legislative finding that the Communist Party is a "Communist-action organization" within the meaning of the Internal Security Act of 1950 and pro-vides that "knowing" members of the Communist Party are "subject to all the provisions and penalties" of that Act. It furthermore sets up a new classification of "Communist-infiltrated organizations" and provides for the imposition of sanctions against them.

We examine these Acts only to determine the congressional plan. Looking to all of them in the aggregate, the conclusion is inescapable that Congress has intended to occupy the field of sedition. Taken as a whole, they evince a congres-sional plan which makes it reasonable to determine that no room has been left for the States to supplement it. Therefore, a state sedition statute is superseded regardless of whether it purports to supplement the federal law. . . .

Second, the federal statutes "touch a field in which the federal interest is so dominant that the federal system [must] be assumed to preclude enforcement of state laws on the same subject." * * * Congress has devised an all-embracing program for resistance to the various forms of totalitarian aggression. Our exter-nal defenses have been strengthened, and a plan to protect against internal subversion has been made by it. It has appropriated vast sums, not only for our own protection, but also to strengthen freedom throughout the world. It has charged the Federal Bureau of Investigation and the Central Intelligence Agency with responsibility for intelligence concerning Communist seditious ac-tivities against our Government, and has denominated such activities as part of a world conspiracy. It accordingly proscribed sedition against all government in the nation—national, state and local. Congress declared that these steps were taken "to provide for the common defense, to preserve the sovereignty of the United States as an independent nation, and to guarantee to each State a repub-lican form of government . . . ." Congress having thus treated seditious conduct as a matter of vital national concern, it is in no sense a local enforcement problem. . . .

Third, enforcement of state sedition acts presents a serious danger of conflict with the administration of the federal program. Since 1939, in order to avoid a hampering of uniform enforcement of its program by sporadic local prosecutions, the Federal Government has urged local authorities not to intervene in such matters, but to turn over to the federal authorities immediately and unevaluated all information concerning subversive activities. . . .

· · ·

. . . [T]he Pennsylvania statute presents a peculiar danger of interference with the federal program. For, as the court below observed:

"Unlike the Smith Act, which can be administered only by federal officers acting in their official capacities, indictment for sedition under the Pennsylvania statute can be initiated upon an information made by a private individual. The opportunity thus present for the indulgence of personal spite and hatred or for furthering some selfish advantage or ambition need only be mentioned to be appreciated. Defense of the Nation by law, no less than by arms, should be a public and not a private undertaking. . . ."

In his brief, the Solicitor General states that forty-two States plus Alaska and Hawaii have statutes which in some form prohibit advocacy of the violent overthrow of established government. These statutes are entitled anti-sedition statutes, criminal anarchy laws, criminal syndicalist laws, etc. Although all of them are primarily directed against the overthrow of the United States Government, they are in no sense uniform. And our attention has not been called to any case where the prosecution has been successfully directed against an attempt to destroy state or local government. Some of these Acts are studiously drawn and purport to protect fundamental rights by appropriate definitions, standards of proof and orderly procedures in keeping with the avowed congressional purpose "to protect freedom from those who would destroy it, without infringing upon the freedom of all our people." Others are vague and are almost wholly without such safeguards. Some even purport to punish mere membership in subversive organizations which the federal statutes do not punish where federal registration requirements have been fulfilled.

* * *

Should the States be permitted to exercise a concurrent jurisdiction in this area, federal enforcement would encounter . . . conflict engendered by different criteria of substantive offenses.

Since we find that Congress has occupied the field to the exclusion of parallel state legislation, that the dominant interest of the Federal Government precludes state intervention, and that administration of state Acts would conflict with the operation of the federal plan, we are convinced that the decision of the Supreme Court of Pennsylvania is unassailable.

* * *

The judgment of the Supreme Court of Pennsylvania is

Affirmed.

Mr. Justice Reed, with whom Mr. Justice Burton and Mr. Justice Minton join, dissenting.

The problems of governmental power may be approached in this case free from the varied viewpoints that focus on the problems of national security. This is a jurisdictional problem of general importance because it involves an asserted limitation on the police power of the States when it is applied to a crime that is punishable also by the Federal Government. As this is a recurring problem, it is appropriate to explain our dissent.

Congress has not, in any of its statutes relating to sedition, specifically barred the exercise of state power to punish the same Acts under state law. . . .

•   •   •

We cannot agree that the federal criminal sanctions against sedition directed at the United States are of such a pervasive character as to indicate an intention to void state action.

. . . [T]he Court states that the federal sedition statutes touch a field "in which the federal interest is so dominant" they must preclude state laws on the same subject.

We look upon the Smith Act as a provision for controlling incitements to overthrow by force and violence the Nation, or any State, or any political subdivision of either. Such an exercise of federal police power carries, we think, no such dominancy over similar state powers as might be attributed to continuing federal regulations concerning foreign affairs or coinage, for example. In the responsibility of national and local governments to protect themselves against sedition, there is no "dominant interest."

We are citizens of the United States and of the State wherein we reside and are dependent upon the strength of both to preserve our rights and liberties. . . .

. . . [T]he Court finds ground for abrogating Pennsylvania's anti-sedition statute because, in the Court's view, the State's administration of the Act may hamper the enforcement of the federal law. . . .

•   •   •

Mere fear by courts of possible difficulties does not seem to us in these circumstances a valid reason for ousting a State from exercise of its police power. Those are matters for legislative determination. . . .

Finally, . . . there is an independent reason for reversing the Pennsylvania Supreme Court. The Smith Act appears in Title 18 of the United States Code, which . . . provides:

"Nothing in this title shall be held to take away or impair the jurisdiction of the courts of several States under the laws thereof."

That declaration springs from the federal character of our Nation. It recognizes the fact that maintenance of order and fairness rests primarily with the States. . . . This Court has interpreted the section to mean that States may provide concurrent legislation in the absence of explicit congressional intent to the contrary. * * * The majority's position in this case cannot be reconciled with that clear authorization of Congress.

The law stands against any advocacy of violence to change established governments. Freedom of speech allows full play to the processes of reason. The state and national legislative bodies have legislated within constitutional limits so as to allow the widest participation by the law enforcement officers of the respective governments. The individual States were not told that they are powerless to punish local acts of sedition, nominally directed against the United States. Courts should not interfere. We would reverse the judgment of the Supreme Court of Pennsylvania.

CHAPTER 10

State Power to Regulate Commerce

INTRODUCTORY ESSAY

The power of Congress to regulate commerce "among the states" is vast but far from exclusive. Constitutional language granting this power is general and open-ended. One of the Supreme Court's most important responsibilities has been to interpret how this broad language relates to the exercise of state power in an endless variety of regulatory settings. No definitive rulings fixing the limits of state authority or the exact point of demarcation between national and state power to regulate commerce have emerged. The process of constitutional interpretation is heavily influenced by changes in the perceived needs and interests of society; and this fact is nowhere better illustrated than in the regulation of commerce. Cases in this area also vividly illustrate the Court's vital function in policing the boundaries of the federal system.

Commerce Clause and the Federal Relationship

The Commerce Clause, as drafted in 1787, represented an attempt to address some of the problems faced by a growing national economy beset with commercial rivalries among largely independent states in a weak confederation. But the affirmative grant of power to Congress was not accompanied by an explicit negation of state power. Although restricting the state power to tax imports and exports (unless that power is authorized by Congress), the Constitution is silent on the nature and extent of state power to regulate commerce. We know that some of the Framers of the Constitution, including Madison, assumed that the commerce power was indivisible—that it was an exclusive grant to the national government, which by implication barred all state action in this field. But experience coupled with the principle of federalism soon made it apparent that this inflexible position was untenable. Nevertheless, it was clear that even in the absence of specific language, the Commerce Clause placed substantial *implied* limits on state power. Over the years those limits have been defined and redefined, not only by Supreme Court decisions but also by the exercise of a congressional power that has traditionally been accorded wide scope in this field.

By applying the Commerce and Supremacy Clauses simultaneously in *Gibbons v. Ogden,* 9 Wheat. 1 (1824), Chief Justice Marshall was able to draw the logical conclusion that an exercise of the commerce power by Congress must prevail over conflicting state legislation. The power of Congress to regulate commerce among the states was plenary; it could be defined by Congress and was subject to no limitations within the Commerce Clause per se. Any restrictions on the power must be derived from other parts of the Constitution, such as the Tenth Amendment and the Due Process Clause, neither of which was deemed applicable in this case.

But suppose Congress has not acted on a matter covered by state legislation in the commerce field. Or suppose state action merely complements existing national policy. Under such circumstances are the states free to act, even if such action has an impact on interstate commerce? The answer to this question is a carefully qualified *yes*—if certain prerequisites are met. The cases presented in this chapter highlight some of the most important and enduring of these prerequisites. They indicate the complex and sometimes inconsistently applied criteria by which the Supreme Court distinguishes between constitutional and unconstitutional state regulation of commerce. These cases also reveal the difficulty of the Court's task in balancing the competing needs of a huge national economy and a decentralized political system in a society demanding both governmental regulation and constitutional rights.

Origins of State Power to Regulate Commerce

In *Gibbons v. Ogden,* it was not necessary for Marshall to deal directly with the scope of state power to regulate commerce. As noted in Chapter 5, the congressional act under which Gibbons was licensed to engage in commercial navigation superseded the steamboat monopoly granted by New York. Marshall acknowledged that the states retained the power to regulate their "completely internal commerce." He also conceded that the states could exercise a broad police power to protect the health and safety of their citizens. But he stopped short of recognizing explicitly that this amounted to a concurrent power to regulate interstate commerce, which the states shared with Congress. Nor did he find it necessary to distinguish precisely between "domestic trade," which a state was free to regulate, and "that commerce which concerns more States than one."

The Supreme Court did not resolve this issue in a formal decision until 1852. Before that time the Court had upheld various state laws directly or indirectly affecting interstate commerce, ruling that they were appropriate exercises of the police power to protect public health, safety, and morality or to promote the general welfare (*Willson v. Blackbird Creek Marsh Co.,* 2 Pet. 245 [1829]; *New York v. Miln,* 11 Pet. 102 [1837]). But the concept of interstate commerce was too all-embracing and the demand for state regulatory activity too strong for the Court to avoid the issue indefinitely. Ultimately it reached the Taney Court in *Cooley v. Board of Wardens,* 12 How. 299 (1852). Justice Benjamin R. Curtis wrote the opinion of the Court, recognizing that the Commerce Clause did not automatically bar all state regulation in this field. At issue was the constitutionality of a Pennsylvania law requiring ships entering or leaving the port of Philadelphia to hire local pilots. This was admittedly a regulation of both interstate and foreign commerce. Nevertheless, it was upheld because it dealt with a "subject" of commerce "imperatively demanding that diversity, which alone can meet the local necessities of navigation." Curtis reasoned that the term commerce covered a multitude of subjects, some requiring national uniformity in their regulation, others calling for the diversity of local control. Since the Constitution did not explicitly prohibit the states from regulating and since Congress in 1789 had purported to authorize state regulation of pilots, he concluded that the law in question was valid. This distinction between local and national aspects of interstate commerce, although far from clear-cut, was a significant addition to constitutional interpretation. Although its application in *Cooley* was expressly limited to the facts of the case, the principle applied soon achieved the status of constitutional doctrine. The Court's attempt to strike a balance between the values of local diversity and those of national uniformity has been apparent in hundreds of decisions since *Cooley*. The Justices have come to use more sophisticated terminology than the local–national dichotomy employed by Curtis. But his perception of the complexity of commerce and the problem of promoting it through regulations appropriate to a federal system remains important to this day.

Elements of dual federalism, emphasizing the relative autonomy of state and national governments, were evident in the *Cooley* doctrine. These factors became even more apparent during the so-called laissez-faire era beginning in the late 1880s and culminating in the late 1930s. During this period dual federalism assumed, more so than before or since, a negative aspect, revealed by the Court's tendency to restrict each sphere of government by invoking the prerogatives of the other. As we have seen, the Court began to use the Tenth Amendment, sometimes in combination with the concept of substantive due process, as justification for limiting the scope of national power to regulate commerce (*United States* v. *E. C. Knight Co.,* 156 U.S. 1 [1895]; *Hammer* v. *Dagenhart,* 247 U.S. 251 [1918]). At the same time it found constitutional support for restricting state regulation as well, even when it extended only to *intrastate* commercial activity.

Thus in *Wabash, St. Louis, and Pacific Railway Co.* v. *Illinois,* 118 U.S. 557 (1886), the Court held that an Illinois regulation of railway rates charged to in-state customers for goods brought from or destined to other states was a violation of the Commerce Clause. It reached this conclusion even though Congress had not legislated on the matter. Clearly the absence of national legislation covering a given subject of commerce was no guarantee that state legislation dealing with that subject would be upheld. This point was clearly implicit in the *Cooley* decision with its distinction between national and local "subjects" of commerce, but it was somewhat obscured by the presence of congressional legislation approving the requirement for ship pilots at issue there. In decisions such as the *Wabash* case, however, the Court drove home the point that congressional silence was not the principal criterion for assessing the constitutionality of state action. Nonetheless, the immediate congressional response to the *Wabash* decision was passage of the Interstate Commerce Act and creation of the Interstate Commerce Commission in 1887.

Even during this period, the Court was willing to defer to the express intent of Congress to leave a subject to state regulation. For example, in August 1890, Congress reacted negatively to a Supreme Court decision handed down three months earlier invalidating an Iowa prohibition law that banned the sale of alcoholic beverages imported from other states. Invoking the "original package doctrine" (see Chapter II) the Court had held that in the absence of congressional permission, Iowa lacked constitutional authority to interfere with the importation and sale of beer by an Illinois brewer (*Leisy* v. *Hardin,* 135 U.S. 100 [1890]). Through passage of the Wilson Act, Congress granted this permission by abolishing the exemption of imported liquor from the police power of the states. The following year the Supreme Court unanimously sustained this legislation by upholding the application of a Kansas prohibition statute to liquor imported from another state (*In re Rahrer,* 140 U.S. 545 [1891]). In 1894 the Court also sustained a Massachusetts prohibition against the manufacture or sale of oleomargarine colored to look like butter. On this occasion, the silence of Congress was interpreted as *consent* rather than opposition to state regulation (*Plumley* v. *Massachusetts,* 155 U.S. 461 [1894]). The Court's ambivalence in ascertaining the meaning of congressional silence in the commerce field prompted Thomas Reed Powell, in a memorable caricature of the process of constitutional interpretation, to distinguish between that silence which is "silent," thereby permitting state regulation, and that silence which is "vocal," and "says that the commerce must be free from state regulation" (Powell, 1937, pp. 338–339).

Tangled Threads of Interpretation

Except for the Court's general inclination to take a more critical view of economic regulation between the mid-1880s and the late 1930s, no consistent historical pattern has emerged in this field since the *Cooley* case. From time to time the Court has attempted to classify state regulations with respect to their "direct" or "indirect" effect upon interstate commerce or the degree to which they "burden" or "discriminate" against it. The "direct-indirect" test has not been in vogue since the late 1930s; but even when it was employed, the Court seemed more concerned about the basic distinction between commerce regulations per se and police power legislation aimed at protecting the health, safety, and general welfare of the community. The Court has become less concerned than was Justice Curtis in the *Cooley* case with the *subject* of commerce being regulated and more concerned with the *means* by which the regulation is implemented. Professor Laurence H. Tribe has aptly described the pragmatic approach that the modern Supreme Court is most likely to follow: "State regulation affecting interstate commerce will be upheld if (a) the regulation is rationally related to a legitimate state end, and (b) the regulatory burden imposed on interstate commerce, and any discrimination against it, are outweighed by the state interest in enforcing the regulation" (Tribe, 1978, p. 326).

This approach has produced results in different cases that are plainly irreconcilable. For instance, in *Southern Pacific Co.* v. *Arizona,* 325 U.S. 761 (1945), the Court invalidated a law limiting the lengths of passenger and freight trains traveling through the state to fourteen and seventy cars respectively. The regulation imposed a substantial burden on interstate commerce, but Arizona defended it as an appropriate safety measure and pointed to the absence of conflicting national legislation on the subject. The Supreme Court, in a divided decision, declared the law unconstitutional. In his opinion for the majority, Chief Justice Stone concluded that "as a safety measure," the law afforded "slight and dubious advantage, if any, over unregulated train lengths." Accordingly, the "serious burden" imposed on interstate commerce was not justified. On the other hand, before this decision the Court had upheld a number of railroad safety measures adopted by the states, including Arkansas' "full crew" laws. These regulations fixed the minimum number of employees required to serve on trains traveling designated distances within the state. The statutes were again sustained more than twenty years after the *Southern Pacific* decision, even though they were no longer clearly appropriate as safety measures. As enacted in 1903 and 1907, they included the requirement of a fireman on each train. By 1968 coal-burning steam engines had been replaced by diesel power, and the continued requirement of a fireman was justified, if at all, only by the consideration of providing local employment. Nevertheless, the Court in an opinion by Justice Black, who had dissented in *Southern Pacific Co.* v. *Arizona,* was willing to defer to state policy. Even if the laws were no longer justifiable as safety measures, Black maintained that it was up to the legislature, not the Court, to change them (*Brotherhood of Locomotive Engineers* v. *Chicago, Rock Island, & Pacific Railroad Co.,* 382 U.S. 423 [1966]).

In the 1938 case of *South Carolina Highway Department* v. *Barnwell,* 303 U.S. 177, the Court sustained a South Carolina statute prescribing maximum weights and widths of trucks using the highways of the state. This measure imposed a substantial burden on interstate commerce, but the Court, through Justice Stone, reasoned that the countervailing safety considerations were more important. Stone pointed to the extensive control that states had traditionally exerted over their public roads (a point that he stressed seven years later in attempting to distinguish the railroad regulation struck down in *Southern Pacific* from the South Carolina restriction). He also pointed out that the highway regulation fell with equal weight on intrastate and interstate truckers—that it did not, in other words, single out businesses engaged in interstate commerce and impose added burdens on them to the advantage of intrastate economic interests. Still, the decision depended heavily on a view of state autonomy in building, maintaining, and controlling highways that was debatable even in 1938 and is open to far more serious challenge now that a nationally subsidized interstate highway system is a reality.

Commerce Clause as a Check on Localism

Any state regulation of interstate commerce aimed squarely at promoting local business interests by curtailing competition from out-of-state firms is unlikely to survive a constitutional challenge that reaches the Supreme Court. Those who drafted the Commerce Clause recognized the importance of promoting a national economy in the United States, and successive generations of Justices have not lost sight of that objective. The 1949 decision in *Hood & Sons* v. *DuMond,* 336 U.S. 525, provides a good illustration of this point. The Supreme Court invalidated a New York administrative decision denying Hood, a Massachusetts corporation, permission to enlarge from three to four the number of milk processing plants that it operated in New York. Writing for the majority, Justice Jackson viewed this limitation on Hood's base of supply as a form of economic isolation that the state was not free to impose. It made no difference in principle that New York placed a ceiling, rather than an absolute ban, on Hood's activities within the state. "Our system, fostered by the Commerce Clause," he asserted, "is that every farmer and every craftsman shall be encouraged to produce by the certainty that he will have free access to every market in the Nation." While this language suggests a bucolic utopia far removed from the experience of American farmers in the twentieth century—perhaps even in the eighteenth—Jackson's emphasis on the *national* economic unit is in the mainstream of constitutional development. Here, as in the *Southern Pacific* case, the absence of national legislation on the matter at issue was not the controlling factor. The state had acted simply to protect local interest, and that action, the Court found, was inconsistent with the negative implications of the Commerce Clause.

In the 1978 case of *Philadelphia* v. *New Jersey*, 437 U.S. 617, the Supreme Court invalidated a state law prohibiting the importation of most solid and liquid wastes from other states. Brushing aside the alleged environmental dangers posed by overuse of New Jersey's limited landfill space, the Court, through Justice Stewart, concluded that however justifiable the objectives of the law might be, the method employed to achieve them could not discriminate against articles of interstate commerce "unless there is some reason, apart from their origin, to treat them differently." The Court saw this attempt to bar out-of-state access to New Jersey's privately owned landfill sites while leaving them open to in-state users as simply another example of "parochial legislation" tending to promote state economic protectionism at the expense of national interests. The problem of preserving adequate landfill space was by no means unique to New Jersey. And yet the state was attempting through this legislation "to isolate itself from a problem common to many by erecting a barrier against the movement of interstate trade."

In a strongly worded dissent, Justice Rehnquist, joined by Chief Justice Burger, accused the majority of presenting New Jersey with a "Hobson's choice" (a choice without alternatives). It would be forced either to curb all landfill operations within the state and come up with some "presently nonexistent solution" for disposing of its own waste or to accept waste from every part of the country. He maintained that the majority was departing from a long line of precedents that had repeatedly recognized the state's authority to protect its citizens against serious health hazards. If New Jersey could prohibit the importation of "diseased meat" or "germ-infested rags," as these precedents indicated, the state should surely be permitted to exclude solid and liquid waste generated outside its borders. He refused to treat the issue as one of economic isolation, insisting that New Jersey was faced with a serious practical problem that, in the interest of public health, justified adopting different policies regarding landfill use by in-state and out-of-state waste producers. It did not follow that because New Jersey "must somehow dispose of its own noxious items," it must also "serve as a depository for those of every other state." The divergent priorities stressed in the majority and dissenting opinions suggest the great variety of factors that can enter into the Court's efforts to balance contending interests in the commerce field.

As the majority opinion in *Philadelphia* v. *New Jersey* indicates, the Court is unlikely to permit a state to conserve its privately controlled natural resources if the conservation effort accords preferential treatment to local consumers. In a 1923 decision the Court invalidated a West Virginia law requiring local natural gas producers to give priority to the orders of in-state, as opposed to out-of-state, customers (*Pennsylvania* v. *West Virginia*, 262 U.S. 553). A state can, of course, assume ownership and direct control of its natural resources without violating the Commerce Clause. But if it seeks to regulate privately owned businesses, even those engaged in the sale of scarce natural resources, the Court is almost certain to condemn any economic policies that result in local favoritism.

Until recently the Court recognized an exception to this general restriction by permitting the states to exercise broad control over the out-of-state shipment of wild animals and fish for commercial sale. But in *Hughes* v. *Oklahoma*, 60 L. Ed. 2d 250 (1979), this exception was abolished. At issue was the constitutionality of a statute providing that Oklahoma minnows, other than those produced in licensed hatcheries, could not be sold outside the state. The law was apparently designed to protect the state's "natural" minnow population. Overruling *Geer* v. *Connecticut*, 161 U.S. 519 (1896), the Court concluded that "challenges under the Commerce Clause to state regulations of wild animals should be considered according to the same general rule applied to state regulations of other natural resources." Writing for the majority, Justice Brennan acknowledged the states' "interests in conservation and protection of wild animals as legitimate local purposes similar to the states' interests in protecting the health and safety of their citizens." In this case, however, these interests did not justify Oklahoma's overt discrimination against interstate commerce. The statute placed "no limits on the numbers of minnows that [could] be taken by licensed minnow dealers," nor did it limit the way in which minnows could be disposed of within the state. The statute simply forbade "the transportation of any commercially significant number of natural minnows . . . out of the state for sale." According to the Court, Oklahoma had chosen "the most discriminatory means even though nondiscriminatory alternatives would seem likely to fulfill the state's purported legitimate local purpose more effectively." State efforts to protect wildlife therefore must be consistent with the principle that "our economic unit is the nation" (*Hood & Sons* v. *DuMond*).

In a dissenting opinion Justice Rehnquist, joined by Chief Justice Burger, conceded that the Oklahoma statutory scheme at issue might not have been "the most artfully designed to accomplish its purpose." Still, he insisted, the range of regulations available to the state was "extremely broad, particularly where, as here, the burden on interstate commerce [was], at most, minimal." He concluded that any minimal burden imposed by requiring that minnows to be sold out of state be purchased from hatcheries was "more than outweighed by Oklahoma's substantial interest in conserving and regulating exploitation of its natural minnow supply."

The Court has been equally skeptical of state regulations that pressure out-of-state businesses into moving the center of their operations to the regulating state. Even when such coercive measures are defended as legitimate health measures, the Court is not easily convinced. In *Dean Milk Co.* v. *Madison*, 340 U.S. 349 (1951), for instance, the Court struck down a purported local health ordinance prohibiting the sale of milk if it came from a farm more than twenty-five miles from Madison,

Wisconsin, or was bottled more than five miles away from the central square of the city. Clearly this measure discriminated against interstate commerce, something that the Court was unwilling to condone, even for health purposes, if "reasonable, nondiscriminatory alternatives, adequate to conserve legitimate local interests" were available. In this instance the Court believed that such alternatives could be found.

Similarly, in 1976 the Court struck down a Mississippi regulation under which the Board of Health prohibited the sale of milk from another state, unless Mississippi milk could be marketed there. The mandatory nature of this reciprocity was held to be an undue burden on interstate commerce and was not justified either as a health measure or as a provision promoting free trade among the states (*Great Atlantic & Pacific Tea Co.* v. *Cottrell*, 424 U.S. 366).

Commerce Clause and the Preemption Doctrine

A broad commitment to national considerations is also evident in the Court's frequent application of the "preemption doctrine" to state regulation of interstate commerce (discussed more fully in Chapter 9). *Burbank* v. *Lockheed Air Terminal*, 411 U.S. 624 (1973), illustrates this tendency. By a 5 to 4 vote the Court held that an aircraft noise abatement ordinance passed by the City Council was preempted by the Federal Noise Control Act of 1972, even though the latter contained no specific preemptive language and there was no evidence that the ordinance placed a heavy burden on interstate commerce. Relying chiefly on the Supremacy Clause, Douglas emphasized the potential safety hazards that could result if a "significant number of municipalities" adopted similar ordinances. The Noise Control Act established a "comprehensive scheme" of aircraft noise regulation, including involvement of the Environmental Protection Agency. It was the "pervasive nature" of this federal regulatory pattern that preempted the Burbank ordinance. Justice Rehnquist, joined by Justices Stewart, White, and Marshall, dissented. He cited the stated intention of Congress in passing the 1972 law not to "alter the balance between state and federal regulation" struck by such earlier measures as the Federal Aviation Act of 1958. This legislation had been drafted with a view toward the continuation of the extensive regulatory power over aircraft noise that state and local governments had traditionally exercised. The dissenters cited considerations of federalism in support of their view that the ordinance should be upheld. They maintained that the "basic constitutional division of legislative competence between the states and Congress" was consistent with democratic values and that this principle should be followed here. They preferred to view this ordinance as a routine exercise of the police power and thought that the inquiry should be confined to the facts of the case, unaffected by speculation about the possible effect of such an ordinance if adopted by other cities. A majority of the Court gave greater weight, however, to the promotion of perceived national interests.

State Promotion of Noneconomic Objectives

The Court has upheld state regulations designed to promote chiefly noneconomic objectives consistent with the police power, even when the regulations would inhibit economic competition. The question is one of degree. If the Court consid-

ers the purpose served by the regulation important and the interference with competition incidental, it will sustain it. For example, in a recent case, a sharply divided
Court upheld a Maryland law authorizing the state to pay a bounty to junk processors for the hulks of abandoned automobiles (*Hughes* v. *Alexandria Scrap Corp.,*
426 U.S. 794 [1976]). To receive the bounty, a dealer had to furnish documentation
of title. However, the documentation requirements were stiffer for out-of-state
processors. A Virginia processor challenged the law as a violation of both the
Commerce Clause and the Equal Protection Clause. (We are concerned here only
with the commerce issue.) Justice Powell, writing for the majority, conceded that
the law had the practical effect of channeling economic benefits to in-state processors. Nevertheless, he concluded: "Nothing in the purposes animating the Commerce Clause forbids a state, in the absence of congressional action, from
participating in the market and exercising the right to favor its own citizens over
others." In a dissenting opinion, Justice Brennan, joined by Justices White and
Marshall, denied that this law differed from the kind of "economic protectionism"
struck down in previous cases. He maintained that the Maryland bounty was an
obvious discrimination against interstate commerce.

The foregoing discussion is far from a complete catalog of Commerce Clause
interpretation as applied to state action. This brief overview should nevertheless be
sufficient to indicate the breadth of choice and the variety of alternatives open to
the Court in this field. No single dominant theme emerges, but it seems that the
Court accords priority to two countervailing considerations: encouragement of the
continued growth of a strong national economy; and promotion of state responsibility under the police power to protect the health, safety, and general welfare of
the citizenry. The simultaneous commitments to national unity and local autonomy are apparent in the Court's case-by-case weighing of alternatives under the
Commerce Clause. In the next chapter we shall examine a similar, but conceptually
distinct, process of judicial choice in the field of state taxation.

Cooley v. Board of Wardens

12 How. 299 (1852)

[The controversy that led to this landmark constitutional decision began when
Aaron Cooley violated a Pennsylvania law by first failing to hire pilots and then
refusing to pay pilotage fees on two of his ships at the port of Philadelphia. The
Board of Port Wardens successfully sued him in a local trial court, and this
judgment was affirmed by the Pennsylvania Supreme Court. Cooley brought his
case to the United States Supreme Court, challenging the pilotage law on several
constitutional grounds. The following excerpts from Justice Curtis' majority

opinion deal with the question of whether this law violated the Commerce Clause.]

Mr. Justice Curtis delivered the opinion of the Court.

. . .

That the power to regulate commerce includes the regulation of navigation, we consider settled. And when we look to the nature of the service performed by pilots, to the relations which that service and its compensations bear to navigation between the several States, and between the ports of the United States and foreign countries, we are brought to the conclusion, that the regulation of the qualifications of pilots, of the modes and times of offering and rendering their services, of the responsibilities which shall rest upon them, of the powers they shall possess, of the compensation they may demand, and of the penalties by which their rights and duties may be enforced, do constitute regulations of navigation, and consequently of commerce, within the just meaning of this clause of the Constitution.

The power to regulate navigation is the power to prescribe rules in conformity with which navigation must be carried on. It extends to the persons who conduct it, as well as to the instruments used. Accordingly, the first Congress assembled under the Constitution passed laws, requiring the masters of ships and vessels of the United States to be citizens of the United States, and established many rules for the government and regulation of officers and seamen. * * * These have been from time to time added to and changed, and we are not aware that their validity has been questioned.

Now, a pilot, so far as respects the navigation of the vessel in that part of the voyage which is his pilotage ground, is the temporary master charged with the safety of the vessel and cargo, and of the lives of those on board, and intrusted with command of the crew. He is not only one of the persons engaged in navigation, but he occupies a most important and responsible place among those thus engaged. And if Congress has power to regulate the seamen who assist the pilot in the management of the vessel, a power never denied, we can perceive no valid reason why the pilot should be beyond the reach of the same power. . . .

Nor should it be lost sight of, that this subject of the regulation of pilots and pilotage has an intimate connection with, and an important relation to, the general subject of commerce with foreign nations and among the several States, over which it was one main object of the Constitution to create a national control. Conflicts between the laws of neighboring states, and discriminations favorable or adverse to commerce with particular foreign nations, might be created by state laws regulating pilotage, deeply affecting that equality of commercial rights, and that freedom from state interference, which those who formed the Constitution were so anxious to secure, and which the experience of more than half a century has taught us to value so highly. . . .

. . .

It becomes necessary, to consider whether this law of Pennsylvania, being a regulation of commerce, is valid.

The Act of Congress of the 7th of August, 1789, * * * is as follows:

"That all pilots in the bays, inlets, rivers, harbors, and ports of the United States, shall continue to be regulated in conformity with the existing laws of the States, respectively, wherein such pilots may be, or with such laws as the States may respectively hereafter enact for the purpose, until further legislative provision shall be made by Congress."

If the law of Pennsylvania, now in question, had been in existence at the date of this Act of Congress, we might hold it to have been adopted by Congress, and thus made a law of the United States, and so valid. Because this Act does, in effect, give the force of an Act of Congress, to the then existing state laws on this subject, so long as they should continue unrepealed by the State which enacted them.

But the law on which these actions are founded was not enacted till 1803. What effect, then, can be attributed to so much of the Act of 1789 as declares that pilots shall continue to be regulated in conformity "with such laws as the States may respectively hereafter enact for the purpose, until further legislative provision shall be made by Congress"?

If the States were devested of the power to legislate on this subject by the grant of the commercial power to Congress, it is plain this Act could not confer upon them power thus to legislate. If the Constitution excluded the States from making any law regulating commerce, certainly Congress cannot regrant, or in any manner reconvey to the States that power. . . . [W]e are brought directly and unavoidably to the consideration of the question, whether the grant of the commercial power to Congress, did per se deprive the States of all power to regulate pilots. This question has never been decided by this court, nor, in our judgment, has any case depending upon all the considerations which must govern this one, come before this court. The grant of commercial power to Congress does not contain any terms which expressly exclude the States from exercising an authority over its subject matter. If they are excluded it must be because the nature of the power, thus granted Congress, requires that a similar authority should not exist in the States. If it were conceded on the one side, that the nature of this power, like that to legislate for the District of Columbia, is absolutely and totally repugnant to the existence of similar power in the States, probably no one would deny that the grant of the power to Congress, as effectually and perfectly excludes the States from all future legislation on the subject, as if express words had been used to exclude them. And on the other hand, if it were admitted that the existence of this power in Congress, like the power of taxation, is compatible with the existence of a similar power in the States, then it would be in conformity with the contemporary exposition of the Constitution * * * and with the judicial construction, given from time to time by this court, after the most deliberate consideration, to hold that the mere grant of such a power to Congress, did not imply a prohibition on the States to exercise the same power; that it is not the mere existence of such a power, but its exercise by Congress, which may be incompatible with the exercise of the same power by the States, and that the States may legislate in the absence of congressional regulations. * * *

. . . [W]hen the nature of a power like this is spoken of, when it is said that the nature of the power requires that it should be exercised exclusively by Congress, it must be intended to refer to the subjects of that power, and to say they are of such a nature as to require exclusive legislation by Congress. Now, the power to regulate commerce, embraces a vast field, containing not only many, but exceedingly various subjects, quite unlike in their nature, some imperatively demanding a single uniform rule, operating equally on the commerce of the United States in every port; and some, like the subject now in question, as imperatively demanding that diversity, which alone can meet the local necessities of navigation.

Either absolutely to affirm, or deny, that the nature of this power requires exclusive legislation by Congress, is to lose sight of the nature of the subjects of this power, and to assert concerning all of them, what is really applicable but to a part. Whatever subjects of this power are in their nature national, or admit only of one uniform system, or plan of regulation, may justly be said to be of such a nature as to require exclusive legislation by Congress. That this cannot be affirmed of laws for the regulation of pilots and pilotage is plain. The Act of 1789 contains a clear and authoritative declaration by the first Congress, that the nature of this subject is such, that until Congress should find it necessary to exert its power, it should be left to the legislation of the States; that it is local and not national; that it is likely to be the best provided for; not by one system, or plan of regulations, but by as many as the legislative discretion of the several States should deem applicable to the local peculiarities of the port within their limits.

• • •

It is the opinion of a majority of the court that the mere grant to Congress of the power to regulate commerce, did not deprive the States of power to regulate pilots, and that although Congress has legislated on this subject, its legislation manifests an intention, with a single exception, not to regulate this subject, but to leave its regulation to the several States. To these precise questions, which are all we are called on to decide, this opinion must be understood to be confined. It does not extend to the question what other subjects, under the commercial power, are within the exclusive control of Congress, or may be regulated by the States in the absence of all congressional legislation; nor to the general question how far any regulation of a subject by Congress may be deemed to operate as an exclusion of all legislation by the States upon the same subject. We decide the precise questions before us, upon what we deem sound principles, applicable to this particular subject in the state in which the legislation of Congress has left it. We go no farther.

• • •

We are of opinion that this state law was enacted by virtue of a power, residing in the State to legislate; that it is not in conflict with any law of Congress; that it does not interfere with any system which Congress has established by making regulations, or by intentionally leaving individuals to their own unrestricted action; that this law is therefore valid, and the judgment of the Supreme Court of Pennsylvania in each case must be affirmed.

MESSRS. JUSTICES McLEAN and WAYNE dissented. MR. JUSTICE DANIEL, although he concurred in the judgment of the court, yet dissented from its reasoning.

• • •

MR. JUSTICE DANIEL:

I agree with the majority in their decision, that the judgments of the Supreme Court of Pennsylvania in these cases should be affirmed, though I cannot go with them in the process or argument by which their conclusion has been reached. . . . The true question here is, whether the power to enact pilot laws is appropriate and necessary, or rather most appropriate and necessary to the State or the federal governments. It being conceded that this power has been exercised by the States from their very dawn of existence; that it can be practically and beneficially applied by the local authorities only; it being conceded, as it must be, that the power to pass pilot laws, as such, has not been in any express terms delegated to Congress, and does not necessarily conflict with the right to establish commercial regulations, I am forced to conclude that this is an original and inherent power in the States, and not one to be merely tolerated, or held subject to the sanction of the federal government.

South Carolina Highway Department v. Barnwell

303 U.S. 177 (1938)

MR. JUSTICE STONE delivered the opinion of the Court.

The Act of the General Assembly of South Carolina * * * prohibits use on the state highways of motor trucks and "semi-trailer motor trucks" whose width exceeds 90 inches, and whose weight including load exceeds 20,000 pounds. . . . The principal question for decision is whether these prohibitions impose an unconstitutional burden upon interstate commerce.

• • •

The district court of three judges, after hearing evidence, . . . enjoined the enforcement of the weight provision against interstate motor carriers on the specified highways, and also the width limitation of 90 inches, except in the case of vehicles exceeding 96 inches in width. . . .

The trial court rested its decision that the statute unreasonably burdens interstate commerce, upon findings, not assailed here, that there is a large amount of motor truck traffic passing interstate in the southeastern part of the United States, which would normally pass over the highways of South Carolina, but which will be barred from the state by the challenged restrictions if enforced, and upon its conclusion that, when viewed in the light of their effect upon interstate commerce, these restrictions are unreasonable.

• • •

South Carolina has built its highways and owns and maintains them. It has received from the federal government, in aid of its highway improvements, money grants which have been expended upon the highways to which the injunction applies. . . .

While the constitutional grant to Congress of power to regulate interstate commerce has been held to operate of its own force to curtail state power in some measure, it did not forestall all state action affecting interstate commerce. Ever since Willson v. Black Bird Creek Marsh Co. * * * it has been recognized that there are matters of local concern, the regulation of which unavoidably involves some regulation of interstate commerce but which, because of their local character and their number and diversity, may never be fully dealt with by Congress. Notwithstanding the commerce clause, such regulation in the absence of Congressional action has for the most part been left to the states by the decisions of this Court, subject to the other applicable constitutional restraints.

The commerce clause, by its own force, prohibits discrimination against interstate commerce, whatever its form or method, and the decisions of this Court have recognized that there is scope for its like operation when state legislation nominally of local concern is in point of fact aimed at interstate commerce, or by its necessary operation is a means of gaining a local benefit by throwing the attendant burdens on those without the state. * * *

But the present case affords no occasion for saying that the bare possession of power by Congress to regulate the interstate traffic forces the states to conform to standards which Congress might, but has not adopted, or curtails their power to take measures to insure the safety and conservation of their highways which may be applied to like traffic moving intrastate. Few subjects of state regulation are so peculiarly of local concern as is the use of state highways. There are few, local regulation of which is so inseparable from a substantial effect on interstate commerce. Unlike the railroads, local highways are built, owned and maintained by the state or its municipal subdivisions. The state has a primary and immediate concern in their safe and economical administration. The present regulations, or any others of like purpose, if they are to accomplish their end, must be applied alike to interstate and intrastate traffic both moving in large volume over the highways. The fact that they affect alike shippers in interstate and intrastate commerce in large number within as well as without the state is a safeguard against their abuse.

From the beginning it has been recognized that a state can, if it sees fit, build and maintain its own highways, canals and railroads and that in the absence of Congressional action their regulation is peculiarly within its competence, even though interstate commerce is materially affected. * * * Congress not acting, state regulation of intrastate carriers has been upheld regardless of its effect upon interstate commerce. * * * With respect to the extent and nature of the local interests to be protected and the unavoidable effect upon interstate and intrastate commerce alike, regulations of the use of the highways are akin to local regulation of rivers, harbors, piers and docks, quarantine regulations, and game laws, which, Congress not acting, have been sustained even though they materially interfere with interstate commerce.

The nature of the authority of the state over its own highways has often been pointed out by this Court. It may not, under the guise of regulation, discriminate against interstate commerce. But "In the absence of national legislation especially covering the subject of interstate commerce, the state may rightly prescribe uniform regulations adapted to promote safety upon its highways and the conservation of their use applicable alike to vehicles moving in interstate commerce and those of its own citizens." * * * This Court has often sustained the exercise of that power although it has burdened or impeded interstate commerce. It has upheld weight limitations lower than those presently imposed, applied alike to motor traffic moving interstate and intrastate. * * * Restrictions favoring passenger traffic over the carriage of interstate merchandise by truck have been similarly sustained, * * * as has the exaction of a reasonable fee for the use of the highways. * * *

In each of these cases regulation involves a burden on interstate commerce. But so long as the state action does not discriminate, the burden is one which the Constitution permits because it is an inseparable incident of the exercise of a legislative authority, which, under the Constitution, has been left to the states.

Congress, in the exercise of its plenary power to regulate interstate commerce, may determine whether the burdens imposed on it by state regulation, otherwise permissible, are too great, and may, by legislation designed to secure uniformity or in other respects to protect the national interest in the commerce, curtail to some extent the state's regulatory power. But that is a legislative, not a judicial function, to be performed in the light of the Congressional judgment of what is appropriate regulation of interstate commerce, and the extent to which, in that field, state power and local interests should be required to yield to the national authority and interest. In the absence of such legislation the judicial function, under the commerce clause . . . stops with the inquiry whether the state legislature in adopting regulations such as the present has acted within its province, and whether the means of regulation chosen are reasonably adapted to the end sought. * * *

. . . [C]ourts do not sit as legislatures, either state or national. They cannot act as Congress does when, after weighing all the conflicting interests, state and national, it determines when and how much the state regulatory power shall yield to the larger interests of a national commerce. And in reviewing a state highway regulation where Congress has not acted, a court is not called upon, as are state legislatures, to determine what, in its judgment, is the most suitable restriction to be applied of those that are possible, or to choose that one which in its opinion is best adapted to all the diverse interests affected. * * * When the action of a legislature is within the scope of its power, fairly debatable questions as to its reasonableness, wisdom and propriety are not for the determination of courts, but for the legislative body, on which rest the duty and responsibility of decision. * * * This is equally the case when the legislative power is one which may legitimately place an incidental burden on interstate commerce. It is not any the less a legislative power committed to the states because it affects interstate commerce, and courts are not any the more entitled, because interstate commerce is affected, to substitute their own for the legislative judgment. * * *

Since the adoption of one weight or width regulation, rather than another, is a legislative not a judicial choice, its constitutionality is not to be determined by weighing in the judicial scales the merits of the legislative choice and rejecting it if the weight of evidence presented in court appears to favor a different standard. * * * Being a legislative judgment it is presumed to be supported by facts known to the legislature unless facts judicially known or proved preclude that possibility. Hence, in reviewing the present determination we examine the record, not to see whether the findings of the court below are supported by evidence, but to ascertain upon the whole record whether it is possible to say that the legislative choice is without rational basis. * * * Not only does the record fail to exclude that possibility, but it shows affirmatively that there is adequate support for the legislative judgment.

. . . . . .

. . . The fact that many states have adopted a different standard is not persuasive. The conditions under which highways must be built in the several states, their construction and the demands made upon them, are not uniform. The road building art, as the record shows, is far from having attained a scientific certainty and precision, and scientific precision is not the criterion for the exercise of the constitutional regulatory power of the states. * * * The legislature, being free to exercise its own judgment, is not bound by that of other legislatures. It would hardly be contended that if all the states had adopted a single standard, none, in the light of its own experience and in the exercise of its judgment upon all the complex elements which enter into the problem, could change it.

. . . . . .

The regulatory measures taken by South Carolina are within its legislative power . . . and the resulting burden on interstate commerce is not forbidden.

Reversed.

MR. JUSTICE CARDOZO and MR. JUSTICE REED took no part in the consideration or decision of this case.

Southern Pacific Co. v. Arizona

325 U.S. 761 (1945)

MR. CHIEF JUSTICE STONE delivered the opinion of the Court.

The Arizona Train Limit Law of May 16, 1912, * * * makes it unlawful for any person or corporation to operate within the state a railroad train of more than fourteen passenger or seventy freight cars, and authorizes the state to recover a money penalty for each violation of the Act. The questions for decision are whether Congress has, by legislative enactment, restricted the power of the states to regulate the length of interstate trains as a safety measure and, if not, whether the statute contravenes the commerce clause of the federal Constitution.

In 1940 the State of Arizona brought suit in the Arizona Superior Court against . . . the Southern Pacific Company to recover the statutory penalties for operating within the state two interstate trains, one a passenger train of more than fourteen cars, and one a freight train of more than seventy cars. [Southern Pacific] answered, admitting the train operations, but defended on the ground that the statute offends against the commerce clause and the due process clause of the Fourteenth Amendment and conflicts with federal legislation. . . .

· · ·

Congress, in enacting legislation within its constitutional authority over interstate commerce, will not be deemed to have intended to strike down a state statute designed to protect the health and safety of the public unless its purpose to do so is clearly manifested * * * or unless the state law, in terms or in its practical administration, conflicts with the Act of Congress, or plainly and palpably infringes its policy. * * *

· · ·

Although the commerce clause conferred on the national government power to regulate commerce, its possession of the power does not exclude all state power of regulation. Ever since Willson v. Black Bird Creek Marsh Co. * * * it has been recognized that, in the absence of conflicting legislation by Congress, there is a residuum of power in the state to make laws governing matters of local concern which nevertheless in some measure affect interstate commerce or even, to some extent, regulate it. * * * Thus the states may regulate matters which, because of their number and diversity, may never be adequately dealt with by Congress. * * * When the regulation of matters of local concern is local in character and effect, and its impact on the national commerce does not seriously interfere with its operation, and the consequent incentive to deal with them nationally is slight, such regulation has been generally held to be within state authority. * * *

But ever since Gibbons v. Ogden, * * * the states have not been deemed to have authority to impede substantially the free flow of commerce from state to state, or to regulate those phases of the national commerce which, because of the need of national uniformity, demand that their regulation, if any, be prescribed by a single authority.* * * Whether or not this long recognized distribution of power between the national and the state governments is predicated upon the implications of the commerce clause itself * * * or upon the presumed intention of Congress, where Congress has not spoken, * * * the result is the same.

In the application of these principles some enactments may be found to be plainly within and others plainly without state power. But between these extremes lies the infinite variety of cases, in which regulation of local matters may also operate as a regulation of commerce, in which reconciliation of the conflicting claims of state and national power is to be attained only by some appraisal and accommodation of the competing demands of the state and national interests involved. * * *

For a hundred years it has been accepted constitutional doctrine that the commerce clause, without the aid of Congressional legislation, thus affords some protection from state legislation inimical to the national commerce, and that in such cases, where Congress has not acted, this Court, and not the state legislature, is under the commerce clause the final arbiter of the competing demands of state and national interests. * * *

Congress has undoubted power to redefine the distribution of power over interstate commerce. It may either permit the states to regulate the commerce in a manner which would otherwise not be permissible * * * or exclude state regulation even of matters of peculiarly local concern which nevertheless affect interstate commerce. * * *

But in general Congress has left it to the courts to formulate the rules thus interpreting the commerce clause in its application, doubtless because it has appreciated the destructive consequences to the commerce of the nation if their protection were withdrawn * * * and has been aware that in their application state laws will not be invalidated without the support of relevant factual material which will "afford a sure basis" for an informed judgment. * * * Meanwhile,

Congress has accommodated its legislation, as have the states, to these rules as an established feature of our constitutional system. There has thus been left to the states wide scope for the regulation of matters of local state concern, even though it in some measure affects the commerce, provided it does not materially restrict the free flow of commerce across state lines, or interfere with it in matters with respect to which uniformity of regulation is of predominant national concern.

Hence the matters for ultimate determination here are the nature and extent of the burden which the state regulation of interstate trains, adopted as a safety measure, imposes on interstate commerce, and whether the relative weights of the state and national interests involved are such as to make inapplicable the rule, generally observed, that the free flow of interstate commerce and its freedom from local restraints in matters requiring uniformity of regulation are interests safeguarded by the commerce clause from state interference.

While this Court is not bound by the findings of the state court, and may determine for itself the facts of a case upon which an asserted federal right depends, * * * the facts found by the state trial court showing the nature of the interstate commerce involved, and the effect upon it of the train limit law, are not seriously questioned. Its findings with respect to the need for and effect of the statute as a safety measure, although challenged in some particulars which we do not regard as material to our decision, are likewise supported by evidence. Taken together the findings supply an adequate basis for decision of the constitutional issue.

The findings show that the operation of long trains . . . is standard practice over the main lines of the railroads of the United States, and that, if the length of trains is to be regulated at all, national uniformity in the regulation adopted, such as only Congress can prescribe, is practically indispensable to the operation of an efficient and economical national railway system. . . . Outside of Arizona, where the length of trains is not restricted, [Southern Pacific] runs a substantial proportion of long trains. In 1939 on its comparable route for through traffic through Utah and Nevada from 66 to 85% of its freight trains were over 70 cars in length and over 43% of its passenger trains included more than fourteen passenger cars.

In Arizona, approximately 93% of the freight traffic and 95% of the passenger traffic is interstate. Because of the Train Limit Law [Southern Pacific] is required to haul over 30% more trains in Arizona than would otherwise have been necessary. The record shows a definite relationship between operating costs and the length of trains, the increase in length resulting in a reduction of operating costs per car. The additional cost of operation of trains complying with the Train Limit Law in Arizona amounts for the two railroads traversing that state to about $1,000,000 a year. The reduction in train lengths also impedes efficient operation. . . .

• • •

The unchallenged findings leave no doubt that the Arizona Train Limit Law imposes a serious burden on the interstate commerce conducted by [Southern

Pacific]. It materially impedes the movement of . . . interstate trains through that state and interposes a substantial obstruction to the national policy proclaimed by Congress, to promote adequate, economical and efficient railway transportation service. * * * Enforcement of the law in Arizona, while train lengths remain unregulated or are regulated by varying standards in other states, must inevitably result in an impairment of uniformity of efficient railroad operation because the railroads are subjected to regulation which is not uniform in its application. Compliance with a state statute limiting train lengths requires interstate trains of a length lawful in other states to be broken up and reconstituted as they enter each state according as it may impose varying limitations upon train lengths. The alternative is for the carrier to conform to the lowest train limit restriction of any of the states through which its trains pass, whose laws thus control the carriers' operations both within and without the regulating state.

If one state may regulate train lengths, so may all the others, and they need not prescribe the same maximum limitation. The practical effect of such regulation is to control train operations beyond the boundaries of the state exacting it because of the necessity of breaking up and reassembling long trains at the nearest terminal points before entering and after leaving the regulating state. The serious impediment to the free flow of commerce by the local regulation of train lengths and the practical necessity that such regulation, if any, must be prescribed by a single body having a nation-wide authority are apparent.

* * *

We think, as the trial court found, that the Arizona Train Limit Law, viewed as a safety measure, affords at most slight and dubious advantage, if any, over unregulated train lengths. . . . Its undoubted effect on the commerce is the regulation, without securing uniformity, of the length of trains operated in interstate commerce, which lack is itself a primary cause of preventing the free flow of commerce by delaying it and by substantially increasing its cost and impairing its efficiency. In these respects the case differs from those where a state, by regulatory measures affecting the commerce, has removed or reduced safety hazards without substantial interference with the interstate movement of trains. Such are measures abolishing the car stove, * * * requiring locomotives to be supplied with electric headlights, * * * providing for full train crews, * * * and for the equipment of freight trains with cabooses. * * *

The principle that, without controlling Congressional action, a state may not regulate interstate commerce so as substantially to affect its flow or deprive it of needed uniformity in its regulation is not to be avoided by "simply invoking the convenient apologetics of the police power." * * *

* * *

. . .[W]e have pointed out that when a state goes beyond safety measures which are permissible because only local in their effect upon interstate commerce and "attempts to impose particular standards as to structure, design, equipment and operation [of vessels plying interstate] which in the judgment of its authorities may be desirable but pass beyond what is plainly essential to safety and seaworthiness, the State will encounter the principle that such requirements, if imposed at all, must be through the action of Congress which can establish a uniform rule. Whether the state in a particular matter goes too far must be left to be determined when the precise question arises."

Here we conclude that the state does go too far. Its regulation of train lengths, admittedly obstructive to interstate train operation, and having a seriously adverse effect on transportation efficiency and economy, passes beyond what is plainly essential for safety since it does not appear that it will lessen rather than increase the danger of accident. * * *

• • •

. . .[South Carolina Highway Department v. Barnwell] was concerned with the power of the state to regulate the weight and width of motor cars passing interstate over its highways, a legislative field over which the state has a far more extensive control than over interstate railroads. In that case . . . we were at pains to point out that there are few subjects of state regulation affecting interstate commerce which are so peculiarly of local concern as is the use of the state's highways. Unlike the railroads local highways are built, owned and maintained by the state or its municipal subdivisions. The state is responsible for their safe and economical administration. Regulations affecting the safety of their use must be applied alike to intrastate and interstate traffic. The fact that they affect alike shippers in interstate and intrastate commerce in great numbers, within as well as without the state, is a safeguard against regulatory abuses. Their regulation is akin to quarantine measures, game laws, and like local regulations of rivers, harbors, piers, and docks, with respect to which the state has exceptional scope for the exercise of its regulatory power, and which, Congress not acting, have been sustained even though they materially interfere with interstate commerce. * * *

The contrast between the present regulation and . . . the highway safety regulation in point of the nature of the subject of regulation and the state's interest in it, illustrate and emphasize the considerations which enter into a determination of the relative weights of state and national interests where state regulation affecting interstate commerce is attempted. Here examination of all the relevant factors makes it plain that the state interest is outweighed by the interest of the nation in an adequate, economical and efficient railway transportation service, which must prevail.

Reversed.

Mr. Justice Rutledge concurs in the result.

Mr. Justice Black, dissenting.

• • •

The determination of whether it is in the interest of society for the length of trains to be governmentally regulated is a matter of public policy. Someone must fix that policy—either the Congress, or the state, or the courts. A century and a half of constitutional history and government admonishes this Court to leave that choice to the elected legislative representatives of the people themselves, where it properly belongs both on democratic principles and the requirements of efficient government.

* * *

There have been many sharp divisions of this Court concerning its authority, in the absence of congressional enactment, to invalidate state laws as violating the Commerce Clause. * * * That discussion need not be renewed here, because even the broadest exponents of judicial power in this field have not heretofore expressed doubt as to a state's power, absent a paramount congressional declaration, to regulate interstate trains in the interest of safety. . . .

* * *

. . . Congress could when it pleased establish a uniform rule as to the length of trains. Congress knew about the Arizona law. It is common knowledge that the Interstate Commerce Committees of the House and the Senate keep in close and intimate touch with the affairs of railroads and other national means of transportation. Every year brings forth new legislation which goes through those Committees, much of it relating to safety. The attention of the members of Congress and of the Senate has been focused on the particular problem of the length of railroad trains. We cannot assume that they were ignorant of the commonly known fact that a long train might be more dangerous in some territories and on some particular types of railroad. The history of congressional consideration of this problem leaves little if any room to doubt that the choice of Congress to leave the state free in this field was a deliberate choice, which was taken with a full knowledge of the complexities of the problems and the probable need for diverse regulations in different localities. I am therefore compelled to reach the conclusion that today's decision is the result of the belief of a majority of this Court that both the legislature of Arizona and the Congress made wrong policy decisions in permitting a law to stand which limits the length of railroad trains. . . .

When we finally get down to the gist of what the Court today actually decides, it is this: Even though more railroad employees will be injured by "slack action" movements on long trains than on short trains, there must be no regulation of this danger in the absence of "uniform regulations." That means that no one can legislate against this danger except the Congress; and even though the Congress is perfectly content to leave the matter to the different state legislatures, this Court, on the ground of "lack of uniformity," will require it to make an express avowal of that fact before it will permit a state to guard against that admitted danger.

We are not left in doubt as to why, as against the potential peril of injuries to employees, the Court tips the scales on the side of "uniformity." For the evil it finds in a lack of uniformity is that it (1) delays interstate commerce, (2) increases its cost and (3) impairs its efficiency. All three of these boil down to the same thing, and that is that running shorter trains would increase the cost of railroad operations. The "burden" on commerce reduces itself to mere cost because there was no finding, and no evidence to support a finding that by the expenditure of sufficient sums of money, the railroads could not enable themselves to carry goods and passengers just as quickly and efficiently with short trains as with long trains. Thus the conclusion that a requirement for long trains will "burden interstate commerce" is a mere euphemism for the statement that a requirement for long trains will increase the cost of railroad operations.

. . .

This record in its entirety leaves me with no doubt whatever that many employees have been seriously injured and killed in the past, and that many more are likely to be so in the future, because of "slack movement" in trains. . . . It may be that offsetting dangers are possible in the operation of short trains. The balancing of these probabilities, however, is not in my judgment a matter for judicial determination, but one which calls for legislative consideration. Representatives elected by the people to make their laws, rather than judges appointed to interpret those laws, can best determine the policies which govern the people. That at least is the basic principle on which our democratic society rests. I would affirm the judgment of the Supreme Court of Arizona.

MR. JUSTICE DOUGLAS, dissenting.

I have expressed my doubts whether the courts should intervene in situations like the present and strike down state legislation on the grounds that it burdens interstate commerce. * * * My view has been that the courts should intervene only where the state legislation discriminated against interstate commerce or was out of harmony with laws which Congress had enacted. * * * It seems to me particularly appropriate that that course be followed here. . . .

. . . [W]e are dealing here with state legislation in the field of safety where the propriety of local regulation has long been recognized. * * * Whether the question arises under the Commerce Clause or the Fourteenth Amendment, I think the legislation is entitled to a presumption of validity. . . .

[As an indication of the Court's continued ambivalence in this area, see *Bibb* v. *Navajo Freight Lines, Inc.,* 359 U.S. 520 (1959). In that case the Court struck down, as a burden on interstate commerce, an Illinois law requiring the use of contoured mudguards on trucks using the state's highways.]

Hood & Sons v. DuMond

336 U.S. 525 (1949)

MR. JUSTICE JACKSON delivered the opinion of the Court.

This case concerns the power of the State of New York to deny additional facilities to acquire and ship milk in interstate commerce where the grounds of denial are that such limitation upon interstate business will protect and advance local economic interests.

H. P. Hood & Sons, Inc., a Massachusetts corporation, has long distributed milk and its products to inhabitants of Boston. . . . Dairies located in New York State since about 1900 have been among the sources of Boston's supply. . . . The area . . . has been developed as a part of the Boston milkshed from which both the Hood Company and a competitor have shipped to Boston.

. . . Hood's entire business in New York, present and proposed, is interstate commerce. This Hood has conducted for some time by means of three receiving depots, where it takes raw milk from farmers. . . . These existing plants have been operated under license from the State and are not in question here as the State has licensed Hood to continue them. The controversy concerns a proposed additional plant for the same kind of operation at Greenwich, New York.

. . . [T]he Agriculture and Markets Law of New York forbids a dealer to buy milk from producers unless licensed to do so by the Commissioner of Agriculture and Markets. For the license he must pay a substantial fee and furnish a bond to assure prompt payment to producers for milk. . . . [T]he Commissioner may not grant a license unless satisfied "that the applicant is qualified by character, experience, financial responsibility and equipment to properly conduct the proposed business." The Hood Company concededly has met all the foregoing tests and license for an additional plant was not denied for any failure to comply with these requirements.

The Commissioner's denial was based on further provisions of this section which require him to be satisfied "that the issuance of the license will not tend to a destructive competition in a market already adequately served, and that the issuance of the license is in the public interest."

• • •

In denying the application for expanded facilities, the Commissioner states his grounds as follows:

"If applicant is permitted to equip and operate another milk plant in this territory, and to take on producers now delivering to plants other than those which it operates, it will tend to reduce the volume of milk received at the plants which lose those producers, and will tend to increase the cost of handling milk in those plants.

"If applicant takes producers now delivering milk to local markets, . . . it will have a tendency to deprive such markets of a supply needed during the short season.

"There is no evidence that any producer is without a market for his milk. There is no evidence that any producers not now delivering milk to applicant would receive any higher price, were they to deliver their milk to applicant's proposed plant.

"The issuance of a license to applicant which would permit it to operate an additional plant, would tend to a destructive competition in a market already adequately served, and would not be in the public interest."

Denial of the license was sustained by the Court of Appeals over constitutional objections duly urged under the Commerce Clause and, because of the importance of the questions involved, we brought the case here by certiorari.

Production and distribution of milk are so intimately related to public health and welfare that the need for regulation to protect those interests has long been recognized and is, from a constitutional standpoint, hardly controversial. Also, the economy of the industry is so eccentric that economic controls have been found at once necessary and difficult. These have evolved detailed, intricate and comprehensive regulations, including price-fixing. They have been much litigated but were generally sustained by this Court as within the powers of the State over its internal commerce as against the claim that they violated the Fourteenth Amendment. * * * As the States extended their efforts to control various phases of export and import also, questions were raised as to limitations on state power under the Commerce Clause of the Constitution.

• • •

. . . New York's regulations, designed to assure producers a fair price and a responsible purchaser, and consumers a sanitary and modernly equipped handler, are not challenged here but have been complied with. It is only additional restrictions, imposed for the avowed purpose and with the practical effect of curtailing the volume of interstate commerce to aid local economic interests, that are in question here. . . .

• • •

This distinction between the power of the State to shelter its people from menaces to their health or safety and from fraud, even when those dangers emanate from interstate commerce, and its lack of power to retard, burden or constrict the flow of such commerce for their economic advantage, is one deeply rooted in both our history and our law.

• • •

The Commerce Clause is one of the most prolific sources of national power and an equally prolific source of conflict with legislation of the state. While the

Constitution vests in Congress the power to regulate commerce among the states, it does not say what the states may or may not do in the absence of congressional action, nor how to draw the line between what is and what is not commerce among the states. Perhaps even more than by interpretation of its written word, this Court has advanced the solidarity and prosperity of this Nation by the meaning it has given to these great silences of the Constitution.

. . . This Court consistently has rebuffed attempts of states to advance their own commercial interests by curtailing the movement of articles of commerce, either into or out of the state, while generally supporting their right to impose even burdensome regulations in the interests of local health and safety. . . .

• • •

[The] principle that our economic unit is the Nation, which alone has the gamut of powers necessary to control of the economy, including the vital power of erecting customs barriers against foreign competition, has as its corollary that the states are not separable economic units. . . . [T]he state may not use its admitted powers to protect the health and safety of its people as a basis for suppressing competition. . . . This Court has not only recognized [the] disability of the state to isolate its own economy as a basis for striking down parochial legislative policies designed to do so, but it has recognized the incapacity of the state to protect its own inhabitants from competition as a reason for sustaining particular exercises of the commerce power of Congress to reach matters in which states were so disabled. * * *

The material success that has come to inhabitants of the states which make up this federal free trade unit has been the most impressive in the history of commerce, but the established interdependence of the states only emphasizes the necessity of protecting interstate movement of goods against local burdens and repressions. We need only consider the consequences if each of the few states that produce copper, lead, high-grade iron ore, timber, cotton, oil or gas should decree that industries located in that state shall have priority. What fantastic rivalries and dislocations and reprisals would ensue if such practices were begun! . . .

Our system, fostered by the Commerce Clause, is that every farmer and every craftsman shall be encouraged to produce by the certainty that he will have free access to every market in the Nation, that no home embargoes will withhold his export, and no foreign state will by customs duties or regulations exclude them. Likewise, every consumer may look to the free competition from every producing area in the Nation to protect him from exploitation by any. Such was the vision of the Founders; such has been the doctrine of this Court which has given it reality.

The State, however, insists that denial of the license for a new plant does not restrict or obstruct interstate commerce, because [Hood] has been licensed at its other plants without condition or limitation as to the quantities it may purchase. Hence, it is said, all that has been denied [Hood] is a local convenience—that of being able to buy and receive at Greenwich quantities of milk it is free to buy at

Eagle Bridge and Salem. It suggests that, by increased efficiency or enlarged capacity at its other plants, [Hood] might sufficiently increase its supply through those facilities.

The weakness of this contention is that a buyer has to buy where there is a willing seller, and the peculiarities of the milk business necessitate location of a receiving and cooling station for nearby producers. . . .

But the argument also asks us to assume that the Commissioner's order will not operate in the way he found that it would as a reason for making it. He found that [Hood & Sons], at its new plant, would divert milk from the plants of some other large handlers in the vicinity, which plants "can handle more milk." This competition he did not approve. He also found it would tend to deprive local markets of needed supplies during the short season. In the face of affirmative findings that the proposed plant would increase [Hood's] supply, we can hardly be asked to assume that denial of the license will not deny . . . access to such added supplies. While the state power is applied in this case to limit expansion by a handler of milk who already has been allowed some purchasing facilities, the argument for doing so, if sustained, would be equally effective to exclude an entirely new foreign handler from coming into the state to purchase.

· · ·

Since the statute as applied violates the Commerce Clause and is not authorized by federal legislation pursuant to that Clause, it cannot stand. The judgment is reversed and the cause remanded for proceedings not inconsistent with this opinion.

It is so ordered.

MR. JUSTICE BLACK, dissenting.

· · ·

The language of this state Act is not discriminatory, the legislative history shows it was not so intended, and the commissioner has not administered it with a hostile eye. The Act must stand or fall on this basis notwithstanding the overtones of the Court's opinion. If [Hood] and other interstate milk dealers are to be placed above and beyond this law, it must be done solely on this Court's new constitutional formula which bars a state from protecting itself against local destructive competitive practices so far as they are indulged in by dealers who ship their milk into other states.

· · ·

Reconciliation of state and federal interests in regulation of commerce always has been a perplexing problem. The claims of neither can be ignored if due regard be accorded the welfare of state and nation. For in the long run the welfare of each is dependent upon the welfare of both. Injury to commercial activities in the states is bound to produce an injurious reaction on interstate commerce, and vice versa. The many local activities which are parts of interstate transactions have given rise to much confusion. The basic problem has always been whether the state or federal government has power to regulate such local activities, whether the power of either is exclusive or concurrent, whether the state has power to regulate until Congress exercises its supreme power, and the extent to which and the circumstances under which this Court should invalidate state regulations in the absence of an exercise of congressional power. This last question is the one here involved.

. . .

There has certainly been no proof here that New York is wrong in believing that its law will rehabilitate farmers, induce more of them to get and stay in the milk business, and thus provide a greater New York production of better milk available for sale both in and out of New York. Should this result follow, interstate commerce will not be burdened, it will be helped. And it seems to me that . . . this Court should not pit its legal judgment against a legislative judgment that is in harmony with the views of persons who have devoted their lives to a practical study of the milk problem.

. . .

The sole immediate result of today's holding is that [Hood] will be allowed to operate a new milk plant in New York. This consequence standing alone is of no great importance. But there are other consequences of importance. It is always a serious thing for this Court to strike down a statewide law. It is more serious when the state law falls under a new rule which will inescapably narrow the area in which states can regulate and control local business practices found inimical to the public welfare. The gravity of striking down state regulations is immeasurably increased when it results as here in leaving a no-man's land immune from any effective regulation whatever. It is dangerous to assume that the aggressive cupidity of some need never be checked by government in the interest of all.

. . .

The basic question here is not the greatness of the commerce clause concept, but whether all local phases of interstate business are to be judicially immunized from state laws against destructive competitive business practices such as those prohibited by New York's law. Of course, there remains the bare possibility Congress might attempt to federalize all such local business activities in the forty-eight states. While I have doubt about the wisdom of this New York law, I do not conceive it to be the function of this Court to revise that state's economic judgments. Any doubt I may have concerning the wisdom of New York's law is far less, however, than is my skepticism concerning the ability of the Federal Government to reach out and effectively regulate all the local business activities in the forty-eight states.

I would leave New York's law alone.

Mr. Justice Murphy joins in this opinion.

Mr. Justice Frankfurter, with whom Mr. Justice Rutledge joins, dissenting.

If the Court's opinion has meaning beyond deciding this case in isolation, its effect is to hold that no matter how important to the internal economy of a State may be the prevention of destructive competition, and no matter how unimportant the interstate commerce affected, a State cannot as a means of preventing such competition deny an applicant access to a market within the State if that applicant happens to intend the out-of-state shipment of the product that he buys. I feel constrained to dissent because I cannot agree in treating what is essentially a problem of striking a balance between competing interests as an exercise in absolutes. . . .

• • •

As I see the central issue, . . . it is whether the difference in degree between denying access to a market for failure to comply with sanitary or book-keeping regulations and denying it for the sake of preventing destructive competition from disrupting the market is great enough to justify a difference in result. . . . In view of the importance that we have hitherto found in regulation of the economy of agriculture, I cannot understand the justification for assigning, as a matter of law, so much higher a place to milk dealers' standards of book-keeping than to the economic well-being of their industry.

• • •

My conclusion, accordingly, is that the case should be remanded to the Supreme Court of Albany County for action consistent with the views I have stated.

Philadelphia v. New Jersey

437 U.S. 617 (1978)

Mr. Justice Stewart delivered the opinion of the Court.

A New Jersey law prohibits the importation of most "solid or liquid waste which originated or was collected outside the territorial limits of the State. . . ." In this case we are required to decide whether this statutory prohibition violates the Commerce Clause of the United States Constitution.

The statutory provision . . . took effect in early 1974. . . . Apart from . . . narrow exceptions, . . . New Jersey closed its borders to all waste from other States.

Immediately affected by these developments were the operators of private landfills in New Jersey, and several cities in other States that had agreements with these operators for waste disposal. They brought suit against New Jersey and its Department of Environmental Protection in state court, attacking the statute and regulations on a number of state and federal grounds. . . . [T]he trial court declared the law unconstitutional because it discriminated against interstate commerce. The New Jersey Supreme Court . . . reversed. It found that [the statute] advanced vital health and environmental objectives with no economic discrimination against, and with little burden upon, interstate commerce, and that the law was therefore permissible under the Commerce Clause of the Constitution. . . .

· · ·

The state court expressed the view that there may be two definitions of "commerce" for constitutional purposes. When relied on "to support some exertion of federal control or regulation," the Commerce Clause permits "a very sweeping concept" of commerce. * * * But when relied on "to strike down or restrict state legislation," that Clause and the term "commerce" have a "much more confined . . . reach." * * *

The state court reached this conclusion in an attempt to reconcile modern Commerce Clause concepts with several old cases of this Court holding that States can prohibit the importation of some objects because they "are not legitimate subjects of trade and commerce." Bowman v. Chicago & Northwestern R. Co. * * * These articles include items "which, on account of their existing condition, would bring in and spread disease, pestilence, and death, such as rags or other substances infected with the germs of yellow fever or the virus of small-pox, or cattle or meat or other provisions that are diseased or decayed, or otherwise, from their condition and quality, unfit for human use or consumption." * * * The state court found that . . . the state regulations * * * banned only "those wastes which can[not] be put to effective use," and therefore those wastes were not commerce at all, unless "the mere transportation and disposal of valueless waste between states constitutes interstate commerce within the meaning of the constitutional provision." * * *

We think the state court misread our cases, and thus erred in assuming that they require a two-tiered definition of commerce. In saying that innately harmful articles "are not legitimate subjects of trade and commerce," the Bowman Court was stating its conclusion, not the starting point of its reasoning. All objects of interstate trade merit Commerce Clause protection; none is excluded by definition at the outset. In Bowman . . . the Court held simply that because the articles' worth in interstate commerce was far outweighed by the dangers inhering in their very movement, States could prohibit their transportation across state lines. Hence, we reject the state court's suggestion that the banning of "valueless" out-of-state wastes . . . implicates no constitutional protection. Just as Congress has power to regulate the interstate movement of these wastes, States are not free from constitutional scrutiny when they restrict that movement. * * *

A

Although the Constitution gives Congress the power to regulate commerce among the States, many subjects of potential federal regulation under that power inevitably escape congressional attention. . . . In the absence of federal legislation, these subjects are open to control by the States so long as they act within the restraints imposed by the Commerce Clause itself. * * * The bounds of these restraints appear nowhere in the words of the Commerce Clause, but have emerged gradually in the decisions of this Court giving effect to its basic purpose. . . .

The opinions of the Court through the years have reflected an alertness to the evils of "economic isolation" and protectionism, while at the same time recognizing that incidental burdens on interstate commerce may be unavoidable when a State legislates to safeguard the health and safety of its people. Thus, where simple economic protectionism is effected by state legislation, a virtually per se rule of invalidity has been erected. * * * The clearest example of such legislation is a law that overtly blocks the flow of interstate commerce at a State's borders. * * * But where other legislative objectives are credibly advanced and there is no patent discrimination against interstate trade, the Court has adopted a much more flexible approach. . . . The crucial inquiry . . . must be directed to determining whether [the New Jersey statute] is basically a protectionist measure, or whether it can fairly be viewed as a law directed to legitimate local concerns, with effects upon interstate commerce that are only incidental.

B

. . .

[Philadelphia] strenuously contend[s] that [New Jersey's law], "while outwardly cloaked 'in the currently fashionable garb of environmental protection,' . . . is actually no more than a legislative effort to suppress competition and stabilize the cost of solid waste disposal for New Jersey residents. . . ."

[New Jersey], on the other hand, [denies that its law] was motivated by financial concerns or economic protectionism. . . .

This dispute about ultimate legislative purpose need not be resolved, because its resolution would not be relevant to the constitutional issue to be decided in this case. Contrary to the evident assumption of . . . the parties, the evil of protectionism can reside in legislative means as well as legislative ends. Thus, it does not matter whether the ultimate aim of [the statute] is to reduce the waste disposal costs of New Jersey residents or to save remaining open lands from pollution, for we assume New Jersey has every right to protect its residents' pocketbooks as well as their environment. And it may be assumed as well that

New Jersey may pursue those ends by slowing the flow of *all* waste into the State's remaining landfills, even though interstate commerce may incidentally be affected. But whatever New Jersey's ultimate purpose, it may not be accomplished by discriminating against articles of commerce coming from outside the State unless there is some reason, apart from their origin, to treat them differently. Both on its face and in its plain effect, [New Jersey's law] violates this principle of nondiscrimination.

The Court has consistently found parochial legislation of this kind to be constitutionally invalid, whether the ultimate aim of the legislation was to assure a steady supply of milk by erecting barriers to allegedly ruinous outside competition, * * * or to create jobs by keeping industry within the State, * * * or to preserve the State's financial resources from depletion by fencing out indigent immigrants. * * * In each of these [instances], a presumably legitimate goal was sought to be achieved by the illegitimate means of isolating the State from the national economy.

• • •

The New Jersey law at issue in this case falls squarely within the area that the Commerce Clause puts off-limits to state regulation. On its face, it imposes on out-of-state commercial interests the full burden of conserving the State's remaining landfill space. . . . [T]he State has overtly moved to slow or freeze the flow of commerce for protectionist reasons. . . . What is crucial is the attempt by one State to isolate itself from a problem common to many by erecting a barrier against the movement of interstate trade.

[New Jersey argues] that not all laws which facially discriminate against out-of-state commerce are forbidden protectionist regulations. In particular, they point to quarantine laws, which this Court has repeatedly upheld even though they appear to single out interstate commerce for special treatment. * * * [In New Jersey's view, the statute] is analogous to such health-protective measures, since it reduces the exposure of New Jersey residents to the allegedly harmful effects of landfill sites.

It is true that certain quarantine laws have not been considered forbidden protectionist measures, even though they were directed against out-of-state commerce. * * * But those quarantine laws banned the importation of articles such as diseased livestock that required destruction as soon as possible because their very movement risked contagion and other evils. Those laws thus did not discriminate against interstate commerce as such, but simply prevented traffic in noxious articles, whatever their origin.

The New Jersey statute is not such a quarantine law. There has been no claim here that the very movement of waste into or through New Jersey endangers health, or that waste must be disposed of as soon and as close to its point of generation as possible. The harms caused by waste are said to arise after its disposal in landfill sites, and at that point, as New Jersey concedes, there is no basis to distinguish out-of-state waste from domestic waste. If one is inherently harmful, so is the other. Yet New Jersey has banned the former while leaving its landfill sites open to the latter. The New Jersey law blocks the importation of waste in an obvious effort to saddle those outside the State with the entire burden of slowing the flow of refuse into New Jersey's remaining landfill sites. That legislative effort is clearly impermissible under the Commerce Clause of the Constitution.

Today, cities in Pennsylvania and New York find it expedient or necessary to send their waste into New Jersey for disposal, and New Jersey claims the right to close its borders to such traffic. Tomorrow, cities in New Jersey may find it expedient or necessary to send their waste into Pennsylvania or New York for disposal, and those States might then claim the right to close their borders. The Commerce Clause will protect New Jersey in the future, just as it protects her neighbors now, from efforts by one State to isolate itself in the stream of interstate commerce from a problem shared by all.

The judgment is reversed.

Mr. Justice Rehnquist, with whom The Chief Justice joins, dissenting.

• • •

The question presented in this case is whether New Jersey must . . . continue to receive and dispose of solid waste from neighboring States, even though these will inexorably increase . . . health problems. . . . The Court answers this question in the affirmative. New Jersey must either prohibit *all* landfill operations, leaving itself to cast about for a presently nonexistent solution to the serious problem of disposing of the waste generated within its own borders, or it must accept waste from every portion of the United States, thereby multiplying the health and safety problems which would result if it dealt only with such wastes generated within the State. Because past precedents establish that the Commerce Clause does not present [New Jersey] with such a Hobson's choice, I dissent.

• • •

. . . The physical fact of life that New Jersey must somehow dispose of its own noxious items does not mean that it must serve as a depository for those of every other State. . . . New Jersey should be free under our past precedents to prohibit the importation of solid waste because of the health and safety problems that such waste poses to its citizens. The fact that New Jersey continues to, and indeed must continue to, dispose of its own solid waste does not mean that New Jersey may not prohibit the importation of even more solid waste into the State. I simply see no way to distinguish solid waste, on the record of this case, from germ-infected rags, diseased meat, and other noxious items.

• • •

. . . I do not see why a State may ban the importation of items whose movement risks contagion, but cannot ban the importation of items which, although they may be transported into the State without undue hazard, will then simply pile up in an ever increasing danger to the public's health and safety. The Commerce Clause was not drawn with a view to having the validity of state laws turn on such pointless distinctions.

. . . The fact that New Jersey has left its landfill sites open for domestic waste does not, of course, mean that solid waste is not innately harmful. Nor does it mean that New Jersey prohibits importation of solid waste for reasons other than the health and safety of its population. New Jersey must out of sheer necessity treat and dispose of its solid waste in some fashion. . . . It does not follow that New Jersey must, under the Commerce Clause, accept solid waste . . . from outside its borders and thereby exacerbate its problems.

. . . Because I find no basis for distinguishing the laws under challenge here from our past cases upholding state laws that prohibit the importation of items that could endanger the population of the State, I dissent.

Burbank v. Lockheed Air Terminal

411 U.S. 624 (1973)

MR. JUSTICE DOUGLAS delivered the opinion of the Court.

• • •

This suit brought by [Lockheed Air Terminal] asked for an injunction against the enforcement of an ordinance adopted by the City Council of Burbank, California, which made it unlawful for a so-called pure jet aircraft to take off from the Hollywood-Burbank Airport between 11 p.m. of one day and 7 a.m. the next day, and making it unlawful for the operator of that airport to allow any such aircraft to take off from that airport during such periods. The only regularly scheduled flight affected by the ordinance was an intrastate flight of Pacific Southwest Airlines originating in Oakland, California, and departing from Hollywood-Burbank Airport for San Diego every Sunday night at 11:30.

The District Court found the ordinance to be unconstitutional on both Supremacy Clause and Commerce Clause grounds. * * * The Court of Appeals affirmed on the grounds of the Supremacy Clause both as respects pre-emption and as respects conflict. * * * The case is here on appeal. * * * We affirm the Court of Appeals.

The Federal Aviation Act of 1958, * * * as amended by the Noise Control Act of 1972, * * * . . . provides in part, "The United States of America is declared to possess and exercise complete and exclusive national sovereignty in the airspace of the United States . . . ." . . . [T]he Administrator of the Federal Aviation Administration (FAA) has been given broad authority to regulate the use of the navigable airspace, "in order to insure the safety of aircraft and the efficient utilization of such airspace . . ." and "for the protection of persons and property on the ground . . . ."

• • •

The Noise Control Act of 1972 . . . provides that the Administrator . . . after consulting with EPA [the Environmental Protection Agency], shall provide "for the control and abatement of aircraft noise and sonic boom, including the application of such standards and regulations in the issuance, amendment, modification, suspension, or revocation of any certificate authorized by . . . [the Act]," as amended, provides that future certificates for aircraft operations shall not issue unless the new aircraft noise requirements are met.

• • •

There is, to be sure, no express provision of pre-emption in the 1972 Act. That, however, is not decisive. As we stated * * *

"Congress legislated here in a field which the States have traditionally occupied. . . . So we start with the assumption that the historic police powers of the States were not to be superseded by the Federal Act unless that was the clear and manifest purpose of Congress. . . . Such a purpose may be evidenced in several ways. The scheme of federal regulation may be so pervasive as to make reasonable the inference that Congress left no room for the States to supplement it. . . . Or the Act of Congress may touch a field in which the federal interest is so dominant that the federal system will be assumed to preclude enforcement of state laws on the same subject. . . . Likewise, the object sought to be obtained by the federal law and the character of obligations imposed by it may reveal the same purpose. . . . Or the state policy may produce a result inconsistent with the objective of the federal statute."

It is the pervasive nature of the scheme of federal regulation of aircraft noise that leads us to conclude that there is pre-emption. . . .

• • •

Our prior cases on pre-emption are not precise guide-lines in the present controversy, for each case turns on the peculiarities and special features of the federal regulatory scheme in question. * * * Control of noise is of course deep seated in the police power of the States. Yet the pervasive control vested in EPA and in FAA under the 1972 Act seems to us to leave no room for local curfews or other local controls. What the ultimate remedy may be for aircraft noise which plagues many communities and tens of thousands of people is not known. The procedures under the 1972 Act are under way. In addition, the Administrator has imposed a variety of regulations relating to takeoff and landing procedures and runway preferences. The Federal Aviation Act requires a delicate balance between safety and efficiency * * * and the protection of persons on the ground. * * * Any regulations adopted by the Administrator to control noise pollution must be consistent with the "highest degree of safety." * * * The interdependence of these factors requires a uniform and exclusive system of federal regulation if the congressional objectives underlying the Federal Aviation Act are to be fulfilled.

If we were to uphold the Burbank ordinance and a significant number of municipalities followed suit, it is obvious that fractionalized control of the timing of take-offs and landings would severely limit the flexibility of the FAA in controlling air traffic flow. The difficulties of scheduling flights to avoid congestion and the concomitant decrease in safety would be compounded. In 1960 the FAA rejected a proposed restriction on jet operations at the Los Angeles airport between 10 p.m. and 7 a.m. because such restrictions could "create critically serious problems to all air transportation patterns." * * * . . . This decision, announced in 1960, remains peculiarly within the competence of the FAA, supplemented now by the input of the EPA. We are not at liberty to diffuse the powers given by Congress to FAA and EPA by letting the States or municipalities in on the planning. If that change is to be made, Congress alone must do it.

Affirmed.

MR. JUSTICE REHNQUIST, with whom MR. JUSTICE STEWART, MR. JUSTICE WHITE, and MR. JUSTICE MARSHALL join, dissenting.

The Court concludes that congressional legislation dealing with aircraft noise has so "pervaded" that field that Congress has *impliedly* pre-empted it, and therefore the ordinance of the city of Burbank here challenged is invalid under the Supremacy Clause of the Constitution. . . .

The Burbank ordinance prohibited jet takeoffs from the Hollywood-Burbank Airport during the late evening and early morning hours. Its purpose was to afford local residents at least partial relief, during normal sleeping hours, from the noise associated with jet airplanes. The ordinance in no way dealt with flights over the city, * * * nor did it categorically prohibit all jet takeoffs during those hours.

[Lockheed Air Terminal does] not contend that the noise produced by jet engines could not reasonably be deemed to affect adversely the health and welfare of persons constantly exposed to it; control of noise, sufficiently loud to be classified as a public nuisance at common law, would be a type of regulation well within the traditional scope of the police power possessed by States and local governing bodies. Because noise regulation has traditionally been an area of local, not national, concern, in determining whether congressional legislation has, by implication, foreclosed remedial local enactments "we start with the

assumption that the historic police powers of the States were not to be superseded by the Federal Act unless that was the clear and manifest purpose of Congress." * * * This assumption derives from our basic constitutional division of legislative competence between the States and Congress; from "due regard for the presuppositions of our embracing federal system, *including the principle of diffusion of power not as a matter of doctrinaire localism but as a promoter of democracy . . . .*" * * * (emphasis added). Unless the requisite pre-emptive intent is abundantly clear, we should hesitate to invalidate state and local legislation for the added reason that "the state is powerless to remove the ill effects of our decision, while the national government, which has the ultimate power, remains free to remove the burden."
* * *

. . .

Considering the language Congress enacted into law, the available legislative history, and the light shed by these on the congressional purpose, Congress did not intend either by the 1958 Act or the 1968 Amendment to oust local governments from the enactment of regulations such as that of the city of Burbank. The 1972 Act quite clearly intended to maintain the status quo between federal and local authorities. The legislative history of the 1972 Act, quite apart from its concern with avoiding additional pre-emption, discloses a primary focus on the alteration of procedures within the Federal Government for dealing with problems of aircraft noise already entrusted by Congress to federal competence. The 1972 Act set up procedures by which the Administrator of the Environmental Protection Agency would have a role to play in the formulation and review of standards promulgated by the Federal Aviation Administration dealing with noise emissions of jet aircraft. But because these agencies have exclusive authority to reduce noise by promulgating regulations and implementing standards directed at one or several of the causes of the level of noise, local governmental bodies are not thereby foreclosed from dealing with the noise problem by every other conceivable method.

A local governing body that owns and operates an airport is certainly not, by the Court's opinion, prohibited from permanently closing down its facilities. A local governing body could likewise use its traditional police power to prevent the establishment of a new airport or the expansion of an existing one within its territorial jurisdiction by declining to grant the necessary zoning for such a facility. Even though the local government's decision in each case was motivated entirely because of the noise associated with airports, I do not read the Court's opinion as indicating that such action would be prohibited by the Supremacy Clause merely because the Federal Government has undertaken the responsibility for some aspects of aircraft noise control. Yet if this may be done, the Court's opinion surely does not satisfactorily explain why a local governing body may not enact a far less "intrusive" ordinance such as that of the city of Burbank.

The history of congressional action in this field demonstrates, I believe, an affirmative congressional intent to allow local regulation. But even if it did not go that far, that history surely does not reflect "the clear and manifest purpose of Congress" to prohibit the exercise of "the historic police powers of the States" which our decisions require before a conclusion of implied pre-emption is reached. Clearly Congress could pre-empt the field to local regulation if it chose, and very likely the authority conferred on the Administrator of the Federal Aviation Administration * * * is sufficient to authorize him to promulgate regulations effectively pre-empting local action. But neither Congress nor the Administrator has chosen to go that route. Until one of them does, the ordinance of the city of Burbank is a valid exercise of its police power.

The District Court found that the Burbank ordinance would impose an undue burden on interstate commerce, and held it invalid under the Commerce Clause for that reason. Neither the Court of Appeals nor this Court's opinion, in view of their determination as to pre-emption, reached that question. The District Court's conclusion appears to be based, at least in part, on a consideration of the effect on interstate commerce that would result if all municipal airports in the country enacted ordinances such as that of Burbank. Since the proper determination of the question turns on an evaluation of the facts of each case, * * * and not on a predicted proliferation of possibilities, the District Court's conclusion is of doubtful validity. The Burbank ordinance did not affect emergency flights, and had the total effect of prohibiting one scheduled commercial flight each week and several additional private flights by corporate executives; such a result can hardly be held to be an unreasonable burden on commerce. . . .

CHAPTER **11**

State Taxing
and Spending Power

INTRODUCTORY ESSAY

As we saw in the preceding chapter, state power to regulate interstate commerce was not clearly recognized when the federal Constitution was written. Marshall skirted the question in *Gibbons* v. *Ogden,* 9 Wheat. 1 (1824), and it was only late in his Chief Justiceship that the issue became indirectly identified with the concept of state police power, which the Supreme Court had begun to evolve at that time. But the state power to regulate local aspects of interstate commerce did not receive official sanction until 1852, in *Cooley* v. *Board of Wardens* (12 How. 299). By contrast, the state power to tax was well established in 1787. The grant of taxing authority to Congress in Article I, Section 8, Clause 1, of the Constitution did not withdraw or transfer it from the states. Taxation simply became one of those concurrent powers exercised broadly by both the national and the state governments. It should be noted that the authority to tax at the local level is derived from the states. Cities, counties, and other units of local government are created and may be abolished by the states, and the scope of their taxing power is largely determined either by state constitutional provisions or by statutes, subject always, of course, to federal constitutional requirements.

Routine aspects of state and local taxation do not often raise serious federal constitutional problems. The states have retained broad discretion under the federal Constitution to tap a variety of revenue sources, the latitude of which has tended to expand as governmental services and accompanying costs have increased. It is only when states or their subdivisions use taxation to block or undermine a federal constitutional principle or objective that the state taxing power is likely to be limited by the Supreme Court. One such principle is the promotion of a *national* economy, embodied in such provisions as the Commerce Clause and the restriction on state taxation of imports and exports. A state tax that unfairly burdens interstate commerce to the advantage of local economic interests is vulnerable to constitutional attack. Our discussion of the state power to regulate commerce touched on this aspect of state taxation. We will now examine two additional problems posed by the federal relationship, both of which have their origins in constitutional principles and both of which reflect the gradual but significant expansion of governmental power.

Reciprocal Tax Immunity

We begin with the doctrine of reciprocal immunity from taxation. In *M'Culloch* v. *Maryland,* 4 Wheat. 316 (1819), Chief Justice Marshall wrote for a unanimous Court that not only does Congress have an implied power to establish a national bank but also a state cannot use its taxing authority to undermine that power. Maryland's attempt to tax the Baltimore branch of the Bank of the United States was, in Marshall's view, inconsistent with the national government's exercise of its implied powers. He based his position squarely on the Supremacy Clause, reasoning that it was not possible to sanction any state tax having the potential to destroy an entity that had been constitutionally created by the national government. It was in this context that he coined the famous phrase "the power to tax involves the power to destroy." In Marshall's view, this reasoning did not apply in reverse—that is, it did not provide justification for imposing restrictions on national taxing power when that power interfered with constitutional objectives pursued by the states. But whether Marshall acknowledged it or not, the logic of his argument did cut both ways in a federal system that recognized two distinct spheres of authority with the states having an avowed right to claim supremacy or at least equality in relation to the national government in certain areas. As the doctrine of dual federalism emerged during the Taney era and in the years following the Civil War, the argument in favor of state immunity from national taxation gained support. In 1871 the Supreme Court embraced it in the case of *Collector* v. *Day,* 11 Wall. 113, holding that the salary of a Massachusetts judge was immune from the federal income tax adopted during the Civil War. The salary of the state judge was treated as an "instrumentality" of state government protected by the Tenth Amendment, just as the bank of the United States had been viewed as an instrumentality of the national government protected by the Supremacy Clause. This reasoning was subsequently applied to exempt from state and federal income taxes the salaries of many officials at all levels of government. Precisely why the salaries of judges and other government officials should be accorded this special protection was never very clear, but the broader principle of reciprocal tax immunity, which *Collector* v. *Day* established, followed logically from the assumptions underlying classical federalism. The gradual decline of reciprocal tax immunity since the 1930s illustrates the wisdom of Holmes' insight that "the life of the law is not logic but experience."

Tax Immunity for "Essential Governmental Functions"

Reciprocal immunity was expanded in *Pollock* v. *Farmers' Loan & Trust Co.,* 157 U.S. 429 (1895) and 158 U.S. 601 (1895) (see Chapter 6), when the Court held that Congress could not tax income generated by state and local securities. Although, as we have noted, this decision was overruled by the Sixteenth Amendment, Congress has not yet seen fit to tax securities of this type. Thus, municipal bonds remain a source of income not taxed by the national government. It is generally recognized, however, that Congress could remove this exemption at any time without serious constitutional challenge.

Reciprocal tax immunity continued to expand through the 1920s, reaching what one commentator has called "ridiculous extremes" (Pritchett, 1977, p. 173). It served, for example, as the basis for striking down a state tax on income accruing to a company that had leased oil lands belonging to American Indians and hence technically classified as federal property (*Gillespie v. Oklahoma,* 257 U.S. 501 [1922]). In its 5 to 4 decision, the Court majority concluded that the lessee was an instrumentality of the United States carrying out the government's "duties to the Indians." In a 1928 case, the states were barred from taxing royalties derived from national patents on the ground that the taxing of royalties would discourage national efforts to promote science and invention (*Long v. Rockwood,* 277 U.S. 142). With the coming of the Great Depression in the 1930s and the attendant demands for more sources of tax revenue, these decisions were overturned (*Fox Film Corp. v. Doyal,* 286 U.S. 123 [1932], overruling *Long v. Rockwood;* and *Helvering v. Mountain Producers Corp.,* 303 U.S. 376 [1938], overruling *Gillespie*). During this period, reciprocal immunity with respect to the exemption of salaries paid to state and federal officials continued to flourish. Decisions in the late 1930s, however, rejected the application of the immunity doctrine to salaries and in *Graves v. New York ex rel. O'Keefe,* 306 U.S. 466 (1939), the Court repudiated the specific holding in *Collector v. Day.* Justice Stone, who along with Justices Holmes and Brandeis had been on the dissenting side during the heyday of reciprocal tax immunity, assumed a leading role in articulating the new approach after 1937. As in many other areas of constitutional law during this period, a combination of societal and personnel changes influenced the Court to fundamentally alter its position on intergovernmental, or reciprocal, tax immunity. In his *Graves* opinion, Justice Stone abandoned the rigid logic of dual federalism and recognized the practical demands imposed on the people by two governments within the same territory, each having the power to tax. As Stanley Friedelbaum has noted, in the "changed climate" of the late 1930s, "Stone stood as the architect of a new philosophy designed to give meaning to . . . cooperative federalism" (Friedelbaum, 1972, p. 232).

Neither the states nor the national government can tax essential governmental functions performed by the other. This is as true today as it was in the 1920s when reciprocal tax immunity was at its peak. The problem, of course, is that of determining at a given time just what constitutes an essential function of government. Obviously, Congress could not impose a tax on such state property as the capitol building or the governor's mansion; nor could a state levy a tax on the distribution to law libraries within its jurisdiction of volumes of the *United States Supreme Court Reports.* But when we move away from the extreme situations suggested by these illustrations, the answers are not so easy. For example, while a state cannot tax federal property directly, it may place a privilege tax on a person or corporation using federal property and may base the tax on the value of such property (*United States v. City of Detroit,* 355 U.S. 466 [1958]). States may also tax federal contractors, even if the burden of the tax is absorbed in the contract price and thus in effect passed on to the government (*Alabama v. King & Boozer,* 314 U.S. 1 [1941]). On the other hand, the Supremacy Clause broadly protects functions of the national government from regulation through the imposition of state taxes or the exercise of the state police power (*United States* v. *Georgia Public Service Commission*, 371 U.S. 285 [1963]). Precise distinctions in this area are the exception rather than the rule. Basically, the Supreme Court has attempted to maximize the discretion of the taxing authority without impairing the performance of essential activities of government. Formal doctrine is less useful to the Court in making specific determination in this field than practical assessments of political or economic reality.

Federal Taxation of State-Owned Business Enterprises

One important aspect of state activity has consistently been excluded from the category of intergovernmental tax immunity. When the state engages in enterprises or activities typically conducted by private business, it loses any serious claim to the privileged status of tax immunity. Thus, as early as 1905, the Supreme Court held that a state-owned liquor monopoly was subject to federal taxation (*South Carolina* v. *United States*, 199 U.S. 437). In the well-known case of *New York* v. *United States* (326 U.S. 572 [1946]), a divided Court upheld a federal tax on the sale of bottled mineral water by a state public benefit corporation, the Saratoga Springs Authority. Announcing the judgment of the Court, Justice Frankfurter found no basis for invoking the doctrine of reciprocal tax immunity. He contrasted the setting of this case with that of *M'Culloch* v. *Maryland,* in which the principle of reciprocal immunity was originally applied. Frankfurter noted the prevailing judicial trend toward a narrowing of the immunity doctrine. For him this tendency did not necessarily imply Supreme Court approval of the particular tax policies adopted by government but rather indicated "an awareness of the limited role of courts in assessing the relative weight of the factors upon which immunity is based." Such a view was consistent with Frankfurter's judicial philosophy, typically labeled as one of self-restraint. In upholding the federal tax, he rejected previous Supreme Court attempts to assign certain kinds of state activities to fixed categories such as "proprietary" or "governmental," finding this formalism unnecessarily restrictive. The tax in question was levied on the *sale* of mineral water. It fell with equal weight on the state of New York and private individuals and imposed no special burden on the state. For him and for Justice Rutledge, who joined his opinion, this nondiscriminatory feature was of critical importance. By contrast, Justice Stone in a concurring opinion, supported by Justices Reed, Murphy, and Burton, played down the importance of the nondiscriminatory nature of the tax. The question for him was not whether it was nondiscriminatory, but whether it unduly interfered with "performance of the state's functions of government." He maintained that in this instance no such interference existed.

Justices Black and Douglas dissented sharply, asserting that the state's sale of mineral water was a legitimate exercise of its sovereign power. In the absence of a constitutional amendment authorizing such a tax, the doctrine of reciprocal immunity should prevail. They feared that the federal taxing power might be used to hamper the delivery of essential governmental services at the state and local level. Black and Douglas were expressing concern about maintaining a necessary degree of balance within the federal system—a concern very similar to that expressed by

Justice Rehnquist thirty years later in the *Usery* case. As Justice Douglas put it, once Congress is permitted to put local governments on its "tax collector's list, their capacity to serve the needs of their citizens is at once hampered or curtailed." The answer to this allegation is, of course, that this is not necessarily true if the available sources of state and local revenue are likewise expanded. The general decline of the reciprocal immunity doctrine on all fronts suggests this expansion. The theoretical premises of the doctrine, as articulated by Marshall, remain intact, but the scope of its practical application is now very narrow. Even in those areas where the national government might constitutionally claim immunity from state taxation, Congress has in recent decades been more and more inclined to authorize such levies or to prescribe payments to the states in lieu of taxes. The Tennessee Valley Authority, for example, currently makes such payments in lieu of property taxes to the state of Tennessee and other states in which its programs of water resource development and electrical power production are in operation.

A recent illustration of the extent of erosion of reciprocal tax immunity is provided by the 1978 decision in *Massachusetts* v. *United States* (435 U.S. 444). Here the Court upheld the imposition of a federal aircraft registration tax on a state-owned helicopter used exclusively for police work. It is difficult to think of a more basic governmental function than that of law enforcement, but the Justices found the tax valid as a "user fee" that did not violate the state's immunity from federal taxation. This ruling is fully consistent with the trend of recent cases. For the purposes of both federal and state taxation, the emphasis is on enlarging, not restricting, the available sources of revenue. (Compare *United States* v. *County of Fresno*, 429 U.S. 452 [1977], in which the Court, over the lone dissent of Justice Stevens, upheld a local property tax on federal forestry service employees whose houses were rented from the government. The tax was imposed only on those renting from owners [in this case the federal government] who were themselves exempt from taxation. Justice White for the majority found the tax nondiscriminatory and concluded that since it fell on individuals and not government, it was no impediment to the work of the forestry service.)

Scope of State Taxing Power: The Rise and Fall of the "Original Package Doctrine"

Article I, Section 10, Clause 2, of the Constitution provides that: "No state shall, without the consent of the Congress, lay any imposts or duties on imports or exports, except what may be absolutely necessary for executing its inspection laws." Like the Commerce Clause, this provision was intended to promote broad national economic interests and minimize the negative influence of parochial state policies. In addition, the Imports-Exports Clause was designed to bar discrimination against both the shipment of goods into the United States from foreign countries and the shipment of American goods destined for foreign markets. Another aim of the clause was to remove the unfair advantage that seaboard states with ports of entry would otherwise have over interior states. Given the legal characteristics of a federal system, however, the Imports-Exports Clause was also theoretically applicable to goods imported from or exported to other states within the Union. Despite some tendency to accord it this broad interpretation beginning in the late 1800s, the clause has usually been confined to the movement of goods between foreign countries and the United States.

The first question the Supreme Court considered in delimiting the scope of state taxing power turned on the definition of the word *import.* At what point, for state tax purposes, does a commodity imported from a foreign country lose its distinct character as an import and thereby become subject to a state's general taxing power? Chief Justice Marshall considered this question in the 1827 case of *Brown* v. *Maryland* (12 Wheat. 419). Maryland required that importers and sellers of goods in designated forms pay a license fee of fifty dollars. The state imposed a financial penalty for failure to comply with this requirement. Brown, a seller of foreign merchandise, challenged the law as violative of the Imports-Exports Clause and the Commerce Clause. The Marshall Court declared the law unconstitutional on both grounds. The Chief Justice interpreted the Imports-Exports Clause as a broad restriction on state power. The fee at issue in this case was aimed exclusively at imports and, on the basis of his analysis, was clearly a violation of the Constitution. But Marshall went one step further and considered a question not directly at issue in this case; namely, at what point does a commodity moving into a state from a foreign jurisdiction lose its distinct character as an import? He answered this question with the following statement:

> When the importer has so acted upon the thing imported, that it has become incorporated and mixed-up with the mass of property within the country, it has perhaps lost its distinctive character as an import, and has become subject to the taxing power of the state; but while remaining the property of the importer, in his warehouse, in the original form or package in which it was imported, a tax upon it is too plainly a duty on imports to escape the prohibition in the Constitution.

The law in question was plainly discriminatory, since it did not apply to the sellers of domestic goods and could easily have been invalidated without reference to this "original package" test. But the state Attorney General, Roger B. Taney (Marshall's successor on the Supreme Court), argued that a simple invalidation of the license fee through strict construction of the language of the Imports-Exports Clause could permanently insulate imported goods from state and local taxation. Marshall's development of the "original package" test, with its emphasis on a cut-off point beyond which the states would be free to tax, appears to have come in response to Taney's argument (for background, see Nowak, Rotunda, and Young, 1977, pp. 268 ff.).

In 1872 the original package dictum was accorded formal constitutional status, and served as the basis for striking down a nondiscriminatory property tax on imported goods that, although no longer in the "stream of commerce," remained in their original packages (*Low* v. *Austin,* 13 Wall. 29). The original package doctrine had the appeal of apparent simplicity, and it acquired, with time, the aura accorded to many of the pronouncements of Chief Justice Marshall. But, as many scholars have pointed out, the doctrine was both mechanical and inconsistent with the purpose of the Imports-Exports Clause, which was simply to prevent discriminatory state taxation on goods moving from or to foreign markets.

The law in general is heavily oriented toward precedent or, to put it less generously, toward imitation of the past. Although this tendency is less pronounced in constitutional law than in other legal subfields, it remains a powerful influence on Supreme Court Justices and on lawyers who argue constitutional cases before them. Perhaps this factor provides sufficient explanation for the durability of the original package doctrine. With advances in technology and great increases in the volume of foreign trade, the doctrine became more and more untenable. By the 1940s legal scholars were calling for its repeal and substitution of a simple test focusing on the question of whether a given state tax was discriminatory. Finally, in the 1976 case of *Michelin Tire Corp.* v. *Wages,* 423 U.S. 276, the Supreme Court adopted this position. It overruled *Low* v. *Austin* and upheld a nondiscriminatory Georgia tax on tires and tubes imported from France and Nova Scotia. Writing for the majority, Justice Brennan took note of the extensive criticism of the original package doctrine and of its alleged departure from the intent of the Framers. He also stated emphatically (lest some might think the Court was unduly influenced by extrajudicial considerations) that the Justices had drawn their own conclusions regarding the inadequacy and inappropriateness of the original package doctrine: "Our independent study persuades us that a nondiscriminatory ad valorem property tax is not the type of state exaction which the Framers of the Constitution or the Court in *Brown* had in mind as being an 'impost' or duty and that *Low* v. *Austin's* reliance upon the *Brown* dictum to reach the contrary conclusion was misplaced." Thus the Court managed to nullify the original package doctrine without challenging Marshall's initial statement of the formula—according respect for judicial tradition in the very act of overruling a constitutional precedent.

The Court has encountered other constitutional problems in determining the scope of state taxing power. These include issues of multiple taxation, the proper basis of assessment, the degree of burden that will be permitted on interstate commerce, and the procedural requirements of due process of law. We are concerned in this chapter, however, only with important aspects of the federal relationship and have chosen not to include these matters. State taxation, like its national counterpart, is used for both revenue-raising and regulatory purposes. For example, certain state-imposed license fees may be upheld even though they apply to interstate as well as intrastate business activities. The question in such cases is whether the state is acting within the legislative scope of its police power. The Supreme Court has not, as a general rule, invalidated a state tax merely because it has a regulatory effect. It has been far more concerned with whether the tax discriminates against interstate or foreign commerce or whether it inhibits an essential function of national government (see Nowak, Rotunda, and Young, 1977, Chapter 11). The constitutional scope of the state taxing power is strongly influenced, even in an age of cooperative federalism, by the objective of maintaining a balance between state and national interests.

New York v. United States

326 U.S. 572 (1946)

MR. JUSTICE FRANKFURTER announced the judgment of the Court and delivered an opinion in which MR. JUSTICE RUTLEDGE joined.

. . . [T]he 1932 Revenue Act * * * imposed a tax on mineral waters. The United States brought this suit to recover taxes assessed against the State of New York on the sale of mineral waters taken from Saratoga Springs, New York. The State claims immunity from this tax on the ground that "in the bottling and sale of the said waters the defendant State of New York was engaged in the exercise of a usual, traditional and essential governmental function." The claim was rejected by the District Court and judgment went for the United States. * * * The judgment was affirmed by the Circuit Court of Appeals for the Second Circuit. The strong urging of New York for further clarification of the amenability of States to the taxing power of the United States led us to grant certiorari. * * *

On the basis of authority the case is quickly disposed of. When States sought to control the liquor traffic by going into the liquor business, they were denied immunity from federal taxes upon the liquor business. * * * And in rejecting a claim of immunity from federal taxation when Massachusetts took over the street railways of Boston, this Court a decade ago said: "We see no reason for putting the operation of a street railway [by a State] in a different category from the sale of liquors." * * * We certainly see no reason for putting soft drinks in a different constitutional category from hard drinks. * * *

One of the greatest sources of strength of our law is that it adjudicates concrete cases and does not pronounce principles in the abstract. But there comes a time when even the process of empiric adjudication calls for a more rational disposition than that the immediate case is not different from preceding cases. The argument pressed by New York and the forty-five other States who, as amici curiae, have joined her deserves an answer.

Enactments levying taxes made in pursuance of the Constitution are, as other laws are, "the supreme Law of the Land." * * * The first of the powers conferred upon Congress is the power "To lay and collect Taxes, Duties, Imposts and Excises. . . ." * * * By its terms the Constitution has placed only one limitation upon this power . . . of laying taxes not here relevant: Congress can lay no tax "on articles exported from any State." * * * Barring only exports, the power of Congress to tax "reaches every subject." * * * But the fact that ours is a federal constitutional system, as expressly recognized in the Tenth Amendment, carries with it implications regarding the taxing power as in other aspects of government. * * * Thus, for Congress to tax State activities while leaving untaxed the same activities pursued by private persons would do violence to the presuppositions derived from the fact that we are a Nation composed of States.

But the fear that one government may cripple or obstruct the operations of the other early led to the assumption that there was a reciprocal immunity of the instrumentalities of each from taxation by the other. It was assumed that there was an equivalence in the implications of taxation by a State of the governmental activities of the National Government and the taxation by the National Government of State instrumentalities. This assumed equivalence was nourished by the phrase of Chief Justice Marshall that "the power to tax involves the power to destroy." * * * To be sure, it was uttered in connection with a tax of Maryland which plainly discriminated against the use by the United States of the Bank of the United States as one of its instruments. What he said may not have been irrelevant in its setting. But Chief Justice Marshall spoke at a time when social complexities did not so clearly reveal as now the practical limitations of a rhetorical absolute. * * * The phrase was seized upon as the basis of a broad doctrine of intergovernmental immunity, while at the same time an expansive scope was given to what were deemed to be "instrumentalities of government" for purposes of tax immunity. As a result, immunity was until recently accorded to all officers of one government from taxation by the other, and it was further assumed that the economic burden of a tax on any interest derived from a government imposes a burden on that government so as to involve an interference by the taxing government with the functioning of the other government. * * *

To press a juristic principle designed for the practical affairs of government to abstract extremes is neither sound logic nor good sense. And this Court is under no duty to make law less than sound logic and good sense. . . . The considerations bearing upon taxation by the States of activities or agencies of the federal government are not correlative with the considerations bearing upon federal taxation of State agencies or activities. The federal government is the government of all the States, and all the States share in the legislative process by which a tax of general applicability is laid. . . . [W]e have moved away from the theoretical assumption that the National Government is burdened if its functionaries, like other citizens, pay for the upkeep of their State governments, and we have denied the implied constitutional immunity of federal officials from State taxes. * * *

• • •

When this Court came to sustain the federal taxing power upon a transportation system operated by a State, it did so in ways familiar in developing the law from precedent to precedent. It edged away from reliance on a sharp distinction between the "governmental" and the "trading" activities of a State, by denying immunity from federal taxation to a State when it "is undertaking a business enterprise of a sort that is normally within the reach of the federal taxing power and is distinct from the usual governmental functions that are immune from federal taxation in order to safeguard the necessary independence of the State." * * * But this likewise does not furnish a satisfactory guide for dealing with such a practical problem as the constitutional power of the United States over State activities. To rest the federal taxing power on what is "normally" conducted by private enterprise in contradiction to the "usual" governmental functions is too shifting a basis for determining constitutional power and too entangled in expediency to serve as a dependable legal criterion. The essential nature of the problem cannot be hidden by an attempt to separate manifestations of indivisible governmental powers. * * *

The present case illustrates the sterility of such an attempt. New York urges that in the use it is making of Saratoga Springs it is engaged in the disposition of its natural resources. And so it is. But in doing so it is engaged in an enterprise in which the State sells mineral waters in competition with private waters, the sale of which Congress has found necessary to tap as a source of revenue for carrying on the National Government. To say that the States cannot be taxed for enterprises generally pursued, like the sale of mineral water, because it is somewhat connected with a State's conservation policy, is to invoke an irrelevance to the federal taxing power. Liquor control by a State certainly concerns the most important of a State's natural resources—the health and well-being of its people. * * * If in its wisdom a State engages in the liquor business and may be taxed by Congress as others engaged in the liquor business are taxed, so also Congress may tax the States when they go into the business of bottling water as others in the mineral water business are taxed even though a State's sale of its mineral waters has relation to its conservation policy.

In the older cases, the emphasis was on immunity from taxation. The whole tendency of recent cases reveals a shift in emphasis to that of limitation upon immunity. They also indicate an awareness of the limited role of courts in assessing the relative weight of the factors upon which immunity is based. Any implied limitation upon the supremacy of the federal power to levy a tax like that now before us, in the absence of discrimination against State activities, brings fiscal and political factors into play. The problem cannot escape issues that do not lend themselves to judgment by criteria and methods of reasoning that are within the professional training and special competence of judges. . . .

We have already held that by engaging in the railroad business a State cannot withdraw the railroad from the power of the federal government to regulate commerce. * * * Surely the power of Congress to lay taxes has impliedly no less a reach than the power of Congress to regulate commerce. There are, of course, State activities and State-owned property that partake of uniqueness from the point of view of intergovernmental relations. These inherently constitute a class by themselves. Only a State can own a Statehouse; only a State can get income by taxing. These could not be included for purposes of federal taxation in any abstract category of taxpayers without taxing the State as a State. But so long as Congress generally taps a source of revenue by whomsoever earned and not uniquely capable of being earned only by a State, the Constitution of the United States does not forbid it merely because its incidence falls also on a State. . . .

The process of Constitutional adjudication does not thrive on conjuring up horrible possibilities that never happen in the real world and devising doctrines sufficiently comprehensive in detail to cover the remotest contingency. Nor need we go beyond what is required for a reasoned disposition of the kind of controversy now before the Court. The restriction upon States not to make laws that discriminate against interstate commerce is a vital constitutional principle, even though "discrimination" is not a code of specifics but a continuous process of application. So we decide enough when we reject limitations upon the taxing power of Congress derived from such untenable criteria as "proprietary" against "governmental" activities of the States, or historically sanctioned activities of Government, or activities conducted merely for profit, and find no restriction upon Congress to include the States in levying a tax exacted equally from private persons upon the same subject matter.

Judgment affirmed.

MR. JUSTICE JACKSON took no part in the consideration or decision of this case.

MR. JUSTICE RUTLEDGE, concurring.

I join in the opinion of MR. JUSTICE FRANKFURTER and in the result. . . . Too much is, or may be, at stake for the nation to permit relieving the states of their duty to support it financially as otherwise, when they take over increasingly the things men have been accustomed to carry on as private, and therefore taxable, enterprise. Competitive considerations unite with the necessity for securing the federal revenue, in a time when the federal burden grows heavier proportionately than that of the states, to forbid that they be free to undermine rather than obligated to sustain the nation's financial requirements.

• • •

MR. CHIEF JUSTICE STONE, concurring.

MR. JUSTICE REED, MR. JUSTICE MURPHY, MR. JUSTICE BURTON and I concur in the result. We are of the opinion that the tax here involved should be sustained and the judgment below affirmed.

. . . But we are not prepared to say that the national government may constitutionally lay a non-discriminatory tax on every class of property and activities of States and individuals alike.

Concededly a federal tax discriminating against a State would be an unconstitutional exertion of power over a coexisting sovereignty within the same framework of government. But our difficulty with the formula, now first suggested as offering a new solution for an old problem, is that a federal tax which is not discriminatory as to the subject matter may nevertheless so affect the State, merely because it is a State that is being taxed, as to interfere unduly with the State's performance of its sovereign functions of government. . . .

If the phrase "non-discriminatory tax" is to be taken in its long accepted meaning as referring to a tax laid on a like subject matter, without regard to the personality of the taxpayer, whether a State, a corporation or a private individual, it is plain that there may be non-discriminatory taxes which, when laid on a State, would nevertheless impair the sovereign status of the State quite as much as a like tax imposed by a State on property or activities of the national government. This is not because the tax can be regarded as discriminatory but because a sovereign government is the taxpayer, and the tax, even though non-discriminatory, may be regarded as infringing its sovereignty.

.   .   .

Since all taxes must be laid by general, that is, workable, rules the effect of the immunity on the national taxing power is to be determined not quantitatively but by its operation and tendency in withdrawing taxable property or activities from the reach of federal taxation. Not the extent to which a particular state engages in the activity, but the nature and extent of the activity by whomsoever performed is the relevant consideration.

Regarded in this light we cannot say that the Constitution either requires immunity of the State's mineral water business from federal taxation, or denies to the federal government power to lay the tax.

MR. JUSTICE DOUGLAS, with whom MR. JUSTICE BLACK concurs, dissenting.

I agree that there is no essential difference between a federal tax on South Carolina's liquor business and a federal tax on New York's mineral water business. Whether South Carolina v. United States reaches the right result is another matter.

Mr. Justice Brandeis stated that "Stare decisis is usually the wise policy, because in most matters it is more important that the applicable rule of law be settled than that it be settled right." * * * But throughout the history of the Court stare decisis has had only a limited application in the field of constitutional law. And it is a wise policy which largely restricts it to those areas of the law where correction can be had by legislation. Otherwise the Constitution loses the flexibility necessary if it is to serve the needs of successive generations.

I do not believe South Carolina v. United States states the correct rule. A State's project is as much a legitimate governmental activity whether it is traditional, or akin to private enterprise, or conducted for profit. * * * A State may deem it as essential to its economy that it own and operate a railroad, a mill, or an irrigation system as it does to own and operate bridges, street lights, or a sewage disposal plant. What might have been viewed in an earlier day as an improvident or even dangerous extension of state activities may today be deemed indispensable. . . . Here a State is disposing of some of its natural resources. Tomorrow it may issue securities, sell power from its public power project, or manufacture fertilizer. Each is an exercise of its power of sovereignty. Must it pay the federal government for the privilege of exercising that inherent power? If the Constitution grants it immunity from a tax on the issuance of securities, on what grounds can it be forced to pay a tax when it sells power or disposes of other natural resources?

. . .

A tax is a powerful, regulatory instrument. Local government in this free land does not exist for itself. The fact that local government may enter the domain of private enterprise and operate a project for profit does not put in in the class of private business enterprise for tax purposes. Local government exists to provide for the welfare of its people, not for a limited group of stockholders. If the federal government can place the local governments on its tax collector's list, their capacity to serve the needs of their citizens is at once hampered or curtailed. The field of federal excise taxation alone is practically without limits. Many state activities are in marginal enterprises where private capital refuses to venture. Add to the cost of these projects a federal tax and the social program may be destroyed before it can be launched. In any case, the repercussions of such a fundamental change on the credit of the States and on their programs to take care of the needy and to build for the future would be considerable. To say the present tax will be sustained because it does not impair the State's functions of government is to conclude either that the sale by the State of its mineral water is not a function of government or that the present tax is so slight as to be no burden. The former obviously is not true. The latter overlooks the fact that the power to tax lightly is the power to tax severely. The power to tax is indeed one of the most effective forms of regulation. And no more powerful instrument for centralization of government could be devised. For with the federal government immune and the States subject to tax, the economic ability of the federal government to expand its activities at the expense of the States is at once apparent. . . .

The notion that the sovereign position of the States must find its protection in the will of a transient majority of Congress is foreign to and a negation of our constitutional system. There will often be vital regional interests represented by no majority in Congress. The Constitution was designed to keep the balance between the States and the nation outside the field of legislative controversy.

. . .

. . . [T]he major objection to the suggested test is that it disregards the Tenth Amendment, places the sovereign States on the same plane as private citizens, and makes the sovereign States pay the federal government for the privilege of exercising the powers of sovereignty guaranteed them by the Constitution.

. . .

Those who agreed with South Carolina v. United States had the fear that an expanding program of state activity would dry up sources of federal revenues and thus cripple the national government. * * * That was in 1905. That fear is expressed again today when we have the federal income tax, from which employees of the States may not claim exemption on constitutional grounds. * * * The fear of depriving the national government of revenue if the tax immunity of the States is sustained has no more place in the present decision than the spectre of socialism, the fear of which, said Holmes, "was translated into doctrines that had no proper place in the Constitution or the common law."

There is no showing whatsoever that an expanding field of state activity even faintly promises to cripple the federal government in its search for needed revenues. If the truth were known, I suspect it would show that the activity of the States in the fields of housing, public power and the like have increased the level of income of the people and have raised the standards of marginal or sub-marginal groups. Such conditions affect favorably, not adversely, the tax potential of the federal government.

Massachusetts v. United States

435 U.S. 444 (1978)

MR. JUSTICE BRENNAN delivered the opinion of the Court.

As part of a comprehensive program to recoup the costs of federal aviation programs from those who use the national airsystem, Congress in 1970 imposed an annual registration tax on all civil aircraft that fly in the navigable airspace of the United States. * * * The constitutional question presented in this case is whether this tax, as applied to an aircraft owned by a State and used by it exclusively for police functions, violates the implied immunity of a state government from federal taxation. We hold that it does not.

I

Since the passage of the Air Commerce Act of 1926, * * * the Federal Government has expended significant amounts of federal funds to develop and strengthen an integrated national airsystem and to make civil air transportation safe and practical. . . .

In 1970, after an extended study of the national airsystem, Congress concluded that the level of annual federal outlays on aviation, while significant, had not been sufficient to permit the national airsystem to develop the capacity to cope satisfactorily with the current and projected growth in air transportation.

To remedy this situation, Congress enacted two laws, * * * which together constitute a comprehensive program substantially to expand and improve the national airport and airway system over the decade beginning July 1, 1970. . . . [One of the Acts] adopted several measures to ensure that federal outlays that benefited the civil users of the airways would, to a substantial extent, be financed by taxing measures imposed on those civil users. . . . Congress conceived . . . of these revenue measures as user fees and calculated that they would produce revenues that would defray a significant and increasing percentage of the civil share of the annual total federal airport and airway expenditures. . . .

The financing measures in the . . . Act are intended to promote two purposes. First, they are designed to serve the congressional policy of having those who especially benefit from Government activity help bear the cost. * * * Second, the financing provisions are intended to ensure that the capacity of the national airsystem would not again be found to be insufficient to meet the demands of increasing use. . . .

. . . The tax challenged in this case imposes an annual "flat fee" . . . on all civil aircraft—including those owned by state and national governments—that fly in the navigable airspace of the United States. . . .

• • •

The Commonwealth of Massachusetts owns several aircraft that are subject to the tax imposed * * * including a helicopter which the Commonwealth uses exclusively for patrolling highways and other police functions. In 1973 the United States notified the Commonwealth that it had been assessed for a tax . . . on this state police helicopter. . . . The Commonwealth refused to pay and the United States thereafter levied on one of the Commonwealth's bank accounts and collected this tax, plus interest and penalties.

. . . [T]he Commonwealth then instituted this action for a refund of the money collected, contending that the United States may not constitutionally impose a tax that directly affects the essential and traditional state function of operating a police force. . . .

• • •

II

A

That the existence of the States implies some restriction on the national taxing power was first decided in Collector v Day. * * * There this Court held that the immunity that federal instrumentalities and employees then enjoyed from state taxation * * * was to some extent reciprocal and that the salaries paid state judges were immune from a nondiscriminatory federal tax. This immunity of state and federal governments from taxation by each other was expanded in decisions over the last third of the 19th Century and the first third of this century, * * * but more recent decisions of this Court have confined the scope of the doctrine.

The immunity of the Federal Government from state taxation is bottomed on the Supremacy Clause, but the States' immunity from federal taxes was judicially implied from the States' role in the constitutional scheme. . . .

As the contours of the principle evolved in later decisions, "cogent reasons" were recognized for narrowly limiting the immunity of the States from federal imposts. * * * The first is that any immunity for the protection of state sovereignty is at the expense of the sovereign power of the National Government to tax. Therefore, when the scope of the States' constitutional immunity is enlarged beyond that necessary to protect the continued ability of the States to deliver traditional governmental services, the burden of the immunity is thrown upon the National Government without any corresponding promotion of the constitutionally protected values. * * * The second . . . is that the political process is uniquely adapted to accommodating the competing demands "for national revenue, on the one hand, and for reasonable scope for the independence of state action, on the other." * * * [T]he Congress, composed as it is of members chosen by state constituencies, constitutes an inherent check against the possibility of abusive taxing of the States by the National Government.

In tacit, and at times explicit, recognition of these considerations, decisions of the Court either have declined to enlarge the scope of state immunity or have in fact restricted its reach. Typical of this trend are decisions holding that the National Government may tax revenue generating activities of the States that are of the same nature as those traditionally engaged in by private persons. * * * It is true that some of the opinions speak of the state activity taxed as "proprietary" and thus not an immune essential *governmental* activity, but . . . in New York v. United States, [the Court] rejected the governmental-proprietary distinction as untenable. . . .

Illustrative of decisions actually restricting the scope of the immunity is the line of cases that culminated in the overruling of Collector v Day. * * * Collector v Day, of course, involved a nondiscriminatory tax that was imposed not directly on the State but rather on the salary earned by a judicial officer. . . . [T]he Court [later] demonstrated that an immunity for the salaries paid key state officials is not justifiable. Although key state officials are agents of the State, they are also citizens of the United States, so their income is a natural subject for income taxation. * * *

. . . The purpose of the implied constitutional restriction on the national taxing power is not to give an advantage to the States by enabling them to engage employees at a lower charge than those paid by private entities, * * * but rather is solely to protect the States from undue interference with their traditional governmental functions. While a tax on the salary paid key state officers may increase the cost of government, it will no more preclude the States from performing traditional functions than it will prevent private entities from perform-ing their missions. * * *

These two lines of decisions illustrate the "practical construction" that the Court now gives the limitation the existence of the States constitutionally im-poses on the national taxing power; "that limitation cannot be so varied or extended as seriously to impair either the taxing power of the government impos-ing the tax . . . or the appropriate exercise of the functions of the government affected by it." * * * Where the subject of tax is a natural and traditional source of federal revenue and where it is inconceivable that such a revenue measure could ever operate to preclude traditional state activities, the tax will be valid. . . .

B

A nondiscriminatory taxing measure that operates to defray the cost of a federal program by recovering a fair approximation of each beneficiary's share of the cost is surely no more offensive to the constitutional scheme than is either a tax on the income earned by state employees or a tax on a State's sale of bottled water. . . . There is no danger that such measures will not be based on benefits conferred or that they will function as regulatory devices unduly burdening es-sential state activities. . . .

• • •

. . . So long as charges do not discriminate against state functions, are based on a fair approximation of use of the system, and are structured to produce revenues that will not exceed the total cost to the Federal Government of the benefits to be supplied, there can be no substantial basis for a claim that the National Govern-ment will be using its taxing powers to control, unduly interfere with, or destroy a State's ability to perform essential services.

• • •

Affirmed.

Mr. Justice Blackmun took no part in the consideration or decision of this case.

Mr. Justice Stewart and Mr. Justice Powell concurred in part and con-curred in the judgment. [Omitted.]

Mr. Justice Rehnquist, with whom The Chief Justice joins, dissenting. [Omitted.]

Brown v. Maryland

12 Wheat. 419 (1827)

MR. CHIEF JUSTICE MARSHALL delivered the opinion of the court.

. . . The indictment charges [Brown] with having imported and sold one package of foreign dry goods without having license to do so. A judgment was rendered against [him] . . . for the penalty which the act prescribes for the offense; and that judgment is now before this court.

The cause depends entirely on the question, whether the legislature of a state can constitutionally require the importer of foreign articles to take out a license from the state, before he shall be permitted to sell a bale or package so imported.

. . . [Brown insists] that the act under consideration is repugnant to two provisions in the constitution of the United States:

1. To that which declares that "no state shall, without the consent of Congress, lay any imposts, or duties on imports or exports, except what may be absolutely necessary for executing its inspection laws."

2. To that which declares that Congress shall have power "to regulate commerce with foreign nations, and among the several states, and with the Indian tribes."

1. The first inquiry is into the extent of the prohibition upon states "to lay any imposts, or duties on imports or exports." The counsel for the state of Maryland would confine this prohibition to the laws imposing duties on the act of importation or exportation. The counsel for [Brown] give them a much wider scope.

• • •

What . . . is the meaning of the words, "imposts, or duties on imports or exports"?

An impost, or duty on imports, is a custom or a tax levied on articles brought into a country, and is most usually secured before the importer is allowed to exercise his rights of ownership over them, because evasions of the law can be prevented more certainly by executing it while the articles are in its custody. It would not, however, be less an impost or duty on the articles, if it were to be levied on them after they were landed. The policy and consequent practice of levying or securing the duty before, or on entering the port, does not limit the power to that state of things, nor, consequently, the prohibition, unless the true meaning of the clause so confines it. What, then, are "imports"? . . . They are the articles themselves which are brought into the country. "A duty on imports," then, is not merely a duty on the act of importation, but is a duty on the thing imported. It is not, taken in its literal sense, confined to a duty levied while the article is entering the country, but extends to a duty levied after it has entered the country. The succeeding words of the sentence which limit the prohibition, show the extent in which it was understood. The limitation is, "except what may be absolutely necessary for executing its inspection laws." Now, the inspection laws, so far as they act upon articles for exportation, are generally executed on land, before the article is put on board the vessel; so far as they act upon importations, they are generally executed upon articles which are landed. The tax or duty of inspection, then, is a tax which is frequently, if not always, paid for service performed on land, while the article is in the bosom of the country. Yet this tax is an exception to the prohibition on the states to lay duties on imports or exports. The exception was made because the tax would otherwise have been within the prohibition.

• • •

From the vast inequality between the different states of the confederacy, as to commercial advantages, few subjects were viewed with deeper interest, or excited more irritation, than the manner in which the several states exercised, or seemed disposed to exercise, the power of laying duties on imports. From motives which were deemed sufficient by the statesmen of that day, the general power of taxation . . . was so far abridged as to forbid them to touch imports or exports, with the single exception which has been noticed. Why are they restrained from imposing these duties? Plainly because, in the general opinion, the interest of all would be best promoted by placing that whole subject under the control of Congress. Whether the prohibition to "lay imposts, or duties on imports or exports," proceeded from an apprehension that the power might be so exercised as to disturb that equality among the states which was generally advantageous, . . . or whatever other motive might have induced the prohibition, it is plain that the object would be as completely defeated by a power to tax the article in the hands of the importer the instant it was landed as by a power to tax it while entering the port. . . . No object of any description can be accomplished by laying a duty on importation, which may not be accomplished with equal certainty by laying a duty on the thing imported in the hands of the importer. . . .

• • •

. . . It might . . . be said, that no state would be so blind to its own interests as to lay duties on importation which would either prohibit or diminish its trade. Yet the framers of our constitution have thought this a power which no state ought to exercise. Conceding, to the full extent which is required, that every state would, in its legislation on this subject, provide judiciously for its own interest, it cannot be conceded that each would respect the interest of others. A duty on imports is a tax on the article, which is paid by the consumer. The great importing states would thus levy a tax on the non-importing states, which would not be less a tax because their interest would afford ample security against its ever being so heavy as to expel commerce from their ports.

This would necessarily produce countervailing measures on the part of those states whose situation was less favorable to importation. For this, among other reasons, the whole power of laying duties on imports was, with a single and slight exception, taken from the states. When we are inquiring whether a particular act is within this prohibition, the question is not, whether the state may so legislate as to hurt itself, but whether the act is within the words and mischief of the prohibitory clause. It has already been shown that a tax on the article in the hands of the importer is within its words; and we think it too clear for controversy, that the same tax is within its mischief. We think it unquestionable, that such a tax has precisely the same tendency to enhance the price of the article as if imposed upon it while entering the port.

The counsel for the state of Maryland insist, with great reason, that if the words of the prohibition be taken in their utmost latitude, they will abridge the power of taxation, which all admit to be essential to the states. . . . These words must therefore be construed with some limitation; and, if this be admitted, they insist, that entering the country is the point of time when the prohibition ceases, and the power of the state to tax commences.

It may be conceded that the words of the prohibition ought not to be pressed to their utmost extent; that in our complex system, the object of the powers conferred on the government of the Union, and the nature of the often conflicting powers which remain in the states, must always be taken into view, and may aid in expounding the words of any particular clause. But, while we admit that sound principles of construction ought to restrain all courts from carrying the words of the prohibition beyond the object the constitution is intended to secure, that there must be a point of time when the prohibition ceases, and the power of the state to tax commences; we cannot admit that this point of time is the instant that the articles enter the country. It is, we think, obvious, that this construction would defeat the prohibition.

The constitutional prohibition on the states to lay a duty on imports—a prohibition which a vast majority of them must feel an interest in preserving—may certainly come in conflict with their acknowledged power to tax persons and property within their territory. The power, and the restriction on it, though quite distinguishable when they do not approach each other, may yet, like the intervening colors between white and black, approach so nearly as to perplex the understanding, as colors perplex the vision in marking the distinction between them. Yet the distinction exists, and must be marked as the cases arise. Till they do arise, it might be premature to state any rule as being universal in its application. It is sufficient for the present to say, generally, that when the importer has so acted upon the thing imported that it has become incorporated and mixed up with the mass of property in the country, it has, perhaps, lost its distinctive character as an import, and has become subject to the taxing power of the state; but while remaining the property of the importer, in his warehouse, in the original form or package in which it was imported, a tax upon it is too plainly a duty on imports to escape the prohibition in the constitution.

• • •

This indictment is against the importer, for selling a package of dry goods in the form in which it was imported, without a license. This state of things is changed if he sells them, or otherwise mixes them with the general property of the state, by breaking up his packages, and traveling with them as an itinerant peddler. In the first case, the tax intercepts the import, as an import, in its way to become incorporated with the general mass of property, and denies it the privilege of becoming so incorporated until it shall have contributed to the revenue of the state. It denies to the importer the right of using the privilege which he has purchased from the United States, until he shall have also purchased it from the state. In the last cases, the tax finds the article already incorporated with the mass of property by the act of the importer. He has used the privilege he had purchased, and has himself mixed them up with the common mass, and the law may treat them as it finds them. . . .

• • •

The principle, then, for which [Brown contends], that the importer acquires a right, not only to bring the articles into the country, but to mix them with the common mass of property, does not interfere with the necessary power of taxation which is acknowledged to reside in the states, to that dangerous extent which the counsel for [Maryland] seem to apprehend. It carries the prohibition in the constitution no farther than to prevent the states from doing that which it was the great object of the constitution to prevent.

But if it should be proved that a duty on the article itself would be repugnant to the constitution, it is still argued that this is not a tax upon the article, but on the person. The state, it is said, may tax occupations, and this is nothing more.

It is impossible to conceal from ourselves that this is varying the form, without varying the substance. It is treating a prohibition which is general, as if it were confined to a particular mode of doing the forbidden thing. All must perceive that a tax on the sale of an article, imported only for sale, is a tax on the article itself. It is true, the state may tax occupations generally, but this tax must be paid by those who employ the individual, or is a tax on his business. . . . [A] tax on the occupation of an importer is . . . a tax on importation. . . . This the state has not a right to do, because it is prohibited by the constitution.

• • •

We think, then, that the act under which [Brown was] indicted, is repugnant to that article of the constitution which declares that "no state shall lay any impost or duties on imports or exports."

2. Is it also repugnant to that clause in the constitution which empowers "Congress to regulate commerce with foreign nations, and among the several states, and with the Indian tribes"?

. . .

What, then, is the just extent of a power to regulate commerce with foreign nations, and among the several states?

If this [commerce] power reaches the interior of a state, and may be there exercised, it must be capable of authorizing the sale of those articles which it introduces. . . . Sale is the object of importation, and is an essential ingredient of that intercouse, of which importation constitutes a part. . . . It must be considered as a component part of the power to regulate commerce. Congress has a right, not only to authorize importation, but to authorize the importer to sell.

If this be admitted—and we think it cannot be denied—what can be the meaning of an act of Congress which authorizes importation, and offers the privilege for sale at a fixed price to every person who chooses to become a purchaser? How is it to be construed, if an intent to deal honestly and fairly, an intent as wise as it is moral, is to enter into the construction? What can be the use of the contract? What does the importer purchase, if he does not purchase the privilege to sell?

. . .

We think, then, that if the power to authorize a sale exists in Congress, the conclusion that the right to sell is connected with the law permitting importation, as an inseparable incident, is inevitable.

If the principles we have stated be correct, the result to which they conduct us cannot be mistaken. Any penalty inflicted on the importer for selling the article in his character of importer must be in opposition to the act of Congress which authorizes importation. Any charge on the introduction and incorporation of the articles into and with the mass of property in the country, must be hostile to the power given to Congress to regulate commerce, since an essential part of that regulation, and principal object of it, is to prescribe the regular means for accomplishing that introduction and incorporation.

. . .

It has been contended, that this construction of the power to regulate commerce, as was contended in construing the prohibition to lay duties on imports, would abridge the acknowledged power of a state to tax its own citizens, or their property within its territory.

We admit this power to be sacred; but cannot admit that it may be used so as to obstruct the free course of a power given to Congress. We cannot admit that it may be used so as to obstruct or defeat the power to regulate commerce. It has been observed, that the powers remaining with the states may be so exercised as to come in conflict with those vested in Congress. When this happens, that which is not supreme must yield to that which is supreme. This great and universal truth is inseparable from the nature of things, and the constitution has applied it to the often interfering powers of the general and state governments, as a vital principle of perpetual operation. It results, necessarily, from this principle, that the taxing power of the states must have some limits. It cannot reach and restrain the action of the national government within its proper sphere. . . .

• • •

We think there is error in the judgment of the Court of Appeals of the State of Maryland, in affirming the judgment of the Baltimore City Court, because the act of the legislature of Maryland, imposing the penalty for which the said judgment is rendered, is repugnant to the constitution of the United States, and, consequently, void. The judgment is to be reversed, and the cause remanded to that court, with instructions to enter judgment in favor of [Brown].

MR. JUSTICE THOMPSON dissented. [Omitted.]

Michelin Tire Corp. v. Wages

423 U.S. 276 (1976)

MR. JUSTICE BRENNAN delivered the opinion of the Court.

. . . [T]he Tax Commissioner and Tax Assessors of Gwinnett County, Ga., assessed ad valorem [according to value] property taxes against tires and tubes imported by [Michelin Tire Corp.] from France and Nova Scotia that were included . . . in an inventory maintained at its wholesale distribution warehouse in the county. [Michelin Tire argued that] . . . taxes assessed against its inventory of imported tires and tubes were prohibited by Art I, § 10, cl 2, of the Constitution, which provides in pertinent part that "No State shall, without the consent of Congress, lay any Imposts or Duties on Imports or Exports, except what may be absolutely necessary for executing its Inspection Laws. . . ." . . . The only question presented is whether the Georgia Supreme Court was correct in holding that the tires were subject to the ad valorem property tax.

• • •

Low v Austin * * * is the leading decision of this Court holding that the States are prohibited by the Import-Export Clause from imposing a nondiscriminatory ad valorem property tax on imported goods until they lose their character as imports and become incorporated into the mass of property in the State. . . .

Scholarly analysis has been uniformly critical of Low v Austin. It is true that Chief Justice Marshall * * * said that ". . . while [the thing imported remains] the property of the importer, in his warehouse, in the original form or package in which it was imported, a tax upon it is too plainly a duty on imports to escape the prohibition in the constitution." Commentators have uniformly agreed that Low v Austin misread this dictum in holding that the Court . . . included nondiscriminatory ad valorem property taxes among prohibited "imposts" or "duties," for the contrary conclusion is plainly to be inferred from consideration of the specific abuses which led the Framers to include the Import-Export Clause in the Constitution. * * *

Our independent study persuades us that a nondiscriminatory ad valorem property tax is not the type of state exaction which the Framers of the Constitution or the Court . . . had in mind as being an "impost" or "duty" and that Low v Austin's . . . contrary conclusion was misplaced.

One of the major defects of the Articles of Confederation, and a compelling reason for the calling of the Constitutional Convention of 1787, was the fact that the Articles essentially left the individual States free to burden commerce both among themselves and with foreign countries very much as they pleased. Before 1787 it was commonplace for seaboard States to derive revenue to defray the costs of state and local governments by imposing taxes on imported goods destined for customers in inland States. At the same time, there was no secure source of revenue for the central government. * * *

• • •

The Framers of the Constitution thus sought to alleviate three main concerns by committing sole power to lay imposts and duties on imports in the Federal Government, with no concurrent state power: the Federal Government must speak with one voice when regulating commercial relations with foreign governments, and tariffs, which might affect foreign relations, could not be implemented by the States consistently with that exclusive power; import revenues were to be the major source of revenue of the Federal Government and should not be diverted to the States, and harmony among the States might be disturbed unless seaboard States, with their crucial ports of entry, were prohibited from levying taxes on citizens of other States by taxing goods merely flowing through their ports to the inland States not situated as favorably geographically.

Nothing in the history of the Import-Export Clause even remotely suggests that a nondiscriminatory ad valorem property tax which is also imposed on imported goods that are no longer in import transit was the type of exaction that was regarded as objectionable by the Framers of the Constitution. For such an exaction, unlike discriminatory state taxation against imported goods as imports, was not regarded as an impediment that severely hampered commerce or constituted a form of tribute by seaboard States to the disadvantage of the interior States.

It is obvious that such nondiscriminatory property taxation can have no impact whatsoever on the Federal Government's exclusive regulation of foreign commerce, probably the most important purpose of the clause's prohibition. By definition, such a tax does not fall on imports as such because of their place of origin. It cannot be used to create special protective tariffs or particular preferences for certain domestic goods, and it cannot be applied selectively to encourage or discourage any importation in a manner inconsistent with federal regulation.

Nor will such taxation deprive the Federal Government of the exclusive right to all revenues from imposts and duties on imports and exports, since that right by definition only extends to revenues from exactions of a particular category; if nondiscriminatory ad valorem taxation is not in that category, it deprives the Federal Government of nothing to which it is entitled. Unlike imposts and duties, which are essentially taxes on the commercial privilege of bringing goods into a country, such property taxes are taxes by which a State apportions the cost of such services as police and fire protection among the beneficiaries according to their respective wealth; there is no reason why an importer should not bear his share of these costs along with his competitors handling only domestic goods. The Import-Export Clause clearly prohibits state taxation based on the foreign origin of the imported goods, but it cannot be read to accord imported goods preferential treatment that permits escape from uniform taxes imposed without regard to foreign origin for services which the State supplies. * * * . . . Taxes imposed after an initial sale, after the breakup of the shipping packages, or the moment goods imported for use are committed to current operational needs are . . . all likely to have an incidental effect on the volume of goods imported; yet all are permissible. * * * What those taxes and nondiscriminatory ad valorem property taxes share, it should be emphasized, is the characteristic that they cannot be selectively imposed and increased so as substantially to impair or prohibit importation.

Finally, nondiscriminatory ad valorem property taxes do not interfere with the free flow of imported goods among the States, as did the exactions by States under the Articles of Confederation directed solely at imported goods. . . . An evil to be prevented by the Import-Export Clause was the levying of taxes which could only be imposed because of the peculiar geographical situation of certain States that enabled them to single out goods destined for other States. In effect, the clause was fashioned to prevent the imposition of exactions which were no more than transit fees on the privilege of moving through a State. A nondiscriminatory ad valorem property tax obviously stands on a different footing, and to the extent there is any conflict whatsoever with this purpose of the clause, it may be secured merely by prohibiting the assessment of even nondiscriminatory property taxes on goods which are merely in transit through the State when the tax is assessed.

. . . [The Import-Export Clause] is not written in terms of a broad prohibition of every "tax." The prohibition is only against States laying "imposts or duties" on "imports." By contrast, Congress is empowered to "lay and collect Taxes, Duties, Imposts, and Excises," which plainly lends support to a reading of the Import-Export Clause as not prohibiting every exaction or "tax" which falls in some measure on imported goods. . . .

. . . [S]ince prohibition of nondiscriminatory ad valorem property taxation would not further the objectives of the Import-Export Clause, only the clearest constitutional mandate should lead us to condemn such taxation. The terminology employed in the clause—"Imposts or Duties"—is sufficiently ambiguous that we decline to presume it was intended to embrace taxation that does not create the evils the clause was specifically intended to eliminate.

• • •

. . . [W]e therefore hold that the nondiscriminatory property tax levied on [Michelin's] inventory of imported tires was not interdicted by the Import-Export Clause of the Constitution. The judgment of the Supreme Court of Georgia is accordingly affirmed.

MR. JUSTICE STEVENS took no part in the consideration or decision of this case.

CHAPTER **12**

Interstate Relations

INTRODUCTORY ESSAY

Federalism entails more than just the relations between the national government and the several states; it also involves relations between the states themselves, referred to as interstate relations. The Framers could well have left this horizontal dimension of their newly devised federal structure to rules and regulations already governing relations between sovereignties in international law. Or they could have relied on the goodwill and cooperative spirit of state officials to facilitate smoothly functioning relations among the states, without writing specific provisions into the Constitution. The Framers were too well aware, though, of the vagaries and pitfalls of relying on either what could have been discretionary international common law applied to state sovereignty or the thin measure of goodwill among staunch, often parochial, states' rightish officials. Indeed, as our discussions have made clear, part of the reason for calling the Constitutional Convention stemmed from the failure of the confederated states to cooperate through either common law or informal interaction. As a consequence, rather than leave interstate matters to providence, the Framers provided a structure for handling what they considered problems in interstate relations, and they did so in the Full Faith and Credit, Privileges and Immunities, and Rendition Clauses of Article IV, the Compact Clause of Article I, and in the clause granting original jurisdiction to resolve disputes between states to the Supreme Court in Article III. These clauses were devised "to help fuse into one nation a collection of independent sovereign states" (*Toomer* v. *Witsell,* 334 U.S. 395 [1948]), a task, as we shall see, reasonably well accomplished.

Full Faith and Credit

The Full Faith and Credit Clause requires that each state recognize and enforce the judgments, public records, and laws of every other state. In addition to asserting this general principle, the Constitution grants Congress the power to enact legislation prescribing the manner in which such full faith and credit will be accomplished. To that end, Congress passed legislation in 1790 and 1804 clearly providing for authentification and effect. As a consequence of this legislation and minor subsequent amendment, little dispute has arisen over this provision of the Constitution.

The most important aspect of full faith and credit is in the area of judicial pronouncements. The goal of unity and good relations between states could hardly be accomplished if a citizen in State A could simply move to State B and thereby avoid any liability incurred by an adverse civil judgment received in State A. Suppose such an event occurred: Ms. Smith sues Mr. Jones in Tennessee and secures a $5,000 judgment in her favor. Mr. Jones promptly moves to California. Rather than lose her money or be forced to retry the whole matter in California, under the provisions of the Full Faith and Credit Clause, Ms. Smith could bring action in the California courts seeking enforcement of the Tennessee judgment. In California, the judge would seek to ascertain that the court records were authentic and that Tennessee properly had jurisdiction. If it could be shown that these claims were true, California would have to use its enforcement machinery to secure Ms. Smith's $5,000 from Mr. Jones and must do so, even if its substantive law would not have led to the granting of such a judgment to Ms. Smith. Thus, California courts have the authority to look only to the jurisdictional power of the Tennessee state court to act and not to the legal basis upon which that court reached judgment. All of this is not simply between Ms. Smith and a California judge. Mr. Jones is allowed to enter the litigation but can defend himself only by challenging the jurisdiction of the Tennessee court, not by challenging the merits of the Tennessee ruling.

Enforcement of a sister state's judicial pronouncements is one aspect of full faith and credit. Another, more problematic aspect concerns the use of one state court's judgment as a defense in another state court action arising from the same set of facts. If Mr. Jones had originally resided in California, but had been sued by Ms. Smith in Tennessee and paid her the awarded damages, Ms. Smith would not be entitled to sue Mr. Jones for the same actions in California. Should she try, Mr. Jones could bring to the California court's attention the judicial pronouncement in Tennessee. Under principles of *res judicata* (matters already settled by judgment are conclusive) and full faith and credit, California must recognize the Tennessee judgment as final and stop the suit of Ms. Smith in California.

Full Faith and Credit in Interstate Divorce Suits

These general rules governing the use of state judicial pronouncements as a defense against actions in another state at one time worked havoc in certain divorce cases. When divorce laws were stricter in some states than in others, it was not inconceivable, for example, for a male spouse to desert a family, secure a divorce quickly in another state (most likely Nevada), and later use that divorce decree as a bar to any divorce action that his wife might bring in his home state. Since the out-of-state "quickie" divorce likely did not include alimony or child support, the abandoned wife was often left to suffer considerable hardship because most states respected the divorce decree of a sister state as a valid defense, leaving the wife with no legal recourse.

Part of the problem stems from the fact that a state, under its police power, legitimately has authority over the marital status of its citizenry. In general, state laws not only prescribe the legal obligation a person acquires upon becoming a party to a marriage but also define for the community how its members can legally relate to the married couple. Thus, when feuding spouses seek a legal dissolution of their marriage in a state court, a state judge is called upon to reach a judgment on their marital status not only for the wife and husband but for the community at large as well. In reaching what is referred to as a judgment *in rem* (a judgment against a thing or a status) as opposed to a judgment *in personam* (a judgment against a person), a court determines whether it has jurisdiction over the status in question by ascertaining if one (or both) of the parties involved has domicile in the state. (In law, domicile is a person's permanent home, a place of residence to which one intends to return.) If a person seeking divorce is domiciled in the state in question, he or she is entitled to a ruling on the status of the marriage. After establishing that the domicile of either party is within the state, a court can assert authority over the marital status of the domiciled citizen. As the excerpted case of *Sosna* v. *Iowa*, 419 U.S. 393 (1975), makes clear, what constitutes proof of domicile for divorce purposes is primarily a state matter. If both parties reside in the same state, no legal problem arises. But, until recently, if spouses were domiciled in separate states, the general rule that within its borders a state can determine the marital status of any one of its citizens, and the corollary rule that the decree of any one state is valid in any other state, served to facilitate the injustice shown in our example.

The Supreme Court struggled with this injustice for some time and finally enunciated a viable policy in the 1948 case of *Estin* v. *Estin*, 334 U.S. 541. The Court's policy until 1906 was based on the rule just stated, simply that a divorce decree granted in either state of the separately domiciled couple must be granted full faith and credit in all other states (*Atherton* v. *Atherton*, 181 U.S. 155 [1901]). This applied even if the defendant spouse received no notice of the suit and was thus unable to be represented. In the face of the simplicity and certainty of this position, the Court altered the general rule determining the validity of interstate divorce decrees in the 1906 case of *Haddock* v. *Haddock*, 201 U.S. 562. In this case, the majority ruled that for a divorce to be valid in other states the hearing had to be *in personam* rather than *in rem*. That is, the defendant spouse had to be served notice and thereby given the opportunity to appear at the hearing. In *Haddock*, Mrs. Haddock, the defendant spouse domiciled in New York, had not been served notice and had not appeared in the Connecticut court in which her husband had secured the challenged divorce. The Court's ruling allowed that since Mrs. Haddock had not been given the opportunity to appear, New York need not give full faith and credit to the Connecticut dissolution. Nonetheless, since Connecticut had the right to govern the marital status of its citizenry, the divorce was effective there. Thus, Mr. and Mrs. Haddock were lawfully wed while in New York and lawfully divorced when in Connecticut, and each divorced and married respectively when living in his or her state of domicile alone. (In response to *Haddock* and other soon-to-be-noted confusions, Justice Jackson averred in *Estin:* "If there is one thing that people are entitled to expect from their lawmakers, it is rules of law that will enable individuals to tell whether they are married and, if so, to whom.")

Between 1906 and 1942 the Court was fortunate in that the states generally ignored the full implications of *Haddock* and continued to recognize out-of-state divorces as valid. Ultimately, though, the difficulties of *Haddock* required a reassessment. In *Williams* v. *North Carolina (Williams I)*, 317 U.S. 287 (1942), and its sequel, *Williams II*, 325 U.S. 226 (1945), the Court did just that. Both cases involved North Carolina's substantial effort to convict and punish the Williamses for bigamy. The Williamses married each other after securing "quickie" Nevada divorces from their respective North Carolina spouses. Once married, they returned to North Carolina only to be charged by that state with bigamy. North Carolina justified its charges by refusing to recognize the Nevada divorce, a position wholly defensible given the failure of both divorcing parties to notify the original North Carolina spouses, per *Haddock*.

In *Williams I* the Court overruled *Haddock* and officially returned to the policy of requiring state recognition of a sister state's divorce decrees (at least temporarily). Undaunted, North Carolina brought the same charges against the Williamses again, but this time asserted that the authority of Nevada to rule on the divorces was not valid since the Williamses had not established a bona fide domicile. Without such authority the Nevada decree was invalid, meaning that the Williamses had never secured a divorce and thus were guilty of bigamy. (Interestingly, this second prosecution proceeded despite the death of one of the original spouses and the marriage of the other.) The Supreme Court upheld North Carolina's right in *Williams II* to determine whether domicile was bona fide and hence whether the Nevada court had actual jurisdiction.

The *Williams* decisions revitalized the very problem to which *Haddock* had been an attempted, but feeble, answer. Finally, in *Estin* v. *Estin* (1948), the Court formulated what has proven to be a viable solution, establishing a divisible divorce: Any state's dissolution of a marriage must be recognized as valid by all other states, but that same decree cannot be conclusive of such matters as alimony, child support, or property disbursement. This ruling has had the effect of foreclosing bigamy prosecutions while minimizing an individual's ability to elude financial and other responsibilities.

Privileges and Immunities

National unification would have been illusive at best, had the Framers limited their governance of interstate relations to a Full Faith and Credit Clause alone. Recognition of sister state documents would have been of little consequence had it been possible to foster ill will through constitutionally permissible state legislation granting special preference to in-state citizens at the expense of citizens of other states. To preclude this possibility for ill will, the Framers included Section 2 of Article IV granting federal protection of the "privileges and immunities" of state citizenship. Section 2 reads: "Citizens of each state shall be entitled to all privileges and immunities of citizens in the several states."*

No doubt the Framers would have preferred to find less cryptic language to express what they had in mind, namely to make it impossible for a state to dis-

---

* This clause is not to be confused with a similar clause in the Fourteenth Amendment that reads: "No state shall make or enforce any law which shall abridge the privileges and immunities of citizens of the United States." This Fourteenth Amendment version protects rights of national citizenship, while the Article IV version protects rights of state citizenship.

criminate unduly against those citizens of other states who happened to be within its borders and to protect such citizens in fairly limited areas of civil and political rights. Yet, the words themselves, particularly outside of any historical context, appear to grant a substantial power to the national government to create and enforce uniform, national civil rights. In practice, the Court has retained a remarkable fidelity to the intent of the Framers despite the potential breadth of the clause used to express that intent. In part this fidelity stems from judicial reliance on an earlier version of the Privileges and Immunities Clause, which appeared in the Articles of Confederation. That more thorough version reads as follows:

> The better to secure and perpetuate mutual friendship and intercourse among the people of the different states in the union, the free inhabitants of each of these states, paupers, vagabonds, and fugitives from justice excepted, shall be entitled to all privileges and immunities of free citizens in the several states: and the people of each state shall have ingress and regress to and from any other state, and shall enjoy therein all the privileges of trade and commerce, subject to the same duties, impositions, and restrictions on the inhabitants thereof respectively. . . .

This language suggests a desire to assure out-of-state citizens equal footing with in-state citizens. It does not leave much room to assume that the intent of the Framers was to foster a national set of civil rights and a police power to enforce those rights.

The limited scope of the Privileges and Immunities Clause, as judicially applied, rests as well on the principles of vertical federalism intended by the Framers. As we have already noted, those at the Constitutional Convention wished to maintain the states as viable political entities and not mere administrative arms of the federal government. Any interpretation of the Privileges and Immunities Clause that granted the national government the expansive power to enforce its own version of civil and political rights would go contrary to this vision of the federal relationship.

Fundamental Immunities

The first major case relying on the Privileges and Immunities Clause remained faithful to a narrow interpretation but reached its conclusion in a potentially problematic manner. In *Corfield* v. *Coryell,* 6 Fed. Cas. 546 (an 1823 circuit court decision), Supreme Court Justice Bushrod Washington argued that Section 2 protects only those privileges and immunities "which are, in their nature, fundamental; which belong of right to the citizens of all free governments." For Washington, these fundamentals included, but were not limited to,

> the right of a citizen of one state to pass through or reside in any other state . . .; to claim the benefit of the writ of *habeas corpus;* to institute and maintain actions of any kind in the courts of the state; to take, hold, and dispose of property; and an exemption from higher taxes or impositions than are paid by other citizens of the state.

Washington's list of fundamental rights is very limited and fails to comport with what the average twentieth-century citizen would consider the rights of a citizen of a free government. Although the list itself appears shy of modern standards, the logic underlying the position could easily be extended to include a more pervasive set of fundamentals that a state could not abridge in the treatment of citizens of other states, and ultimately in the treatment of its own citizens.

Equality of Rights

Subsequent rulings have not enlarged upon Washington's list nor used his assumption as a building block for an expansive federal role in the protection of civil rights. (What centralizing experiences have occurred have stemmed from constitutional sources other than the Privileges and Immunities Clause.) This nationalizing potential, in fact, led post-*Corfield* courts to shift their focus from defining fundamental rights to determining whether equality of rights was being granted state citizen and noncitizen alike. As Tribe (1978) has suggested, after the Civil War the clause was initially interpreted to mean that whatever rights a state granted to its own citizens "shall be the measure of the rights of citizens of other states" when in that state (Slaughterhouse Cases, 16 Wall. 36 [1873]). A state law could be held in opposition to the Privileges and Immunities Clause not for denying a fundamental right per se, but for according a fundamental right to an in-state citizen and denying it to an out-of-stater. While the distinction between fundamental and nonfundamental rights still informed the discussion, the fact that the test was equality or inequality helped to minimize the need to develop a comprehensive specification of fundamental rights (Tribe, 1978, p. 407). Indeed, the Court asserted its unwillingness to define fundamental rights and its intention to proceed on a case-by-case basis. This policy created some uncertainty for litigants but gave the Court control over determining which are the fundamental rights guaranteed to citizens of the several states and which are the nonfundamental rights that states can grant to their own citizens but deny to citizens of other states.

Reasonable Differential Treatment

As the last component suggests, the Privileges and Immunities Clause does not preclude all differential treatment of out-of-state citizens within a state. Indeed, after the Slaughterhouse Cases the Court began to allow even discriminations involving "fundamental" rights if it could be shown that such discriminations were not "reasonably . . . characterized as hostile to the rights of citizens of other states" (*Blake* v. *McClung,* 172 U.S. 256 [1898]). This reasonableness factor has allowed different state standards governing the practice of certain professions to stand as not violative of the Privileges and Immunities Clause. Thus, out-of-state doctors, lawyers, and other professionals may be required to prove their competency before being allowed to practice in a state while lesser competency requirements may be demanded of state citizens. Tuition rates can also be higher for out-of-state students as can charges for fishing and hunting licenses. These discrepancies are viewed as reasonable discriminations; a state can impose them in part because valid interests of the state justify the differential treatment and not solely the out-of-state status. Along these lines, the Court allowed Iowa to maintain its one-year durational requirement before a new resident can secure an Iowa divorce (*Sosna* v. *Iowa*).

In *Toomer* v. *Witsell,* the Court had incorporated these exceptions more formally. The case involved a South Carolina law designed to limit commercial shrimping by nonresident shrimpers within the three-mile zone off South Carolina's coast. The Court decided that South Carolina had violated the Privileges and Immunities Clause by its choice to charge an out-of-state shrimper a license fee 100 times that of an in-state shrimper. The Court said:

> Like many other Constitutional provisions, the Privileges and Immunities Clause is not absolute . . . it does not preclude disparity of treatment in the many situations where there are perfectly valid independent reasons for it . . . it does bar discriminations against citizens of other states where there is no substantial reason for the discrimination beyond the mere fact that they are citizens of other states.

To justify discrimination against out-of-staters, states must now show that the discrimination serves certain reasonably important state interests. The Court also requires the state to show why it cannot use other, less restrictive alternatives to accomplish the goal in question. *Toomer* thus shifts the litigant's burden of showing what and how a fundamental right has been violated to a requirement that the state prove reasonableness of discrimination and the absence of other alternatives to accomplish the goal of concern. The failure of Alaska to demonstrate the reasonableness of its position served to justify the Court's decision in *Hicklin* v. *Orbeck,* 437 U.S. 518 (1978), striking down an Alaska statute requiring employers to give preferential treatment to the employment of Alaska residents.

Rendition

The Full Faith and Credit Clause does not extend to criminal laws; that is, no state need enforce the criminal laws of a sister state or respect those laws as defense in prosecution. Such a position has its roots in the Anglo-American concept of due process, which requires trial in the district where the crime was committed. Most courts hold that only the court of the district in which the crime was committed has the authority to try an individual. Complete reliance on this tradition at the outset of the nation could have allowed any of the several states to become havens for fugitives from the justice of a neighboring state. The Framers therefore included a Rendition Clause in Article IV. That clause states:

> A person charged in any state with treason, felony, or other crime, who shall flee from justice, and be found in another state, shall on demand of the executive authority of the state from which he fled, be delivered up, to be removed to the state having jurisdiction of the crime.

Pursuant to this clause, Congress in 1793 passed legislation delineating the manner of rendition and obligating governors to comply with the extradition requirements. Those provisions, both statutory and constitutional, were presumed to cover any and all violations of a state's criminal law and required a governor to deliver a fugitive to a requesting state even if the fugitive's acts would not have been criminal in the governor's state. This presumption was validated in the 1861 case of *Kentucky v. Dennison,* 24 How. 66, even though the final outcome in that case belies that holding.

Kentucky v. Dennison

Kentucky v. Dennison involved Kentucky's effort to force Ohio Governor Dennison to render up a free black named William Lago. Lago had been indicted by Kentucky for the crime of aiding the escape of slaves and had fled to Ohio in the hopes of avoiding prosecution. Kentucky called upon Governor Dennison, following all the necessary procedures outlined in the 1793 statute, in good faith that it would secure Lago. Dennison refused to extradite Lago on the grounds that the Kentucky crime in question was not a crime covered by the Constitution. Kentucky sued for a writ of *mandamus* to force Dennison's delivery of Lago.

The Supreme Court was ultimately called upon to resolve this explosive question in the delicate days before the Civil War. The Court held that Dennison was wrong in refusing to deliver Lago. Neither the Constitution nor the 1793 statute granted gubernatorial discretion to determine which crimes were extraditable. Hence, Dennison had a clear duty and obligation to comply with Kentucky's request for Lago. Even so, the Court, possibly aware of the improbability of compliance, asserted that since the statute had no provisions for enforcement nor was the federal system designed to allow the national government to force state officials to comply with federal choices, the Court would not issue the writ of *mandamus.* The Court essentially held that a governor's duty to return fugitives is mandatory in principle, discretionary in fact. The Court has recently made clear that the decision to return a prisoner is an exclusively state *executive* function. State courts cannot, as announced in *Michigan* v. *Doran,* 58 L. Ed. 2d 521 (1979), prevent the return of a prisoner on the prisoner's claim that the state seeking the defendant lacks probable cause to bring the charges.

The policy position in *Dennison* has remained intact. Because orderly rendition has been the norm, no real challenges have come to the Court's attention since 1861. Moreover, Congress has remedied any real problems by making it a federal crime to flee across state borders to avoid prosecution. Under this 1934 law, FBI agents can arrest a fugitive and return that person to the state of origin either to be tried for the federal offense or to be released to local authorities.

Interstate Compacts

Both the Full Faith and Credit Clause and the Privileges and Immunities Clause were designed to minimize any friction that might be generated by hostile state officials and state citizens. The Compact Clause, in contrast, was more positive in nature. By not precluding the states from reaching agreements among themselves, the Framers opened the door to an important form of interstate cooperation. The relevant portions of Article I's Compact Clause require that "no state shall without the consent of Congress . . . enter into any agreement with another state or with a foreign power." Through an agreement coupled with the requisite congressional consent, New York and New Jersey, for example, have been able to manage New York City's port authority in a much more efficient and effective manner. Other states have joined cooperatively to regulate the use of oil, gas, water, and other natural resources, including water power. Civil defense compacts have arisen, as well, to facilitate the prompt and effective handling of emergencies. Indeed, an increasing number of broad-range mutual interests have been attended to through this means of cooperation.

The clause would appear to be rather straightforward. No compact or agreement can be undertaken by a state independently; that is, Congress must approve all interstate agreements. Despite what appears to be obvious, the Supreme Court has sustained as valid several agreements not approved by Congress, most notably in the recent Multistate Tax Compact Case, 434 U.S. 452 (1978).

In 1967 a Multistate Tax Compact went into effect among seven original adopting states. Since 1967 a total of twenty-three states have participated at various times, some remaining, some withdrawing; the 1978 membership was nineteen. The purpose of the Compact is to reduce the inefficiency inherent in the separate, single-state tax administration of multistate businesses. The Compact established a commission to study tax systems, to develop greater uniformity in state and local taxation, to make recommendations for the adoption of uniform administrative regulations across states, and to function as the member states' auditing agent for the determination of multistate business tax liability, among other things. All commission recommendations require adoption by the member state before they become effective. U.S. Steel Corp. and other large corporations, sensing that the commission's activities worked to their disadvantage, challenged the commission and its alleged powers by arguing that since Congress never consented to the Compact it was invalid and unreasonably burdened interstate commerce.

The Supreme Court sustained the Compact as valid despite the absence of congressional consent. The Court relied primarily on the 1893 case of *Virginia* v. *Tennessee*, 148 U.S. 503. In this early case, the Court sustained a compact between Virginia and Tennessee that resolved a border dispute, ruling that it was valid under tacit approval by Congress. In the 1893 opinion, Justice Field added that not all compacts require approval by Congress, tacit or otherwise. Compacts regulating the sale of merchandise, border agreements, an agreement to combat immediate invasion were all matters not requiring congressional consent because such compacts did not tend to "increase the political power of the states, which may encroach upon or interfere with the just supremacy of the United States." The policy established by the Court held that the border agreed upon by Virginia and Tennessee did not expand the power of these states with respect to the national government and was thus constitutional. In the Multistate Tax Compact Case, because the taxing authority remained in the hands of each state and because all regulations promulgated by the commission were ineffectual until state statutes authorized them, the Compact did not expand state power at the expense of federal power. Indeed, the Compact gave no single state any greater power than it possessed independently. As such, the Compact could be no greater burden on interstate commerce than were those state taxations of multistate businesses already sustained as constitutional.

Compacts that are granted congressional approval function as treaties; that is, they are the supreme law of the land. Once approved, the terms of the compact are binding on all parties, preventing a state from unilaterally withdrawing and from using its internal domestic policy to avoid compliance with the terms of the compact. In the 1952 case of *West Virginia ex rel. Dyer* v. *Sims,* 341 U.S. 22, the Court overruled the West Virginia State Supreme Court's holding that West Virginia's compact commitments were contrary to the West Virginia constitution.

Supreme Court Jurisdiction of Disputes Between States

Should the available remedies outlined in the foregoing sections fail to resolve an interstate dispute, the issue can ultimately be litigated in the United States Supreme Court (assuming, of course, that the controversy in question meets the requirements of standing to sue). Article III is interpreted as granting the Court original and exclusive jurisdiction in matters involving disputes between states. (When a state sues the United States or a subdivision of another state, the Court's original jurisdiction is not exclusive, thus allowing the Court, at times, to refer these disputes to lower federal courts and await the opportunity to handle the matter upon appeal.) When the Court does function as a court of first instance in disputes between states, it usually does not "hear" the case as would a trial court. Rather, the Court appoints a special master to ascertain the facts of the case and recommend judgment. The Court usually proceeds to a consideration of the master's report and decides accordingly, often simply supporting the conclusions rendered by the special master.

In disputes between states the Court must ascertain that the matter in question is really between two states and that the state's participation is not simply a ruse to get around the Eleventh Amendment's limitation on citizens from one state suing another state. The Court did, in fact, decline to hear a dispute allegedly between New Hampshire and Louisiana in 1883 for that very reason (*New Hampshire* v. *Louisiana,* 108 U.S. 76). A group of New Hampshire citizens nominally transferred ownership of their Louisiana bonds to New Hampshire. New Hampshire then sued Louisiana in the Supreme Court to recover the losses the bondholders suffered when Louisiana defaulted on its bonds. Without this transfer, of course, New Hampshire's citizens had no recourse to secure their money, given the Eleventh Amendment. The Court saw through New Hampshire's action and refused to decide the matter. When citizens give full and clear title to defaulted state bonds to a state, however, the Court will adjudicate the matter, as it did in *South Dakota* v. *North Carolina,* 192 U.S. 286 (1904).

Compliance

Once the Court asserts jurisdiction and resolves a dispute, there is always the delicate issue of compliance with the Court's judgment. Should a state disobey a Supreme Court ruling, it is unclear what steps the Court would or could take to secure compliance. A series of cases between Virginia and West Virginia beginning in 1907 and ending in 1918 raised this very concern (*Virginia* v. *West Virginia*, 206 U.S. 290 [1907]; 209 U.S. 514 [1908]; 220 U.S. 1 [1911]; 222 U.S. 17 [1911]; 231 U.S. 89 [1913]; 234 U.S. 117 [1914]; 238 U.S. 202 [1915]; 241 U.S. 531 [1916]; 246 U.S. 565 [1918]). In 1906 Virginia brought suit against West Virginia for monies due Virginia as part and parcel of a debt retirement agreement reached when West Virginia was established as a state out of what was then Virginia state territory. By 1915 the Supreme Court had clearly decided in favor of Virginia, but West Virginia still refused to pay and appeared in no particular rush to do so. In 1918 the Court announced yet another judgment in the matter, asserting the existence of enforcement powers and the justification for their use and avowing that they would be brought to bear if West Virginia continued in its recalcitrance. Aside from a vague reference to a possible act of Congress to handle the matter or continued Court action, it was unclear just what powers would be invoked. The Court, in fact, scheduled reargument on the very issue of what enforcement powers ought to be used, only to be relieved of the whole matter when West Virginia finally complied. Noncompliance remains a very real problem for the Court should states begin to doubt the authority of the Court to resolve particular kinds of disputes.

Estin v. Estin

334 U.S. 541 (1948)

Opinion of the Court by MR. JUSTICE DOUGLAS announced by MR. JUSTICE REED.

This case . . . presents an important question under the Full Faith and Credit Clause of the Constitution. * * * It is whether a New York decree awarding [Mrs. Estin] $180 per month for her maintenance and support in a separation proceeding survived a Nevada divorce decree which subsequently was granted [Mr. Estin].

The parties were married in 1937 and lived together in New York until 1942 when the husband left the wife. There was no issue [no children] of the marriage. In 1943 she brought an action against him for a separation. He entered a general appearance. The court, finding that he had abandoned her, granted her a decree of separation and awarded her $180 per month as permanent alimony. In January 1944 he went to Nevada where in 1945 he instituted an action for divorce. She was notified of the action . . . but entered no appearance in it. In May, 1945, the Nevada court, finding that [Mr. Estin] had been a bona fide resident of

Nevada since January 30, 1944, granted him an absolute divorce. . . . The Nevada decree made no provision for alimony, though the Nevada court had been advised of the New York decree.

Prior to that time [Mr. Estin] had made payments of alimony under the New York decree. After entry of the Nevada decree he ceased paying. Thereupon [Mrs. Estin] sued in New York for a supplementary judgment for the amount of the arrears. [Mr. Estin] appeared in the action and moved to eliminate the alimony provisions of the separation decree by reason of the Nevada decree. The [New York] Court denied the motion and granted [Mrs. Estin] judgment for the arrears. * * *

We held in Williams v. North Carolina * * * (1) that a divorce decree granted by a State to one of its domiciliaries is entitled to full faith and credit in a bigamy prosecution brought in another State, even though the other spouse was given notice of the divorce proceeding . . . and (2) that while the finding of domicile by the court that granted the decree is entitled to *prima facie* weight, it is not conclusive in a sister State but might be relitigated there. * * * The latter course was followed in this case, as a consequence of which the . . . Court of New York found, in accord with the Nevada court, that [Mr. Estin] "is now and since January, 1944, has been a bona fide resident of the State of Nevada."

[Mr. Estin's] argument therefore is that the tail must go with the hide—that since by the Nevada decree, recognized in New York, he and [Mrs. Estin] are no longer husband and wife, no legal incidence of the marriage remains. We are given a detailed analysis of New York law to show that the New York courts have no power either by statute or by common law to compel a man to support his ex-wife, that alimony is payable only so long as the relation of husband and wife exists, and that in New York, as in some other states * * * a support order does not survive divorce.

The difficulty with that argument is that the highest court in New York has held in this case that a support order can survive divorce and that this one has survived [this] divorce. That conclusion is binding on us, except as it conflicts with the Full Faith and Credit Clause. . . . The only question for us is whether New York is powerless to make such a ruling in view of the Nevada decree.

. . . The requirements of procedural due process were satisfied and the domicile of the husband in Nevada was foundation for a decree effecting a change in the marital capacity of both parties in all the other States of the Union, as well as in Nevada. * * * But the fact that marital capacity was changed does not mean that every other legal incidence of the marriage was necessarily affected.

. . . An absolutist might quarrel with the result and demand a rule that once a divorce is granted, the whole of the marriage relation is dissolved, leaving no roots or tendrils of any kind. But there are few areas of the law in black and white. The greys are dominant and even among them the shades are innumerable. For the eternal problem of the law is one of making accommodations between conflicting interests. This is why most legal problems end as questions of degree. That is true of the present problem under the Full Faith and Credit Clause. The question involves important considerations both of law and of policy which it is essential to state.

The situations where a judgment of one State has been denied full faith and credit in another State, because its enforcement would contravene the latter's policy, have been few and far between. * * * The Full Faith and Credit Clause is not to be applied, accordion-like, to accommodate our personal predilections. It substituted a command for the earlier principles of comity and thus basically altered the status of the States as independent sovereigns. * * * It ordered submission by one State even to hostile policies reflected in the judgment of another State, because the practical operation of the federal system, which the Constitution designed, demanded it. The fact that the requirements of full faith and credit, so far as judgments are concerned, are exacting, if not inexorable, * * * does not mean, however, that the State of the domicile of one spouse may . . . enter a decree that changes every legal incidence of the marriage relationship.

Marital status involves the regularity and integrity of the marriage relation. It affects the legitimacy of the offspring of marriage. It is the basis of criminal laws, as the bigamy prosecution in Williams v. North Carolina dramatically illustrates. The State has a considerable interest in preventing bigamous marriages and in protecting the offspring of marriages from being bastardized. The interest of the State extends to its domiciliaries. The State should have the power to guard its interest in them by changing or altering their marital status and by protecting them in that changed status throughout the farthest reaches of the nation. For a person domiciled in one State should not be allowed to suffer the penalties of bigamy for living outside the State with the only one which the State of his domicile recognizes as his lawful wife. And children born of the only marriage which is lawful in the State of his domicile should not carry the stigma of bastardy when they move elsewhere. These are matters of legitimate concern to the State of the domicile. . . . In no other way could the State of the domicile have and maintain effective control of the marital status of its domiciliaries.

Those are the considerations that have long permitted the State of the matrimonial domicile to change the marital status of the parties by an ex parte divorce proceeding [a divorce proceeding with only one of the parties present]. . . . In this case New York evinced a concern with this broken marriage when both parties were domiciled in New York and before Nevada had any concern with it. New York was rightly concerned lest the abandoned spouse be left impoverished and perhaps become a public charge. The problem of her livelihood and support is plainly a matter in which her community had a legitimate interest. The New York court, having jurisdiction over both parties, undertook to protect her by granting her a judgment of permanent alimony. Nevada, however, apparently follows the rule that dissolution of the marriage puts an end to a support order. * * * But the question is whether Nevada could under any circumstances adjudicate rights of [Mrs. Estin] under the New York judgment when she was not personally served or did not appear in the proceeding.

●　●　●

. . . The Nevada decree that is said to wipe out [Mrs. Estin's] claim for alimony under the New York judgment is nothing less than an attempt by Nevada to restrain [her] from asserting her claim under that judgment. That is an attempt to exercise an in personam jurisdiction over a person not before the court. That may not be done. Since Nevada had no power to adjudicate [Mrs. Estin's] rights in the New York judgment, New York need not give full faith and credit to that phase of Nevada's judgment. A judgment of a court having no jurisdiction to render it is not entitled to the full faith and credit which the Constitution and statute of the United States demand. * * *

The result in this situation is to make the divorce divisible—to give effect to the Nevada decree insofar as it affects marital status and to make it ineffective on the issue of alimony. It accommodates the interests of both Nevada and New York in this broken marriage by restricting each State to the matters of her dominant concern.

●　●　●

Affirmed.

Mr. Justice Frankfurter, dissenting. [Omitted.]

Mr. Justice Jackson, dissenting.

If there is one thing that the people are entitled to expect from their lawmakers, it is rules of law that will enable individuals to tell whether they are married and, if so, to whom. Today many people who have simply lived in more than one state do not know, and the most learned lawyer cannot advise them with any confidence. The uncertainties that result are not merely technical, nor are they trivial; they affect fundamental rights and relations such as the lawfulness of their cohabitation, their children's legitimacy, their title to property, and even whether they are law-abiding persons or criminals. In a society as mobile and nomadic as ours, such uncertainties affect large numbers of people and create a social problem of some magnitude. It is therefore important that, whatever we do, we shall not add to the confusion. I think that this decision does just that.

●　●　●

. . . [T]he question is whether the New York judgment of separation or the Nevada judgment of divorce controls the present obligation to pay alimony. The New York judgment of separation is based on the premise that the parties remain husband and wife, though estranged, and hence the obligation of support, incident to marriage, continues. The Nevada decree is based on the contrary premise that the marriage no longer exists and so obligations dependent on it have ceased.

The Court reaches the Solomon-like conclusion that the Nevada decree is half good and half bad under the full faith and credit clause. It is good to free the husband from the marriage; it is not good to free him from its incidental obligations. Assuming the judgment to be one which the Constitution requires to be recognized at all, I do not see how we can square this decision with the command that it be given *full* faith and credit. . . . [I]f we are to hold this divorce good, I do not see how it can be less good than a divorce would be if rendered by the courts of New York.

As I understand New York law, if, after a decree of separation and alimony, the husband had obtained a New York divorce against his wife, it would terminate her right to alimony. If the Nevada judgment is to have *full* faith and credit, I think it must have the same effect that a similar New York decree would have. I do not see how we can hold that it must be accepted for some purposes and not for others, that he is free of his former marriage but still may be jailed, as he may in New York, for not paying the maintenance of a woman whom the Court is compelled to consider as no longer his wife.

Sosna v. Iowa

419 U.S. 393 (1975)

Mr. Justice Rehnquist delivered the opinion of the Court.

. . . Carol Sosna married Michael Sosna on September 5, 1964, in Michigan. They lived together in New York between October 1967 and August 1971, after which date they separated but continued to live in New York. In August 1972, [Carol Sosna] moved to Iowa with her three children, and the following month she petitioned the District Court of Jackson County, Iowa, for a dissolution of her marriage. Michael Sosna, who had been personally served with notice of the action when he came to Iowa to visit his children, made a special appearance to contest the jurisdiction of the Iowa court. The Iowa court dismissed the petition for lack of jurisdiction, finding that Michael Sosna was not a resident of Iowa and [his wife] had not been a resident of the State of Iowa for one year preceding the filing of her petition. In so doing the Iowa court applied the provisions of

[the] Iowa Code * * * requiring that [anyone seeking a divorce] be "for the last year a resident of the state."

. . .

The durational residency requirement under attack in this case is a part of Iowa's comprehensive statutory regulation of domestic relations, an area that has long been regarded as a virtually exclusive province of the States. . . .

The statutory scheme in Iowa, like those in other States, sets forth in considerable detail the grounds upon which a marriage may be dissolved and the circumstances in which a divorce may be obtained. Jurisdiction over a petition for dissolution is established by statute in "the county where either party resides," * * * and the Iowa courts have construed the term "resident" to have much the same meaning as is ordinarily associated with the concept of domicile. * * * . . .

The imposition of a durational residency requirement for divorce is scarcely unique to Iowa, since 48 States impose such a requirement as a condition for maintaining an action for divorce. As might be expected, the periods vary among the States and range from six weeks to two years. The one-year period selected by Iowa is the most common length of time prescribed.

[Carol] Sosna contends that the Iowa requirement of one year's residence is unconstitutional for two separate reasons: *first,* because it establishes two classes of persons and discriminates against those who have recently exercised their right to travel to Iowa; * * * and, *second,* because it denies a litigant the opportunity to make an individualized showing of bona fide residence and therefore denies such residents access to the only method of legally dissolving their marriage. * * *

State statutes imposing durational residency requirements were of course invalidated when imposed by States as a qualification for welfare payments, * * * for voting, * * * and for medical care. * * * But none of those cases intimated that the States might never impose durational residency requirements, and such a proposition was in fact expressly disclaimed. What those cases had in common was that the durational residency requirements they struck down were justified on the basis of budgetary or record-keeping considerations which were held insufficient to outweigh the constitutional claims of the individuals. But Iowa's divorce residency requirement is of a different stripe. [Sosna] was not irretrievably foreclosed from obtaining some part of what she sought, as was the case with the welfare recipients, . . . the voters, . . . or the indigent patient. . . . She would eventually qualify for the same sort of adjudication which she demanded virtually upon her arrival in the State. Iowa's requirement delayed her access to the courts, but, by fulfilling it, a plaintiff could ultimately obtain the same opportunity for adjudication which she asserts ought to be hers at an earlier point in time.

Iowa's residency requirement may reasonably be justified on grounds other than purely budgetary considerations or administrative convenience. * * * A decree of divorce is not a matter in which the only interested parties are the State as a sort of "grantor," and a plaintiff such as [Sosna] in the role of "grantee." Both spouses are obviously interested in the proceedings, since it will affect their marital status and very likely their property rights. Where a married couple has minor children, a decree of divorce would usually include provisions for their custody and support. With consequences of such moment riding on a divorce decree issued by its courts, Iowa may insist that one seeking to initiate such a proceeding have the modicum of attachment to the State required here.

Such a requirement additionally furthers the State's parallel interests in both avoiding officious intermeddling in matters in which another State has a paramount interest, and in minimizing the susceptibility of its own divorce decrees to collateral attack. A State such as Iowa may quite reasonably decide that it does not wish to become a divorce mill for unhappy spouses who have lived there as short a time as [Sosna] had when she commenced her action in the state court after having long resided elsewhere. Until such time as Iowa is convinced that [she] intends to remain in the State, it lacks the "nexus between person and place of such permanence as to control the creation of legal relations and responsibilities of the utmost significance." * * * Perhaps even more importantly, Iowa's interests extend beyond its borders and include the recognition of its divorce decrees by other States under the Full Faith and Credit Clause of the Constitution, Art IV, § 1. . . . [T]he State asked to enter such a decree is entitled to insist that the putative divorce plaintiff satisfy something more than the bare minimum of constitutional requirements before a divorce may be granted. The State's decision to exact a one-year residency requirement as a matter of policy is therefore buttressed by a quite permissible inference that this requirement not only effectuates state substantive policy but likewise provides a greater safeguard against successful collateral attack than would a requirement of bona fide residence alone. This is precisely the sort of determination that a State in the exercise of its domestic relations jurisdiction is entitled to make.

We therefore hold that the state interest in requiring that those who seek a divorce from its courts be genuinely attached to the State, as well as a desire to insulate divorce decrees from the likelihood of collateral attack, requires a different resolution of the constitutional issue [presented than was the case in matters of welfare rights, voting, and indigent patients].

Affirmed.

Mr. Justice White, dissenting. [Omitted.]

Mr. Justice Marshall, with whom Mr. Justice Brennan joins, dissenting.

The Court today departs sharply from the course we have followed in analyzing durational residency requirements. . . .

. . . [A]ny classification that penalizes exercise of the constitutional right to travel is invalid unless it is justified by a compelling governmental interest. As recently as last Term we held that the right to travel requires that States provide the same vital governmental benefits and privileges to recent immigrants that they do to long-time residents. * * * Although we recognized that not all durational residency requirements are penalties upon the exercise of the right to travel interstate, we held that free medical aid, like voting * * * and welfare assistance, * * * was of such fundamental importance that the State could not constitutionally condition its receipt upon long-term residence. . . .

. . . [T]he Court has employed what appears to be an ad hoc balancing test, under which the State's putative interest in ensuring that its divorce plaintiffs establish some roots in Iowa is said to justify the one-year residency requirement. I am concerned not only about the disposition of this case, but also about the implications of the majority's analysis for other divorce statutes and for durational residency requirement cases in general.

• • •

The Court proposes three defenses for the Iowa statute: first, the residency requirement merely delays receipt of the benefit in question—it does not deprive the applicant of the benefit altogether; second, since significant social consequences may follow from the conferral of a divorce, the State may legitimately regulate the divorce process; and third, the State has interests both in protecting itself from use as a "divorce mill" and in protecting its judgments from possible collateral attack in other States. In my view, the first two defenses provide no significant support for the statute in question here. Only the third has any real force.

. . . Iowa's residency requirement, the Court says, merely forestalls access to the courts; applicants seeking welfare payments, medical aid, and the right to vote, on the other hand, suffer unrecoverable losses throughout the waiting period. This analysis, however, ignores the severity of the deprivation suffered by the divorce petitioner who is forced to wait a year for relief. * * * The injury accompanying that delay is not directly measurable in money terms like the loss of welfare benefits, but it cannot reasonably be argued that when the year has elapsed, the petitioner is made whole. The year's wait prevents remarriage and locks both partners into what may be an intolerable, destructive relationship. . . .

. . . I find the majority's second argument no more persuasive.
. . . [I]n this case, I fail to see how any legitimate objective of Iowa's divorce regulations would be frustrated by granting equal access to new state residents. To draw on an analogy, the States have great interests in the local voting process and wide latitude in regulating that process. Yet one regulation that the States may not impose is an unduly long residence requirement. * * * To remark, as the Court does, that because of the consequences riding on a divorce decree "Iowa may insist that one seeking to initiate such a proceeding have the modi-

cum of attachment to the state required here" is not to make an argument, but merely to state the result.

The Court's third justification seems to me the only one that warrants close consideration. Iowa has a legitimate interest in protecting itself against invasion by those seeking quick divorces in a forum with relatively lax divorce laws, and it may have some interest in avoiding collateral attacks on its decree in other States. These interests, however, would adequately be protected by a simple requirement of domicile—physical presence plus intent to remain—which would remove the rigid one-year barrier while permitting the State to restrict the availability of its divorce process to citizens who are genuinely its own.

• • •

. . . [E]ven a one-year period does not provide complete protection against collateral attack. It merely makes it somewhat less likely that a second State will be able to find "cogent evidence" that Iowa's determination of domicile was incorrect. But if the Iowa court has erroneously determined the question of domicile, the year's residence will do nothing to preclude collateral attack. . . .

. . . [I]n one sense the year's residency requirement may technically increase rather than reduce the exposure of Iowa's decrees to collateral attack. Iowa apears to be among the States that have interpreted their divorce residency requirements as being of jurisdictional import. Since a State's divorce decree is subject to collateral challenge in a foreign forum for any jurisdictional flaw that would void it in the State's own courts, * * * the residency requirement exposes Iowa divorce proceedings to attack both for failure to prove domicile and for failure to prove one year's residence. If nothing else, this casts doubt on the majority's speculation that Iowa's residency requirement may have been intended as a statutory shield for its divorce decrees. In sum, concerns about the need for a long residency requirement to defray collateral attacks on state judgments seem more fanciful than real. If, as the majority assumes, Iowa is interested in assuring itself that its divorce petitioners are legitimately Iowa citizens, requiring petitioners to provide convincing evidence of bona fide domicile should be more than adequate to the task.

I conclude that the course Iowa has chosen in restricting access to its divorce courts unduly interferes with the right to "migrate, resettle, find a new job, and start a new life." * * *

Hicklin v. Orbeck

437 U.S. 518 (1978)

Mr. Justice Brennan delivered the opinion of the Court.

In 1972, professedly for the purpose of reducing unemployment in the State, the Alaska Legislature passed an Act entitled "Local Hire Under State Leases." * * * The key provision of "Alaska Hire," as the Act has come to be known, is the requirement that "all oil and gas leases, easements or right-of-way permits for oil or gas pipeline purposes, . . . to which the state is a party" contain a provision "requiring the employment of qualified Alaska residents" in preference to non-residents. * * * This employment preference is administered by providing persons meeting the statutory requirements for Alaskan residency with certificates of residence—"resident cards"—that can be presented to an employer covered by the Act as proof of residency. * * * [Hicklin and others], desirous of securing jobs covered by the Act but unable to qualify for the necessary resident cards, challenge Alaska Hire as violative of both the Privileges and Immunities Clause of Art IV, § 2 and the Equal Protection Clause of the Fourteenth Amendment.

I

Although enacted in 1972, Alaska Hire was not seriously enforced until 1975, when construction on the Trans-Alaska Pipeline was reaching its peak. At that time, the State Department of Labor began issuing residency cards and limiting to resident cardholders the dispatchment to oil pipeline jobs. On March 1, 1976, in response to "numerous complaints alleging that persons who are not Alaska residents have been dispatched on pipeline jobs when *qualified* Alaska residents were available to fill the jobs." * * * Edmund Orbeck, the Commissioner of Labor, . . . issued a Cease and Desist Order to all unions supplying pipeline workers enjoining them "to respond to all open job calls by dispatching *all qualified* Alaska residents before *any* non-residents are dispatched." * * * As a result, [Hicklin and others], all but one of whom had previously worked on the pipeline, were prevented from obtaining pipeline-related work. . . .

• • •

II

[Hicklin's] principal challenge to Alaska Hire is made under the Privileges and Immunities Clause of Art IV, § 2: "The Citizens of each State shall be entitled to all Privileges and Immunities of Citizens in the several States.". . . The purpose of the Clause * * * is "to place the citizens of each State upon the same footing with citizens of other States, so far as the advantages resulting from citizenship in those States are concerned. It relieves them from the disabilities of alienage in other States; it inhibits discriminating legislation against them by other States; it gives them the right of free ingress into other States, and egress from them; it insures to them in other States the same freedom possessed by the citizens of those States in the acquisition and enjoyment of property and in the pursuit of happiness; and it secures to them in other States the equal protection of their laws. It has been justly said that no provision in the Constitution has tended so strongly to constitute the citizens of the United States one people as this."

[The Hicklin et al.] appeal to the protection of the Clause is strongly supported by this Court's decisions holding violative of the Clause state discrimination against nonresidents seeking to ply their trade, practice their occupation, or pursue a common calling within the State. . . . [In 1870 this Court] recognized that a resident of one State is constitutionally entitled to travel to another State for purposes of employment free from discriminatory restrictions in favor of state residents imposed by the other State.

Again, Toomer v Witsell, * * * the leading modern exposition of the limitations the Clause places on a State's power to bias employment opportunities in favor of its own residents, invalidated a South Carolina statute that required nonresidents to pay a fee one hundred times greater than that paid by residents for a license to shrimp commercially in the three-mile maritime belt off the coast of that State. The Court reasoned that although the Privileges and Immunities Clause "does not preclude disparity of treatment in the many situations where there are perfectly valid independent reasons for it," * * * "[i]t does bar discrimination against citizens of other States where there is no substantial reason for the discrimination beyond the mere fact that they are citizens of other States." * * * A "substantial reason for the discrimination" would not exist, the Court explained, "unless there is something to indicate that non-citizens constitute a peculiar source of the evil at which the [discriminatory] statute is aimed." * * * Moreover, even where the presence or activity of nonresidents causes or exacerbates the problem the State seeks to remedy, there must be a "reasonable relationship between the danger represented by non-citizens, as a class, and the . . . discrimination practiced upon them." * * * . . .

Even assuming that a State may validly attempt to alleviate its unemployment problem by requiring private employers within the State to discriminate against nonresidents, . . . it is clear that under the Toomer analysis . . . Alaska Hire's discrimination against nonresidents cannot withstand scrutiny under the Privileges and Immunities Clause. For although the statute may not violate the Clause if the State shows "something to indicate that non-citizens constitute a peculiar source of the evil at which the statute is aimed," * * * and, beyond this, the State "has no burden to prove that its laws are not violative of the . . . Clause," * * * certainly no showing was made on this record that nonresidents were "a peculiar source of the evil" Alaska Hire was enacted to remedy, namely

Alaska's "uniquely high unemployment." * * * What evidence the record does contain indicates that the major cause of Alaska's high unemployment was not the influx of nonresidents seeking employment, but rather the fact that a substantial number of Alaska's jobless residents—especially the unemployed Eskimo and Indian residents—were unable to secure employment either because of their lack of education and job training or because of their geographical remoteness from job opportunities; and that the employment of nonresidents threatened to deny jobs to Alaska residents only to the extent that jobs for which untrained residents were being prepared might be filled by nonresidents before the residents' training was completed.

Moreover, even if the State's showing is accepted as sufficient to indicate that nonresidents were "a peculiar source of evil," Toomer . . . compel[s] the conclusion that Alaska Hire nevertheless fails to pass constitutional muster. For the discrimination the Act works against nonresidents does not bear a substantial relationship to the particular "evil" they are said to present. Alaska Hire simply grants all Alaskans, regardless of their employment status, education, or training, a flat employment preference for all jobs covered by the Act. A highly skilled and educated resident who has never been unemployed is entitled to precisely the same preferential treatment as the unskilled, habitually unemployed Arctic Eskimo enrolled in a job training program. If Alaska is to attempt to ease her unemployment problem by forcing employers within the State to discriminate against nonresidents—again, a policy which may present serious constitutional questions—the means by which she does so must be more closely tailored to aid the unemployed the Act is intended to benefit. Even if a statute granting an employment preference to unemployed residents or to residents enrolled in job training programs might be permissible, Alaska Hire's across-the-board grant of a job preference to all Alaskan residents clearly is not.

. . . Alaska contends that because the oil and gas that is the subject of Alaska Hire is *owned* by the State, this ownership of itself is sufficient justification for the Act's discrimination against nonresidents, and takes the Act totally without the scope of the Privileges and Immunities Clause. As the State sees it "the privileges and immunities clause [does] not apply, and was never meant to apply, to decisions by the states as to how they would permit, if at all, the use and distribution of the natural resources which they own. . . ." * * * We do not agree that the fact that a State owns a resource, of itself, completely removes a law concerning that resource from the prohibitions of the Clause. . . . Rather than placing a statute completely beyond the Clause, a State's ownership of the property with which the statute is concerned is a factor—although often the crucial factor—to be considered in evaluating whether the statute's discrimination against noncitizens violates the Clause. Dispositive though this factor may be in many cases in which a State discriminates against nonresidents, it is not dispositive here.

The reason is that Alaska has little or no proprietary interest in much of the activity swept within the ambit of Alaska Hire; and the connection of the State's oil and gas with much of the covered activity is sufficiently attenuated so that it cannot justifiably be the basis for requiring private employers to discriminate against nonresidents. . . . Alaska Hire extends to employers who have no connection, whatsoever, with the State's oil and gas, perform no work on state land, have no contractual relationship with the State, and receive no payment from the State. The Act goes so far as to reach suppliers who provide goods or services to subcontractors who, in turn, perform work for contractors despite the fact that none of these employers may themselves have direct dealings with the State's oil and gas or ever set foot on state land. Moreover, the Act's coverage is not limited to activities connected with the extraction of Alaska's oil and gas. It encompasses . . . "employment opportunities at refineries and in distribution systems utilizing oil and gas obtained under Alaska leases." * * * The only limit of any consequence on the Act's reach is the requirement that "the activity which generates the employment must take place inside the state." Although the absence of this limitation would be noteworthy, its presence hardly is; for it simply prevents Alaska Hire from having what would be the surprising effect of requiring potentially covered out-of-state employers to discriminate against residents of their own State in favor of nonresident Alaskans. In sum, the Act is an attempt to force virtually all businesses that benefit in some way from the economic ripple effect of Alaska's decision to develop her oil and gas resources to bias their employment practices in favor of the State's residents. We believe that Alaska's ownership of the oil and gas that is the subject matter of Alaska Hire simply constitutes insufficient justification for the pervasive discrimination against nonresidents that the Act mandates.

. . .

. . . [T]he breadth of the discrimination mandated by Alaska Hire goes far beyond the degree of resident bias Alaska's ownership of the oil and gas can justifiably support. . . . As Mr. Justice Cardozo observed, * * * the Constitution "was framed upon the theory that the peoples of the several states must sink or swim together, and that in the long run prosperity and salvation are in union and not division."

Reversed.

United States Steel Corp.
v. Multistate Tax Commission

434 U.S. 452 (1978)

Mr. Justice Powell delivered the opinion of the Court.

The Compact Clause of Art I, § 10, cl 3, of the Constitution provides that "No State shall, without the Consent of Congress, . . . enter into any Agreement or Compact with another State, or with a foreign Power . . . ." The Multistate Tax Compact, which established the Multistate Tax Commission, has not received congressional approval. This appeal requires us to decide whether the Compact is invalid for that reason. . . . [The Court also considered whether the Compact violated the Commerce Clause and the Fourteenth Amendment.]

I

The Multistate Tax Compact was drafted in 1966 and became effective, according to its own terms, on August 4, 1967, after seven States had adopted it. By the inception of this litigation in 1972, 21 States had become members. . . .

• • •

. . . [T]he Multistate Tax Compact . . . symbolized the recognition that, as applied to multistate businesses, traditional state tax administration was inefficient and costly to both State and taxpayer. In accord with that recognition, Art I of the Compact states four purposes: (1) facilitating proper determination of state and local tax liability of multistate taxpayers, including the equitable apportionment of tax bases and settlement of apportionment disputes; (2) promoting uniformity and compatibility in state tax systems; (3) facilitating taxpayer convenience and compliance in the filing of tax returns and in other phases of tax administration; and (4) avoiding duplicative taxation.

To these ends, Art VI [of the Compact] creates the Multistate Tax Commission, composed of the tax administrators from all the member States. . . . [It] authorizes the Commission (i) to study state and local tax systems; (ii) to develop and recommend proposals for an increase in uniformity and compatibility of state and local tax laws; . . . (iii) to compile and publish information that may assist member States in implementing the Compact and taxpayers in complying with the tax laws; and (iv) to do all things necessary and incidental to the administration of its functions pursuant to the Compact.

Articles VII and VIII detail more specific powers of the Commission. Under Art VII, the Commission may adopt uniform administrative regulations . . . relating to specified types of taxes. These regulations are advisory only. Each member State has the power to reject, disregard, amend, or modify any rules or regulations promulgated by the Commission. They have no force in any member State until adopted by that State in accordance with its own law.

Article VIII . . . authorizes any member State . . . to request that the Commission perform an audit on its behalf. The Commission, as the State's auditing agent, may seek compulsory process in aid of its auditing power in the courts of any State that has adopted Art VIII. Information obtained by the audit may be disclosed only in accordance with the laws of the requesting State. Moreover, individual member States retain complete control over all legislation and administrative action affecting the rate of tax, the composition of the tax base, . . . and the means and methods of determining tax liability and collecting any taxes determined to be due.

· · ·

In 1972, [U.S. Steel Corp. et al.] brought this action on behalf of all . . . multistate taxpayers threatened with audits by the Commission. . . . Their complaint challenged the constitutionality of the Compact on . . . grounds [that] the Compact, never having received the consent of Congress, is invalid under the Compact Clause. . . .

· · ·

II

Article I, § 10, cl 1, of the Constitution—the Treaty Clause—declares that "No State shall enter into Any Treaty, Alliance or Confederation . . . ." Yet Art I, § 10, cl 3—the Compact Clause—permits the States to enter into "agreements" or "compacts," so long as congressional consent is obtained. The Framers clearly perceived compacts and agreements as differing from treaties. The records of the Constitutional Convention, however, are barren of any clue as to the precise contours of the agreements and compacts governed by the Compact Clause. This suggests that the Framers used the words "treaty," "compact," and "agreement" as terms of art, for which no explanation was required and with which we are unfamiliar. Further evidence that the Framers ascribed precise meanings to these words appears in contemporary commentary.

Whatever distinct meanings the Framers attributed to the terms in Art I, § 10, those meanings were soon lost. In 1833, Mr. Justice Story perceived no clear distinction among any of the terms. Lacking any clue as to the categorical definitions the Framers had ascribed to them, Justice Story developed his own theory. Treaties, alliances and confederations, he wrote, generally connote military and political accords and are forbidden to the States. Compacts and agreements, on the other hand, embrace "mere private rights of sovereignty: such as questions of boundary; interests in land situate in the territory of each other; and other internal regulations for the mutual comfort and convenience of States bordering on each other." * * * In the latter situations, congressional consent was required . . . "in order to check any infringement of the rights of the national government." * * *

• • •

. . . [I]n Virginia v Tennessee . . . the Court held that Congress tacitly had assented to the running of a boundary between the two States. In an extended dictum, however, Justice Field took the Court's first opportunity to comment upon the Compact Clause. . . .

• • •

. . . [Justice Field maintained that as] the Compact Clause could not have been intended to reach every possible interstate agreement, it was necessary to construe the terms of the Compact Clause by reference to the object of the entire section in which it appears.

> "Looking at the clause in which terms 'compact' or 'agreement' appear, it is evident that the prohibition is directed to the formation of any combination tending to the increase of political power in the States, which may encroach upon or interfere with the just supremacy of the United States." * * *

. . . While [no subsequent] cases explicitly applied the Virginia v Tennessee test, they reaffirmed its underlying assumption: not all agreements between States are subject to the strictures of the Compact Clause. . . .

• • •

This was the status of the Virginia v Tennessee test until two Terms ago, when we decided New Hampshire v Maine. * * * In that case we specifically applied the test and held that an interstate agreement locating an ancient boundary did not require congressional consent. We reaffirmed Justice Field's view that the "application of the Compact Clause is limited to agreements that are 'directed to the formation of any combination tending to the increase of political power in the States, which may encroach upon or interfere with the just supremacy of the United States.'" * * * This rule states the proper balance between federal and state power with respect to compacts and agreements among States.

[U.S. Steel Corp. et al.] maintain that history constrains us to limit application of this rule to bilateral agreements involving no independent administrative body. They argue that this Court never has upheld a multilateral agreement creating an active administrative body with extensive powers delegated to it by the States, but lacking congressional consent. It is true that most multilateral compacts have been submitted for congressional approval. But this historical practice, which may simply reflect considerations of caution and convenience on the part of the submitting States, is not controlling. . . .

[U.S. Steel et al.] further urge that the pertinent inquiry is one of potential, rather than actual, impact upon federal supremacy. We agree. But the multilateral nature of the agreement and its establishment of an ongoing administrative body do not, standing alone, present significant potential for conflict with the principles underlying the Compact Clause. The number of parties to an agreement is irrelevant if it does not impermissibly enhance state power at the expense of federal supremacy. As to the powers delegated to the administrative body, we think these also must be judged in terms of enhancement of state power in relation to the Federal Government. * * * We turn, therefore, to the application of the Virginia v Tennessee rule to the Compact before us.

III

On its face the Multistate Tax Compact contains no provisions that would enhance the political power of the member States in a way that encroaches upon the supremacy of the United States. . . . This pact does not purport to authorize the member States to exercise any powers they could not exercise in its absence. Nor is there any delegation of sovereign power to the Commission: each State retains complete freedom to adopt or reject the rules and regulations of the Commission. Moreover, . . . each State is free to withdraw at any time. Despite this apparent compatibility of the Compact with the interpretation of the Clause established by our cases, [U.S. Steel et al.] argue that the Compact's effect is to threaten federal supremacy.

[They] contend . . . that the Compact encroaches upon federal supremacy with respect to interstate commerce. This argument, as we understand it, has four principal components. It is claimed, first, that the Commission's use in its audits of "unitary business" and "combination of income" methods for determining a corporate taxpayer's income creates a risk of multiple taxation for multistate businesses. Whether or not this risk is a real one, it cannot be attributed to the existence of the Multistate Tax Commission. When the Commission conducts an audit at the request of a member State, it uses the methods adopted by that State. Since [U.S. Steel et al.] do not contest the right of each State to adopt these procedures if it conducted the audits separately, they cannot be heard to complain that a threat to federal supremacy arises from the Commission's adoption of the unitary business standard in accord with the wishes of the member States. Indeed, to the extent that the Commission succeeds in promoting uniformity in the application of state taxing principles, the risks of multiple taxation should be diminished.

[The] second contention as to enhancement of state power over interstate commerce is that the Commission's regulations provide for apportionment of nonbusiness income. This allegedly creates a substantial risk of multiple taxation, since other States are said to allocate this income to the place of commercial domicile. We note first that the regulations of the Commission do not require the apportionment of nonbusiness income. They do define business income, which is apportionable under the regulations, to include elements that might be regarded as nonbusiness income in some States. * * * But again there is no claim that the member States could not adopt similar definitions in the absence of the Compact. Any State's ability to exact additional tax revenues from multistate businesses cannot be attributed to the Compact; it is the result of the State's freedom to select, within constitutional limits, the method it prefers.

The third aspect of the Compact's operation said to encroach upon federal commerce power involves the Commission's requirement that multistate businesses under audit file data concerning affiliated corporations. [U.S. Steel argues] that the costs of compiling financial data of related corporations burden the conduct of interstate commerce for the benefit of the taxing States. Since each State presumably could impose similar filing requirements individually, however, [they] again do not show that the Commission's practices, as auditing agent for member States, aggrandize their power or threaten federal control of commerce. Moreover, to the extent that the Commission is engaged in joint audits, [U.S. Steel's] filing burdens well may be reduced.

[U.S. Steel's] final claim of enhanced state power with respect to commerce is that the "enforcement powers" conferred upon the Commission enable that body to exercise authority over interstate business to a greater extent than the sum of the States' authority acting individually. This claim also falls short of meeting the standard of Virginia v Tennessee. Article VIII of the Compact authorizes the Commission to require the attendance of persons and the production of documents in connection with its audits. The Commission, however, has no power to punish failures to comply. It must resort to the courts for compulsory process, as would any auditing agent employed by the individual States. The only novel feature of the Commission's "enforcement powers" is the provision in Art VIII permitting the Commission to resort to the courts of any State adopting that Article. Adoption of the Article, then, amounts to nothing more than reciprocal legislation for providing mutual assistance to the auditors of the member States. Reciprocal legislation making the courts of one State available for the better administration of justice in another has been upheld by this Court as a method "to accomplish fruitful and unprohibited ends." * * * [U.S. Steel makes] no showing that increased effectiveness in the administration of state tax laws, promoted by such legislation, threatens federal supremacy. * * *

• • •

We conclude that [this] constitutional challenge to the Multistate Tax Compact fails . . . .

Affirmed.

Mr. Justice White, with whom Mr. Justice Blackmun joins, dissenting.

The majority opinion appears to concede, as I think it should, that the Compact Clause reaches interstate agreements presenting even *potential* encroachments on federal supremacy. In applying its Compact Clause theory to the circumstances of the Multistate Tax Compact, however, the majority is not true to this view. For if the Compact Clause has any independent protective force at all, it must require the consent of Congress to an interstate scheme of such complexity and detail as this. The majority states it will watch for the mere *potential* of harm to federal interests, but then approves the Compact here for lack of *actual* proved harm.

The Constitution incorporates many restrictions on the powers of individual States. Some of these are explicit, some are inferred from positive delegations of power to the Federal Government. In the latter category falls the federal authority over interstate commerce. The individual States have long been permitted to legislate, in a nondiscriminatory manner, over matters affecting interstate commerce, where Congress has not exerted its authority, and where the federal interest does not require a uniform rule. * * *

. . .

The Compact Clause, however, is directed to joint action by more than one State. If its only purpose in the present context were to require the consent of Congress to agreements between States that would otherwise violate the Commerce Clause, it would have no independent meaning. The Clause must mean that some actions which would be permissible for individual States to undertake are not permissible for a group of States to *agree* to undertake.

. . .

Congressional consent to an interstate compact may be expressed in several ways. . . .

. . .

In the present case, it would not be possible to infer approval from the congressional reaction to the Multistate Tax Compact. Indeed, the history of the Congress and the Compact is a chronicle of jealous attempts of one to close out the efforts of the other.

On the congressional side of this long-lived battle, bills to approve the Compact have been introduced 12 separate times, but all have faltered before arriving at a vote. . . .

For its part, the Multistate Tax Commission has made no attempt to disguise its purpose. . . . The Commission lists as one of its "major goals" the desire to "guard against restrictive federal legislation and other federal action which impinges upon the ability of state tax administrators to carry out the laws of their States effectively." . . .

A hostile stalemate characterizes the present position of the parties. . . . No one could view this history and conclude that the Congress has acquiesced in the Multistate Tax Compact.

. . .

It might be argued that Congress could more clearly have expressed its federal interest by passing a statute pre-empting the field, possibly in the form of an alternative apportionment formula. To hold Congress to the necessity of such action, however, accords no force to the Compact Clause independent of the Commerce Clause. . . . If the way to show a "*potential* federal interest" requires an exercise of the actual federal commerce power, then the purposes of the Compact Clause, and the Framers' deep-seated and special fear of agreements between States, would be accorded absolutely no respect.

Virginia v Tennessee quite clearly holds that not all agreements and compacts must be submitted to the Congress. The majority's phraseology of the test as "potential impact upon federal supremacy" incorporates the Virginia v Tennessee standard. Nor do I disagree that many interstate agreements are legally effective without congressional consent. "Potential impact upon federal supremacy" requires some demonstration of a federal interest in the matter under consideration, and a threat to that interest. In very few cases, short of a direct conflict, will the record of congressional and executive action demonstrate as clearly as the record in the present case that the Federal Government considers itself to have a valid interest in the subject matter. . . .

It seems to me, however, that even if a realistic potential impact on federal supremacy failed to materialize at one historic moment, that should not mean that an interstate compact or agreement is forever immune from congressional disapproval on an absolute or conditional basis. Yet the majority's approach appears to be that, because the instant agreement is, in the majority's view, initially without the Clause, it will *never* require congressional approval. The majority would approve this Compact without congressional ratification purely on the basis of its form: that no power is conferred upon the Multistate Tax Commission that could not be independently exercised by a member State. Such a view pretermits the possibility of requiring congressional approval in the future should circumstances later present even more clearly a potential federal interest, so long as the form of the Compact has not changed. That consequence fails to provide the ongoing congressional oversight that is part of the Compact Clause's protections.

· · ·

The Compact Clause is an important, intended safeguard within our constitutional structure. It is functionally a conciliatory rather than a prohibitive clause. All it requires is that Congress review interstate agreements that are capable of affecting federal or other States' rights. In the Court's decision today, a highly complex multistate compact, detailed in structure and pervasive in its effect on the important area of interstate and international business taxation, has been legitimized without the consent of Congress. If the Multistate Tax Compact is not a compact within the meaning of Art I, § 10, then I fear there is very little life remaining in that section of our Constitution.

I respectfully dissent.

PART V

SCOPE OF ADMINISTRATIVE POWER: THE BURGEONING BUREAUCRACY

CHAPTER 13

Delegation
of Legislative Power

INTRODUCTORY ESSAY

As we have already noted, the national government's role in the American political experience has changed considerably since the Philadelphia Convention. At the outset and throughout most of the nineteenth century, American national government was limited in scope. With few exceptions, it was a government primarily dominated by a Congress enacting basically self-executing laws. With the passage of the Interstate Commerce Act in 1887 and the concomitant establishment of the Interstate Commerce Commission (ICC), the nature of that once "unobtrusive" government evolved to incorporate ever more explicit and complex regulation. Today the national government is as responsible for the nation's social, economic, and physical well-being as it once was for the health of the body politic alone (see Lowi, 1969).

This expansion in scope and responsibility has made the twentieth-century law-making task all the more difficult, particularly for Congress to undertake alone. In an increasingly complex society characterized by technological sophistication and economic interdependence, the sheer magnitude of the problems demanding congressional attention and the practical difficulties of the day-to-day regulation required by many solutions serve as obvious constraints on the ability of Congress to legislate comprehensively, much less effectively. Indeed, this complexity and attendant impracticality, coupled with the politics of the legislative process, make it difficult for Congress to fashion rules whose enforcement can be foreseen with any measure of precision. At the same time, the deliberate, tortoiselike pace of the legislative process makes it all but impossible for Congress to respond quickly to changing circumstances, making meaningful, up-to-date rules and regulations virtually inconceivable. As a result, Congress has been forced, though not wholly unwillingly, to turn to the executive branch, the judicial branch (occasionally), and a hybrid creation known as independent regulatory agencies, not only to enforce and construe law, but to create it as well. For instance, Congress created the Federal Communications Commission and allowed it to establish rules regulating the use of the radio and television airwaves. And Supreme Court Justices are allowed to make rules regulating civil and criminal procedure for the entire federal court system (subject to a modest and rarely invoked legislative veto). This process of conferring upon an administrative agency or executive or judicial officer certain "tasks and powers the legislature would and could itself exercise" (Lowi, 1969, p. 126) is known as the delegation of legislative powers.

The Nondelegability Doctrine

While practical considerations have made it necessary for Congress to delegate some of its rule-making power, the process does not comport well with either legal or political theory. In the first place, the legality of delegation is placed in question by Article I's rather clear designation that *all* legislative power be vested in Congress. Setting rates for rail transport, specifying criminal and civil procedure in federal courts, devising regulations regarding product packaging, and specifying air routes, while not the most exciting of legislative concerns, are nonetheless exertions of legislative power. In granting the Interstate Commerce Commission, the Supreme Court, the Federal Trade Commission, and the Civil Aeronautics Board, respectively, the power to establish these rules, Congress, at first glance, appears to have violated one of the central tenets of American constitutional law: separation of powers. In *J. W. Hampton & Co.* v. *United States,* 276 U.S. 394 (1928), Chief Justice Taft went so far as to say:

> [I]n carrying out that Constitutional division into three branches it is a breach of the national fundamental law if Congress gives up its legislative power and transfers it to the President, or to the judicial branch, or if by law attempts to vest itself of either executive or judicial power.

Essentially, the argument is this: If the Constitution is to limit the power of those holding office under its authority, then how the Constitution divides that power must be taken seriously and any transfers of power must be considered unconstitutional.

In addition to contravening the separation of powers, the delegation of legislative power is viewed by some as contrary to the long-standing common law maxim of agency: *Delegata potestas non potest delegari.* Roughly translated, the maxim means that power once delegated cannot be redelegated. In the context of legislative power, the maxim applies to any congressional redelegation of the authority originally delegated to Congress by the Constitution or the people. Congress serves as the agent of the people, and in that capacity, as would be expected of any agent, it ought not to pass its responsibility to someone else. In the *Second Treatise,* John Locke relied on this concept when he asserted that "the legislative neither must nor can transfer the power of making laws to anybody else, or place it anywhere but where the people have."

Both of these legal rationales for nondelegability are bolstered by two tenets of political theory that have attained almost hallowed status in American politics: (1) representative democracy and (2) government by consent of the governed. Of course, both of these concepts assume a contract theory of government, much as contractual assumptions underpin the common law concept of agency. The governmental contract in American politics embodies the granting of discretionary lawmaking power (with limits) to a body of officeholders democratically selected and expected to represent the will of the people. Under such a contract, were representatives to exert legislative powers not to the liking of the governed, the governed could easily determine political responsibility and simply oust at the next election those legislators who failed to govern according to the wishes of the governed. Neither representative democracy nor consent of the governed is fulfilled, however, if democratically chosen representatives transfer the lawmaking power elsewhere. Under this system of delegation, rules once made by elected representatives are made by administrators not subject to electoral control and, hence, those rules are no longer formed by representatives with the consent of the governed. Broad transfers of discretionary lawmaking power, then, violate both tenets of political theory by limiting the effectiveness of the electoral check on legislative power as originally contracted (see Barber, 1975).

The concept of due process of law has also been used as a ground to support nondelegation. The rationale behind its use is closely tied to the contractual matters just discussed, but the due process basis for holding a prohibition on delegation is more a matter of protecting the private citizen than an abstraction of political philosophy. Due process of law has a long history as a vehicle through which to secure both substantive and procedural rights for private citizens. At its core, the concept requires that government not act capriciously or arbitrarily when it affects the lives, liberties, and properties of its citizens. Courts have usually argued that capricious and arbitrary actions of government and government officials will be minimized if officials, legislatures, and courts follow procedure and act as prescribed by law. To a certain extent, it appears to be a violation of a person's rights to due process of law if the rules being applied against that person have been created by an administrator acting under delegated powers, when the power to delegate is not authorized by law in the first place. In a nutshell, the application of due process in this context is sustained by the belief that only a "representative legislature" ought to make rules governing individual actions and affecting individual rights and only this kind of legislature ought to be able to make those rules with virtually total discretion (Barber, 1975, p. 34).

Due process concerns are particularly relevant if a citizen is adversely affected by a fine or jail sentence prescribed by a delegatee or an agent who is simply another private citizen and not an official of the government. Part of the Supreme Court's displeasure with the Bituminous Coal Conservation Act of 1935 stemmed from a provision that granted a group of private coal producers and miners the power to make rules fixing hours and wages for miners across the entire industry. In holding that this delegation violated the Due Process Clause of the Fifth Amendment, the Court declared that this was "legislative delegation in its most obnoxious form; for it is not even delegation to an official or an official body, presumptively disinterested, but to private persons whose interests may be and often are adverse to the interests of others in the same business" (*Carter* v. *Carter Coal Co.*, 298 U.S. 238 at 311 [1936]).

Nondelegability in Practice

In light of the foregoing discussion, it is easy to see how the Court might be caught in a bind between a collection of theories calling for nondelegability, on the one hand, and a realistic appraisal of modern governance demanding delegation, on the other. At first the Court allowed itself to sustain obvious delegations of legislative power by claiming they were really not delegations at all. This approach of keeping the all-inclusive nondelegation principle intact while allowing some delegations proved untenable. Ultimately the Court replaced this legal fiction by relaxing the all-inclusiveness assumption of nondelegability; that is, it maintained that although the theories clearly prohibit some kinds of delegations, they do not cover all delegations. In so doing, the Court allowed itself to pay homage to the time-honored legal and philosophic traditions that undergird the notion of nondelegability while meeting more forthrightly the obvious congressional need to share the awesome, potentially paralyzing burden of modern-day lawmaking.

Under more recent policy, what differentiates permissible from impermissible delegation is the degree of rule-making discretion Congress transfers to the delegatee. For the most part the Court now holds that as long as the delegatee is not granted virtually unfettered discretion (such being the essence of legislative power and hence an exclusively congressional function), the delegation is acceptable. To make sure that broad, open-ended transfers of discretion are not made, the Court requires Congress to provide intelligible standards to guide the agent granted the particular rule-making power. By clearly informing the agent of the subject matter to be dealt with and by providing recognizable standards to guide rule-making, Congress, according to the Court, retains enough of a guiding hand in what the agent can and cannot do so as not to violate, in any serious fashion at least, the principle of separation of powers. This call for standards does more than curb potential abdications of congressional responsibility. It also enables courts to play a more clear-cut role in limiting any rule-making excesses that an overly zealous agent might exercise. The Court's role in this type of oversight further safeguards the principle of separation of powers as well as the due process rights of the citizenry (Tribe, 1978, pp. 284–291).

Our discussion so far suggests that there is but one type of delegation. In point of fact, though, there are two kinds of legislation Congress can enact to delegate power. One is called "contingency legislation" and the other "sublegislation" or "filling-up-the-details legislation." Contingency legislation has proven the least problematic for the Court. In this kind of delegation, Congress outlines with some precision the regulation or law but grants to an officer or agent the power to determine when the legislation will take effect. The power to determine whether or not the legislation is to take effect is usually limited to a determination of particular facts that activate the legislation. This kind of legislation basically delegates a fact-finding power, rather than granting any rule-making discretion per se.

The Supreme Court initially sustained contingency legislation in *Brig Aurora* v. *United States,* 7 Cranch 382, decided in 1813. The case arose in connection with American efforts to remain neutral during the Napoleonic Wars. One measure designed to assure this neutrality was the Non-Intercourse Act of 1809. The Act granted the President the power to invoke an embargo against either Great Britain or France; which of these two nations would be the target of the embargo depended upon the President's determination of specific facts. If the President found that either Great Britain or France had ceased "to violate neutral commerce" vis-à-vis American ships, then he was free to invoke an embargo against whichever party continued to violate American neutrality. President Madison determined that France was the first to comply and thus instituted the embargo against Great

Britain. The Act was held constitutional and not violative of the nondelegation doctrine since the act of fact-finding was not viewed as an exertion of legislative power. Clearly Congress had said what was to be done, had set the policy. Because the President had simply determined a set of facts preordained by Congress and thereby activated the law's effect, legislative power had not been delegated to him.

Some eighty years later the Court ruled in a similar fashion in *Field* v. *Clark*, 143 U.S. 649 (1892). The Court upheld the Tariff Act of 1890, which granted the imposition of tariffs on certain imported products if the country sending the products placed a tariff on American goods viewed as "reciprocally unequal and unreasonable." It was left to the President to determine whether or not another nation's tariffs were reciprocally unequal and unreasonable. Here, again, the Court viewed the delegation as simply a fact-finding power and not a legislative one. Speaking for the majority, Justice Harlan noted:

> The Act . . . does not in any real sense invest the President with the power of legislation . . . he had no discretion in the premises . . . only to the enforcement of the policy established by Congress. As [enforcement] was absolutely required when the President ascertained the existence of a particular fact, it cannot be said that in ascertaining that fact and in issuing his proclamation, in obedience to the legislative will, he exercised the function of making laws. Legislative power was exercised when Congress declared that [enforcement] should take effect upon a named contingency.

Of course, the Court failed to acknowledge the degree of ostensibly "legislative" discretion the President had in determining what constituted the "unequal and unreasonable" tariff whose imposition would cause the legislative policy to go into effect. The Court seemed satisfied by the fact that Congress had set the specific rates of tariff, thus minimizing presidential discretion.

In 1928, however, the Court sustained contingency tariff legislation that not only allowed presidential discretion in deciding when to apply the tariff but also granted the President the power to flexibly set the tariff rate as well. In *J. W. Hampton & Co.* v. *United States,* the Court ruled the Tariff Act of 1922 constitutional. In the Act Congress granted the President the power to make the Act effective if inequality obtained and to set a tariff rate believed to approximate the equality desired. The Court recognized the discretionary character of the delegation, by arguing:

> If Congress shall lay down by legislative act an intelligible principle to which the person or body authorized to fix such rates is directed to conform such legislative action is not a forbidden delegation of legislative power.

In part, the delegations in *Brig Aurora, Field,* and *Hampton* deal with foreign affairs. In 1936 in *United States* v. *Curtiss–Wright Export Corp.,* 299 U.S. 304, the Court stated more explicitly that continuing delegations of legislative power regulating matters involving foreign affairs must be assessed on different grounds than delegations involving domestic matters. As noted in Chapter 8, the Court has recognized that the Chief Executive possesses independent powers in foreign affairs; because of his independent powers in that area, delegations of foreign affairs powers do not violate the principle of separation of powers. In *Curtiss–Wright* the

Court ruled that a grant of power to Roosevelt to prohibit the sale of arms to Bolivia and Paraguay if he found that such prohibition would contribute to the establishment of peace was not an unconstitutional contingency delegation of legislative power. In 1965, in *Zemel* v. *Rusk,* 381 U.S. 1, the Court supported this view again by saying: "Congress—in giving the Executive authority over matters of foreign affairs—must of necessity paint with a brush broader than that it customarily wields in domestic affairs."

In the domestic sphere, and particularly within the realm of the second category of congressional delegations, the Court has approached the issue from a slightly different angle. The first consideration of a congressional delegation of "sublegislative" power occurred in the 1825 case of *Wayman* v. *Southard,* 10 Wheat. 1. Here, Marshall's Court upheld a congressional grant of power to the judiciary to specify its own rules of procedure. Marshall, speaking for the majority, presented two justifications for the validity of the delegation. In the first place he saw a distinction between important subjects with which Congress alone could deal and subjects of less interest with which its agents could deal. Secondly, in the latter category, Marshall believed that if Congress enacted a general provision, agents of Congress could "fill in the details." The transfer of the power to create rules of procedure from Congress to the judiciary was justifiable in this instance because (1) the subject was of "less interest" and (2) the judiciary was merely "filling in the details" of a general provision.

Of the two justifications, the latter survived to guide subsequent Court policy in the area. Initially the "fill in the details" rationale served to continue the legal fiction that what was delegation was really not delegation after all (Barber, 1975). For instance, in *United States* v. *Grimaud,* 220 U.S. 506 (1910), the Court sustained a grant of rule-making power over grazing in national forests to the Secretary of Agriculture as a conferrence of "administrative function and not delegating to him legislative power."

More explicit recognition of the validity of congressional delegation in conjunction with closer attention to the standards upon which delegatees were to act came not only with *J. W. Hampton & Co.* in contingency legislation, but also with two cases striking down "sublegislative" delegations in 1935. In *Panama Refining Co.* v. *Ryan,* 293 U.S. 388 (1935), the Court ruled that the National Industrial Recovery Act's grant of power to Roosevelt to exclude from interstate commerce oil produced in violation of state regulation was an unconstitutional delegation of legislative power. Rather than argue that this grant of power was illegal as a violation of a blanket prohibition on delegation, the Court said that

> legislation must often be adapted to complex conditions involving a host of details with which the national legislature cannot deal directly . . . [The Constitution does not deny that Congress needs] . . . flexibility and practicality . . . to perform its function in laying down principles and establishing standards, while leaving selected instrumentalities the making of subordinate rules within prescribed limits and the determination of facts to which the policy as declared by the legislature is to apply.

While recognizing the validity of delegations regarding the details of policy application, the Court argued that when discretionary functions were delegated, they had to be accompanied by reasonably clear congressional standards. From the majority's perspective the grant of discretion to the President to regulate "hot oil" in interstate commerce had been "without standard or rule, to be dealt with as he pleased." As such, it was an unacceptable delegation of legislative power.

Later in 1935 the Court again ruled a congressional grant of rule-making power to the President unconstitutional on grounds of nondelegability. In the National Industrial Recovery Act (NIRA) challenged in *Panama Refining Co.,* Congress had sought to deal with the Depression by granting to the President the power to establish "codes of fair competition" for a broad range of industries. These codes, developed in some instances by an industry itself in conjunction with executive officials and ultimately approved by the President, were enforceable against all industries by criminal prosecution and/or civil process. A conviction on several violations of an executive- and industry-created Live Poultry Code brought to the Supreme Court the case of *Schechter Poultry Corp.* v. *United States,* 295 U.S. 495 (1935). The rule-making entailed in the creation of these codes obviously involved a delegation of legislative power. At issue was whether the necessary standards for such a delegation had been met. While the preamble to the NIRA had announced purposes such as to curb "unfair competition," increase productivity, and "otherwise rehabilitate industry," the granting of the power to fix codes carried no standards satisfactory to the Court. Indeed, the Court asserted that the NIRA granted "virtually unfettered" discretion to the President to enact "laws for the government of trade and industry throughout the country." As such, the NIRA could not stand the nondelegability test, even in its more modern form.

The *Panama Refining Co.* and *Schechter Poultry Corp.* cases stand out as the only two instances where the Court struck down a delegation of legislative power to governmental officials. As noted earlier, in 1936 the Court, in *Carter* v. *Carter Coal Co.,* also ruled portions of the Bituminous Coal Conservation Act unconstitutional for delegating legislative power to private citizens. We would be remiss if we did not place these striking symbols of the nondelegation doctrine in a broader context. These cases are part and parcel of the famous battle between the Court and President Roosevelt over the best way to salvage an economy ravaged by the Depression. The newly formed Democratic coalition elected to office in 1932 sought new solutions to the painful economic crisis that had begun with the stock market crash of 1929. The proposed solutions employed touches of Keynesian economics that called for governmental intervention in the economy, including some forms of regulation and control of free enterprise. These new solutions flew in the face of long-standing laissez-faire notions about limiting governmental involvement in the economy. In 1935 the Court was composed of four stalwart supporters of this laissez-faire view who could count on the support of fellow travelers on the Court enough of the time to form a solid majority in opposition to Roosevelt's New Deal. As we have noted elsewhere, this majority effectively curtailed the bulk of Roosevelt's efforts until the 1937 "switch in time that saved nine." In this light, it would be easy to conjecture that the *Panama* and *Schechter* decisions relied on the nondelegability thesis as a convenient way to block the New Deal. While this is no doubt part of the explanation, it is also true that the National Industrial Recovery Act was not an ideal piece of legislation. The rush to overcome a crisis may well have led Congress in 1933 to rely excessively on executive solutions rather than pass more deliberate and less justifiably suspect legislation.

Beyond these three cases, the Court has seen its way clear to sustain delegation after delegation, particularly since 1937. With little else to go on, one might conclude that Congress learned its lesson from the slap on the wrist provided by the three 1935 decisions and thereafter was careful to stipulate the standards of delegation with greater precision. In a technical sense, this is true. Congress does include direct standards in most delegating legislation, but at the same time the Court has loosened its strict attention to standards and found such assertions as "just and reasonable," "public interest," and "public convenience, interest, or necessity" sufficiently intelligible to guide delegatees and pass constitutional muster. Congress can now delegate pretty much as it pleases; the Court will, as often as not, either simply ignore questions of delegation, work diligently to find (if not create) standards, or narrowly interpret statutes to avoid issues of delegation altogether.

For instance, in the 1974 case of *National Cable Television Association* v. *United States,* 415 U.S. 336, the Supreme Court narrowly interpreted a grant of power to the Federal Communications Commission (FCC) to collect fees from cable television companies so as to avoid the possible conclusion that Congress had delegated its general taxing power to the FCC. In the Independent Offices Appropriation Act of 1952 Congress had authorized the head of each federal agency to set fees the agency head considered to be fair and equitable but tied in some way to the "value to the recipient" of the regulation. In light of this, the FCC had set a yearly fee of 30 cents per cable television subscriber ostensibly to pay part of the cost of the benefits the federal government conferred by virtue of its regulation. The Court held that the grant of power to agency heads to charge and set a fee was a constitutional delegation of power since the charge in question was strictly a fee and not a tax. Objecting to the FCC's assessment, Justice Marshall, in dissent, chastised the Court for "beclouding" the issue of whether this fee ought to be charged or what was or was not an appropriate fee for the FCC to charge by dredging up the "dead issue of nondelegability." For Marshall, the

> notion that the Constitution narrowly confines the power of Congress to delegate authority to administrative agencies, which was briefly in vogue in the 1930s, has been virtually abandoned by the Court for all practical purposes, at least in the absence of a delegation creating the danger of overbroad, unauthorized, and arbitrary application of criminal sanctions in an area of [constitutionally] protected freedoms. (*United States* v. *Robel,* 389 U.S. 258 [1967].)

Marshall underscored his position in his majority opinion in *Federal Energy Administration* v. *Algonquin SNG, Inc.,* 426 U.S. 548 (1976). In this case a challenge was made to a presidential action raising the license fees on imported crude oil. The power to do so stemmed from the Trade Expansion Act of 1962 as amended in 1974, which allowed the President to take any actions he deemed necessary to adjust the importation of articles believed to threaten to impair the national security. In 1975, President Ford, after an investigation by the Secretary of the Treasury, raised the license fees on imported crude oil so as to minimize the nation's present, continued, and possibly increasing reliance on foreign crude oil and thereby reduce the threat such reliance on foreign energy sources might have to national security. The challenge asserted that this was an unconstitutional delegation of legislative powers. Relying on *J. W. Hampton & Co.,* the Court concluded that raising the license fees was a constitutional action and that such a delegation met all the requirements for clear standards sufficient to rebut any attack on the delegation doctrine. According to the Court, the President's options were not unbounded. Indeed, by the terms of the statute he could act only to the extent "he deems necessary to adjust the imports of such article and its derivatives so that such imports will not threaten to impair the national security." Furthermore, because necessity makes it all but unreasonable and impractical to compel Congress to outline detailed rules, the Court believed there was no real problem of an unconstitutional delegation of legislative powers.

These two cases from the 1970s illustrate the Court's willingness to sustain fairly broad delegations of legislative powers. Chapter 14 will outline the indirect means employed by the Court to control the burgeoning bureaucracy.

J. W. Hampton & Co. v. United States

276 U.S. 394 (1928)

Mr. Chief Justice Taft delivered the opinion of the court.

J. W. Hampton, Jr. & Company made an importation into New York of barium dioxide which the collector of customs assessed at the dutiable rate of 6 cents per pound. This was 2 cents per pound more than that fixed by statute. * * * The rate was raised by the collector by virtue of the proclamation of the President * * * issued under . . . authority of . . . the Tariff Act of September 21, 1922, * * * which is the so-called flexible tariff provision. Protest was made and an appeal was taken. . . . The case came . . . before the United States customs court. * * * A majority held the act constitutional. Thereafter the case was appealed to the United States court of customs appeals. On the 16th day of October, 1926, the Attorney General certified that in his opinion the case was of such importance as to render expedient its review by this court. Thereafter the judgment of the United States customs court was affirmed. * * * On a petition to this court for certiorari, . . . the writ was granted. * * *

• • •

The issue here is as to the constitutionality of [the Tariff Act] upon which depends the authority for the proclamation of the President and for 2 of the 6 cents per pound duty collected from [J. W. Hampton]. The contention of the taxpayers is . . . that the section is invalid in that it is a delegation to the

President of the legislative power, which by article 1, § 1 of the Constitution, is vested in Congress, the power being that declared in § 8 of article 1, that the Congress shall have power to lay and collect taxes, duties, imposts, and excises. . . .

. . . It seems clear what Congress intended by [the Act]. Its plan was to secure by law the imposition of customs duties on articles of imported merchandise which should equal the difference between the cost of producing in a foreign country the articles in question and laying them down for sale in the United States, and the cost of producing and selling like or similar articles in the United States, so that the duties not only secure revenue but at the same time enable domestic producers to compete on terms of equality with foreign producers in the markets of the United States. It may be that it is difficult to fix with exactness this difference, but the difference which is sought in the statute is perfectly clear and perfectly intelligible. Because of the difficulty in practically determining what that difference is, Congress seems to have doubted that the information in its possession was such as to enable it to make the adjustment accurately, and also to have apprehended that with changing conditions the difference might vary in such a way that some readjustments would be necessary to give effect to the principle on which the statute proceeds. To avoid such difficulties, Congress adopted . . . the method of describing with clearness what its policy and plan was and then authorizing a member of the executive branch to carry out its policy and plan and to find the changing difference from time to time and to make the adjustments necessary to conform the duties to the standard underlying that policy and plan. As it was a matter of great importance, it concluded to give by statute to the President . . . the function of determining the difference as it might vary. . . .

• • •

The well-known maxim "delegata potestas non potest delegari" [that which is delegated cannot be redelegated], applicable to the law of agency in the general and common law, is well understood and has had wider application in the construction of our Federal and state Constitutions than it has in private law. Our Federal Constitution and state Constitutions of this country divide the governmental power into three branches. The first is the legislative, the second is the executive, and the third is the judicial, and the rule is that in the actual administration of the government Congress or the legislature should exercise the legislative power, the President or the state executive, the governor, the executive power, and the courts or the judiciary the judicial power, and in carrying out that constitutional division into three branches it is a breach of the national fundamental law if Congress gives up its legislative power and transfers it to the President, or to the judicial branch, or if by law it attempts to invest itself or its members with either executive power or judicial power. This is not to say that the three branches are not co-ordinate parts of one government and that each in the field of its duties may not invoke the action of the two other branches in so far as the action invoked shall not be an assumption of the constitutional field of action of another branch. In determining what it may do in seeking assistance from another branch, the extent and character of that assistance must be fixed according to common sense and the inherent necessities of the governmental coordination.

The field of Congress involves all and many varieties of legislative action, and Congress has found it frequently necessary to use officers of the executive branch, within defined limits, to secure the exact effect intended by its acts of legislation, by vesting discretion in such officers to make public regulations interpreting a statute and directing the details of its execution, even to the extent of providing for penalizing a breach of such regulations. * * *

Congress may feel itself unable conveniently to determine exactly when its exercise of the legislative power should become effective, because dependent on future conditions, and it may leave the determination of such time to the decision of an executive. . . .

. . . [O]ne of the great functions conferred on Congress by the Federal Constitution is the regulation of interstate commerce and rates to be exacted by interstate carriers for the passenger and merchandise traffic. The rates to be fixed are myriad. If Congress were to be required to fix every rate, it would be impossible to exercise the power at all. Therefore, common sense requires that in the fixing of such rates, Congress may provide a Commission, as it does, called the Interstate Commerce Commission, to fix those rates, after hearing evidence and argument concerning them from interested parties, all in accord with a general rule that Congress first lays down that rates shall be just and reasonable considering the service given and not discriminatory. . . .

• • •

It is conceded by counsel that Congress may use executive officers in the application and enforcement of a policy declared in law by Congress and authorize such officers in the application of the congressional declaration to enforce it by regulation equivalent to law. But it is said that this never has been permitted to be done where Congress has exercised the power to levy taxes and fix customs duties. The authorities make no such distinction. The same principle that permits Congress to exercise its rate-making power in interstate commerce by declaring the rule which shall prevail in the legislative fixing of rates, and enables it to remit to a rate-making body created in accordance with its provisions the fixing of such rates, justifies a similar provision for the fixing of customs duties on imported merchandise. If Congress shall lay down by legislative act an intelligible principle to which the person or body authorized to fix such rates is directed to conform, such legislative action is not a forbidden delegation of legislative power. If it is thought wise to vary the customs duties according to changing conditions of production at home and abroad, it may authorize the Chief Executive to carry out this purpose. . . .

Schechter Poultry Corp. v. *United States*

295 U.S. 495 (1935)

Mr. Chief Justice Hughes delivered the opinion of the court.

[Schechter Poultry Corp. et al.] were convicted in the District Court of the United States for the Eastern District of New York on eighteen counts of an indictment charging violations of what is known as the "Live Poultry Code," and on an additional count for conspiracy to commit such violations. . . .

The Circuit Court of Appeals sustained the conviction on the conspiracy count and on sixteen counts for violation of the code. . . . On the respective applications of the defendants * * * . . . this Court granted writs of certiorari. * * *

• • •

The "Live Poultry Code" was promulgated under § 3 of the National Industrial Recovery Act. That section . . . authorizes the President to approve "codes of fair competition." Such a code may be approved for a trade or industry, upon application by one or more trade or industrial associations or groups, if the President finds (1) that such associations or groups "impose no inequitable restrictions on admission to membership therein and are truly representative," and (2) that such codes are not designed "to promote monopolies or to eliminate or oppress small enterprises and will not operate to discriminate against them, and will tend to effectuate the policy" * * * of the act. Such codes "shall not permit monopolies or monopolistic practices." As a condition of his approval, the President may "impose such conditions (including requirements for the making of reports and the keeping of accounts) for the protection of consumers, competitors, employes and others, and in furtherance of the public interest, and may provide such exceptions to and exemptions from the provisions of such code as the President in his discretion deems necessary to effectuate the policy herein declared." Where such a code has not been approved, the President may prescribe one, either on his own motion or on complaint. Violation of any provision of a code (so approved or prescribed) "in any transaction in or affecting interstate or foreign commerce" is made a misdemeanor punishable by a fine of not more than $500 for each offense, and each day the violation continues is to be deemed a separate offense.

The "Live Poultry Code" was approved by the President on April 13, 1934. . . .

The declared purpose is "To effect the policies of title I of the National Industrial Recovery Act." . . .

•   •   •

The code fixes the number of hours for workdays. It provides that no employee, with certain exceptions, shall be permitted to work in excess of forty (40)
hours in any one week, and that no employee, save as stated, "shall be paid in
any pay period less than at the rate of fifty (50) cents per hour." . . . [The code
also limits child labor practices and creates administrative procedures for the
execution of the code's provisions.]

The seventh article, containing "trade practice provisions," prohibits various
practices which are said to constitute "unfair methods of competition." . . .

•   •   •

Of the eighteen counts of the indictment upon which the defendants were
convicted, aside from the count for conspiracy, two counts charged violation of
the minimum wage and maximum hour provisions of the code; . . . ten counts,
respectively, were that [Schechter, in selling] to retail dealers and butchers, had
permitted "selections of individual chickens taken from particular coops and half
coops."

Of the other six counts, one charged the sale to a butcher of an unfit chicken;
two counts charged the making of sales without having the poultry inspected or
approved in accordance with regulations or ordinances of the City of New York;
two counts charged the making of false reports or the failure to make reports
relating to the range of daily prices and volume and sales for certain periods; and
the remaining count was for sales to slaughterers or dealers who were without
licenses required by the ordinances and regulations of the City of New York.

First. Two preliminary points are stressed by the government with respect to
the appropriate approach to the important questions presented. We are told that
the provision of the statute authorizing the adoption of codes must be viewed in
the light of the grave national crisis with which Congress was confronted. Undoubtedly, the conditions to which power is addressed are always to be considered when the exercise of power is challenged. Extraordinary conditions may call
for extraordinary remedies. But the argument necessarily stops short of an attempt to justify action which lies outside the sphere of constitutional authority.
Extraordinary conditions do not create or enlarge constitutional power. The
Constitution established a national government with powers deemed to be adequate, as they have proved to be both in war and peace, but these powers of the
national government are limited by the constitutional grants. Those who act
under these grants are not at liberty to transcend the imposed limits because they
believe that more or different power is necessary. Such assertions of extra-consti-
tutional authority were anticipated and precluded by the explicit terms of the
Tenth Amendment, "The powers not delegated to the United States by the
Constitution, nor prohibited by it to the States, are reserved to the States respectively, or to the people."

The further point is urged that the national crisis demanded a broad and intensive co-operative effort by those engaged in trade and industry, and that this necessary co-operation was sought to be fostered by permitting them to initiate the adoption of codes. But the statutory plan is not simply one for voluntary effort. It does not seek merely to endow voluntary trade or industrial associations or groups with privileges or immunities. It involves the coercive exercise of the law-making power. The codes of fair competition which the statute attempts to authorize are codes of laws. If valid, they place all persons within their reach under the obligation of positive law, binding equally those who assent and those who do not assent. Violations of the provisions of the codes are punishable as crimes.

Second. The question of the delegation of legislative power[:] . . . The Constitution provides that "all legislative powers herein granted shall be vested in a Congress of the United States, which shall consist of a Senate and House of Representatives." * * * And the Congress is authorized "to make all laws which shall be necessary and proper for carrying into execution" its general power. * * * The Congress is not permitted to abdicate or to transfer to others the essential legislative functions with which it is thus vested. We have repeatedly recognized the necessity of adapting legislation to complex conditions involving a host of details with which the National Legislature cannot deal directly. We pointed out in the Panama Ref. Co. Case that the Constitution has never been regarded as denying to Congress the necessary resources of flexibility and practicality, which will enable it to perform its function in laying down policies and establishing standards, while leaving to selected instrumentalities the making of subordinate rules within prescribed limits and the determination of facts to which the policy as declared by the Legislature is to apply. But . . . the constant recognition of the necessity and validity of such provisions, and the wide range of administrative authority which has been developed by means of them, cannot be allowed to obscure the limitations of the authority to delegate, if our constitutional system is to be maintained. * * *

Accordingly, we look to the statute to see whether Congress has overstepped these limitations—whether Congress in authorizing "Codes of Fair Competition" has itself established the standards of legal obligation, thus performing its essential legislative function, or, by the failure to enact such standards, has attempted to transfer that function to others.

The aspect in which the question is now presented is distinct from that which was before us in the case of the Panama Company. There, the subject of the statutory prohibition was defined. * * * That subject was the transportation in interstate and foreign commerce of petroleum and petroleum products which are produced or withdrawn from storage in excess of the amount permitted by State authority. The question was with respect to the range of discretion given to the President in prohibiting that transportation. * * * As to the "Codes of Fair Competition," . . . the question is more fundamental. It is whether there is any adequate definition of the subject to which the codes are to be addressed.

What is meant by "fair competition" as the term is used in the act? Does it refer to a category established in the law, and is the authority to make codes limited accordingly? Or is it used as a convenient designation for whatever set of laws the formulators of a code for a particular trade or industry may propose and the President may approve (subject to certain restrictions), or the President may himself prescribe, as being wise and beneficent provisions for the government of the trade or industry in order to accomplish the broad purposes of rehabilitation, correction and expansion which are stated [in the Act]?

The act does not define "fair competition." "Unfair competition" as known to the common law is a limited concept. Primarily, and strictly, it relates to the palming off of one's goods as those of a rival trader. * * * In recent years its scope has been extended. It has been held to apply to misappropriation as well as misrepresentation, to the selling of another's goods as one's own—to misappropriation of what equitably belongs to a competitor. * * * Unfairness in competition has been predicated on acts which lie outside the ordinary course of business and are tainted by fraud, or coercion, or conduct otherwise prohibited by law. * * * But it is evident that in its widest range "unfair competition," as it has been understood in the law, does not reach the objectives of the codes which are authorized by the National Industrial Recovery Act. The codes may, indeed, cover conduct which existing law condemns, but they are not limited to conduct of that sort. The government does not contend that the act contemplates such a limitation. It would be opposed both to the declared purposes of the act and to its administrative construction.

The Federal Trade Commission Act * * * introduced the expression "unfair methods of competition," which were declared to be unlawful. That was an expression new in the law. Debate apparently convinced the sponsors of the legislation that the words "unfair competition," in the light of their meaning at common law, were too narrow. We have said that the substituted phrase has a broader meaning; that it does not admit of precise definition, its scope being left to judicial determination as controversies arise. * * * What are "unfair methods of competition" are thus to be determined in particular instances, upon evidence, in the light of particular competitive conditions and of what is found to be a specific and substantial public interest. * * * To make this possible Congress set up a special procedure. A commission, a quasi-judicial body, was created. Provision was made for formal complaint, for notice and hearing, for appropriate findings of fact supported by adequate evidence, and for judicial review to give assurance that the action of the Commission is taken within its statutory authority. * * *

In providing for codes, the National Industrial Recovery Act dispenses with this administrative procedure and with any administrative procedure of an analogous character. But the difference between the code plan of the Recovery Act and the scheme of the Federal Trade Commission Act lies not only in procedure but in subject matter. We cannot regard the "fair competition" of the codes as antithetical to the "unfair methods of competition" of the Federal Trade

Commission Act. The "fair competition" of the codes has a much broader range and a new significance. The Recovery Act provides that it shall not be construed to impair the powers of the Federal Trade Commission, but, when a code is approved, its provisions are to be the "standards of fair competition" for the trade or industry concerned, and any violation of such standards in any transaction in or affecting interstate or foreign commerce is to be deemed "an unfair method of competition" within the meaning of the Federal Trade Commission Act. * * *

For a statement of the authorized objectives and content of the "codes of fair competition" we are referred repeatedly to the "declaration of policy" in * * * the Recovery Act. Thus, the approval of a code by the President is conditioned on his finding that it "will tend to effectuate the policy of this title." * * * The President is authorized to impose such conditions "for the protection of consumers, competitors, employes and others, and in furtherance of the public interest, and may provide such exceptions to and exemptions from the provisions of such code as the President in his discretion deems necessary to effectuate the policy herein declared." * * * The "policy herein declared" is manifestly that set forth. . . . That declaration embraces a broad range of objectives. Among them we find the elimination of "unfair competitive practices." But even if this clause were to be taken to relate to practices which fall under the ban of existing law, either common law or statute, it is still only one of the authorized aims described. * * * It is there declared to be "the policy of Congress"—

"to remove obstructions to the free flow of interstate and foreign commerce which tend to diminish the amount thereof; and to provide for the general welfare by promoting the organization of industry for the purpose of co-operative action among trade groups, to induce and maintain united action of labor and management under adequate governmental sanctions and supervision, to eliminate unfair competitive practices, to promote the fullest possible utilization of the present productive capacity of industries, to avoid undue restriction of production (except as may be temporarily required), to increase the consumption of industrial and agricultural products by increasing purchasing power, to reduce and relieve unemployment, to improve standards of labor, and otherwise to rehabilitate industry and to conserve natural resources."

. . . [Under these provisions], whatever "may tend to effectuate" these general purposes may be included in the "codes of fair competition." We think the conclusion is inescapable that the authority sought to be conferred * * * was not merely to deal with "unfair competitive practices" which offend against existing law, and could be the subject of judicial condemnation without further legislation, or to create administrative machinery for the application of established principles of law to particular instances of violation. Rather, the purpose is clearly disclosed to authorize new and controlling prohibitions through codes of laws which would embrace what the formulators would propose, and what the President would approve, or prescribe, as wise and beneficent measures for the government of trades and industries in order to bring about their rehabilitation,

correction and development, according to the general declaration of policy. * * *
Codes of laws of this sort are styled "codes of fair competition."

• • •

The question, then, turns upon the authority which * * * the Recovery Act
vests in the President to approve or prescribe. . . . Congress cannot delegate
legislative power to the President to exercise an unfettered discretion to make
whatever laws he thinks may be needed or advisable for the rehabilitation and
expansion of trade or industry. * * *

Accordingly we turn to the Recovery Act to ascertain what limits have been
set to the exercise of the President's discretion. *First,* the President, as a condition
of approval, is required to find that the trade or industrial associations or groups
which propose a code "impose no inequitable restrictions on admission to membership" and are "truly representative." That condition, however, relates only to
the status of the initiators of the new laws and not to the permissible scope of such
laws. *Second,* the President is required to find that the code is not "designed to
promote monopolies or to eliminate or oppress small enterprises and will not
operate to discriminate against them." And to this is added a proviso that the
code "shall not permit monopolies or monopolistic practices." But these restrictions leave virtually untouched the field of policy envisaged * * * and in that
wide field of legislative possibilities the proponents of a code, refraining from
monopolistic designs, may roam at will and the President may approve or disapprove their proposals as he may see fit. That is the precise effect of the further
finding that the President is to make—that the code "will tend to effectuate the
policy of this title." While this is called a finding, it is really but a statement of an
opinion as to the general effect upon the promotion of trade or industry of a
scheme of laws. These are the only findings which Congress has made essential in
order to put into operation a legislative code having the aims described in the
"Declaration of Policy."

Nor is the breadth of the President's discretion left to the necessary implications of this limited requirement as to his findings. As already noted, the President in approving a code may impose his own conditions, adding to or taking
from what is proposed, as "in his discretion" he thinks necessary "to effectuate
the policy" declared by the act. Of course, he has no less liberty when he prescribes a code on his own motion or on complaint, and he is free to prescribe one
if a code has not been approved. The act provides for the creation by the President of administrative agencies to assist him, but the action or reports of such
agencies, or of his other assistants—their recommendations and findings in relation to the making of codes—have no sanction beyond the will of the President,
who may accept, modify or reject them as he pleases. . . .

• • •

To summarize and conclude upon this point: * * * the Recovery Act is
without precedent. It supplies no standards for any trade, industry or activity. It

does not undertake to prescribe rules of conduct to be applied to particular states of fact determined by appropriate administrative procedure. Instead of prescribing rules of conduct, it authorizes the making of codes to prescribe them. For that legislative undertaking, § 3 sets up no standards, aside from the statement of the general aims of rehabilitation, correction and expansion. * * * In view of the scope of that broad declaration, and of the nature of the few restrictions that are imposed, the discretion of the President in approving or prescribing codes, and thus enacting laws for the government of trade and industry throughout the country, is virtually unfettered. We think that the code-making authority thus conferred is an unconstitutional delegation of legislative power.

[The Court also considered Commerce Clause questions and concluded that the attempted regulation of intrastate activities exceeded the constitutional grant of power to regulate interstate commerce.]

Mr. Justice Cardozo, concurring.

The delegated power of legislation which has found expression in this code is not canalized within banks that keep it from overflowing. It is unconfined and vagrant. . . .

. . . Here, in the case before us, is an attempted delegation not confined to any single act nor to any class or group of acts identified or described by reference to a standard. Here in effect is a roving commission to inquire into evils and upon discovery correct them.

I have said that there is no standard, definite or even approximate, to which legislation must conform. Let me make my meaning more precise. If codes of fair competition are codes eliminating "unfair" methods of competition ascertained upon inquiry to prevail in one industry or another, there is no unlawful delegation of legislative functions when the President is directed to inquire into such practices and denounce them when discovered. . . . Delegation in such circumstances is born of the necessities of the occasion. The industries of the country are too many and diverse to make it possible for Congress, in respect of matters such as these, to legislate directly with adequate appreciation of varying conditions.
. . .

But there is another conception of codes of fair competition, their significance and function, which leads to very different consequences, though it is one that is struggling now for recognition and acceptance. By this other conception a code is not to be restricted to the elimination of business practices that would be characterized by general acceptance as oppressive or unfair. It is to include whatever ordinances may be desirable or helpful for the well-being or prosperity of the industry affected. In that view, the function of its adoption is not merely negative, but positive: the planning of improvements as well as the extirpation of abuses. What is fair, as thus conceived, is not something to be contrasted with what is unfair or fraudulent or tricky. The extension becomes as wide as the field of industrial regulation. If that conception shall prevail, anything that Congress may do within the limits of the commerce clause for the betterment of business may be done by the President upon the recommendation of a trade association by calling it a code. This is delegation running riot. No such plenitude of power is susceptible of transfer. The statute, however, aims at nothing less, as one can learn both from its terms and from the administrative practice under it. Nothing less is aimed at by the code now submitted to our scrutiny.

The code does not confine itself to the suppression of methods of competition that would be classified as unfair according to accepted business standards or accepted norms of ethics. It sets up a comprehensive body of rules to promote the welfare of the industry, if not the welfare of the nation, without reference to standards, ethical or commercial, that could be known or predicted in advance of its adoption. . . . Even if the statute itself had fixed the meaning of fair competition by way of contrast with practices that are oppressive or unfair, the code outruns the bounds of the authority conferred. What is excessive is not sporadic or superficial. It is deep-seated and pervasive. The licit and illicit sections are so combined and welded as to be incapable of severance without destructive mutilation.

· · ·

I am authorized to state that Mr. Justice Stone joins in this opinion.

CHAPTER **14**

Exercise of Administrative Power

INTRODUCTORY ESSAY

Constitutional standards applicable to the delegation of legislative authority place very little actual restraint on administrative power in the United States. The non-delegation doctrine, rooted in the constitutional principle of separation of powers, is admittedly of great theoretical significance; but it stands as a practical judicial check only on the most irresponsible and directionless transfers of legislative power to executive and administrative agencies. It is important to keep in mind that the decision in *Schechter Poultry Corp.* v. *United States,* 295 U.S. 495 (1935), marked the last occasion on which the Supreme Court invoked the nondelegation doctrine as a basis for invalidating an act of Congress. That decision, it is true, has not been overruled; but its underlying theme of skepticism regarding governmental supervision of the economy has long since been abandoned by the Supreme Court. Although some have called for the revival of the *Schechter* Rule (see Lowi, 1969, Chapter 5), most students of administrative law doubt that judicial standards regarding the delegation of legislative power are of much practical importance. (See, for example, Gellhorn and Byse, 1974, Chapter 2.)

We have commented frequently on the judicial revolution of 1937 and what it signified for the way the Supreme Court functions within the American political system. The turnabout was reflected in the Court's growing acceptance of a greatly enlarged governmental role, federal and state, in economic regulation and social welfare. But this accommodation to the reality of "big government" was to some extent counterbalanced by a growing tendency to protect civil rights and liberties and to strengthen the rights of persons accused of crime. The Justices appointed by Franklin D. Roosevelt were convinced of the need for positive government at all levels. But like their more conservative predecessors, they put a high premium on individual rights. The difference lay in the nature of the rights protected. Prior to 1937 the emphasis of the Court majority was on rights identified with traditional institutions of private property—especially corporate property devoted to business activity. After 1937 the emphasis shifted to protection of First Amendment freedoms of expression, guarantees of racial equality, and the tightening of procedural requirements imposed on law enforcement practices. While our attention in this chapter is directed toward the growth of bureaucratic power largely outside the areas of freedom of expression and criminal justice, it is essential to remember that the Supreme Court has, since the late 1930s, greatly expanded the scope of constitutional restriction in these and other areas of civil rights and liberties.

As we have seen, the Court-packing proposal that FDR introduced early in 1937 was followed within a few months by major Supreme Court decisions upholding broad federal and state regulatory power. This judicial approval went far beyond the sanctioning of economic supervision. It included recognition of an expanded social service commitment by government. The Court's upholding of all aspects of the vast social security system in 1937 was a particularly important indication of its posture toward the rapidly growing federal bureaucracy (see *Steward Machine Co. v. Davis*, 301 U.S. 548 [1937], discussed in Chapter 6).

While governmental activity was growing at an unprecedented rate, the Supreme Court appeared to bow to the inevitable problems of overwhelming size in government by showing less and less willingness to review the details of administrative activity. It no longer seriously questioned the scope of administrative authority. (The sheer size of the federal administrative bureaucracy prevents any detailed review at the Supreme Court level and probably even at lower levels of the judicial system.) Although the Court was reluctant to deal with substantive issues of administrative power, it began to take an active interest, along with lower federal courts, in developing standards of procedural regularity for reviewing administrative action. This focus on procedural as opposed to substantive questions has continued down to the present, although the Court has sometimes failed to differentiate clearly between the two.

Since the 1930s the constitutional focus of Supreme Court review of administrative action has been on the requirements of due process of law. Historically, due process has been accorded both a substantive and a procedural meaning. Broadly speaking, the concept of substantive due process deals with the question of *what* government can do. It centers on the reasonableness of governmental activity in a given area. In American constitutional law the concept of substantive due process dates only from the mid-nineteenth century. It provided the primary conceptual justification for the Court's defense of property rights during the forty-year period culminating in FDR's Court-packing venture. More recently substantive due process (which went into eclipse after 1937) has been somewhat revitalized as a constitutional basis for the right of privacy (see, for example, *Griswold* v. *Connecticut*, 381 U.S. 479 [1965], which invalidates a state law barring the use of contraceptives; and *Roe* v. *Wade*, 410 U.S. 113 [1973], which limits state authority to impose criminal penalties in connection with abortions).

Procedural due process, rooted in the English common law tradition, is concerned with *how* government accomplishes its legitimate objectives—how it exercises its power within its acknowledged range of responsibility. Procedural due process is by far the older and more fully developed of the two concepts. It affords a wider and more clearly defined set of choices in the exercise of judicial review.

Perhaps because most judges feel more comfortable and confident in dealing with questions of procedure and less at home with attempts to determine the most appropriate or reasonable administrative policy, the Supreme Court has chosen a relatively limited role in reviewing administrative decisions. Some critics have asserted that the single greatest failure of the Supreme Court in the second half of the twentieth century has been its inability or unwillingness to establish effective judicial controls on the exercise of bureaucratic power. Others have argued, on the contrary, that given the vast range of specialized and technically complex governmental activity in modern society, a limited supervisory role by Justices—who are, of necessity, generalists—is inevitable. It is not our purpose to defend or challenge either of these positions but, rather, to examine, through a few representative decisions, the nature of Supreme Court interpretation of administrative decision-making. In doing so, we move somewhat beyond the traditional categories of constitutional law typically included in a casebook for students. A great many Supreme Court cases involving administrative agencies are based on statutory interpretation rather than on provisions of the Constitution. But this distinction should not obscure the fact that a great deal of the power exercised by modern government in the United States is bureaucratic power. A study of the allocation of constitutional power would be unnecessarily limited if it did not at least touch on the Supreme Court's function in deciding cases arising from the process of bureaucratic decision-making. Problems of bureaucratic power in the United States are not confined to the national government. They permeate the political system at every level from the White House to city hall, from the Department of Education to the county school superintendent's office. Often the responsibilities for carrying out a national administrative program are shared by the federal government and the states. The Social Security Administration provides a ready example. The Supreme Court is most concerned with questions of federal bureaucratic power, and our brief discussion accordingly emphasizes cases arising from federal agency action.

Constitutional and Statutory Review

When we speak of judicial review of administrative action, it is necessary to distinguish between constitutional and statutory review. Both types of review are applicable to administrative action. Thus we are dealing here with a far broader conception of judicial review than that developed in our discussion of *Marbury* v. *Madison,* 1 Cranch 137 (1803). Of course, administrative policy, like other governmental action, is subordinate to provisions of the Constitution. The Supreme Court may have occasion to strike down an administrative regulation because it conflicts with the Due Process Clause of the Fifth Amendment or some other constitutional provision. Far more often, however, judicial review of administrative action, both by the Supreme Court and other tribunals such as the Court of Appeals for the District of Columbia, is based on statutory provisions. These provisions may be either general or specific, defining the responsibilities of a particular agency or establishing basic procedural requirements for all agencies. An example of a specific statutory review is provided by the Social Security Act of 1935, creating the Social Security Administration and detailing its functions. General statutory review, on the other hand, is illustrated by such legislation as the Administrative Procedure Act (APA) of 1946. This act sets forth in detail the procedural standards required of virtually all federal agencies in their formulations of administrative policy.

In addition to constitutional and statutory review, a separate category of nonstatutory judicial review should be noted. This type of review is based on writs of equity dating from the early English legal tradition. The injunction, discussed in

Chapter 2, is a common form through which nonstatutory review is exercised. It is true that statutes may authorize the issuance of injunctions, but the existence of such statutes is not a prerequisite to the exercise of this type of review. (For background, see Shapiro, 1968, Chapter 1.) The cases included in this chapter may be more fully understood if this difference is kept in mind.

Statutory Interpretation

We have chosen two recent cases to illustrate the kinds of administrative policies that may result in Supreme Court review of statutory requirements. In *United States v. Bisceglia*, 420 U.S. 141 (1975), the Court considered the question of whether the Internal Revenue Service had statutory authority to issue a "John Doe" summons to a bank vice president in connection with its investigation of certain questionable deposits. Each of the two deposits under investigation consisted of $20,000 in $100 bills. This money, which the Commercial Bank of Middlesboro, Kentucky, had deposited in a branch of the Federal Reserve Bank, was in badly deteriorated physical condition, possibly indicating that it had been stored for a long time under abnormal conditions. When this information was routinely reported to the IRS, that agency, suspecting that the money had never been reported for tax purposes, but having no evidence to substantiate this suspicion, initiated an inquiry. The first step was issuance of the John Doe warrant calling for production of books and records that would indicate who had made the deposits.

Writing for a majority of seven, Chief Justice Burger held that the IRS had acted within its statutory authority under the Internal Revenue Code of 1954 in issuing the summons. Burger concluded that authorization of the IRS to investigate "all persons . . . who may be liable to pay any internal revenue tax" and to issue a summons to "any person" to acquire relevant information was a sufficiently broad grant of power to cover persons not identified when the investigation began. He pointed out that the IRS had a legitimate interest in large or unusual cash transactions like the one at issue here. "It would seem elementary," he concluded, "that no meaningful investigation of such events could be conducted if the identity of the persons involved must first be ascertained . . . not always an easy task."

In a sharply worded dissent, Justice Stewart, joined by Justice Douglas, read the same statutory language to require far more specific identification of the person or persons being summoned. For him the applicable statutory language indicated "unmistakably that the summons power is a tool for the investigation of particular taxpayers." He maintained that the general duties of the IRS are much broader than its summons authority. If such a limitation were not recognized, the summons power could be used "methodically to force disclosure of whole categories of transactions and closely monitor the operations of myriad segments of the economy on the theory that the information thereby accumulated might facilitate the assessment and collection of some kind of a federal tax from somebody." Stewart and Douglas feared that the majority opinion authorized "exactly that." A note of deep suspicion regarding the unbridled power of the IRS was apparent in this and many of Justice Douglas' later dissents. That theme has become popular in campaign oratory and editorial commentary but has not yet been embraced by a Supreme Court majority.

Another problem of judicial review stemming from statutory provisions arises when Congress approves policies that directly conflict with each other. A classic illustration is provided by the 1978 case of *Tennessee Valley Authority* v. *Hill*, 437 U.S. 153. In 1967 the Tennessee Valley Authority (TVA) began work on the Tellico Dam and Reservoir Project, using funds specifically appropriated by Congress for this purpose. The project was controversial from the beginning—favored by land developers and electrical power interests, and opposed by environmental groups because of its allegedly needless destruction of a rare and valuable natural river setting. Construction was delayed through legal challenges brought under the National Environmental Policy Act requiring, among other things, the submission of an Environmental Impact Statement. It was not until 1973 that the TVA was able to convince a United States district court that it had met this requirement. In that year Congress passed the Endangered Species Act. Shortly thereafter, a University of Tennessee professor of zoology identified a small fish, commonly known as the "snail darter," as an endangered species whose habitat in the Little Tennessee River would be destroyed by completion of the reservoir. Since it was determined that the snail darter could live only in this potentially affected portion of the river, the Secretary of the Interior, pursuant to provisions of the Endangered Species Act, declared it to be the fish's "critical habitat" and stated that all federal agencies (including the TVA) must act so as not to destroy or modify this critical habitat. Environmental groups immediately went back to court to enjoin completion of the Tellico dam project. Although finding that creation of the reservoir might totally wipe out the snail darter, U.S. District Court Judge Robert Taylor refused to grant the injunction and dismissed the complaint. Work continued on the Tellico project, but when it was nearing completion, the Court of Appeals for the Sixth Circuit reversed the district court ruling and remanded the case with instructions that a permanent injunction be issued to halt any activities that would destroy or modify the snail darter's critical habitat. The TVA obtained Supreme Court review of this decision on a writ of certiorari, and in a 6 to 3 ruling, the Supreme Court affirmed.

Chief Justice Burger wrote the majority opinion, holding that the Endangered Species Act clearly prohibited the TVA, under the circumstances of this case, from impounding the river, even though the project was well under way when the Act was passed and the snail darter was declared an endangered species. It made no difference that Congress had continued to appropriate money for the project even after action was taken by the Secretary of the Interior to protect the snail darter. Continuance of appropriations, in the Court's view, did not amount to an implied repeal of the Endangered Species Act as it related to the Tellico project.

Burger made it abundantly clear that this holding did not imply the Court's approval of the practical result produced by application of the requirements spelled out in the Endangered Species Act. He quoted at length from a passage attributed to Sir Thomas More in the play *A Man for All Seasons*. The thrust of More's statement is summed up in his comment: "I know what's legal, not what's right. And I'll stick to what's legal. . . . I'm not God." Expressing agreement with the Court of Appeals, Burger concluded that "in our constitutional system the commitment to the separation of powers is too fundamental for us to preempt congressional action by judicially decreeing what accords with 'commonsense and the public weal.'"

The dissenters were far less deferential toward formal statutory requirements. Justice Powell, joined by Justice Blackmun, contended that the Endangered Species

Act should not be interpreted to reach such an impractical result. He thought it the "duty of the Court to adopt a permissible construction that accords with some modicum of commonsense and the public weal." He was confident that Congress would soon amend the Act so as to avoid the waste of the over $50 million already committed to the Tellico project. He thought, however, that it was not "the province of this Court to force Congress into otherwise unnecessary action by interpreting a statute to produce a result no one intended." In a short dissent, Justice Rehnquist maintained that the district court acted within its proper discretion in initially refusing to enjoin construction of the dam.

In its statutory review of administrative action, the Supreme Court, and other courts similarly engaged, can be expected to give major attention to the supposed legislative intent underlying the passage of the law in question. But, as the TVA case amply illustrates, legislative intent is an elusive concept. It is seldom self-evident in a complex controversy when competing objectives and commitments are at stake. The issues are often so complex that judicial deference to legislative intent is at least understandable as a justification for avoiding direct involvement in the policy-making process. But in the very act of interpreting legislative intent in an area where goals pursued by legislators are in conflict, the Court makes choices, forces further decisions on other participants in the political system—in short, participates in the formulation of public policy. Indeed, Congress and the President later saw fit to authorize TVA expenditures for the completion of the Tellico dam. The fact that the Court may formulate policy indirectly and negatively rather than directly and affirmatively makes little, if any, difference.

Due Process and Administrative Action

In constitutional, as opposed to statutory, review the Supreme Court has emphasized standards of procedural due process in determining the basic fairness of challenged administrative decisions. These standards include the requirement of notice and an opportunity to be heard. They also call for procedural regularity by condemning arbitrary decisions. In spite of the attention given these procedural requirements, a majority of the Justices have traditionally accorded wide latitude to administrative discretion. For example, in *Mathews* v. *Eldridge,* 424 U.S. 319 (1976), the Court upheld procedures under which social security disability benefits can be initially terminated without an evidentiary hearing. George Eldridge, who was originally disabled due to "chronic anxiety and back strain," was informed by official letter that, according to medical reports, his disability no longer existed and that benefit payments would be terminated. Although procedures provided for ample notification, opportunity for the beneficiary to reply, and an evidentiary hearing prior to final termination, the payments could be stopped initially without such a hearing. Provision was also made for retroactive payments to any recipient whose disability was later determined not to have ended. But Eldridge was concerned with the initial decision to terminate, contending that the Due Process Clause of the Fifth Amendment required that such a decision be accompanied by the right to an evidentiary hearing. He relied on the 1970 decision in *Goldberg* v. *Kelly,* 397 U.S. 254, which recognized the right to an evidentiary hearing prior to the termination of welfare benefits.

Justice Powell, for a six-member majority, rejected Eldridge's argument and distinguished the *Goldberg* ruling. Conceding that a "property interest" in the form of benefit payments was at stake here, and that an evidentiary hearing would be required before *final* termination, he nevertheless concluded that a hearing was not required prior to the actual cessation of payments. As the dissenters, Justices Brennan and Marshall pointed out, this distinction between initial and final termination did not take into account the actual hardship imposed on real people, including Eldridge himself. As a direct result of the termination of his benefits, there was a foreclosure on his home. The family's furniture was repossessed, and Eldridge, his wife, and their children were forced to sleep in one bed. But such practical considerations are not often permitted to influence the fastidious application of constitutional principles by appellate judges, far removed from the sights and smells of economic reality.

Justice Powell maintained that since economic necessity was not a necessary precondition to the receipt of social security disability payments, "the potential deprivation . . . is generally likely to be less" than in the case of a welfare recipient whose benefits are based squarely on economic need. The dissenters viewed this argument as purely speculative and, as previously noted, pointed out that it was totally erroneous when applied to the facts of this case. Powell also asserted that medical judgments regarding disability were more likely to be accurate than decisions regarding the justified termination of welfare payments. He noted further that *Goldberg* v. *Kelly* departed from established practice in other areas by recognizing the right to a pretermination hearing in the first place. Whatever one thinks of the Court's decision on the merits (and our skepticism is openly acknowledged), the ruling underscores the Court's basic reluctance to disturb well-established administrative procedures. In this case the presumption of constitutionality accorded acts of Congress was freely applied to administrative procedures adopted in carrying out a congressionally created program.

By contrast with the permissive approach followed in *Mathews* v. *Eldridge*, the Court in *Hampton* v. *Mow Sun Wong*, 426 U.S. 88 (1976), declared unconstitutional a century-old policy inaugurated by the Civil Service Commission and followed by a number of other agencies, providing for the exclusion of aliens from most federal jobs. In promulgating this policy, the Civil Service Commission was acting under rule-making authority delegated by Congress to the President and in turn by the President to the Commission. Neither Congress nor the President had specifically authorized the policy, but both had acquiesced in it from its inception in 1883. The *Mow Sun Wong* case arose as a class action brought by five permanently resident aliens, all of whom had been denied federal employment in spite of their acknowledged qualifications for the jobs they were seeking. (For further background, see "The Supreme Court, 1975 Term," *Harvard Law Review* 90, 1976, pp. 105-114.)

Justice Stevens wrote the majority opinion in this case. He conceded that either Congress or the President might have the authority to withhold federal employment from aliens for broad foreign policy, national security, or economic reasons. Such a decision, he suggested, could be insulated from constitutional attack by virtue of the "political questions doctrine." But when, as here, an agency acts of its own discretion, under general rule-making authority but without specific directives from President or Congress, its action can be justified only if it furthers purposes with which the agency is "properly concerned." The Civil Service Commission could not invoke those broad foreign policy or economic objectives that might support the President or Congress in banning aliens from federal employment. The one legitimate objective cited by the Commission, that of administrative convenience, was not alone sufficient to overcome the due process argument against such a policy. The essential point to emphasize in the *Mow Sun Wong* decision is that although the Court invalidated an agency regulation on constitutional grounds, it left the way open for reinstatement of the employment prohibition via congressional act or presidential order. On September 8, 1976, just three months after the decision, President Ford took this action unilaterally, thereby giving retroactive executive sanction to the substance of the Commission's regulation.

As we become more conscious of the pervasive and growing governmental power wielded by administrative agencies, the courts may come under greater pressure, through an increased volume of litigation, to place tighter legal controls on bureaucratic authority. But no pronounced trend of this kind is yet apparent. There is general agreement, even within the ranks of government officialdom, that many bureaucrats abuse their power and in general make life unnecessarily difficult through the proliferation of endless trivial requirements and petty formalities. But the complaint is generalized, undirected, and for the most part unaccompanied by specific proposals for the kinds of legal solutions that courts can provide. Tension continues to exist between the divergent modes of decision-making fostered by the adversary system and the less formal but often equally cumbersome administrative process. It is unrealistic to expect that this tension will diminish with the mere passage of time. The Supreme Court has marked out important procedural due process standards applicable to administrative agencies. While its decisions may seldom result in the outright rejection of given administrative policies, we can expect these procedural standards to be of continuing constitutional significance as the Court further refines and sharpens them.

United States v. Bisceglia

420 U.S. 141 (1975)

MR. CHIEF JUSTICE BURGER delivered the opinion of the Court.

We granted certiorari to resolve the question whether the International Revenue Service has statutory authority to issue a "John Doe" summons to a bank or other depository to discover the identity of a person who has had bank transactions suggesting the possibility of liability for unpaid taxes.

I

On November 6 and 16, 1970, the Commercial Bank of Middlesboro, Kentucky, made two separate deposits with the Cincinnati Branch of the Federal Reserve Bank of Cleveland, each of which included $20,000 in $100 bills. The evidence is undisputed that the $100 bills were "paper thin" and showed signs of severe disintegration which could have been caused by a long period of storage under abnormal conditions. As a result the bills were no longer suitable for circulation and they were destroyed by the Federal Reserve in accord with established procedures. Also in accord with regular Federal Reserve procedures, the Cincinnati Branch reported these facts to the Internal Revenue Service.

It is not disputed that a deposit of such a large amount of high denomination currency was out of the ordinary for the Commercial Bank of Middlesboro. . . . This fact, together with the uniformly unusual state of deterioration of the $40,000 in $100 bills, caused the Internal Revenue Service to suspect that the transactions relating to those deposits may not have been reported for tax purposes. An agent was therefore assigned to investigate the matter.

After interviewing some of the bank's employees, none of whom could provide him with information regarding the two $20,000 deposits, the agent issued a "John Doe" summons directed to [Bisceglia], an executive vice president of the Commercial Bank of Middlesboro. The summons called for production of "[t]hose books and records which will provide information as to the person(s) or firm(s) which deposited, redeemed, or otherwise gave to the Commercial Bank $100 bills. . . ." This, of course, was simply the initial step in an investigation which might lead to nothing or might reveal that there had been a failure to report money on which federal estate, gift or income taxes were due. [Bisceglia], however, refused to comply with the summons even though he has not seriously argued that compliance would be unduly burdensome.

In due course, proceedings were commenced in United States District Court for the Eastern District of Kentucky to enforce the summons . . . . [Bisceglia] was ordered to comply with the summons . . . .

The Court of Appeals reversed . . . . We disagree and reverse the judgment of the Court of Appeals.

* * *

II

. . . [O]ur tax structure is based on a system of self-reporting. There is legal compulsion to be sure, but basically the Government depends upon the good faith and integrity of each potential taxpayer to disclose honestly all information relevant to tax liability. Nonetheless, it would be naive to ignore the reality that some persons attempt to outwit the system, and tax evaders are not readily identifiable. Thus, * * * the Internal Revenue Service [has] a broad mandate to investigate and audit "persons who *may* be liable" for taxes and * * * [also has] the power to "examine any books, papers, records or other data which may be relevant . . . and to summon . . . any person having possession . . . of books of account . . . relevant or material to such inquiry." Of necessity, the investigative authority . . . provided [the IRS] is not limited to situations in which there is probable cause, in the traditional sense, to believe that a violation of the tax laws exists. * * * The purpose of the statutes is not to accuse, but to inquire. Although such investigations unquestionably involve some invasion of privacy, they are essential to our self-reporting system, and the alternatives could well involve far less agreeable invasions of house, business, and records.

We recognize that the authority vested in tax collectors may be abused, as all power is subject to abuse. However, the solution is not to restrict that authority so as to undermine the efficacy of the federal tax system, which seeks to assure that taxpayers pay what Congress has mandated and prevents dishonest persons from escaping taxation and thus shifting heavier burdens to honest taxpayers. Substantial protection is afforded by the provision that an Internal Revenue Service summons can be enforced only by the courts. * * * Once a summons is challenged it must be scrutinized by a court to determine whether it seeks information relevant to a legitimate investigatory purpose and is not meant "to harass the taxpayer or to put pressure on him to settle a collateral dispute, or for any other reason reflecting on the good faith of the particular investigation." * * * . . . [T]he federal courts have taken seriously their obligation to apply this standard to fit particular situations, either by refusing enforcement or narrowing the scope of the summons. * * *

. . . [T]he power to summon and inquire in cases such as the instant one is not unprecedented. For example, had [Bisceglia] been brought before a grand jury under identical circumstances there can be little doubt that he would have been required to testify and produce records or be held in contempt. * * * . . .

• • •

III

Against this background, we turn to the question whether the summons issued . . . was authorized by the Internal Revenue Code of 1954. Of course, the mere fact that the summons was styled "In the matter of the tax liability of John Doe" is not sufficient grounds for denying enforcement. The use of such fictitious names is common in indictments * * * and other types of compulsory process. Indeed, the courts of appeals have regularly enforced Internal Revenue Service summonses which did not name a specific taxpayer who was under investigation. * * * [Bisceglia] undertakes to distinguish these . . . on the ground that they involved situations in which either a taxpayer was identified or a tax liability was known to exist as to an unidentified taxpayer. However, while they serve to suggest the almost infinite variety of factual situations in which a "John Doe" summons may be necessary, it does not follow that these cases define the limits of the Internal Revenue Service's power to inquire concerning tax liability.

. . . [Sections of the Internal Revenue Code permit] the Internal Revenue Service to investigate and inquire after "*all* persons . . . who *may* be liable to pay *any* internal revenue tax . . . ." To aid in this investigatory function, [the Code] authorizes the summoning of "*any* . . . person" for the taking of testimony and examination of books which may be relevant for "ascertaining the correctness of *any* return, . . . determining the liability of *any* person . . . or collecting *any* such liability . . . ." Plainly, this language is inconsistent with an interpretation that would limit the issuance of summonses to investigations which have already focused upon a particular return, a particular named person, or a particular potential tax liability.

Moreover, such a reading of the Internal Revenue Service's summons power ignores the fact that it has a legitimate interest in large or unusual financial transactions, especially those involving cash. The reasons for that interest are too numerous and too obvious to catalog. . . .

It would seem elementary that no meaningful investigation of such events could be conducted if the identity of the persons involved must first be ascertained, and that is not always an easy task. Fiduciaries and other agents are understandably reluctant to disclose information regarding their principals, as [Bisceglia] was in this case. Moreover, if criminal activity is afoot the persons involved may well have used aliases or taken other measures to cover their tracks. Thus, if the Internal Revenue Service is unable to issue a summons to determine the identity of such persons, the broad inquiry authorized * * * will be frustrated in this class of cases. Settled principles of statutory interpretation require that we avoid such a result absent unambiguous direction from Congress. * * * No such congressional purpose is discernible in this case.

We hold that the Internal Revenue Service was acting within its statutory authority in issuing a summons to respondent for the purpose of identifying the person or persons who deposited 400 decrepit $100 bills with the Commercial Bank of Middlesboro within the space of a few weeks. Further investigation may well reveal that such person or persons have a perfectly innocent explanation for the transactions. It is not unknown for taxpayers to hide large amounts of currency in odd places out of a fear of banks. But on this record the deposits were extraordinary and no meaningful inquiry can be made until [Bisceglia] complies with the summons as modified by the District Court.

We do not mean to suggest by this holding that [Bisceglia's] fears that the * * * summons power could be used to conduct "fishing expeditions" into the private affairs of bank depositors are trivial. . . .

Congress has provided protection from arbitrary or capricious action by placing the federal courts between the government and the person summoned. The District Court in this case conscientiously discharged its duty to see that a legitimate investigation was being conducted and that the summons was no broader than necessary to achieve its purpose.

The judgment of the Court of Appeals is reversed and the cause is remanded to it with directions to affirm the order of the District Court.

Mr. Justice Blackmun, with whom Mr. Justice Powell joins, concurring. [Omitted.]

Mr. Justice Stewart, with whom Mr. Justice Douglas joins, dissenting.

• • •

Congress has carefully restricted the summons power to certain rather precisely delineated purposes:

> "ascertaining the correctness of any return, making a return where none has been made, determining the liability of any person for any internal revenue tax or the liability at law or in equity of any transferee or fiduciary of any person in respect of any internal revenue tax, or collecting any such liability." * * *

This provision speaks in the singular—referring to "the correctness of any return" and to "the liability of any person." The delineated purposes are jointly denominated an "inquiry" concerning "the person liable for tax or required to perform the act," and the summons is designed to facilitate the "[e]xamination of books and witnesses" which "may be relevant or material to such inquiry." * * * This language indicates unmistakably that the summons power is a tool for the investigation of particular taxpayers.

• • •

. . . Every day the economy generates thousands of sales, loans, gifts, purchases, leases, deposits, mergers, wills, and the like which—because of their size or complexity—suggest the possibility of tax problems for somebody. Our economy is "tax relevant" in almost every detail. Accordingly, if a summons could issue for any material conceivably relevant to "taxation"—that is, relevant to the general *duties* of the IRS—the Service could use the summons power as a broad research device. The Service could use that power methodically to force disclosure of whole categories of transactions and closely monitor the operations of myriad segments of the economy on the theory that the information thereby accumulated might facilitate the assessment and collection of some kind of a federal tax from somebody. * * * And the Court's opinion today seems to authorize exactly that.

But Congress has provided otherwise. The Congress *has* recognized that information concerning certain classes of transactions is of peculiar importance to the sound administration of the tax system, but the legislative solution has not been the conferral of a limitless summons power. Instead, various special-purpose statutes have been written to require the reporting or disclosure of particular kinds of transactions. * * * Meanwhile, the scope of the summons power itself has been kept narrow. Congress has never made that power coextensive with the Service's broad and general canvassing duties. * * * Instead, the summons power has always been restricted to the particular purposes of individual investigation. * * *

Thus, a financial or economic transaction is not subject to disclosure through summons merely because it is large or unusual or generally "tax relevant"—but only when the summoned information is reasonably pertinent to an ongoing investigation of somebody's tax status. This restriction checks possible abuses of the summons power in two rather obvious ways. First, it guards against an overbroad summons by allowing the enforcing court to prune away those demands which are not relevant to the particular, ongoing investigation. * * * Second, the restriction altogether prohibits a summons which is wholly unconnected with such an investigation.

The Court today completely obliterates the historic distinction between the general duties of the IRS, and the limited purposes for which a summons may issue. * * * . . . [T]he Court approves enforcement of a summons having no investigatory predicate. The sole premise for this summons was the Service's theory that the deposit of old worn-out $100 bills was a sufficiently unusual and interesting transaction to justify compulsory disclosure of the identities of all the large-amount depositors at [Bisceglia's] bank over a one-month period. That the summons was not incident to an ongoing, particularized investigation, but was merely a shot in the dark to see if one might be warranted, was freely conceded by the IRS agent who served the summons.

The Court's opinion thus approves a breathtaking expansion of the summons power. There are obviously thousands of transactions occurring daily throughout the country which, on their face, suggest the *possibility* of tax complications for the unknown parties involved. These transactions will now be subject to forced disclosure at the whim of any IRS agent, so long only as he is acting in "good faith." * * *

· · ·

The Court's attempt to justify this extraordinary departure from established law is hardly persuasive. The Court first notes that a witness may not refuse testimony to a grand jury merely because the grand jury has not yet specified the "identity of the offender." * * * This is true but irrelevant. The IRS is not a grand jury. It is a creature not of the Constitution but of legislation and is thus peculiarly subject to legislated constraints. * * *

The Court next suggests that this expansion of the summons power is innocuous, at least on the facts of this case, because the Bank Secrecy Act of 1970 itself compels banks to disclose the identity of certain cash depositors. * * * Aside from the fact that the summons at issue here forces disclosure of some deposits not covered by the Act and its attendant regulations, the argument has a more basic flaw. If the summons authority * * * allows preinvestigative inquiry into any large or unusual bank deposit, the 1970 Act was largely redundant. The IRS

could have saved Congress months of hearings and debates by simply directing
* * * summonses on a regular basis to the Nation's banks, demanding the iden-
tities of their large cash depositors. . . .

· · ·

I would affirm the judgment of the Court of Appeals.

[Subsequent disclosure of the bank records, in compliance with the Supreme
Court's ruling, provided no basis for a further IRS investigation. No prosecutions
for tax evasion or any other crime were undertaken.]

Tennessee Valley Authority v. Hill

437 U.S. 153 (1978)

MR. CHIEF JUSTICE BURGER delivered the opinion of the Court.

The questions presented in this case are (a) whether the Endangered Species
Act of 1973 requires a court to enjoin the operation of a virtually completed
federal dam—which had been authorized prior to 1973—when, pursuant to
authority vested in him by Congress, the Secretary of the Interior has determined that operation of the dam would eradicate an endangered species; and (b)
whether continued congressional appropriations for the dam after 1973 constituted an implied repeal of the Endangered Species Act, at least as to the particular dam.

I

The Little Tennessee River originates in the mountains of northern Georgia
and flows through the national forest lands of North Carolina into Tennessee,
where it converges with the Big Tennessee River near Knoxville. . . .

In this area of the Little Tennessee River the Tennessee Valley Authority, a
wholly owned public corporation of the United States, began constructing the
Tellico Dam and Reservoir Project in 1967, shortly after Congress appropriated
initial funds for its development. . . . When fully operational, the dam would
impound water covering some 16,500 acres—much of which represents valuable
and productive farmland—thereby converting the river's shallow, fast-flowing
waters into a deep reservoir over 30 miles in length.

The Tellico Dam has never opened, however, despite the fact that construction has been virtually completed and the dam is essentially ready for operation.
Although Congress has appropriated monies for Tellico every year since 1967,
progress was delayed, and ultimately stopped, by a tangle of lawsuits and admin-

istrative proceedings. After unsuccessfully urging TVA to consider alternatives to damming the Little Tennessee, local citizens and national conservation groups brought suit in the District Court, claiming that the project did not conform to the requirements of the National Environmental Policy Act of 1969 (NEPA). * * * After finding TVA to be in violation of NEPA, the District Court enjoined the dam's completion pending the filing of an appropriate Environmental Impact Statement. * * * The injunction remained in effect until late 1973, when the District Court concluded that TVA's final Environmental Impact Statement for Tellico was in compliance with the law. * * *

A few months prior to the District Court's decision dissolving the NEPA injunction, a discovery was made in the waters of the Little Tennessee which would profoundly affect the Tellico Project. Exploring the area around Coytee Springs, which is about seven miles from the mouth of the river, a University of Tennessee ichthyologist, Dr. David A. Etnier, found a previously unknown species of perch, the snail darter, or Percina Imostoma tanasi. . . .

The moving force behind the snail darter's sudden fame came some four months after its discovery, when the Congress passed the Endangered Species Act of 1973. * * * This legislation, among other things, authorizes the Secretary of the Interior to declare species of animal life "endangered" and to identify the "critical habitat" of these creatures. When a species or its habitat is so listed, the following portion of the Act—relevant here—becomes effective:

> "The Secretary [of the Interior] shall review other programs administered by him and utilize such programs in furtherance of the purposes of this Act. All other Federal departments and agencies shall, in consultation with and with the assistance of the Secretary, utilize their authorities in furtherance of the purposes of this Act by carrying out programs for the conservation of endangered species and threatened species listed pursuant to section 4 of this Act and *by taking such action necessary to insure that actions authorized, funded, or carried out by them do not jeopardize the continued existence of such endangered species and threatened species or result in the destruction or modification of habitat of such species* which is determined by the Secretary, after consultation as appropriate with the affected States, to be critical." * * * (emphasis added).

In January 1975, [Hill] and others petitioned the Secretary of the Interior to list the snail darter as an endangered species. . . . [T]he Secretary formally listed the snail darter as an endangered species on November 10, 1975. * * * . . . [T]he Secretary determined that the snail darter apparently lives only in that portion of the Little Tennessee River which would be completely inundated by the reservoir created as a consequence of the Tellico Dam's completion. * * * The Secretary went on to explain the significance of the dam to the habitat of the snail darter.

> "[T]he snail darter occurs only in the swifter portions of shoals over clean gravel substrate in cool, low-turbidity water. Food of the snail darter is almost exclusively snails which require a clean gravel substrate for their survival. *The proposed impound-*

ment of water behind the proposed Tellico Dam would result in total destruction of the snail darter's habitat." * * * (emphasis added).

Subsequent to this determination, the Secretary declared the area of the Little Tennessee which would be affected by the Tellico Dam to be the "critical habitat" of the snail darter. * * * Using these determinations as a predicate, and notwithstanding the near completion of the dam, the Secretary declared that pursuant to * * * the Act, "all Federal agencies must take such action as is necessary to insure that actions authorized, funded, or carried out by them do not result in the destruction or modification of this critical habitat area." * * * This notice, of course, was pointedly directed at TVA and clearly aimed at halting completion or operation of the dam.

During the pendency of these administrative actions, other developments of relevance to the snail darter issue were transpiring. Communication was occurring between the Department of the Interior's Fish and Wildlife Service and TVA with a view toward settling the issue informally. These negotiations were to no avail, however, since TVA consistently took the position that the only available alternative was to attempt relocating the snail darter population to another suitable location. . . .

Meanwhile, Congress had also become involved in the fate of the snail darter. Appearing before a Subcommittee, . . . TVA representatives described the discovery of the fish and the relevance of the Endangered Species Act to the Tellico Project. * * * . . . [TVA's] position . . . [was] that the Act did not prohibit the completion of a project authorized, funded, and substantially constructed before the Act was passed. TVA also described its efforts to transplant the snail darter, but contended that the dam should be finished regardless of the experiment's success. . . . Congress then approved the TVA general budget, which contained funds for continued construction of the Tellico Project.

In February 1976, * * * [Hill] filed the case now under review, seeking to enjoin completion of the dam and impoundment of the reservoir on the ground that those actions would violate the Act by directly causing the extinction of the species Percina Imostoma tanasi. The District Court denied [Hill's] request for a preliminary injunction and set the matter for trial. . . .

• • •

Trial was held in the District Court on April 29 and 30, 1976, and on May 25, 1976, the court entered its memorandum opinion and order denying [Hill his] requested relief and dismissing the complaint. . . .

• • •

Thereafter, in the Court of Appeals, [Hill] argued that the District Court had abused its discretion by not issuing an injunction in the face of "a blatant statutory violation." * * * That court agreed, and on January 31, 1977, it reversed, remanding "with instructions that a permanent injunction issue halting all activities incident to the Tellico Project which may destroy or modify the critical habitat of the snail darter." * * * . . .

• • •

We granted certiorari * * * to review the judgment of the Court of Appeals.

II

We begin with the premise that operation of the Tellico Dam will either eradicate the known population of snail darters or destroy their critical habitat. [TVA] does not now seriously dispute this fact. In any event, * * * the Secretary of the Interior is vested with exclusive authority to determine whether a species such as the snail darter is "endangered" or "threatened" and to ascertain the factors which have led to such a precarious existence. * * * Congress has authorized—indeed commanded—the Secretary to "issue such regulations as he deems necessary and advisable to provide for the conservation of such species." * * * As we have seen, the Secretary promulgated regulations which declared the snail darter an endangered species whose critical habitat would be destroyed by creation of the Tellico Reservoir. . . .

Starting from the above premise, two questions are presented: (a) would TVA be in violation of the Act if it completed and operated the Tellico Dam as planned?; (b) if TVA's actions would offend the Act, is an injunction the appropriate remedy for the violation? For the reasons stated hereinafter, we hold that both questions must be answered in the affirmative.

A

It may seem curious to some that the survival of a relatively small number of three-inch fish among all the countless millions of species extant would require the permanent halting of a virtually completed dam for which Congress has expended more than $100 million. The paradox is not minimized by the fact that Congress continued to appropriate large sums of public money for the project, even after congressional appropriations committees were apprised of its apparent impact upon the survival of the snail darter. We conclude, however, that the explicit provisions of the Endangered Species Act require precisely that result.

One would be hard pressed to find a statutory provision whose terms were any plainer than those . . . of the Endangered Species Act. Its very words affirmatively command all federal agencies "to *insure* that actions *authorized, funded,* or *carried out* by them do not *jeopardize* the continued existence" of an endangered species or "*result* in the destruction or modification of habitat of such species . . . ." * * * (Emphasis added.) This language admits of no exception. Nonetheless, [TVA] urges, as do the dissenters, that the Act cannot reasonably be interpreted as applying to a federal project which was well under way when Congress passed the Endangered Species Act of 1973. To sustain that position, however, we would be forced to ignore the ordinary meaning of plain language. It has not been shown, for example, how TVA can close the gates of the Tellico Dam without "carrying out" an action that has been "authorized" and "funded" by a federal agency. Nor can we understand how such action will *"insure"* that the snail darter's habitat is not disrupted. Accepting the Secretary's determinations, as we must, it is clear that TVA's proposed operation of the dam will have precisely the opposite effect, namely the *eradication* of an endangered species.

Concededly, this view of the Act will produce results requiring the sacrifice of the anticipated benefits of the project and of many millions of dollars in public funds. But examination of the language, history and structure of the legislation under review here indicates beyond doubt that Congress intended endangered species to be afforded the highest of priorities.

· · ·

The legislative proceedings in 1973 are, in fact, replete with expressions of concern over the risk that might lie in the loss of *any* endangered species. . . . Congress was concerned about the *unknown* uses that endangered species might have and about the *unforeseeable* place such creatures may have in the chain of life on this planet.

· · ·

As it was finally passed, the Endangered Species Act of 1973 represented the most comprehensive legislation for the preservation of endangered species ever enacted by any nation. Its stated purposes were "to provide a means whereby the ecosystems upon which endangered species and threatened species depend may be conserved," and "to provide a program for the conservation of such . . . species. . . ." * * * In furtherance of these goals, Congress expressly stated * * * that "all Federal departments and agencies *shall* seek *to conserve endangered species and threatened species* . . . ." * * * (Emphasis added.) Lest there be any ambiguity as to the meaning of this statutory directive, the Act specifically defined "conserve" as meaning "to use and the use of *all methods and procedures which are necessary* to bring *any endangered species* to the point at which the measures provided pursuant to this Act are no longer necessary." * * * (Emphasis added.)

· · ·

It is against this legislative background that we must measure TVA's claim that the Act was not intended to stop operation of a project which, like Tellico Dam, was near completion when an endangered species was discovered in its path. While there is no discussion in the legislative history of precisely this problem, the totality of congressional action makes it abundantly clear that the result we reach today is wholly in accord with both the words of the statute and the intent of Congress. The plain intent of Congress in enacting this statute was to halt and reverse the trend toward species extinction, whatever the cost. This is reflected not only in the stated policies of the Act, but in literally every section of the statute. . . .

It is not for us to speculate, much less act, on whether Congress would have altered its stance had the specific events of this case been anticipated. In any event, we discern no hint in the deliberations of Congress relating to the 1973 Act that would compel a different result than we reach here. . . .

. . .

In passing the Endangered Species Act of 1973, Congress was also aware of certain instances in which exceptions to the statute's broad sweep would be necessary. Thus, . . . [the Act] creates a number of limited "hardship exemptions," none of which would even remotely apply to the Tellico Project. . . .

Notwithstanding Congress' expression of intent in 1973, we are urged to find that the continuing appropriations for Tellico Dam constitute an implied repeal of the 1973 Act, at least insofar as it applies to the Tellico Project. . . .

There is nothing in the appropriations measures, as passed, which state that the Tellico Project was to be completed irrespective of the requirements of the Endangered Species Act. These appropriations, in fact, represented relatively minor components of the lump sum amounts for the *entire* TVA budget. To find a repeal of the Endangered Species Act under these circumstances would surely do violence to the "cardinal rule . . . that repeals by implication are not favored."
* * *

. . .

Perhaps mindful of the fact that it is "swimming upstream" against a strong current of well-established precedent, TVA argues for an exception to the rule against implied repealers in a circumstance where, as here, appropriations committees have expressly stated their "understanding" that the earlier legislation would not prohibit the proposed expenditure. We cannot accept such a proposition. Expressions of committees dealing with requests for appropriations cannot be equated with statutes enacted by Congress, particularly not in the circumstances presented by this case. . . .

. . .

B

Having determined that there is an irreconcilable conflict between operation of the Tellico Dam and the explicit provisions * * * of the Endangered Species Act, we must now consider what remedy, if any, is appropriate.

. . .

Here we are urged to view the Endangered Species Act "reasonably," and hence shape a remedy "that accords with some modicum of commonsense and the public weal." * * * But is that our function? We have no expert knowledge on the subject of endangered species, much less do we have a mandate from the people to strike a balance of equities on the side of the Tellico Dam. Congress has spoken in the plainest of words, making it abundantly clear that the balance has been struck in favor of affording endangered species the highest of priorities, thereby adopting a policy which it described as "institutionalized caution."

Our individual appraisal of the wisdom or unwisdom of a particular course consciously selected by the Congress is to be put aside in the process of interpreting a statute. Once the meaning of an enactment is discerned and its constitutionality determined, the judicial process comes to an end. We do not sit as a committee of review, nor are we vested with the power of veto. The lines ascribed to Sir Thomas More by Robert Bolt are not without relevance here:

> "The law, Roper, the law. I know what's legal, not what's right. And I'll stick to what's legal. . . . I'm *not* God. The currents and eddies of right and wrong, which you find such plain-sailing, I can't navigate, I'm no voyager. But in the thickets of the law, oh there I'm a forester. . . . What would you do? Cut a great road through the law to get after the Devil? . . . And when the last law was down, and the Devil turned round on you—where would you hide, Roper, the laws all being flat? This country's planted thick with laws from coast to coast—Man's laws, not God's—and if you cut them down . . . d'you really think you could stand upright in the winds that would blow then? Yes, I'd give the Devil benefit of law, for my own safety's sake." * * *

We agree with the Court of Appeals that in our constitutional system the commitment to the separation of powers is too fundamental for us to pre-empt congressional action by judicially decreeing what accords with "commonsense and the public weal." Our Constitution vests such responsibilities in the political Branches.

Affirmed.

Mr. Justice Powell, with whom Mr. Justice Blackmun joins, dissenting.

• • •

In my view, [the Endangered Species Act] cannot reasonably be interpreted as applying to a project that is completed or substantially completed when its threat to an endangered species is discovered. Nor can I believe that Congress could have intended this Act to produce the "absurd result"—in the words of the District Court—of this case. If it were clear from the language of the Act and its legislative history that Congress intended to authorize this result, this Court would be compelled to enforce it. It is not our province to rectify policy or political judgments by the Legislative Branch, however egregiously they may disserve the public interest. But where the statutory language and legislative history, as in this case, need not be construed to reach such a result, I view it as the duty of this Court to adopt a permissible construction that accords with some modicum of commonsense and the public weal.

• • •

Today the Court, like the Court of Appeals below, adopts a reading of * * * the Act that gives it a retroactive effect and disregards 12 years of consistently expressed congressional intent to complete the Tellico Project. With all due respect, I view this result as an extreme example of a literalist construction, not required by the language of the Act and adopted without regard to its manifest purpose. Moreover, it ignores established canons of statutory construction.

The starting point in statutory construction is, of course, the language [of the Act] itself. * * * I agree that it can be viewed as a textbook example of fuzzy language, which can be read according to the "eye of the beholder." The critical words direct all federal agencies to take "such action [as may be] necessary to insure that actions authorized, funded, or carried out by them do not jeopardize the continued existence of . . . endangered species . . . or result in the destruction or modification of [a critical] habitat of such species . . . ." [Hill]—as did the Sixth Circuit—read these words as sweepingly as possible to include all "actions" that any federal agency ever may take with respect to any federal project, whether completed or not.

The Court today embraces this sweeping construction. * * * Under the Court's reasoning, the Act covers every existing federal installation, including great hydroelectric projects and reservoirs, every river and harbor project, and every national defense installation—however essential to the Nation's economic health and safety. The "actions" that an agency would be prohibited from "carrying out" would include the continued operation of such projects or any change necessary to preserve their continued usefulness. The only precondition, according to [Hill], to thus destroying the usefulness of even the most important federal project in our country would be a finding by the Secretary of the Interior that a continuation of the project would threaten the survival or critical habitat of a newly discovered species of water spider or amoeba.

• • •

The critical word in [the Act] is "actions" and its meaning is far from "plain." It is part of the phrase: "actions authorized, funded, or carried out." In terms of planning and executing various activities, it seems evident that the "actions" referred to are not all actions that an agency can ever take, but rather actions that the agency is *deciding whether* to authorize, to fund, or to carry out. In short, these words reasonably may be read as applying only to *prospective actions*. . . .

This is a reasonable construction of the language and also is supported by the presumption against construing statutes to give them a retroactive effect. . . . Similarly under * * * the Endangered Species Act, at some stage of a federal project, and certainly where a project has been completed, the agency no longer has a reasonable choice simply to abandon it. When that point is reached, as it was in this case, the presumption against retrospective interpretation is at its strongest. The Court today gives no weight to that presumption.

The Court recognizes that the first purpose of statutory construction is to ascertain the intent of the legislature. * * * The Court's opinion reviews at length the legislative history, with quotations from Committee reports and statements by Members of Congress. The Court then ends this discussion with curiously conflicting conclusions.

... While the Court's review of the legislative history establishes that Congress intended to require governmental agencies to take endangered species into account in the planning and execution of their programs, there is not even a hint in the legislative history that Congress intended to compel the undoing or abandonment of any project or program later found to threaten a newly discovered species.

If the relevant Committees that considered the Act, and the Members of Congress who voted on it, had been aware that the Act could be used to terminate major federal projects authorized years earlier and nearly completed, or to require the abandonment of essential and long-completed federal installations and edifices, we can be certain that there would have been hearings, testimony, and debate concerning consequences so wasteful, so inimical to purposes previously deemed important, and so likely to arouse public outrage. The absence of any such consideration by the Committees or in the floor debates indicates quite clearly that no one participating in the legislative process considered these consequences as within the intendment of the Act.

• • •

I have little doubt that Congress will amend the Endangered Species Act to prevent the grave consequences made possible by today's decision. Few, if any, Members of that body will wish to defend an interpretation of the Act that requires the waste of at least $53 million * * * and denies the people of the Tennessee Valley area the benefits of the reservoir that Congress intended to confer. There will be little sentiment to leave this dam standing before an empty reservoir, serving no purpose other than a conversation piece for incredulous tourists.

But more farreaching than the adverse effect on the people of this economically depressed area is the continuing threat to the operation of every federal project, no matter how important to the Nation. If Congress acts expeditiously, as may be anticipated, the Court's decision probably will have no lasting adverse consequences. But I had not thought it to be the province of this Court to force Congress into otherwise unnecessary action by interpreting a statute to produce a result no one intended.

MR. JUSTICE REHNQUIST, dissenting. [Omitted.]

Mathews v. Eldridge

424 U.S. 319 (1976)

MR. JUSTICE POWELL delivered the opinion of the Court.

The issue in this case is whether the Due Process Clause of the Fifth Amendment requires that prior to the termination of Social Security disability benefit payments the recipient be afforded an opportunity for an evidentiary hearing.

Cash benefits are provided to workers during periods in which they are completely disabled under the disability insurance benefits program created by the 1956 amendments to * * * the Social Security Act. * * * . . . . Eldridge was first awarded benefits in June 1968. In March 1972, he received a questionnaire from the state agency charged with monitoring his medical condition. Eldridge completed the questionnaire, indicating that his condition had not improved and identifying the medical sources, including physicians, from whom he had received treatment recently. The state agency then obtained reports from his physician and a psychiatric consultant. After considering these reports and other information in his file the agency informed Eldridge by letter that it had made a tentative determination that his disability had ceased in May 1972. The letter included a statement of reasons for the proposed termination of benefits, and advised Eldridge that he might request reasonable time in which to obtain and submit additional information pertaining to his condition.

In his written response, Eldridge disputed one characterization of his medical condition and indicated that the agency already had enough evidence to establish his disability. The state agency then made its final determination that he had ceased to be disabled in May 1972. This determination was accepted by the Social Security Administration (SSA), which notified Eldridge in July that his benefits would terminate after that month. The notification also advised him of his right to seek reconsideration by the state agency of this initial determination within six months.

Instead of requesting reconsideration Eldridge commenced this action challenging the constitutional validity of the administrative procedures established by the Secretary of Health, Education, and Welfare for assessing whether there exists a continuing disability. He sought an immediate reinstatement of benefits pending a hearing on the issue of his disability. * * * The Secretary moved to dismiss on the grounds that Eldridge's benefits had been terminated in accordance with valid administrative regulations and procedures and that he had failed to exhaust available remedies. . . .

* * *

. . . [The] District Court held that prior to termination of benefits Eldridge had to be afforded an evidentiary hearing of the type required for welfare bene-ficiaries under * * * the Social Security Act. * * * . . . [T]he Court of Appeals for the Fourth Circuit affirmed. . . . We reverse.

* * *

Procedural due process imposes constraints on governmental decisions which deprive individuals of "liberty" or "property" interests within the meaning of the Due Process Clause of the Fifth or Fourteenth Amendment. The Secretary does not contend that procedural due process is inapplicable to terminations of Social Security disability benefits. He recognizes, as has been implicit in our prior decisions, * * * that the interest of an individual in continued receipt of these benefits is a statutorily created "property" interest protected by the Fifth Amendment. * * * Rather, the Secretary contends that the existing administra-tive procedures . . . provide all the process that is constitutionally due before a recipient can be deprived of that interest.

This Court consistently has held that some form of hearing is required before an individual is finally deprived of a property interest. * * * The "right to be heard before being condemned to suffer grievous loss of any kind, even though it may not involve the stigma and hardships of a criminal conviction, is a principle basic to our society." * * * The fundamental requirement of due process is the opportunity to be heard "at a meaningful time and in a meaningful manner." * * * Eldridge agrees that the review procedures available to a claimant before the initial determination of ineligibility becomes final would be adequate if dis-ability benefits were not terminated until after the evidentiary hearing stage of the administrative process. The dispute centers upon what process is due prior to the initial termination of benefits, pending review.

In recent years this Court increasingly has had occasion to consider the extent to which due process requires an evidentiary hearing prior to the deprivation of some type of property interest even if such a hearing is provided thereafter. In only one case, Goldberg v Kelly, * * * has the Court held that a hearing closely approximating a judicial trial is necessary. In other cases requiring some type of pretermination hearing as a matter of constitutional right the Court has spoken sparingly about the requisite procedures. . . .

These decisions underscore the truism that " '[d]ue process,' unlike some legal rules, is not a technical conception with a fixed content unrelated to time, place, and circumstances." * * * "[D]ue process is flexible and calls for such procedural protections as the particular situation demands." * * * Accordingly, resolution of the issue whether the administrative procedures provided here are constitution-ally sufficient requires analysis of the governmental and private interests that are affected. * * * More precisely, our prior decisions indicate that identification of the specific dictates of due process generally requires consideration of three distinct factors: first, the private interest that will be affected by the official action; second, the risk of an erroneous deprivation of such interest through the procedures used, and the probable value, if any, of additional or substitute procedural safeguards; and finally, the Government's interest, including the function involved and the fiscal and administrative burdens that the additional or substitute procedural requirement would entail. * * *

• • •

Despite the elaborate character of the administrative procedures provided by the Secretary, the courts below held them to be constitutionally inadequate, concluding that due process requires an evidentiary hearing prior to termination. In light of the private and governmental interests at stake here and the nature of the existing procedures, we think this was error.

Since a recipient whose benefits are terminated is awarded full retroactive relief if he ultimately prevails, his sole interest is in the uninterrupted receipt of this source of income pending final administrative decision on his claim. . . .

Only in Goldberg has the Court held that due process requires an evidentiary hearing prior to a temporary deprivation. It was emphasized there that welfare assistance is given to persons on the very margin of subsistence. . . . Eligibility for disability benefits, in contrast, is not based upon financial need. Indeed, it is wholly unrelated to the worker's income or support from many other sources, such as earnings of other family members, workmen's compensation awards, tort claims awards, savings, private insurance, public or private pensions, veterans' benefits, food stamps, public assistance, or the "many other important programs, both public and private, which contain provisions for disability payments affecting a substantial portion of the work force . . . ." * * *

As Goldberg illustrates, the degree of potential deprivation that may be created by a particular decision is a factor to be considered in assessing the validity of any administrative decisionmaking process. * * * The potential deprivation here is generally likely to be less than in Goldberg, although the degree of difference can be overstated. . . . [T]o remain eligible for benefits a recipient must be "unable to engage in substantial gainful activity." * * *. . . .

As we recognized last Term, . . . "the possible length of wrongful deprivation of . . . benefits [also] is an important factor in assessing the impact of official action on the private interests." The Secretary concedes that the delay between a request for a hearing before an administrative law judge and a decision on the claim is currently between 10 and 11 months. Since a terminated recipient must first obtain a reconsideration decision as a prerequisite to invoking his right to an evidentiary hearing, the delay between the actual cut off of benefits and final decision after a hearing exceeds one year.

In view of the torpidity of this administrative review process, * * * and the typically modest resources of the family unit of the physically disabled worker, the hardship imposed upon the erroneously terminated disability recipient may be significant. Still, the disabled worker's need is likely to be less than that of a welfare recipient. In addition to the possibility of access to private resources, other forms of government assistance will become available where the termination of disability benefits places a worker or his family below the subsistence level. * * * In view of these potential sources of temporary income, there is less reason here than in Goldberg to depart from the ordinary principle, established by our decisions, that something less than an evidentiary hearing is sufficient prior to adverse administrative action.

An additional factor to be considered here is the fairness and reliability of the existing pretermination procedures, and the probable value, if any, of additional procedural safeguards. Central to the evaluation of any administrative process is the nature of the relevant inquiry. * * * In order to remain eligible for benefits the disabled worker must demonstrate by means of "medically acceptable clinical and laboratory diagnostic techniques" * * * that he is unable "to engage in any substantial gainful activity by reason of any *medically determinable* physical or mental impairment . . . ." * * * (emphasis supplied). In short, a medical assessment of the worker's physical or mental condition is required. This is a more sharply focused and easily documented decision than the typical determination of welfare entitlement. In the latter case, a wide variety of information may be deemed relevant, and issues of witness credibility and veracity often are critical to the decisionmaking process. . . .

By contrast, the decision whether to discontinue disability benefits will turn, in most cases, upon "routine, standard, and unbiased medical reports by physician specialists," * * * concerning a subject whom they have personally examined. . . . To be sure, credibility and veracity may be a factor in the ultimate disability assessment in some cases. But procedural due process rules are shaped by the risk of error inherent in the truthfinding process as applied to the generality of cases, not the rare exceptions. The potential value of an evidentiary hearing, or even oral presentation to the decisionmaker, is substantially less in this context than in Goldberg.

* * *

A further safeguard against mistake is the policy of allowing the disability recipient's representative full access to all information relied upon by the state agency. In addition, prior to the cut off of benefits the agency informs the recipient of its tentative assessment, the reasons therefor, and provides a summary of the evidence that it considers most relevant. Opportunity is then afforded the recipient to submit additional evidence or arguments, enabling him to challenge directly the accuracy of information in his file as well as the correctness of the agency's tentative conclusions. These procedures * * * enable the recipient to "mold" his argument to respond to the precise issues which the decisionmaker regards as crucial.

• • •

In striking the appropriate due process balance the final factor to be assessed is the public interest. This includes the administrative burden and other societal costs that would be associated with requiring, as a matter of constitutional right, an evidentiary hearing upon demand in all cases prior to the termination of disability benefits. The most visible burden would be the incremental cost resulting from the increased number of hearings and the expense of providing benefits to ineligible recipients pending decision. No one can predict the extent of the increase, but the fact that full benefits would continue until after such hearings would assure the exhaustion in most cases of this attractive option. Nor would the theoretical right of the Secretary to recover undeserved benefits result, as a practical matter, in any substantial offset to the added outlay of public funds. . . . [E]xperience with the constitutionalizing of government procedures suggests that the ultimate additional cost in terms of money and administrative burden would not be insubstantial.

Financial cost alone is not a controlling weight in determining whether due process requires a particular procedural safeguard prior to some administrative decision. But the Government's interest, and hence that of the public, in conserving scarce fiscal and administrative resources, is a factor that must be weighed. At some point the benefit of an additional safeguard to the individual affected by the administrative action and to society, in terms of increased assurance that the action is just, may be outweighed by the cost. Significantly, the cost of protecting those whom the preliminary administrative process has identified as likely to be found undeserving may in the end come out of the pockets of the deserving since resources available for any particular program of social welfare are not unlimited. * * *

But more is implicated in cases of this type than ad hoc weighing of fiscal and administrative burdens against the interests of a particular category of claimants. The ultimate balance involves a determination as to when, under our constitutional system, judicial-type procedures must be imposed upon administrative action to assure fairness. We reiterate the wise admonishment of Mr. Justice Frankfurter that differences in the origin and function of administrative agencies "preclude wholesale transplantation of the rules of procedure, trial, and review which have evolved from the history and experience of courts." * * * The judicial model of an evidentiary hearing is neither a required, nor even the most effective, method of decisionmaking in all circumstances. The essence of due process is the requirement that "a person in jeopardy of serious loss [be given] notice of the case against him and opportunity to meet it." * * * All that is necessary is that the procedures be tailored, in light of the decision to be made, to "the capacities and circumstances of those who are to be heard," * * * to insure that they are given a meaningful opportunity to present their case. In assessing what process is due in this case, substantial weight must be given to the good-faith judgments of the individuals charged by Congress with the administration of social welfare programs that the procedures they have provided assure fair consideration of the entitlement claims of individuals. * * * This is especially so where, as here, the prescribed procedures not only provide the claimant with an effective process for asserting his claim prior to any administrative action, but also assure a right to an evidentiary hearing, as well as to subsequent judicial review, before the denial of his claim becomes final. * * *

We conclude that an evidentiary hearing is not required prior to the termination of disability benefits and that the present administrative procedures fully comport with due process.

The judgment of the Court of Appeals is reversed.

MR. JUSTICE BRENNAN, with whom MR. JUSTICE MARSHALL concurs, dissenting.

. . . I agree with the District Court and the Court of Appeals that, prior to termination of benefits, Eldridge must be afforded an evidentiary hearing of the type required for welfare beneficiaries. * * * I would add that the Court's consideration that a discontinuance of disability benefits may cause the recipient to suffer only a limited deprivation is no argument. It is speculative. Moreover, the very legislative determination to provide disability benefits, without any prerequisite determination of need in fact, presumes a need by the recipient which is not this Court's function to denigrate. Indeed, in the present case, it is indicated that because disability benefits were terminated there was a foreclosure upon the Eldridge home and the family's furniture was repossessed, forcing Eldridge, his wife and children to sleep in one bed. * * * Finally, it is also no argument that a worker, who has been placed in the untenable position of having been denied disability benefits, may still seek other forms of public assistance.

MR. JUSTICE STEVENS took no part in the consideration or decision of this case.

1789	*Jay*	Rutledge, J.	Cushing	Wilson	Blair		
1790–91	*Jay*	Rutledge, J.	Cushing	Wilson	Blair	Iredell	
1792	*Jay*	Johnson, T.	Cushing	Wilson	Blair	Iredell	
1793–94	*Jay*	Paterson	Cushing	Wilson	Blair	Iredell	
1795	*Rutledge, J.*	Paterson	Cushing	Wilson	Blair	Iredell	
1796–97	*Ellsworth*	Paterson	Cushing	Wilson	Chase, S.	Iredell	
1798–99	*Ellsworth*	Paterson	Cushing	Washington	Chase, S.	Iredell	
1800	*Ellsworth*	Paterson	Cushing	Washington	Chase, S.	Moore	
1801–03	*Marshall, J.*	Paterson	Cushing	Washington	Chase, S.	Moore	
1804–05	*Marshall, J.*	Paterson	Cushing	Washington	Chase, S.	Johnson, W.	
1806	*Marshall, J.*	Livingston	Cushing	Washington	Chase, S.	Johnson, W.	
1807–10	*Marshall, J.*	Livingston	Cushing	Washington	Chase, S.	Johnson, W.	Todd
1811–12	*Marshall, J.*	Livingston	Story	Washington	Duvall	Johnson, W.	Todd
1823–25	*Marshall, J.*	Thompson	Story	Washington	Duvall	Johnson, W.	Todd
1826–28	*Marshall, J.*	Thompson	Story	Washington	Duvall	Johnson, W.	Trimble
1829	*Marshall, J.*	Thompson	Story	Washington	Duvall	Johnson, W.	McLean
1830–34	*Marshall, J.*	Thompson	Story	Baldwin	Duvall	Johnson, W.	McLean

Year										
1835	*Marshall, J.*	Thompson	Story	Baldwin	Duvall	Wayne	McLean			
1836	*Taney*	Thompson	Story	Baldwin	Barbour	Wayne	McLean		McKinley	
1837–40	*Taney*	Thompson	Story	Baldwin	Barbour	Wayne	McLean	Catron	McKinley	
1841–44	*Taney*	Thompson	Story	Baldwin	Daniel	Wayne	McLean	Catron	McKinley	
1845	*Taney*	Nelson	Woodbury	(vacant)	Daniel	Wayne	McLean	Catron	McKinley	
1846–50	*Taney*	Nelson	Woodbury	Grier	Daniel	Wayne	McLean	Catron	McKinley	
1851–52	*Taney*	Nelson	Curtis	Grier	Daniel	Wayne	McLean	Catron	McKinley	
1853–57	*Taney*	Nelson	Curtis	Grier	Daniel	Wayne	McLean	Catron	Campbell	
1858–60	*Taney*	Nelson	Clifford	Grier	Daniel	Wayne	McLean	Catron	Campbell	
1861	*Taney*	Nelson	Clifford	Grier	(vacant)	Wayne	McLean	Catron	Campbell	
1862	*Taney*	Nelson	Clifford	Grier	Miller	Wayne	Swayne	Catron	Davis	
1863	*Taney*	Nelson	Clifford	Grier	Miller	Wayne	Swayne	Catron	Davis	Field
1864–65	*Chase, S.P.*	Nelson	Clifford	Grier	Miller	Wayne	Swayne	Catron	Davis	Field
1866–67	*Chase, S.P.*	Nelson	Clifford	Grier	Miller	Wayne	Swayne	Catron	Davis	Field
1868–69	*Chase, S.P.*	Nelson	Clifford	Grier	Miller	(vacant)	Swayne	(ended)	Davis	Field
1870–71	*Chase, S.P.*	Nelson	Clifford	Strong	Miller	Bradley	Swayne		Davis	Field
1872–73	*Chase, S.P.*	Hunt	Clifford	Strong	Miller	Bradley	Swayne		Davis	Field
1874–76	*Waite*	Hunt	Clifford	Strong	Miller	Bradley	Swayne		Davis	Field
1877–79	*Waite*	Hunt	Clifford	Strong	Miller	Bradley	Swayne		Harlan	Field
1880	*Waite*	Hunt	Clifford	Woods	Miller	Bradley	Swayne		Harlan	Field
1881	*Waite*	Hunt	Gray	Woods	Miller	Bradley	Matthews		Harlan	Field
1882–87	*Waite*	Blatchford	Gray	Woods	Miller	Bradley	Matthews		Harlan	Field
1888	*Fuller*	Blatchford	Gray	Lamar, L.	Miller	Bradley	Matthews		Harlan	Field
1889	*Fuller*	Blatchford	Gray	Lamar, L.	Miller	Bradley	Brewer		Harlan	Field
1890–91	*Fuller*	Blatchford	Gray	Lamar, L.	Brown	Bradley	Brewer		Harlan	Field

523

Year	Chief Justice								
1892	*Fuller*	Blatchford	Gray	Lamar, L.	Brown	Shiras	Brewer	Harlan	Field
1893	*Fuller*	Blatchford	Gray	Jackson, H.	Brown	Shiras	Brewer	Harlan	Field
1894	*Fuller*	White	Gray	Jackson, H.	Brown	Shiras	Brewer	Harlan	Field
1895–97	*Fuller*	White	Gray	Peckham	Brown	Shiras	Brewer	Harlan	Field
1898–1901	*Fuller*	White	Gray	Peckham	Brown	Shiras	Brewer	Harlan	McKenna
1902	*Fuller*	White	Holmes	Peckham	Brown	Shiras	Brewer	Harlan	McKenna
1903–05	*Fuller*	White	Holmes	Peckham	Brown	Day	Brewer	Harlan	McKenna
1906–08	*Fuller*	White	Holmes	Peckham	Moody	Day	Brewer	Harlan	McKenna
1909	*Fuller*	White	Holmes	Lurton	Moody	Day	Brewer	Harlan	McKenna
1910–11	*White, E.*	Van Devanter	Holmes	Lurton	Lamar, J.	Day	Hughes	Harlan	McKenna
1912–13	*White, E.*	Van Devanter	Holmes	Lurton	Lamar, J.	Day	Hughes	Pitney	McKenna
1914–15	*White, E.*	Van Devanter	Holmes	McReynolds	Lamar, J.	Day	Hughes	Pitney	McKenna
1916–20	*White, E.*	Van Devanter	Holmes	McReynolds	Brandeis	Day	Clarke	Pitney	McKenna
1921	*Taft*	Van Devanter	Holmes	McReynolds	Brandeis	Day	Clarke	Pitney	McKenna
1922	*Taft*	Van Devanter	Holmes	McReynolds	Brandeis	Day	Sutherland	Pitney	McKenna
1923–24	*Taft*	Van Devanter	Holmes	McReynolds	Brandeis	Butler	Sutherland	Sanford	McKenna
1925–29	*Taft*	Van Devanter	Holmes	McReynolds	Brandeis	Butler	Sutherland	Sanford	Stone
1930–31	*Hughes*	Van Devanter	Holmes	McReynolds	Brandeis	Butler	Sutherland	Roberts	Stone
1932–36	*Hughes*	Van Devanter	Cardozo	McReynolds	Brandeis	Butler	Sutherland	Roberts	Stone
1937	*Hughes*	Black	Cardozo	McReynolds	Brandeis	Butler	Sutherland	Roberts	Stone
1938	*Hughes*	Black	Cardozo	McReynolds	Brandeis	Butler	Reed	Roberts	Stone
1939	*Hughes*	Black	Frankfurter	McReynolds	Douglas	Butler	Reed	Roberts	Stone
1940	*Hughes*	Black	Frankfurter	McReynolds	Douglas	Murphy	Reed	Roberts	Stone
1941–42	*Stone*	Black	Frankfurter	Byrnes	Douglas	Murphy	Reed	Roberts	Jackson, R.
1943–44	*Stone*	Black	Frankfurter	Rutledge, W.	Douglas	Murphy	Reed	Roberts	Jackson, R.

Year									
1945	*Stone*	Black	Frankfurter	Rutledge, W.	Douglas	Murphy	Reed	Burton	Jackson, R.
1946–48	*Vinson*	Black	Frankfurter	Rutledge, W.	Douglas	Murphy	Reed	Burton	Jackson, R.
1949–52	*Vinson*	Black	Frankfurter	Minton	Douglas	Clark	Reed	Burton	Jackson, R.
1953–54	*Warren*	Black	Frankfurter	Minton	Douglas	Clark	Reed	Burton	Jackson, R.
1955	*Warren*	Black	Frankfurter	Minton	Douglas	Clark	Reed	Burton	Harlan
1956	*Warren*	Black	Frankfurter	Brennan	Douglas	Clark	Reed	Burton	Harlan
1957	*Warren*	Black	Frankfurter	Brennan	Douglas	Clark	Whittaker	Burton	Harlan
1958–61	*Warren*	Black	Frankfurter	Brennan	Douglas	Clark	Whittaker	Stewart	Harlan
1962–65	*Warren*	Black	Goldberg	Brennan	Douglas	Clark	White, B.	Stewart	Harlan
1965–67	*Warren*	Black	Fortas	Brennan	Douglas	Clark	White, B.	Stewart	Harlan
1967–69	*Warren*	Black	Fortas	Brennan	Douglas	Marshall, T.	White, B.	Stewart	Harlan
1969	*Burger*	Black	Fortas	Brennan	Douglas	Marshall, T.	White, B.	Stewart	Harlan
1969–70	*Burger*	Black	(vacant)	Brennan	Douglas	Marshall, T.	White, B.	Stewart	Harlan
1970–71	*Burger*	Black	Blackmun	Brennan	Douglas	Marshall, T.	White, B.	Stewart	Harlan
1972–75	*Burger*	Powell	Blackmun	Brennan	Douglas	Marshall, T.	White, B.	Stewart	Rehnquist
1975–79	*Burger*	Powell	Blackmun	Brennan	Stevens	Marshall, T.	White, B.	Stewart	Rehnquist

JUSTICES BY APPOINTING PRESIDENT
AND POLITICAL PARTY AFFILIATION

Washington

John Jay (1745–1829) Federalist
John Rutledge (1739–1800) Federalist
William Cushing (1732–1810) Federalist
James Wilson (1724–1798) Federalist
John Blair (1732–1800) Federalist
James Iredell (1751–1799) Federalist
Thomas Johnson (1732–1819) Federalist
William Paterson (1745–1806) Federalist
Samuel Chase (1741–1811) Federalist
Oliver Ellsworth (1745–1807) Federalist

Adams, J.

Bushrod Washington (1762–1829) Federalist
Alfred Moore (1755–1810) Federalist
John Marshall (1755–1835) Federalist

Jefferson

William Johnson (1771–1834) Republican
Henry Livingston (1757–1823) Republican
Thomas Todd (1765–1826) Republican

Madison

Gabriel Duvall (1752–1844) Republican
Joseph Story (1779–1845) Republican

Monroe

Smith Thompson (1768–1843) Republican

Adams, J. Q.

Robert Trimble (1776–1828) Republican

Jackson

John McLean (1785–1861) Democrat (later Republican)
Henry Baldwin (1780–1844) Democrat
James M. Wayne (1790–1867) Democrat
Roger B. Taney (1777–1864) Democrat
Philip P. Barbour (1783–1841) Democrat
John Catron (1778–1865) Democrat*

Van Buren

John McKinley (1780–1852) Democrat
Peter V. Daniel (1784–1860) Democrat

Tyler

Samuel Nelson (1792–1873) Democrat

*While Catron was nominated by Jackson on Jackson's last day in office, Van Buren, upon taking office, approved the nomination and Senate confirmation followed on the fourth day of Van Buren's presidency.

Polk
Levi Woodbury (1789–1851) Democrat
Robert C. Grier (1794–1870) Democrat

Fillmore
Benjamin R. Curtis (1809–1874) Whig

Pierce
John A. Campbell (1811–1889) Democrat

Buchanan
Nathan Clifford (1803–1881) Democrat

Lincoln
Noah H. Swayne (1804–1884) Republican
Samuel F. Miller (1816–1890) Republican
David Davis (1815–1886) Republican (later Democrat)
Stephen J. Field (1816–1899) Democrat
Salmon P. Chase (1808–1873) Republican

Grant
William Strong (1808–1895) Republican
Joseph P. Bradley (1813–1892) Republican
Ward Hunt (1810–1886) Republican
Morrison Waite (1816–1888) Republican

Hayes
John Marshall Harlan (1833–1911) Republican
William B. Woods (1824–1887) Republican

Garfield
Stanley Matthews (1824–1889) Republican

Arthur
Horace Gray (1828–1902) Republican
Samuel Blatchford (1820–1893) Republican

Cleveland
Lucius Q.C. Lamar (1825–1893) Democrat
Melville W. Fuller (1833–1910) Democrat

Harrison
David J. Brewer (1837–1910) Republican
Henry B. Brown (1836–1913) Republican
George Shiras, Jr. (1832–1924) Republican
Howell E. Jackson (1832–1895) Democrat

Cleveland
Edward D. White (1845–1921) Democrat
Rufus W. Peckham (1838–1909) Democrat

McKinley
Joseph McKenna (1843–1926) Republican

Roosevelt, T.
Oliver Wendell Holmes (1841–1935) Republican
William R. Day (1849–1923) Republican
William H. Moody (1853–1917) Republican

Taft
Horace H. Lurton (1844–1914) Democrat
Charles E. Hughes (1862–1948) Republican
Willis Van Devanter (1859–1941) Republican
Joseph R. Lamar (1857–1916) Democrat
Mahlon Pitney (1858–1924) Republican

Wilson
James C. McReynolds (1862–1946) Democrat
Louis D. Brandeis (1856–1941) Democrat
John H. Clarke (1857–1945) Democrat

Harding
William H. Taft (1857–1930) Republican
George Sutherland (1862–1942) Republican
Pierce Butler (1866–1939) Democrat
Edward T. Sanford (1865–1930) Republican

Coolidge
Harlan F. Stone (1872–1946) Republican

Hoover
Owen J. Roberts (1875–1955) Republican
Benjamin N. Cardozo (1870–1938) Democrat

Roosevelt, F. D.
Hugo L. Black (1886–1971) Democrat
Stanley F. Reed (1884–   ) Democrat
Felix Frankfurter (1882–1965) Independent
William O. Douglas (1898–   ) Democrat
Frank Murphy (1890–1949) Democrat
James F. Byrnes (1879–1972) Democrat
Robert H. Jackson (1892–1954) Democrat
Wiley B. Rutledge (1894–1949) Democrat

Truman
Harold H. Burton (1888–1964) Republican
Fred M. Vinson (1890–1953) Democrat
Tom C. Clark (1899–1977) Democrat
Sherman Minton (1890–1965) Democrat

Eisenhower
Earl Warren (1891–1974) Republican
John Marshall Harlan (1899–1971) Republican
William J. Brennan, Jr. (1906–   ) Democrat
Charles E. Whittaker (1901–1973) Republican
Potter Stewart (1915–   ) Republican

Kennedy
Byron R. White (1917–   ) Democrat
Arthur J. Goldberg (1908–   ) Democrat

Johnson
Abe Fortas (1910–   ) Democrat
Thurgood Marshall (1908–   ) Democrat

Nixon
Warren E. Burger (1907–   ) Republican
Harry A. Blackmun (1908–   ) Republican
Lewis F. Powell, Jr. (1907–   ) Democrat
William H. Rehnquist (1924–   ) Republican

Ford
John Paul Stevens (1920–   ) Republican

CONSTITUTION OF THE UNITED STATES

We the People of the United States, in Order to form a more perfect Union, establish Justice, insure domestic Tranquillity, provide for the common defence, promote the general Welfare, and secure the Blessings of Liberty to ourselves and our Posterity, do ordain and establish this Constitution for the United States of America.

Article. I.

Section. 1. All legislative Powers herein granted shall be vested in a Congress of the United States, which shall consist of a Senate and House of Representatives.

Section. 2. The House of Representatives shall be composed of Members chosen every second Year by the People of the several States, and the Electors in each State shall have the Qualifications requisite for Electors of the most numerous Branch of the State Legislature.

No Person shall be a Representative who shall not have attained to the age of twenty five Years, and been seven Years a Citizen of the United States, and who shall not, when elected, be an Inhabitant of that State in which he shall be chosen.

Representatives and direct Taxes shall be apportioned among the several States which may be included within this Union, according to their respective Numbers, which shall be determined by adding to the whole Number of free Persons, including those bound to Service for a Term of Years, and excluding Indians not taxed, three fifths of all other Persons. The actual Enumeration shall be made within three Years after the first Meeting of the Congress of the United States, and within every subsequent Term of ten Years, in such Manner as they shall by Law direct. The number of Representatives shall not exceed one for every thirty Thousand, but each State shall have at Least one Representative; and until such enumeration shall be made, the State of New Hampshire shall be entitled to chuse three, Massachusetts eight, Rhode-Island and Providence Plantations one, Connecticut five, New-York six, New Jersey four, Pennsylvania eight, Delaware one, Maryland six, Virginia ten, North Carolina five, South Carolina five, and Georgia three.

When vacancies happen in the Representation from any State, the Executive Authority thereof shall issue Writs of Election to fill such Vacancies.

The House of Representatives shall chuse their Speaker and other Officers; and shall have the sole Power of Impeachment.

Section. 3. The Senate of the United States shall be composed of two Senators from each State, chosen by the Legislature thereof, for six Years; and each Senator shall have one Vote.

529

Immediately after they shall be assembled in Consequence of the first Election, they shall be divided as equally as may be into three Classes. The Seats of the Senators of the first Class shall be vacated at the Expiration of the second Year, of the second Class at the Expiration of the fourth Year, and of the third Class at the Expiration of the sixth Year, so that one third may be chosen every second Year; and if Vacancies happen by Resignation, or otherwise, during the Recess of the Legislature of any State, the Executive thereof may make temporary Appointments until the next Meeting of the Legislature, which shall then fill such Vacancies.

No Person shall be a Senator who shall not have attained to the Age of thirty Years, and been nine Years a Citizen of the United States, and who shall not, when elected, be an Inhabitant of that State for which he shall be chosen.

The Vice President of the United States shall be President of the Senate but shall have no Vote, unless they be equally divided.

The Senate shall chuse their other Officers, and also a President pro tempore, in the Absence of the Vice President, or when he shall exercise the Office of President of the United States.

The Senate shall have the sole Power to try all Impeachments. When sitting for that Purpose, they shall be on Oath or Affirmation. When the President of the United States is tried the Chief Justice shall preside: And no Person shall be convicted without the Concurrence of two thirds of the Members present.

Judgment in Cases of Impeachment shall not extend further than to removal from Office, and disqualification to hold and enjoy any Office of honor, Trust or Profit under the United States: but the Party convicted shall nevertheless be liable and subject to Indictment, Trial, Judgment and Punishment, according to Law.

Section. 4. The Times, Places and Manner of holding Elections for Senators and Representatives, shall be prescribed in each State by the Legislature thereof; but the Congress may at any time by Law make or alter such Regulations, except as to the Places of chusing Senators.

The Congress shall assemble at least once in every Year, and such Meeting shall be on the first Monday in December, unless they shall by Law appoint a different Day.

Section. 5. Each House shall be the Judge of the Elections, Returns and Qualifications of its own Members, and a Majority of each shall constitute a Quorum to do Business; but a smaller Number may adjourn from day to day, and may be authorized to compel the Attendance of absent Members, in such Manner, and under such Penalties as each House may provide.

Each House may determine the Rules of its Proceedings, punish its Members for disorderly Behaviour, and, with the Concurrence of two thirds, expel a Member.

Each House shall keep a Journal of its Proceedings, and from time to time publish the same, excepting such Parts as may in their Judgment require Secrecy; and the Yeas and Nays of the Members of either House on any question shall, at the Desire of one fifth of those Present, be entered on the Journal.

Neither House, during the Session of Congress, shall, without the Consent of the other adjourn for more than three days, nor to any other Place than that in which the two Houses shall be sitting.

Section. 6. The Senators and Representatives shall receive a Compensation for their Services to be ascertained by Law, and paid out of the Treasury of the United States. They shall in all Cases, except Treason, Felony and Breach of the Peace, be privileged from Arrest during their Attendance at the Session of their respective Houses, and in going to and returning from the same; and for any Speech or Debate in either House, they shall not be questioned in any other Place.

No Senator or Representative shall, during the Time for which he was elected, be appointed to any civil Office under the Authority of the United States, which shall have been created, or the Emoluments whereof shall have been encreased during such time; and no Person holding any Office under the United States, shall be a Member of either House during his Continuance in Office.

Section. 7. All Bills for raising Revenue shall originate in the House of Representatives; but the Senate may propose or concur with amendments as on other Bills.

Every Bill which shall have passed the House of Representatives and the Senate, shall, before it becomes a law, be presented to the President of the United States: If he approve he shall sign it, but if not he shall return it, with his Objections to that House in which it shall have originated, who shall enter the Objections at large on their Journal, and proceed to reconsider it. If after such Reconsideration two thirds of that House shall agree to pass the Bill, it shall be sent, together with the Objections, to the other House, by which it shall likewise be reconsidered, and if approved by two thirds of that House, it shall become a Law. But in all such Cases the Votes of both Houses shall be determined by yeas and Nays, and the Names of the Persons voting for and against the Bill shall be entered on the Journal of each House respectively. If any Bill shall not be returned by the President within ten Days (Sunday excepted) after it shall have been presented to him, the Same shall be a Law, in like Manner as if he had signed it, unless the Congress by their Adjournment prevent its Return, in which Case it shall not be a Law

Every Order, Resolution, or Vote to which the Concurrence of the Senate and House of Representatives may be necessary (except on a question of Adjournment) shall be presented to the President of the United States; and before the Same shall take Effect, shall be approved by him, or being disapproved by him, shall be repassed by two thirds of the Senate and House of Representatives, according to the Rules and Limitations prescribed in the Case of a Bill.

Section. 8. The Congress shall have Power To lay and collect Taxes, Duties, Imposts and Excises, to pay the Debts and provide for the common Defence and general Welfare of the United States; but all Duties, Imposts and Excises shall be uniform throughout the United States;

To borrow Money on the credit of the United States;

To regulate Commerce with foreign Nations, and among the several States, and with the Indian Tribes;

To establish an uniform Rule of Naturalization, and uniform Laws on the subject of Bankruptcies throughout the United States;

To coin Money, regulate the Value thereof, and of foreign Coin, and fix the Standard of Weights and Measures;

To provide for the Punishment of counterfeiting the Securities and current Coin of the United States;

To establish Post Offices and post Roads;

To promote the Progress of Science and useful Arts, by securing for limited Times to Authors and Inventors the exclusive Right to their respective Writings and Discoveries;

To constitute Tribunals inferior to the supreme Court;

To define and punish Piracies and Felonies committed on the high Seas, and Offenses against the Law of Nations;

To declare War, grant Letters of Marque and Reprisal, and make Rules concerning Captures on Land and Water;

To raise and support Armies, but no Appropriation of Money to that Use shall be for a longer Term than two Years;

To provide and maintain a Navy;

To make Rules for the Government and Regulation of the land and naval Forces;

To provide for calling forth the Militia to execute the Laws of the Union, suppress Insurrections and repel Invasions;

To provide for organizing, arming, and disciplining, the Militia, and for governing such Part of them as may be employed in the Service of the United States, reserving to the States respectively, the Appointment of the Officers, and the Authority of training the Militia according to the discipline prescribed by Congress;

To exercise exclusive Legislation in all Cases whatsoever, over such District (not exceeding ten Miles square) as may, by Cession of Particular States, and the Acceptance of Congress, become the Seat of the Government of the United States, and to exercise like Authority over all Places purchased by the Consent of the Legislature of the State in which the Same shall be, for the Erection of Forts, Magazines, Arsenals, dock-Yards and other needful Buildings;—And

To make all Laws which shall be necessary and proper for carrying into Execution the foregoing Powers and all other Powers vested by this Constitution in the Government of the United States, or in any Department or Officer thereof.

Section. 9. The Migration or Importation of such Persons as any of the States now existing shall think proper to admit, shall not be prohibited by the Congress prior to the Year one thousand eight hundred and eight, but a Tax or duty may be imposed on such Importation, not exceeding ten dollars for each Person.

The Privilege of the Writ of Habeas Corpus shall not be suspended, unless when in Cases of Rebellion or Invasion the public Safety may require it.

No Bill of Attainder or ex post facto Law shall be passed.

No Capitation, or other direct, Tax shall be laid, unless in Proportion to the Census of Enumeration herein before directed to be taken.

No Tax or Duty shall be laid on Articles exported from any State.

No Preference shall be given by any Regulation of Commerce or Revenue to the Ports of one State over those of another; nor shall Vessels bound to, or from, one State, be obliged to enter, clear or pay Duties in another.

No Money shall be drawn from the Treasury, but in Consequence of Appropriations made by Law; and a regular Statement and Account of the Receipts and Expenditures of all public Money shall be published from time to time.

No Title of Nobility shall be granted by the United States: And no Person holding any Office of Profit or Trust under them, shall, without the Consent of the Congress, accept of any present, Emolument, Office, or Title, of any kind whatever, from any King, Prince or foreign State.

Section. 10. No State shall enter into any Treaty, Alliance, or Confederation; grant Letters of Marque and Reprisal; coin Money; emit Bills of Credit; make any Thing but gold and silver Coin a Tender in Payment of Debts; pass any Bill of Attainder, ex post facto Law, or Law impairing the Obligation of Contracts, or grant any Title of Nobility.

No State shall, without the Consent of the Congress, lay any Imposts or Duties on Imports or Exports, except what may be absolutely necessary for executing it's inspection Laws: and the net Produce of all Duties and Imposts, laid by any State on Imports or Exports, shall be for the Use of the Treasury of the United States; and all such Laws shall be subject to the Revision and Controul of the Congress.

No State shall, without the Consent of Congress, lay any Duty of Tonnage, keep Troops, or Ships of War in time of Peace, enter into any Agreement or Compact with another State, or with a foreign Power, or engage in War, unless actually invaded, or in such imminent Danger as will not admit of delay.

Article. II.

Section. 1. The executive Power shall be vested in a President of the United States of America. He shall hold his Office during the Term of four Years, and, together with the Vice President, chosen for the same Term, be elected, as follows:

Each State shall appoint, in such Manner as the Legislature thereof may direct, a Number of Electors, equal to the whole Number of Senators and Representatives to which the State may be entitled in the Congress: but no Senator or Representative, or Person holding an Office of Trust or Profit under the United States, shall be appointed an Elector.

The Electors shall meet in their respective States, and vote by Ballot for two Persons, of whom one at least shall not be an Inhabitant of the same State with themselves. And they shall make a List of all the Persons voted for, and of the Number of Votes for each; which List they shall sign and certify, and transmit sealed to the Seat of the Government of the United States, directed to the President of the Senate. The President of the Senate shall, in the presence of the Senate and House of Representatives, open all the Certificates, and the Votes shall then be counted. The Person having the greatest Number of Votes shall be the President, if such Number be a Majority of the whole Number of Electors appointed; and if there be more than one who have such Majority, and have an equal Number of Votes, then the House of Representatives shall immediately chuse by Ballot one of them for President; and if no Person have a Majority, then from the five highest on the List the said House shall in like Manner chuse the President. But in chusing the President, the Votes shall be taken by States, the Representatives from each State having one Vote; a quorum for this Purpose shall consist of a Member or Members from two thirds of the States, and a Majority of all the States shall be necessary to a Choice. In every Case, after the Choice of the President, the Person having the greatest Number of Votes of the Electors shall be the Vice President. But if there should remain two or more who have equal Votes, the Senate shall chuse from them by Ballot the Vice President.

The Congress may determine the Time of chusing the Electors, and the Day on which they shall give their Votes; which Day shall be the same throughout the United States.

No person except a natural born Citizen, or a Citizen of the United States, at the time of the Adoption of this Constitution, shall be eligible to the Office of President; neither shall any person be eligible to that Office who shall not have attained to the Age of thirty five Years, and been fourteen Years a Resident within the United States.

In Case of the Removal of the President from Office, or of his Death, Resignation, or Inability to discharge the Powers and Duties of the said Office, the Same shall devolve on the Vice President, and the Congress may by Law provide for the Case of Removal, Death, Resignation or Inability, both of the President and Vice President, declaring what Officer shall then act as President, and such Officer shall act accordingly, until the Disability be removed, or a President shall be elected.

The President shall, at stated Times, receive for his Services, a Compensation, which shall neither be increased nor diminished during the Period for which he shall have been elected, and he shall not receive within that Period any other Emolument from the United States, or any of them.

Before he enter on the Execution of his Office, he shall take the following Oath or Affirmation:—"I do solemnly swear (or affirm) that I will faithfully execute the Office of President of the United States, and will to the best of my Ability, preserve, protect and defend the Constitution of the United States."

Section. 2. The President shall be Commander in Chief of the Army and Navy of the United States, and of the Militia of the several States, when called into the actual Service of the United States; he may require the Opinion, in writing, of the principal Officer in each of the executive Departments, upon any Subject relating to the Duties of their respective Offices, and he shall have Power to grant Reprieves and Pardons for Offenses against the United States, except in Cases of Impeachment.

He shall have Power, by and with the Advice and Consent of the Senate, to make Treaties, provided two thirds of the Senators present concur; and he shall nominate, and by and with the Advice and Consent of the Senate, shall appoint Ambassadors, other public Ministers and Consuls, Judges of the supreme Court, and all other Officers of the United States, whose Appointments are not herein otherwise provided for, and which shall be established by Law: but the Congress may by Law vest the Appointment of such inferior Officers, as they think proper, in the President alone, in the Courts of Law, or in the Heads of Departments.

The President shall have Power to fill up all Vacancies that may happen during the Recess of the Senate, by granting Commissions which shall expire at the End of their next Session.

Section. 3. He shall from time to time give to the Congress Information on the State of the Union, and recommend to their Consideration such Measures as he shall judge necessary and expedient; he may, on extraordinary Occasions, convene both Houses, or either of them, and in Case of Disagreement between them, with Respect to the Time of Adjournment, he may adjourn them to such Time as he shall think proper; he shall receive Ambassadors and other public Ministers; he shall take Care that the Laws be faithfully executed, and shall Commission all the Officers of the United States.

Section. 4. The President, Vice President and all Civil Officers of the United States, shall be removed from Office on Impeachment for, and Conviction of, Treason, Bribery, or other high Crimes and Misdemeanors.

Article. III.

Section. 1. The judicial Power of the United States, shall be vested in one supreme Court, and in such inferior Courts as the Congress may from time to time ordain and establish. The Judges, both of the supreme and inferior Courts, shall hold their Offices during good Behaviour, and shall, at stated Times, receive for their Services, a Compensation, which shall not be diminished during their Continuance in Office.

Section. 2. The judicial Power shall extend to all Cases, in Law and Equity, arising under this Constitution, the Laws of the United States, and Treaties made, or which shall be made, under their Authority;—to all Cases affecting Ambassadors, other public ministers and Consuls;—to all Cases of admiralty and maritime Jurisdiction;—to Controversies to which the United States shall be a Party;—to Controversies between two or more States;—between a State and Citizens of another State;—between Citizens of different States;—between Citizens of the same State claiming Lands under Grants of different States, and between a State, or the Citizens thereof, and foreign States, Citizens or Subjects.

In all Cases affecting Ambassadors, other public Ministers and Consuls, and those in which a State shall be Party, the supreme Court shall have original Jurisdiction. In all the other Cases before mentioned, the supreme Court shall have appellate Jurisdiction, both as to Law and Fact, with such Exceptions, and under such Regulations as the Congress shall make.

The Trial of all Crimes, except in Cases of Impeachment, shall be by Jury; and such Trial shall be held in the State where the said Crimes shall have been committed; but when not committed within any State, the Trial shall be at such Place or Places as the Congress may by Law have directed.

Section. 3. Treason against the United States, shall consist only in levying War against them, or in adhering to their Enemies, giving them Aid and Comfort. No Person shall be convicted of Treason unless on the Testimony of two Witnesses to the same overt Act, or on Confession in open Court.

The Congress shall have Power to declare the Punishment of Treason, but no Attainder of Treason shall work Corruption of Blood, or Forfeiture except during the Life of the Person attainted.

Article. IV.

Section. 1. Full Faith and Credit shall be given in each State to the public Acts, Records, and judicial Proceedings of every other State. And the Congress may by general Laws prescribe the Manner in which such Acts, Records and Proceedings shall be proved, and the Effect thereof.

Section. 2. The Citizens of each State shall be entitled to all Privileges and Immunities of Citizens in the several States.

A Person charged in any State with Treason, Felony, or other Crime, who shall flee from Justice, and be found in another State, shall on Demand of the executive Authority of the State from which he fled, be delivered up, to be removed to the State having Jurisdiction of the Crime.

No Person held to Service or Labour in one State, under the Laws thereof, escaping into another, shall, in Consequence of any Law or Regulation therein, be discharged from such Service or Labour, but shall be delivered up on Claim of the Party to whom such Service or Labour may be due.

Section. 3. New States may be admitted by the Congress into this Union; but no new State shall be formed or erected within the Jurisdiction of any other State; nor any State be formed by the Junction of two or more States, or Parts of States, without the Consent of the Legislatures of the States concerned as well as of the Congress.

The Congress shall have Power to dispose of and make all needful Rules and Regulations respecting the Territory or other Property belonging to the United States; and nothing in this Constitution shall be so construed as to Prejudice any Claims of the United States, or of any particular State.

Section. 4. The United States shall guarantee to every State in this Union a Republican Form of Government, and shall protect each of them against Invasion; and on Application of the Legislature, or of the Executive (when the Legislature cannot be convened) against domestic Violence.

Article. V.

The Congress, whenever two thirds of both Houses shall deem it necessary, shall propose Amendments to this Constitution, or, on the Application of the Legislatures of two thirds of the several States, shall call a Convention for proposing Amendments, which, in either Case, shall be valid to all Intents and Purposes, as Part of this Constitution, when ratified by the Legislatures of three fourths of the several States, or by Conventions in three fourths thereof, as the one or the other Mode of Ratification may be proposed by the Congress; Provided that no Amendment which may be made prior to the Year One thousand eight hundred and eight shall in any Manner affect the first and fourth Clauses in the Ninth Section of the first Article; and that no State, without its Consent, shall be deprived of it's equal Suffrage in the Senate.

Article. VI.

All Debts contracted and Engagements entered into, before the Adoption of this Constitution, shall be as valid against the United States under this Constitution, as under the Confederation.

This Constitution, and the Laws of the United States which shall be made in Pursuance thereof; and all Treaties made, or which shall be made, under the Authority of the United States, shall be the supreme Law of the Land; and the Judges in every State shall be bound thereby, any Thing in the Constitution or Laws of any State to the Contrary notwithstanding.

The Senators and Representatives before mentioned, and the Members of the several State Legislatures, and all executive and judicial Officers, both of the United States and of the several States, shall be bound by Oath or Affirmation, to support this Constitution;

but no religious Test shall ever be required as a Qualification to any Office or public Trust under the United States.

Article. VII.

The Ratification of the Conventions of nine States, shall be sufficient for the Establishment of this Constitution between the States so ratifying the Same.

AMENDMENT [I.]

Congress shall make no law respecting an establishment of religion, or prohibiting the free exercise thereof; or abridging the freedom of speech, or of the press; or the right of the people peaceably to assemble, and to petition the Government for a redress of grievances.

AMENDMENT [II.]

A well regulated Militia, being necessary to the security of a free State, the right of the people to keep and bear Arms, shall not be infringed.

AMENDMENT [III.]

No Soldier shall, in time of peace be quartered in any house, without the consent of the Owner, nor in time of war, but in a manner to be prescribed by law.

AMENDMENT [IV.]

The right of the people to be secure in their persons, houses, papers, and effects, against unreasonable searches and seizures, shall not be violated, and no Warrants shall issue, but upon probable cause, supported by Oath or affirmation, and particularly describing the place to be searched, and the persons or things to be seized.

AMENDMENT [V.]

No person shall be held to answer for a capital, or otherwise infamous crime, unless on a presentment or indictment of a Grand Jury, except in cases arising in the land or naval forces, or in the Militia, when in actual service in time of War or public danger; nor shall any person be subject for the same offence to be twice put in jeopardy of life or limb; nor shall be compelled in any criminal case to be a witness against himself, nor be deprived of life, liberty, or property, without due process of law; nor shall private property be taken for public use, without just compensation.

AMENDMENT [VI.]

In all criminal prosecutions, the accused shall enjoy the right to a speedy and public trial, by an impartial jury of the State and district wherein the crime shall have been committed, which district shall have been previously ascertained by law, and to be informed of the nature and cause of the accusation; to be confronted with the witnesses against him; to have compulsory process for obtaining witnesses in his favor, and to have the Assistance of Counsel for his defence.

AMENDMENT [VII.]

In Suits at common law, where the value in controversy shall exceed twenty dollars, the right of trial by jury shall be preserved, and no fact tried by a jury, shall be otherwise re-examined in any Court of the United States, than according to the rules of the common law.

AMENDMENT [VIII.]

Excessive bail shall not be required, nor excessive fines imposed, nor cruel and unusual punishments inflicted.

AMENDMENT [IX.]

The enumeration in the Constitution, of certain rights, shall not be construed to deny or disparage others retained by the people.

AMENDMENT [X.]

The powers not delegated to the United States by the Constitution, nor prohibited by it to the States, are reserved to the States respectively, or to the people.

AMENDMENT [XI.]

The Judicial power of the United States shall not be construed to extend to any suit in law or equity, commenced or prosecuted against one of the United States by Citizens of another State, or by Citizens or Subjects of any Foreign State.

AMENDMENT [XII.]

The Electors shall meet in their respective states and vote by ballot for President and Vice President, one of whom, at least, shall not be an inhabitant of the same state with themselves; they shall name in their ballots the person voted for as President, and in distinct ballots the person voted for as Vice-President, and they shall make distinct lists of all persons voted for as President, and of all persons voted for as Vice-President, and of the number of votes for each, which lists they shall sign and certify, and transmit sealed to the seat of the government of the United States, directed to the President of the Senate;—The President of the Senate shall, in the presence of the Senate and House of Representatives, open all the certificates and the votes shall then be counted;—The person having the greatest number of votes for President, shall be the President, if such number be a majority of the whole number of Electors appointed; and if no person have such majority, then from the persons having the highest numbers not exceeding three on the list of those voted for as President, the House of Representatives shall choose immediately, by ballot, the President. But in choosing the President, the votes shall be taken by states, the representation from each state having one vote; a quorum for this purpose shall consist of a member or members from two-thirds of the states, and a majority of all the states shall be necessary to a choice. And if the House of Representatives shall not choose a President whenever the right of choice shall devolve upon them, before the fourth day of March next following, then the Vice-President shall act as President, as in the case of the death or other constitutional disability of the President—The person having the greatest number of votes as Vice-President, shall be the Vice-President, if such number be a majority of the whole number of Electors appointed, and if no person have a majority, then from the two highest numbers on the list, the Senate shall choose the Vice-President; a quorum for the purpose shall consist of two-thirds of the whole number of Senators, and a majority of the whole number shall be necessary to a choice. But no person constitutionally ineligible to the office of President shall be eligible to that of Vice-President of the United States.

AMENDMENT XIII.

SECTION 1. Neither slavery nor involuntary servitude, except as a punishment for crime whereof the party shall have been duly convicted, shall exist within the United States, or any place subject to their jurisdiction.

SECTION 2. Congress shall have power to enforce this article by appropriate legislation.

AMENDMENT XIV.

SECTION 1. All persons born or naturalized in the United States and subject to the jurisdiction thereof, are citizens of the United States and of the State wherein they reside. No State shall make or enforce any law which shall abridge the privileges or immunities of citizens of the United States; or shall any State deprive any person of life, liberty, or property, without due process of law; nor deny to any person within its jurisdiction the equal protection of the laws.

SECTION. 2. Representatives shall be apportioned among the several States according to their respective numbers, counting the whole number of persons in each State, excluding Indians not taxed. But when the right to vote at any election for the choice of electors for President and Vice President of the United States, Representatives in Congress, the Executive and Judicial officers of a State, or the members of the Legislature thereof, is denied to any of the male inhabitants of such State, being twenty-one years of age, and citizens of the United States, or in any way abridged, except for participation in rebellion, or other crime, the basis of representation therein shall be reduced in the proportion which the number of such male citizens shall bear to the whole number of male citizens twenty-one years of age in such State.

SECTION 3. No person shall be a Senator or Representative in Congress, or elector of President and Vice President, or hold any office, civil or military, under the United

States, or under any State, who, having previously taken an oath, as a member of Congress, or as an officer of the United States, or as a member of any State legislature, or as an executive or judicial officer of any State, to support the Constitution of the United States, shall have engaged in insurrection or rebellion against the same, or given aid or comfort to the enemies thereof. But Congress may by a vote of two-thirds of each House, remove such disability.

SECTION 4. The validity of the public debt of the United States, authorized by law, including debts incurred for payment of pensions and bounties for services in suppressing insurrection or rebellion, shall not be questioned. But neither the United States nor any State shall assume or pay any debt or obligation incurred in aid of insurrection or rebellion against the United States, or any claim for the loss or emancipation of any slave; but all such debts, obligations and claims shall be held illegal and void.

SECTION 5. The Congress shall have the power to enforce, by appropriate legislation, the provisions of this article.

AMENDMENT XV.

SECTION. 1. The right of citizens of the United States to vote shall not be denied or abridged by the United States or by any State on account of race, color, or previous condition of servitude.

SECTION 2. The Congress shall have power to enforce this article by appropriate legislation.

AMENDMENT XVI.

The Congress shall have power to lay and collect taxes on incomes, from whatever source derived, without apportionment among the several States, and without regard to any census or enumeration.

AMENDMENT [XVII.]

The Senate of the United States shall be composed of two Senators from each State, elected by the people thereof, for six years; and each Senator shall have one vote. The electors in each State shall have the qualifications requisite for electors of the most numerous branch of the State legislatures.

When vacancies happen in the representation of any State in the Senate, the executive authority of such State shall issue writs of election to fill such vacancies: *Provided,* That the legislature of any State may empower the executive thereof to make temporary appointments until the people fill the vacancies by election as the legislature may direct.

This amendment shall not be so construed as to affect the election or term of any Senator chosen before it becomes valid as part of the Constitution.

AMENDMENT [XVIII.]

SECTION. 1. After one year from the ratification of this article the manufacture, sale, or transportation of intoxicating liquors within, the importation thereof into, or the exportation thereof from the United States and all territory subject to the jurisdiction thereof for beverage purposes is hereby prohibited.

SEC. 2. The Congress and the several States shall have concurrent power to enforce this article by appropriate legislation.

SEC. 3. This article shall be inoperative unless it shall have been ratified as an amendment to the Constitution by the legislatures of the several States, as provided in the Constitution, within seven years from the date of the submission hereof to the States by the Congress.

AMENDMENT [XIX.]

The right of citizens of the United States to vote shall not be denied or abridged by the United States or by any State on account of sex.

Congress shall have power to enforce this article by appropriate legislation.

AMENDMENT [XX.]

SECTION 1. The terms of the President and Vice President shall end at noon on the 20th day of January, and the terms of Senators and Representatives at noon on the 3d day of January, of the years in which such terms would have ended if this article had not been ratified; and the terms of their successors shall then begin.

SEC. 2. The Congress shall assemble at least once in every year, and such meeting shall begin at noon on the 3d day of January, unless they shall by law appoint a different day.

SEC. 3. If, at the time fixed for the beginning of the term of the President, the President elect shall have died, the Vice President elect shall become President. If a President shall not have been chosen before the time fixed for the beginning of his term, or if the President elect shall have failed to qualify, then the Vice President elect shall act as President until a President shall have qualified; and the Congress may by law provide for the case wherein neither a President elect nor a Vice President elect shall have qualified, declaring who shall then act as President, or the manner in which one who is to act shall be selected, and such person shall act accordingly until a President or Vice President shall have qualified.

SEC. 4. The Congress may by law provide for the case of the death of any of the persons from whom the House of Representatives may choose a President whenever the right of choice shall have devolved upon them, and for the case of the death of any of the persons from whom the Senate may choose a Vice President whenever the right of choice shall have devolved upon them.

Sec. 5. Sections 1 and 2 shall take effect on the 15th day of October following the ratification of this article.

Sec. 6. This article shall be inoperative unless it shall have been ratified as an amendment to the Constitution by the legislatures of three-fourths of the several States within seven years from the date of its submission.

Amendment [XXI.]

Section. 1. The eighteenth article of amendment to the Constitution of the United States is hereby repealed.

Sec. 2. The transportation or importation into any State, Territory or possession of the United States for delivery or use therein of intoxicating liquors, in violation of the laws thereof, is hereby prohibited.

Sec. 3. This article shall be inoperative unless it shall have been ratified as an amendment to the Constitution by conventions in the several States, as provided in the Constitution, within seven years from the date of the submission hereof to the States by the Congress.

Amendment [XXII.]

Section 1. No person shall be elected to the office of the President more than twice, and no person who has held the office of President, or acted as President, for more than two years of a term to which some other person was elected President shall be elected to the office of the President more than once. But this Article shall not apply to any person holding the office of President, when this Article was proposed by the Congress, and shall not prevent any person who may be holding the office of President, or acting as President, during the term within which this Article becomes operative from holding the office of President or acting as President during the remainder of such term.

Sec. 2. This Article shall be inoperative unless it shall have been ratified as an amendment to the Constitution by the legislatures of three-fourths of the several States within seven years from the date of its submission to the States by the Congress.

Amendment [XXIII.]

Section 1. The District constituting the seat of Government of the United States shall appoint in such manner as the Congress may direct:

A number of electors of President and Vice President equal to the whole number of Senators and Representatives in Congress to which the District would be entitled if it were a State, but in no event more than the least populous State; they shall be in addition to those appointed by the States, but they shall be considered, for the purposes of the election of President and Vice President, to be electors appointed by a State; and they shall meet in the District and perform such duties as provided by the twelfth article of amendment.

Sec. 2. The Congress shall have power to enforce this article by appropriate legislation.

Amendment [XXIV.]

Section 1. The right of citizens of the United States to vote in any primary or other election for President or Vice President, for electors for President or Vice President, or for Senator or Representative in Congress, shall not be denied or abridged by the United States or any State by reason of failure to pay any poll tax or other tax.

Section. 2. The Congress shall have power to enforce this article by appropriate legislation.

Amendment [XXV.]

Section 1. In case of the removal of the President from office or of his death or resignation, the Vice President shall become President.

Section. 2. Whenever there is a vacancy in the office of the Vice President, the President shall nominate a Vice President who shall take office upon confirmation by a majority vote of both Houses of Congress.

Section. 3. Whenever the President transmits to the President pro tempore of the Senate and the Speaker of the House of Representatives his written declaration that he is unable to discharge the powers and duties of his office, and until he transmits to them a written declaration to the contrary, such powers and duties shall be discharged by the Vice President as Acting President.

Section. 4. Whenever the Vice President and a majority of either the principal officers of the executive departments or of such other body as Congress may by law provide, transmit to the President pro tempore of the Senate and the Speaker of the House of Representatives their written declaration that the President is unable to discharge the powers and duties of his office, the Vice President shall immediately assume the powers and duties of the office as Acting President.

Thereafter, when the President transmits to the President pro tempore of the Senate and the Speaker of the House of Representatives his written declaration that no inability exists, he shall resume the powers and duties of his office unless the Vice President and a majority of either the principal officers of the executive department or of such other body as Congress may by law provide, transmit within four days to the President pro tempore of the Senate and the Speaker of the House of Representatives their written declaration that the President is unable to discharge the powers and duties of his office. Thereupon Congress shall decide the issue, assembling within forty-eight hours for that purpose if not in session. If the Congress, within twenty-one days after receipt of the latter written declaration, or, if Congress is not in session, within twenty-one days after Congress is required to assemble, determines by two-thirds vote of both Houses that the President is unable to discharge the powers and duties of his office, the Vice President shall continue to discharge the same as Acting President; otherwise, the President shall resume the powers and duties of his office.

AMENDMENT [XXVI]

SECTION 1. The right of citizens of the United States, who are eighteen years of age or older, to vote shall not be denied or abridged by the United States or by any State on account of age.

SECTION 2. The Congress shall have power to enforce this article by appropriate legislation.

PROPOSED AMENDMENT XXVII

Proposing an amendment to the Constitution of the United States relative to equal rights for men and women.

Resolved by the Senate and House of Representatives of the United States of America in Congress assembled (two-thirds of each House concurring therein), That

The following article is proposed as an amendment to the Constitution of the United States, which shall be valid to all intents and purposes as part of the Constitution when ratified by the legislatures of three-fourths of the several States within seven years from the date of its submission by the Congress:

"Section 1. Equality of rights under the law shall not be denied or abridged by the United States or by any State on account of sex.

"Section 2. The Congress shall have the power to enforce, by appropriate legislation, the provisions of this article.

"Section 3. This amendment shall take effect two years after the date of ratification."

BIBLIOGRAPHY

Abernathy, M. Glenn. *Civil Liberties Under the Constitution.* 3rd ed. New York: Harper & Row, 1977.

Abraham, Henry J. *The Judicial Process: An Introductory Analysis of the Courts of the United States, England, and France.* 3rd ed. New York: Oxford University Press, 1975.

Antieau, Chester J. *Modern Constitutional Law.* 2 vols. Rochester, N.Y.: Lawyers Cooperative Publishing Company, 1969.

Association of American Law Schools. *Selected Essays on Constitutional Law 1938-1962.* St. Paul, Minn.: West Publishing Company, 1963.

Barber, Sotirios A. *The Constitution and the Delegation of Congressional Power.* Chicago: University of Chicago Press, 1975.

Berger, Raoul. *Congress v. the Supreme Court.* Cambridge: Harvard University Press, 1969.

Berger, Raoul. *Impeachment: The Constitutional Problems.* Cambridge: Harvard University Press, 1973.

Cardozo, Benjamin N. *The Nature of the Judicial Process.* New Haven: Yale University Press, 1921.

Chase, Harold W., and Ducat, Craig R. (Eds.). *Constitutional Interpretation.* St. Paul, Minn.: West Publishing Company, 1974.

Congressional Quarterly. "Constitutional Standard for Presidential Impeachment." *Congressional Quarterly Weekly Report,* March 1974.

Congressional Quarterly. *The Supreme Court: Justice and the Law.* Washington, D.C.: Congressional Quarterly, 1977.

Cortner, Richard C. *The Apportionment Cases.* Knoxville: University of Tennessee Press, 1970.

Cortner, Richard C. *The Jones and Laughlin Case.* New York: Knopf, 1970.

Cortner, Richard C., and Lytle, Clifford M. (Eds.). *Modern Constitutional Law.* New York: Free Press, 1971.

Corwin, Edward S. *The Doctrine of Judicial Review.* Princeton: Princeton University Press, 1914.

Corwin, Edward S. *Essays in American Constitutional History.* Ed. by Alpheus T. Mason and G. Garvey. New York: Harper & Row, 1964.

Cox, Archibald. *The Role of the Supreme Court in American Government.* New York: Oxford University Press, 1976.

Cushman, Robert E., and Cushman, Robert F. *Cases in Constitutional Law.* New York: Appleton-Century-Crofts, 1963.

Dixon, Robert G., Jr. *Democratic Representation.* New York: Oxford University Press, 1968.

Federal Judicial Center. "Report of the Study Group on the Caseload of the Supreme Court." 57 F.R.D. 573 (1972).

Frankfurter, Felix. *The Commerce Clause Under Marshall, Taney and Waite.* Chapel Hill: University of North Carolina Press, 1937.

Freund, Paul A. (Ed.). *History of the Supreme Court of the United States.* 11 vols. New York: Macmillan, 1971–

Friedelbaum, Stanley H. (Ed.). *Contemporary Constitutional Law: Case Studies in the Judicial Process.* Boston: Houghton Mifflin, 1972.

Gellhorn, Walter, and Byse, Clark. *Administrative Law.* 6th ed. Chicago: Foundation Press, 1974.

Goebel, Julius, Jr. *Antecedents and Beginnings to 1801.* Vol. 1, *History of the Supreme Court of the United States,* ed. by Paul A. Freund. New York: Macmillan, 1971.

Goldman, Sheldon, and Sarat, Austin (Eds.). *American Court Systems: Readings in Judicial Process and Behavior.* San Francisco: W. H. Freeman and Company, 1978.

Grossman, Joel B., and Wells, Richard S. (Eds.). *Constitutional Law and Judicial Policy Making.* New York: Wiley, 1972.

Gunther, Gerald. *Constitutional Law.* 9th ed. Chicago: Foundation Press, 1975.

Haines, Charles G. *The Role of the Supreme Court in American Government and Politics, 1789-1835.* Berkeley: University of California Press, 1957.

Hamilton, Alexander. *The Federalist,* No. 78. In *The Federalist Papers.* New York: Atherton Books, 1966.

Hamilton, John C. *Works of Alexander Hamilton.* New York: C. S. Francis and Co., 1851.

Holcombe, Arthur N. *The Constitutional System.* Rev. ed. Glenview, Ill.: Scott, Foresman, 1969.

House Judiciary Committee. "Excerpts From Impeachment Study." *New York Times,* February 22, 1974.

Howard, J. Woodford. "On the Fluidity of Judicial Choice." *American Political Science Review* 62 (1968): 43-57.

Jacob, Herbert. *Justice in America: Courts, Lawyers, and the Judicial Process.* 3rd ed. Boston: Little, Brown, 1978.

Johnson, Lock, and McCormick, James. "The Making of International Agreements: A Reappraisal of Congressional Involvement." *Journal of Politics* 40 (1978): 468-478.

Kallenbach, Joseph E. *The American Chief Executive: The Presidency and the Governorship.* New York: Harper & Row, 1966.

Kelly, Alfred H., and Harbison, Winfred A. *The American Constitution: Its Origins and Development.* 4th ed. New York: Norton, 1970.

King, Willard L. *Melville Weston Fuller: Chief Justice of the United States, 1888-1910.* Chicago: University of Chicago Press, 1967.

Konefsky, Samuel J. *The Legacy of Holmes and Brandeis: A Study in the Influence of Ideas.* New York: Macmillan, 1956.

Kutler, Stanley I. (Ed.). *The Supreme Court and the Constitution: Readings in American Constitutional History.* New York: Norton, 1977.

Labovitz, John R. *Presidential Impeachment.* New Haven: Yale University Press, 1978.

Library of Congress, Congressional Research Service. *The Constitution of the United States: Analysis and Interpretation.* Washington, D.C.: U.S. Government Printing Office, 1973.

Lockhart, William B., Kamisar, Yale, and Choper, Jesse H. *The American Constitution.* 3rd ed. St. Paul, Minn.: West Publishing Company, 1970.

Lowi, Theodore J. *The End of Liberalism.* New York: Norton, 1969.

Lytle, Clifford M. *The Warren Court and Its Critics.* Tuscon: University of Arizona Press, 1968.

McCloskey, Robert G. (Ed.). *Essays in Constitutional Law.* New York: Random House, 1957.

Madison, James. *Letters and Other Writings of James Madison.* Ed. by Phillip R. Fendall. Philadelphia: Lippincott, 1865.

Mason, Alpheus T., and Beaney, William M. (Eds.). *American Constitutional Law, Introductory Essays and Selected Cases.* 6th ed. Englewood Cliffs, N.J.: Prentice-Hall, 1978.

Meeker, Leonard C. "The Legality of United States Participation in the Defense of Vietnam." *Department of State Bulletin* 54 (1966): 474-483.

Mendelson, Wallace. "Mr. Justice Douglas and Government by the Judiciary." *Journal of Politics* 38 (1976): 918-937.

Mendelson, Wallace (Ed.). *The Constitution and the Supreme Court.* 2nd ed. New York: Dodd, Mead, 1965.

Miller, Samuel F. *Lectures on the Constitution.* New York: Banks and Brothers, 1891.

Mullen, William F. *Presidential Power and Politics.* New York: St. Martin's Press, 1976.

Murphy, Walter F. *Elements of Judicial Strategy.* Chicago: University of Chicago Press, 1964.

Murphy, Walter F., and Pritchett, C. Herman (Eds.). *Courts, Judges and Politics.* 2nd ed. New York: Random House, 1974.

Nowak, John E., Rotunda, Ronald D., and Young, J. Nelson. *Constitutional Law.* St. Paul, Minn.: West Publishing Company, 1977.

Powell, Thomas Reed. "The Still Small Voice of the Commerce Clause." *Proceedings of the National Tax Association* 337 (1937): 338-339.

Pritchett, C. Herman. *The American Constitution.* 3rd ed. New York: McGraw-Hill, 1977.

Pritchett, C. Herman. *Congress Versus the Supreme Court, 1957-1960.* Minneapolis: University of Minnesota Press, 1961.

Rathjen, Gregory, and Spaeth, Harold. "Access to the Federal Courts: An Analysis of Burger Court Policy Making." *American Journal of Political Science* 23 (1979): 360-383.

Roche, John P. "Judicial Self-Restraint." *American Political Science Review* 49 (1955): 762-772.

Rodell, Fred. *Nine Men: A Political History of the Supreme Court From 1790 to 1955.* New York: Random House, 1955.

Rohde, David, and Spaeth, Harold. *Supreme Court Decision Making*. San Francisco: W. H. Freeman and Company, 1976.

Roosevelt, Theodore. *Autobiography*. New York: Macmillan, 1913.

Saye, Albert B. (Ed.). *American Constitutional Law—Text and Cases*. 2nd ed. St. Paul, Minn.: West Publishing Company, 1979.

Schmidhauser, John R. *Constitutional Law in the Political Process*. Chicago: Rand McNally, 1963.

Schubert, Glendon. *Judicial Policy Making*. Chicago: Scott, Foresman, 1965.

Schubert, Glendon (Ed.). *Constitutional Politics*. New York: Holt, Rinehart and Winston, 1960.

Schwartz, Bernard. *Constitutional Law*. 2nd ed. New York: Macmillan, 1972.

Scigliano, Robert. *The Supreme Court and the Presidency*. New York: Free Press, 1971.

Scott, Kenneth E. "Standing in the Supreme Court: A Functional Analysis." *Harvard Law Review* 86 (1973): 645-692.

Shapiro, Martin. *The Supreme Court and Administrative Agencies*. New York: Free Press, 1968.

Shapiro, Martin, and Hobbs, Douglas S. *The Politics of Constitutional Law*. Cambridge, Mass.: Winthrop, 1974.

Spaeth, Harold J. *Supreme Court Policy Making: Explanation and Prediction*. San Francisco: W. H. Freeman and Company, 1979.

Spaeth, Harold J. *The Warren Court: Cases and Commentary*. San Francisco: Chandler, 1966.

Stephens, Otis H. *The Supreme Court and Confessions of Guilt*. Knoxville: University of Tennessee Press, 1973.

"The Supreme Court, 1975 Term." *Harvard Law Review* 90 (1976): 1-282.

"The Supreme Court, 1976 Term." *Harvard Law Review* 91 (1977): 1-301.

"The Supreme Court, 1977 Term." *Harvard Law Review* 92 (1978): 1-339.

Swisher, Carl B. *American Constitutional Development*. 2nd ed. Boston: Houghton Mifflin, 1954.

Swisher, Carl B. *The Growth of Constitutional Power in the United States*. Phoenix Edition. Chicago: University of Chicago Press, 1963.

Taft, William Howard. *Our Chief Magistrate and His Powers*. New York: Columbia University Press, 1916.

Tribe, Laurence H. *American Constitutional Law*. Mineola, N.Y.: Foundation Press, 1978.

Tribe, Laurence H. "Unraveling *National League of Cities:* The New Federalism and Affirmative Rights to Essential Government Services." *Harvard Law Review* 90 (1977): 1065-1104.

Warren, Charles. *The Supreme Court in United States History*. 2 vols. Rev. ed. Boston: Little, Brown, 1926.

Wasby, Stephen L. *Continuity and Change: From the Warren Court to the Burger Court*. Pacific Palisades, Calif.: Goodyear, 1976.

White, G. Edward. *The American Judicial Tradition: Profiles of Leading American Judges*. New York: Oxford University Press, 1976.

GLOSSARY

abstention   The doctrine under which the U.S. Supreme Court and other federal courts choose not to decide on, or interfere with, state cases even when empowered to do so. This doctrine is typically invoked when a case can be decided on the basis of state law.

adjudication   The process of judging wherein a court determines the issues and pronounces judgment in a case.

ad valorem   "According to the value." Referring to a tax or duty guaranteed according to the assessed value of the subject matter taxed.

adversary proceeding   A legal action involving parties with adverse or opposing interests. A basic aspect of the American legal system, the adversary proceeding provides the framework within which most constitutional cases are decided. For an exception to this generalization, see *ex parte* below.

advisory opinion   This broad term refers to a judicial opinion, not involving adverse parties in a "case or controversy," given at the request of the legislature or the executive. It has been long-standing policy of the U.S. Supreme Court not to render such opinions.

affirm   To uphold, confirm, or ratify the decision of a lower court on appeal or certiorari to the U.S. Supreme Court.

amicus curiae   "Friend of the court." An individual or organization allowed to take part in a judicial proceeding, not as one of the adversaries, but as a party interested in the outcome. Usually an amicus curiae files a brief in support of one side or the other, but occasionally takes a more active part in the argument of the case.

appeal   A distinct stage in a continuing judicial proceeding in which the losing party requests a higher court to review the record and decision of a lower court. In theory, the U.S. Supreme Court grants an appeal "as a matter of right." But the requirement that a "substantial federal question" be presented in the case under review in fact gives the Court ample discretion in determining whether to grant an appeal.

appellant   The losing party in a judicial action who appeals to a higher court.

appellee   The party against whom a case is appealed to a higher court. This term was used in early U.S. Supreme Court decisions, but has been replaced by the term *respondent.*

assign   To transfer or grant a legal right.

assignee   One to whom a legal right is transferred.

bona fide   "In good faith." Made or acting without deceit or fraud.

case or controversy   Article III of the U.S. Constitution extends the federal judicial power to actual cases or controversies, not to hypothetical or abstract questions of law.

certification   A procedure under which a lower court requests a decision by a higher court on specified questions in a case, pending a final decision by the lower court.

certiorari   "To be informed." A petition similar to an appeal, but may be granted or refused at the discretion of the appellate court.

civil action   A judicial proceeding, outside the criminal law, by which an individual seeks to enforce his or her rights or to obtain redress for wrongs.

class action   A lawsuit brought by one or more parties on behalf of themselves and others similarly situated.

collateral attack   An effort to avoid or challenge the integrity of a judicial decision in another judicial proceeding.

collateral estoppel   Being barred from making a claim in one judicial proceeding that has been disproved by the facts presented in another, earlier proceeding.

comity   Courtesy; respect; civility. A matter of goodwill and tradition, rather than of right, wherein one jurisdiction respects the judgment of another.

common law   A system of legal rules and principles first developed by English judges prior to the colonization of America and accepted as a basic aspect of the American legal system. The common law is not a fixed system, but an ever changing body of rules and principles articulated by judges and applied to changing needs and circumstances.

criminal action   A judicial action brought by the government against a person charged with the commission of a crime.

decision on the merits   A judicial decision that reaches the subject matter of a case and decides upon it with finality.

declaratory judgment   A judicial ruling conclusively declaring the rights, duties, or status of the parties, but imposing no additional order, restriction, or requirement on them.

defendant   The party against whom a legal action or proceeding is brought. The term is used in both civil and criminal cases.

dismissal   A judicial order terminating a case, putting it out of court.

doctrine   A legal principle or rule developed through judicial decisions.

domicile   A person's permanent home and principal establishment, as recognized by law.

duty   A person's legal obligation, either to another person or to the community. If one person has a right to something, another person has a duty to avoid interfering with that right.

equity   Historically, a system of rules, remedies, customs, and principles devised by English judges to supplement the common law. Because the common law served only to recompense after injury, equity was devised to prevent injuries that could not be repaired or recompensed after the fact. See *irreparable injury* below.

exclusionary rule   A basis for excluding relevant evidence from a trial. In American constitutional law this term usually refers to the exclusion of evidence obtained by illegal means. Such evidence is excluded regardless of its reliability or importance.

ex parte   "On or from one side only." An application to a court, made by one party without giving notice to the adverse party. In American constitutional law this term often appears in connection with a habeas corpus proceeding.

ex rel.   "On the relation or information of." Usually designating the name of a person on whose behalf the government is bringing legal action against another party.

extradition   The surrender of a person by one state or country at the request of another for trial or punishment on criminal charges, either before or after conviction.

habeas corpus   "You have the body." A judicial order issued to an official holding someone in custody, requiring the official to bring the prisoner to court for the purpose of allowing the court to determine whether that person is being held legally.

in camera   "In a chamber." In private. Referring to a judicial hearing or trial from which the public is excluded.

injunction   A judicial order requiring a person to do, or to refrain from doing, a designated thing.

in personam   "Against a person." Referring to a legal action brought to enforce rights against a person.

in re   "In the matter of." In the transaction; concerning.

in rem   "Against a thing," as a right, status, or property. Referring to a legal action brought to enforce rights in a thing against the entire world.

irreparable injury   An injury for which the award of money may not be adequate compensation and which may require the issuance of an injunction to fulfill the requirements of justice.

judgment   A judicial decision regarding the rights and claims of the parties in a lawsuit. In a criminal case the court's formal declaration to the accused regarding the legal consequences of a determination of guilt.

jurisdiction   The geographical area within which, the subject matter with respect to which, and the persons over whom a court can properly exercise its power.

justiciability   The quality of appropriateness for judicial decision. A justiciable dispute is one that can be effectively decided by a court.

liability   A broad legal term connoting debt, responsibility, or obligation. The condition of being bound to pay a debt or to discharge an obligation. This responsibility can be either civil or criminal.

litigant   A party to, or participant in, a legal action.

mandamus   "We enjoin." A judicial writ or order commanding a public official or an organization to perform a specified duty.

moot   Referring to a question that does not involve rights currently at issue in, or pertinent to, the outcome of a case.

obiter dicta   "Something said in passing." Incidental statements in a judicial opinion that are not binding and are unnecessary to support the decision.

overrule   To supersede or overturn. In constitutional law this term usually refers to the superseding of a previous judicial decision by a later decision. A decision may be overruled by the court that originally rendered it or by a higher court in the same judicial system. The term can also refer to the court's denial of an objection by counsel.

parens patriae   "Father of the country." A doctrine embracing the power of a government to take care of dependent children and legally incompetent persons, or in some cases a government functioning as general guardian of its people.

party   A person taking part in a legal transaction. This term includes plaintiffs and defendants in lawsuits, but has a far broader legal connotation.

per curiam   "By the court." Referring to an opinion authorized by a court collectively, usually not identified with the name of any particular member of the court.

petition   A written request, usually addressed to a court, asking for a specified action. Sometimes the term indicates written requests in an ex parte proceeding, where there is no adverse party. In some jurisdictions the term refers to the first pleading in a lawsuit.

petitioner   In U.S. Supreme Court cases this term usually refers to the party who seeks review via a writ of certiorari.

plaintiff   The party initiating legal action; the complaining party.

plenary   Full; complete. The term is often used with reference to the nature and extent of governmental powers enumerated in the federal Constitution.

police power   The government's authority to make and enforce laws designed to protect the public health, safety, morality, and general welfare of the people. In American constitutional law this term was originally applied to state power, but has come to refer to broad governmental authority at all levels.

political   Referring to a question that a court believes to be appropriate for decision by the legislative or the executive branch of government. A question deemed by a court to be improper for judicial decision.

precedent   A judicial decision on a point of law giving direction or authority for later cases presenting the same legal problem, although involving different parties.

preemption   In constitutional law the doctrine under which a field, previously open to action by the states, may be brought by the U.S. Congress within the primary or exclusive control of the national government.

prima facie   "At first glance; on the face of it." Referring to a point that will be considered true if uncontested or unrefuted.

privilege   In general, an activity or a claim that a person may engage in or enjoy without interference. The term is often used interchangeably with *right* in American constitutional law, as with reference to the "privileges and immunities" clauses of Article IV and the Fourteenth Amendment of the U.S. Constitution.

quash   To annul, set aside, overthrow, suppress. The term is used with reference to action by a court.

remand   To send back, as from a higher court to a lower court for the lower court to take specified action in a case or to follow proceedings designated by the higher court.

remedy   The means through which a legal right is enforced or an injury is redressed.

res judicata   "Things decided." A thing or matter decided by a judgment, connoting the firmness and finality of the judgment as it affects the parties to the lawsuit. Use of the term has the general effect of bringing litigation on a contested point to an end.

respondent   The party against whom an appeal is taken to a higher court.

reverse   To annul or set aside, as when an appellate court reverses the decision of a lower court. The appellate court may either substitute its own judgment or remand the case to the lower court with instructions regarding further proceedings in the matter.

review   Examination by an appellate court of the decision of a lower court.

right   Anything to which a person has a just and valid legal claim. Every legal right carries with it a corresponding duty.

show cause   A court order requiring a person to appear in court and explain why certain judicial action should not be taken.

standing to sue   A court's determination that parties to a case deserve to have their controversy heard and decided. In general, a court requires a degree of personal interest or stake in the outcome.

stare decisis   "To stand by decided matters." The principle that past decisions should stand as precedents for future decisions. This principle, which stands for the proposition that precedents are binding on later decisions, is presumably followed less rigorously in constitutional law than in most other branches of the law.

stay   To postpone, hold off, or stop execution of a judgment.

subpoena   "Under penalty." A judicial order requiring a person to appear in court in connection with a designated proceeding.

subpoena duces tecum   "Under penalty you shall bring with you." A judicial order requiring a party to bring certain described records, papers, books, or documents to court.

summary proceeding   In the work of the U.S. Supreme Court the term is used to indicate cases decided without oral argument. In contempt cases a short proceeding, without a jury, in which the judge serves as prosecutor, fact finder, and sentencer.

sustain   To grant, uphold, or support.

third party   A person not directly connected with a legal proceeding, but potentially affected by its outcome.

vacate   To set aside or annul, as when an appellate court vacates the judgment of a lower court.

writ   A judicial order authorizing or requiring the performance of a designated action.

TABLE OF CASES

Cases preceded by an asterisk are excerpted in this volume.

Alabama v. *King & Boozer,* 314 U.S. 1 (1941), 418

Anderson v. *Dunn,* 6 Wheat. 204 (1821), 152

*Ashwander v. *Tennessee Valley Authority,* 297 U.S. 288 (1936), 92, 139–140

*Association of Data Processing Service Organizations v. *Camp,* 397 U.S. 150 (1970), 86, 87, 110–115

Atherton v. *Atherton,* 181 U.S. 155 (1901), 444

*Bailey v. *Drexel Furniture Co.,* 259 U.S. 20 (1922), 222, 242–246, 253

*Baker v. *Carr,* 369 U.S. 186 (1962), 5, 19, 28, 30, 90, 127–139, 326

Barenblatt v. *United States,* 360 U.S. 109 (1959), 146, 147

Barlow v. *Collins,* 397 U.S. 159 (1970), 86, 87

Bibb v. *Navajo Freight Lines, Inc.,* 359 U.S. 520 (1959), 400

Blake v. *McClung,* 172 U.S. 256 (1898), 447

Bloom v. *Illinois,* 391 U.S. 194 (1968), 45

Bolling v. *Sharpe,* 347 U.S. 497 (1954), 18

Bowman v. *Chicago & Northwestern Railway Co.,* 125 U.S. 165 (1888), 407, 408

Brandenburg v. *Ohio,* 395 U.S. 444 (1969), 88, 121

Branzburg v. *Hayes,* 408 U.S. 665 (1972), 45

Brig Aurora v. *United States,* 7 Cranch 382 (1813), 478, 479

Broadrick v. *Oklahoma,* 413 U.S. 610 (1973), 92

Brotherhood of Locomotive Engineers v. *Chicago, Rock Island, & Pacific Railroad Co.,* 382 U.S. 423 (1966), 382

Brown v. *Board of Education,* 347 U.S. 483 (1954), 18, 41, 60, 62, 63, 65, 68, 92, 347–348

554

Brown v. *Board of Education,* 349 U.S. 294 (1955), 41, 60, 62

*Brown v. *Maryland,* 12 Wheat. 419 (1827), 421, 433–438

*Buckley v. *Valeo,* 424 U.S. 1 (1976), 224, 261–267, 278

*Burbank v. *Lockheed Air Terminal,* 411 U.S. 624 (1973), 385, 411–415

Burdick v. *United States,* 236 U.S. 79 (1915), 283

Carter v. *Carter Coal Co.,* 298 U.S. 238 (1936), 178, 200, 202, 344, 477, 481

Champion v. *Ames,* 188 U.S. 321 (1903), 177

Chapman, In re, 166 U.S. 661 (1897), 153

Cheff v. *Schnackenberg,* 384 U.S. 373 (1966), 45

Child Labor Tax Case: See *Bailey* v. *Drexel Furniture Co.*

Chisholm v. *Georgia,* 2 Dall. 419 (1793), 42

Codispoti v. *Pennsylvania,* 418 U.S. 506 (1974), 45

Cohens v. *Virginia,* 6 Wheat. 264 (1821), 17, 340, 348

Colegrove v. *Green,* 328 U.S. 549 (1946), 90, 127, 128, 131, 132, 135

Collector v. *Day,* 11 Wall. 113 (1871), 348, 417, 418, 430, 431

Communist Party v. *Subversive Activities Control Board,* 351 U.S. 115 (1956), 40

*Cooley v. *Board of Wardens,* 12 How. 299 (1852), 379, 380, 381, 386–389, 416

*Cooper v. *Aaron,* 358 U.S. 1 (1958), 18, 41, 59–64

Corfield v. *Coryell,* 6 Fed. Cas. 546 (1823), 446, 447

Daniel v. *Paul,* 395 U.S. 298 (1969), 179

Dean Milk Co. v. *Madison,* 340 U.S. 349 (1951), 384

Debs, In re, 158 U.S. 564 (1895), 273

DeFunis v. *Odegaard,* 416 U.S. 312 (1974), 83

Dombrowski v. *Pfister,* 380 U.S. 479 (1965), 87, 88, 118, 119, 120, 121

Dred Scott Case: See *Scott* v. *Sanford*

Duncan v. *Kahanamoku,* 327 U.S. 304 (1944), 318

Eakin v. *Raub,* 12 Sergeant and Rawle 330 (1823), 15

*Eastland v. *United States Servicemen's Fund,* 421 U.S. 491 (1975), 148, 166–171

*Estin v. *Estin,* 334 U.S. 541 (1948), 444, 445, 452–456

Fay v. *Noia,* 372 U.S. 391 (1963), 88

Federal Energy Administration v. *Algonquin SNG, Inc.,* 426 U.S. 548 (1976), 482

Field v. *Clark,* 143 U.S. 649 (1892), 479, 485

Flast v. *Cohen,* 392 U.S. 83 (1968), 85, 98, 99, 100, 101, 102, 104, 105

Fletcher v. *Peck,* 6 Cranch 87 (1810), 17

Flint v. *Stone Tracy Co.,* 220 U.S. 107 (1911), 220

Fox Film Corp. v. *Doyal,* 286 U.S. 123 (1932), 418

Frothingham v. *Mellon,* 262 U.S. 447 (1923), 85, 98, 99, 100, 104, 247

Fry v. *United States,* 421 U.S. 542 (1975), 342

Furman v. *Georgia,* 408 U.S. 256 (1972), 284, 303, 305, 307

Garland, Ex parte, 4 Wall. 333 (1867), 284

Garner v. *United States,* 424 U.S. 648 (1976), 225

Geer v. *Connecticut*, 161 U.S. 519 (1896), 384

General Motors Leasing Corp. v. *United States*, 429 U.S. 338 (1977), 225

*Gibbons v. *Ogden*, 9 Wheat. 1 (1824), 174, 175, 177, 178, 181–188, 206, 340, 363, 379, 395, 416

Gillespie v. *Oklahoma*, 257 U.S. 501 (1922), 418

Glidden Co. v. *Zdanok*, 370 U.S. 530 (1962), 40

Goldberg v. *Kelly*, 397 U.S. 254 (1970), 499, 500, 517, 518, 519

*Goldfarb v. *Virginia State Bar*, 421 U.S. 773 (1975), 6, 180, 213–217

Gomillion v. *Lightfoot*, 364 U.S. 339 (1960), 131

Graves v. *New York ex rel. O'Keefe*, 306 U.S. 466 (1939), 418

Great Atlantic & Pacific Tea Co. v. *Cottrell*, 424 U.S. 366 (1976), 385

Griswold v. *Connecticut*, 381 U.S. 479 (1965), 84, 495

*Grossman, Ex parte, 267 U.S. 87 (1925), 45, 70–74, 284

Grosso v. *United States*, 390 U.S. 62 (1968), 225

Haddock v. *Haddock*, 201 U.S. 562 (1906), 444, 445

*Hammer v. *Dagenhart*, 247 U.S. 251 (1918), 177, 222, 244, 344, 356–360, 363, 380

Hampton v. *Mow Sun Wong*, 426 U.S. 88 (1976), 500, 501

*J. W. Hampton & Co. v. *United States*, 276 U.S. 394 (1928), 476, 479, 480, 482, 483–485

Hardin v. *Kentucky Utilities Co.*, 390 U.S. 1 (1968), 112

Heart of Atlanta Motel v. *United States*, 379 U.S. 241 (1964), 179, 209

Helvering v. *Davis*, 301 U.S. 619 (1937), 224

Helvering v. *Mountain Producers Corp.*, 303 U.S. 376 (1938), 418

*Hicklin v. *Orbeck*, 437 U.S. 518 (1978), 448, 461–464

Hipolite Egg Co. v. *United States*, 220 U.S. 45 (1911), 178

Hirabayashi v. *United States*, 320 U.S. 81 (1943), 330, 331

Hoke v. *United States*, 227 U.S. 308 (1913), 177

Home Building & Loan Association v. *Blaisdell*, 290 U.S. 398 (1934), 344

*Hood & Sons v. *DuMond*, 336 U.S. 525 (1949), 382, 384, 401–406

Hughes v. *Alexandria Scrap Corp.*, 426 U.S. 794 (1976), 386

Hughes v. *Oklahoma*, 60 L. Ed. 2d 250 (1979), 384

Humphrey's Executor v. *United States*, 295 U.S. 602 (1935), 279, 299, 301

Hylton v. *United States*, 3 Dall. 171 (1796), 14, 219, 230, 231, 235

Jacobellis v. *Ohio*, 378 U.S. 184 (1964), 91n

*Katzenbach v. *McClung*, 379 U.S. 294 (1964), 179, 180, 208–213

Kennedy v. *Sampson*, 511 F. 2d 430 (1974), 285

Kentucky v. *Dennison*, 24 How. 66 (1861), 449

Kilbourn v. *Thompson*, 103 U.S. 168 (1881), 144, 149, 152, 158

Knowlton v. *Moore*, 178 U.S. 41 (1900), 220

Konigsberg v. *State Bar of California*, 353 U.S. 252 (1957), 40

*Korematsu v. *United States*, 323 U.S. 214 (1944), 273, 318, 319, 329–336

Leisy v. *Hardin,* 135 U.S. 100 (1890), 381

Linda R. S. v. *Richard D.,* 410 U.S. 208 (1973), 87

Long v. *Rockwood,* 277 U.S. 142 (1928), 418

Low v. *Austin,* 13 Wall. 29 (1872), 421, 422, 438, 439

Luther v. *Borden,* 7 How. 1 (1849), 89, 129, 130

McCardle, Ex parte, 7 Wall. 506 (1869), 39, 40, 47, 57-59

McCray v. *United States,* 195 U.S. 27 (1904), 221, 222, 236-241, 245

M'Culloch v. *Maryland,* 4 Wheat. 316 (1819), 143, 173, 174, 340, 348, 349-355, 417, 419

McGrain v. *Daugherty,* 273 U.S. 135 (1927), 145, 150-155, 158

Mapp v. *Ohio,* 367 U.S. 643 (1961), 89, 123, 126

Marbury v. *Madison,* 1 Cranch 137 (1803), 6, 14, 15, 16, 19-26, 30, 34, 46, 63, 98, 102, 174, 219, 496

Marchetti v. *United States,* 390 U.S. 39 (1968), 225

Marshall v. *Gordon,* 243 U.S. 521 (1917), 153

Martin v. *Hunter's Lessee,* 1 Wheat. 304 (1816), 17, 348

Maryland v. *Wirtz,* 392 U.S. 138 (1968), 346

Massachusetts v. *Laird,* 400 U.S. 886 (1970), 316, 325-329

Massachusetts v. *Mellon,* 262 U.S. 447 (1923), 325, 326

Massachusetts v. *United States,* 435 U.S. 444 (1978), 420, 429-432

Mathews v. *Eldridge,* 424 U.S. 319 (1976), 499, 500, 516-521

Mayberry v. *Pennsylvania,* 400 U.S. 455 (1971), 45

Merryman, Ex parte, 17 Fed. Cas. 144 (1861), 317, 318

Michelin Tire Corp. v. *Wages,* 423 U.S. 276 (1976), 422, 438-441

Michigan v. *Doran,* 58 L. Ed. 2d 521 (1979), 449

Milligan, Ex parte, 4 Wall. 2 (1866), 318, 327

Missouri v. *Holland,* 252 U.S. 416 (1920), 312, 313

Morehead v. *New York ex rel. Tipaldo,* 298 U.S. 587 (1936), 344

Mulford v. *Smith,* 307 U.S. 38 (1939), 224

Multistate Tax Compact Case: See *United States Steel Corp.* v. *Multistate Tax Commission*

Munn v. *Illinois,* 94 U.S. 113 (1877), 343

Myers v. *United States,* 272 U.S. 52 (1926), 278, 279, 280, 299

National Cable Television Association v. *United States,* 415 U.S. 236 (1974), 482

National Labor Relations Board v. *Jones & Laughlin Steel Corp.,* 301 U.S. 1 (1937), 38, 179, 195-203

National League of Cities v. *Usery,* 426 U.S. 833 (1976), 179, 342, 346, 347, 348, 366-372, 420

Neagle, In re, 135 U.S. 1 (1890), 272, 273

Nebbia v. *New York,* 291 U.S. 502 (1934), 344

New Hampshire v. *Louisiana,* 108 U.S. 76 (1883), 451

New York v. *Miln,* 11 Pet. 102 (1837), 343, 379

New York v. *United States,* 326 U.S. 572 (1946), 419, 423-429, 431

New York Times v. *United States* [Pentagon Papers Case], 403 U.S. 713 (1971), 311

Nixon Tapes Case: See *United States* v. *Nixon*

Ogden v. *Saunders*, 12 Wheat. 213 (1827), 342

Okanogan Indians v. *United States* [Pocket Veto Case], 279 U.S. 655 (1929), 285

Oregon v. *Mitchell*, 400 U.S. 112 (1970), 42

Panama Refining Co. v. *Ryan*, 293 U.S. 388 (1935), 480, 481, 488, 489

*Pennsylvania v. *Nelson*, 350 U.S. 497 (1956), 40, 347, 348, 372-377

Pennsylvania v. *West Virginia*, 262 U.S. 553 (1923), 40, 384

Pentagon Papers Case: See *New York Times* v. *United States*

*Philadelphia v. *New Jersey*, 437 U.S. 617 (1978), 383, 384, 406-411

Plessy v. *Ferguson*, 163 U.S. 537 (1896), 92

Pocket Veto Case: See *Okanogan Indians* v. *United States*

Pollock v. *Farmers' Loan & Trust Co.*, 157 U.S. 429 (1895), 417

*Pollock v. *Farmers' Loan & Trust Co.*, 158 U.S. 601 (1895), 17, 42, 220, 226-236, 417

Powell v. *McCormack*, 395 U.S. 486 (1969), 30, 90, 91, 281, 327

Prize Cases, 2 Bl. 635 (1863), 316, 328, 329

Rahrer, In re, 140 U.S. 545 (1891), 381

Reid v. *Covert*, 351 U.S. 487 (1956), 313

Rizzo v. *Goode*, 423 U.S. 362 (1976), 88

Roe v. *Wade*, 410 U.S. 113 (1973), 495

*Schechter Poultry Corp. v. *United States*, 295 U.S. 495 (1935), 178, 200, 202, 481, 486-493, 494

*Schick v. *Reed*, 419 U.S. 256 (1974), 284, 302-307

Schlesinger v. *Reservists Committee*, 418 U.S. 208 (1974), 86

Scott v. *Sanford* [Dred Scott Case], 19 How. 393 (1857), 17, 42, 340

Shreveport Rate Case, 234 U.S. 342 (1914), 178

Sierra Club v. *Morton*, 405 U.S. 727 (1972), 86, 107, 108, 109, 110

Simon v. *Eastern Kentucky Welfare Rights Organization*, 426 U.S. 26 (1976), 87

*Singleton v. *Wulff*, 428 U.S. 106 (1976), 84, 93-97

Slaughterhouse Cases, 16 Wall. 36 (1873), 447

Sonzinsky v. *United States*, 300 U.S. 506 (1937), 222

*Sosna v. *Iowa*, 419 U.S. 393 (1975), 444, 448, 456-460

South Carolina v. *Katzenbach*, 383 U.S. 301 (1966), 326

South Carolina v. *United States*, 199 U.S. 437 (1905), 419, 427, 428

*South Carolina Highway Department v. *Barnwell*, 303 U.S. 177 (1938), 382, 390-394, 398

South Dakota v. *North Carolina*, 192 U.S. 286 (1904), 451

*Southern Pacific Co. v. *Arizona*, 325 U.S. 761 (1945), 381, 382, 383, 394-400

Springer v. *United States*, 102 U.S. 586 (1881), 220

Stafford v. *Wallace*, 258 U.S. 495 (1922), 178

Steel Seizure Case: See *Youngstown Sheet & Tube Co.* v. *Sawyer*

*Steward Machine Co. v. Davis, 301 U.S. 548 (1937), 224, 256-261, 345, 495

*Stone v. Powell, 428 U.S. 465 (1976), 88, 89, 122-127

Sturgis v. Crowninshield, 14 Wheat. 122 (1819), 342

Swift and Company v. United States, 196 U.S. 375 (1905), 178

*Taylor v. Hayes, 418 U.S. 488 (1974), 45, 74-79

*Tennessee Valley Authority v. Hill, 437 U.S. 153 (1978), 498, 499, 507-515

Texas v. White, 7 Wall. 700 (1869), 340

Toomer v. Witsell, 334 U.S. 395 (1948), 442, 448, 462, 463

Train v. City of New York, 420 U.S. 35 (1975), 275, 276

United States v. Belmont, 301 U.S. 324 (1937), 314

*United States v. Bisceglia, 420 U.S. 141 (1975), 497, 501-507

*United States v. Butler, 297 U.S. 1 (1936), 222, 223, 224, 246-256, 344

United States v. City of Detroit, 355 U.S. 466 (1958), 418

United States v. County of Fresno, 429 U.S. 452 (1977), 420

*United States v. Curtiss-Wright Export Corp., 299 U.S. 304 (1936), 309, 319, 320-324, 479-480

*United States v. Darby, 312 U.S. 100 (1941), 179, 204, 344, 345, 360-366

United States v. Doremus, 249 U.S. 86 (1919), 222, 245

United States v. Georgia Public Service Commission, 371 U.S. 285 (1963), 419

United States v. Grimaud, 220 U.S. 506 (1910), 480

United States v. Kahriger, 345 U.S. 22 (1953), 218, 225

*United States v. E. C. Knight Co., 156 U.S. 1 (1895), 176, 177, 180, 188-195, 380

United States v. Midwest Oil Co., 236 U.S. 459 (1915), 273

*United States v. Nixon [Nixon Tapes Case], 418 U.S. 683 (1974), 12, 14, 19, 27-33, 34, 282, 311

United States v. Pink, 315 U.S. 203 (1942), 314

*United States v. Richardson, 418 U.S. 166 (1974), 85, 97-105

United States v. Robel, 389 U.S. 258 (1967), 482

United States v. Rumely, 345 U.S. 41 (1953), 147, 159, 161

*United States v. Students Challenging Regulatory Agency Procedures, 412 U.S. 669 (1973), 86, 105-110

United States v. United States District Court, 407 U.S. 297 (1972), 311

*United States Steel Corp. v. Multistate Tax Commission [Multistate Tax Compact Case], 434, U.S. 452 (1978), 450, 465-471

Veazie Bank v. Fenno, 8 Wall. 531 (1869), 221, 245

Virginia v. Tennessee, 148 U.S. 503 (1893), 450, 467, 468, 469, 471

Virginia v. West Virginia I, 206 U.S. 290 (1907), 452

Virginia v. West Virginia II, 209 U.S. 514 (1908), 452

Virginia v. West Virginia III, 220 U.S. 1 (1911), 452

Virginia v. West Virginia IV, 222 U.S. 17 (1911), 452

Virginia v. *West Virginia V,* 231 U.S. 89
   (1913), 452

Virginia v. *West Virginia VI,* 234 U.S.
   117 (1914), 452

Virginia v. *West Virginia VII,* 238 U.S.
   202 (1915), 452

Virginia v. *West Virginia VIII,* 241 U.S.
   531 (1916), 452

Virginia v. *West Virginia IX,* 246 U.S.
   565 (1918), 452

Wabash, St. Louis, and Pacific Railway Co.
   v. *Illinois,* 118 U.S. 557 (1886), 380

Watkins v. *United States,* 354 U.S. 178
   (1957), 146, 147, 156–166

Wayman v. *Southard,* 10 Wheat. 1
   (1825), 480

Weeks v. *United States,* 232 U.S. 383
   (1914), 88, 123

Weiner v. *United States,* 357 U.S. 349
   (1958), 279, 298–301

Wesberry v. *Sanders,* 376 U.S. 1 (1964),
   90n

West Virginia ex rel. Dyer v. *Sims,* 341
   U.S. 22 (1952), 451

Whitney v. *California,* 274 U.S. 357
   (1927), 87, 121

Wickard v. *Filburn,* 317 U.S. 111 (1942),
   180, 203–208, 211

Williams v. *North Carolina [Williams I],*
   317 U.S. 287 (1942), 445, 453, 454

Williams v. *North Carolina [Williams II],*
   325 U.S. 226 (1945), 445, 453, 454

Willson v. *Blackbird Creek Marsh Co.,* 2
   Pet. 245 (1829), 342, 379, 391,
   395

Worcester v. *Georgia,* 6 Pet. 515 (1832),
   41

Yates v. *United States,* 354 U.S. 298
   (1957), 40

Yellin v. *United States,* 374 U.S. 109
   (1963), 147

Younger v. *Harris,* 401 U.S. 37 (1971),
   88, 115–122

Youngstown Sheet & Tube Co. v. *Sawyer*
   [Steel Seizure Case], 343 U.S. 579
   (1952), 273, 275, 285–298, 310,
   327, 328, 329

Zemel v. *Rusk,* 381 U.S. 1 (1965), 480